ÆSCHYLUS AND ATHENS

A BACCHANT

ÆSCHYLUS
AND
ATHENS

A STUDY IN THE SOCIAL ORIGINS
OF DRAMA

GEORGE THOMSON

Professor of Greek in the University of Birmingham
and formerly Fellow of King's College, Cambridge

HASKELL HOUSE PUBLISHERS LTD.
Publishers of Scarce Scholarly Books
NEW YORK. N. Y. 10012
1972

First Published 1940

HASKELL HOUSE PUBLISHERS LTD.
Publishers of Scarce Scholarly Books
280 LAFAYETTE STREET
NEW YORK. N. Y. 10012

Library of Congress Catalog Card Number: **73-186307**

Standard Book Number 8383-0723-X

Printed in the United States of America

PREFACE TO THE FIRST EDITION

THIS is an attempt to reinterpret the plays of Æschylus, on which I have been working for many years, in the light of the general evolution of Greek society and in particular the transition from tribal society to the state. The range it covers is so wide that I should have been glad to spend more time on it, but in the immediate future research is likely to be difficult, and therefore I have decided to publish it without further delay.

The books to which I owe most are, in my special field, the works of Jane Harrison and Ridgeway, and the earlier works of Cornford, and, more generally, Morgan's *Ancient Society*, Engels' *Origin of the Family*, and Caudwell's *Illusion and Reality*. Other obligations are acknowledged in the notes and references.

I must also mention a special debt to my friends the peasant-fishermen of the Blasket Island in West Kerry, who taught me, among many other things that could not have been learnt from books, what it is like to live in a pre-capitalist society. It is true that nominally they fall within the orbit of the capitalist system, because they are liable for rent, but most of them refuse to pay it; and in general their traditions, especially their poetry, date from a time when social relations were profoundly different from those in which I have been brought up.

These, then, are the principal sources to which I am indebted for what is new in the present work—apart from the political events of the last ten years, which have forced me, in common with many others, to reorientate my whole attitude to life.

I wish to thank Mrs. H. F. Stewart for the drawings, and the Syndics of the Cambridge University Press for permission to reproduce, in Chapters XV and XVII, material from my editions of the *Oresteia* and *Prometheus Bound*.

GEORGE THOMSON.

September, 1940.

PREFACE TO THE SECOND EDITION

Looking back on this piece of work after five years, I regard it as a preliminary sketch of an extensive field which needs to be systematically re-explored. There are many details I would like to modify, but in general both the method and the results have stood the test of further research, which I hope to publish in due course. Meanwhile, the book is still in demand, and accordingly it is now reissued with only a few minor corrections and additions.

GEORGE THOMSON.

September, 1945.

CONTENTS

PAGE

INTRODUCTION   I

Tragedy and democracy—the relativity of ideas—Morgan on primitive Greek society—comparative anthropology—evolutionism and diffusionism—historical linguistics—prospects of classical research.

PART ONE

TRIBAL SOCIETY

I. TOTEMISM   II

Economic classification of modern tribes—Australian totemism —the increase ceremony—the totemic taboo—mimetic magic— descent from the totem—segmentation of the primitive horde— appropriation and production—decline of totemism—division of labour—modes of reckoning descent—their economic significance —origin of exogamy—tribal co-operation—totemic ancestor worship—chieftaincy and divinity—nature gods—totemism in Greece—clan emblems—the clan feast—initiation and marriage —the sacred marriage—ritual of the god-king.

II. EXOGAMY   23

Primitive Indo-European culture—the classificatory system of relationship—Morgan's theory of group marriage—the Indo-European classificatory system—the Greek phratry—matrilineal descent in prehistoric Greece—Zeus and Hera—Greek terms for brother—co-operation and competition—property in cattle— Jewish law of inheritance—collapse of exogamy—homicide— Erinyes.

III. PROPERTY   37

Land tenure in the Homeric poems—allotment of land in the Old Testament—allotment of land in prehistoric Greece— reservations of land—allotment and reservation of booty and food—reservation the reward of military service—Attic law of inheritance—Moira a symbol of primitive communism—allotment of functions among the gods—Greek craft clans—the Moirai as spinners—magic of clothes and names—totemic designs on swaddling bands—daímon—birth, marriage and death —the Greek clan name—Moirai as ancestral spirits—Norns— Moira, Erinys, Dike—Moira and Zeus—Nomos.

PART TWO

FROM TRIBE TO STATE

IV. MONARCHY   59

Minoan culture—Greek dialects—pre-Hellenic elements in Greek religion—social organisation of the Achæans—vassalage— rulers and people—Achæan society reflected in Olympus—society and religion—myth and ritual—evolution of epic—Iliad and Odyssey—decline of the monarchy—Hesiod.

PAGE

V. ARISTOCRACY 69
The Dorian conquest—serfdom—development of the *témenos*—
appropriation of the land—aristocratic priesthood—aristocratic
law of homicide—early history of Attica—Eupatridai—laws of
Drakon—early history of Ionia—landlord and peasant in Hesiod
—Moira and Metron—choral lyric—Ionian science—society and
the cosmos—Anaximander.

VI. TYRANNY 85
Meidas and Gyges—the coinage—rise of the merchant class—
aristocratic attitude to trade—Solon—the middle class and the
mean—Peisistratos—historical function of the tyranny—Theognis
and the democratic revolution.

PART THREE

ORIGIN OF DRAMA

VII. INITIATION 97
Age grades—primitive ideas of birth and death—birth and death
in initiation—purifications and ordeals—the Men's House—
secret societies—ritual dramas—initiation at Sparta—in Crete—
at Athens—cutting of the hair—human sacrifice at initiation—
birth of Zeus—Kouretes—birth and death of Dionysus—adoption—deification—bull-roarer—Pelops—origin of the Olympian
Games—death of the old king—*prytaneîon*—initiation at Eleusis—
the Eleusinian Mysteries and the Olympian Games—relation of
the Mysteries to primitive initiation.

VIII. DIONYSUS 130
Dionysus and Apollo—original form of initiation—initiation in
ancient China—the *Natureingang*—peasant festivals of modern
Europe—Frazer's theory—*eiresiône* and *phármakos*—Bacchants o.
Euripides—Agrionia—myth of Lykourgos—immersion in water
—marriage of Dionysus—daughters of Proitos—Io—Hera and
the cow—the Dionysiac *thíasos*.

IX. ORPHISM 151
Dionysus and the tyranny—Arion—Thracian origin of Orphism
—the mining industry—Orphism and the Hesiodic *Theogony*—
Dike—Love—Orphic eschatology—soul and body—Ananke—
the Wheel—Diodoros on the mines—Orphic myths—Orphic
thíasoi—Orphism and the democratic movement.

X. DITHYRAMB 165
First day of the City Dionysia—*pompé, agón, kômos*—Dionysus as
a bull—Arion and the dithyramb—Archilochos—hymn of the
Kouretes—god, priest and poet—daughters of Eleuther—*pompé*
and *stásimon*—Dionysiac passion-play—ritual vestiges in tragedy.

XI. TRAGEDY 175
Evolution of the third actor—of the second—the Messenger—
Xanthos and Melanthos—comic elements in the *Bacchants*—

hypokrités and *exárchon*—origin of the actor—secularisation of
mystic ritual—strophic form—the refrain—*kommós* and *agón*—
anagnórisis—*stichomýthia*—riddles—the stage—mediæval liturgy-
plays—Peisistratos and the dithyramb—origin of drama in the
ritual of the totemic clan.

PART FOUR

ÆSCHYLUS

XII. DEMOCRACY 199
Phratry and citizenship—rules of inheritance in Attica, Gortyna
and Sparta—status of women at Sparta—in primitive Attica—
reorganisation of the Attic tribal system—reform of the calendar
—Aristotle on the Attic tribal system—*isonomía*—Pythagoras—
political significance of early Pythagoreanism—relation to
Orphism—Calvinism—Pythagorean doctrine of the mean—
Alkmaion—Hippokrates—victory of the middle class.

XIII. ATHENS AND PERSIA 220
Rise of the Persian Empire—Kleisthenes and Persia—Miltiades
—Marathon—Themistokles—disunity of the Greeks—Salamis—
fall of Themistokles—revolt of the Spartan serfs—fall of Kimon
—Athenian imperialism.

XIV. TETRALOGY 232
Competitions at the City Dionysia—origin of *leitourgía*—satyr-play
—Pickard-Cambridge on Aristotle—ritual obscenity—origin of
comedy—Peloponnesian drama—Lenaia—ritual basis of Attic
comedy—the trilogy.

XV. ORESTEIA 245
Life of Æschylus—the surviving plays—House of Atreus—
Agamemnon—*Choephoroi*—mythical symbolism—Apollo and the
Erinyes—purification of Orestes—*Eumenides*—What is justice?—
Apollo and the *exegetaí*—Erinyes and Semnai—*métoikoi*—Pana-
thenaic procession.

XVI. EARLIER PLAYS 298
Myth of Io—Danaides—*Suppliants*—Why do the Danaides reject
the match?—endogamy in Egypt—Æschylus and endogamy—
Aristotle on quarrels about heiresses—trial of Hypermnestra—
Thesmophoria—discovery of agriculture—*Persians*—Æschylus
and the single tragedy—*Seven against Thebes*—from clan to state.

XVII. PROMETHEIA 317
Discovery of fire—Prometheus in Hesiod—mystical allusions—
cults of Prometheus—Herakles—Is Prometheus in the wrong?—
popular view of the tyrant—Zeus a tyrant—characterisation of
Prometheus—wisdom through suffering—origins of civilisation
—structure of the *Prometheus Bound*—*Prometheus Unbound*—*Prometheus the Fire-bearer*—Moschion—Kritias—Pythagoras on the
social function of religion—Protagoras—Philemon—Diogenes—
Shelley

PAGE

XVIII. AFTER ÆSCHYLUS 347
    Evolution of the single tragedy—slave labour—imperialism—
    contradictions in Athenian democracy—*sophrosýne*—function of
    money—money in Greek thought—decay of the chorus—*deus ex
    machina*—*peripéteia*—relation of Sophokles to Æschylus—*Elektra*—
    Œdipus Tyrannus—the thought of Sophokles—Euripides—*Ion*—
    Bacchants—degradation of family life—*Medea*—destruction of
    Melos—*Trojan Women*—idealism and materialism—Moira,
    Ananke, Tyche—end of Greek tragedy.

XIX. PITY AND FEAR 372
    Aristotle's *Poetics*—*kátharsis*—epilepsy—ritual of the Korybantes
    —primitive theory of possession—possession in the cults of
    Dionysus—hysteria among primitive peoples—psychological
    origin of Orphic and Dionysiac cults—religious hysteria at Eleusis
    —*Ion* of Plato—the poet is possessed—the actor—tragedy and the
    Mysteries—social function of *kátharsis*—of the arts.

APPENDIX I. NOTE ON THE CLASSIFICATORY SYSTEM . . . 387
APPENDIX II. INDO-EUROPEAN TERMS OF RELATIONSHIP . . . 402
NOTES AND REFERENCES 418
BIBLIOGRAPHY 456
CHRONOLOGICAL TABLE 465
INDEX 469

DIAGRAMS

THE CLASSIFICATORY SYSTEM OF RELATIONSHIP 24
HISTORY OF INITIATION 128
EVOLUTION OF THE ACTOR 174
RITUAL PATTERN OF GREEK TRAGEDY 192
EVOLUTION OF GREEK POETRY 196

ILLUSTRATIONS

A BACCHANT (from an Attic vase painting) . . . . *frontispiece*
A SOLDIER WITH EMBLAZONED SHIELD (from an Attic vase
    painting) . . . . *page* 9
SLAVES DIGGING FOR POTTER'S CLAY (from a Corinthian clay tablet) 57
DIONYSUS AND SATYRS (from an Attic vase painting) . . . 95
THE OWL OF ATHENA (from an Attic coin) 197
MAPS OF GREECE . . . . *end-papers*

INTRODUCTION

GREEK tragedy was one of the distinctive functions of Athenian democracy. In its form and its content, in its growth and its decay, it was conditioned by the evolution of the social organism to which it belonged.

In the Ægean basin, split up into innumerable islands and valleys, the centralisation of political power was difficult, and the political units tended to remain autonomous. External expansion being thus restricted, their internal development was proportionately intense. In the democratic city-state, ancient society rose, on a scale necessarily minute, to its highest point. These states had advanced so rapidly that they carried with them copious traditions of the past, and their autonomy favoured the persistence of alternative versions of the same events, which provided abundant material for comparison and analysis. Moreover, surrounded as they were by primitive peoples, thoughtful citizens did not fail to perceive that their own ancestors had once lived as these barbarians lived now.[1] And, finally, the success of the democratic movement predisposed its exponents towards enquiry into its origins, while the strenuous opposition which it had encountered taught them to regard conflict, whether between man and man or man and nature, as the driving-force of human progress. The result was a view of evolution at once rational and dynamic.

Æschylus was a democrat who fought as well as wrote. The triumph of democracy over the internal and external enemies allied against it was the inspiration of his art. He was a leading citizen of the most advanced community in Greece; he was also, as a member of the old Attic nobility, the heir to local traditions which had their roots far back in the society of the primitive tribe.[2] The fundamental question which engrossed him all his life was this—how had the tribal society enshrined in those traditions evolved into the democratic city-state which he had helped to establish? It is a question that must

concern us, too, if we wish to understand his art, and it is at
the same time so vital to the understanding of European
civilisation as to invest his art with a permanent historical
importance.

The Greek view of life was not, as sometimes represented,
the expression of qualities inherent in the Greeks as such; it
was the rich and varied response of a heterogeneous people to
the complex and continuous growth of Greek society itself as
determined by the special conditions of its material and
historical environment. The use that men make of their
leisure, their ideas of the physical world, of right and wrong,
their art, philosophy and religion, vary and develop in accordance with variations and developments in their social relations
which in turn are ultimately determined by their mode of
securing their material subsistence. This is not to deny that
there exists an objective reality, or that some men have formed
a truer idea of it than others; but every idea of it is relative in
so far as it starts from conscious or unconscious assumptions
determined by the position of the man himself in the world he
contemplates.

To that extent, therefore, not only was the Greek view of
life relative, but so is our view of the Greek view. Our view
cannot be wholly objective, and the professed impartiality of
some modern scholars is an illusion; but it will be more or less
objective in proportion as we recognise and analyse our own
preconceptions. We must become conscious of our prejudices
in order to correct them. The historian of the past is a citizen
of the present. Those who as citizens are averse or indifferent
to contemporary social changes will seek in the civilisation of
ancient Greece something stable and absolutely valuable,
which will both reflect and fortify their attitude of acquiescence.
Others, who cannot acquiesce, will study the history of Greece
as a process of continuous change, which, if it can be made to
reveal its underlying laws, will help them to understand, and so
direct, the forces making for change in the society of to-day. To
such as these, the study of Æschylus, who was a revolutionary
poet, will be especially congenial, and the preconceptions with
which they approach him, being akin to his own, will be a
positive advantage.

It is known that, in common with other civilised peoples, the Greeks had once been organised in tribes. The precise nature of their tribal institutions is a question which the internal evidence is in itself too fragmentary to solve. Yet for a proper understanding of the city-state it is imperative to ascertain, not only what it was and what it was becoming, but also what it had ceased to be. The internal evidence must therefore be studied in the light of what is known of tribal institutions in general. This principle was applied to early Greek history with important results by Morgan in the nineteenth century, and by some of his predecessors, such as Millar and Ferguson, in the eighteenth, but, despite all the material that has accumulated since then, it has been so far neglected by recent historians, especially in this country, that most of them are not even acquainted with the results already obtained.

By classifying the surviving tribes of modern times according to their predominant mode of food production, some valuable correlations have been established between material culture and social institutions, and, with certain reservations, these results can be applied to the problems of archæology. In some departments of Greek archæology, important work along these lines has already been done by Harrison, Ridgeway, Cook and others, but, owing largely to their neglect of Morgan, their use of the anthropological evidence was insufficiently systematic. This explains, though without justifying, recent scepticism as to the validity of their method. Thus, writing of the origins of tragedy, which is one of the problems to be investigated in this book, Pickard-Cambridge remarks: "All the arguments that can be drawn from the Australian bush, Central Africa, and other remote regions can prove nothing about Greek tragedy in default of all evidence from Greece itself."[3] This provincialism goes far to explain why the problem of the origin of Greek tragedy remains unsolved. There is plenty of evidence in Greece itself for eyes that have been trained to recognise it.

The comparative study of social evolution is complicated by two factors, both making for uneven development. In the first place, the growth of many primitive communities has been retarded by economic difficulties of their habitat. The lower hunting tribes of contemporary Australia have failed to advance beyond the mode of production left behind in Europe at the close of the palæolithic epoch; but, though their economic development has been arrested, their social institutions have not remained stationary—they have continued to develop, but only in directions determined by that mode of production. It would, consequently, be premature to argue without further analysis from the social organisation of contemporary Australia to that of palæolithic Europe; but it would be equally mistaken to deny the possibility of co-ordinating the two sets of data.

In the second place, the more backward peoples have been continuously subjected to the cultural influence of the more advanced, with the result that their development has been accelerated, deflected, or obstructed. In extreme cases the peoples themselves have been destroyed. The complications arising from the operation of this factor cannot be fully resolved until we have worked out a theory of cultural diffusion, but meanwhile it may be observed that their significance can easily be exaggerated.[4] Since the function of all social institutions, alien or indigenous, is to satisfy some need, the origin of this or that custom is not explained by saying that it was borrowed from abroad. As Ferguson remarked, "nations borrow only what they are nearly in a condition to have invented themselves."[5]

The successive phases of evolution through which the ancient Greeks had passed are stratified, not only in their material remains, but in their language. The comparative study of the Indo-European languages has already reached a point at which it is possible to draw certain general conclusions concerning the culture of the people that spoke the parent-speech. When this study has been co-ordinated with that of other groups of languages, the science of historical linguistics will be raised to a new level of efficiency. Even now, in so limited a field as Greek, the concerted application of historical linguistics and social anthropology can yield new and important results.

It has sometimes been said, especially in recent years, that the possibilities of further research in classical studies are limited. I believe that they are as limitless in this as in any other branch of science, historical or physical; but, if we are to exploit them, we must emancipate ourselves from traditional methods, which served well in their time but are now exhausted. The art of Æschylus, like all art, must be studied as a product of social evolution, and for that purpose the departmentalism of classical research, and the barriers between classical research and other branches of the historical sciences, must be broken down. This is a task of some difficulty for those who have been brought up in the old convention, but it must be undertaken. We live in a period of disintegration, cultural and social, but out of this is already emerging the prospect of a new integration. By directing our study of Æschylus to this end, we can hope to achieve, as he achieved, a true harmony between theory and practice, between poetry and life.

Lastly, a few words about the plan of this book. The four parts into which it is divided correspond to the main stages of the argument, which, despite ramifications, is continuous. Part One begins with an analysis of the economic and social structure of the primitive tribe, and the conclusions reached are applied to the interpretation of tribal survivals in early Greece. Part Two covers the transition from tribal society to the city-state, and relates the development of poetry and science to the early history of the class struggle. Part Three resumes from Part One the history of primitive initiation, which is then applied to the growth of mystical religion and the origin of tragedy. In Part Four these various threads—political, ideological, artistic—are drawn together for the interpretation of Æschylus and, after dealing more briefly with the subsequent history of Greek tragedy, the book ends with a discussion of the function of the arts in relation to the psychological effects of the class struggle.

There are times when the reader may feel that the detail devoted to particular problems is disproportionate. In general, technical matter has been confined to the notes, but some of my conclusions, being new and at the same time vital, demanded full investigation in the text. It will be as well to indicate at the outset which these are and what value I place upon them.

In Chapter I an attempt is made to discover the origin of totemism, but I wish it to be understood that this part of my

BA

argument is provisional. The only points on which I am prepared at the present stage to insist are two—that totemism is
an integral feature of the tribal system and that the true theory
of its origin must include a solution of the contradiction between
the present practice of Australian tribes and their ancestral
traditions.

In Chapter II it is contended that the Indo-European
terminology of kinship was originally classificatory. The
evidence is set out in Appendix II. Apart from its bearing on
the history of Indo-European culture, this conclusion affords,
in my opinion, a striking confirmation of Morgan's general
theory of the classificatory system.

In Chapter III the mythical concept of the Moirai, the Greek
goddesses of Fate, is interpreted as a symbol of primitive communism. This conclusion has been reached by applying the
principle that what ultimately determines man's consciousness
is his social being. The same principle is applied in Chapters
IX and XII to Orphism and Pythagoreanism, and in Chapter
XVIII to the Aristotelian doctrine of *peripéteia*.

In Chapters X and XI Aristotle's account of the origin of
tragedy is vindicated by a comparative study of the primitive
secret society, followed by a dialectical analysis of the internal
evidence. One reason why his account of the matter has been
called in question by modern scholars is that they have been
confronted by a contradiction which their empirical method
is powerless to resolve. If tragedy and dithyramb were originally the same, how is it that they are actually so different? The
answer is that they became different precisely because they had
once been the same.

The interpretation of Æschylus in Chapters XV–XVII,
parts of which have been already published, is my own,
although it has its roots in the work of Headlam and Sheppard.
In Chapter XVII I have illustrated by the myth of Prometheus
the principle that myths retain their vitality in proportion as
they readapt themselves to changes in the structure of society.
This is an important principle of mythological analysis, which
requires to be more fully worked out. In the myth of Prometheus it is relatively easy to strip the primitive kernel of its
accretions, because it bears so directly on the class struggle,

but in others it is more difficult. In Chapter VIII I have assumed that the Dionysiac myths persisted with little modification of their primitive form. I believe that this assumption is correct, the explanation being that they drew their vitality from Orphism, which was itself a revival of the primitive cults of Dionysus, but I am aware that it requires further argument.

The book suffers from one fundamental weakness—the lack of a systematic investigation into the economic structure of early Greek society. Heichelheim's *Wirtschaftsgeschichte des Altertums*, which contains much valuable material, appeared too late for me to absorb it as fully as it deserves. Perhaps, even here, I shall have achieved something if I have convinced specialists in economics of the urgency of the task that awaits them. Indeed, throughout the book my main object has been to inspire my readers, especially those who are alive to the need for new methods in the study of ancient society, with a sense of the wide and fertile country that lies ready for them to cultivate.

PART ONE

TRIBAL SOCIETY

SOLDIER WITH EMBLAZONED SHIELD

I

TOTEMISM

THE surviving tribes of modern times have been assigned to the following categories in virtue of their predominant mode of food-production: Lower Hunters (food-gathering and hunting); Higher Hunters (hunting and fishing); Pastoral (two grades); Agricultural (three grades).[1] The higher hunting grade is distinguished from the lower by the use of the bow in addition to the spear. In the second pastoral grade stock-raising is supplemented by agriculture. Of the three agricultural grades, the first is characterised by garden tillage, the second by field tillage, and in the third field tillage is supplemented by stock-raising. The last marks a stage in the development of the tribe at which its social and political structure is already in dissolution.

This classification is, of course, an abstraction. The categories are not mutually exclusive. Thus, food-gathering is maintained among the higher hunters and hunting throughout the pastoral and agricultural grades, but in each case with diminishing importance. Nor do they constitute a strict chronological sequence. Stock-raising and tillage have been universally preceded by hunting, and that in turn by food-gathering, but the relation between stock-raising and tillage is variable, being largely determined by geographical factors. Some parts of the world are rich in domesticable animals, others in cultivable plants. Others, again, are rich in both, and in these the two modes of production may have been combined from the beginning in the form of mixed farming.

The characteristic religion of tribal society in its more primitive phases is totemism. Each clan of which the tribe is composed is associated with some natural object, which is called its "totem." The clansmen regard themselves as akin to their totem-species and as descended from it. They are forbidden to eat it,[2] and perform a traditional ceremony designed to increase its numbers. Members of the same totem may not intermarry.

Totemism survives most completely among the lower hunting tribes of Australia; it is also found in forms more or less degenerate among more advanced tribes in America, Melanesia, Africa, India and other parts of Asia; and among the Indo-European, Semitic and Chinese peoples there are numerous traditions and institutions which have been assigned to a totemic origin. All these peoples are, or have been, organised in tribes, and therefore the view that they too were formerly totemic will be considerably strengthened if it can be shown that totemism is an inherent feature of the tribal system. In studying this subject, the Australian evidence is of primary importance, since it represents the most primitive stratum of which we have direct knowledge. Even in Australia, however, the form in which totemism has survived is not, as we shall see, its original form. If from an analysis of the present form of Australian totemism we can deduce its original form, and relate both to a coherent process of economic and social change, the result may be regarded as an approximation to the history of totemism, not only in Australia, but in other parts of the world.

The great majority of Australian totems are edible species of plants and animals.[3] The remainder are mostly natural objects, like stones and stars, or natural processes, like rain and wind. These inorganic totems are secondary, being formed by analogy after the totemic system had fully developed. In seeking the origin of the system, we must concentrate on the plants and animals, and the fact that most of these are edible entitles us to presume that its origin is connected with the food supply.

The ceremonies for the increase of the totem species are performed at the beginning of the breeding season at a prescribed spot, called the "totem centre," on the hunting-ground of the clan to which the totem belongs. The totem centre is usually situated at an actual breeding place of the species in question.[4] This point has been established by recent observers, but its significance has not been appreciated. If we ask what brought the ancestors of the wallaby clan to the spot where ceremonies for the increase of wallabies are now performed, the answer can only be that they came there to eat wallabies.

At the present time the members of the clan are forbidden to eat, though not necessarily to kill, their totem species; but to this rule there are significant exceptions. Among some of the Central tribes, at the performance of the increase ceremony, the headman of the clan is not only permitted but obliged to eat a little of the species.[5] As he explains, he must "get the totem inside him" in order to perform his magic. That this ritual infraction of the taboo is derived from the general practice of earlier times is proved by the tribal traditions, in which the clan ancestors are represented as feeding habitually or exclusively on their totem species.[6] These traditions show that formerly, so far from being tabooed, particular species had been the principal source of food supply. They point to a time when the extremely low level of technique had imposed severe restrictions on the quest for food, resulting in a specialised diet. The totemic clan had its origin in a horde of food-gatherers attracted to the breeding ground of a particular species of animal or plant, which became its staple food. It remains to be seen how this state of affairs was transformed into its opposite.

The increase ceremonies are designed to represent dramatically the growth or gathering of the totem, if it is a plant, or, if it is an animal, its distinctive habits, gestures and cries, and in some cases the act of catching it and killing it. It is probable that the original function of such performances was practice in the behaviour of the species, whose habits had to be studied before it could be caught. At a later stage, owing to improvements in technique, this function was superseded by that of a magical rehearsal, in which, by mimicking in anticipation the successful operation of the quest for food, the clansmen evoked in themselves the collective and concerted energy requisite for the real task. Primitive magic is founded on the notion that, by creating the illusion that you control reality, you can actually control it. It is an illusory technique complementary to the deficiencies of the real technique. Owing to the low level of production, the subject is as yet imperfectly conscious of the objectivity of the external world, and consequently the performance of the preliminary rite appears as the cause of success in the real task; but at the same time, as a guide to action, magic embodies the valuable truth that the external world can in fact be changed by man's subjective attitude towards it. The huntsmen whose energies have been stimulated and organised by the mimetic rite are actually better huntsmen than they were before.

Each member of the clan has a strong sense of affinity or even identity with his totem species. The men who lived on wallabies, thriving when they thrived, starving when they starved, and dramatically impersonating them in order to control them, were literally flesh of their flesh and blood of their blood, and they expressed this distinctive relationship by saying that they *were* wallabies. Consequently, when the authority exercised by their oldest members was projected in the form of ancestor worship, the ancestors were worshipped in the form of wallabies.[7]

It may therefore be inferred that the first stage in the evolution of totemism was the segmentation of the primitive horde, which divided in order to gain access to the principal sources of food supply. So long as the new groups thus created lost touch with one another, the change was merely quantitative—two hordes instead of one; but at some stage, comparable to a biological mutation, this change became qualitative. Instead of continuing to obtain their food independently by simple appropriation, they became integrated as a complex of interdependent clans, each producing for the others; and this principle of co-operation, on which the whole structure of tribal society is founded, was maintained by means of a taboo on eating the totem species. Each unit became a totemic clan, whose function was to produce a supply of its own species for the other clans. How this interchange of products was effected will be discussed later.

As the technique of production improved and new sources of food became available, these initial restrictions disappeared. In this way, having lost its economic basis, totemism was transformed into an exclusively magico-religious system providing a sanction for the established structure of society. The hunting of wallabies being no longer a specialised technique, the function of the wallaby-men in relation to their totem species became purely magical—by performing the traditional ceremonies to make the wallabies increase and multiply for the benefit of the other clans.[8] Meanwhile, the ceremonies themselves were adapted and developed. From being representations of the activities of the totem species as such, they became commemorations of events in the life of the clan ancestors, still conceived in their totemic form, and so served to reinforce the social code by transmitting to the youth the traditional history of the clan. With the further decline of the clan as an economic unit, even this function disappeared. All that remained was a sense of kinship inspired by common descent, a distinctive ancestral cult, the practice of exogamy, and a purely formal taboo on eating a particular species of animal or plant. These are the characteristic features of the clan in the more advanced stages of tribal society, and they can all be traced in the records of ancient Greece.

Membership of the clan was determined by descent. The earlier anthropologists believed that descent was traced through the mother before it was traced through the father. This view has been rejected by most contemporary authorities, though not by all. I believe that it is essentially correct.

Many instances are recorded from modern tribes of transition from matrilineal to patrilineal descent, but none of the reverse process at all.[9] This in itself creates a presumption that the former is the earlier. Descent through the mother preponderates slightly in the hunting grades, but in the higher grades it declines, very rapidly in the pastoral, slowly in the agricultural.[10] This suggests that the mode of reckoning descent is correlated with the mode of production.

Each of these modes of production is marked by a distinctive division of labour between the sexes. In the pre-hunting stage there was no production, only simple appropriation of seeds, fruit and small animals, and therefore there can have been no division of labour at all. With the invention of the spear, however, hunting became the men's task, while the women continued the work of food-gathering.[11] This division is universal among hunting tribes, and it was doubtless dictated in the first instance by the relative immobility of mothers. Hunting led to the domestication of animals, and accordingly cattle-raising is normally men's work.[12] On the other hand, the work of food-gathering, maintained, as we have seen, by the women, led to the cultivation of seeds in the vicinity of the tribal settlement; and accordingly garden tillage is almost universally women's work. Finally, when garden tillage had given place to field tillage and the hoe to the cattle-drawn plough, the work of agriculture was transferred to the men. These ever-shifting tensions between the sexes correspond to the gradual transition from matrilineal to patrilineal descent. The process began with hunting—hence the rather high incidence of patrilineal descent among modern tribes whose progress has been arrested at that stage; it was intensified by the introduction of stock-raising, but in the first phase of agriculture it received a temporary check.

Among the hunting tribes of Australia, where the two modes of descent are almost equally balanced, the incidence of patrilineal descent increases in proportion to the complexity of the elaborate system of exogamy peculiar to that continent[13] —a system which has grown in some areas within living memory;[14] and, since the simple forms are more primitive than the complex, it seems to follow that descent through the mother is more primitive than descent through the father. Other evidence points in the same direction. Thus, in two widely separated tribes, of which we happen to have exceptionally full information, we find elaborate regulations requiring the married men to hand over either the whole or the best part of their catch to their wives' parents. Similar regulations are found in Melanesia, and they point to a state of society in which the men went to live with the clan to which their wives belonged— a matrilineal clan centred in the women.[15]

Another Australian tribe, the Yukumbil, has a tradition to the effect that formerly, when the men went hunting, they took their wives and children with them, but later they left the children behind in charge of an old woman.[16] This tradition is in accord with what has just been said about the sexual division of labour which followed from the development of hunting. When the first camp was formed, the immobility of the women and the prolonged absences of the men required that it should be in their charge. The clan was centred in the women, and the children belonged to the clan into which they were born.

I have argued that the evolution of the tribe, or group of exogamous clans, out of the primitive horde, which was, of course, endogamous,[17] was determined by the advance from simple appropriation to co-operative production, and that the economic interdependence of the clans in the new system was secured by the taboo on the totem species, which obliged each clan to hand over to the others a share of the food it obtained on its own hunting ground. It remains to consider why the clans were exogamous. Why did they not continue to inbreed like the parent-horde? To answer this question we must recapitulate our argument. We have seen reason to believe that each clan subsisted originally on a specialised diet; that the men lived with the clan into which they married, and were obliged to surrender their products to the members of that clan. Thus, the practice of getting husbands from other clans enabled each to extend its diet by obtaining access to foods which it did not produce itself. The initial function of exogamy was to circulate the food supply.

The tribe is a multicellular organism which was evolved out of the primitive horde on the basis of a division of labour conditioned by the low level of production, effected by the rule of exogamy and the totemic taboo, supplemented by mimetic magic, and projected ideologically in the form of zoomorphic ancestor worship.

The keystone of this system was co-operation. So long as the concerted efforts of the whole community were necessary to maintain it at the bare level of subsistence, it was impossible for a few to live on the labour of the many,[18] and the only social inequality was the prestige earned by individual merit. It is true that from an early period a privileged status was enjoyed by the oldest members, who, as the Greek proverb says, were weak in action, wise in counsel, but such privileges were dependent on the general consent.[19] These primitive communities were democratic to a degree that Greek society never was.

Among the lower hunting tribes, the institution of totemism, though it has moved far from its origin in the actual technique of production, is still a coherent system of practices and beliefs as definite and stable as the structure of the tribes themselves. It has grown up with the tribe, and with the tribe it declines. When, owing to economic changes that will be examined later, the structure of the tribe disintegrates, the idea that men and animals are kin decays, and the mimetic rite, with its wild cries, abandoned gestures, and ecstatic rhythm, dissolves into a multiplicity of collateral activities, out of which emerge the arts of poetry, music, and the dance.

The ancestor-worship characteristic of the early phases of tribal society is at once an expression and a confirmation of the authority exercised by the tribal elders. It is magical rather than religious. No prayers are addressed to the totem, only commands.[20] The worshippers simply impose their will on it by the compelling force of the ritual act, and this principle of compulsion corresponds to a condition of society in which the community is still supreme over each and all of its members. The more advanced forms of worship develop in response to the rise of a ruling class—hereditary magicians, priests, chiefs and kings. The totem is now tended with prayer and propitiation, it assumes human shape, and becomes a god. The god is to the community at large what the chief or king is to his subjects. The idea of godhead springs from the reality of kingship; but in the human consciousness, split as it now is by the cleavage in society, this relation is inverted. The king's power appears to be derived from God, and his authority is accepted as being the will of God. Thus, the reality is strengthened by the idea which has grown out of it. Each acts upon the other.

As the royal clan extends its rule, the totem gods of subordinate clans are annexed and absorbed into its own, which thus becomes the god of the tribe, or of the league of tribes, or eventually of the state.[21] Yet this new god still bears the marks of his origin. He is still regarded as incarnate, or capable of being incarnated, in his animal form, or the animal accompanies him as his traditional attendant, or myths are invented in which the clan ancestor is described as the son of the clan animal or of a woman who had lain with the clan god in his animal form. Religious symbolism is still permeated with reminiscences of the animal origin of the godhead.

With the development of tillage, the sky, as the source of rain, and the earth, as the receptacle of seeds, assume a new and universal importance, embracing the common interests of a whole area of tribes; yet even the new sky gods and earth goddesses that emerge out of these conditions usually betray some marks of a pre-anthropomorphic origin. The Greek Zeus is descended from the Indo-European sky god, and was probably anthropomorphic before the Greek-speaking peoples entered Greece; yet some of his characteristics point to a very primitive, perhaps original, association with the oak. Moreover, owing to the fusion of cultures brought about by migrations, federations, invasions and wars of conquest, it often happened that, even after he had become anthropomorphic, the god assimilated totemic elements from the more primitive strata with which he had been brought in contact. Thus, the Greek Zeus has a variety of origins. To the Achæan conquerors, he is a sky god with all the characteristics of a patriarchal pastoral monarch, but to the backward hill tribes of Arcadia he is Zeus Lykaios, almost certainly totemic, and to the people of Praisos in C·ete, who had a taboo on sow's flesh, it was a sow that gave him birth.[22]

It is therefore unfortunate that in studying the question of totemic survivals in Greek religion most scholars have confined their attention to the animal associations of the gods. The deities of the Greek pantheon are all the product of a long and complex process involving the fusion of tribes into peoples, the subjugation of one people by another, the propagation and aggregation of an unknown variety of cultures. In these conditions, to ask, as many have done, whether this or that god was originally Hellenic or pre-Hellenic, totemic or non-totemic, is to ask a question that has no meaning. The clearest evidence of totemism lies in a different direction.

Kreousa, the mother of Ion, belonged to the clan of the Erechtheidai.[23] When she exposed her child, she adorned it with a gold necklace fashioned in the likeness of a pair of snakes; and in doing this she was following the traditional custom of her clan. It is a common practice among primitive tribes to mark children with scars, tattoos, paint or ornaments representing the clan totem.[24] In this case the custom was explained as a tribute to the memory of the Erichthonios, who was the grandfather of Erechtheus. Erechtheus was said to have been a man with a snake's tail; and his grandfather, according to one tradition, had been guarded at birth by a pair of snakes, while in another he was himself born in the form of a snake. In other words, the emblem of the Erechtheidai was a snake, and their clan ancestor was a snake man. The snake was the totem of the clan. Another snake clan was the Spartoi of Thebes, sprung from the dragon slain by Kadmos; and on the tomb of Epameinondas was a shield emblazoned with the figure of a dragon in token of his membership of that clan.[25] The great Attic clans all had their traditional emblems, which they carried on their shields—the *triskelés* (swastika) of the Alkmaionidai, the horse of the Peisistratidai, the ox-head of the Eteoboutadai and others not yet identified.[26] The significance of the *triskelés* is unknown. The horse of the Peisistratidai is evidently to be connected with their descent from the horse-god Poseidon. The ox-head has been identified by its appearance on Attic coins just at the time when the faction of Lykourgos, who belonged to the Eteoboutadai, was at the height of its power. The Eteoboutadai claimed descent from Boutes the Oxherd, and they held the priesthood of the Diipolia, famous for its ritual slaughter of an ox, which is clearly derived from the communal feast of a totemic clan.[27] Another Attic clan, the Euneidai, who held the priesthood of Dionysos Melpomenos, traced their descent through Hypsipyle to Dionysus, the god of wine; and in one of their legends, when Hypsipyle was on the point of being put to death, she was saved by the unexpected appearance of her sons, who proved their identity by revealing the emblem of their clan, which was a golden vine. Finally, the Ioxidai of Lycia, descended from Theseus, were forbidden to burn asparagus, which they worshipped in memory of their ancestress Perigoune, who had sought refuge in a bed of asparagus when pursued by Theseus. The last example is perhaps the most remarkable. The taboo on the totem species has survived, and the species is still worshipped in its totemic form.

In pastoral society, cattle are used principally for milk, not for meat, and therefore the flesh of domestic animals,

especially female, is commonly tabooed.[28] The totemic taboo
has thus acquired a new economic function. Meanwhile, the
increase ceremony of the hunting period has been transformed
into the common meal at which the clansmen, together with
the spirits of their dead, reunite from time to time under the
presidency of their chief and partake sacramentally of meat
from their sacred herds. Here we see the germ of the Diipolia,
and also of the feasts of the Achæans described by Homer.
Nestor regales his people on the flesh of bulls, which he has
sacrificed to the tribal god, Poseidon.[29] Many centuries later, the
totemic sacrifice reappears in the ritual of the Orphic brotherhoods, in which, by eating the flesh and drinking the blood of
the bull Dionysus, men whom the class-struggle had humbled
and oppressed fed on the illusion of a lost equality.

We have seen that one function of the totemic rite had been
to transmit to the rising generation the traditions of the clan.
Year by year those who had reached puberty were initiated
into adult life by special ceremonies designed to instruct them
in the social code, as expressed in sexual and dietary taboos,
and to impress them with a sense of the inviolability of tribal
custom as expounded by the elders.[30] The significance of this
crucial change—at once physical, mental and social—was
expressed in the idea, which underlies all such ceremonies, that
in becoming man or woman the child was born again.

Initiation was followed by marriage. It is probable that in
the earliest period of tribal society the only restrictions on the
mating of the sexes were those imposed by the rule of exogamy;
and it is also possible that, in the stage of food-gathering, sexual
intercourse was confined to the productive seasons of the year.[31]
The significance of these yearly marriages was enhanced by the
subjective attitude of the partners, who saw in them the effi-
cient cause of the seasonal process of which they were a part—
they were performed as mimetic acts of ritual designed to
promote the fertility of Nature; and at a later period, when the
relations of the sexes had become monogamous, this magical
function persisted in the ceremonial union or sacred marriage
of a selected pair.

So long as they have pasture, cattle feed and breed of
themselves, but by comparison with cattle-raising the work of

CA

tilling, sowing and reaping is slow, arduous and uncertain. It requires patience, foresight, faith. Accordingly, agricultural society is characterised by the extensive development of magic. The clan structure survives as a pattern for the formation of secret sodalities,[32] out of which arise organised priesthoods and eventually a god-king with the special function of promoting by mimetic magic the annual sequence from seedtime to harvest.[33] His office begins by being annual, and he is consecrated by a coronation rite, based on the rites of initiation, which signifies that he is born again, no longer man, but god. In a series of ritual acts he has intercourse with a priestess, marks out the soil for distribution among the clans, turns the first sod with his sacred hoe, cuts the first ear of corn with his sacred sickle and, finally, at harvest he is put to death, to be replaced at the new year by a successor of unimpaired vitality. This elaborate system of agricultural magic was understood to mean that the fertility of the soil and the prosperity of the people depended on the physical vigour of the king, but objectively it was the magical manifestation of the high degree of centralised control without which organised agriculture would have been impossible. That is its positive side, but it has also a negative aspect in that magic, which began as an aid to real technique, is now becoming an obstruction.

The ritual of the god-king can be clearly traced in ancient Egypt and Babylonia, and also to some extent in Greece—for example, in the sacred marriage and ritual ploughing at Eleusis. It is probable therefore that some of the pre-Achæan monarchies, such as that of the Attic Kekrops, were of this agrarian and hieratic type.

These questions will be resumed after we have considered more closely the tribal institutions of early Greece and the causes which led to their decline.

EXOGAMY

THE Indo-European languages are derived from the speech of a people which occupied some part of the Eurasian plain between the Baltic and the Caspian in the latter part of the third millennium B.C. The first appearance of Greek-speaking tribes in the Ægean basin has been provisionally dated about 1800 B.C.[1] At the end of the third millennium, the original people had broken up, migrating south, east and west, and the parent speech split into derivative languages, from which are descended the Indo-European languages actually surviving or preserved in written records.

Attempts to identify the original people by the evidence of archæological remains are at present too conjectural to build on,[2] but we can draw certain conclusions about their culture from a comparative analysis of the linguistic data. This evidence suggests that, at the time of their dispersal, the primitive Indo-Europeans were a predominantly pastoral people with some knowledge of agriculture; that they were organised in clans and perhaps also in village settlements under some form of chieftaincy or kingship; that descent was reckoned in the male line, and that the women went to live with the clan into which they married. Thus, speaking in terms of the classification adopted in the last chapter, we may assign them to the Second Pastoral Grade. Further light is shed on their social history by a study of their terms of kinship.

In primitive languages all over the world terms of relationship are used in a way which to us is very strange. When I speak of my father, I refer to the man who begot me; but, when a primitive tribesman speaks of his father, he may be referring to his father's brother. His terminology does not distinguish between the two. With us, the term father denotes a physiological relationship determined by parenthood; in the primitive tribe it denotes a collective social relationship. And so with

THE CLASSIFICATORY SYSTEM OF RELATIONSHIP

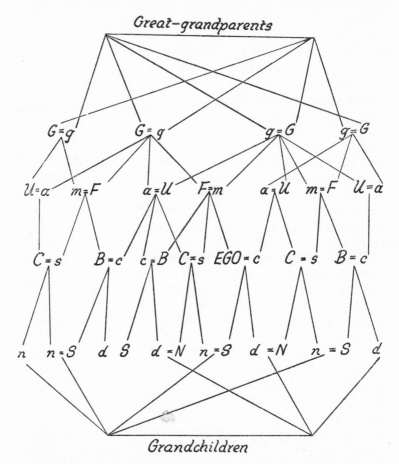

G grandfather, g grandmother, U uncle and father-in-law, a aunt and mother-in-law, F father, m mother, C male cousin, c female cousin, B brother, s sister, N nephew, n niece, S son, d daughter. EGO is a man. With EGO as a woman, the brother's children are nephew and niece and the sister's are son and daughter.

the other terms. This is what is called the classificatory system.[3] Its details vary among different peoples, but it is everywhere based on the same principle, which may be briefly explained as follows.

The term for "father" is applied not only to the actual father, but to the father's brothers, to the father's father's brothers' sons, to the father's father's father's brother's sons' sons, and so on. The term for "mother" is applied to the actual mother, to the mother's sisters, to the mother's mother's sisters' daughters, and so on. The terms for "brother" and "sister" are applied to the children of all those who are called "fathers" and "mothers."

On the other hand, while my father's brothers are my "fathers," my mother's brothers are denoted by a different term, which may be translated "uncle." The same term is applied to my father's mother's brothers' sons, and so on. Similarly, while my mother's sisters are my "mothers," my father's sisters are my "aunts," and the same term is applied to my mother's father's sisters' daughters, and so on.

The children of my father's brothers and of my mother's sisters are my "brothers" and "sisters," but the children of my father's sisters and mother's brothers are denoted by terms which in the most primitive types of the system are identical with the terms for "brother-in-law" and "wife," if I am a man, or for "husband" and "sister-in-law," if I am a woman. In the accompanying diagram these terms are translated male and female "cousin." Similarly, if I am a man, my brother's children are my "sons" and "daughters," but my sister's children are my "nephews" and "nieces"; and, conversely, if I am a woman, my brother's children are my "nephews" and "nieces," while my sister's children are my "sons" and "daughters." Lastly, my father-in-law is denoted by the same term as my mother's brother, and my mother-in-law by the same term as my father's sister.

This terminology is clearly designed to express the relationships characteristic of a community divided into two exogamous and intermarrying groups. My father and his brothers and sisters belong to Group A; my mother and her brothers and sisters belong to Group B. My father's brothers are married to my mother's sisters, my father's sisters to my mother's brothers. With patrilineal descent, I belong to Group A; with matrilineal descent, to Group B. In either case, in my own generation, the members of my group are my "brothers" and "sisters," while those of the other group are my male and female "cousins." The generation below my own is divided in the same way between my "sons" and "daughters," on the one hand, and my "nephews" and "nieces," on the other. Lastly, my father-in-law is denoted by the same term as my mother's brother because he *is* my mother's brother; my mother-in-law is denoted by the same term as my father's sister because she *is* my father's sister. In many parts of the world the marriage system connoted by this terminology still survives. Where it does not, its former existence is proved by the survival of the terminology designed to express it.

The same reasoning suffices to explain the classificatory principle itself. A man applies to his wife's sisters the same term as he applies to his wife, and a woman applies to her husband's brothers the same term as she applies to him. Her sisters are not his wives, nor are his brothers her husbands; yet he calls her sisters "wives," and she calls his brothers "husbands." The nomenclature does not correspond to the reality. Accordingly, it was inferred by Morgan, who discovered the classificatory system, that this nomenclature is a survival from a previous condition in which it did correspond to the reality—a society in which, in each generation, the brothers of each group were mated collectively to the sisters of the other. On that assumption, the whole system explains itself. If each brother is husband to each sister, the offspring of this collective union will be the children of all: each man will stand to the children in the relation of father, each woman in the relation of mother. It will be seen that in such conditions the terminology does not express consanguinity as such but social relationships as determined by marriage.

Morgan's theory of the classificatory system was accepted in principle by Howitt, Rivers, Spencer and Gillen, but at the present day it is rejected by most authorities in western Europe and America.[4] The principal objections urged against it are discussed in Appendix I. They all come from empiricists who have not felt the need of defining their philosophical stand-point. The theory has been reasserted by the anthropologists of the Soviet Union, who maintain that it has only been abandoned elsewhere because its implications are incompatible with the bourgeois attitude to contemporary society. Morgan's readers will remember that his argument led him to a remarkable prediction of the socialist revolution.

The opposition to Morgan on this issue has been strengthened by the assumption, which, despite some remarks of his own,[5] has passed without question, that there is no trace of the classificatory system in the Indo-European group of languages. So far from this assumption being correct, the Indo-European terminology, including some well-known anomalies hitherto unsolved, is completely and coherently explained on the hypothesis that it is derived from the classificatory system. The evidence will be found in Appendix II. This conclusion is of considerable importance for the cultural history of the Indo-European-speaking peoples, because it shows that their tribal institutions were of the same character as those of other branches of the human race.

It was argued in the last chapter that the first stage in the evolution of the tribe was the segmentation of the primitive horde into two exogamous units. This is the stage reflected in the classificatory system. The subsequent stages varied in different parts of the world. In parts of Melanesia, India, and America the tribe consists of so many phratries and each phratry of so many clans. As Morgan showed, the phratry, in North America at least, is a group of interrelated clans created by the segmentation of a single original clan. At present the exogamous unit is the clan, but there is reason to believe that it was formerly the phratry.[6]

The Indo-European tribal system belonged to the same type. Among the Greeks, the tribe, phratry and clan are represented by the *phylé*, *phratría*, and *génos*; among the Romans by the *tribus*, *curia*, and *gens*.[7] The Dorian Greeks were divided into three tribes, the Ionians into four. The subdivisions of the Dorian tribes have not yet been precisely determined, but each of the four Ionian tribes was composed of so many phratries and each phratry of so many clans. Moreover, it appears that among the Greeks, as among the North American Indians, the phratry was originally exogamous. The evidence for this conclusion lies in the special Greek usage of the primitive Indo-European term for brother.

The Greek *phráter*, derived from the Indo-European **bhrātēr*, which in the other languages yielded the term for "brother," denoted not a brother but a fellow-member of the phratry. At Athens, when a boy came of age, he was formally admitted to his father's phratry at the feast of the Apatouria, which means the feast of men "of the same fathers."[8] In what sense were the *phráteres* "brothers" and sons "of the same fathers"? At Sparta, where the boys were organised in sodalities called *agélai*, the term *kásios*, which is a variant of *kásis*, "brother," was applied to all the brothers and male cousins in the same *agéla*, and another variant of the same word, *káses*, was used at Sparta to denote a man "of one's own generation." The Ionian *phráteres* and the Dorian *kásioi* were originally, in each generation, the sons of the same father, the sons of the father's brothers, the sons of the father's father's brother's sons, and so on. They were brothers in the classificatory sense. The greater part of this conclusion was reached by Kretschmer, working solely on the internal evidence without reference to the classificatory system.[9]

The Greek phratry was based on patrilineal descent. So, too, as we have just remarked, was the society of the Indo-European people at the time of its dispersal. Moreover, the ideal society of the Homeric Olympus, which was modelled, as we shall see later, on the real world, was strongly patriarchal. But there is another side to this picture, which we must now proceed to examine.

In the historical period, the people of Lycia were still matrilineal, both in succession and descent, and this feature of Lycian society is reflected in the tradition of Bellerophon, who migrated from Argos to Lycia, where he married the king's daughter and at the same time succeeded to a share in the kingdom. This form of succession, in which royal privilege is held by right of marriage, is remarkably common in the Greek genealogies. Thus, we are told that Temenos, one of the leaders of the invading Dorians, announced his intention of leaving his kingdom to Deiphontes, who had married his daughter Hyrnetho. He was then murdered by his own sons, but the people insisted on giving the kingdom to Deiphontes. This tradition plainly embodies a conflict between matrilineal and patrilineal succession. Equally significant is the myth of the Calydonian hunt. When Meleager handed over the boar to Atalanta, his mother's brothers took it from her on the ground that, if he relinquished it, it belonged to them "by right of birth." Meleager belonged to his mother's clan, which insisted on the booty he had acquired remaining in it. Further, in an Attic tradition we are expressly told that before the reign of King Kekrops women had enjoyed equal rights with men, there had been no marriage and children had been named after the mother.[10]

The people of Lycia had close traditional connections with the pre-Dorian peoples of Crete. It is clear from the archæological remains of Minoan Crete and Mycenæ that the women of this period enjoyed a social status far superior to their position in historical Greece.[11] Moreover, Minoan theology differed profoundly from the Homeric. The gods of Homer are entirely anthropomorphic; the Minoan are largely animal. The Homeric Olympus is ruled by Zeus and Hera, the monogamous pair, with the male as the dominant partner. The principal cult of Minoan society was the worship of a mother goddess, with a subordinate male partner, her son or her consort or both. For these reasons it is now generally agreed that the institutions of Minoan society were, to an extent not yet precisely defined, matrilineal.

This contrast between the Homeric tradition and the realities that lay behind it is very striking, and it is not the only one. For reasons which will appear in a later chapter, such fundamental institutions of primitive society as the tribe, the clan, initiation, which are clearly traceable in Greece both before and after Homer, are hardly mentioned in the Homeric poems. Therefore, when Homer presents us with Zeus and Hera as husband and wife, we shall do well to remember the remark of Herodotus, that it was Homer and Hesiod who made the Greek theogony. As Cook has shown, the Homeric view of Zeus and Hera is a reconstruction of two earlier traditions in which these partners were entirely unrelated.[12] In the one, the consorts were Hera and Herakles, with the goddess as the dominant partner; in the other they were Zeus and Dione, with the god as the dominant partner. The first pair is Minoan, the second Indo-European. Zeus and Dione are both Greek in name, and their joint worship can be traced to Dodona, the district which according to Aristotle, was the original home of the Hellenes.[13] The fusion of peoples resulting from the Indo-European immigration was symbolised in the union of the immigrant father god with the indigenous mother goddess, the precedence given to the former marking the decline in the status of women.

It is, of course, true that the interpretation of mythological data is often uncertain, but fortunately the present case does not rest on mythology alone. It is supported by evidence of a peculiarly precise and rigorous kind, which places the main conclusion beyond question.

The I.E. *bhrātēr, "brother," has survived in that sense in all the derivative languages except Greek and Hittite; and similarly the I.E. *su̯esōr, "sister," has survived in all except Greek and Modern Albanian. These three languages are all known to have been deeply affected by non-Indo-European speech—Hittite by Sumerian and Akkadian, Albanian by Turkish, Greek by the pre-Greek languages of the Ægean basin. The Greek derivatives of I.E. *bhrātēr and *su̯esōr are phráter and éor. The first of these is used, as we have seen, to denote a fellow-member of the phratry; the second survives only in a gloss of Hesychios.[14] The Greek for brother and sister is adelphós and adelphé, properly phráter ádelphos and éor ádelphos, a brother or sister "of the same womb" as opposed to (phráter —éor) ópatros, a brother or sister "by the same father." In Homeric Greek we also find kasígnetos and kasignéte, used in such a way as to indicate that they too originally connoted relationship through the mother. This evidence, which was collected by Kretschmer, is decisive.[15] After their entry into the Ægean, the Greek-speaking peoples adopted matrilineal descent, and the new significance of phráter and éor was indicated by the use of descriptive epithets, which eventually supplanted them. They retained, however, the patrilineal organisation of the phratry, and in that connection the term *phráter* survived. The women had no organisation corresponding to the phratry, and consequently the term *éor* disappeared. The linguistic data are completely explained on this hypothesis, and on any other they are unintelligible.

Some archæologists, while recognising this distinction between the Indo-European and non-Indo-European peoples of the Ægean, have tended to assume that its significance was primarily racial.[16] This is a misapprehension. The patrilineal institutions of the primitive Indo-Europeans are explained by their mode of production, which was predominantly pastoral. It has already been pointed out that pastoral society is characterised by a marked tendency towards patrilineal descent. Moreover, at a later stage of our enquiry we shall find reason to believe that, at a still earlier period, Indo-European society had been matrilineal. In the same way, the subsequent decline of mother-right in Greece is not a matter of race, but belongs to the common history of the whole population.

It is characteristic of hunting tribes that the huntsman does not appropriate his catch, but brings it home to be distributed.[17] So long as the technique of hunting was too low to permit of individual production, consumption as well as production was necessarily collective.[18] But when men began to hunt singly, there arose a contradiction between the mode of production, which was now individual, and the mode of consumption, which was still collective; and in this contradiction lay the germ of private property. Similarly, a man tended to claim what he had acquired with his own hands for himself and his immediate relatives, and in this claim lay the germ of the individual family.[19] But it was a long time before these disruptive tendencies became strong enough to disturb the outward structure of society. Their first effect was to intensify clan co-operation, which was extended in every direction, covering the whole field of social life.[20] Clan was bound to clan by an elaborate system of reciprocal services, out of which arose a spirit of constructive rivalry, each vying with the others for prestige. The man who had acquired a surplus of game or plunder signalised his success by inviting another clan to feast with his own. Such an invitation was also a challenge, because it imposed on the clan that accepted it a moral obligation to return it, if possible with interest. Failure to do so meant loss of prestige. At a later stage, if the obligation was not returned, it might be commuted into some form of labour service. The clans were no longer equal. Co-operation had been transformed into competition.

In parts of North America, these tendencies have developed into the system known as "potlatch." They can be clearly traced in Chinese tradition, and more faintly in the exchange of gifts which is a feature of the Homeric poems. When Glaukos exchanged shields with Diomedes, gold for bronze, Homer can only explain it by saying that Glaukos lost his head; but it is more likely that Glaukos was expecting a return such as Mentes promised Telemachos after being presented with an heirloom. It is easy to see how these hospitable exchanges might develop into barter.[21]

The growth of private ownership derived a powerful impetus from the domestication of cattle. Game is perishable and land is immovable, but wealth in the form of cattle is durable and easy to steal or to exchange.[22] Being necessarily nomadic, pastoral tribes are quick to increase their wealth by cattle raids and war; and since warfare, which had grown out of hunting, was waged by the men, it reinforced the tendency, already inherent in pastoral society, for wealth to accumulate in their hands. Constantly on the move, these turbulent tribes plunder one district after another. The male captives are killed, the women are carried off as chattels, their skill at the lqom being measured in terms of cattle. But warfare requires unity of leadership, and consequently these tribes develop a type of kingship which is primarily not magical, but military. In reward for their successful leadership, the kings receive the lion's share of the spoils, and the wealth thus amassed promotes social inequalities which shake the whole fabric of tribal society, beginning at the top. The details of this process will be studied in the next chapter. At present we are concerned with its effect on the rules of inheritance.

The Jewish tribes which eventually settled in the land of Canaan were a pastoral people of this character. As Robertson Smith has shown, it is probable that the Semitic stock was originally matrilineal, but when the Jews took to agriculture they were already strongly patriarchal. All property, real and personal, was transmitted in the male line. The land was inalienable; the acquired goods were distributed among the sons.[23] But what happened if a man had no sons? In the Book of Numbers (xxvii. 8) we read: "If a man die, and have no son, then ye shall cause his inheritance to pass unto his daughter." This meant that the usufruct passed to the man she married, who, of course, would belong to another clan. Accordingly it was enacted (xxxvi. 8): "And every daughter that possesseth an inheritance in any tribe of the children of Israel, shall be wife unto one of the family of the tribe of her father, that the children of Israel may enjoy every man the inheritance of his fathers." The word which in the English version is translated "family" means properly a clan.[24] The heiress was compelled to marry into her own clan. Only in that way could the property be retained in the male line. The principle of exogamy, on which the structure of the tribal system depends, and with it the liberty of the woman, have been sacrificed to the interests of private property.

In Greece this process was slower to develop, because, as we have seen, the tendency to father-right had been temporarily reversed, but it is at least possible that the breakdown of exogamy had begun among the ruling families before the Dorian conquest. A remarkable feature of the pre-Dorian genealogies is the large number of instances in which a man marries the daughter of his brother or father's brother;[25] but, since the historical value of these genealogies is open to question, it is better not to rely on them. Clearer evidence of the explosive effects of the new wealth derived from the plunder of Minoan Greece is provided by traditions of the same period relating to homicide within the kin.

Tribal society recognises two major crimes—incest and witchcraft.[26] Incest is violation of the rules of exogamy; witchcraft is the misapplication for individual ends of magic, which was designed for the service of the community. Manslaughter between clans is common, but it is not a crime—that is to say, it is not punished by the community at large but settled by the clans to which the individuals concerned belong. The manner of its settlement is a matter of some importance.

When a man has been killed, his fellow clansmen must avenge him. The obligation is instantaneous and absolute. It is entirely irrespective of the circumstances of the case. The clan to which the victim belonged apply to the clan of the offender for compensation. If suitable compensation is granted, the affair is at an end. If not, the victim's clansmen seek out the offender and kill him; or, if they cannot kill him, they kill another member of his clan. In the latter case, the other clan is now placed under the same obligation, and so there arises a vendetta, which may last for generations.[27]

These laws can be studied in detail among the higher hunting and agricultural tribes of North America; they can also be traced among the primitive Germanic tribes and among the Greeks. In Attic law, the terms for "prosecution" and "defence" mean properly to pursue and to flee,[28] and even in the historical period prosecution for homicide was left to the initiative of the victim's kinsmen.[29] In the Homeric poems, the manslayer has the alternatives of paying compensation or leaving the country. Compensation is given in movable goods, though the mythological evidence suggests that in earlier times it had also taken the form of labour service.[30]

But what happened when a man killed a fellow clansman? So long as the clan was based on collective ownership, compensation was impossible, but at the same time one of the principal causes of crime was absent, and therefore homicide within the clan was extremely rare. In Greece, however, during the period we are considering, as among the Germans in the last period of the Roman Empire, it became common. Enriched by wars of conquest, the ruling families embroiled themselves in internecine struggles of succession and inheritance.[31]

The clan owed its solidarity to the fact that, so long as the technique of production was too low for the individual to be self-sufficient, he could only exist as a member of a co-operative group. Throughout the history of tribal society, clan kinship is of all ties the most sacred. The horror excited by homicide within the clan is well described by Grönbech, writing of the primitive Norsemen. After explaining that homicide between clans is "not a crime against life itself, not even to be reckoned as anything unnatural," he goes on:

On the other hand, from the moment we enter into the
clan, the sacredness of life rises up in absolute inviolability,
with its judgment upon bloodshed as sacrilege, blindness,
suicide. The reaction comes as suddenly and unmistakably
as when a nerve is touched by a needle.[32]

Among the Norsemen, the man who had killed a fellow
clansman was cursed and cast out of the clan. He became an
outlaw. Unless, as sometimes happened, he was adopted into
another clan, he ceased to exist as a member of society.[33] Cut
off from the clan, in which alone he had had his being, he went
mad and died of starvation. So in Greece. The man who had
killed a fellow clansman was hounded out of the community,
pursued by the curses of his kinsfolk, or, as they expressed it,
by his victim's avenging spirits, the Erinyes or Arai, who
drove him mad and sucked his blood until he was nothing but
a heap of bones.[34]

These Erinyes were conceived of as snakes. In Greece, as
elsewhere, the snake became a generalised symbol for the
spirits of the dead—the reason being doubtless that the snake
casts its slough and so appears to renew its life. In the legend of
Œdipus, as treated by the Attic poets, the Erinys embodies the
curse inherited from Laios by his son and his son's sons. In
Pindar the sons of Œdipus are destroyed by the Erinys in retribution for their father's parricide. That was the Dorian
tradition, being recorded as such by Herodotus. In the *Odyssey*,
however, the Erinys that persecuted Œdipus was his mother's,
and in other legends the function of the Erinyes is to avenge
the manslaughter of a kinsman in the female line. Thus, they
were invoked by Althaia against her son Meleager, who had
murdered her brother; they persecuted Alkmaion for the
murder of his mother, Eriphyle, and Orestes for the murder of
Clytemnestra.[35] The Erinyes were the ancestral spirits of a
community which traced descent through the mother, and
their prominence in these traditions of the Mycenean Age
reflects the dynastic conflicts precipitated in the ruling class
of a matrilineal society by the rapid growth of property.

The word *erinýs* is probably not Indo-European, and there
are other indications pointing to an Ægean origin. In the

Homeric poems, and again in the mystical tradition of Eleusis, the Erinyes appear also as punishers of perjury.[36] The crime of perjury presupposes the ordeal by oath, which, as Diamond has shown, marks an advanced stage in the development of law. It does not appear until the growing interests of property and trade have prompted the publication of a written code—as, for example, in the Hittite Code, and even there it is only employed in default of independent evidence. Now, in the Code of the Cretan city of Gortyna, the ordeal by oath is prescribed more extensively than in any other ancient code before the development of what Diamond defines as mature law. Moreover, in the Greek tradition the institution of this ordeal was ascribed to the Cretan lawgiver, Rhadamanthys.[37] There is no difficulty in supposing that the legal system of Minoan Crete, which left a deep impression on the folk memory of the Greeks, had advanced to this point, but the high development of law at Gortyna, which was not a great commercial city, is an apparent anomaly that requires to be explained. The explanation seems to be that Minoan culture was in part absorbed by the Greek-speaking conquerors of Crete.

It may be concluded therefore that the Indo-European immigrants into the Ægean took over the cult of the Erinyes when they adopted matrilineal descent. At the same time, as we shall see in the next chapter, they were not without ancestral spirits of their own.

III

PROPERTY

WHEN the Homeric chieftain counts his possessions, he enumerates his household goods, his slaves, and his livestock, but he does not mention the pastures on which his cattle graze, and it is at least doubtful whether he regards even the land he cultivates as his own, except where it is a gift from his people. That so many modern readers have failed to appreciate this fact is due to the influence of an environment in which private property has come to be regarded as a self-evident and unchallengeable right. Yet, even in England, it is little more than a century since the peasants were driven by the Enclosure Acts from the last of the common fields, and in the Middle Ages, before the first enclosures, there was no private ownership of land as we understand it.[1]

Nilsson maintains that the Homeric similes belong to the latest stratum in the evolution of the poems.[2] In one of these, two men are described, with measures in their hands, dividing equally a piece of common ploughland.[3] Modern commentators have been at pains to reconcile this passage with their preconceptions by interpreting it to mean that two brothers are dividing their father's estate; but the men are not described as brothers, and, if the land had been their father's estate, it would not have been described as common.[4] The natural interpretation of the words is that the land is being divided for use, not for ownership, and this accords with a recognised feature of primitive land tenure in other parts of Europe and elsewhere. With the notable exception of Ridgeway, modern scholars have failed to see that the Homeric evidence on this subject can only be understood in the light of a comparative analysis of land tenure in primitive society generally. This is one of the urgent tasks awaiting the attention of archæologists, and, of course, it is far too complex to be attempted here. There is, however, an alternative approach. If it is true that men's ideas about the world are ultimately conditioned by their economic relations, it should be possible to discover something about those relations by examining the ideas in which they are reflected.

The three Fates—*Moîrai* in Greek, *Parcæ* in Latin, *Nornen* in German—are still part of the common stock of the European literary tradition. They are the goddesses who sit and spin the thread of human destiny, ordaining for each man at birth the principal events of his life, and especially the last of all—his death. The present chapter will be devoted to an analysis of this conception.

The basic meaning of the word *moîra* is a share or portion. As John the Deacon remarked in his commentary on Hesiod, the Moirai (goddesses of Fate) are "dispensations" or "divisions."[5] With *moîra* is associated another word, *láchos*, a portion given or received by the process of casting lots. One of the Moirai bore the name of Lachesis, the goddess of Allotment. In this sense *láchos* is synonymous with *klêros*, which, commonly used of a lot or holding of land, originally denoted a piece of wood used for casting lots.[6]

The Attic clan of the Gephyraioi was descended from a branch of the stock of Kadmos which had settled in Boiotia, where "it was allotted the portion of Tanagra."[7] Whether this expression is intended literally is more than we can say; but we know that elsewhere it has been customary for immigrant tribes to cast lots for the occupied territory. It will be remembered how the tribes of Israel occupied the Promised Land:

> Speak unto the children of Israel and say unto them, When ye are passed over Jordan into the land of Canaan, then ye shall drive out all the inhabitants of the land from before you. . . . And ye shall dispossess the inhabitants of the land and dwell therein; for I have given you the land to possess it. And ye shall divide the land by lot for an inheritance among your families; and to the more ye shall give the more inheritance, and to the fewer ye shall give the less inheritance: every man's inheritance shall be in the place where his lot falleth; according to the tribes of your fathers ye shall inherit (Num. xxxiii. 51–4).

And Joshua said unto the children of Israel, How long are

ye slack to go to possess the land which the Lord God of your
fathers hath given you? Give out from among you three men
from each tribe: and I will send them, and they shall rise
and go through the land, and describe it according to the
inheritance of them; and they shall come again to me. . . .
Ye shall therefore describe the land into seven parts, and
bring the description hither to me, that I may cast lots for
you here before the Lord our God (Joshua xviii. 3–6).

The land was to be distributed by lot among the tribes, and
the territory of each tribe was to be subdivided by lot among
the "families" or clans.[8]

In the seventh Olympian, Pindar relates how the island
of Rhodes was divided into three *moîrai* by the sons of Helios.
That these three *moîrai* correspond to the three immigrant
tribes is clear from the Homeric version of the same tradition.[9]
That they were distributed by lot is not expressly stated, but
it may be inferred from the myth, which Pindar relates in the
same poem, of the origin of the island. When the Olympian
gods cast lots for the newly-conquered world, Helios was
absent and so left without a *klêros*.[10] The omission was
rectified by assigning to him the island of Rhodes, then
beneath the sea, which he had already descried rising to the
surface, and this arrangement was ratified by an appeal to
Lachesis.[11]

The same myth, though without mention of Helios and
Rhodes, is related in the *Iliad*.[12] The sons of Kronos divided
the world into three *moîrai*, for which they cast lots, and Zeus
was warned by Poseidon that he must keep within his *moîra*.
Similarly, we are told by Hesiod that Hekate received from
Zeus a *moîra* of land and sea, retaining in perpetuity the share
allotted to her at the time of the original division or *dasmós*.[13]

The evidence of mythology is supported by historical tradition. After their conquest of the Peloponnese, the Dorian
chieftains divided the country into three portions, for which
they cast lots.[14] It is probable therefore that the portion of
Tanagra was allotted to the descendants of Kadmos in the
same way.

In the *Odyssey*, when King Nausithoos led the Phæacians
to their new home, he "divided the ploughlands."[15] According

to Herodotus, the people of Kyrene invited settlers from Greece to participate in a "re-division of the land."[16] Some time later the territory of Kyrene was again divided by an arbitrator from Arcadia, who divided the land into three *moîrai* and the inhabitants into three tribes. These tribes were artificial units created for the purpose of dividing the land. Even after its basis in kinship had crumbled away, the tribal system still seemed the necessary foundation for any form of ordered society. Thus, when the dispossessed Attic peasants of the time of Solon demanded a re-division of the land,[17] their demand was an appeal to ancient tribal practice; and similarly the Athenian institution of the *klerouchía*, in which conquered territory was divided among settlers from Athens, marked the persistence, in new conditions, of the tribal conception of land settlement.

Besides dividing the ploughlands, King Nausithoos "made temples." Besides distributing the land among the tribes, the arbitrator of Kyrene reserved certain estates for the king as chief priest of the community; and the Athenians assigned similar reservations to the priesthood in their settlement of Lesbos.[18] These reservations, or *teméne*, were estates "set apart" for the use of priests, chiefs and kings.[19]

The Homeric evidence shows clearly that, while power or privilege was in the gift of the king, land was in the gift of the people, who bestowed on their leaders, in reward for military service, estates which differed from the others in that they were not assigned by lot to tribe or clan, but by special gift to an individual.[20] Thus, Bellerophon was rewarded by the King of Lycia with royal honours, while the people bestowed on him a *témenos* of the best arable land. Æneas was warned by Achilles, whom he had come to fight, that, even if he should win, he could not hope for royal honours from Priam, who had sons of his own to provide for, nor for a *témenos* from the people. In the same way, the elders of Aitolia (presumably the chiefs of the clans) tried to induce Meleager to fight for them by offering him a *témenos* of the most fertile land in the country. Appropriation of the land cannot have proceeded far in a community in which the most fertile part of it could be bestowed by common consent on an individual. The Homeric *témenos* represents the germ of private property in land developing within a collective tribal system.

Booty was distributed in the same way.[21] Just as the island of Rhodes, allotted to Helios, is described by Pindar as his *láchos* or *géras*, his lot or his privilege, so the same terms—*moîra* or *láchos*, *géras* or *timé*—are applied to the share of the spoils allotted to each warrior. The process of distribution is called, as before, a *dasmós*; and just as the king received a *témenos* which was "set apart" for him, so in the distribution of booty he received a "chosen gift" reserved from the general allotment.[22] And here, too, the ultimate authority seems to have been vested in the people. "How can the Achæans give you a *géras*?" Achilles cries to Agamemnon, who has demanded a substitute for Chryseis. "The spoils we have taken have already been divided, and it would not be right for the people to bring them together again."[23] Nevertheless, it appears that the king was in a position to assign other shares to his vassals, and he is sometimes accused of keeping more than his share to himself.[24] He is beginning to claim as a right what was properly a gift from his people. The same ambiguity appears in respect of the kingship itself. Once assigned to a particular family, it tended to become hereditary, because military leadership is a specialised occupation, but it was still subject to popular ratification. Telemachos hoped to succeed to his father's kingdom, but all he claimed as his right was the inheritance of his personal property. When the sons of Temenos murdered their father in order to keep the kingship in the family, the people restored it to Deiphontes.[25]

In the year 484 B.C. the Athenian people proposed to distribute a surplus from the silver mines among the whole citizen body, but Themistokles persuaded them to devote it to the construction of a fleet instead.[26] The collective distribution characteristic of tribal society had become incompatible with the interests of the state. It is an illuminating incident, because it shows how tenaciously the common people had clung to the primitive conception of property.

As it was with land and booty, so it was with food. In ancient times, so Plutarch writes, when meals were administered by Moira or Lachesis on the principle of equality, everything was

decently and liberally arranged; and in support of this contention he points out that the old word for a meal meant properly a division.[27] His etymology is correct: *daís* is cognate
with *dasmós*. The *moîrai* of meat were divided equally and distributed originally by lot;[28] but the chine, which was the choicest
portion, was reserved as a *géras* for the chief who presided at
the meal. When Menelaos invited his guests to sit down to
table at Sparta, he handed to them the chine which the attendants had set before him. The swineherd Eumaios paid the
same compliment to the disguised Odysseus—a dramatic touch,
because he gave his lord the lordly portion without knowing
who he was.[29]

Plutarch goes on to remark that the equality of the common
meal was destroyed in course of time by the growth of luxury
(he should, rather, have said the growth of property) but persisted in the public distribution of meat at state sacrifices.[30]
These state sacrifices, on which vast sums were spent under
the Athenian democracy, served an economic need, because
they provided the lower classes with their only opportunity of
eating roast meat; and the principle on which they rested—
that the citizens met to share food with their god—shows that
they were derived from the communal feast of the primitive
clan.[31]

Lastly, the conditions on which the king or chief enjoyed
all these privileges are stated in a famous passage of the *Iliad*:[32]
"Why have the people of Lycia conferred on us the highest
honours—pride of place and precedence in food and drink?
They regard us as gods, and they have bestowed on us a
témenos of rich ploughland. Therefore we must be foremost in
the fray, that the people may say, These kings of ours, who
feed on our fat herds and quaff our choicest wine, can fight."
Royal honours were the gift of the people granted in recognition of military service.[33]

After the democratic revolution, the use of the lot became
an integral element in the administration of the Athenian state,
and Greek writers are unanimous in regarding it as a distinctive
characteristic of a democratic constitution.[34] It may therefore
be added to those other elements in ancient democracy which
we have already traced back to a tribal origin. The truth is

that ancient democracy was essentially the reassertion by the common people of their lost equality.[35]

All the key-words we have been considering—*moîra, klêros, láchos, dasmós*—reappear in the terminology of the Greek laws of inheritance.[36] The property that a man inherits from his father is his *klêros*, or in poetry his *moîra*. In earlier times, the father had divided his property among his sons before he died, and we learn from a passage in the *Odyssey* that this *dasmós* had been effected by lot. In Attic law, the property was inherited by the sons; in default of sons, by the daughters; in default of children, by the brothers; in default of any close relative, by the fellow clansmen. Similar rules of priority are prescribed in the Code of Gortyna and in Hebrew Law; and, as Morgan pointed out, we have only to reverse the order to see that they correspond to the gradual restriction of the right of inheritance from the circle of the clan to the individual family, thus marking the transition from collective to private ownership.[37] Even in democratic Athens, this transition had not been completed. The right of testamentary disposition, which is one of the characteristics of mature law, was only recognised in default of legitimate issue.[38] Thus the son's claim on his father's property was the last vestige of the time when all property had been owned collectively by the clan. And the transition had proceeded so surreptitiously that the regulations governing the disposal of private property were still expressed in terms that had their origin in primitive communism.

It may therefore be concluded that in its application to food, booty and land the idea of Moira reflects the collective distribution of wealth through three successive stages in the evolution of tribal society. Oldest of all was the distribution of food, which goes back to the hunting period. Next came the distribution of chattels and inanimate movables acquired by warfare, which was a development of hunting; and, last, the division of land for the purposes of agriculture.

The use of the lot was, of course, a guarantee of equality. The goods were divided as equally as possible, and then the portions were distributed by a process which, since it lay outside human control, was impartial. And for the same reason it was regarded as magical, as an appeal to the Moirai or spirits of the Lot, who determined each man's portion. With the growth of private property, the use of the lot became increasingly restricted, and the popular conception of the Moirai was modified accordingly. They became the goddesses who determined for each man his lot in life.

Besides these divisions of wealth, the word *moîra* was also applied to divisions of function. Here again we find traces of a social order which had vanished from the real world reflected in the ideal world of Olympus.

Before making war on the Titans, Zeus swore to the gods that, if victorious, he would not only respect the privileges of those who already had privileges, but bestow others on those who at present had none. The result was that, when the war was over, he was invited to assume the sovereignty.[39] Zeus became king in reward for military service. After becoming king, he assigned to the gods their several privileges or functions.[40] The *géras* of Hephaistos was fire; the *moîra* allotted to Atlas was to hold up the sky; the *moîra* of the nymphs was to care for mortals in early manhood; to Apollo was assigned music and dancing, while lamentation was the *láchos* of Hades. Once Aphrodite, whose *moîra* or *timé* was love-making, was caught working at the loom, and Athena protested to Zeus that, since Aphrodite had stolen her *kléros*, she would no longer pursue the vocation which she had received from the Moirai. In Æschylus, the Erinyes accuse Apollo of robbing them of the *láchos* which the Moirai had bestowed on them at birth; and Asklepios was punished for the same reason—in seeking to raise the dead, he had trespassed on the *moîra* of Hades.

In the earliest phase of tribal society the only division of labour had been sexual, but, with the development of stock-raising, tillage and handicrafts, specialised occupations tended to become hereditary in particular clans. In ancient Greece we meet with many such craft clans: the Homeridai (rhapsodes), the Asklepiadai (physicians), the Iamidai, Branchidai and Krontidai (soothsayers), the Euneidai (lyre-players), the Kerykes and Theokerykes (heralds).[41] At Sparta, the heralds all belonged to the clan of the Talthybiadai: as Herodotus remarks, heraldry was the *géras* of the clan.[42] And there are many other clans whose name bears a vocational significance:

the Poimenidai (herdsmen), Aigeirotomoi (hewers of poplar), Bouzygai (ox-spanners), Phreorychoi (well-diggers), Daidalidai and Kropidai (sculptors); Hephaistiadai, Aithalidai, Eupyridai and Pelekes (armourers and smiths).

Discussing the Attic craft clans, one contemporary historian declares that they must have been guilds and, considering it improbable that such guilds could have existed in primitive Attica, he concludes that "these names were fancy choices."[43] No doubt many of them were guilds—that is to say, professional associations to which admission was obtained by some form of co-option; but, as Grönbech has shown, the guild is descended from the clan.[44] The mediæval guild is simply an advanced form of the craft clan. The only structural difference between them is that membership of the guild is not determined by birth, except in so far as the son becomes eligible by following his father's vocation; and even the primitive clan commonly admits strangers by adoption. Since the craft clan is a widespread feature of the higher stages of tribal society, there is no difficulty in supposing that it existed in primitive Attica; and, even if it did not, at least there existed the primitive clans out of which the craft clans subsequently evolved. If this historian had given any attention to the history of primitive society, he would have had no need to resort to fancies.

The Asklepiadai claimed descent from Asklepios, the god of physicians; the Iamidai from Apollo, the god of prophets; the Kerykes from Hermes, the god of heralds; the Talthybiadai and Theokerykes from the herald Talthybios; the Daidalidai from Daidalos, the sculptor; the Bouzygai from Bouzyges, said to have been the first man to harness cattle to the plough.[45] In all these cases the vocation of the clan coincides with the traditional function of the eponymous god or hero from whom it claims descent.

Here again endless confusion has been introduced by recent historians owing to their ignorance of the structure of the primitive clan. Of the clans just mentioned, some certainly— the Homeridai and Asklepiadai, for example—and others probably were guilds in the historical period. So far as their origins are concerned, that point, as we have seen, is immaterial; but it is not established by the fact that their first ancestor is mythical. Wade-Gery defines the Athenian *génos* as "a group of Athenians connected by fictional common ancestry—fictional, because the alleged ancestor is always mythical."[46] This is simply a *non sequitur*. The fact that the first ancestor of the clan is mythical does not disprove its claim to common descent. If it did, the common descent characteristic of totemic clans throughout the world would be a fiction, because in these cases the first ancestor is not a human being at all. These current misapprehensions would be easier to excuse if the true nature of the clan, in Greece and elsewhere, had not been explained sixty years ago by Morgan.

The physician Asklepios is a mythical projection of the human physician. Apollo as prophet and Hermes as herald were fashioned in the image of real prophets and real heralds. If Talthybios was a historical person, which is doubtful, he belonged to the clan which subsequently named itself after him. The hero Bouzyges is nothing more than an impersonation of the traditional function of the Bouzygai. According to Herodotus, it was Homer and Hesiod who "gave the gods their titles, distinguished their privileges and crafts, and fixed their form."[47] Some of these attributes may have been older than Herodotus allows, but his essential point is correct—they were derivative, not primitive. Invading tribes had overrun the Ægean, and so the sons of Kronos conquered the world; the invading tribes had divided the land by lot, and so the sons of Kronos divided the world; the kings of these tribes owed their sovereignty to military service, and so did the King of Olympus. The parallel will be pursued in the next chapter. In the same way, the division of labour among the gods, as it appears in the Homeric poems, is simply the reflex of the division of labour which had been effected in the real world by the primitive system of clan crafts—a system in which a man's vocation in life was determined by the clan into which he was born.

This brings us to the important question: how did the Moirai become spinners—Klotho, Atropos and Lachesis?

Klotho, who is spinning personified, is the oldest of the three, because, while Homer speaks of the Moirai collectively as Klothes, he never mentions the other two.[48] Atropos appears in later literature as the "goddess of the abhorrèd shears who

slits the thin-spun life"—an image apparently based on the
process of cutting the web from the loom. "I have rolled up
like a weaver my life: he will cut me off from the loom."[49]
But this notion is not found in early Greek literature,[50] nor does
it conform to the meaning of the word as the Greeks interpreted it—she who cannot be turned back, whose thread cannot be unspun.[51] And even this interpretation, which can be
traced back to Æschylus, is not easily reconciled with the
operations of spinning or weaving. It is not hard for the spinner
to unwind what she has spun, nor for the weaver to unravel
what she has woven. Penelope is a standing instance to the
contrary. It is possible therefore that this interpretation rests
on a false etymology. The word is based on the idea of turning
(*trépo*)—of that there is no doubt; it may be, however, that the
prefix is not privative but intensive. In that case, Atropos is
simply a variant of *átraktos*, with interchange of *p* and *k*
—not "she who cannot be turned," but the Turner—a personification of the spindle.

There remains Lachesis, the goddess of Allotment. Her
place by the side of Klotho and Atropos suggests that originally she, too, must have carried some connotation germane to
the art of spinning—either the allotment of the unworked
wool among the spinners or, what comes to the same thing, the
amount of wool required to fill the spindle.[52]

How then did these Klothes or Moirai become spinners of
destiny? The answer must be sought in the function of their
human prototypes. We must also observe—the tradition is
insistent on this point—that a man's destiny is spun by the
Moirai at the time of his birth.[53] What were the women of the
clan engaged in spinning at the birth of a child? To this question there seems to be only one answer. They were making
its clothes.

The primary function of clothes is, of course, to protect the
body, but among primitive peoples this function is commonly encrusted with magical practices and beliefs founded on
the notion that there exists an intimate relation between a
man's clothes and his life. The same idea underlies the custom
of decorating the body by scarification, tattooing, painting,
and the use of detachable ornaments.[54]

In ancient Greece the newborn child was wrapped in swaddling bands and adorned with amulets such as necklaces and rings. These articles were known collectively as *gnorísmata*, or tokens, because they were sufficiently distinctive to identify the child.[55] When an unwanted child was exposed, its tokens were exposed with it. This was done even when, so far from hoping it might survive, its parents were determined it should perish. Thus, when the infant Cyrus was handed over to a shepherd with instructions that it was to be left a prey for the wild beasts of the hills, it was richly attired in embroidered linen and ornaments of gold; and, when the shepherd substituted for it his own stillborn child, he transferred these tokens from the one to the other.[56] The custom of exposing the tokens cannot therefore in general have been prompted by the hope of subsequent recovery, although in particular cases that may have been a secondary motive; and the fact that the child was not simply killed, but left to die, and its clothes abandoned with it, suggests that at one time exposure was a ritual act based partly on the belief that the child's life was bound up with its clothes, which bore the marks of its origin.

Were these marks totemic? The question is worth raising, because it is a widespread practice among primitive tribes to mark the children by tattooing or other means with the totemic sign of the clan to which they belong.

The Arabic *wasm* is a mark branded on camels. According to Robertson Smith, it was originally a totemic sign placed, not only on camels, but on their owners.[57] Moreover, as he points out, the word itself is cognate with *ism*, which is the Arabic for name. Now, precisely the same equation is found in Indo-European. The Latin *nota* and *nomen*, the Greek *onotázo* and *ónoma*, are derived from the same base.[58] Some scholars have hesitated to accept this equation, because its significance is not immediately apparent. But the Semitic analogy makes it plain. The mark and the name are the same thing, both representing, the one in graphic and the other in spoken form, the clan totem incarnate in the bearer. This explains why in primitive society the name is universally hedged round with taboos.[59]

Is there any evidence that the *gnorísmata* were totemic? The

Spartoi of Thebes had two emblems—the snake and the spear. The story was that the body of every member of this clan was marked with a spear from birth; but, since birth-marks are not hereditary, it has been plausibly suggested that the spear was a totemic tattoo.[60] The clearest instance, however, is the snake necklace exposed with the infant Ion. As we remarked in the first chapter, the snake was the totem of the clan.

In the *Oresteia*, Orestes proves his identity to his sister by showing her a garment she had woven for him as a child—probably, as the scholiast observes, his swaddling bands; and in it are animal designs.[61] These animal designs were a traditional *motif* in the metal ornaments and embroidered swaddling bands in which infants were attired. There are several instances in the comedies of Menander.[62] Syriskos is examining the tokens of a foundling: "Here's an iron ring plated with gold, and on the seal is carved—is it a bull or a goat?" And again: "Doris, go and fetch the casket with the embroideries in it—you know, the one I gave you to keep. . . . Isn't this a he-goat or an ox or some such beast? . . . That's the attire they found me in as a child." These animal designs on the *gnorísmata* are clearly derived from an earlier custom of marking the child with the totem of its clan.

The significance of the totemic emblem was twofold. It signified that the child that bore it was a reincarnation of the clan ancestor, and had inherited by right of birth the traditional duties and privileges of the clan. Therefore, as mythical projections of the women who wove the swaddling-bands embroidered with the clan-totem the Moirai represented the authority of ancestral custom which determined from birth the part allotted to the individual in the life of the tribe.

The connection between Moira and the clan totem is established by another line of argument. The *daímon* of the Orphics and Pythagoreans was the guardian spirit assigned to every man at birth who decided all the crucial issues of his life. This is the function of the Egyptian *ka*, the Mexican *nagual*, and the North American *manitoo*—all individual totems evolved out of the collective totem of the clan, with which in many cases they are combined.[63] And besides this individual *daímon*, we also find traces of a hereditary *daímon*, the *daímon génnes* of Æschylus, or *daímon* of the clan.⁶⁴ Further, the words *daímon* and *moîra* are constantly associated in such a way as to indicate that their meaning is essentially the same.⁶⁵ The Greek for "trying one's luck" is "to ascertain one's *moîra*," or, alternatively, "to put one's *daímon* to the test." Empedokles says that there are two kinds of *daímones* or *moîrai* that inaugurate man's life at birth. Iphigeneia cries out in the same breath against the evil *daímon* which brought her from the womb and the Moirai who delivered her mother of a child so miserable. That this significance of *daímon* is fundamental is proved by its etymology; for *daímon* is cognate with *daís*, a meal, and with *dasmós*, a division—it is the Apportioner or ancestral spirit who determines each man's *moîra*.

The functions of the Moirai were not confined to birth.⁶⁶ They were also associated with re-birth, with marriage and with death. At Athens, when a man returned home after being reported dead and duly lamented by his kinsfolk, he was readmitted to the community by a ceremony consisting of a mimic birth, and he was described as *deuterópotmos*, one who had received a second *pótmos*—*pótmos* being synonymous with *moîra* in the sense of that which "falls to one's lot." In myth, it was the Moirai who attended at the bridal bed of Zeus and Hera. In cult, the Greek bride offered a lock of her hair to Artemis and the Moirai. Antiphon says of the bridal night that "this night inaugurates a new *pótmos*, a new *daímon*."⁶⁷ And, finally, the phrase *moîra thanátou* (portion of death), corresponding to *moîra biótoio* and *moîra gámou* (portion of life, portion of marriage), shows that man had his portion in death as well as life.⁶⁸ All this will become clear when we have had an opportunity of examining the interconnection in primitive thought of the ideas relating to birth, adoption, initiation, marriage and death.

I have argued that the Moirai originated as a symbol of the economic and social functions characteristic of the primitive tribe—the sharing of food, the sharing of booty, the sharing of land, and the division of labour between the clans. These functions were maintained under the direction of the tribal elders, the accepted exponents of ancestral custom. If, therefore, the Moirai symbolised the authority of ancestral custom, it becomes pertinent to enquire why they were conceived in female form.

Among the arguments advanced by Robertson Smith in support of his contention that the Semitic peoples were originally matrilineal is the fact that in the Semitic languages tribal units are treated as feminine. "If," he says, "at the time when the use of genders was taking shape, the effective bond of blood had been reckoned through the father, it is simply incredible that the tribal unity could have been personified as the mother of the stock."[69] The same argument applies to Greek. The normal type of the clan name is based on the element -*ida*-, which is an extension of the suffix -*id* by another suffix, -*a*. Both these suffixes are feminine, and in the dialects of north-west Greece clan names of this type were actually declined as feminine.[70] Thus, the typical Greek clan name, which in historical times was applied exclusively to men, was originally restricted to the women.

A tribe in which the principle of mother-kin is fully operative has the following characteristics.[71] The children belong to the mother's clan. When they grow up, the men marry women of other clans and go to live with the clan into which they marry. The women remain in their own clan. Therefore the descent of the clan is traced through the women and its affairs are administered by the women. If therefore the Moirai represented the authority of tribal custom as vested in the elders of the clan, and if those elders were women, then we may say that in origin the Moirai were simply the ancestral spirits of the clan.

So, as we have seen, were the Erinyes. Were the Moirai and the Erinyes originally identical? I think not. True, they had much in common. Both were female; both were worshipped exclusively by the female sex.[72] If, as we have suggested, the Erinyes were of Ægean origin, their sex is explained by the matrilineal institutions of pre-Hellenic Greece. The name of the Moirai, on the other hand, is Indo-European. Yet, as we saw in the last chapter, the Indo-European immigrants into Greece were patrilineal. This apparent contradiction can be resolved on the hypothesis that the origin of the Moirai lies in the primitive culture of the Indo-European peoples before their dispersal; and this hypothesis is supported by some independent evidence.

In the first place, there is a striking resemblance between the Greek Moirai and the Germanic Norns. They, too, were associated with birth, marriage and death; they, too, were spinners of fate.[73] The Germans cannot have derived this conception directly from the Greeks; nor is it likely that they derived it through Latin, because the Roman concept of the Parcæ as spinners was merely a literary borrowing from Greek and as such confined to the educated classes. If the Parcæ, as spinners, had exercised any influence on popular thought, we should expect to find traces of it in the widespread Gallic and Germanic cults of the Matres Deæ.[74] Yet, though the evidence is plentiful, there is only one instance in which these deities are identified with the Parcæ, and none in which they are represented as spinners. The Norns require closer investigation than they have yet received, but, with this reservation, it may be suggested that their affinities with the Moirai must be due to a common Indo-European origin.

In the second place, the significance of Moira in relation to the sharing of food shows that the idea had its roots in the hunting period—a stage which, at the time of the dispersal, Indo-European society had left far behind; and, as we saw in the first chapter, one of the characteristics of that stage is the relatively high incidence of matrilineal descent. It appears therefore that in the idea of Moira we have one of the oldest traditions of the Indo-European peoples.

Unlike the Erinyes, the Moirai have no animal associations. This too follows naturally from the hypothesis I have advanced. As ancestral spirits of a matrilineal society, the Erinyes maintained their connection with the female ancestors; but when, before its dispersal, the Indo-European-speaking people adopted patrilineal descent, the Moirai ceased to represent the ancestors, who were now men, and so were cut off from their totemic origin.

Yet, though their origins were distinct, their functions are closely related. Æschylus says that in the beginning the world was ruled by "the threefold Moirai and the unforgetting Erinyes."[75] The women of Thebes cry out against "Moira, giver of evil and the shade of Œdipus, the black Erinys." When Agamemnon repented of having robbed Achilles of his *géras* or *moîra*, he attributed his blunder to the malice of Zeus, Moira and Erinys. In the post-Homeric period, Moira is often replaced in this connection by Dike, or Justice. Thus, when Agamemnon and Menelaos have refused burial, which is the *moîra* of the dead, to the body of Ajax, the dead man's kinsman utters a curse upon them in which he invokes Zeus, Erinys, and Dike, "who brings to fulfilment." The epithet *telesphóros*, which is here applied to Dike, was also a traditional epithet of Moira. In the *Oresteia*, the parents who have been struck down by their children cry out on the name of Dike and on the thrones of the Erinyes. Finally, Herakleitos says that, if the Sun were to exceed his *métra* or measures, he would be detected by the Erinyes, the ministers of Dike.[76] In a later chapter we shall find that these "measures" are really "portions," the idea of *métron* being a post-Homeric development of *moîra*.

These passages make it clear, first, that the function ascribed in Attic poetry to Dike had previously belonged to Moira, and, secondly, that both were functionally related to the Erinyes. The nature of their relationship appears to be that, whereas Moira or Dike is offended by violation of the established portions or limits set to human conduct, the actual punishment of the offender is effected by the agency of the Erinyes. The Moirai decree what shall be, and the Erinyes see to it that their decrees are carried out. This traditional co-operation between the Moirai and Erinyes corresponds to the fusion of cultures which underlies Greek civilisation, and the superior authority enjoyed by the Moirai reflects the dominance of the Indo-European element in it.

In explaining his blunder, Agamemnon coupled with Moira and Erinys the name of Zeus. How did Zeus stand in relation to the Moirai? According to Æschylus, when Zeus first became king, he was powerless to override the authority of the Moirai. In the Homeric poems, Zeus stands to the Moirai in the same equivocal relationship as the king stood to his people. When Sarpedon is about to die, Zeus is sorely tempted to save him, which suggests that he could if he would, but he desists when Hera indignantly warns him that, if he violates the decrees of Fate, other gods will seek to do the same.[77] On the other hand, such stereotyped phrases as *moîra theôn* and *epeklósanto theoí* imply that the authority of the Moirai is already fading before the growing power of the gods,[78] and their eventual subordination is revealed at a later period in the cult title *moiragétes*, "leader of the Moirai," borne by Zeus at Olympia and by Apollo at Delphi.[79] The new gods have conquered. The tribe has been superseded by the state.

Having explained their sex, we have no difficulty in understanding why the function of the Moirai was symbolised by the spindle. Spinning was the women's task. So, before the development of field tillage, was agriculture. The significance of Moira in this connection is clearly brought out when we contrast it with another element in Greek thought which had its origin in the work of the men.

In pastoral society, the men tend the flocks, the women work the wool which the men bring home. The notion of pasture underlies a word whose social importance eventually eclipsed that of Moira—the word *nómos*.[80] This too originally signified a division or portion, but, whereas *moîra* was applied primarily to cultivated land, *nómos* was confined to pasture. Now, private property was naturally much slower to develop in uncultivated land than in cultivated. Long after the *moîra* of the clan had been split up into family holdings, the pastures remained common, their use being regulated by customary rights. In this way the word *nómos* acquired the sense of a common usage or acknowledged custom, and so at a still later stage custom as by law established. Thus, both Moira and Nomos have their roots in the economic relations of tribal society; but, whereas at the beginning of the historical period the primitive significance of Moira is already in decay, the idea of Nomos does not reach maturity until long afterwards in the democratic city-state. The decline of Moira and the rise of Nomos correspond to the transition from the matrilineal tribe to the patrilineal state.

We have not yet finished with the idea of Moira. After its first roots in the social organism have withered, it sends out fresh roots, through which it renews its vitality by adapting itself to the new modes of thought set in motion by the ever-changing organism on which it feeds; and so the continuity which underlies its successive transformations is simply the continuity of society itself.

PART TWO

FROM TRIBE TO STATE

SLAVES DIGGING FOR
POTTER'S CLAY

IV

MONARCHY

THE earliest settlers in Crete were probably of North
African origin, belonging to the same stock as the primitive
inhabitants of Lower Egypt.[1] They were joined at an early
period by immigrants from Cyprus and Asia Minor. Their
social and cultural development was continuously stimulated
by contacts with the advanced states of Egypt and the East,
and by the middle of the second millennium B.C. they had
built up a highly organised, commercial, theocratic state
centred in the city of Knossos. The commercial connections of
Minoan Crete radiated all over the Mediterranean, and its
relations with Lycia, the Cyclades, and parts of the Greek
mainland were particularly close. The legends of Argos and
Attica suggest that these areas had at one time been ruled from
Knossos or at least subjected to tribute. All this presupposes
command of the sea and an advanced state organisation; and
these are precisely the features of the Minoan age which
impressed themselves most deeply on the Greek tradition. The
sea power of Minos is mentioned by Thucydides as a historical
fact,[2] and his fame as a legislator survived in the mystical tradition, which made him the supreme judge of the dead who
allotted to each soul its portion in eternal life.[3]

This high degree of social organisation was not reproduced
outside Crete itself. The cities of the mainland—Orchomenos,
Thebes, Argos, Tiryns and Mycenæ—were comparatively small
and isolated military strongholds, whose massive walls frowned
menacingly over the surrounding plains. Soon after the middle
of the second millennium the city of Knossos was destroyed,
and the centre of power shifted to Mycenæ, whose ruling
dynasty exercised an uncertain hegemony over its neighbours.
The power of these dynasties rested mainly on conquest and
plunder. There was a protracted war between Mycenæ and

59

Thebes. It was a period of intense social disturbance, culminating in maritime raids of marauding bands as far as the borders of Egypt and in the siege of Troy. It was brought to an end by the incursion of the Dorian tribes (1000 B.C.), which plundered the plunderers and established new dynasties in Thessaly, the Peloponnese and Crete itself. After the Dorian conquest, more settled conditions supervened. The wealth of Minoan civilisation had been exhausted.

The origin of these pre-Dorian dynasties is uncertain, but it is probable that many of them spoke Greek. The distribution of dialects in historical Greece suggests that Greek speech had been carried into the Ægean basin in three successive movements.[4] The first brought Ionic to Boiotia, Attica and the northern Peloponnese. This is the period in which the political influence of Crete was at its height—a fact which is reflected by the absorption into Greek of a large and important alien element, including the words for "brother" and for "king." The second movement, associated with the fall of Knossos (1450 B.C.), brought the parent dialect of Æolic and Arcadic to Thessaly, the Peloponnese, Crete, Rhodes and Cyprus. It is highly probable that this was the speech of the Achæan princes described in the Homeric poems. The third movement was the spread of Doric, which overlaid the Achæan dialects throughout the Peloponnese, except the Arcadian highlands, and extended overseas as far as Crete, Rhodes and the Lycian seaboard. Meanwhile, Æolic and Ionic were carried across the Ægean to the northern and central coasts of Asia Minor by fugitives from the Dorian conquest.

The same process is reflected, though naturally with less precision, in the history of religion. The cults of Earth at Dodona and Delphi, of Demeter at Eleusis and in Argos and Arcadia, of Athena in Boiotia, Attica and Sparta and of Hera in Argos, Arcadia and Elis—all these are pre-Hellenic.[5] At Dodona, Earth was joined at an early date by Zeus; at Delphi she was superseded by Apollo, who has both northern and Ægean connections. The supremacy of Athena in Attica, of Hera in Argos, and of Demeter in Arcadia, was disputed by Poseidon, and at Olympia Hera gave way to Zeus. Since the name of Zeus is certainly Indo-European, and since most of

the Achæan dynasties claimed descent from him, it is likely
that they were instrumental in diffusing his worship through
the Peloponnese and overseas to Crete.

Beginning with peaceful infiltration, the process became
progressively more violent, and the Achæan period was
catastrophic. These northern invaders, disguising their obscure
origin under the royal name of Zeus, had pillaged the rich
treasuries of Mycenæ, Sparta and Minoan Crete. Their tribal
organisation must have been far from primitive when they
entered the Ægean, but hitherto the germs of decay had been
working slowly from within. Now, in the clash of conquest, the
accumulated intensity of the contradiction between the old
structure of society and its transformed content precipitated a
convulsion, out of which, after the Dorian conquest, there
emerged a new and different structure. Henceforward the community was divided against itself between those who produced
wealth and those who enjoyed it. It was this internal opposition
which, by multiplying the divisions of labour, rendered possible the immense technical and cultural advances which
marked the transition from barbarism to civilisation. But this
opposition was not static—it was a struggle, intensely and
incessantly accelerating the whole *tempo* of social change. The
interval between the Achæan conquests and contemporary
Europe is but an insignificant fraction of the countless ages
that had elapsed since the emergence of those conquering tribes
out of the primitive horde.

The social organisation of the Achæans has been reconstructed from the archæological remains with the aid of the
Homeric poems.[6] The king lives in a palace on some rocky
eminence, surrounded by the dwellings of his vassals. The relation between king and vassal is such as we find in similar conditions among the primitive Germans 2,000 years later. In
reward for military service, the vassal holds in fee the rule of
some portion of the conquered territory, and in return he takes
up arms for the king when called on to do so. Such was the
relation of Bellerophon to the King of Lycia, of Phoinix to
the father of Achilles; and we remember how Odysseus endeavoured, but in vain, to evade military service. The vassal
is entitled to be consulted on matters of policy and to feed at

the royal table. There are many such councils in the *Iliad*, and in the *Odyssey* the offence of the suitors lies in their abuse of a recognised privilege. Finally, each vassal stood in the relation of king to vassals of his own. Odysseus was a vassal of Agamemnon's, but to the princes of Ithaca he was king.

The revolutionary feature of this relationship is that it is personal, independent of kinship, and therefore anti-tribal.[7] The resulting conflict among the ruling chiefs between personal and tribal loyalties has already been discussed, and it explains a remarkable feature of the Homeric poems. We learn from a single verse of the *Iliad* that the Achæan army, like those of Athens and Sparta many centuries later, was organised on a tribal basis; but the fact is mentioned incidentally, and it is never mentioned again. This reticence on the subject of tribal institutions does not mean that they had ceased to exist, but that the poems belonged to the tradition of a ruling class which instinctively made little of the loyalties it had defied.[8] The common soldiers continued to be marshalled phratry by phratry, but the vassal followed his lord.

This distinction between the *esthloi*—rich, well-armed, valiant and so "good"—and the *kakoi*, who simply followed their leaders, is not yet so rigid as it was eventually to become, because the power of the chiefs is based on wealth in the form of plunder, not yet on land, and such wealth can be lost as easily as won.[9] Nevertheless, it is already recognisable. When Thersites was bold enough to raise his voice against the war, Odysseus thrashed him. The upstart was given a salutary lesson. Achilles declared he would rather be a serf among the living than a king among the dead; and meanwhile, as we learn from Hesiod, the serf fortified himself against the wrongs of this world with the hope that they would be punished in the next. The community is divided against itself. Its outlook is no longer unified.

The characteristics of these Achæan princes—their social organisation, their personal ideals, their attitude to the common people—are all mirrored in the stories told to them by their poets about their gods.

The dwelling of Zeus is on the cloud-capped peak of Olympus.[10] In the beginning, as cloud-gatherer and thunderer, he

had dwelt alone, the other gods residing elsewhere—Hera in
Argos, Aphrodite in Paphos, Athena in the House of Erechtheus; but now they have been gathered together in a single
celestial city—Zeus in the central palace, the others in the surrounding mansions built for them by Hephaistos. The supremacy of Zeus is recognised, though in practice it is often challenged. He summons his subordinates to councils, at which the
affairs of mankind are discussed, and entertains them to meat,
wine and music. These gods are selfish, unscrupulous, passionate, intensely alive to all delights of the senses. In one
thing only are they divided from their worshippers—they can
never die; and of that privilege they are extremely jealous.
Mortals must not aspire above their mortal state, or they will
be blasted with the thunderbolt. As the common people are
to their chiefs, so are the chiefs to their gods.[11] These Achæans
expressed their sense of the limitations to their control of
natural forces by personifying those forces as a class of supernatural beings which controlled them in the same way as they
controlled their subject class. The Achæan Olympus was the
mythical mirror of social reality.[12]

It will be remembered that, in the hunting tribe, the authority of the elders had been projected as ancestor worship, and
that later, when power was concentrated in the hands of a
chief or king, a god was worshipped in the king's image. The
further evolution of human society promoted an increasing
complexity in the relations of the divine powers believed to
govern it. Some gods were subordinated to others: wars between tribes and peoples were waged again in heaven. The
galaxy of totemic emblems which made up the royal insignia of
the Pharaohs was a crystallised symbol of the fusion and subordination of originally independent tribes which had led to
the unification of the kingdom; and the ever-shifting relations
between the rival cities of the Tigris and Euphrates are reflected in the composite and unstable Babylonian pantheon.
In the same way, the suzerainty of Zeus over his turbulent
Olympians reproduces the organisation of Achæan Greece
under the loose hegemony of the royal house of Atreus.

Myth was created out of ritual. The latter term must be
understood in a wide sense, because in primitive society

everything is sacred, nothing profane. Every action—eating, drinking, tilling, fighting—has its proper procedure, which being prescribed, is holy. In the song and dance of the mimetic rite, each performer withdrew, under the hypnotic effect of rhythm, from the consciousness of reality, which was peculiar to himself, individual, into the subconscious world of fantasy, which was common to all, collective, and from that inner world they returned charged with new strength for action. Poetry and dancing, which grew out of the mimetic rite, are speech and gesture raised to a magical level of intensity. For a long time, in virtue of their common origin and function, they were inseparable. The divergence of poetry from dancing, of myth from ritual, only began with the rise of a ruling class whose culture was divorced from the labour of production. In Greece, as among the primitive Germans, this class was a military aristocracy which ruled by right of conquest, and its first product was in both cases the art of epic poetry. After the battle was over, tired but contented, the warriors forgot their fatigue as they listened to a lay, chanted by one of themselves or later by a minstrel, in honour of their victory. The function of these lays was not to prepare for action, like that of choral poetry, but to relax after action, and therefore they were less tense, less concentrated, less sacral. Moreover, their themes were not the collective traditions of clan or tribe, but the exploits of individuals; and therefore their technique was freer from convention, more open to innovations.

Behind Greek epic there probably lies the custom of collective chanting, such as we find among some of the North American tribes, but if so it has left no traces. The decisive stage in the evolution of epic was the rise of the military dynasties, which furnished the art of song with new themes and a new technique. The new themes were the wars of conquest, and the new technique was the lay sung by a trained minstrel at the feasts to which the king entertained his vassals. From this point the evolution of the art can be traced in written records. As Chadwick has shown in his masterly study of the subject, the history of Greek and of Teutonic epic presents a number of common features, which enable us to relate both to their social environment.[13]

The themes of the Teutonic lays were originally contemporary. The minstrel sings to-day of the victory of yesterday. Thanks to his training, the metrical form of the lay has become a second language to him, in which he is as fluent as in ordinary speech. The court minstrel is a vassal of the king, whose power he consolidates by perpetuating the memory of his achievements.

The Homeric poems do not belong to this stage, but they point back to it.[14] We hear little about minstrelsy in the *Iliad*, because its theme is actual fighting, but on one occasion Achilles consoles himself in idleness by singing of "the glories of men," which must mean their exploits in battle, and the Olympian banquet in the first book concludes with songs and dances from Apollo and the Muses. In the *Odyssey*, Phemios sings of the homecoming of the Achæans, Demodokos of the Trojan horse, and we are expressly told that contemporary themes are the most popular. We also hear of a minstrel at Mycenæ, to whom Agamemnon had entrusted the guardianship of his Queen—evidently a vassal of high standing.

The Homeric poems themselves belong to the second stage. The Achæan monarchies have succumbed to the Dorian invaders, and the wealthy families of Thessaly and the Peloponnese have fled to Asia Minor, taking their cultural traditions with them. There they found new kingdoms, formed partly from the indigenous population and partly from the refugees now swarming across the Ægean. These new settlements are petty agricultural states, in which the king is merely the principal landowner. In these conditions, the minstrels no longer sing of contemporary victories, because there are none to sing of, and so they turn back to the idealised traditions of the past.

It was in this environment, with the monarchy already in decline, that Greek epic matured. It may be assumed that the lays which these emigrants had brought with them were already of a high artistic order. Now they were brought to perfection. The major factor underlying the last phase in the evolution of the *Iliad* and *Odyssey* is this uneventful period of concentration on a number of rich and already well-handled themes by craftsmen who had behind them a centuries-old tradition, formed under the influence of Minoan civilisation, which they now re-fashioned all the more boldly because it had been uprooted from the country of its origin. The masterly construction of these poems is so impressive that it has been adduced as evidence of single authorship; but there is no reason why the same effect should not have been produced over a number of generations in the conditions of oral transmission. One may still encounter among the peasantry sagas or folk-tales which are artistically perfect—not because they are the work of a conscious artist, but because in the course of centuries they have been progressively shaped and polished by a sort of natural erosion, which has worn away excrescences and fashioned by slow degrees a final unity. And the hereditary poets of the Homeridai *were* conscious artists, cultivated and refined, who perfected the traditional material by infusing into it their own personal outlook.

In the same way, the tragic intensity with which the story of the *Iliad* is imagined arises out of the historical conditions in which the poem had evolved. The Achæan dynasties had risen and fallen while it was being composed. These sophisticated poets of Smyrna and Chios were far removed from the semi-barbarous robber chiefs of whom they wrote. The result was a dynamic tension between themselves and their material; and so deeply had they absorbed their material that this tension appears as something internal in the heroes of the story. "If," says Sarpedon to his vassal, "we were destined to live for ever like the gods and never grow old or die, I should not send you into battle nor would I go myself; but, since in any case we are encompassed on every side by a thousand deaths and dangers, let us go—to give glory, or to win it."[15] That is not the voice of a robber chief. The Achilles who drew his sword upon the king, sulked in his tent, sobbed like a child, spurned the offer of cities, rolled in the dust for grief, dragged his enemy's corpse at the tail-piece of his chariot and begged the aged Priam to go for fear he should be seized by a sudden paroxysm and kill him—that is the authentic Achæan chief, the restless cattle-raider, the pillager of Knossos. But Achilles is doomed; so is Agamemnon, and Ajax. The empire they carved out by robbery and rapine has been swept away, to be remembered in melodious hexameters by the quiet and sensitive poets of Ionia, who loved to note the movement of sheep stampeded in the fold, the long sweep of scythes in the grass or the deft grace of a woman's fingers at the loom. And so, as they see him, Achilles is tormented by foreknowledge of his future. "Shall I go home to Phthia and live out my life in uneventful ease, or die young in battle and live for ever on the lips of poets?" That is the dilemma of the *Iliad*, which crystallises in a single masterpiece five centuries of revolutionary change.

In the *Odyssey*, which is later than the *Iliad*, the technique is the same, but the material is less traditional—the scenes in Ithaca must be largely fiction; and the tone is gentler, less heroic. If, as Nilsson has maintained,[16] the stories about the Phœnicians belong to the late eighth century, when maritime trade was just beginning to revive, it may be inferred that one of the main themes of the poem—the fear and fascination of the sea—was evoked by the early beginnings of the commercial movement which was soon to precipitate a new crisis completing the evolution of the city-state.

The art of epic had grown up with the monarchy, and with the monarchy it declined. The king had been needed to lead the tribes in war, and, when the wars were at their height, the Greek kingdoms became federated under a supreme monarchy at Mycenæ; but this system rapidly collapsed, not merely because it was threatened by the Dorians, but because it was unable to adapt itself to a peacetime basis. The instability of the Achæan kingship is apparent in the Homeric poems. Even on the field of battle, Agamemnon is unable to control his strongest vassal, and meanwhile his palace at home has been seized by a usurper. In the generations following the Trojan War, the Achæan federation dissolved into a multitude of petty principalities, in each of which, as the pressure of military needs relaxed, the king was forced to share his privileges with his vassals, until nothing was left of his office but the name.[17]

When the royal courts broke up, the minstrels went out among the people, taking with them their traditional technique and adapting their themes to their new environment. Composed for a rich and leisured aristocracy, the Homeric poems had been designed to please; but the peasants to whom these minstrels now addressed themselves had no use for poetry unless it could help to fill hungry mouths. The poetry of Hesiod was designed to teach. In the *Works and Days*, the peasants received instruction in farming, star-reading, weather lore, charms and omens, and generally how to make the best of their hard lot; in the *Theogony*, they were told of the origin of the world, and how by violence and cunning the Olympians had subjugated the gods of the Golden Age, when all men had lived contentedly without having to win their bread in the sweat of their brows. In the poetry of Hesiod, the peasants were urged to "work, work, work," and at the same time they were fed on folk-memories of primitive communism.[18]

ARISTOCRACY

To placate Achilles, Agamemnon offered him, among other things, seven townships in Messenia, inhabited by people rich in flocks and herds, who, he said, would honour him with gifts like a god.[1] These townships were evidently royal demesnes which the king wished to bestow on a vassal because they were too far from his capital to be ruled directly. This method of organising conquered territory is analogous to the feudal system of western Europe, being based on a similar gradation of rank from the king through his vassals and his vassals' vassals to the serfs. It represents an advance on the *témenos*, because it implies that the land belonged, in fact if not in name, to the sovereign. It did not last, because in peacetime, as we have seen, the centrifugal tendencies of the local chiefs were too strong for it, and it was swept away by the Dorian invaders.

When the Dorians entered the Peloponnese, their tribal organisation was still largely intact.[2] The tribal assembly, composed of the adult men, was still able to assert its authority. That is shown by the treatment of the sons of Temenos and by the subsequent history of the Spartan *apélla*. Similarly, at Sparta, the effective administrative body was for a long time the *gerousía*, the council of tribal elders. The function of the Spartan kingship remained essentially military and, though in the historical period the office was hereditary, the part played by the assembly after the death of Temenos shows that the succession had once been subject to popular ratification.

The Dorian settlement of Sparta derived its distinctive character from the fact that the tribal system, confined to the conquerors, who formed a small minority of the total population, was thereby converted, with little internal change, into a rigidly exclusive ruling caste. Since their numbers were few, the Spartans could only hold down the serfs by maintaining their military organisation in a state of constant readiness, and the basis of that organisation was tribal. For the same reason, they had to close their own ranks against the disruptive inequalities that would follow from the growth of private property. Accordingly, they did everything in their power to maintain among themselves the tribal principle of common ownership. The land was divided into family estates, but these estates were inalienable, and their function was, by exploiting the serfs who worked them to the extent of 50 per cent. of the produce,[3] to provide each Spartan with his contribution to the collective food supply, for they continued to eat in common. At the same time, they set their faces against the development of trade, and refused to publish a code of laws, without which organised commerce was impossible. In this way a system which had evolved on the basis of equality was transformed into an instrument of class domination. Its structure was still tribal, but in function it had become a state.

Notwithstanding these precautions, inequalities did develop. The law against alienation was evaded, and there arose a class of landless Spartans. The internal pressure thus set up was met by a policy of cautious expansion. It had to be cautious, because a defeat in war would have presented the serfs with the opportunity for which they were always waiting.[4] And for the same reason Spartan foreign policy was guided by the determination to maintain so far as possible the supremacy of the landowning class in other states.

In Thessaly and Crete the subject population was treated by their Dorian conquerors in the same way, although the actual form of serfdom appears to have been rather less severe.[5] In Crete we find a similar system of common meals and family estates, but, thanks no doubt to its maritime position, its social organisation was in some respects more advanced, or at least had become so by the fifth century. In that period, and perhaps earlier, the Dorians of Gortyna had a code of written laws, which, though more primitive than the Attic Code of Solon, implies a considerable development of private property. As I have already remarked, the legal institutions of Dorian Crete may have owed something to the influence of Minoan culture.

It was only in these three areas that the domination of the Dorians was complete. In Sikyon and Argolis, besides the three Dorian tribes, there was a fourth, composed of pre-Dorian elements, and this implies that the pre-Dorian population had not been reduced to serfdom by the act of conquest.[6] The Dorian aristocracies of these areas were weaker, and therefore less successful in resisting the growth of trade.

In other parts of Greece—in Attica and Ionia—the new social system which emerged after the wars of invasion was not based on a racial and cultural cleavage such as divided the Dorians from their subjects. By the end of the seventh century B.C. the Attic landowners had succeeded in reducing their peasantry to a condition worse than serfdom, but, since they were themselves bound to the peasantry by a common culture and by the common ties of tribe and clan, the process took a long time, and it engendered among the peasantry a fierce resentment. The Spartans had won the land by the sword; the Attic nobles had to steal it.

The germ of property in land was, as we have seen, the *témenos*. This germ was bound to develop, because it was economically progressive.[7] Under the tribal system, the land belonging to the clan had either been worked collectively or else divided family by family and periodically re-distributed. These two methods correspond to successive stages in the development of agriculture. Originally, the land had been worked collectively because that was the only way in which it could be worked, and similarly the division into family holdings reflects the rising efficiency of the smaller unit. And, naturally, the smaller unit emerged first among the ruling classes. The *témenos* usually consisted of the best land; not being liable to re-distribution, it could be enclosed and so better protected; and the chief who owned it could cultivate it with the labour of slaves brought home from the wars. Nor were the economic advantages of enclosure lost on the common people. The small man could not hope for a *témenos*, but he could clear and enclose a piece of waste land, which became his by acquisition. This is the *eschatié*, of which there are already instances in the *Odyssey*.[8] His supply of slave labour was limited, but after the Dorian invasions cheap hired labour was available from thousands of detribalised and demoralised outcasts, who could be put to work on the harvest and then turned adrift for the winter.[9]

In these conditions the effect of appropriation was both to enhance the value and to extend the area of the cultivated land.

It was, however, only a matter of time before this process of expansion reached its limit, and then the ownership of land began to concentrate. By loans of seed and stock after a bad season, the big landowner became a creditor of the small, and after a succession of bad seasons the smallholder reached the point at which he could only redeem his debt by surrendering his holding or tying himself to his creditor by some system of annual tribute. He lost his land or became a serf.

The *témenos* was primarily a reward for military service, but it might also be dedicated to the service of a god. Indeed, since the chief was commonly a priest, the two types were not strictly distinguishable.[10] The assignation of *teméne* to priestly families was one of the principal means by which the land passed into the control of the nobility. Just as the god had a chief to be his servant, so he demanded a house to dwell in and cornfields for his maintenance. In many cases the produce of his *témenos* was supplemented by the receipt of tithes. The origin of the tithe lay in the contributions made to the common meal shared by the clan with its god; but the priests had now become the accepted intermediaries between the people and their god, who accordingly shared his meals with them alone.[11]

The priesthood was already well organised in the Mycenean period. That is clear from the antiquity of such clan cults as those of the Branchidai at Miletos and the Eumolpidai at Eleusis, and the priesthood of Apollo at Delphi, which was recruited from a limited number of noble families.[12] But it was only in the eighth and seventh centuries B.C. that religion was consciously organised as a means of reinforcing the economic domination of the landowning class. The process was the more difficult to resist in that it involved no open break with the past, because the clan chief had always been recognised as a religious leader. The clan cult now became a hereditary office confined to the chieftain's family, and, as the largest land-owners, the clan chiefs combined against their clans, using their religious authority to secure their material interests. In virtue of that authority, they became the accepted interpreters of ancestral traditions and customary rights, the accepted judges of civil disputes; and, since in an agricultural economy these disputes were concerned almost exclusively with land, their interests as landowners were well protected. Thus, by extending the privileges accorded to them under the tribal system, they had converted that system into the state.

This transition from tribe to state manifests itself very clearly in the development under the aristocracy of the law of homicide. In tribal society, as already explained (p. 34), homicide within the clan was punished by excommunication, while homicide between clans imposed on the victim's clan the obligation of obtaining satisfaction from the offender's. In both cases the initiative rested with the clan. But now, in the new conditions created by the appropriation of the land, the clan is divided against itself. Accordingly, the obligation to avenge is abolished, except in so far as the initiative in prosecution is still left to the victim's kinsmen, and all acts of manslaughter are treated indiscriminately as crimes punishable by excommunication.

We saw that, in tribal society, the man who had been excommunicated for manslaughter within the clan might be admitted by adoption into another clan. This is quite clear in the Germanic evidence,[13] and in Greece it can be traced in the customs relating to the reception of suppliants. The suppliant was a *hikétes*, one "who comes" to you—a stranger; and the act of supplication was in essence an appeal to be adopted. Thus, after entering the royal palace of the Phæacians, Odysseus clasped the knees of the Queen and then squatted on the hearth, whereupon the King took his hand and led him to a seat at table vacated for the purpose by his favourite son.[14] The suppliant could hardly have said more clearly, Let me be your child, or rather, I *am* your child. He asks to be adopted, and, when his appeal is granted, he is treated as a kinsman.

This adoption of the outcast explains another feature of the aristocratic law of homicide. The manslayer was excommunicated, but he could be readmitted to the community by being purified.[15] This too was a ritual act performed by the priesthood, who thus reserved to themselves full discretion in the treatment of crimes of violence. But, as we shall see when we examine the ritual of initiation, the practice of purification, like adoption, is based on the idea of regeneration or re-birth. Both features therefore—excommunication and purification—were derived from tribal society, and in both cases the change effected under the aristocracy was to transfer the initiative from the clan to the state. The idea of kinship was too deeply rooted in men's minds to be simply set aside, and so the nobles said to the people, We are all one kin, and therefore all homicide is a crime against the kin to be dealt with by the accredited authorities.[16] The tribal conception of kinship has been widened, but the class division has deepened.

This development of criminal law, reached in Attica early in the seventh century, owed much to the political influence of the priesthood of Apollo at Delphi, which worked in close co-operation with Sparta and became the religious stronghold of the aristocracy, as conscious of its social function and proportionately as powerful as the mediæval Papacy.[17] For the common people, it meant, not merely a break with immemorial traditions, but a complete surrender to their rulers in the treatment of a crime to which incentives grew with the growth of private property.

Let us now turn to the early history of Attica, which developed differently from Sparta and more slowly than Ionia. Attica was one of the few parts of the mainland which passed without much disturbance through the period of invasions, and consequently its traditions take us back a long way into the Mycenean Age. Though much still remains obscure, this subject has been greatly clarified by Wade-Gery's careful analysis of the evidence from Thucydides and Aristotle.[18]

Under Kekrops and his successors, Attica had been a loose federation of scattered tribal communities, each with its own chiefs (árchontes) and its own prytaneîon or council house—an institution of which we shall have more to say in a later chapter. There was also at Athens, under the presidency of the Athenian king, a Royal Council, to which these chiefs belonged; but in peacetime they did not attend it, being content with their local autonomy. This we learn from Thucydides, who thus confirms the evidence of the Homeric poems that the basis of the early kingship was military.[19]

In course of time, for the reasons we have given, these local chiefs developed common interests distinct from those of their followers. They began to reside in Athens, where they attended the Council regularly in the new *prytaneîon* built by King Theseus, and the local councils disappeared. Local autonomy was superseded by centralised control. The chiefs had combined to form a governing class. Henceforward the state was administered by officials, still called *árchontes*, elected by and from the families descended in the male line from the original members of the reconstituted Council. The Council itself was composed of *árchontes* whose term of office had expired with the addition of others co-opted from the same families. In this way there arose the ruling caste of the Eupatridai.

In the Attic tradition these changes were all concentrated in the reign of Theseus, but in point of fact they must have extended over several centuries. The decline of the kingship, in particular, was very gradual. The office was first made elective within the royal clan, then it was thrown open to the rest of the Eupatridai, then its tenure was reduced to ten years and finally to one. This last stage was only reached at the beginning of the seventh century. Even after that, the *árchon basileús*, as he was now called, continued to perform priestly functions derived from the kingship and to preside over the Council.

As Wade-Gery has shown, the accounts given by Thucydides and Aristotle of these developments, though independent, are quite consistent. There can be little doubt that they are essentially correct—except in respect of chronology. Here the tradition has been deflected by the claim put forward by Athenian nationalists in the fifth century that the founder of their democracy was Theseus. The centralisation of Attica was regarded as a democratic reform forced upon reluctant local chiefs, and the decline of the monarchy as a crowning act of self-abnegation on the part of Theseus himself, who, after thrusting their new honours on the Eupatridai, abdicated!

The subjective element in Thucydides and Aristotle is easily eliminated, but unfortunately Wade-Gery has introduced preconceptions of his own, which, being contemporary, are more insidious. Thus, when he asks why it was that membership of the Council was confined to the Eupatridai, and gives as his answer that "its functions were such as in an aristocratic

society could only be properly performed by hereditary *áristoi*,"
he seems to be in danger of forgetting that it was these *áristoi*
who, in pursuit of their own interests, had made society aristocratic.[20] It is necessary to resist the uncritical assumption that
the governing class owes its power to a natural capacity for
government.

There are signs that in the period following the Dorian invasion Attica made some progress in the development of overseas
trade,[21] which was perhaps assisted by the disorganisation of the
Peloponnese; but this movement appears to have been checked
in the seventh century by competition from Aigina, which was
more favourably situated on the trans-Ægean trade route.
About 632 B.C. a nobleman named Kylon (the name of his
clan is unknown), who had married a daughter of Theagenes,
tyrant of Megara, attempted to set up a tyranny at Athens.
Since the power of Theagenes appears to have been based on
the woollen trade,[22] it is possible that Kylon too had commercial
connections; but, if so, the mercantile interests at Athens were
not yet strong enough to challenge the landowners successfully,
for Kylon's attempt was abortive. After taking sanctuary in
the temple of Athena Polias, he was put to death at the instigation of Megakles, the leader of the Alkmaionidai, who was
árchon at the time. Kylon's brother and family were sentenced
to perpetual banishment, but his adherents secured the
banishment of the Alkmaionidai as well for violating the
sanctuary.[23] A few years later, the Eupatridai published a code
of laws, drawn up by Drakon, and, since they are not likely
to have taken such a step on their own initiative, it is possible
that this too was the result of pressure from the merchant class.[24]
Apart from the provisions for homicide, which have already
been discussed, all we know of the Code of Drakon is that
petty thefts of agricultural produce were made a capital offence
and that in general it was said to have been written in blood.

Turning to the cities of the Asiatic coast, we find ourselves
again in a very different situation. In the first place, these
communities are all new, being founded by emigrants from
the mainland in accordance with the traditional method of
occupying conquered territory; but they differed from the
Dorian settlements of the Peloponnese in that the newcomers,

who were themselves a mixed lot, fused more completely with the indigenous population, which was non-Greek.

In the second place, these states had important geographical connections, continental and maritime. The Asiatic hinterland was dominated by the wealthy commercial kingdoms of Phrygia, Maionia and, later, Lydia, which in turn were in contact with Babylonia and Assyria. The influence of Oriental art can be traced even in the Homeric poems.[25] Moreover, as we learn from the *Odyssey*, Phœnician traders were already active in the Ægean, and from them the Asiatic Greeks acquired the technique of trade, including the alphabet.

So far as can be gathered from the Homeric poems, down to the end of the eighth century the economy of Ionia remained primarily agricultural, but in the ensuing period maritime trade and colonisation developed so rapidly and widely— ranging from the Crimea to southern Italy, Sicily and North Africa—that the struggle for the land was of relatively brief duration. Landless men were encouraged to seek their fortunes overseas.[26] The internal stresses set up by appropriation of the land found an outlet in colonial expansion, which in turn weakened the position of the landowners by multiplying the possibilities of trade. By the end of the seventh century, in the leading cities of Ionia, political control had been wrested from the landed aristocracy by the tyrant or merchant prince, whose historical function will be examined in the next chapter. What we have to consider now is the effect of the economic and social changes underlying the rise of the aristocracy on Greek poetry and thought.

The poetry of Hesiod, who lived in eighth-century Boiotia, is particularly valuable as a record of his times, because he was not himself a member of the ruling class. He was a yeoman farmer, the son of an immigrant from Kymai on the other side of the Ægean, and it was doubtless from there that he derived his training in the epic tradition. His attitude to the peasantry is at once protective and repressive. He is alive to the growing intensity of competition and to the sufferings inflicted by the rapacity of the ruling landowners; but, since his aim is con- servative—to maintain the established order—he appeals to each class in turn to moderate its claims. The nobles are

warned not to abuse their powers—above all, not to give
"crooked judgments"; the peasants are exhorted to make the
best of their lot by industry and thrift, and to remember that
it is better to enjoy what you have than to covet what you
lack. This attitude is crystallised in some proverbs which now
appear for the first time: Nothing too much; do not strive overmuch; measure in all things is best; suffering teaches sense.[27]
He reminds us of the mediæval schoolmen, whose outlook is
voiced by Chaucer's Parson: "I wot well there is degree above
degree, as reason is, and skill it is that men do their devoir
thereas it is due, but certes extortions and despite of your under-
lings is damnable."[28] The England of Chaucer's Parson was
also based on an agricultural economy, in which the peasant
was bound by similar obligations to his lord.

This proverbial doctrine of "measure" or *métron* does not
appear in the Homeric poems. The nearest approach to it is
the passage in which Poseidon warns Zeus to keep within his
moîra;[29] but in general, as we have seen in our discussion of
this subject, what *moîra* connotes is the positive right enjoyed
by each member of the community to a share in the products
of his labour. The idea of *métron* is *moîra* in a new guise, with
a significant shift of emphasis to its negative aspect: so much
and no more. In the Homeric poems, the word is used only in
a concrete sense of an instrument for measurement or a measured quantity of corn or oil or wine. Under the landed aristocracy, the serf was bound to pay over a fixed portion of his produce to his lord, and the lord must not demand, nor the serf
retain, more than his due.[30] The economic relations characteristic of an agricultural economy are projected as a moral
precept, which in turn invests those relations with an apparently external sanction.

The same idea runs through aristocratic poetry from Alkman
to Pindar. The formula, "Know thyself," inscribed on the
entrance to Apollo's temple at Delphi,[31] is simply a variant of
"Nothing too much": it means that you must recognise your
mortal limitations and not invite divine retribution by aspiring
too high and seeking to become a god. It is an inherent element
in this outlook that all passionate longings are dangerous and
reprehensible. In Pindar, who clung to his aristocratic ideals

in an age in which their social foundation had been largely swept away,[32] the Olympian gods and goddesses, though outwardly the same as Homer's, have lost their irresponsible gaiety—they are splendid to look at, majestic, but they are heartless.

After Hesiod, the art of epic gradually ceased to be creative, but out of it emerged the elegiac couplet, based on the epic hexameter and the epic dialect. Elegiac poetry is mainly secular, and in this respect too it maintains the epic tradition. Much more important, however, and more distinctive of the aristocracy, is the art of choral lyric.

The Achæan chiefs, rewarded by the people for their leadership in war with the lion's share of the spoils, broke loose from the shackles of tribe and clan into an impetuous career of self-assertion; and accordingly their poetry, the epic, was secular, dynamic, individualistic. These chiefs had now been succeeded by sedentary landowners who had combined against the people in a close corporation cut off from the labour of production. They too had ruptured the clan ties between them and their subjects, but in their own ranks each family sedulously maintained its traditional cult as the emblem of its hereditary privileges. Accordingly, aristocratic poetry is religious, static, collective, and in structure more primitive than epic. Its most characteristic form, the choral ode, is in fact directly descended from the ancestral rite of the totemic clan.

The choral ode is a hymn, a processional chant, a dirge for the dead, or a song of triumph for a victory at the Games. Its essence is still the ritual act—the act of sacrifice or dedication or acclaiming the victor on his return to the ancestral home. The centre of the Pindaric ode is the myth, set in between praise of the victor at the opening and the close, and the function of this myth is to celebrate the ancestral glories of his clan. Similarly, in keeping with the static unity of the class for which they are composed, the structure of these odes is severely formal and entirely undramatic. In diction, too, they are far removed from epic. The diction of Homer is simple, spontaneous, free from self-conscious artifice; it is the medium of a community in which social distinctions have not yet petrified into caste. Something of the same fluency is found in the choral odes of

Alkman, who composed for the Spartans at a time when they had not yet become conscious of their historic mission. The mature Sparta is seen in the fragments of Stesichoros—solemn, martial, grandiloquent; and these tendencies are perfected by Pindar, in whose hands the formal, elevated tone of ritual is raised to the highest pitch of elaborate, self-conscious, fastidious, aristocratic art.

The development of aristocratic poetry was most rapid, as we should expect, along the seaboard of Aiolis and Ionia. That the long collective choral ode had once existed on the coast of Asia Minor is clear from the records of Alkman of Sardis and Terpandros of Lesbos; but these poets migrated to Sparta, and in Asia Minor itself the choral ode contracted into the monody—the personal lyrics of Alkaios and Sappho. They both belonged to the old nobility, but in the Lesbos of their day the political supremacy of the landowners was already collapsing and consequently the social barriers between them and the people were breaking down.[33] The Sapphic ode has the simplicity and intensity of the folk-song refined and enriched by the sensitive individualism of a small but enlightened aristocratic circle.

But the greatest achievement of the Greek aristocracy—greater than their poetry—was Ionian science. This movement was confined to the Asiatic seaboard, because it was only there that, thanks to the rapid growth of trade, their vitality had been renewed by fresh contact with the labour of production. Ionian science was the work of a mercantile aristocracy. Its founder, Thales, was himself a merchant who had travelled widely and is said to have made a corner in oil.[34] Of the two sciences which he developed, geometry and astronomy, the first had been called into being by the demands of agriculture and architecture, the second by the need for an adequate technique of navigation in the development of overseas trade. In both he did little more than introduce to the Greeks knowledge that he had acquired from contact with Egypt and Babylonia;[35] but none the less he was serving an immediate need, and in this way he laid the foundations for the Ionian school of philosophy, which aimed at co-ordinating the results obtained from these techniques in a single theory of the origin and growth of the universe. It is significant that this final stage was only reached when Ionian commerce was in decline. The work of Anaximander (611–547 B.C.) was done during the destructive civil wars which followed the collapse of the tyranny at Miletos.

The fundamental question to which these philosophers addressed themselves was the problem of change: how had the world come to be what it was? This question was fundamental, because the ancient structure of human society, which, though never at rest, had maintained an unbroken continuity from the first segmentation of the primitive horde to the Greek settlement of the Asiatic seaboard on the basis of tribe and clan, had now been shattered by the class struggle.[36] As we saw in our analysis of Moira, this structure was the mould in which Greek thought had taken shape; but that mould was now breaking up, and the traditional modes of thought which had been fashioned to express it were defied by the new social structure that was superseding it. It was this abrupt contradiction between inherited ideas and contemporary reality that impelled the Ionian aristocracy to call in question the origin and evolution of the world in which they lived. The traditional ideas were co-ordinated for the first time as a consciously applied scientific method.

The word they used for the world order was *kósmos*. The primary connotation of this word was social, and that connotation still survived in a number of political terms—the *kósmoi* of Crete and the *kosmopóleis* of Lokroi. In the *Iliad*, the verb *kosméo* is used in two senses only—the marshalling of troops for battle and the settlement of tribes on occupied territory; and these two senses were really the same, because the troops were marshalled in tribes and phratries. Thus, the Ionian philosophers described the world order in terms of the tribal order.[37] In reducing the world to order, they proceeded, naturally and inevitably, from the conception of order inherent in their traditional modes of thought.

The tribal structure of society had evolved by organic division of an undifferentiated primary nucleus. The primitive horde had segmented into clans, the clans into groups of clans. These units within units were held together in an intricate network of co-operation and competition, mutual rivalries and reciprocal services. The clans collaborated in the work of production, competed in the struggle for prestige. They were united by intermarriage, divided by the vendetta. The tension set up by the interaction of these contrary forces—co-operation and competition, combination and opposition, attraction and repulsion—was the dynamic of the tribal system, which survived until the growth of private property destroyed its internal equilibrium. In Greece, it had received its first shock during the wars of conquest, which threw up a ruling class of military leaders—a class which had subsequently solidified as a land-owning aristocracy. And nowhere had the forces of disruption developed so swiftly as in Ionia. The Ionian settlers of the Asiatic coast, like the Dorian conquerors of Sparta, had organised themselves on a tribal basis, which they reproduced in their colonies overseas; but, whereas the Spartan conquerors were able to close their ranks, the Ionian Greeks had seen their system dissolve almost before their eyes in the crucible of trade.

Anaximander taught that the physical universe was composed of a number of substances, which had been brought into being by motion out of what he called *to ápeiron*, the boundless, that which is spatially infinite and qualitatively indeterminate.[38] In other words, the universe had evolved by differentiation out of a single original nucleus. And, just as the world order has been brought into being by differentiation, so it is destroyed by assimilation. The derivative substances are continuously encroaching upon one another, with the result that they lose their identity by reabsorption into the undifferentiated primary matter out of which they have emerged. In the words of Anaximander, "they render unto one another the penalty of their injustice according to the ordering of time."

All this has been explained by Cornford—one of the few modern scholars to grapple seriously with the origins of Ionian thought.[39] His account is substantially complete except for one point. The statement of Anaximander's which has just been quoted clearly rests on the idea of *métron*, the notion that due observance of prescribed "measures" or limitations is necessary for the maintenance of the established order; and, as we have seen, this notion is merely the aristo-cratic reinterpretation of the primitive idea of *moîra*. Cornford is therefore quite right in relating the secondary substances of Anaximander to the *moîrai* of Greek tribal society. And his conclusion is confirmed by a scrutiny of the expression used for "paying the penalty"—*didónai díken kai tísin*, corresponding to the Latin *poenas dare*. Now, as Calhoun has pointed out, the phrase *díken didónai* (of which *tísin didónai* is merely an Ionic variant) is used only in reference to private suits, derived from primitive self-help; and, moreover, it is used primarily of giving satisfaction or compensation for homicide.[40] Thus, Anaximander has described the encroachment of one sub-stance on another in terms of a feud or vendetta between rival clans.

It seems clear, therefore, that Anaximander's theory of the physical universe was essentially a conscious realisation of the implications inherent in primitive thought. It was the charac-teristic outlook of primitive man crystallised and formulated at the moment when primitive society was passing away. And it was an intellectual achievement of the first magnitude. We have only to compare Anaximander's consistent materialism and his organic view of evolution with the obscurantist cosmo-logy of Plato and the later Pythagoreans to see that the advance from tribe to state involved loss as well as gain. And, further, having determined the philosopher's position in the world he was endeavouring to explain, we can see where his method failed him. Applying it to the origin of life, he said that man was descended from animals of another species (an idea implicit in totemism) and that life first arose out of the moist element as it was evaporated by the sun. This, too, was a masterly conclusion, to which he was led by actual observa-tion; for he had found fossilised sea-shells above sea-level, and one of the features of Ionia is the advance of the coastline round the estuaries owing to the accumulation of alluvial deposits—a feature so marked that the coastal plain ad-joining the city of Smyrna was once described as "a gift from Poseidon."[41] Organic life, therefore, arose out of the encroachment of the dry element on the moist. But at this point Anaximander was faced with an insoluble contradiction; for his social preconceptions had impelled him to assume that the process of encroachment was destructive. Further progress in the understanding of human evolution was impossible until those preconceptions had been superseded as a result of further progress in society itself.

VI

TYRANNY

THE economic and political changes of the seventh and sixth centuries B.C.—the growth of trade, the rise of a merchant class, the building of towns—were intensified by a technical advance of far-reaching significance which these changes had promoted. The story of Meidas, the Phrygian king who turned all that he touched into gold, is still remembered as a popular fable; and equally famous in antiquity was Gyges of Lydia, who, with the aid of his gold ring, which had a magic seal, made himself invisible, stole into the king's palace, killed the king and became king himself.[1] Both these myths have a historical foundation. It was the merchants of Phrygia and· Lydia, exploiting the gold and silver mines of Sipylos and Tmolos, who invented the coinage. Meidas and Gyges were merchant-princes who used their financial position to seize the royal power. These money-made kings were so different from the kings of the past that they were called by a new name— *týrannoi*, or tyrants.

The fable of Gyges embodies the final step in the evolution of the coinage—the use of metal stamped with the emblem of a prominent merchant as a guarantee of value. Iron spits and gold and silver utensils had long been employed to facilitate exchange, but their circulation had been limited by their bulk and by the lack of a recognised standard. In general, trade had been dependent on barter, which meant that it was confined for the most part to the satisfaction of immediate needs. In contrast to these rudimentary expedients, the new coins were light, standardised and state-guaranteed. Like Gyges' ring, they penetrated everywhere. In the words of Herakleitos, who taught that fire is the primary substance of which the world is made, "fire is exchanged for all things and all things for fire, just as gold for goods and goods for gold."[2]

In one city after another, as the use of money spread, the

merchants challenged the political privileges of the old nobility, who drew their power from birth and their wealth from land. Sappho and Alkaios had seen the overthrow of the Penthilidai by the tyrant Pittakos, who had married into a noble family; the Basilidai of Ephesos had fallen about the same time; and at the end of the seventh century Thrasyboulos was tyrant at Miletos. Meanwhile, on the mainland, the Bakchiadai of Corinth had been overthrown by Kypselos, and a little later tyrannies were set up by Orthagoras at Sikyon and Theagenes at Megara. Of these early tyrants, several are known to have belonged to the merchant class, and all belonged to cities situated on the trans-Ægean trade route.[3]

In Attica the development of the tyranny was slower and is therefore easier to follow. The Athenians had played little part in the colonial expansion of the seventh century, and therefore the internal struggle for the land became all the more intense.

Freedom for trade meant freedom from the control of the Eupatridai, who in turn saw the economic basis of their power being undermined by money. Faced with the competition of these *nouveaux riches*, the landowners recouped themselves by intensifying their exploitation of the peasantry. The result was, however, that, by driving the peasants to clamour for a re-division of the land, they played into the hands of their rivals, who took advantage of agrarian unrest to extort concessions for themselves. In so far as both were opposed to the land-owning aristocracy, the merchants and the peasants had a common interest; but the peasants suffered acutely from the introduction of money,[4] and the worst landowners of all were not the nobles, whose relations with the peasants were at least traditional and personal, but the merchants themselves, who had no use for tradition and managed their estates on a strictly commercial basis. These estates they had acquired either as speculators by buying out the impoverished *noblesse*—for one of the first effects of money had been to facilitate the alienation of land—or else by marrying into the noble families and so securing a share in their political privileges.

The attitude of the aristocracy to these developments is revealed in their poetry. Landed wealth comes from God, who sends the rain from heaven, and is therefore honourable

and enduring, but wealth won by trade is man-made, hazard-
ous and unstable.[5] The losses of a bad season can be made good,
with God's grace, in the following year, but a squall at sea may
sink the merchant's ship with all his capital. The pursuit of
riches is dangerous, because it invites the jealousy of heaven.
Ambition tempts man to overreach himself. He loses what he
has in his eagerness for more. Led on by the lure of winged
hopes, he is a child in chase of a bird. The gods are also jealous
of those who marry above their station. That was the sin of
Ixion, as related by Pindar. Infatuated by the honours which
the gods had conferred on him, he attempted to ravish the
Queen of Heaven, but he embraced only a cloud and was then
hurled into Tartarus.[6]

In Attica, the first great crisis came early in the sixth century.
The peasants were on the verge of insurrection. The lowest
class were permitted to retain only one-sixth of their produce.[7]
Preyed on by usurers, whose rates of interest soared to 50 per
cent., they had been forced to sell their land, their children,
themselves. Many had been driven overseas, many were beggars
or slaves, homeless in fields once their own. The Eupatridai
perceived that, if they were to avert a peasant revolt, they must
enlist the co-operation of the merchants, who were as alarmed
as they were at the threat to property. Accordingly, Solon, a
member of the Eupatridai who had been actively engaged in
trade, was entrusted with dictatorial powers (593 B.C.).

If Solon had been a revolutionary, he would have made
himself tyrant and so perhaps have anticipated the progress of
his people by more than a generation; but, of course, if that
had been his intention, he would not have been appointed.
The Eupatridai knew their man.

First, he relieved the economic pressure on the peasantry
with the minimum of change. By cancelling outstanding debts
and prohibiting enslavement for debt, he evaded the demand
for a re-division of the land. He did nothing to modify the
sixth-part system or to restrict current rates of interest. The
smallholder was still exposed to the depredations of the usurer,
still in danger of being driven off the land. That was no doubt
part of Solon's intention, because, so long as the peasantry was
attached to the soil, it was not available as a source of cheap

labour for the development of industry. This factor was of great importance for the merchant class at a time when the industrial exploitation of slave labour had hardly begun. It was in this period, moreover, that the Athenians began to work the silver mines of Laurion, and the main source of labour must have been the peasants driven off the land.

Further, Solon gave the working class a voice in the government by reviving the popular assembly, which since the decay of the tribal system had ceased to function. It was this body that elected, though not from its own members, the *árchontes* and other officers of state. It also met as a court of justice to try cases other than homicide. The revival of the assembly can hardly have been of direct benefit to the peasants, who were naturally too poor to travel to Athens for its meetings, but it improved considerably the position of the artisans, who could now settle their own legal disputes. On the other hand, by the side of the Assembly, Solon created a new body, the Council of the Four Hundred, from which the working class was excluded, and the Assembly could only vote on resolutions placed before it by the Council. His motive in instituting this body was to put a check both on the working class and on the Council of the Areopagus, which was the name now borne by the old Council of the Eupatridai. The class which gained by this innovation was therefore the new middle class.

Having saved the Eupatridai from expropriation, Solon was in a position to demand something in return. They surrendered their claim tŏ serve as *árchontes* by right of birth. The qualification for administrative office and subsequent membership of the Council of the Areopagus was fixed in terms of landed property. This meant that wealthy merchants could now become *árchontes* by investing their capital in land, and it was a substantial breach in the aristocratic monopoly; but, since a merchant turned landowner tended to become a landowner in his outlook and interests, it did not meet the full demands of the merchant class. As Wade-Gery has put it:

> Under Solon, the new rich had been prepared to buy land in order to enter the governing class; they turned themselves into country gentlemen . . . presumably by converting

personal into real property. But after a little time those who had done so ranked and felt as "landlords," solid with the old aristocracy; and the new rich maintained the right of a merchant, as a merchant, to enter the governing class without becoming a country gentleman first.[8]

The institution of the Council of the Four Hundred by the side of the Council of the Areopagus reflected the growing differentiation between religious and secular interests in consequence of the development of trade. Nevertheless, although no longer composed exclusively of Eupatridai, the latter remained the stronghold of reaction. Besides its jurisdiction in cases of homicide, it had the right to prosecute in cases where the popular court had declined to do so, and it exercised over the observance of the laws a general supervision which must have been the more effective for being undefined.

The general significance of Solon's reforms emerges very clearly from Adcock's remarks on his attitude to the working class:[9]

> The effect of his limitations on the Assembly was to keep administration and the initiative in policy in the hands of the well-to-do or middle classes. It was true that years of aristocratic government had left the commons politically uneducated, the easy dupes of ambitious leaders, and Solon's poems show him well aware of the dangers of their uninstructed hopes. But the alternative, to deny to the commons all political power, was a greater evil and a greater danger, and Solon might hope that the new economic order would keep the poorer Athenians too busy or too contented to lend themselves to faction. Given that little power which was enough, the people might not be misled into grasping at more. And both policy and justice demanded that, if they did not really govern, they should be protected from misgovernment and injustice.

When Solon claimed that he had given the people a measure of power that was neither too much nor too little, he made a significant contribution to the development of Greek thought.[10] The motto of the old aristocracy, nothing too much, had set an upper limit to man's earthly lot, but no lower limit. Solon claimed to have found the mean, and was thus the first to express the characteristic outlook of the rising middle class.

During the next thirty years, as wealth in personal property continued to grow, the aristocratic front began to crack. Solon himself had been a landowner who turned to trade, and now other noble families followed suit—above all, the Alkmaionidai, who had commercial connections with Sardis, the great *entrepôt* for the hinterland of Asia Minor, and the Peisistratidai, who were interested in the mines of Laurion. Each of these princely houses cultivated its own political following. Megakles, son of Alkmaion, organised the merchants and artisans of the ports, Peisistratos the mining population. They were both opposed by Lykourgos of the Eteoboutadai, at the head of the big landowners, and at the same time they were in competition with one another. So long as the opposition was divided, the established régime survived. Twice Peisistratos attempted to seize power, but both times he was driven out by combination of his opponents. He employed his second exile in developing important financial interests in the silver mines of Mount Pangaion in Thrace; and, meanwhile, in 546, Sardis had fallen to the Persians. This must have been a blow to his rival, Megakles. Six years later he made his third attempt, and this time he was successful.[11]

Like other tyrannies, the rule of Peisistratos was necessarily autocratic, because a strongly centralised monarchy was the only safeguard against a counter-revolution. In the absolute character of his rule, as in his championship of the new middle class, he bears a recognisable relationship to the English Tudors.

He used the lands vacated by the exiled grandees to solve the agrarian problem. The peasants were settled on the confiscated estates with government assistance as small proprietors. Their demands were satisfied. This was an enduring achievement. Meanwhile, his vigorous commercial policy in developing the coinage and the export trade ensured the continued support of the merchants, and his comprehensive programme of public works, including the demolition of the old city wall and the construction of an aqueduct, which is a sure sign of the urban revolution, gave employment to the working class in addition to the demands of private enterprise in shipbuilding, pottery and metallurgy. A century later, Sparta still had the appearance of a village; Athens was already a city.

These social changes necessarily involved a transformation of the religious and cultural life of the community, and under Peisistratos this, too, was consciously directed. He completed the temple of Athena Polias and reorganised the Panathenaia as a great national festival. He gave official recognition to the worship of Dionysus, who hitherto had been scarcely recognised as an Olympian, in order to offset the exclusive clan cults of the aristocracy, and he founded or reorganised the festival of the City Dionysia, which in civic splendour was soon to outshine even the Panathenaia. And, finally, he instituted public recitals by Ionian minstrels of the Homeric poems, which now became known in Attica for the first time. The aim underlying all these cultural innovations was to reinforce the commercial expansion of the new city-state by fostering a spirit of national self-consciousness.

The success of Peisistratos was due primarily to his correct estimate of the objective possibilities of the situation with which he had to deal. It was indeed fortunate for him that his rule coincided with the Persian advance to the Ægean, which freed him from the commercial competition of Ionia, but he was quick to turn his good fortune to account. In foreign policy, his most important achievement was the occupation of Sigeion on the Hellespont. Control of the Dardanelles thus became for the Athenians one of their vital interests, ensuring them of a plentiful supply of cheap corn, and so enabling them to support a far larger industrial population than they could have done from their own resources at the existing level of production. This policy had, of course, its negative side. It depressed the home market and discouraged the improvement of agricultural technique; but, so long as Athens was able to control the Hellespont and absorb the influx into the towns, it was justified.

Peisistratos died in 528 and was succeeded by his two sons, Hipparchos and Hippias. Hipparchos was assassinated nine years later in the course of a personal vendetta. Athenians of the next century persuaded themselves that the assassins of Hipparchos were responsible for the overthrow of the tyranny, but in point of fact Hippias remained in power for another eight years. His growing unpopularity during the latter part of his reign, though doubtless accentuated by personal factors, was due primarily to the changes taking place in the balance of political forces. In strengthening the middle classes, Peisistratos had done his work so thoroughly that they now felt strong enough to dispense with a protective dictatorship. Consequently, they grew increasingly impatient of the expenses it entailed, while Hippias became involved in financial difficulties, which he could only meet by still further exactions. Thus, having begun as a progressive force, the tyranny had become an obstacle to progress. The final blow came in 512, when Hippias was deprived by the Persian conquest of Thrace of his main source of revenue. He was expelled two years later.

It was not, however, the progressive forces that actually effected his overthrow, but a combination of his opponents on the other side—Kleisthenes, the son of his father's enemy, Megakles, who was playing his own hand, and the other exiled aristocrats, who saw in the weakening of the tyranny an opportunity for a counter-revolution. For many years past the Alkmaionidai had been assiduously repairing their fortunes, and, in particular, they secured an enormous contract for rebuilding the temple at Delphi, which had been destroyed by fire.[12] Kleisthenes used his influence at Delphi to break the friendly relations which Peisistratos had cultivated with Sparta, and in 510 he entered Attica with the Spartan King at the head of a Spartan army. It was evidently intended by his allies that the tyranny of Hippias should be followed by a restoration of the aristocracy, but Kleisthenes aimed at taking his place. When his aims became apparent, the aristocratic leader Isagoras appealed to Sparta to intervene a second time. Kleisthenes replied by appealing to the people. He put through a number of democratic reforms in the teeth of the aristocrats and enfranchised hundreds of resident aliens and slaves. The result was that, when the Spartan King reappeared in Attica to restore the *ancien régime*, with Isagoras acting as informer, he was shut up together with his troops in the Akropolis and only released on the understanding that he would desist from

further intervention. It was a great victory for the people.
The function of the Greek tyranny was transitional. By forcing and holding a breach in the rule of the aristocracy, it
enabled the middle class to consolidate its forces for the final
stage in the democratic revolution, which involved the overthrow of the tyranny itself. That is why, in Greek tradition, it
was almost unanimously condemned. It was denounced in
advance by the aristocrats because it was progressive, and in
retrospect by the democrats because it had become reactionary.
The only poets who have anything to say in its favour are
Pindar and Simonides, who served their patrons for pay.
Doubtless the first poets at the City Dionysia were warm in
their praises of Peisistratos, but their writings have perished;[13]
and to the contemporaries of Æschylus the tyranny meant,
above all, Hippias, who, after his expulsion, joined forces with
the national enemy in the hope of being restored as the puppet
of a foreign power. And, finally, since it was everywhere transitional and in many states had been terminated by a successful
counter-revolution, it came to symbolise in popular imagination the spectacular rise to power of the man who, having
amassed great riches, forgets that he is mortal and is lured by
divine wrath to self-destruction. Behind this tradition there lies
a consciousness of the treacherous mobility of money, which
turns king into beggar as rapidly as beggar into king.

The violent resistance which the democratic movement had
encountered is vividly mirrored in the poetry of Theognis.
True to type, this reactionary *bon vivant* identified civilisation
with the privileges of his class:[14]

> Shame has perished; pride and insolence have conquered
> justice and possess the earth. . . . The city is still a city, but
> the populace is changed: once they knew nothing of laws,
> wrapped their flanks in goatskins and dwelt like deer beyond
> the walls; but now they are nobles and the one-time nobles
> base—O who can bear the sight? . . . Grind them hard and
> let their yoke be heavy—that is the way to make them love
> their masters. . . . The mass of the people knows one virtue,
> wealth; nothing else avails. . . . Not to be born is best, nor
> look upon the sunshine; or once born to hasten through the
> gates of death and lie beneath a heap of earth.

Because the old caste system has broken down; because the serfs are no longer content to be burdened like asses; because, too, the old unwritten code of personal allegiance and liberality has been translated into cash—therefore civilisation has perished. But civilisation did not wait for Theognis. The old culture, it is true, was breaking up, but only because new aspirations, new values, new ideas were bursting into life.

PART THREE

ORIGIN OF DRAMA

DIONYSUS AND SATYRS

VII

INITIATION

IN the primitive hunting tribe, besides the sexual division of labour already noted, the members of the community are graded according to age as children, adults and elders.[1] The children assist the women in the work of food-gathering; the men hunt and fight; the elders are the councillors of the tribe. The transition from one grade to another is effected by rites of initiation. The most important of these is the initiation of boys at puberty, which is at once an introduction to full tribal status and a preparation for marriage. The initiation of girls is similar, but usually less elaborate. It is also less widely attested, because primitive women are naturally loth to reveal to male anthropologists secrets which they guard from their own men; and the status of women in our own society is such that few have the opportunity of becoming anthropologists.[2]

The function of initiation—to admit the child to the status of adult—is expressed in primitive thought as a belief that the child dies and is born again. To understand this conception, we must discard modern notions of the nature of birth and death. In primitive society, the newborn child is regarded as one of its ancestors come to life again. That is why, in many parts of the world, including Greece, it is or has been the custom to name the child after one of its grandparents.[3] At puberty the child dies as a child and is born again as a man or woman. The adult is transformed in the same way into an elder, and at death the elder enters the highest grade of all, that of the totemic ancestors, from which in due course he re-emerges to pass through the whole cycle again. Birth is death and death is birth. They are complementary and inseparable aspects of an eternal process of change, which includes not merely birth and death as we understand them but also the growth and decay of the power to beget and to give birth. As Cureau has remarked in his study of the African negro, "the

97

natives hold that every serious event in physical life is equivalent to death followed by resurrection."[4]

This mode of thought is expressed concretely in a universal feature of primitive initiation—the mimetic or symbolic death and resurrection of the novice.[5] The ceremony takes various forms. Some are highly realistic, comprising both the act of killing him and his birth from a woman; in others he is supposed to be swallowed and disgorged by a god or spirit. This element is so fundamental that it can be readily recognised in the more attenuated forms characteristic of the higher stages of tribal society. Such is the magic sleep or dream, in which the novice is laid to rest as a child and, after being possessed of an ancestral spirit, awakes as a man. Such, too, it may be conjectured, is the custom, common to many initiation ceremonies, of dressing the boy as a girl or the girl as a boy, on the principle that in order to acquire a new identity the novice must first escape from the old.[6] In many tribes, when the boys are taken away to be initiated, their mothers mourn for them as dead, and, when they return, they behave like infants, as though unable to speak or walk or recognise their friends. At the same time they receive a new name, which in primitive thought is equivalent to a new identity.[7] Just as the naming of a newborn child after one of its forbears originally signified that it was the reincarnation of the man whose name it bore, so the assumption of a new name at initiation signifies that the novice has been born again.

Besides these dramatic representations of the death and resurrection, the novice is usually subjected to a surgical operation consisting in the amputation of some part of his body— the removal of the foreskin, if it is a boy, or of the clitoris, if it is a girl; the knocking out of a tooth; the amputation of a finger; the cutting of the hair or of a lock of hair. Of these operations, the most primitive are circumcision and tooth-extraction, both of which are found in Australia, but never in combination. This suggests that they were all originally different methods of achieving a common object. What that object was is a question that lies beyond our present purpose; but it may be observed that, since the amputated part is carefully preserved,[8] there is a parallel between these rites and the burial of the dead, whose bodies are preserved, in whole or in part, in order that they may be born again.

The remaining rites of initiation fall into two categories, which may be taken together because they cannot always be distinguished—purification and ordeals. The novices are washed in water or blood, they bathe in a stream or in the sea, or they are scorched in front of a fire; they run races, sometimes with painful handicaps; they engage in sham fights, often with fatal consequences; they are scourged until they are unconscious; their ears and noses are bored, their flesh gashed or tattooed. The physical pain incidental to most of these rites is universally explained as a trial of strength or test of endurance, in which failure means disqualification or disgrace; and there can be no doubt that the severity of these ordeals has been consciously accentuated by the elders in order to terrify the novice into a habit of permanent obedience. It is probable, however, that their original function was purification or mortification. Just as pollution is disease and disease is death, so purification is a renewal of life.

Finally, the novice receives instruction in the customs and traditions of the tribe. This is done by homilies and catechisms, by the performance of dramatic dances, and by the revelation of sacred objects, whose significance is at the same time explained. The whole ceremony is strictly secret. It is performed at a distance from the tribal settlement, usually on a specially prepared ceremonial ground, from which all members of the community except the elders and their initiated assistants have been warned away, often on pain of death. In many tribes the actual initiation is preceded by a period of seclusion, which may last for months, and when the novices return to the settlement they are strictly forbidden to reveal to the uninitiated anything that they have done or seen or heard.

Among most hunting tribes, initiation is followed immediately by marriage, which therefore is not marked by any ritual distinct from initiation itself. That explains why the marriage rite of many primitive peoples closely resembles initiation. This is especially true of the woman's part in it, because in her case the postponement of marriage after puberty is rare. The men, on the other hand, are usually obliged, in the higher grades of tribal society, to undergo a further period of probation before they can marry. This interval is spent in the Men's House, which has been described by Hutton Webster as follows:[9]

> The Men's House is usually the largest building in a tribal settlement. It belongs in common to the villagers; it serves as a council chamber or town hall, as a guest-house for strangers, and as the sleeping resort of the men. . . . When marriage and the exclusive possession of a woman do not follow immediately upon initiation into the tribe, the institution of the Men's House becomes an effective restraint upon the sexual proclivities of the unmarried youth. It then serves as a club-house for the bachelors. . . . An institution so firmly established and so widely spread may be expected to survive by devotion to other uses, as the earlier ideas which led to its foundation fade away. As guard posts where the young men are confined on military service and are exercised in the arts of war, these houses often become a serviceable means of defence. The religious worship of the community often centres in them. Often they form the theatre of dramatic representations. . . . The presence, then, in a primitive community of the Men's House in any one of its numerous forms points strongly to the existence, now or in the past, of secret initiation ceremonies.

In general, initiation is associated with the tribe as a whole, but the evidence of the lower hunting tribes in Australia and New Guinea points clearly to an antecedent stage in which it had been centred in the totemic clan. The transfer of these rites from clan to tribe corresponds to the consolidation of the tribal system; and, conversely, when that system begins to disintegrate, initiation loses its tribal character, either falling into decay, in which case the rites become perfunctory and disconnected, still generally practised, but domestic in character and often performed long before puberty, or else, retaining their original cohesion, they form the basis of the magical sodality or secret society, which is the old clan in a new and modified form. Moreover, as Webster has shown, the rise of these societies and the decline of the clan are both correlated with the development of social inequalities:[10]

Initiation ceremonies, such as we have been studying, retain their democratic and tribal aspects only in societies which have not emerged from that primitive stage in which all social control is in the hands of the tribal elders. The presence of ceremonies of this character throughout Australia and New Guinea is to be associated with the absence of definite and permanent chieftainships in these islands. . . . In Melanesia and Africa, political centralisation has resulted to a large degree in the establishment of chieftainships powerful over a considerable area and often hereditary in nature, but this process has not continued so far as to make possible the entire surrender to the tribal chiefs of those functions of social control which in the earlier stages of society rest with the elders alone. . . . With developing political centralisation such functions tend to become obsolete and the religious and dramatic aspects of the societies assume the most important place. This last stage is reached both in Polynesia and in North America.

In the secret society the structure of the clan is perpetuated and transformed. It has a distinctive totem, a distinctive tradition, and a distinctive ritual; it derives its unity from the strong sense of solidarity which animates its members; and in many cases it has magico-economic functions to perform—the propagation of animals used for food, the making of rain, the promotion of the harvest. On the other hand, its membership is not based on consanguinity, but on community of religious experience, beginning with the rite of initiation. In other words, the qualification for admission is not birth, but re-birth. Accordingly, the totem is no longer hereditary, but acquired by initiation.

The candidate for admission, who is usually but not invariably an adolescent, goes out alone into the forest, where he spends many days or weeks or months in complete solitude, fasting, sleeping, and dreaming of the animal concerned, which thus becomes his individual totem or guardian spirit, the power that shapes his destiny and determines all the crucial issues of his life. When he returns home, he is an initiate and as such receives a new name. Among the Kwakiutl Indians the novices return in a state of temporary insanity, induced both by their physical privations and by the strength of their belief

HA

that the guardian spirit has actually entered their bodies and possessed them. The spirit is then exorcised by songs and dances performed by the society and designed to signify that the newly initiated member has died and been born again. The same idea underlies the ritual associated with what in North America has become the principal function of these societies—the healing of the sick. In the Ojibwa fraternities, the patient whose spirit has been exorcised becomes thereby an initiate, and in the Tsiahk fraternity of the Cape Flattery Indians the patient has to be initiated before he can be cured. He is restored to health by being born again.

The power of these sodalities is derived primarily, of course, from their monopoly of certain forms of magic; but at this stage of human society magic has become far more than a supplement to the technique of production. The privileges enjoyed by the initiated have lost their economic foundation and are exercised more or less consciously for the purpose of social exploitation. In Mexico and Peru, the most advanced areas of primitive America, this hypertrophy of magic, which is a constant tendency in the development of agriculture, reduced the people to a state of absolute subjection to a blood-thirsty theocracy, whose progressive refinement of human sacrifice was only terminated by the extinction of their culture in the even greater horrors of the Spanish conquest.

Finally, a universal feature of these sodalities, not only in America, but in Africa and Polynesia, is the periodical performance of some kind of ritual drama, in which the actors impersonate the tribal ancestors, often in their totemic form. Thus, the Katcina sodalities of the Hopi Indians perform a masked dance of the ancestors, who are regarded as still active members of the community and charged by means of the dance with the duty of sending rain and making the crops grow. Such ritual resembles mature drama in that it is performed before an audience and represents an action, while its association with the ancestral spirits and its economic function relate it no less clearly to the mimetic rite of the primitive hunting clan.

We saw in an earlier chapter how the mimetic dance of the totemic clan, which originated as part of the actual technique of production and represented the actions of the totem species, passed into a dramatisation of the activities of the clan ancestors conceived as animals (p. 15). In this way the ritual gave rise to a myth, which reproduced all its features in a narrative form. It is often said in such cases that the myth is the explanation of the ritual; but, at least in its earlier phases, it is rather the spoken form of the ritual act—the collective expression of the unforgettable experience periodically shared by the participants in the rite itself. Later, when the clan system is in decay, the myth may detach itself from the rite and develop independent features of its own. Even these, however, are largely inspired by ritual, because in primitive society almost every experience assumes the form of some ritual act. Or else, maintaining their original relationship, both myth and ritual survive in the drama of the magical fraternity, which preserves, as we have seen, the structure of the clan. In these conditions, since the fraternity is secret, the myth becomes a mystery, which is revealed to the uninitiated only in its outward and visible form, its inner meaning being reserved for "those who understand." Lastly, when the fraternity itself declines, its dramatic function is usually the most persistent. The society of mystics becomes a guild of actors, whose plays have lost their esoteric significance, but still retain to some extent the character of a mystery, which somehow renews life.

Our next task is to examine in the light of these conclusions the evidence relating to analogous institutions in ancient Greece. This consists principally in rites performed during adolescence or early manhood, in myths relating to the birth of Zeus and Dionysus, in the ritual origins of certain festivals, in the cults of mystical religion, and, finally, in the origins of drama.

The traditional education of the Spartan youth, which has become a byword for austerity, has been described at length by Plutarch.[11]

The newborn child was taken to the elders of the tribe, who decided whether it was to be reared or exposed. Boys remained in the care of their parents until they were seven, when they were enrolled in one of the *agélai* or "herds," led by one of themselves. The members of the *agéla* lived a communal life strictly disciplined and constantly supervised by the elders.

They shaved their heads, wore coarse cloaks and walked bare-foot. They spent the day in athletic exercises, including mock fights. During the summer they slept on rushes which they gathered from the Eurotas and had to pluck by hand without using knives. In winter the rushes were replaced by leaves of the herb called wolf's-bane. After their twelfth year they were allowed only a single cloak, which they wore summer and winter, and were forbidden to anoint themselves or bathe except on rare and specified occasions. Each of the more promising was assigned to a man called his "lover," with whom he entered into an intimate relationship which lasted throughout life. At the age of seventeen they were promoted from the *agéla* to the *boúa*, or "herd of oxen," under the leader-ship of an *eíren*—that is, a man in his second year of adult status. The *eíren* supervised their games, fights and preparations for meals, for which they had to steal fuel and food without being detected.[12] After supper he remained with them, teaching them songs and questioning them about public affairs. The boy who gave a wrong answer had his thumb bitten by the *eíren*. Among the songs they learnt was their part in a festival of three choirs, the first being supplied by themselves, the second by the men, and the third by the elders. The elders began, "Once we were young and brave and strong"; the men answered, "So are we now, so come and try"; the boys ended, "But we'll be strongest by and by." At eighteen the boy became a *melleíren*, and at some time during the next two years he was subjected to the severest test of all—the public scourging of all the *melleírenes* at the altar of Artemis Orthia. Plutarch records that he had himself seen several boys die without a murmur during this barbarous ordeal.

At twenty the *melleíren* became an *eíren* and was admitted to the *pheidítion* or *philítion*, a club-house where the men partook of common meals provided by contributions from their *klêroi* and from the produce of the hunt. Boys were allowed to attend on these occasions after being warned by the oldest man present that "through this"—pointing to the door—"no words go out." Marriage was not permitted immediately after the attainment of manhood, while those who remained unmarried beyond a certain period, the length of which is not stated, were subject to various penalties and disabilities. Even after marriage, the men continued to eat and sleep at the club-house.

Of the training for girls we know less, but they too were organised in *agélai* for practice in dancing and running for the public festivals, which were witnessed by the men and were the recognised occasion for proposals of marriage.[13] The bride was carried off by her husband with a pretence of force. She was attended by an older woman, who cut her hair, dressed her in man's clothes, and then left her in the dark. Later in the night she was visited by her husband, who lay with her and then returned to spend the rest of the night at the club-house. Plutarch says that the women did not marry for some time after puberty, and this accords with the evidence that their education, too, was strictly controlled by the state.

According to Aristotle, the institutions of Dorian Crete were more archaic than the Spartan, and in support of this contention he points out that the *andreîon*, or "men's house," which is what the Cretans called the place of the men's common meals, was the old name of the Spartan *pheidítion*.[14] In Crete, too, the boys used to attend at these meals, wearing coarse cloaks, but they did not enter the *agéla* until seventeen, which was the age at which the Spartan boys entered the *boúa*. In the *agéla* they were inured to physical hardships, trained in hunting and running, also in mock fights, in which one *agéla* was set against another, and in the national war dance, traditionally ascribed to the Kouretes and representing a march into battle to the music of lyre and flute. The importance of foot-racing is indicated by the terms *dromeîs* and *apodrómoi*, "runners" and "non-runners," which were used to distinguish members of the *agélai* from their juniors.

The Cretan boy, too, had his lover, whom he acquired in the following manner. Having given three days' notice of his intention, the lover went with his boon companions to the boy's home and with their assistance carried him off from his relatives, who pursued them as far as the Men's House. After that he was free to take the boy with him into any part of the country he pleased. For two months the boy lived entirely with his new companions, spending most of the time in hunting. When the period of seclusion was over, he received from his lover the gifts of a warrior's costume, an ox and a drinking-cup, returned to his home, sacrificed the ox to Zeus, and entertained his comrades from the Men's House to a feast.

We are informed by Strabo that "all those promoted from the *agéla* were obliged to marry at the same time." This means that marriage was a state-controlled and public ceremony comprising all those who belonged to the same age grade. Nothing of importance has been recorded of the Cretan training for girls, except that they married at puberty, but continued to live with their parents "until they were old enough to keep house."

Some of the details in this evidence will acquire significance from subsequent stages of our enquiry, but the general character of the two systems is already clear. In both countries the crucial period in the transition from boyhood to manhood began at the age of seventeen. The transition itself seems to have been effected at Sparta by the ordeal of flagellation, in Crete by the two months of seclusion. One would like to know more of what happened during those months, but it is plain that the gifts which the boy received at the end of that period were intended to signify that he was now a man and as such entitled to eat with men.

That the Dorian discipline of Sparta and Crete was largely unique in the Greek world is clear from the unfailing interest which it excited among other Greeks. It is natural that such customs should have been better preserved by that branch of the Greek race which was the last to enter the Ægean, and especially by the Spartans, who, for the reasons given in an earlier chapter, were the most conservative aristocracy in Greece. Nevertheless, the existence of *agélai* among the Ionians is attested by inscriptions from Miletos and Smyrna, and the training of boys at Athens, though less austere than the Spartan, followed the same lines.

At the annual feast of the Apatouria, the names of legitimate and adopted children born during the year were enrolled by the father on the register of the phratry to which he belonged, and on the third day of the festival ceremonies were performed on behalf of the children admitted in previous years —the dedication of a lock of their hair to Artemis, and for the

girls a sacrifice called the *gamelía* or "bridal sacrifice," implying that its object was to get husbands for them. It was also
customary at this festival for the boys to compete in recitations
of poetry before the adult members of the phratry.[15]

The Athenian educational system was reorganised in the
latter part of the fourth century B.C. and the evidence relating
to it is mostly late.[16] It is probable, however, that its essential
features go back to an earlier period, and in the oath of allegiance taken by the novices, which is one of the surviving docu-
ments, there are elements which must be archaic.[17] The boys
were trained in gymnastics under the supervision of a *gymnasíarchos*, an officer whose tribal origin will appear in a later
chapter.[18] At the age of eighteen they became *épheboi*, corresponding to the Spartan *melleírenes*, and were sent away for
two years' military service on the frontiers. During this period
they wore a distinctive cloak, originally black or dun in colour,
later white. At the end of their military service they underwent an examination (*dokimasía*) and were admitted to full
civic status. After the collapse of the city-state as an autonomous
unit, their military duties were eventually abolished and superseded by training in athletics and philosophy, which attracted
to Athens well-to-do young men from all parts of the Roman
Empire. In this development of the Athenian discipline we
discern the thread connecting the age grades of tribal initiation
with the academic degrees of the modern university.

The rough cloaks of the Spartan and Cretan boys were doubtless explained as appropriate to their strenuous life, but the
distinctive colours of the Athenian cloak suggest that all three
had a ritual origin. Black or dun was the traditional colour of
mourning in all parts of Greece except Argos, where it was
white. It is possible therefore that we have here a vestige of
the primitive belief in the death of the child at initiation.

The same belief seems to underlie the custom of cutting the
hair.[19] At Sparta, the boy's head was close-cropped from the
time he entered the *agéla* until he became an *eíren*, and the
girl's hair was cut on the wedding night immediately before
the coming of the bridegroom. At Athens, the hair was dedicated on the third day of the Apatouria, which was called the
koureôtis heméra, perhaps in allusion to this rite. The custom is

not recorded in Crete, but that is almost certainly an accident, because there is abundant evidence, both literary and epigraphical, that in ancient Greece, as in many other parts of the world, the hair was cut on two distinct occasions—the attainment of puberty by a boy or the marriage of a girl and the death of a relative.[20] It is true that the same rite was sometimes performed on other occasions, especially recovery from sickness or escape from danger; but we have already seen that in primitive society every crisis in life is apt to be regarded in the light of initiation. At Gytheion in Laconia there was a local tradition, evidently primitive, that, after the murder of his mother, Orestes recovered his sanity by biting off one of his fingers, and at the same time he shore his hair as a thankoffering to the Erinyes.[21] Here the cutting of the hair is associated with a still more primitive rite of the same nature. As we shall see in a later chapter, the idea that the restored Orestes had in some sense been born again can be traced in the *Oresteia* of Æschylus (p. 280).[22] The crisis may be puberty, conversion, danger, disease or death, but in each case it is an occasion demanding the renewal of life.

Before examining the myths relating to the birth of Zeus and Dionysus, we must add to our account of primitive initiation a further detail. We saw that in one form of the rite it was pretended that the novice was killed and eaten by a spirit, who afterwards disgorged him as a man. In some tribes, it appears, this is or has been more than a pretence. One of the novices is really killed and his flesh eaten by the others.[23] At the present day, this practice of cannibalism at initiation is exceptional, and so perhaps it has always been, because, of course, since the idea of a mimic death is inherent in initiation, we have no right to assume that a pretence of cannibalism is necessarily derived from the reality; but we have to admit the possibility, which must be judged in the light of the other evidence.

When Rhea gave birth to Zeus on Mount Ida in Crete, she concealed him from her father Kronos, who had been in the habit of devouring his offspring, and replaced him by a stone wrapped in swaddling-bands, which Kronos swallowed instead. She played the same trick when she gave birth to Poseidon, the substitute in his case being a foal.[24] The horse was one of the animal forms of Poseidon, and the stone substituted for Zeus is clearly the thunder-stone.[25] This indicates that the legend has its roots in the lowest stratum of religion.

The infant Zeus was entrusted by Rhea to the Kouretes, who danced around it, beating their drums and clashing their spears on their shields in order that its cries might not reach the ears of Kronos.[26] There is reason to believe, as Rendel Harris has shown, that this war dance of the Kouretes was originally a bee dance.[27] The Kouretes were reputed to have invented the art of bee-keeping, and, while under their protection, the infant Zeus was fed by the daughters of Melisseus, the "bee-man"; but this element in the myth, though of great importance for the origin of the cult of Zeus, does not concern us now. To finish the story, when Zeus grew up, he forced his father to disgorge the stone, and also the other children, with whose aid he then overthrew him and hurled him into Tartarus.[28]

This legend was associated with an actual cult at Palaikastro in Crete, where the mystery of the god's birth was enacted by a secret society called the Kouretes, and the rites included a hymn in which the god was invoked as "greatest *koûros*" to march and rejoice in dance and song for the incoming year.[29] The word *koûros* means a boy or young man, and from it is derived the name of the Kouretes, which is used in the Homeric poems as a common noun synonymous with *koûros*.

From this evidence Jane Harrison concluded that "the Kouretes are young men who have been initiated themselves and will initiate others, will instruct them in tribal duties and tribal dances, steal them away from their mothers, make away with them by some pretended death, and, finally, bring them back as newborn, grown youths, full members of their tribe."[30] In reaching this conclusion, Jane Harrison was apparently unaware that it was actually the custom in historical Crete for boys to be stolen from their homes and secluded in the wilds by initiated men, and that the Kouretes were the traditional inventors of the war dance practised by the boys in preparation for this event.

Objection might be raised to this interpretation on the ground that, when Zeus was committed to the care of the

Kouretes, he was not a boy approaching puberty, but an infant; but this discrepancy can, I think, be explained. In the first place, as we have already remarked, when the practice of initiation declines, the rites tend to be performed at an earlier age. An example close at hand is the Jewish rite of circumcision, which, originally performed in preparation for marriage, now takes place a few days after birth.³¹ If such displacements can occur in the ritual itself, it is clear that they would occur even more easily in myths that had lost contact with their ritual origin. Further, it appears that, like other divine children, such as Hermes in the Homeric hymn, the infant Zeus grew with prodigious rapidity. Kallimachos tells us that, after being entrusted to the Kouretes, the child soon became a youth, the down appearing swiftly on his chin, and that while still a child he had already imagined all things perfect; while Aratos goes even further and says that the infant grew up in the space of a year.³²

The Kouretes were closely associated, and indeed confused, with other analogous organisations—the Korybantes, who worshipped the mother goddess of western Asia Minor, and the Daktyloi of Ida, magicians who were credited with the discovery of iron. In some versions of the birth of Zeus, the Kouretes are displaced by the Korybantes, and both are connected with iron-working. The oldest piece of iron hitherto known in Greece was found in Crete among other objects dating from the second Middle Minoan period, and in Asia Minor iron was well-known to the Hittites at least as far back as the thirteenth century B.C. and probably long before.³³ Like all new techniques, the working of iron must have been regarded in the first instance as a mystery, the function of a magical fraternity; and therefore this accords with the other evidence to the effect that the myths relating to the Kouretes, Korybantes, and Daktyloi, embody the folk-memory of primitive initiatory societies in prehistoric Crete and Asia Minor.

There are many versions of the birth of Dionysus, some derived from the Phrygian Sabazios, others from the Egyptian Osiris. For the present I shall confine myself to the two main centres of the Greek tradition—Thebes and Crete.³⁴

Zeus fell in love with Semele, the daughter of Kadmos, and

promised her anything she asked. Deluded by Hera, she asked him to woo her as he had wooed Hera; whereupon, appearing in a fiery chariot, he hurled his thunderbolt, and Semele died of fright. Snatching her unborn child from the flames, Zeus sewed it up in his thigh, and from there in due time Dionysus was born. So far the Theban myth. Enraged at the honours which Zeus was bestowing on the child, Hera suborned the Titans and persuaded them to destroy it. Accordingly, having provided themselves with attractive toys—a *kônos* or spinning-top, a *rhómbos*, and golden apples from the Hesperides—the Titans enticed the child from the Kouretes, in whose charge it had been placed, tore it in pieces, threw the limbs into a cauldron, boiled and ate them. This part of the myth was enacted in the Cretan ritual of Zagreus and in the Orphic mysteries. When Zeus discovered what had happened, he blasted the Titans with his thunderbolt, and in some way— the tradition varies at this point—the dead child was brought to life again.

The birth of Dionysus from the thigh of Zeus introduces a new complication. This part of the myth corresponds to Kronos's treatment of his children and to the Orphic myth of Phanes, who was swallowed by Zeus and re-born as his son. The re-birth of Phanes is clearly a symbol of adoption. It is no doubt a hieratic construct, with no immediate foundation in ritual, but such mythography presupposes a traditional pattern, supplied in this case by the myth of Kronos, which we have just explained as a symbol of initiation. What, then, was there in common between initiation and adoption? The answer is that in primitive society they are virtually identical.[35] Strangers are adopted into the clan by the act of being born again. Thus, the Jewish rite of circumcision, which was performed soon after birth on a legitimate child, was also performed on strangers of any age as a rite of adoption.[36] In the Icelandic sagas, the adopted stranger is explicitly described as having been born again, and he receives a new name, as at initiation. When Herakles ascended to Olympus, Hera sat on a couch, took him to her bosom, and passed him through her clothes to the ground in imitation of childbirth.[37] Diodoros, who records this myth, adds that similar rites were still practised for the adoption of strangers by the barbarians, and numerous parallels might be cited, not only from primitive tribes, but from mediæval and modern Europe.

Even so, the treatment of Dionysus by Zeus cannot be regarded as a simple act of adoption, because Zeus was the acknowledged father. It was not an adoption, but a deification. In one version we are expressly told that the purpose of the thunderbolt was to make both mother and child immortal. As Cook has shown, the thunderbolt of Zeus was originally conceived as inflicting death in order to confer immortality.[38] Similarly, when Demeter wished to immortalise the infant Demophoon, she buried it in the fire—an act which the child's mother naturally resented as calculated to kill it.[39] The child had to die in order that it might live for ever. "That which thou sowest is not quickened, except it die."[40] Deification is a form of adoption, and adoption is a form of initiation.

The Titans who abducted Dionysus in order to eat him appear at first sight to have little in common with the Kouretes, who abducted Zeus in order to save him from being eaten; but it is a commonplace of mythology that such extreme antinomies are apt to conceal an underlying affinity, and in the present instance our suspicions are confirmed by a myth of the birth of Epaphos, in which the villains, whom Hera persuades to make away with the child, are the Kouretes.[41] The contradiction is simply the mythical expression of the ambivalent nature of the rite itself.

The same conclusion is reached from an examination of the toys with which the child was lured away. The Golden Apples of the Hesperides are a folk-tale motive, but the *kônos* and *rhómbos* are derived from ritual. The *kônos* was probably a spinning top of the familiar type, the *rhómbos* was a piece of wood attached to a string by which it was spun in the air, and both were used in mystical rites to imitate thunder. In fact, as Andrew Lang pointed out long ago, the *rhómbos* is identical with the bull-roarer used by modern savages to produce rain and to terrify the novices at initiation.[42] Thus, in the Wiradthuri tribe of Australia, only the initiated may actually see a bull-roarer, and the uninitiated believe that it is the voice of a spirit. At the crisis of initiation, which takes place in darkness, the old men close round the novices, whirling their bull-roarers in the air. When the crisis is over, the instruments are revealed to them and their use explained. That is the *anakálypsis*, the revelation of the sacred objects; and that is the ceremony of which a faint memory lingers in the toys which the Titans displayed to Dionysus. And, if we ask why the bull-roarer should play so prominent a part in initiation, the answer may be given in the words of a Wiradthuri headman, who declared that the sound of the bull-roarer was the voice of a spirit calling on the rain to fall and everything to grow anew.[43]

Finally, Dionysus was boiled and eaten.[44] He was not the only one. Medea told the daughters of Pelias that they could make their aged father young again by boiling him. Failing to carry conviction, she took an old ram, cut it up, threw the pieces into a cauldron of boiling water, and produced out of the cauldron a lamb. Ino, sister to Semele and foster-mother to Dionysus, whom she is said to have brought up as a girl, threw her own child, Melikertes, into a cauldron, then snatched up the cauldron with the dead child in it and leapt into the sea. By that means both became immortal, the mother being re-named as Leukothea, the child as Palaimon. Thetis boiled all her children regularly, until at the birth of Achilles the misguided father intervened. This story was told by Hesiod, and, according to the scholiast who records it, Thetis wanted to see whether the child was mortal, but we may suspect that her real motive was rather to ensure that it would be immortal.[45] Most famous of all, however, is the boiling of Pelops, and that brings us to the origin of the Olympian Games. In this part of my argument I shall follow the steps of Weniger and Cornford.[46]

When Pelops was a child, his father Tantalos invited the gods to a feast, to be provided by contributions from each of the participants. Tantalos himself contributed the flesh of his son, whom he cut up, boiled in a cauldron, and served up as meat before his unsuspecting guests. When Zeus discovered the nature of the dish that had been laid before them, he directed that the child should be put back in the cauldron and so restored to life. This was done, and the child was lifted out of the cauldron by Klotho, whom we have already met as a goddess of birth. Here she is a goddess of re-birth. Tantalos was blasted with the thunderbolt.

As for Pelops, as soon as the bloom of manhood appeared on his cheeks, he resolved to marry Hippodameia, daughter of Oinomaos, the King of Elis. Hippodameia had already had thirteen suitors, all of whom had perished in the ordeal which the father imposed on every candidate for his daughter's hand. The ordeal was a chariot race. The suitor drove one chariot, with his prospective bride beside him; the father pursued him in another, overtook him, and killed him. Pelops, however, took the precaution of bribing the King's charioteer to remove one of the linch-pins. The result was that the King's chariot crashed, and the King himself was killed by Pelops with a thrust of his spear. So Pelops married Hippodameia and succeeded to her father's kingdom.

In the historical period, the Olympian Games were celebrated in every fourth year at alternate intervals of forty-nine and fifty months. When one celebration fell in the month of Apollonios, the next would be held four years later in the ensuing month of Parthenios. This arrangement is clearly based on the bisection of an octennial cycle, which is the shortest period in which the Greek lunar year of 354 days could be made to coincide with the solar year of $365\frac{1}{4}$ days. In eight years the difference between the two amounted to exactly ninety days, which were made up by intercalating three months of thirty days each. Translated into myth, this reconciliation of the solar and lunar reckonings appeared as a union of Sun and Moon, which, as Frazer has shown, is a common form of the sacred marriage. In this case the celestial pair were impersonated by Pelops and Hippodameia.

The race of Pelops was a chariot race, but we know from the local traditions of Olympia that in the earliest period the only contest had been a foot race. Moreover, the octennial cycle underlying the Olympian calendar presupposes a considerable knowledge of astronomy. It must have superseded an earlier cycle corresponding to the annual sequence of the seasons, which in the octennial reckoning is ignored. For these reasons Weniger conjectured that, prior to the introduction of that reckoning, the festival was annual. This conjecture will receive further support when we have examined the women's festival at Olympia.

To return to the local tradition, it must be remembered, as Weniger and Cornford have pointed out, that the two priestly clans of Olympia, the Iamidai and the Klytiadai, who had administered the festival from time immemorial, were still in office at the time when Pausanias, who records the tradition, visited Olympia in the second century A.D. There is no reason therefore to question its authenticity on the ground that the form in which we have it is late. According to this tradition, when Rhea gave birth to Zeus, she entrusted the child "to the Daktyloi of Ida, or the Kouretes, as they were also called," who travelled from Crete to Olympia and there amused themselves by running a race, the winner being crowned with wild olive, which was so abundant "that they used to sleep on its leaves while they were still green."[47]

The leaves, we observe, had to be still green. In other words, the practice had a ritual significance, and the reader will already have recalled the practice of the Spartan boys, who, after *their* day's racing, used to sleep on rushes from the Eurotas. That too had a ritual significance, because the use of a knife was prohibited. And here it may be added that, after being escorted to the *prytaneîon* or town hall, the Olympian victor was pelted with leaves. This is usually interpreted as a fertility rite, and so in a sense it was, but that does not go to the heart of the matter. At Sparta, we are told, the custom was to place no offerings in the tomb of the dead, only the body itself wrapped in a purple soldier's cloak and laid on leaves of olive.[48] The magical virtue of these leaves, for living and dead alike, was newness of life.

As we have already remarked, the Games were celebrated in the months of Apollonios and Parthenios alternately. This feature is unique. The Pythian Games, too, were held at alternate intervals of forty-nine and fifty months, but the intercalations were so arranged that the festival always fell in the same month of the year. The reason for the irregularity at Olympia is that, when the Games were reorganised on the octennial cycle, they collided with the women's festival of the

Heraia. This part of Weniger's argument may be given in the form in which it has been summarised by Cornford:

> It is highly probable that these games of virgins (*parthénia*) gave its name to the month Parthenios, and were in honour of Hera Parthenos—Hera, whose virginity was perpetually renewed after her sacred marriage with Zeus. It is also probable that they were held at the new moon—that is, on the first day of Parthenios. Further, if these games gave that month its name, in that month they must always have fallen. Thus the octennial period of the Heraia is of the usual straightforward type, which keeps always to the same month. The natural inference is that the Heraia were first in the field, and that, when the men's games were fixed at the same season, it was necessary to avoid this older fixed festival. At the same time, if the games of Zeus were allowed to be established regularly in the middle of the preceding month, Apollonios, it was obvious that the Heraia would sink into a mere appendage. Zeus, on the other hand, was not inclined to yield permanent precedence to Hera. The deadlock was solved by a characteristic compromise. The octennial period for the Games of Zeus was so arranged that in alternate Olympiads they should fall fourteen days before, and fourteen days after, the Heraia (on Apollonios 14/15 and Parthenios 14/15). By this device of priestly ingenuity the honour of both divinities was satisfied, and so the inconvenient variation of the months for the Olympic festival is explained.

The hypothesis that the Heraia was originally annual and the older of the two is confirmed by a remarkable feature of the festival itself, which neither Weniger nor Cornford has explained. The festival was held every fourth year under the supervision of a sodality called the Sixteen Women, who wove a robe for Hera in honour of the occasion and provided two choirs, one for Hippodameia, the other for Physkoa, a local bride of Dionysus.[49] This suggests that the festival goes back in part to a time when there was no Hera and no Hippodameia, only Physkoa, a girl who "made things grow." The main contest at the festival consisted in three foot races for girls. The winners were crowned with wild olive and received a share of the cow which was sacrificed to Hera. Now, these three foot races were run in order of age, the youngest running first and the eldest last. The inference seems clear. When the festival was annual, there had been only one race, run by all the girls who had reached puberty during the current year. When it became quadrennial, provision had to be made for the girls who had reached puberty during the first two of the three full years which had elapsed since the last celebration of the festival, but priority was given to the third group as being pre-eminently the girls of the year.

To sum up our argument, the men's foot race, which was the nucleus of the Olympia, was an annual ordeal or *agón* to determine who should be the *koûros* of the year. The women's foot race of the Heraia was an ordeal of precisely the same nature, the winner being the *koûre* of the year. Both were ordeals of initiation, but for the winners they were more than that—initiation and deification as well. Accordingly, when the two festivals were co-ordinated, the winning pair became partners in the sacred marriage—the Pelops and Hippodameia of the year.

There still remains a further question. What became of the winning pair at the end of their year? We know what frequently happened in such cases from the evidence amassed by Frazer in his encyclopædic study of the sacred marriage in the *Golden Bough*.[50] As he has demonstrated, the king was originally divine—he was regarded as god, or, it would be better to say, he *was* god, the idea of divinity being merely a projection of the magical powers with which he had been invested by the rite of coronation. That this rite was indistinguishable from what later came to be regarded as deification has been made still clearer by Hocart's study of the subject, from which it also emerges that coronation is only a specialised rite of initiation.[51] Like the boy at the threshold of manhood, the candidate for divine honours has to die and be born again. Further, since the magical control of the crops, which it is his function to exercise,[52] is a task of tremendous difficulty and importance, on which the life of the community depends, it is essential that the person to whom it is entrusted should himself be in the prime of life; and since that condition is transitory, his tenure of office is limited to a single cycle, from seed-time to harvest. At the end of the year he is killed—or, rather, not killed, but sent to rejoin his fellow gods after accomplishing his task on earth. And, lastly, since these magical powers are dependent on physical strength, his successor is commonly chosen by ordeal of combat, in which he is challenged and overthrown by a younger and stronger man. This feature appears at Olympia in a tradition recorded by Plutarch. "In ancient times," he says, "there was also held an ordeal of single combat, which ended only in the slaughter of the vanquished."[53]

The myth of Pelops may therefore be interpreted as a symbol of the specific form which primitive initiation had assumed in prehistoric Olympia. It consisted of two parts—initiation into manhood and initiation into kingship. The first was effected by a ceremony in which the novices were believed to be devoured by the gods as children and restored as men. The second was effected by a competitive ordeal (originally a foot race, later a chariot race), the winner being acclaimed as the god-king of the year. And, lastly, at the end of the year, the god-king was killed by his successor.

Even in historical times, the Olympian victor was regarded with superstitious veneration and invested with honours that might be described as either royal or divine. At Olympia itself he was crowned with olive and feasted in the *prytaneîon*. On his return to his native city, he was dressed in purple and drawn by white horses in a triumphal procession through a breach in the walls. At Sparta, he marched by the side of the kings into battle, evidently in the belief that his proximity would carry them to victory. At Athens, he enjoyed the right of eating in the *prytaneîon* at the public cost for the rest of his life, and after death he was worshipped as a hero, less mortal than divine. Unless we remember all this, we are not in a position to appreciate the anxious insistency with which in many odes Pindar warns the victor at the Games not to seek too much, not to peer too far into the future, not to aspire to become a god. Even in the Altis at Olympia, where, next to Delphi, the Greek aristocracy felt most at home, they were confronted with this strange contradiction, which was only accepted because it was ineradicable and because it could be piously cloaked in the trappings of ancient priestcraft.

The course of our argument has carried us a long way from the initiation ceremonies of the primitive tribe, but the same thread runs right through to the end. The *prytaneîon* of the Greek city-state was not merely an eating-place at which distinguished citizens and strangers were publicly entertained; it was the sacred hearth of the community, which at Athens was kindled annually by the victors in the torch races of the *épheboi*.[54] As Hutton Webster remarked, "an institution so firmly established and so widely spread" as the Men's House "may be expected to survive by devotion to other uses as the earlier ideas which led to its foundation fade away."

It may therefore be asserted with some confidence that Cornford was right in rejecting Ridgeway's view that the Olympian Games were originally a festival of the dead. It is true that the institution of athletic contests at the funerals of distinguished men is attested by the Homeric poems and by the actual practice of historical times; but Cornford's own view has now been amplified and extended in such a way that puberty and death appear as events of the same order, both fitting occasions for a ritual that brings newness of life.

Our knowledge of the Eleusinian Mysteries is derived largely from the Hellenistic period or later, but at a number of vital points the tradition can be traced through Plato, Aristophanes and Æschylus to the Homeric Hymn to Demeter, and it is carried still further, into the Mycenean period, by the evidence of archæological remains.[55]

On the other hand, it is clear that by the fifth century B.C. the primitive character of the cult had been radically altered by successive accretions and reorganisations. Originally, it appears, it was the property of a single clan, the Eumolpidai, which was joined at an early period by the Kerykes. The great service of Demeter to mankind, which the Mysteries were believed to commemorate, was the discovery of agriculture.[56] The same service was commemorated at Athens itself in the festival of the Thesmophoria, which had much in common with the Mysteries of Eleusis and moreover was reserved to women. It is possible therefore that the cult of Eleusis was originally of the same type. Indeed, the myth of the Eleusinian Demeter, who revealed the art of agriculture herself, but

taught the use of the plough through the medium of her foster-
son, Triptolemos, seems to reflect a transition from matrilineal
to patrilineal descent, which, as we saw in an earlier chapter
(p. 16), is associated with the advance from garden tillage to
field tillage. One function of the Eumolpidai, undoubtedly
ancient, was the ceremonial ploughing of the Rharian plain,
which suggests that the clan had once been a royal one with
functions similar to those studied by Hooke and others in early
Babylonia and Egypt. Throughout the prehistoric period, the
cult was local, strangers being admitted only by adoption, but
in the sixth century, perhaps under Peisistratos, who rebuilt
the Hall of Initiation, it was taken over by the growing Attic
state and thrown open to all persons of Greek speech, even
including slaves.[57] There can be no doubt that the tyrant's
interest in Eleusis was prompted by the same motives as his
patronage of the Orphic movement. Aristotle says that it was
characteristic of democracy to reduce the number and broaden
the basis of the old aristocratic cults.[58] The evolution of the
Mysteries was therefore part and parcel of the evolution of the
Attic state. Beginning as a local cult in a small and primitive
tribal community, it reflected successively the early kingship,
based on agrarian magic, the religious exclusiveness of the
aristocracy, and, finally, under the impetus of the democratic
revolution, the intrusion of state control.

For these reasons we are compelled to make considerable
reservations before accepting the important hypothesis propounded by Foucart, that the Eleusinian Mysteries were
borrowed from Egypt.[59] There is much to be said in its favour.
There was an Attic tradition that agriculture had been introduced from Egypt; there are striking resemblances between the
myths of Demeter and Dionysus and the myths of Isis and
Osiris; and an Eleusinian tomb of the tenth or ninth century
B.C. has been found to contain an image of Isis, made of
Egyptian porcelain, together with other Egyptian objects
belonging to the same cult. This evidence proves that the cult
of Demeter had been subjected at one period to Egyptian
influence; but the precise extent of that influence can only be
determined after an investigation of the social origins of
mystical religion as such. It is this part of the problem that

Foucart neglects. The history of Egypt shows that the cult of Osiris originated in the needs of primitive agriculture, and that it was further developed in response to the social stresses set up by the struggle between the monarchy, the aristocracy, and the people, which came to a head under Ikhnaton. Indeed, the so-called "democratisation of Osiris," which accompanied the rise of a middle-class bureaucracy under the anti-aristocratic kings of the eighteenth Dynasty, was a development of the same order as the process which broadened the basis of the Eleusinian Mysteries 1,000 years later.[60] Religious ideas are borne by trade winds far afield, but they only take root in soils ready to receive them, and their subsequent growth is determined primarily by the conditions of their immediate environment. In order to assess the significance of the features common to the two cults, it is necessary to relate both to the general history of agriculture and to relate their points of divergence to the special history of the two areas. It is only when that has been done that we shall be in a position to treat the question of diffusion as a separable factor.

The Great Mysteries of Eleusis were celebrated annually in the month of Boedromion, which coincided approximately with our September and immediately preceded the month in which the crops were sown for the ensuing year. We are told by Plutarch that in primitive Attica the sowing had taken place earlier than it did in historical times, and so we may infer that the Mysteries were originally designed to synchronise with the beginning of the agricultural year.[61]

The man or woman who wished to be admitted to the Great Mysteries had first of all to be initiated at the Little Mysteries of Agra, which were said to have been founded by Demeter for the benefit of Herakles.[62] When Herakles was about to descend into Hades, he went to Eleusis and asked to be initiated, but was rejected on the ground that he was a stranger. Accordingly, he was adopted into the community by Demeter at Agra, and then his request was granted. The Little Mysteries were celebrated in the month of Anthesterion, corresponding to the latter part of February and the first part of March, when the last summer's wine matured. After participating in these Mysteries, the candidate was not initiated at Eleusis in the following autumn, but had to wait at least until the following year. This interval was evidently a period of probation, like the two years spent at Sparta in the *melleírenes* and at Athens in the *épheboi*. We are also told that the cloak worn by the candidate during his initiation might not be changed, but had to be worn continuously until it fell off.[63]

On the fourteenth day of Boedromion the *épheboi* marched to Eleusis and on the next escorted the sacred objects, possibly images of Demeter and Persephone, from there to Athens. On the following day, the candidates assembled at Athens in the presence of the *hierophántes* and the *daidoûchos*, the high priests of the Eumolpidai and the Kerykes, who issued a solemn proclamation in which they warned the unworthy to depart. Barbarians and unpurified homicides were explicitly disqualified.

Next followed purification. The candidate procured a pig, drove it down to the shore, and bathed with it in the sea. The pig was then slaughtered, and its blood spilt over the candidate, who sat on a low seat, his head veiled. On the analogy of primitive initiation, we may conjecture that the pig's blood was a substitute for the candidate's own, and the significance of the veil is explained when we find that it was worn by both parties at marriage, and that at death it was both placed over the head of the corpse and worn by the relatives as a sign of mourning. In the present instance it was perhaps associated with the myth of Demeter, who is described in the Homeric Hymn as sitting veiled in mourning for her daughter.[64]

The next stage in the proceedings is obscure. It consisted apparently of a sacrifice and an intrusive element from the cult of Asklepios at Epidauros. The candidates are also described as "staying at home." Then, on the nineteenth, singing and dancing through the fields, the great procession set out for Eleusis, escorting the image of Iakchos, which seems to be another intrusive element, derived from the cult of Dionysus. Various ceremonies were performed on the way, including the exchange of imprecations and obscene jests at the bridge over the Kephissos. This is a primitive fertility rite of world-wide distribution, but, not being specially connected with initiation, it need not detain us now. It appears that the procession included those who had only been initiated at Agra in the preceding spring as well as those whose probation was now completed; and consequently, on their arrival at Eleusis, the pilgrims fell into two grades—the *mýstai*, who had to wait another year before proceeding further, and the *epóptai*, who were admitted to the Hall of Initiation (*telestérion*), where the secrets of Eleusis were revealed to them.

What precisely it was that was "seen and heard" on this occasion is a matter of conjecture. It seems clear, however, that there was a sacred marriage enacted by the high priest and priestess, and a ritual drama symbolising the journey of the soul to the judgment seat. One of the most striking features of the ceremony, which can be traced as far back as Æschylus, was the sudden blaze of torchlight which illuminated the darkness and transformed the sorrow of the onlookers into joy.[65] It is also stated that an ear of corn was revealed to them as a sign of their salvation. The other features, deduced from the symbolism of the Homeric Hymn, are too uncertain to be relied on.

The initiates were under a vow to divulge nothing of what they had heard or seen, and the silence thus imposed on them was expressed in the mystical symbol of "the golden key on the tongue." Now, in the Egyptian ritual of the dead, after the body had been purified, the lips were touched by a sacred object called the *Pesesh-Kef*. This ceremony was called the Opening of the Mouth, and it ensured that the dead man would be born again in the Underworld. This certainly looks like a case of direct contact between the two cults, particularly when we find that another variant of the same symbol, "the great ox on the tongue," was associated with Pythagoreanism, which also had connections with Egypt.[66] Yet even here we had better reserve judgment, because we are informed by Spencer and Gillen that in Central Australia to this day the elders of the Arunta tribe release the young men from the ban of silence by touching their lips with a sacred object.[67]

The main reason why our evidence for the actual content of the Eleusinian Mysteries is so slight is probably not that the secrets were so well kept, but that they were so well known. The habitual and casual familiarity with which such writers as Æschylus and Plato allude to these matters presupposes in their public a general and intimate knowledge, and shows that many of the mystical formulæ had passed into the common currency of everyday Attic speech. These half-veiled allusions, of which Greek literature is full, can be made to reveal, if not the ritual itself, at least the subjective attitude of the mystic, which is almost equally significant.

The Eleusinian initiate differed from other men in that he had "brighter hopes" of the future—the hope of a "better lot" in the life hereafter, when, "delivered from the evils" of mortality, he would obtain the crown of glory and live in the blessed company of the gods. The impression left on his mind by his experience of the mystical rites is vividly described by Plutarch:[68]

> At first wanderings and wearisome hurryings to and fro, and unfinished journeys half-seen as through a darkness; then before the consummation itself all the terrors, shuddering and trembling, sweat and wonder; after which they are confronted by a wonderful light, or received into pure regions and meadows, with singing and dancing and sanctities of holy voices and sacred revelations, wherein, made perfect at last, free and absolved, the initiate worships with crowned head in the company of those pure and undefiled, looking down on the impure, uninitiated multitude of the living as they trample one another under foot and are herded together in thick mire and mist.

It was the same experience that inspired the famous allegory in which Plato likened the soul of man to a charioteer.[69] The chariot has wings, and is drawn by two horses, one good, the other bad, one drawing it aloft into the celestial heights, the other dragging it down to earth. The soul drives on, struggling and sweating. Chariots crash and collide, horses are crippled and wings broken, as competitors are trampled down and fall out of the race. But, when the race has been won, then the soul is admitted into the mystery of mysteries, perfect, delivered, blest, gazing in a clear light on the celestial vision. In later literature this image became a commonplace, and passed into Christianity. "Throughout life," says Plutarch, "the soul is engaged in an athletic contest, and, when the contest is over, it meets with its reward." "Come," says Porphyry, "let us strip

and step into the racecourse for the Olympia of the soul!"[70]
"Know ye not," St. Paul asks the Corinthians, "that they
which run in a race run all, but one receiveth the prize? Even so
run, that ye may attain. . . . Now they do it to receive a
corruptible crown; but we an incorruptible."[71] Plutarch and
Porphyry were no doubt drawing consciously on Plato; but it is
important to observe that the image was not invented by Plato,
being found in Æschylus and Sophokles.[72] In fact, it was not a
literary invention at all, but was firmly rooted in the mystic
ritual. Thus, one of the sacred formulæ which the Orphics
hoped to recite in the other world was, "With swift feet I have
attained unto the crown desired."[73] And the same idea underlies the terminology of Eleusis, which we must now examine.

The successive grades of initiation in the Eleusinian Mysteries are described by Theon of Smyrna as follows:[74]

> The parts of initiation are five. The first is purification.
> The mysteries are not open to anyone who wishes to partake
> of them, some being warned to keep away, such as those who
> have unclean hands or unintelligible speech, and even those
> who are not debarred must first receive purification. Next
> after purification is the administration of the rite. The third
> is the so-called *epopteía*. The fourth, which is also the end of
> the *epopteía*, is the crowning and laying-on of the garland,
> which empowers him, after becoming a *hierophántes* or
> *daidoûchos* or other official, to administer the rite to others.
> And the fifth and last is the blessedness which comes of en-
> joying the love of the gods and feasting with the gods.

The writer is concerned to show that there are five grades,
because that number is necessary to his argument, but, as he
admits himself, the third and fourth are really one, and in
other writers the initial purification is not counted as a grade
of initiation at all, but regarded as preliminary. The five grades
of Theon may therefore be reduced to three: *mýesis* or initiation, *epopteía*, and *eudaimonía* or spiritual bliss.

The rank of *epóptes* was attained, as we have seen, in the
second year after initiation at the Little Mysteries of Agra. The
word *epóptes* means both an "onlooker" and a "supervisor."
As an onlooker, the *epóptes* was permitted to behold the secret
rites enacted in the Hall of Initiation. As a supervisor, he

administered those rites to others. He corresponds, therefore, to the Spartan *eíren*, who, in his second year of manhood, was put in charge of the boys during the period immediately preceding their ordeal at the altar of Artemis.

Now, the same word was also used at Olympia to denote a steward or supervisor at the games.[75] There is no need to suppose that the Eleusinian use of this term was derived from Olympia any more than the Olympian from Eleusis, because both have now been traced independently to their common origin in the primitive ritual of initiation. At both places, the *epóptai* were, or had been, like the *koúretes* of the Cretan myth, the men who, having been initiated themselves, superintended the initiation of others. At Olympia, the ordeal of initiation was a race; at Eleusis it had become a passion play in which the crisis of change was projected as a terrifying drama of the soul on its journey through death to salvation.

That the Greeks themselves were conscious of the significance underlying this double application of the term *epóptes* is clear from another passage in Plutarch, who is again expounding mystical doctrine in terms of an athletic contest:[76]

> According to Hesiod, the souls which have been delivered from birth and are at leisure thenceforward from the body, as it were free and fully absolved, are the guardian spirits (*daímones epimeleîs*) of mankind. Athletes who have given up training on account of their age do not entirely forgo their old delight in bodily contests, but still enjoy watching others at their practices, running alongside and cheering them onward. So too those who have ceased from the contests of life and by virtue of soul become spirits (*daímones*) do not lose all interest in the affairs and discussions and studies of earthly life, but show their goodwill and sympathetic zeal to others engaged in exercising themselves for the same purpose, setting forth with them and shouting encouragement as they see them draw near and at last touch the hoped-for goal.

And again we are reminded of the New Testament:[77]

> Therefore let us also, seeing we are compassed about with so great a cloud of witnesses, lay aside every weight, and the sin which doth so easily beset us, and let us run with patience

the race which is set before us, looking unto Jesus the author and perfecter of our faith, who for the joy that was set before him endured the cross, despising shame, and hath sat down at the right hand of the throne of God.

The cloud of witnesses are the *epóptai*. So for that matter are the Old Blues, now equipped with bicycles; for there can be little doubt that further research would show that the organisation of the modern university, for work and play alike, goes back ultimately to the same source.

The third grade was *eudaimonía*, and it is clear, both because the Greeks counted it blasphemy to apply that word to worldly prosperity, and because here it is expressly associated with admission to the company of the gods, that this grade was only attained after death. We recall the divine honours accorded to the Olympian victor, and again we find that the analogy was consciously worked out. This time it is Plato, protesting against the idea that the reward of the righteous had anything in common with the notorious revelry that followed a victory at the games:[78]

> Even more dashing are the blessings which Mousaios and his son make the gods bestow on the righteous. They claim to take them down to Hades, where they seat them on couches and prepare a banquet of the saints, and there with crowned heads they drink for all time, as though an eternity of drunkenness were virtue's fairest reward.

The rite of initiation was called a *teleté*, and the preliminaries to it were *protéleia*. The same terms were used to describe the marriage rite. Marriage was constantly regarded as a mystery, and the parties to it as initiates. The initiate was described as *téleios*, complete or perfect, and the same term was applied to those who had attained married status, also to Zeus and Hera as patrons of matrimony.[79] Both these connotations are derivative. The primary meaning of *téleios* is "full-grown" or "mature." They are derived therefore from the time when initiation and marriage had both taken place at puberty.

One of the formulæ recited at marriage was, "I have fled the worse and found the better." The same formula was used in the Mysteries of Attis, which reached Athens from Asia

HISTORY OF INITIATION

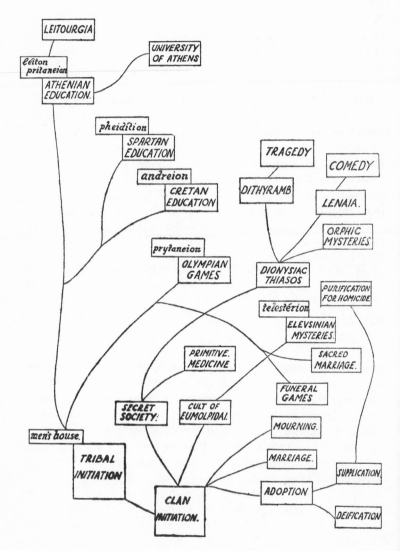

Minor in the fourth century B.C.[80] We are not told that it was employed at Eleusis, but it is evidently based on the idea of "deliverance *or* flight from evil." Its significance in the marriage rite is clearly connected with the notion, to which we referred in a previous chapter (p. 50), that marriage was the inauguration of a new *moîra* or *daímon*; and in the same chapter we referred to the Attic custom relating to the *deuterópotmos*, the man who, having been mistakenly mourned as dead, was readmitted to the community by a mimetic birth, which conferred on him a second *moîra*. Now, in the language of the Mysteries, the term *téleios* is frequently combined with the word *holókleros*, which has precisely the same mystical significance, but means literally "endowed with a whole portion," *kléros* being a synonym of *moîra*. We may say therefore that the function of both the rite of marriage and initiation into the Mysteries was originally to invest the child at puberty with a new *moîra*. The child was born again.

Putting this evidence together, we conclude that the sense in which the mystic had been "made perfect" by initiation was that he had been invested with a new *moîra* for the life after death. As we have already observed, the hope of the mystic was for a better lot, a better portion or *moîra*, in the other world. The same idea is implicit in the word *eudaimonía*, applied to the state of bliss resulting from possession of a good *daímon* after the soul had been delivered from mortality. Thus, the mystical doctrine reproduces the pattern of tribal initiation at every point. At the same time, the old pattern has been charged with an entirely new meaning. In the Mysteries, a ritual which had been designed as a preparation for life has been transformed into a preparation for death. There lies the essence of all mystical religions. How this profound change in man's outlook on the world had been brought about is a question to which we shall address ourselves after we have tried to penetrate the mysteries of Dionysus.

VIII

DIONYSUS

THE myths of Greece form an infinite series, one running into another with little regard for the particular divinity to which they happen to be attached. The thread that unites them is ritual, which is older than the gods.

The gods of the Greek pantheon are each the product of an infinite complex of local cults, which only yielded a unified concept after the atomic structure of tribal society had been merged into the broad strata of economic classes. Even then the concept varied from class to class and from district to district. The Homeric Artemis is a graceful virgin huntress; yet at Ephesos, only a few miles from Smyrna, one of the main centres of the Homeric tradition, the same goddess was worshipped as a many-breasted mother not yet fully anthropomorphic.[1] The Homeric pantheon was already, when it attained its final form, an abstraction with little validity outside the circle of a narrow ruling class. Four centuries later, when commercial intercourse had laid the basis for a new pantheon, modelled on the Homeric but different, Apollo and Dionysus stand at opposite poles, the one for the aristocratic ideal of static perfection—for *Mass*, as Nietzsche expressed it, the other for popular enthusiasm, for *Uebermass*.[2] This differentiation belonged only to the last stage of their evolution, and the earlier stages still survived in ritual. At Delphi, the orgiastic cult of the Thyiades was devoted to Apollo as well as Dionysus; Dionysus as well as Apollo was a musician and a prophet; and such Apolline festivals as the Lampadaphoria at Thebes and the Staphylodromia at Sparta were Dionysiac in everything but name. Nor were the affinities of Dionysus restricted to Apollo. In Crete he was identified with Zeus; in Thrace he was a war-god like Ares; in the Argive myth of the daughters of Proitos the antiquarians were unable to agree whether it was Dionysus or Hera that drove the women mad. And where the evidence permits us to press our analysis a step further back, these gods—Apollo, Dionysus, Hera—all disappear, leaving us with the mimetic ritual of the totemic clan. *Im Anfang war die Tat.*

In the present chapter, therefore, we shall reverse the method adopted by Farnell, who studied the cults of Greek religion by classifying them according to gods, and we shall only pursue the personality of Dionysus as far as the argument requires. After resuming our account of primitive initiation and extending it to parts of the world where it survives only in the seasonal festivals of a detribalised peasantry, we shall follow it into the ritual of the ancient Greek secret society, which was mainly but not exclusively Dionysiac.

The prize of victory at Olympia was a crown of wild olive. In the prehistoric past, when the games were still ordeals of initiation, this plant had been endowed with the magical virtue of communicating that newness of life without which the child could not be born again as man or woman. The human community had fertilised itself by a simple act of physical contact with the fertility of Nature. Conversely, it was necessary that the human community should propagate in order that nature might increase and multiply. The two beliefs were complementary and ultimately identical, both being inspired by an intense realisation of the interdependence of human society and its material environment.

The initiation ceremonies of Australia are the most primitive that have survived; yet their very elaboration proves that they are the outcome of a long process of evolution. As we remarked in the Introduction, the economic development of these tribes has been arrested, but their social institutions have continued to develop in directions in which they still have a functional value. The question therefore arises whether it is possible to penetrate behind these Australian ceremonies to a still more primitive form of initiation.

We have seen that the period of probation interposed in the more advanced tribes between initiation and marriage is not an original element, and that the content of the marriage rite indicates that it was once identical with initiation. From this it may be inferred that in the earliest phase of tribal society the sexes mated at puberty, as they still do in Australia. At that stage initiation was simply initiation into sexual life—the first ritual act of physical union. We have also seen that the classificatory system of relationship is based on a principle which points to unrestricted intercourse within each generation between men and women belonging to different exogamous groups. To these considerations we may now add a third, to which Robertson Smith has drawn attention.[3] The rudest communities of which we have direct knowledge live at an economic level so low that sexual intercourse tends to be restricted to that part of the year in which food is most plentiful; and if this restriction operates now, it must have operated far more forcibly in the earliest phase of all, when the tribe was still in process of evolving out of the primitive horde. This means that initiation was originally an annual summer celebration for a clearly-defined and comprehensive age group consisting of all those of both sexes who had just reached puberty. The rite of human death and rebirth is thus traced back to a form in which it is inseparable from the death and rebirth of vegetation. Human life moved in unison with Nature. The same pulse throbbed in both.

This aspect of initiation is not very prominent in the Australian ceremonies, perhaps because our knowledge of them is confined for the most part to objective descriptions of the actual rites; but it is brought out very clearly in the spring festivals of the ancient Chinese peasantry, which are of considerable importance for the interpretation of peasant customs in other parts of the globe. The account which follows is from Granet. It is especially valuable for its indication of the subjective attitude of the participants, deduced from their traditional songs.[4]

For long centuries, initiations were celebrated in the rural assemblies at the same time as espousals to inaugurate the new season. Learned rituals still speak of the spring festivals when "girls and boys rejoiced in a crowd." The gloss adds: "[then] majority is granted to the boys; [then] wives are taken." Life can only awake by virtue of the combined forces of the two sexes. Only a festival of youth can arouse the spring.

Initiations and espousals were accomplished under the control of the whole community. They held their sittings in places set apart from domestic occupation and profane uses. In a wide untrammelled landscape, boys and girls, freed from customary restraints, learnt contact with nature. Waters flowed in the brooks set free by the melting of the ice; springs which had been bound by winter burst from the fountains which had once more come to life; the thawed ground opened to let the grass appear; the animals peopled it, all springing from their retreats. The time of seclusion was over and that of universal interpenetration was come. Earth and sky could commune, and the rainbow was the sign of their union. Closed groups could now enter into alliance, sexual corporations encounter each other. In a landscape which was at once venerable and new, where from time immemorial their ancestors had been at once initiated into social and sexual life, the young people were united. . . .

One of the most important games of the spring festivals was the crossing of rivers, which was performed half-naked and immediately before the unions in the fields. Shivering from contact with the living waters, the women then felt themselves to be penetrated as it were with floating souls. The sacred fountains, long dried up, awoke anew as though the coming of spring had set free their waters from an underground prison where winter had enchained them. . . . By the act of crossing the rivers, their deliverance was celebrated, fertile rains were drawn down upon the land, and upon oneself the spring of fertilisation. The Chinese never ceased to pray at the same time and by the same rites for births to enrich their families and rain to make the seed to spring. Rains and reincarnations were at first obtained by the sexual games. But in the end it was believed that water possessed a female nature, and that women alone could retain the virtue by which it was possible to obtain rain. In the same way they imagined that virgins could become mothers by simple contact with the sacred rivers. It was in fact a time when births were acquired at the sole profit of the wives and when the only incarnations were those of maternal ancestors. . . .

These festivals consisted of communions, orgies and games. . . . Gatherings, assemblies, hunts, became the opportunities for rivalry in dance and song. This may still be found in our own day amongst the backward populations of
KA

southern China. Their greatest festivals are those in which the boys and girls of neighbouring villages form a line abreast and cut the fern, singing extempore songs. On these jousts depend the prosperity of the year and the people's happiness. In the same way, in the ancient festivals of China, the young people who gathered for the games believed that they were obeying a command of Nature, and working together with her. Their dances and songs correspond to the cries of birds seeking a mate, the flight of insects as they pursued each other. "The grasshopper in the meadow and the one on the little hill hops. Until I have seen my lord—my restless heart, ah, how it beats!—but as soon as I see him—as soon as I am united to him—then my heart will be at peace."

The special importance of this ancient Chinese peasant poetry lies in the fact that, whereas its ritual origin is abundantly clear, so too is its affinity to the *Natureingang* poetry of mediæval Europe—the love-songs of the Goliards and Vagantes, poor clerks and wandering scholars, the German Minnesinger and the Provençal troubadours.[5]

> Letabundus rediit avium concentus,
> ver iocundum prodiit, gaudeat iuventus,
> nova ferens gaudia; modo vernant omnia
> Phebus serenatur,
> redolens temperiem, novo flore faciem
> Flora renovatur.[6]

That these songs too have their origin in agrarian ritual is now generally recognised, and indeed the ritual itself still survives in the decadent forms of the modern European May and harvest festivals.[7] This ritual is important for our present purpose, because I believe that it throws light on certain elements in the worship of Dionysus. It has, of course, been thoroughly examined by Mannhardt and Frazer, and my only reason for taking up the matter here is that one of its central features—the idea of death and resurrection—has not been adequately interpreted.

I shall concentrate on the two festivals, celebrated in the spring or early summer, which are called "Carrying out

Death" and "Bringing in the Summer." In many parts of
Europe only one of these elements is represented, but elsewhere
they are found in combination, and there is no doubt that they
are both integral parts of a single celebration. After a brief
summary of the essential elements in each, I shall call attention
to some details, taken from particular examples, which illustrate their general significance.

A puppet called Death is carried out of the village by a
party of young men or girls, while the onlookers praise it or
curse it or pelt it with stones. It is then hung on a tree, or burnt,
or thrown into a stream, or torn to pieces in the fields, the party
scrambling for the remains. The puppet is always made to
represent a human being, and is often dressed in women's
clothes. Sometimes the part of Death is played by one of the
villagers, and then a pretence is made of killing him. Where
the two ceremonies are combined, the party may spend the
whole night in the woods, and then there is usually sexual
licence. Next follows the bringing in of summer. Boughs are
cut in the woods, or a whole tree is felled, and with these the
party returns to the village and makes a house-to-house collection for food or money, blessing those who give and cursing
those who refuse. The collection is sometimes followed by a
feast. The boughs are eventually hung over the doors or set
up in the cattle-stalls or in the fields, where they are believed
to bring fertility to women, cattle and crops. The tree is frequently accompanied by a puppet representing a boy or girl,
or by a real boy or girl dressed up in foliage. It is erected in
the village as a maypole, around which are held dances, races
and games of various sorts, the winners often being acclaimed
as the king or queen of the year. In some places the king of the
previous year is subjected to an ordeal or suffers a mock execution. The participants in the festival are usually the young
people of the village—the boys or the girls or both; but there
is a rather high proportion of instances in which the celebrations are reserved to women.

In parts of Transylvania, a willow is felled, garlanded and
set up in the village.[8] Old and sick persons spit on it and say,
"You will soon die, but let us live." Next morning, a young
man dressed up in leaves and called the Green George is

carried to a stream as though to be drowned, but at the last moment a puppet made of branches is thrown into the stream in his stead. In Upper Lusatia the puppet is dressed in the veil worn by the last bride and a shirt from the house in which the last death occurred. In Bohemia it is burnt by children, who sing as it burns:

> Now carry we Death out of the village,
> The new Summer into the village.
> Welcome, dear Summer, green little corn!

At Spachendorf in Silesia, the puppet is carried to a field, stripped, and torn to pieces by the crowd, everyone struggling to secure a wisp of the straw of which it is made. The wisps are brought home and placed in the mangers, where it is believed they make the cattle thrive.

Essentially similar to these spring festivals, though usually less elaborate, is the French and German custom of the Harvest May. A branch or tree, decorated with ears of corn, is brought home on the last waggon from the harvest field and fastened on to the farmhouse roof, where it remains for the rest of the year.

Frazer interprets these festivals as follows. Death and Summer are really identical, being different aspects of the vegetation spirit which year by year dies and is born again. Originally the vegetation spirit was embodied in a tree, but gradually it became anthropomorphic—first a puppet adorned with leaves and then a human being similarly adorned and associated with a tree. The mock execution which the human being sometimes undergoes is derived from an earlier custom of human sacrifice, in which the old king was actually killed by the new.

Of the essential identity of the two figures there can be no question. It is proved by many of the songs sung on the occasion, and it is brought out very clearly in some Russian forms of the festival.[9] In Little Russia, a girl called the Kostrubonko lies down as though dead. Mourners move round her and sing:

> Dead, dead is our Kostrubonko!
> Dead, dead is our dear one!

Suddenly the girl springs to her feet, and the mourners rejoice:

Come to life, come to life is our Kostrubonko!
Come to life is our dear one!

Thus far, therefore, Frazer is certainly right, but the remainder
of his interpretation is open to serious objections.

In the first place, it is surely over-simplified. The tree is
undoubtedly a primitive element, going back to a remote past;
but it is hardly probable on general grounds that the form of
a pre-anthropomorphic cult should have been preserved almost
intact, with the transition to anthropomorphism so neatly
stratified, by the peasantry of modern Europe. Nor is there
any independent reason to suppose that the versions in which
the tree is replaced by a tree-man are less primitive than the
others. Moreover, in certain respects, notwithstanding their
underlying affinity, the two figures are very different. Summer
is always a tree or a tree-man, and it has been plausibly suggested that the former was a phallic symbol.[10] In that case the
two elements are distinct and there is no reason to derive one
from the other, the tree-man being the carrier of the phallus.
Death, on the other hand, is almost invariably a puppet, which
in most cases is not specially associated with trees at all, while
in some it is clearly a substitute for a human being. There
are really no grounds for believing that the puppet is pre-
anthropomorphic.

Finally, in view of what was said in the last chapter, it is
rash to assume that a rite of mimic death presupposes an
antecedent stage in which the death was actual. In default of
independent evidence, the feigned death, whether in myth or
in ritual, is adequately explained on the hypothesis that it is
derived from rites of initiation, in which, as we have seen, a
mimic death—not a real death—is an essential element. Thus,
the mock execution of the old king need be no more than a
confused reminiscence of a forgotten initiatory ordeal; and this
interpretation becomes almost necessary when we find that the
mock death is often followed by a mock resurrection. The case
of Kostrubonko has already been quoted. In Saxony, after
being put to death, the king is restored to life by a doctor.[11]
On Frazer's hypothesis, this feature must be explained as a
mock sacrifice substituted for a real sacrifice; but the magic

doctor belongs to a very widespread tradition, which can be traced in Greek comedy and again in the drama of mediæval Europe, and it seems much simpler to suppose that it is nothing more than a folk memory of the mock death and resurrection inherent in the ritual of initiation.

I would suggest therefore an interpretation of these festivals, which, while less simple and obvious, is perhaps for that reason likely to be nearer the truth. At the beginning of spring, the boys and girls of the community go out in procession to the woods and meadows. Their departure is an occasion for mourning, because the boys will return as men and the girls will be maidens no more. Out in the woods they carry branches which they have torn from the trees, and crown their heads with leaves. By this means they assimilate the generative powers just reviving in field and forest, and in the course of the night they perform for the first time the act of sexual union. Next morning they return, carrying with them the emblems of their new status. There are games, contests and trials of strength, and the winning pair are venerated as bride and bridegroom in the sacred marriage of the year. The festival ends with a communal meal.

From one point of view, therefore, the purpose is to impregnate the rising generation by contact with the first spring blossoms; but at the same time the human community must fertilise itself in order to renew the fertility of Nature, and eventually, as the structure of society changes, this aspect becomes dominant. The rite is still performed by the young—a festival of youth is still needed to arouse the spring, but the special significance of their part in it, particularly their ritual death and resurrection, is no longer understood. One of their number suffers a mimic death and resurrection, or a puppet is killed in his stead; and the puppet becomes a symbol for the hunger and sickness of the winter that is past. Similarly, the virtues which they have assimilated by contact with the boughs are restricted to the boughs themselves and finally concentrated in the village maypole. And so the festival degenerates into a traditional pastime, the meaningless *débris* of a forgotten ritual.

The customs of Bringing in the Summer and the Harvest May can, of course, be traced, in a form almost equally decadent, among the ancient Greek peasantry. In Samos, at the festival of Apollo, the children used to beg from door to door with a song of precisely the same type as those still used in central Europe, and they carried the *eiresióne*—a branch garlanded with wool.[12] We are also told that throughout Greece the farmers used to honour Dionysus by setting up in their fields a tree-stump.[13] On the other hand, the *eiresióne* was also carried at the Athenian festival of the Oschophoria, which was officially recognised by the state and administered by the clan of the Phytalidai. The principal events were races for the *épheboi*, a procession led by two young men disguised as women, and a communal feast. Moreover, in Greece as in Italy and elsewhere, the negative element in the primitive ritual, corresponding to the Carrying out of Death, acquired fresh vitality as a ceremony of public atonement. Thus, in Asiatic Greece, in time of plague or famine, a slave or criminal (*pharmakós*) was escorted out of the city; after being given a meal of cheese, figs and barley bread, he was whipped on the genital organs with branches of wild trees, burnt to death on a pile of timber taken from wild trees and his ashes scattered to the winds.[14] Here the element of mortification has been developed along independent lines, but the idea of regeneration clearly underlies the manner of his whipping. Frazer says that "it was not unnatural to stimulate his reproductive powers in order that these might be transmitted in full activity to his successor"; but in the present instance there is no trace of a successor. His reproductive powers were stimulated in order to restore health and plenty.

We saw in the last chapter that initiation was an essential feature in the formation of all secret magical societies, and we have now seen that its origins are inseparable from the origins of agriculture. Our next task is to investigate the worship of Dionysus, which was largely in the hands of secret societies and largely concerned with agricultural magic. I shall begin with the myth of the death of Pentheus as it is presented in the *Bacchants* of Euripides.

It will be remembered that in punishment for his persecution of the worshippers of Dionysus, Pentheus was lured to his death by the god himself. Seized with a desire to see the

Bacchants at their secret rites, he disguises himself at the god's direction in women's clothes, and, thus attired, he is led through the streets of Thebes, the laughing-stock of the people. When they reach the pinewood where the Bacchants are resting before their celebrations, Pentheus asks for a point of vantage from which he can view the spectacle. The god bends down one of the trees, sets Pentheus on its top, and releases it. Then the god disappears, and a voice is heard summoning the Bacchants to punish the sinner who has violated their seclusion. Catching sight of Pentheus in the tree-top, they pelt him with sticks and stones; then, at the bidding of his own mother, Agaue, who with her sisters Ino and Autonoe is among the celebrants, they tear up the tree by the roots and bring it to the ground. Pentheus implores his mother to spare his life, but she does not even recognise him. "She is the priestess who inaugurates the slaughter." With superhuman strength, she wrenches off one of his shoulders. The other women close round. Ino seizes an elbow, Autonoe the feet. Eventually Agaue snatches the head, impales it on her thyrsus or ivy-wreathed wand, and races back in triumph to the city, where she sets it on the roof of the palace. "A wreath freshly plucked have we brought from the hills to the palace, a prey full of blessings." Agaue is the victor, because it was she who struck the first blow. She declares that her fellow-worshippers acclaim her as "blessed Agaue," calls on her father to rejoice in the daughter whom God has blessed, and finally summons her kinsfolk to a feast.

The death of Pentheus was interpreted many years ago by Bather, working on the materials collected by Mannhardt and Frazer.[15] As he pointed out, the myth is founded on ritual, and the ritual on which it is founded belongs to the same type as the customs of Carrying out Death and Bringing in the Summer, the only difference being that here the puppet and the maypole are replaced by a single human victim. To Bather's able analysis, which should be studied in detail, I would merely add a few points that bring these Bacchants into closer relation with what was said in the last chapter concerning secret societies and mystical religion.

At the beginning of the play, having arrived at Thebes after their journey from the east, they open the choral part as follows:

Who is there? who approaches? Let him go hence, let him leave us, and let all lips be at rest, hushed in silence! We shall now praise Dionysus in accord with long custom.

Then they begin a hymn:

Blessèd are they that lead pure lives and have learned by God's grace mysteries, sanctified, made clean, joined in a holy band which roams on the hills with fleet foot, filled with the breath of Bacchus. . . . And with wands high in the air, all heads crowned with the ivy, they adore him, Dionysus.

They spend the night in the woods, some stretched against the stems of pine trees, others with their heads pillowed on a bed of oak leaves. The death of Pentheus is described as an *agón* or ordeal, both from his own point of view and from that of the Bacchants. He leaves the town under the escort or *pompé* of the god. Agaue returns home in a triumphal procession or *kômos*, and she carries the prize of victory, in virtue of which she is acclaimed as *mákar* or *eudaímon*, and her victory is celebrated by a feast.[16]

In the light of the preceding chapter, these details explain themselves. At the beginning of the celebrations the uninitiated are warned away; the reward of initiation is *eudaimonía*; the initiates sleep the sleep of initiation in contact with regenerating leaves; and the remainder follows the same ritual pattern that we have already traced in the Mysteries of Eleusis and the Olympian Games.

It cannot, of course, be doubted that behind the myth of Pentheus there lies a real death. The totemic sacrament of the primitive clan has been transformed from a simple act of magical communion into the bloody sacrifice of a secret society. Pentheus was torn to pieces by the Bacchants as an embodiment of Dionysus, who was torn to pieces by the Titans; or, rather, the death of Dionysus was a mythical projection of the actual death reflected in the myth of Pentheus. In the myth of Dionysus, the death is followed by a resurrection; but in the ritual itself, after the substitution of a human victim, this element was necessarily eliminated, except in so far as the victim's death conferred newness of life on all in contact with his flesh and blood. This in itself is an indication that human sacrifice is not an inherent element in ritual of this type; and a further indication is provided by the words in which Agaue describes the head of Pentheus after she has brought it home. It is, she says, a wreath freshly plucked for the palace—implying that the prize of victory had once been a bunch of foliage and nothing more. The incarnations of Dionysus took many forms in different parts of Greece. In Macedonia it was a snake that was torn to pieces, in Crete a bull, in other places a fawn; and at Orchomenos in Boiotia, only a few miles from Thebes, we are told that "the women possessed by the Bacchic frenzy fell upon the ivy, tearing it to pieces in their hands and devouring it." This we learn from Plutarch, a native of Boiotia.[17] For these reasons we shall refrain from the assumption that such ritual is in general founded on human sacrifice, but shall regard that element as a derivative one, which emerged sporadically, especially in theocratic communities such as Boiotia must have been in the Mycenean period, when the priest kings of Orchomenos were among the most powerful in Greece.

It is strange that so little attention has been paid to Bather's analysis of this myth. Nilsson mentions it, and was evidently impressed by it, because he discusses it incidentally in a footnote, but he concludes: "It seems to me bold to look for a cult practice behind *every* detail of a myth, especially one expounded in poetry."[18] This comment is not very helpful, because, since Nilsson acknowledges the validity of Bather's general method, which indeed he has applied himself to other problems of Greek mythology with conspicuous success, the only criterion in limiting its application must be the strength of the evidence. As Bather pointed out, the same story is told in great detail by Nonnos, who was doubtless familiar with the plays of Euripides, but, although the essential elements are the same in both, the two versions are not identical and may be presumed therefore to derive from a common tradition. It is, of course, true that Euripides and Nonnos were poets, but so were Homer, Hesiod, Pherekydes, Stesichoros and the other writers to whom, directly or indirectly, we owe almost all we know about Greek myths; and the more one studies Greek poetry, the more intensely one realises how profoundly it differs from the modern poetry of western Europe in being so firmly rooted in popular tradition.

We shall now pass in review other evidence relating to these societies or *thíasoi* of Dionysus, which, though fragmentary and confused, becomes at least clearer on the hypothesis we have suggested.

The rending of the ivy at Orchomenos took place during the festival of the Agrionia, and Plutarch records other details of the same festival. "In our country," he says, "at the feast of the Agrionia, the women seek Dionysus as though he had run away; then they give up the search and say that he has fled to the Muses and is in hiding with them; and a little while afterwards, when the supper is at an end, they ask one another riddles and conundrums." And again: "Every year, at the Agrionia, the women called the Oleiai are pursued with a sword by the priest of Dionysus, who, if he catches the hindmost, is permitted to kill her, as was in fact done by the priest Zoilos within living memory." This was written in the first century of our era.[19] In the same passage Plutarch refers to the myth of the daughters of Minyas, king of Orchomenos. Seized with a mad desire for human flesh, they cast lots, and the sister on whom the lot fell gave her son to be torn in pieces. It is clear therefore that at Orchomenos the custom of human sacrifice not only existed in prehistoric times, but was revived occasionally throughout the historical period.

At Orchomenos, therefore, the god ran away and the women went in search of him. This implies that he was subsequently found and brought home. The women tore and devoured the ivy, which was presumably the god whom they had recovered. There was also a ritual pursuit, in which one of their number was killed. The significance of this feature will become clearer in the sequel, but it was evidently an initiatory ordeal, like the foot race run by the Dionysiades at Sparta, and the practice at Alea in Arcadia, where at the beginning of the festival of Dionysus the women were scourged "in the same manner as the Spartan *épheboi*."[20]

Further light is thrown on these details, and fresh details are brought to light, by several local myths which are admittedly based on ritual. They involve Hera as well as Dionysus, yet they are all so closely interrelated that it will be best to give them in full before disentangling the details.

The first is from Tanagra in Boiotia, where it was told in explanation of the local cult of Dionysus. Before the celebrations began, the women went down to the sea in order to purify themselves, and while swimming they were assaulted by the sea god Triton. They cried out to Dionysus, who wrestled with Triton and overcame him.[21]

The second is from Naxos. The nurses of Dionysus were attacked on Mount Drios in Thessaly by the Thracian Boutes (ox-man). They fled to the sea, but one of them, named Koronis, was caught and carried off by Boutes, who took her to Naxos and forced her to cohabit with him until he was driven mad by Dionysus and drowned himself in a well.[22] The last detail reappears in Attica, where Dionysus was welcomed by Ikarios, who was then murdered and his body buried under a tree or thrown into a well; and at Argos, where the king Perseus threw Dionysus himself into the marshes of Lerna.[23] We remember, too, that, when the Bacchants of Thrace had torn Orpheus to pieces, they threw his head into the sea.

The third is from Thrace, and is recorded in the *Iliad*.[24] Lykourgos was a king of the Edonoi and a son of Dryas (the oak-man). He pursued the nurses of Dionysus, who cast their wands to the ground and fled, smitten as they went by the murderous Lykourgos with his *boúplex*. Terrified by his shouts, Dionysus himself sought refuge in the sea, where Thetis took him to her bosom. Lykourgos was blinded by the gods and died soon afterwards. The story is also told by Sophokles in a form which indicates that the shouting of Lykourgos consisted of ritual imprecations. It is uncertain whether his *boúplex* was an ox-goad or a pole-axe, but, since he is described as "murderous" or "manslaying," it was more probably the latter. In another version, after chasing Dionysus into the sea, he imprisoned the Bacchants (as Pentheus does in Euripides), but they were miraculously released. Lykourgos went mad and killed his own son with a blow from his axe, mistaking him for a vine. After mutilating his body, he recovered his senses, but some time afterwards he was torn to pieces on Mount Pangaion.[25]

The flight of the women from Boutes and Lykourgos plainly

corresponds to the ritual pursuit in the feast of the Agrionia at Orchomenos, but in both cases it is a flight to the sea. In the tradition from Tanagra the women purify themselves by bathing in the sea, while the legends of Orpheus and Ikarios, the fate of Boutes in Thessaly and of Dionysus himself at Argos, suggest that the head of the victim or a puppet was thrown into the water. In these myths the main emphasis is on the purificatory character of the rite—the carrying out of the god; but the myth of Perseus is probably to be connected with an actual rite known to have been practised in Argos, where the god was summoned out of a bottomless marsh by a blast of trumpets.[26]

Immersion in water is a purification, but it is also a regeneraation. In the same way, the scourging of the *pharmakós* was designed not merely to expel disease and death but to induce health and life. It is probable therefore that the immersion of these women worshippers of Dionysus was related to a more general practice of the same kind.[27] Greek brides used to bathe before marriage in the river or in water brought from the river. This too was a purification, but at the same time it was believed to promote the bride's fertility. The waters of the nuptial bath are expressly described as "life-giving," and the same idea underlies the formula recited by the brides of the Troad when they bathed in the River Scamander—"Scamander, take my virginity!" This implies that at one time, in Greece as in China, it had been believed that the girl was actually impregnated by contact with the living waters. So long as sexual intercourse was collective and began at puberty, the physiological significance of paternity had been neither significant nor apparent.[28] And, surely, these girls who, having bathed in the river, become brides are the prehistoric human originals of the nymphs of Greek mythology and folklore—the "brides" who are wedded to the river gods and bear heroic sons.

Thus, the bathing of the women in the cult of Dionysus might be a rite either of initiation or of marriage. Probably it was both. The initiates of the *thiasos* were brides of Dionysus.

The capture of Koronis on Mount Drios in Thessaly corresponds to the capture of the hindmost of Orchomenos, but in this case the captive was not killed, but ravished by her captor. Koronis was a native of Naxos, where she appears as one of the god's nurses in the local legend of his birth; and, moreover, it was in Naxos, on another Mount Drios, that Dionysus disappeared with Ariadne after ravishing her from Theseus.[29] This suggests that, at least in some cases, the purpose of the ritual pursuit was to choose a bride for the god. We know that Dionysus had a bride at Olympia (p. 116), and also at Athens, where, in a building called the Boukolion, or cattle-stall, he was united annually in a sacred marriage with the wife of the *árchon basileús*, the priestly successor of the ancient Athenian kings.

Argos, as well as Orchomenos, had a festival called the Agrionia, which was there consecrated to one of the daughters of Proitos. As Bather observed, these three daughters of Proitos bear a remarkable resemblance to the three daughters of Minyas. When Dionysus came to Argos, the women refused to be initiated, whereupon they went mad, killed the babes at their breasts and devoured their flesh. The daughters of Proitos wandered in distraction all over the Peloponnese, pursued by the priest Melampous, who was a native of Orchomenos and a kinsman of Minyas; and during the pursuit one of the sisters died. The others were purified by Melampous, the off-scourings being thrown into the River Anigros, and then they recovered their senses.[30]

In another version of the same myth, the deity whom the daughters of Proitos had offended was not Dionysus, but Hera, by whom, we are told, they were transformed into cows.[31] This seems to show, as Nilsson has remarked, that they had something in common with Io. Io was a priestess of Hera at Argos. Zeus fell in love with her, whereupon she was transformed into a cow and put out to pasture in the meadows of Lerna under the keen eyes of an oxherd called Argos. Eventually, after a long pursuit, Zeus restored her to her right shape and mind by a touch of his hand, and by the same touch she conceived a child. According to Æschylus, her union with Zeus took place in Egypt, but this version betrays the influence of the Egyptian myth of Isis and Osiris, and, according to local traditions, her child was born no further afield than Euboia, the isle of "fair oxen."[32]

The myth of Io is clearly founded on a sacred marriage, the

bride being the priestess of Hera, the bridegroom apparently the priest of Zeus in the guise of a bull; for, as Cook points out, the oxherd Argos is *panóptes*, "all-seeing," which was a traditional epithet of Zeus and the sun, and he is described by Apollodoros as wearing a bull's hide. Further, the keen eyes of Argos and the crescent horns of Io suggest that the marriage was also regarded as a union of sun and moon such as we have already encountered at Olympia. Lastly, an obscure but evidently ancient Argive tradition runs as follows.[33] A herdsman named Haliakmon was tending his cattle on Mount Kokkygion when he chanced to see Zeus in the act of embracing Hera. The sight drove him mad, and he threw himself into the River Karmanor, which was thereafter called the Haliakmon. Later, when Zeus ravished Io, he was pursued by her father, Inachos, who struck him from behind and cursed him. For this offence Inachos was driven mad and threw himself into the Haliakmon, which was thereafter called the Inachos. It appears therefore that the marriage of Zeus with Hera or Io was in some way connected with a ritual pursuit and with immersion in the river.

If the sacred marriage underlying the myth of Io was regarded as a union of sun and moon, we may be sure that this aspect was not the original one, but rather a reflection of calendar reforms introduced by the priesthood with advancing astronomical knowledge. And behind this marriage of sun and moon there lies a marriage of bull and cow. What precisely does this mean? In the first place, as Cook has explained, the ceremony consisted of a dance in which, appropriately disguised, the priest and priestess simulated the copulation of cattle.[34] But why did they act in this manner? The conventional answer to this question—that they did so because Zeus and Hera were respectively associated with the bull and the cow—explains nothing and inverts the true relation of myth and ritual. Zeus and Hera were associated with the bull and the cow because their human representatives were accustomed to act in this manner. If the partners in this dance pretended to be a bull and a cow, the reason must be that at a still earlier period they had actually been a bull and a cow. This is a hard saying, but it can be interpreted.

Behind the worship of Hera at Argos there lies the cult of a sacred cow. It is possible that the Hera seen by Haliakmon in the embrace of Zeus was really a cow in the herd he was tending at the time—one of the sacred cows, which was being mounted by the bull. In any case, a cult of this kind must be derived ultimately from the ritual of a totemic clan. These priestesses of Hera were descended from the women of a cow clan, who had expressed their sense of affinity to the sacred animal in the form of the belief that they *were* cows. As such, they performed a traditional dance in which they promoted the fertility of their herds by means of mimetic magic.

When we meet Hera at the beginning of written literature she is still "cow-faced" (*boôpis*) and has other vestigial connections with the sacred animal, but she has long assumed a human shape and, in consequence, acquired many new and independent characteristics. Her clan origin is naturally not attested directly; but we have already seen how, when the tribal system disintegrates, clan cults merge into tribal cults, and we are told by Plutarch that in ancient times, when it was still a country of village communities, the district of Megara, to the north of Argos, was inhabited by a people of which one section was called the Heraeis, which means the people of Hera.[35] We may say therefore that our hypothesis is not only necessary in order to explain the internal evidence of myth and ritual, but is in accord with the conclusions to which we have been led by our study of primitive religion.

The same considerations can now be applied to the origins of Dionysus. The *thíasoi* which we have been studying were variously associated with the vine, the ivy, the fig, the bull, the goat, the snake, the fawn; and we know from the evidence of vase paintings that at least two of these, the ivy and the fawn, were employed as totemic emblems, being tattooed on the arms of the members of the *thíasos*.[36] Moreover, we are informed by the lexicographer Photius that the verb *nebrizo* meant alternatively "to wear the fawn skin or to rend and devour the fawn, in imitation of the passion of Dionysus."[37] These bacchants, who tore and devoured the fawn, were clad in fawn skins and marked with the sign of the fawn. In other words they *were* fawns, they belonged to a fawn clan—not, it is true, a clan of the most primitive type, a component unit of the tribe, but a secret society, which, like the secret societies of all primitive peoples, had evolved out of the clan and preserved many of its totemic, magico-economic and initiatory functions.

A remarkable feature of these *thíasoi* is that, excepting the priest at their head, their membership is confined to women. We hear of a male *thíasos*, the Meliastai, in Arcadia, and another, the Dionysiastai, in Rhodes, but nothing of consequence is known about them; and at Patrai, on the north coast of the Peloponnese, the god's cult was in the charge of a sacred college consisting of nine men and nine women.[38] In myth, Dionysus is frequently attended by satyrs as well as bacchants and mænads, but the appearance of satyrs in actual cult is confined to the dramatic festivals, and their association with Dionysus is comparatively late.[39] It appears, therefore, that in the earliest period these Dionysiac cults were for the most part reserved to women. And so in many cases they remained. The Oleiai of Orchomenos were women, and so were the Thyiades of Delphi, the Dionysiades of Sparta, the Dysmainai of Mount Taygetos.[40] Even where the *thíasos* had broken down and its cult merged in a popular festival, the celebrations seem to have been conducted mainly by women. These festivals are described by Diodoros, writing in the first century B.C.:[41] "Every other year, in many Greek towns, it is the custom for women to gather together in companies of Bacchus, the girls carrying the thyrsus and worshipping the god with wild, ecstatic cries, while the married women sacrifice in groups, indulge in Bacchic revels, and in general sing hymns to Dionysus in imitation of the Mænads, his ancient ministers."

There were, of course, in many Greek states public cults of Dionysus, from which the men were in no way excluded; yet it is clear that one at least of these, and the most widely diffused, had in former times been confined to women. The Attic feast of the Lenaia fell in the month of Gamelion, which had formerly been called Lenaion, after the feast, and we know from inscriptions that there was a month called Lenaion in the calendars of several Ionian states—Smyrna, Ephesos, Lampsakos, Samos, Delos, Kyzikos.[42] From this it may be inferred that the Lenaia was an ancient Ionian festival, and its name

LA

is evidently related to Lenai, the "mad women," synonymous with Mainades, Thyiades, Dysmainai, all of which are characteristic designations of the Dionysiac *thiasos*. The festival itself is only known to us in the form which it had assumed in fifth-century Attica, where the men's part in it was at least as great as the women's. It is clear therefore that in Attica the worship of Dionysus had been modified in consequence of changes in the relations of the sexes. The nature of these changes will be examined when we resume our account of the democratic revolution, but before leaving the subject of Dionysus we must complete our enquiry into mystical religion.

IX

ORPHISM

THE religious reforms introduced by Peisistratos were explained in the last chapter but one as an integral part of his general policy. In order to break down the political privileges of the old nobility, he had to weaken their control of religion, which they had used as an instrument of class domination; and this end he achieved by giving official encouragement and support to the cults of those sections of the people whose interests he represented—in particular, the worship of Dionysus. This of course implies that the cults of Dionysus were popular, non-aristocratic—an assumption which has now been confirmed by an examination of their content. They were very ancient—older, in fact, than the god to whose name they were attached—and they consisted of a primitive form of agricultural magic. It was natural that such cults should have survived among the peasantry, who continued to till the soil, rather than among the aristocracy, who had withdrawn from the productive labour of society.

Peisistratos was not the first tyrant to pursue a policy of this kind. Some seventy or eighty years before him, Periandros of Corinth had entertained at his court a poet, Arion, from Methymna in Lesbos, who under his patronage invented the dithyramb, a form of choral ode consecrated to Dionysus;[1] and a generation later Kleisthenes, tyrant of Sikyon, had transferred to Dionysus the chief part of a cult which had previously belonged to the Argive hero Adrastos.[2] At Sikyon, in addition to the three Dorian tribes, there was a fourth, drawn from the pre-Dorian elements which had been subjugated at the time of the Dorian conquest, and it was from this tribe that the tyranny derived its principal support. It is clear therefore that, in substituting Dionysus for the Argive hero of the Dorian aristocracy, Kleisthenes was actuated by the same motives as Peisistratos.

Under the tyranny, the worship of Dionysus was brought to town, and its agrarian character was consequently transformed. The new Athenian festival of the City Dionysia was a product of the urban revolution, in virtue of which it acquired a number of characteristics that mark it off sharply from its ultimate origins in the Attic countryside. These new characteristics will have to be carefully examined, but first of all it is necessary to enquire more closely into the religious aspect of the urban revolution.

During the sixth century B.C., a new cult of Dionysus, which may be conveniently described as Orphism, was disseminated with missionary ardour, not only on the mainland and in the islands, but in the colonies beyond the Adriatic. Before asking what it was and why it spread so far, let us consider where it came from and what route it followed.

The story of Arion is told by Herodotus.[3] After spending a long time at the court of Periandros in Corinth, he emigrated to the west, where he made a lot of money. Desiring to return to Corinth, he hired a Corinthian ship and set sail from Taras in southern Italy. On the voyage the sailors plotted to take his life and steal his money. Arion discovered the plot and implored them to spare his life, but they replied that he must choose between killing himself outright, in which case they would bury him ashore, and leaping overboard. Eventually, anxious to hear a singer of such celebrity, they were prevailed upon to let him sing one last song. Attired in his ritual costume, Arion took up his lyre, sang his song, and then leapt into the sea, where he was carried on the back of a dolphin safe to shore at Cape Tainaron.

This is not history, but myth. Dionysus himself, on vase paintings of the period, is represented sailing the seas on board a ship escorted by dolphins. Orpheus, too, was a celebrated singer whose music charmed the creatures of the wild. Dionysus himself leapt into the sea, as we saw in the last chapter, and the head of Orpheus was thrown into the sea after he had been torn in pieces by the Bacchants. Cape Tainaron, where Arion reappeared after he had been reported dead, was one of the entrances to Hades, and it was there that Orpheus descended to the underworld.[4]

Yet, despite its mythical character, the setting of the story has a historical significance. It is known that Corinth was the first city on the mainland to institute a tyranny, and it was an *entrepôt* for trade between the Ægean and the west; nor is there any reason to doubt that the dithyramb was introduced there by a poet from Lesbos, where the tyrant Pittakos was probably contemporary with Periandros. Moreover, it was at Lesbos that the head of Orpheus was said to have been thrown up by the sea, the head itself, we are told, being preserved there as a sacred relic; and it was at Methymna in Lesbos, Arion's native town, that some fishermen were said to have hauled up in their nets a mask of olive wood representing the head of Dionysus. The conclusion to which this evidence points is that the Dionysiac revival originated in Thrace, whence it was carried by trade across the Ægean to Corinth and so to Italy and Sicily.

Its Thracian origin is hardly open to doubt. Thrace had always been a centre of Dionysiac worship. The name of Dionysus has been interpreted by Kretschmer as the Thraco-Phrygian equivalent of *Dios koûros*,[5] and the myth of Orpheus is securely located in the country round Mount Pangaion in Thrace.[6] It was on Mount Pangaion that both Orpheus and Lykourgos, the mythical king of the Edonoi, met their death. This mountain had other, more mundane, associations. It was equally famous for its gold and silver mines, which at this period were the richest accessible to the Greeks.

The Orphics were already established at Athens in the time of Peisistratos, whose patronage was enjoyed by their leader, Onomakritos, the author of a book called *Initiations*.[7] The dithyramb was introduced during the same period by Lasos of Hermione, a town in Argos whose inhabitants were of pre-Dorian origin. As we have seen, the dithyramb had long been known at Corinth, and, since early Attic drama bears the marks of Peloponnesian influence, it is possible that Orphism reached Athens from the same quarter; but there was another route open to it, and more direct.

The relation of the Peisistratidai to the mining industry has been elucidated by Ure in his study of the tyranny.[8] In the course of his struggle with Megakles and Lykourgos, Peisistratos had organised the Hillmen, who were miners of Laurion, the mines being worked mainly at this period by free labour, and it was with their support that he made himself tyrant. As we have seen, he was driven out twice by his opponents before he succeeded in consolidating his position, and he spent his second exile collecting funds at Mount Pangaion in Thrace. After his second restoration he proceeded, in the words of Herodotus, "to root his tyranny with large numbers of mercenaries and with revenues of money gathered partly from the home country and partly from the River Strymon," which flows under Mount Pangaion through the mining district.

The populations of mining districts in all parts of the world have always been mixed, because local labour is insufficient to meet the demands of an industry that requires so many hands. We know that the population of Laurion was mixed in the fifth century, and we may presume that it was so in the sixth. We also know that, in the time of Hipparchos, there was a large Greek element in the mining population of the Strymon, which doubtless included Attic miners from Laurion. Since the Peisistratidai were associated so closely with both centres, there must have been migration of workers in both directions. Finally, not only was Mount Pangaion and the surrounding district the cradle of Orphism, but not far from Laurion, in the heart of the Attic mining area, was the village of Semachidai, which had a shrine of Dionysus, called the Semacheion, and a local tradition of the coming of the god. Here, then, was an avenue leading straight to Athens from Thrace, and accordingly we may infer that this was at least one of the channels through which the Orphic movement entered Attica.

It would seem therefore that Orphism was carried to Attica, as it had been to Corinth and the west, in the wake of industry and trade. It was an outgrowth of the urban revolution.[9] If so, we should be able to recognise in it the type of religion that these social conditions would naturally produce; but before examining the content of Orphism, we must see whether any more can be said about the composition of the working class in sixth-century Attica.

Down to this period, it is agreed, the slave population had been small. Under an agricultural economy, the demand for labour was restricted, except at a few critical periods of the year, such as the harvest, when it was met by the employment of casual free labour. With the growth of trade, however, it became constant and almost unlimited, chiefly for transport, quarrying and the mines. In the fifth century, slaves were plentiful and cheap, but in the sixth, before the Persian wars had opened up the east, the main source of labour, at least in Attica, was the peasantry. In this period, the miners of Laurion were men, and no doubt women and children as well, who had been driven off the land. For these reasons the Orphic movement is likely to have reflected the outlook of a dispossessed peasantry. Now, we have already learnt something of the peasant outlook from the poetry of Hesiod, and we may therefore begin our account of Orphic teaching by comparing its exposition of the origin of the world with the view expounded in the Hesiodic *Theogony*.

According to Hesiod, in the beginning there was the Void. Then Earth came into being, and Love. Out of the Void sprang Erebos and Night, and Night gave birth to Aither and Day. Earth gave birth to Heaven, to whom in turn she bore Ocean, Rhea, Kronos and the Titans. Kronos overthrew his father Heaven and was overthrown by his own son Zeus.[10] According to the Orphics, in the beginning there was Time. Then Aither and the Void came into being, and from them Time fashioned a silver egg, out of which sprang Phanes, or Love. The parentage of Zeus is the same as in Hesiod, but, having come to power, he swallows Phanes and so identifies himself with him. By Persephone he becomes the father of Dionysus, whose death at the hands of the Titans has been described in an earlier chapter (p. 111). When the Titans were blasted by the thunderbolt, they were still reeking with the blood of Dionysus, and from this blend of blood and ashes the human race is sprung. That is why the nature of man is partly good and partly bad. It is divided against itself.

Time, the egg, the swallowing of Phanes, the passion of Dionysus and the origin of mankind—all these are Orphic innovations, the last of them, we are told, being invented by Onomakritos, the *protégé* of Peisistratos at Athens. Yet, notwithstanding these important innovations, it is clear that the

Orphics were building on the Hesiodic tradition. To Homer they owed almost nothing, but their debt to Hesiod was profound. This is in itself enough to indicate in what direction the origins of the movement are to be sought.

In the Homeric poems, the word *dike* means a way, a custom, what is fitting, and in a few passages a judgment. In Hesiod it is used to denote the abstract idea of justice, which is personified as a goddess who sits at the right hand of Zeus and informs him of the wickedness of the nobles who give crooked judgments. The Hesiodic use of the word is an extension of the Homeric, but it is an extension which has been effected by the peasants, who, oppressed as they were, developed the abstraction because they needed it. In the Orphic writings, Dike reappears beside the throne of Zeus.[11] She also appears in the poetry of Solon, whose reformist attitude to the peasantry had brought him into contact with the same stratum in the development of thought.[12]

Finally, the Orphic conception of Love, derived as we have seen from Hesiod, represents a principle that involved a direct challenge to aristocratic thought. To the nobility Love was a dangerous thing, because it implied desire, ambition, discontent. As we saw in our account of Anaximander, the tendency of aristocratic thought was to divide, to keep things apart. To the Orphics, Love was a thing to be revered, because it implied the reunion of what had been sundered, the recovery of what had been lost. In the philosophy of Empedokles, an Orphic of the west, it is Love that brings the world together, Strife that forces it apart, and the world is best when Love overcomes Strife.[13] The tendency of popular thought was to unite.

The core of Orphism lay in its mystical teaching, which was part of its heritage from the agrarian magic of Dionysus. The agricultural origins of mystical religion have already been discussed in connection with the Mysteries of Eleusis. What we have to consider now is the specific character of Orphic mysticism. It is a difficult question, because, once established at Athens, the Orphic movement was brought in close contact with Eleusis, and, owing to their fundamental affinities, the two cults reacted on one another to such an extent that it is not always possible to distinguish them.

The cult of Eleusis enjoyed the official patronage of the state.[14] Securely harnessed to the established order, it served as a medium through which the thwarted aspirations of class society could find expression along channels which led away from conscious realisation of their causes. The Orphics, on the other hand, were organised in small and scattered units, based on the Dionysiac *thiasos*, which were bound together by personal ties, and their mysticism was consequently more individualistic. Not being state-controlled, they developed more fully and consistently the essential function of mystical religion, which is, as we have seen, to renounce life except in so far as it can be made a preparation for death.

Life is a penance by which man atones for the sin of the Titans. The immortal part of him is encased in the mortal; the soul is imprisoned in the body. The body is the tomb of the soul. We are chattels of the gods, who will release us, when it so pleases them, from the prison house of life. All life is a rehearsal for death, for it is only through death that the soul can hope to escape from its imprisonment, to be delivered from the evils of the body. Life is death and death is life. After death the soul is brought to judgment. If it has corrupted itself so deeply by contact with the body that the sin is past cure, it is consigned to eternal torment in the prison house of Tartarus. If its sin is curable, it is purged and chastised, then sent back to earth to renew its penance. When it has lived three lives unspotted of the body, it is released for ever and goes to join the celestial company of the blessed.

Such is the Orphic doctrine of the soul as we find it in Plato. It must have taken some time to achieve so conclusive a formulation, and in the sixth century, no doubt, it was still rudimentary; but through it runs one clear thread—the idea that man is to God and body to soul what the slave is to his master. As Plato says, the soul is by rights the ruler and master, the body its subject and its slave.[15] This dichotomy of human nature, which through Parmenides and Plato became the basis of idealist philosophy, was something new in Greek thought. To the scientists of Miletos, as to the Achæan chiefs and to the primitive savage, the soul was simply that in virtue of which we breathe and move and live; and although, the laws of motion being imperfectly understood, no clear distinction was drawn between organic and inorganic matter, the basis of this conception is essentially materialist. The worlds of Milesian cosmology are described as gods because they move, but they are none the less material. Nowhere in Milesian philosophy, or in the Homeric poems, is there anything that corresponds to this Orphic conception of the soul as generically different from the body, the one pure, the other corrupt, the one divine, the other earthly. So fundamental a revolution in human consciousness only becomes intelligible when it is related to a change equally profound in the constitution of human society; and what that change was is clearly revealed by the symbolism in which the doctrine was expounded.

In an earlier chapter the idea of Moira was traced to the principle that all the members of society are entitled to an equal share in the product of their collective labour. In the period we have now reached, when the last vestiges of tribal society are being rapidly swept away, there arises by the side of Moira the Orphic figure of Ananke, or Necessity. In literature, Ananke makes her first recorded appearance in the writings of Herakleitos and Parmenides, both of whom were influenced by Orphism.[16] Herakleitos couples the two figures as being virtually identical; Parmenides gives the same attributes to Moira, Dike and Ananke. A century later, in Plato's *Republic*, Ananke usurps the place of Moira and is even equipped with her spindle.[17] What is the significance of Ananke?

Throughout Greek literature, from Homer onwards, the ideas of *anánke*, "necessity," and *douleía*, "slavery," are intimately connected, the former being habitually employed to denote both the state of slavery as such and the hard labours and tortures to which slaves are subjected.[18] The sight of slaves harnessed for transport or toiling under the lash suggested the image of a drove of oxen, and accordingly we find that *zygón*, "yoke," is the metaphor traditionally associated with both *douleía* and *anánke*; and in a painting of the Orphic underworld we see Sisyphos rolling his stone uphill, while over him, lash in hand, stands the slave-driver Ananke.[19] Ananke represents the principle that the labouring members of society are denied all share in the product of their labour beyond the minimum necessary to keep them labouring. When Moira became Ananke, she was transformed into her opposite.

One of the formulæ which the Orphics learnt for recital after the soul had left the body, was: "I have flown off the wheel of grief and misery."[20] This wheel, which is variously described as the Wheel of Birth, the Wheel of Fate and the Wheel of Necessity, is clearly descended from the totemic cycle of birth and death; but the primitive concept has been invested with a new meaning, expressed in a contemporary symbol.[21] The wheel was a common instrument of torture used for the chastisement of slaves. The victim was tied hand and foot to the wheel, which was then revolved. Therefore, to fly off the wheel of birth was to be released, delivered, to find escape, to gain a breathing space, from the miseries of mortality. This doctrine of deliverance from labour or from evil, which we have already met at Eleusis, is now charged with an allusion to a grim reality.

Having determined the origin of Orphic symbolism, we must guard against a hasty conclusion as to the social composition of the movement. In the course of its long history, Orphism penetrated into all classes of society, influencing democrats like Euripides, aristocrats like Plato, and respectable bourgeois like Plutarch. When the Greek city-state had passed the zenith of its development, and mystical religion was drawing fresh vitality from the diffusion of idealism, pessimism and social desperation, men of all classes expressed their sense of disunion in terms of the deepening cleavage in society. There is consequently no reason to suppose that, even in its earliest period, the Orphic movement was a slave movement. At the same time the distinctive character of Orphic symbolism does confirm the conclusion to which we have been tending, that the movement drew its initial inspiration from the sufferings of the peasantry, turned off the land and enslaved or driven into industry by the urban revolution. The clearest guide in this matter is the early history of Christianity.

Ever since the conversion of the Emperor Constantine, Christianity has been, in its official form, as distinct from revolutionary heresies, a religion of the ruling class; yet, like Orphism, it began among the workers and it retains to this day the marks of its humble origin. We still sing in the Magnificat, forgetful of its social implications, "The hungry he hath filled with good things, and the rich he hath sent empty away." We still adhere to the doctrine of redemption, which originally connoted the action of a slave in purchasing his liberty. We still bend the knee before the Cross, which, like the Orphic Wheel, was once the symbol of a contemporary reality.

With this proviso, let us see whether it is possible to form any idea of what life was like in the mines of Thrace and Laurion. Direct evidence is lacking. At the end of the second century B.C., when there was an unsuccessful revolt, the number of slaves employed in the Attic mines ran, we are told, into tens of thousands.[22] In 413 B.C., during the Peloponnesian War, 20,000 Attic slaves deserted to the Spartans, and a large proportion of these were probably miners.[23] Under the tyranny, a century earlier, the number employed in the mines was doubtless much smaller. Of the conditions in which they worked, all that is known is what we can infer from the account given by Diodoros in the first century B.C. of conditions in the gold and silver mines of Egypt and Spain. This evidence, though indirect, is not so remote as at first sight it appears, because it is clear that, in these Egyptian and Spanish mines, the actual labour of extracting the ore from the rock, which is the part of the process that concerns us, was entirely unskilled, and is therefore unlikely to have altered.[24]

On the borders of Egypt, and in the adjacent districts of Arabia and Ethiopia, there are many large gold-mines worked intensively at great expense of misery and money. The rock is black, with rifts and veins of marble so dazzling white that it outshines everything. This is where the gold is prepared by the overseers of the mines with a multitude of labourers. To these mines the Egyptian kings send condemned criminals, captives in war, also those who have fallen victim to false accusations or been imprisoned for incurring the royal displeasure, sometimes with all their kinsfolk—both for the punishment of the guilty and for the profits which accrue from their labour. There they throng, all in chains, all kept at work continuously day and night. There is no relaxation, no means of escape; for, since they speak a variety of languages, their guards cannot be corrupted by friendly conversation or casual acts of kindness. Where the gold-bearing rock is very hard, it is first burned with fire, and, when it has been softened sufficiently to yield to their efforts, thousands upon thousands of these unfortunate wretches are set to work on it with iron stone-cutters under the direction of the craftsman who examines the stone and instructs them where to begin. The strongest of those assigned to this luckless labour hew the marble with iron picks. There is no skill in it, only force. The shafts are not cut in a straight line but follow the veins of the shining stone. Where the daylight is shut out by the twists and turns of the quarry, they wear lamps tied to their foreheads, and there, contorting their bodies to fit the contours of the rock, they throw the quarried fragments to the ground, toiling on and on without intermission under the pitiless overseer's lash. Young children descend the shafts into the bowels of the earth, laboriously gathering the stones as they are thrown down, and carrying them into the open air at the shaft-head, where they are taken from them by men over thirty years, each receiving a prescribed amount, which they break on stone mortars with iron pestles into pieces as small as a vetch. Then they are handed on to women and older men, who lay them on rows of grindstones, and standing in groups of two and three they pound them to powder as fine as the best wheaten flour. No one could look on the squalor of these wretches, with not even a rag to cover their loins, without feeling compassion for their plight. They may be sick, or maimed, or aged, or weakly women, but there is no indulgence, no respite. All alike are kept at their labour by the lash, until, overcome by hardships, they die in their torments (*en taîs anánkais*). Their misery is so great that they dread what is to come even more than the present, the punishments are so severe, and death is welcomed as a thing more desirable than life.

It is not for the citizens of an empire which still employs children in mines and factories to point an accusing finger at the Roman;[25] but it is necessary for us to remember the blood and tears that were shed on the raw materials of Greek art.

The account of the Spanish mines is equally illuminating.[26]

The workers in these mines produce incredible profits for the owners, but their own lives are spent underground in the quarries wearing and wasting their bodies day and night. Many die, their sufferings are so great. There is no relief, no respite from their labours. The hardships to which the overseer's lash compels them to submit are so severe that, except for a few, whose strength of body and bravery of soul enable them to endure for a long time, they abandon life, because death seems preferable.

In this passage, apparently without noticing it, Diodoros has slipped into the traditional phraseology of Orphism.

Surely, these are the realities that first inspired the imagery that underlies so many Orphic parables and fables of this life and the next—the Platonic Cave, in which men are chained hand and foot from childhood and have never seen the daylight; or the topography of Tartarus, with its subterranean torrents of water, mud, fire, brimstone; or the upper regions, under a clear sky, where the souls of the righteous are at rest.[27]

Those who are judged to have lived lives of outstanding purity, these are they who are liberated and delivered from the subterranean regions as from a prison, and they are brought up to dwell on the surface of the earth; while those who have purified themselves sufficiently by the pursuit of wisdom, enjoy eternal life, free altogether from the body, in the fairest land of all, which would be hard to describe even if there were time to do it. And so, Simmias, for these reasons we must do everything in our power to attain to virtue and wisdom while we live. The prize is fair and the hope is great.

Plato was not a miner—far from it—but he was drawing on an old tradition. Surely it was in the mines that men first thought of life as a prison house and of the body as the tomb of the soul.[28]

In ritual, the Orphics seem to have maintained the traditions of the Dionysiac *thíasos*. It is probable, though not quite certain, that the animal sacrament persisted in a modified form, which was interpreted as a means of reuniting the banished soul with its divine original.[29] Admission was still by initiation of the type already described, but the Orphic hierarchy of degrees was possibly less elaborate than the Eleusinian. On the other hand, the Orphic *thíasoi* were not confined to women. Not only were men freely admitted, but at least in Attica, if we may judge from the *Hippolytos* of Euripides, they were encouraged to remain celibate. It is probable that in this matter the Orphics were influenced by local conditions, which varied greatly in different states; but the myth of Orpheus himself, who is said to have incurred the hostility of the Bacchants by initiating a band of armed men, suggests that the admission of men was an early and memorable innovation.[30]

So far as we can judge, Orphism was never, even in its early days, a revolutionary movement. It did not seek to change the world, but to escape from it. In this respect, like the Lutheran movement of sixteenth-century Germany, it reflected the incapacity of an uprooted peasantry to organise effectively. It voiced a deep protest, but it made no demands, and so it served to divert the pressure of material needs by otherworldly promises.

To appreciate the crudity of the Orphic theogony, we have only to compare it with the scientific theory that was being worked out in the same period by the philosophers of Miletos. Nevertheless, it would be a mistake to conclude that the Orphic movement was a retrograde step in the evolution of Greek thought.

In the first place, the primitive character of Orphism was due entirely to its class origin. The ruling class of Ionia had risen to a far higher level, but only because it was the ruling class. They lived on the proceeds; the others paid the price. Moreover, it must be remembered that the scientists and philosophers were only a section of that class. At Miletos itself, the heart of Ionian enlightenment, the priestly clan of the Branchidai, whose cult of Apollo exercised a political influence second only to that of the other Apollo at Delphi, owed their power to the skilful manipulation of oracles.[31] These Milesian nobles had outgrown superstition in their private lives, but there was no question of abandoning it as an instrument of public policy. We do not know from what source the prophets of Miletos drew their inspiration. At Delphi, the oracles were delivered by a priestess after she had intoxicated herself by chewing laurel leaves and inhaling vegetable gases from a fissure in the rock.

In the second place, as we have already observed, the Orphics issued a challenge to the time-honoured code of aristocratic morality. Hope is dangerous, love is dangerous, it is dangerous to strive overmuch, dangerous to emulate the gods; keep measure in all things, rest content with what you have. The Orphics delivered men from these timid and intimidating lies. They could not rest content with what they had because they had nothing, and their hopes were as infinite as their desires. All life was strife and struggle, and if man would only run the race with courage, there was none so humble or debased but he might win the prize of glory and become a god. In all this the Orphics revealed—in an inverted, mystical form —the objective potentialities of the democratic movement, and it remained for the people, aroused out of its lethargy, to translate their mysticism into action.

X

DITHYRAMB

LET us now examine the ritual of the City Dionysia, founded or re-founded by Peisistratos. The form in which we know it dates only from the fifth century, and it was reorganised at the end of the sixth. The antiquity of particular elements is therefore uncertain, but for our purpose this does not present a difficulty, because in ritual even innovations tend to conform to a pre-existing pattern.[1]

The festival was celebrated at the end of March, in the month of Elaphebolion, the beginning of spring, when the sea was subsiding after the winter storms, and when traders and visitors from other parts of Greece were beginning to appear in the streets. It lasted for at least five days, possibly six. The present chapter will be mainly concerned with the first.

On the first day, the image of Dionysos Eleuthereus was removed from the temple in which it was housed throughout the year and carried out of the city to a shrine near the Akademia on the road to Eleutherai, a village on the frontier between Attica and Boiotia. The story was that the image had originally belonged to Eleutherai, from whence it was transferred to Athens, and that this part of the festival was a commemoration of that event. The image was escorted by the *épheboi* marching in armour and followed by a brilliant procession, which included animals for sacrifice, unmarried girls carrying on their heads baskets containing the sacrificial implements, and the general public, men and women, natives and foreigners, all gaily attired, the rich driving in chariots, many of them wearing crowns or masks. In the market-place a halt was made while a chorus performed before the statues of the Twelve Gods. Then the procession pursued its course as far as the Akademia. The image was deposited on a low altar, hymns were sung in praise of the god, and the animals were sacrificed. The chief of these was a bull offered on behalf of the state and described in an official inscription as being "worthy of the god."[2] Details are lacking, but, if the normal procedure was followed, the beast was slaughtered, roasted and cut up into *moîrai*, which were then distributed among the official representatives of the state. There were many other victims beside the bull, some also provided by the state, others offered on behalf of civic organisations or individual citizens. The celebrants were also supplied with wine, and, after the feast was over, they reclined by the roadside on beds of ivy leaves, drinking and merry-making.[3] At nightfall the procession returned to the city by torchlight, but instead of being restored to its temple, the image of Dionysus was escorted by the *épheboi* to the theatre and set up on an altar in the middle of the orchestra, where it remained until the end of the festival.

There is no reason to question the tradition that this image had been transferred to Athens from Eleutherai. On the contrary, it is confirmed by independent evidence, which will be examined in due course. At the same time, it is permissible to doubt whether the procession was simply a commemoration of that event and nothing more, because, taken together, the first day's programme constitutes a ritual sequence which explains itself.

In our study of tribal initiation, we observed that the ceremony consisted of three parts. The boy was taken away from the settlement, subjected to an ordeal, and then restored to the community as a man. In Greek, these three stages appear as the *pompé*, or "send-off," the *agón*, "ordeal" or "contest," and the *kômos* or "triumphal return." In our account of the Olympian Games (pp. 115–18), we saw that the *agón* was represented by the athletic contests, and that the victors, after being crowned, were escorted in a triumphal procession or *kômos* to the *prytaneîon* of Olympia, where they were feasted. To this account we may now add that one of the entrances to the Altis, where the contests were held, was called the *pompike hodós*, the Processional Road, which was the entrance used for the purpose of a *pompé* or procession.[4] What this procession consisted of we are not told, but it may be assumed to have included the competitors who were about to take part in the athletic contests. The Olympian festival consisted therefore of a *pompé*, an *agón* and a *kômos*. Finally, in our account of the *Bacchants* of Euripides, we observed that Dionysus was described as the escort or *pompós* of Pentheus; that, after leaving the city, the Bacchants spent the night sleeping on oak leaves; that the sacrifice of Pentheus was described as an *agón*, and the triumphal return of the Bacchants to the city as a *kômos* (p. 141).

At the City Dionysia, the procession from the city is expressly described in an Athenian law as a *pompé*, and the return as a *kômos*.⁵ The only doubt that arises is in regard to the *agón*, which is not mentioned in the law, but I think it can be shown that the *agón* is represented in this case by the sacrifice which took place after the conclusion of the *pompé*. The *agón* of the Bacchants was also at the same time a sacrifice, Pentheus being the victim, Agaue "the priestess who began the slaughter." And the parallel is really closer than that, because there is reason to believe that the bull of the City Dionysia performed the same function as the human victim of the Bacchants.

The bull was one of the commonest incarnations of Dionysus. As Plutarch says, images of Dionysus in the form of a bull existed in many parts of Greece,⁶ and we have seen that, when the Kouretes of Crete tore and devoured the bull, they believed that they were eating their god. The women of Elis, at a festival of Dionysus, sang a hymn which has been partly recorded by Plutarch:⁷ "Come, hero Dionysus, to the holy temple of the people of Elis, come to the temple with the Charites, raging with bull's feet, worthy Bull, worthy Bull!" In this hymn the bull is expressly identified with the god, and presumably the animal which is being addressed is ready to be sacrificed. That presumption is confirmed by a remarkable vase painting, which portrays a Dionysiac *pompé* or procession.⁸ The procession is led by a bull, escorted by attendants carrying vine sprays, and followed by Dionysus himself seated in a waggon. It has even been suggested that the subject of this painting is the actual procession at the City Dionysia; but, without committing ourselves so far as that (the vine sprays are against it), we may say that, whatever the occasion may have been, Dionysus is here present both in his own person and in the bull, just as he was present in the *Bacchants* both in his own person and in that of Pentheus. Lastly, the words of the hymn from Elis, "worthy bull," recall the Athenian inscription already quoted, which stated that the victim sacrificed at the City Dionysia was a bull "worthy of the god." This was evidently a ritual formula. For these reasons it is safe to conclude that the sacrifice of the bull at the City Dionysia, like that of Pentheus in the *Bacchants*, was a sacrament, the bull being the incarnation of the god.

The remaining days of the festival were devoted to the contests in the theatre. These, too, were described as an *agón*, the significance of which will become clear when we have discovered their origin.[9] They were of two kinds—the dramatic competitions and the dithyrambs. There were two dithyrambic competitions—one between five choirs of boys, the other between five choirs of men. The men's choirs were not introduced until after the fall of the tyranny.

In the form which it had assumed under the democracy at Athens, the dithyramb was a hymn, in honour of Dionysus, but not necessarily about him, sung to the accompaniment of a flute by a choir of fifty boys or men grouped in a circle round the altar in the centre of the orchestra. That this was not its primitive form is certain. But what *was* its primitive form? In exploring this question, we must remember that, so far as our knowledge goes, the majority of the dithyrambs composed in the fifth century were designed for performance at Athens; yet the dithyramb had had a long history, and it had a wide distribution.

The origin of the dithyramb is attributed by Pindar in one of his poems to Corinth, in others to Thebes and to Naxos. Having many patrons to serve, he did not hesitate to give different answers to the same question. Thebes and Naxos both claimed to be the birthplace of Dionysus. The claim of Corinth to the dithyramb rested on the story of Arion, recounted in the last chapter. "Arion," says Herodotus, "was the first man of whom we have knowledge to compose, name and produce a dithyramb in Corinth." This statement, reproduced by Suidas in a somewhat different form, is understood by Pickard-Cambridge to mean that Arion "first produced a chorus which kept to a definite spot (e.g. a circle round an altar) instead of wandering like revellers at random; and he made their song a regular poem, with a definite subject from which it took its name." This is the accepted interpretation, and it is almost certainly correct.

Arion belonged to the latter part of the seventh century. We also hear of dithyrambs composed at an early period by Bakchiadas of Sikyon, where the worship of Dionysus was encouraged under the tyrant Kleisthenes (*c.* 590 B.C.), and by Archilochos of Paros, who sang: "I know how, thunderstruck with wine, to lead the dithyramb, the fair strain of Dionysus."[10] As the *exárchon*, or leader, Archilochos may be presumed to have improvised a series of stanzas, after each of which his companions sang a refrain; but, of course, it does not follow in the least that the artistic standard of this improvised revel song was low. Primitive poetry is a magical utterance issuing spontaneously from a state of ecstasy or elation, and that state is often induced by drink. The interconnection of inspiration, improvisation and intoxication can still be studied in the peasant poetry, which often reaches a degree of technical elaboration far higher than our own, of modern Europe. Let us not be misled in this matter by Pickard-Cambridge, who, in commenting on the words, "thunderstruck with wine," declares: "Archilochos may have led off the revel song in that state; it may be doubted if he composed it so, or indeed if it was 'composed' at all." That is what comes of judging Greek poetry by the canons of Greek verse composition.

The evidence of Archilochos is confirmed by Æschylus, who lived at a time when, at least in Athens, the dithyramb had long ceased to be a revel song. "It is fitting," he says, "that the mingled notes of the dithyramb should accompany Dionysus in his *kômos*."[11] This gives us a further clue. Without pressing the *kômos* too closely, we may surely infer that the dithyramb began as a processional sung on the occasion of the ritual sequence which we have traced in the Dionysiac *thíasos* and in the opening festivities of the City Dionysia. A victim is conducted in procession to a certain spot, there it is sacrificed, and then the procession returns.

At the City Dionysia, not only was the principal victim a bull, but a bull was the prize of victory at the dithyrambic contests. Moreover, it appears that the winning poet was mounted in a chariot and escorted in a triumphal procession, which included, we may suppose, the bull he had just received as a prize. Thus, addressing himself after having won fifty such victories, Simonides writes: "Fifty times, for training a lovely choir of men, thou didst mount the bright chariot of glorious Victory."[12] We may also suppose that the bull was sacrificed by the poet, who then gave a feast to his friends.

Pindar describes the dithyramb as "the bull-driving dithyramb."[13] In what sense did the dithyramb "drive the bull"? The current answers to this question are admittedly unsatisfactory. Pindar may possibly have meant that it was in virtue of the winning dithyramb that the victorious poet was able to drive his bull home. In that case, he was alluding to the contemporary festival at Athens. But it seems more likely that the epithet was traditional. If the dithyramb was originally a processional sung on the occasion we have described, it was the song sung when the bull was being driven to the sacrifice.

The situation implied by the hymn of the women of Elis is rather different. There the women seem to be at the temple awaiting the arrival of the procession. We are reminded of another hymn, in which the Kouretes of Crete greeted the arrival of their god:[14] "Hail, greatest *koûros*, Kronios, lord of all, . . . thou hast come at the head of thy *daímones*. Come for the year to Dikte, and rejoice in the song that we weave for thee with mingled pipe and harp and sing as we take our stand about thy altar!" It is noteworthy that this hymn consists of a series of stanzas interpellated with a recurrent refrain. The text, which is incomplete, contains no reference to a sacrifice, and the god invoked is Zeus, not Dionysus, to whom however the Cretan Zeus is closely akin. Of course, we cannot assert that either of these hymns was a dithyramb. All we can say is that they closely resemble what, in the light of other evidence, the primitive dithyramb appears to have been.

The association of the dithyramb with the bull reminds us of the myths of Boutes, the ox-man, and of Lykourgos, who wielded an ox-goad or an axe for slaughtering oxen. From one point of view, each of these figures clearly stands for the priest at the head of the *thíasos*; but from another, since both of them suffered what was also done to their god, they appear to impersonate Dionysus. This ambiguity, which was evidently

an inherent feature of the cult, is reproduced by Euripides in the *Bacchants*, where Dionysus is at once the leader of the *thíasos* and its god.

What was the relation, in the mature dithyramb, of the poet to his choir? At the City Dionysia, the expenses of production were defrayed by the state, with the exception of the flute-player, who had to be provided by the poet himself.[15] This regulation implies that in earlier times the flute-player's function had been performed by the poet in his own person. The poet had once been the leader of the choir, like Archilochos at Paros, improvising the stanzas and accompanying the refrains. And this comes near to saying that he was originally the officiating priest, who impersonated the god.

If, as our argument suggests, the dithyramb began as a musical accompaniment of the procession of the Dionysiac *thíasos*, it follows that the singers were originally women. The hymn of the women of Elis cannot be used as evidence in this connection, because it is not expressly described as a dithyramb; but we have already remarked that at the City Dionysia the boys' choirs were older than the men's, and there is one piece of evidence which perhaps carries us a step further into the past.[16] It is an epigram celebrating a victory won by a poet otherwise unknown with a choir provided from the Attic tribe of Akamantis, and it begins: "Often in the past, in the choirs of the tribe of Akamantis, the Horai, the Dionysiades, cried Alleluia on the occasion of ivy-carrying dithyrambs, and shaded the hair of skilful poets with headbands of blooming roses." It is natural to connect these Horai with other mythical projections of the female votaries of Dionysus, such as the Mousai and the Charites, especially since they are described as Dionysiades, which was the name of a real *thíasos* at Sparta; and it is difficult to understand why they should be thus associated with past performances of the dithyramb unless the performers had once been women.

The villagers of Eleutherai, to whom the Athenians said the image of Dionysos Eleuthereus originally belonged, had another image of the god which was a replica of the one they had surrendered. This is recorded by Pausanias, who had seen both.[17] In the same village was located the myth of the daughters of

Eleuther, who, after beholding a vision of the god clad in a goat-skin, slighted him, and were driven mad. They were cured when their father in response to an oracle instituted the worship of Dionysos Melanaigis, Dionysus of the Black Goat-skin. This tradition helps to explain how the goat came to be associated with the City Dionysia; for at the tragic contests, as distinct from the dithyrambic, the prize was not a bull, but a goat. And further it indicates that the cult of Dionysos Eleuthereus had once belonged to a woman's *thíasos* of the normal type. Indeed, it may well have been this *thíasos* that gave the village its name; for *hai eleútherai* is equivalent to *hai aphetaí*, women who have been "set free" or "let loose," like the daughters of Proitos or Io, who were turned adrift in the open country after the god had driven them mad.

It appears therefore that the dithyramb had originally belonged to the Dionysiac *thíasos* of women. The first stage in its evolution as an art-form was the decline of the *thíasos* which followed the declining social status of women. The second stage was reached when, instead of being sung as a processional, it was brought to a stand at an altar, and so became a *stásimon* or standing-song—a "station" in fact.[18] We have seen how the procession of the City Dionysia made just such a stand at the altars of the Twelve Gods in the market-place and again at the altar on which the image was deposited at the end of the *pompé*. And if it is asked what was the theme of this *stásimon*, it must surely have been in the first instance the myth corresponding to the rite which was about to be celebrated—the passion of Dionysus. And finally, since there is reason to think that the leader of the choir impersonated the god, it is plain that we have here the germ of a ritual drama. When the leader of the dithyramb begins to speak in character to his chorus, the dithyramb is becoming a passion-play. As Aristotle said, the art of tragedy was evolved "from the leaders of the dithyramb."[19]

At this critical point in its evolution, the primitive dithyramb segmented, and the two forms that emerged out of it developed by dissimilation. Since they were coexistent, each limited the development of the other. They could only grow in contrary directions. In one, the music dominated the words, the leader became the instrumentalist, and the mimetic element was suppressed. In the other, the words became so dominant as to shake themselves free of their musical integument, while the leader became an actor, then two actors, and finally three. Yet, long after it had grown wings, there still clung to the art of tragedy fragments of the chrysalis that had once secreted it. An examination of the extant plays suggests that, before Æschylus, they had normally begun and ended with a passage from the chorus as it entered or left the orchestra.[20] In these two elements we can discern the last vestiges of the *pompé* and the *kômos*, and by the same reasoning we are led to the conclusion that the performance which began and ended in this way was, in origin and essence, an *agón*—an ordeal or contest, a purge or purification which renewed life.

EVOLUTION OF THE ACTOR

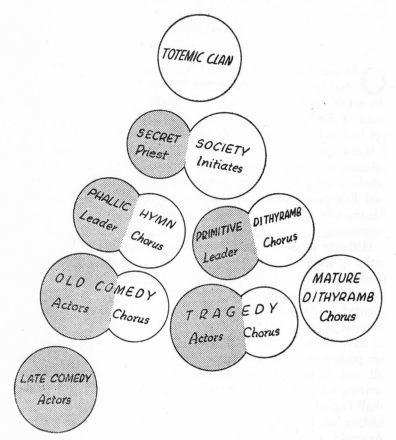

XI

TRAGEDY

Our next task is to bridge the gap of at least half a century that lies between the critical moment at which we left the art of tragedy at the end of the last chapter and the earliest work of Æschylus. This is the most difficult problem we have yet had to face, because not only is the evidence fragmentary, it is also for the most part of dubious quality. For an adequate solution we must wait until fresh light has been thrown on the whole subject by a comparative study of primitive, Oriental and European drama, such as has never yet been attempted. Meanwhile we must do our best with the resources at our command.

Hitherto we have been tracing the course of tragedy in the order of its development. That procedure must now be abandoned. Almost all that we know of Greek tragedy in this period is what can be inferred from the surviving plays, supplemented by Aristotle's *Poetics*. How precious that supplement is may be judged from the fact that, of the 250 odd plays known to have been written by Æschylus, Sophokles and Euripides, we possess only thirty-three, whereas Aristotle possessed them all, not to mention an unknown number of plays by other writers, which have completely disappeared. That being so, we shall regard as a crucial test of any reconstruction of the early history of tragedy its compatibility with the evidence of Aristotle, who, besides being incomparably better informed than we are, was the masterly exponent of a scientific method. Beginning with a study of the actor, we shall proceed to an examination of the chorus, and then, after adverting to Aristotle's analysis of the tragic climax, we shall conclude with some remarks about the stage. In all this our attention will be concentrated on the history of tragedy before Æschylus. At the end of the chapter much will still remain to be accounted for, but this must be reserved until we have resumed our history of Athens.

Aristotle informs us that the second actor was introduced by Æschylus, the third by Sophokles.[1] This number was never exceeded. Of the seven surviving plays of Æschylus, the third actor is employed only in the last four—the trilogy of the *Oresteia*, and the *Prometheus Bound*, which was probably the last of all. Since the introduction of the third actor lies well within the period covered by the surviving plays, it should be possible to follow the way in which his function was developed; and the knowledge thus gained may throw light on the development of the second actor.[2]

The full use of the third actor is seen in those dialogues in which three characters are present on the stage and each converses freely with both the others. There are many such in Sophokles and Euripides, but in Æschylus the interchange is never completely reciprocal. Thus, in the *Choephoroi*, Pylades is present when Orestes discloses himself to Clytemnestra, but his part is confined to answering a question addressed to him by Orestes; during the trial in the *Eumenides*, Athena converses with Apollo, and Apollo is addressed by Orestes, but nothing passes between Orestes and Athena until the trial is over, and by that time Apollo's part is at an end. In the *Agamemnon*, Kasandra is present during the dialogue between Agamemnon and Clytemnestra, but says nothing at all; and similarly in the prologue of the *Prometheus Bound* the hero remains silent until Might and Hephaistos have gone. In these two cases the silent character is introduced for the sake of the sequel. The only other dialogue of this type is in the *Antigone*, the earliest of the extant plays of Sophokles, where Antigone remains silent during the dialogue between Kreon and the Guard and then engages with Kreon after the Guard has gone. In all three instances the silence is, of course, dramatically effective, and Æschylus in particular was famous for his dramatic silences, but the absence of such effects from the later plays shows that they are a sign of immaturity.

Let us now apply the same considerations to the development of the second actor. For this purpose we turn to the three earliest of the surviving plays, all by Æschylus—the *Suppliants* (about 495 B.C.), the *Persians* (472 B.C.) and the *Seven against Thebes* (467 B.C.).

The *Seven* opens with a speech from the King to his people, represented by the audience. A messenger enters, gives his report, and withdraws. The King prays for victory, and the scene ends. This can hardly be called a dialogue. Later in the play the Messenger delivers a series of speeches, describing in turn the appearance of the enemy champions, each of whom is about to attack one of the seven gates; the King replies to each with a description of the defending champion; and each pair of speeches is followed by a passage from the Chorus in strophic lyric. This may be called a dialogue, but, since it consists entirely of set speeches, it is of a very formal character. On the other hand, both King and Messenger, when alone on the stage, converse freely with the Chorus.

In the *Persians*, when the Messenger arrives with news of the defeat at Salamis, the Queen is on the stage, but he delivers his message to the Chorus, who reply in strophic lyric. At length the Queen, after declaring that grief had rendered her speechless, questions the Messenger, and there ensues a dialogue between them, in which the Chorus take no part. Later in the play, the Queen is again on the stage when the ghost of Darius appears, but the ghost addresses the Chorus, who reply in strophic lyric as before. On this occasion the Queen's silence is unmotivated. Then follows a dialogue in which the ghost converses first with the Queen, the Chorus remaining silent, and later with the Chorus, the Queen remaining silent. Clearly, the dramatist has not yet learnt to manage a dialogue in which the two actors and the Chorus converse together. On the other hand, though earlier than the *Seven*, this play is marked by greater freedom in the handling of dialogues between the actors. The reason is perhaps that it is self-contained, whereas the *Seven* is the third play of a continuous trilogy; for, when we examine the Æschylean trilogy in detail, we shall find that the third play is the least elaborately constructed.

In the *Suppliants*, though there are several dialogues between one of the actors and the Chorus, there is only one between the actors—the King's altercation with the Herald; and it is significant that the Herald is probably speaking from she orchestra. Earlier in the play, Danaos is present throughout the King's long interview with the Chorus, but he takes no part until the end, when he addresses a short speech to the King, and even then he is met with a reply in which the King refers to him in the third person. The silence of Danaos in this scene, protracted and unmotivated, is extremely crude. Indeed, throughout the play his function is mainly that of a messenger; and, even as a messenger, he reports little that could not have been reported by the King. It may be suspected that Danaos has been introduced chiefly for the sake of the second and third plays of the trilogy, in which he must have had a prominent part. So far as the first is concerned, it would have suffered little if it had been written for a single actor.

We saw that, in the *Persians*, when the Messenger brings the news, and again when the ghost appears, there follows a dialogue between the actor, speaking in iambic trimeters or trochaic tetrameters, and the Chorus, who reply in strophic lyric. There are three dialogues of this type in the *Suppliants*—where the Chorus appeal to the King, and again to Danaos, and where they are assaulted by the Herald. In the *Seven against Thebes* there are two, while the description of the champions, in which two actors are involved, is an elaboration of the same principle. It is probable therefore that at an earlier period the actor's part had been largely of this character. And perhaps we may go even further. In the *Suppliants*, where the Chorus is assaulted by the Herald, the latter begins in lyric, like the Chorus itself—it is only later that he drops into iambic. It is possible, as Kranz has suggested, that this technique dates from a time when there had been no spoken part at all, only a lyrical exchange between chorus and actor.

The problem which Æschylus set himself by his introduction of the second actor was how to reorientate the actors towards each other and away from the chorus. By solving it, he revolutionised the relationship of stage to orchestra, because he was then able to develop the plot through the actors alone without the intervention of the chorus. Now, we learn from Aristotle that the actor's part was originally played by the poet;[3] and it is easy to see that, if Æschylus took the part himself, he was in a peculiarly strong position for grappling with the problem of developing it—a pretty example of the unity of theory and practice. And further, if the actor was the poet, engaged in a lyrical exchange with the chorus, we are not far removed from the primitive dithyramb, which was based, as we have seen, on precisely this relationship. As Aristotle said, the art of tragedy was derived from the leaders of the dithyramb.

The characters of Greek tragedy were mostly drawn from a limited number of traditional types, each of them distinguished by a conventional costume—the king, the queen, the prophet, the herald, the messenger, and so on. The most important is the king, of whom more will be said later, but in one respect the most remarkable is the messenger. This type differs from the others in that, with one exception (the Corinthian Messenger of Sophokles), it is never individualised. The function of messenger is, of course, sometimes performed by another character, such as Danaos in the *Suppliants* and the Phrygian slave in the *Orestes*; but, where the messenger appears as such, he lacks personality. The most conspicuous example is the *Seven against Thebes*, in which (apart from the spurious finale) the King and the Messenger are the only acting parts. The King and the Chorus are both well characterised, but the Messenger, who has a long part and is on and off throughout the play, remains a speaking voice and nothing more. The explanation appears to be that this type is an archaic and perfunctory element, which, being designed for the merely technical purpose of reporting what has happened off stage, has remained in its primitive condition. When there was only one actor, and the hero was killed in the course of the play, his death was reported in an undramatic narrative.

In the light of these considerations it is not difficult to envisage the outline of a pre-Æschylean tragedy. The chorus entered with a song or recitative, and after taking up their positions round the altar they sang a *stásimon*. Then the hero appeared, explained his identity and expounded the situation in a dialogue with the chorus. Then he disappeared, and, after another *stásimon* from the chorus, a messenger entered to announce the hero's death. There followed a lament, the messenger retired, and the chorus left the orchestra in the same manner as they had entered.

At this point we must pause to meet a difficulty. If tragedy arose out of the worship of Dionysus, its plots must originally have been drawn from the myths of Dionysus. That follows from our argument, and it is confirmed by the Greek tradition, which is quite clear on this point. But we are told by Aristotle that its plots were for a long time "small" and its diction "ridiculous."[4] How are these two traditions to be reconciled? The difficulty has been expressed by Pickard-Cambridge in his remarks on Thespis, the traditional founder of tragedy, who is said to have written a play on the myth of Pentheus.[5] "The language of Thespis," he says, "may have been in some ways rude and grotesque; but the story of Pentheus . . . must always have been tragic." This is a questionable assumption.

One of the myths of Eleutherai concerned a duel between Xanthos (Fair Man) and Melanthos (Dark Man) in which the former was slain by his opponent with the help of Dionysos Melanaigis. As Usener has explained, this myth is founded on a ritual drama of a well-known type, in which Summer is killed by Winter; and Farnell has even maintained that in this drama of Eleutherai we have the prototype of Athenian tragedy.[6] Farnell's view must be rejected, for two reasons. In the first place, there is nothing to show that it was played in this form, or indeed in any form, during the critical period of the sixth century B.C.; and further, so far as it can be reconstructed from the myth, it involves three actors and no chorus. It lies off the direct line of descent. On the other hand, it is a Dionysiac subject—the stuff of which tragedy was made; and, moreover, it is clearly a subject that would lend itself to boisterous treatment. We have only to think of our own mumming-plays derived from the same origin, such as the duel between St. George and Captain Slasher.[7]

But could the story of Pentheus have been treated in this way? There is positive evidence that it had been. There can be no doubt that the scene in the *Bacchants* of Euripides, where Pentheus appears immediately before his death dressed up in woman's finery, with his belt unfastened and a curl out of place, which the god laughingly puts straight, is intentionally ridiculous; and, as Bather pointed out, the comic treatment of this stage in the myth is explained by the corresponding stage

in the ritual.[8] Pickard-Cambridge's attitude on this matter
springs from a misunderstanding of the nature of primitive
religion. The idea that such things as laughter, ribaldry and
obscenity have no place in divine worship has little validity
outside the narrow circle of our own Protestant tradition.

Further, if the diction of tragedy was originally ridiculous,
that quality was in keeping with its metrical form. The measure
originally employed was the trochaic tetrameter[9]—a light and
tripping rhythm which Æschylus and Euripides continued to
use occasionally for imparting animation to the dialogue; but in
general it was superseded by the iambic trimeter, which was
nearer to the rhythm of common speech. Both these metres
were of popular origin, and the iambic was closely associated
with the lampoon, which was certainly ridiculous.

It is clear therefore that there is no real discrepancy in our
evidence at this point, although at a later stage of our enquiry
we shall have to face the question as to why in the later period
the comic element was eliminated.

Let us now examine the tragic actor from a different point of
view. The Greek for an actor was *hypokritēs*, corresponding to
the verb *hypokrinomai*, which, except when it is used of acting,
means always either "answer" or "interpret." Was the Greek
actor an answerer or an interpreter? Whom did he answer or
what did he interpret? This problem has been mishandled by
modern scholars, who have assumed it is merely a matter of
choosing between the two.[10] Before we can do that, we must
explain why the two senses were covered by a single word.

In the *Iliad*, the Trojans see an omen—an eagle carrying a
snake. Polydamas explains what he understands the omen to
mean, and concludes: "That is how a diviner would *interpret* it."
In the *Odyssey*, Penelope has had a dream; she says to Odysseus,
"*Interpret* my dream"; and Odysseus replies, "It is not possible
to *interpret* your dream." There is no question what the verb
means in these three passages. In another passage of the *Odyssey*,
an eagle is seen carrying a goose. Peisistratos turns to Menelaos
and asks him: "Is this omen intended for you or for us?"
Menelaos ponders, wondering "how he should *interpret* it (or
answer) aright."[11] In this last passage, where the word might be
translated either way, the essential unity of the two senses is

NA

clearly revealed: *hypokrínomai* means to "interpret a dream or omen" or alternatively to "answer an enquiry about a dream or omen." It was a ritual term, describing a function of the priesthood.

In the generalised sense of "answer," the verb *hypokrínomai* is found only once in the *Iliad* and once in the *Odyssey*, the normal word for "answer" being *ameíbomai*, which occurs many hundreds of times. It follows that the generalised usage of *hypokrínomai* was only just beginning in Homeric Greek. In Ionic it became the dominant usage, but in Attic *hypokrínomai* is only used of "acting," being the verb corresponding to the substantive *hypokrités*, and the idea of "answer" is expressed by another formation from the same root, *apokrínomai*. It may be inferred that in Attic *hypokrínomai* lost its original sense when the corresponding substantive acquired the sense of "actor."

The problem is now reduced to this: when the word *hypokrités* was first applied to the actor, did it connote *hypokrínomai* in its primitive sense of "interpret" or in its derivative sense of "answer"? Now, in Attic, there is no evidence that *hypokrínomai* ever meant "answer" or that *hypokrités* ever meant an "answerer." The verb is only used in the sense corresponding to the substantive, and the substantive is always used of an actor or declaimer, except in one passage of Plato.[12] This passage is instructive. Plato is discussing the exact meaning of the word *prophétes*. Some people, he says, speak of *prophétai* as though they were the same as *mánteis*, "prophets," but this usage is incorrect: the *prophétai* are not prophets, but interpreters (*hypokritaí*) of enigmatical utterances and appearances. Now, since Plato is here concerned to point out the strict sense of the word *prophétes*, we must presume that he is being equally strict in his use of *hypokrités*—that is to say, he is aware that the latter was originally applied, like *krités*, to an interpreter of oracles, dreams, or omens.

The current Attic for interpreter in this sense was *hermeneús*, the origin of which is uncertain. The Ionic was *exegetés*, which was also the title of a priesthood at Eleusis. The Eleusinian *exegetaí* were exponents of the *legómena*, the "things said" at the Mysteries, and in that way they interpreted the *drómena*, the "things done" in the symbolic ritual. Now, the word *exegetés* means primarily a "leader." It is therefore synonymous with *exárchon*, which is the term used by Archilochos and Aristotle of the leader of the dithyramb. These considerations suggest that the *hypokrités* and the *exárchon* were originally identical.

The *exárchon* was the poet-leader of the dance and song of the dithyrambic chorus, descended from the god-priest of the Dionysiac *thíasos*. How did he become an interpreter? The *thíasos* was a secret society, and consequently its ritual was a mystery, which only those who had been initiated into the secret were able to understand. Accordingly, when this ritual became a drama in the full sense of the word, a mimetic rite performed by initiates before an uninitiated audience, it needed an interpreter. Let us suppose that the guild of Eleutherai is performing a choral dance before a crowd of spectators. The dance is designed to symbolise the wanderings of the daughters of Eleuther after they have been driven mad by Dionysus. The performers understand this, but the spectators do not. Accordingly, at some point, the leader comes forward and says in plain language, "I am Dionysus, and these are the daughters of Eleuther, whom I have driven mad." In doing this, the leader is already an interpreter, and he is on the way to becoming an actor. Tragedy was derived from the leaders of the dithyramb.

The art of tragedy has now been traced back to a point at which it makes contact with the most advanced ritual dramas of the North American Indians; for it will be remembered that, though these dramas were sometimes performed in public, their inner meaning was understood only by the initiated members of the secret society that performed them. On this point Hutton Webster writes as follows:[13]

> The rites, in part secret, in part public, constitute a rude but often very effective dramatisation of the myths and legends. Usually only the members of the particular society which performs the rites understand their significance. The actors, masked or costumed, represent animals or divine beings whose history the myths recount.

Among the North American Indians, the growth of drama was arrested at the critical point, the reason being that the social status of the secret societies was sufficiently secure to resist secularisation. In Attica, where the Dionysiac *thíasos* was in decline, it only survived by becoming a guild of actors.

The choral odes of Greek tragedy are constructed on the rhythmical pattern known as antistrophic form. A rhythmical system (*strophé*), or stanza as we should call it, is introduced and repeated; then a second system is introduced and repeated in the same way, and so on. The ode falls therefore into a series of pairs (AA BB CC). Sometimes each pair is followed by an *ephýmnion* or refrain (AA*x* BB*x* CC*x*).

The structure of the mature dithyramb is different. It is based on what is known as triadic form. A system is introduced, repeated, and followed by a second system, called the *epoidós* or "after-song"; then the first system is reintroduced, again repeated, and followed by a repetition of the *epoidós*; and so on. The dithyramb, therefore, is founded on a single triad continuously repeated (AAB AAB AAB). The *epoidós* is employed occasionally in tragedy, but only at the end of the ode as a *coda*. The triad is said to have been invented by Stesichoros, and it is the dominant form, not only of the dithyramb, but of the later aristocratic choral lyric. Nearly all the odes composed by Pindar and Bakchylides for victories at the games are triadic.

Lastly, there is the form known as monostrophic, consisting of the continuous repetition of a single system (AAA). This is used occasionally by Pindar and Bakchylides in their victory odes, and by the latter in a few of his dithyrambs. Before the invention of the triad, it had been the dominant form of the aristocratic convention. All the extant odes of Alkman, Sappho and Alkaios belong to this type.

We must endeavour to reconstruct the origin and growth of these conventions. In the first place, we observe that of the three forms the antistrophic is the most flexible, because, since each pair is different from the last, the rhythm of the ode can be varied and developed. It is therefore the most dramatic. Secondly, the reason why, in both antistrophic and triadic form, the systems are grouped in pairs must be that the ode was, or had once been, antiphonal.[14] Thirdly, the dithyramb belongs to the aristocratic convention, being either triadic or monostrophic. Which of these two forms is the more primitive? The answer seems to be that neither is primitive, but both have a common origin.

In the *Iliad*, the women of Troy perform a dirge over the body of Hector.[15] They are led by Andromache, Hecuba and Helen. Each of these "leads off" in turn with praise of the dead man, and each solo is followed by a general wail. The word used to describe the function of the leaders is the word applied by Aristotle and Archilochos to the leaders of the dithyramb (*exárchontes*). The ritual basis of this performance is plainly a series of improvised solos from the leaders followed in each case by a refrain from the chorus, and it may be assumed that the solos conformed to a common rhythmical pattern. As treated by Homer, the solos are the vital element, the refrains being merely perfunctory. This subordination of the refrain to the solo, of the many to the few, corresponds to the distinction between the people and the nobility or the laity and the priesthood. Moreover, if we eliminate the popular element entirely, we are left with a series of improvised solos on a repeated musical pattern. This is the aristocratic *skólion* or drinking-song.[16] Seated round the table, one after another of the banqueters sings a stanza, improvising the words to a repeated musical accompaniment. And if we adapt this convention to the conscious art of an individual poet, we have the monostrophic ode of Sappho, Alkaios and Alkman.

Later, the *epoidós* reappears in the aristocratic tradition—not however as a popular refrain but as an artistic elaboration. The ode is now sung by two semi-choruses—the strophe by the first, the antistrophe by the second, and the *epoidós* by the two together. After the practice of antiphony is abandoned, the triad is maintained as the basis of the rhythmical structure, and it passes from the aristocratic ode to the mature dithyramb. Finally, in tragedy, the triad is superseded by the antistrophic pair. On the other hand, the tragedians continue to make occasional use of the refrain, which, owing to the changed significance of *epoidós*, is now known as the *ephýmnion*. It may be inferred that they derived this element from the primitive dithyramb.

This reconstruction involves the assumption that, although

absent from the older aristocratic tradition, the *epoidós* was primitive, and consisted originally of a refrain. We must remember that the convention we have been examining was an artistic one. The traditional hymns used in the everyday service of the gods must have been simpler and more primitive. Of these hymns we know little, but what we do know is significant. The Hymn of the Kouretes, to which we referred in the last chapter, is a monostrophic ode with a refrain attached to each strophe; and the refrain in the hymn to Dionysus sung by the women of Elis—"worthy Bull, worthy Bull"—is described by Plutarch in terms which show that he regarded it as an *epoidós*.[17]

The word *epoidós* had two meanings. In a technical sense, it was applied to the third member of the triad, and in this application it was understood to mean an "after-song." But it was also used in a non-technical sense of a charm, spell, or incantation. In this sense it was synonymous with *epoidé*. The idea of incantation takes us back to primitive magic, and shows that the original significance of *epoidós* was not an "after-song" but a song "sung over" somebody, like the wail of the Trojan women over the body of Hector or the spell recited over the sick man to heal him or over the sinner to effect his damnation. Indeed, we may go further and say that the primitive refrain *was* an incantation. In the *Oresteia* of Æschylus the Erinyes perform a magical dance with the object of effecting the death and damnation of the matricide. The dance is a *stásimon* of the normal type except that the first member of each antistrophic pair is followed by an *ephýmnion*, which is repeated at the end of the second, and it is through these refrains, sung as the Erinyes leap round their victim, that the magic operates. The refrain is used by Æschylus in the same way in the first *stásimon* of the *Suppliants*, where the fugitives are cursing their pursuers and calling down a storm upon them before they can reach harbour. These refrains are simply the incantations of mimetic magic. They are the primitive kernel out of which, by the stages already indicated, the Greek chorus had evolved.

The choral odes of Greek tragedy are of three kinds—the *párodos*, sung while the chorus is entering the orchestra; the *stásimon*, sung after they have taken up their positions; and the *kommós*. Of the first two, which conform to the normal anti-strophic structure, nothing further need be said, but the third is rather different. We have already encountered one example of the *kommós* in the lyrical exchange between the Herald and the Chorus in the *Suppliants* of Æschylus, and in discussing that passage we referred to the view advanced by Kranz that in these lyrical exchanges we have the nucleus of tragic dialogue. The *kommós* is a lament in which the chorus and one or more of the actors participate, and its normal place is immediately before or after the tragic crisis. It is properly a "beating of the breast"—that is to say, a *thrênos* or lament; but it is noteworthy that the word is never used in Attic prose except as a technical term to describe this part of a tragedy. It was therefore an archaic word, and that accords with Kranz's view that what it denoted was a primitive feature of the tragic convention. There are other indications that point in the same direction.

In the simplest type of *kommós* the actor sings a strophe, which is followed by another from the chorus, then the actor sings his antistrophe and the chorus sing theirs (ABAB CDCD). If we eliminate the antistrophic principle, which as we have seen was probably no older than tragedy itself, this structure reduces itself to a monostrophic solo with refrains (A*b* A*b* A*b*); and that, according to our argument, was the form of the primitive dithyramb. Further, it is evident both from the rhythm to which it was set (normally pæonic) and in some cases from the accompanying words that the dance-movement of the *kommós* was excited and impassioned. We know next to nothing of how the musical modes were employed in Greek tragedy, but it seems possible that the *kommós* was further distinguished by the use of the excited Phrygian mode, described as *éntheos* or "possessed"; and we know that this was the mode employed in the dithyramb.[18]

Thus, the climax of the tragedy, corresponding to the crucial moment, the *agón*, in the passion of Dionysus, was commonly cast in a distinctive form which embodied the remains of the primitive dithyramb—a musical dialogue between the leader and his *thíasos*.

In his analysis of tragic plots, Aristotle distinguishes the complex from the simple plot as one in which the change of fortune coincides with a *peripéteia* or an *anagnórisis* or both. What he meant by the former term is a fundamental question which we shall not attempt to answer at this stage. The *anagnórisis* or recognition he defines as "a change from ignorance to knowledge, resulting in friendship or hatred on the part of the characters marked out for good fortune or for ill."[19] He divides these recognitions into four categories according to the means by which they are effected—by tokens, by deliberate self-revelation, by some inadvertent cry or action, and by inference.

His remarks on this subject make it clear, not only that the recognition was a constant and radical feature of the convention, but that one of its commonest forms, which he regards as the crudest, was recognition by means of hereditary tokens. Two examples of this type are known to us from the extant plays—the recognition of Orestes by his embroidered swaddling-bands, and the recognition of Ion by the *gnorísmata* in which he had been exposed as an infant. The significance of these two cases has already been explained, and Aristotle mentions others which clearly belong to the same type—the spear of the Spartoi (p. 49), and the star of the Pelopidai— another traditional birthmark. What was the origin of the *anagnórisis*?

It is agreed that the themes of early tragedy were drawn from the myths of Dionysus, and I have argued that the original theme was the god's death. It is also known that in the fifth century the Dionysiac cycle was no more prominent in tragedy than other mythical cycles. We may now go a step farther. It stands to reason that, before the early tragedians began to draw on other cycles, they must have made full use of the Dionysiac. They must have dramatised, not only the death of Dionysus, but his birth and his resurrection. This, as I have said, stands to reason, and it is supported by the analogy of the mediæval mystery-plays.[20] The nucleus of these was the *Quem quæritis* of the Three Maries in the Easter liturgy. This nucleus was developed by the dramatisation of other elements in the Easter myth—the meeting of the Maries with the angel, with the apostles, and with Christ himself. The second stage was reached when the same process was applied to the myth of the Nativity, and in the third the themes range from the Creation and the Fall to Daniel and Nebuchadnezzar.

For these reasons it is permissible to conjecture that the theme of the recognition is derived from the self-revelation of the god after his re-birth or resurrection. His appearance was followed, we may suppose, by an interrogation on the part of the chorus, at the end of which he proved his identity by revealing to them the sacred objects or mystical symbols associated with his cult. This conjecture derives some additional support from another feature of the convention which has still to be examined.

No characteristic of Greek tragedy is more familiar than the set passages of line-for-line question and answer which are called in Greek *stichomýthia*. Throughout its history this feature retained its severely formal character, except that Sophokles and Euripides sometimes relaxed it to the extent of permitting a change of speaker in the middle of the verse. To our ears the effect is often incongruous or even absurd, as for example at the crisis of the *Agamemnon*; and, if the Athenians accepted it, it was mainly, we must suppose, because it was a fundamental, and therefore primitive, feature of the convention.

These formal dialogues are equally remarkable for their content. Not only do they proceed by the symmetrical arrangement of question and answer, but it often appears, especially in Æschylus, as though the speakers were more concerned to veil their meaning than to elucidate it. "Thy utterance is a riddle—speak in plain words."[21] Such verses are typical. Sometimes the utterance takes the actual form of a riddle. Thus, in the *Choephoroi*, after the murder of Aigisthos, when Clytemnestra asks the slave what the shouting is about, the slave declares darkly, "The living, I tell you, are being killed by the dead," and Clytemnestra replies, "Ah me, a riddle, yet I read its meaning."[22] The full effect of her reply is lost in translation, because the word she uses—*xynêka*, "I understand"—recalls the term commonly applied to initiates—*hoi xynetoí*, "those who understand," those who have been admitted into the mystical secrets. Here then is a riddle, which we must try to solve.

The riddle is as deeply imbedded in Indo-European folklore as it is widespread among primitive peoples at the present day. The data collected by Schulz, which would repay closer analysis, suggest that it formed originally the spoken part of an initiatory test or ordeal.[23] For the present however I must confine myself to the evidence from ancient Greece, which is sufficient to establish provisionally the immediate point at issue.

The riddle was defined by Klearchos of Soloi as "a humorous problem requiring the use of intelligence in discovering the solution and propounded for the sake of a penalty or reward."[24] The normal Greek type may be illustrated by the riddle of the Sphinx, by reading which Œdipus became king of Thebes:[25]

> A thing there is whose voice is one,
> Whose feet are four and two and three;
> So mutable a thing is none
> That moves in earth or sky or sea;
> When on most feet this thing doth go,
> Its strength is least, its pace most slow.

The essential feature is that the thing to be identified is described in symbolical and apparently contradictory terms.

The Sphinx was a female monster who dwelt on Mount Phikion, Phix being the Æolic form of her name. The legend about her relations with the royal house of Thebes is recorded by Pausanias.[26] She learnt her riddle from Laios, who had presumably learnt it from his father, for we are told that originally it was given by the Delphic Oracle to his great-grandfather, Kadmos, the founder of the dynasty. Laios had sons by other women besides his queen, and accordingly, when one of them wished to lay claim to the succession, he was sent up into the mountain, where the Sphinx asked him her riddle, and, if he failed to solve it, he was put to death. This legend implies some form of initiation into the secrets of a royal clan.

At Sparta, it will be remembered, the boys used to be questioned by the *eiren* after supper about public affairs, and, if they gave him a wrong answer, he bit them on the thumb (p. 104). It seems probable that these questions too were originally concerned with initiatory secrets, for we have seen that one of the primitive rites of initiation, which can be traced in the legend of Orestes, is the amputation of a finger (p. 108). Athenaios records that in ancient times riddles used to be asked at drinking-parties for the purpose of educating the young, and he refers to a passage of Diphilos describing three girls of Samos asking one another riddles at a drinking-party during the festival of Adonis. Finally, Plutarch says that, at the Theban festival of the Agrionia, it was the custom for the women, after they had returned from their search for the lost Dionysus, to ask one another riddles after supper.[27]

This evidence suggests that, at least in Greece, the custom of asking riddles was a traditional pastime derived from catechism in the secrets of initiation, the purpose being to test the novice's knowledge of the mystical symbols. It is possible therefore, since so much in Greek tragedy goes back to initiation, that the *stichomýthia* are a vestige of such catechisms; and it is easy to see how the identification of the god might be used as a means of expounding those symbols in the course of a ritual drama.

Finally, we have to see whether anything of value can be extracted from what we know of the stage on which the actors acted. Unfortunately this is very little. Of the stage as it was in the time of Æschylus no trace remains, probably because it was made of timber. Judging from the remains of the earliest stone buildings, which date from the end of the fifth century according to Puchstein, or according to Dörpfeld from the middle of the fourth, it seems probable that the old wooden structure was a long building with wings at either end projecting towards the orchestra, and that the stage was a narrow platform running in front of this building from wing to wing.[28] The front of the building therefore served as a background to the stage, and in it were doors leading from the stage to the actors' changing-rooms. The depth of the stage is unknown, but it cannot have been very high, because we know that the actors conversed freely with the chorus and that there was easy access from stage to orchestra.

The stage was called *skené*, a term also applied to the front of the building behind the stage and to the stage-buildings as a whole. The primary meaning of *skené* is a "tent," and it is also used of the tilt or awning of a covered waggon. This is important, because we are told by Horace that Thespis and his actors used to tour the Attic countryside in a waggon.[29] We also know that waggons were a regular feature of the Dionysiac *kômos*. All this hangs together, and tells us something worth knowing about Attic drama before the institution of the official contests at the City Dionysia. Thespis is said to have won the tragic prize (a goat) about 534 B.C., which was the time when the festival was being organised by Peisistratos.

RITUAL PATTERN OF GREEK TRAGEDY

Primitive Initiation	Greek Initiation	Tragedy
Departure as child	*pompé*	*párodos*
Death and resurrection	*agón* *sparagmós*	*peripéteia* *kommós*
Revelation of sacred objects	*anakálypsis*	*anagnórisis*
Catechism	*ainígmata* *dokimasía*	*stichomýthia*
Return as adult	*kômos*	*éxodos*

If the tradition preserved by Horace is genuine—and, although Horace would not be a reliable authority in himself, it has everything else in its favour—it provides us with an important link in the chain we have been trying to reconstruct. After it had ceased to be the ritual of a secret society, and before it secured a footing in Athens, Dionysiac drama was in the hands of a guild or guilds of actors, who toured the country villages. No doubt, these guilds were still organised on a religious basis, derived from the organisation of the *thíasos*, and their performances were still invested with a religious significance and associated with the welfare of the crops; but it is fairly clear that, if they had remained in this environment, they would have degenerated into the peasant mummery with which we are still familiar in modern Europe. This then was the period in which were developed those qualities of boisterousness and crudity which Aristotle noted as characteristic of early tragic diction.

In his study of the mediæval English stage, Chambers has shown that, with the rise of the bourgeoisie in the thirteenth and fourteenth centuries, the so-called liturgical plays, which had grown out of the ritual of the mediæval Church, were transferred from the clergy to the bourgeois guilds, from the cathedral to the market-place, and at the same time their themes were secularised.[30] The English drama had fundamental elements in common with the Greek; for these liturgical plays were influenced by the mumming-play, folk-dance and other performances derived from the agrarian ritual of the Germanic tribes; and, after being secularised, the drama was further developed by the patronage of the Tudor monarchy. But there is one radical difference, of profound importance for the history of both. In England, the Church stood for the feudal nobility, and its liturgy, as the ritual of a ruling class, had long been stabilised in a rigid form inimical to change. For this reason, the impulse to dramatisation, which came in the first instance from the peasantry, who instinctively sought to turn the liturgy into something useful—into mimetic magic—was only carried forward in the face of strenuous opposition from the ecclesiastical authorities; and for the same reason, when these plays were taken over by the bourgeoisie, the rivals of the feudal nobility, and later patronised by the Tudors as leaders of the bourgeoisie, the drama was developed in conscious opposition to religious ritual, of which it rapidly became entirely independent. In Attica, on the other hand, the worship of Dionysus, out of which the drama evolved, had always been popular, and was therefore revived and reorganised by the tyrants in opposition to the clan-cults of the old nobility. Consequently, when the drama was brought to Athens, the tendency towards secularisation, which had set in with the dissipation of the Dionysiac mysteries among the peasantry, was reversed. Instead of continuing to move away from

ritual, it was brought back into it; and thereafter throughout its history it remained first and foremost a divine service,
which, once established on its new ritual pattern, imposed on
its exponents a severe artistic discipline. That is one reason
why Athenian tragedy is technically more perfect than
Elizabethan.

We have seen that in his religious policy Peisistratos was
pursuing a consciously realised objective. The same is true of
his attitude to the drama. When he instituted the tragic contests, his aim was not merely to gratify the tastes and interests
of the Athenian merchants and artisans, but to use the art-
form which the people had created as a means of raising their
cultural level and welding them into a nation. Just as the new
art-form was an expression of the progress already made, so
under his direction it became a stimulus to further progress.
Athenian tragedy was from the beginning inseparably bound
up with the material and social advancement of the Athenian
people.

He also saw that, if the Athenians were to develop a distinctive national culture, they must absorb the culture of other
Greek states, especially those which at this time were more
advanced than they were. It was for this purpose that he instituted the public recitation of Ionian epic, thus throwing open
to Athenian dramatists a storehouse of richly elaborated traditional material. But the most striking testimony to his far-
sightedness is the history of the mature dithyramb.

Under the tyrants, Athens rapidly became the principal
centre in Greece for the performance of dithyrambs, yet almost
all the dithyrambic poets known to us were foreigners—Lasos
of Hermione, Hypodikos of Chalkis, Pindar of Thebes,
Simonides and Bakchylides of Keos, all of whom wrote mainly
for the City Dionysia.[31] Why did the Athenian tyrants do so
much to encourage an art-form for which their own poets, preoccupied with tragedy, showed little inclination? The reason
must surely be that they appreciated its value for the development of tragedy. In the Peloponnese, at Corinth and Sikyon,
the popular movement, and with it the Dionysiac revival, had
begun much earlier than at Athens; and moreover its characteristic art-form, the dithyramb, had been assisted from the

outset by close contact with the choral tradition of the Dorian aristocracy—a tradition which had never taken root in Attica. By establishing the dithyramb at the City Dionysia, the tyrants made this tradition accessible to the Athenian dramatists, who were thus able to infuse it into their treatment of the tragic chorus.

Thus, while the power came from the people, it was their leader who made them conscious of it and so enabled them to use it. Without this union of mass-impetus with individual leadership, the art of tragedy could not have advanced as rapidly as it did, and so would not have been ready to take full advantage of the tremendous stimulus it was shortly to receive from the democratic revolution.

Our argument up to this point may be recapitulated as follows. The Dionysiac *thíasos* was a secret magical society which preserved in modified form the structure and functions of the totemic clan, out of which it had evolved during the later phases of tribal society. It was composed of women led by a male priest. Its principal rite, derived from initiation, contained three elements—an orgiastic exodus into the open country, a sacrament in which a victim was torn to pieces and eaten raw, and a triumphant return. This ritual was projected as a myth of the passion of Dionysus. Since its function was to promote the fertility of the soil, it persisted only among the peasantry, and so at a later stage became closely identified with the popular movement against the landed nobility. In some parts of Greece, owing to changes in the social relations of the sexes, the ritual passed into the control of the men and underwent further modification. It ceased to be secret, and began to disintegrate. The orgiastic procession became a hymn, which was developed most rapidly in the Peloponnese; the sacrament became a passion-play, developed principally in Attica, where the popular movement, after beginning later, progressed further. From the first arose the dithyramb, from the second tragedy. Both were urbanised and consciously directed by the tyrants, the former maturing under the influence of aristocratic lyric. Thus, looking back over our argument, we may say definitely that the art of tragedy was descended, remotely but directly, and with each stage in its evolution conditioned by the evolution of society itself, from the mimetic rite of the primitive totemic clan.

EVOLUTION OF GREEK POETRY

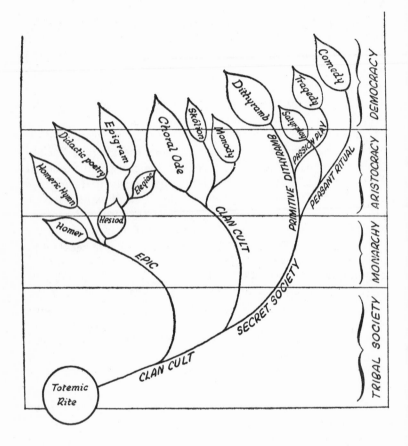

PART FOUR

ÆSCHYLUS

*Reproduced by kind permission of Graf Leo Maria Lanckoroński
from his book, "Schönes Geld der Alten Welt," Munich, 1935.*

THE OWL OF ATHENA

XII

DEMOCRACY

THERE had been little outward change in the constitution
of Athens under the tyrants, who had maintained their
control of the administration by filling the executive offices with
their own nominees. After the expulsion of Hippias and the
defeat of the counter-revolution attempted by Isagoras, a new
constitution was drawn up with the object of placing the rights
won by the people on a secure foundation.

Athens had now passed from a simple agricultural to a
monetary economy. The hereditary privileges of the landowning class had been abolished; the claims of birth had been
subordinated to the claims of property. These changes had
already led to profound modifications in the laws of inheritance
and in the social relations of the sexes; and now the last
remnants of the old tribal system, based on kinship, which had
become a fetter on the new economic and social realities, were
swept away. On the other hand, since the revolution thus
effected consisted largely in the recovery by the common
people of the equality which they had enjoyed under the tribal
system, it was accompanied by the revival, in new and vastly
different conditions, of some of the characteristic institutions of
tribal society, such as the popular assembly, the common
festivals, and the use of the lot. And lastly, since the driving
force of the revolution had been the new middle class of
merchants and artisans, the rise of this class to power was
marked by the development of a new and distinctive outlook
on society and on the world.

How the leading families of the primitive Attic clans established themselves as a ruling caste has already been described;
but, although impaired by this development, which destroyed
the solidarity of the clan, the structure of the tribal system
maintained itself right down to the period we have now
reached. The organisation of the army under the four tribal

199

chiefs (*phylobasileîs*), elected from the Eupatridai, was tribal;[1] and, what is still more important, the enjoyment of civic rights was dependent on membership of one of the phratries. Since the phratries were groups of clans, this meant that the citizen body was still a tribal community, composed of those who belonged to the primitive Attic clans. It was at this point that the pressure against the tribal structure was strongest, and it came from the new middle class.

The industrial development of Attica had been hampered in its early stages by shortage of labour. That, as we have seen, is why Solon had done nothing to check the dispossession of the peasantry; and for the same reason he had passed laws against idleness and encouraged the immigration of foreign artisans. These immigrants, however, could only acquire civic rights by obtaining admission to the phratries, and consequently the policy of the landowning aristocracy was to keep the phratries closed. There has been preserved from this period a law stipulating that membership of the phratry should not be restricted to clansmen. This has been claimed as proof that Aristotle was wrong in saying that the Attic phratry consisted simply of so many clans;[2] but, of course, it proves that Aristotle was right, because it stands to reason that, if non-clansmen had not originally been excluded, there would have been no need for a law enforcing their admission. It is clear, however, that this law was largely ineffectual. We are informed by Aristotle that among the strongest supporters of Peisistratos were those who, being of impure descent, were afraid of losing their citizenship—that is to say, descendants of immigrant artisans who had been admitted to the phratries, but were in danger of being expelled by the agrarian party. How much this class owed to the tyranny is shown by the fact that, when it fell, one of the first acts of Isagoras was to disfranchise a large number of citizens who were unable to prove pure Athenian descent, and shortly afterwards, when the Spartan King entered Attica, no less than 700 families, supporters of Kleisthenes, were expelled. It is clear therefore that down to the time when it seized power under the leadership of Kleisthenes the rapidly growing class of merchants and artisans was still insecure in its possession of the franchise owing to the influence

of the landlords in the phratries; and therefore in the new constitution the political functions of the phratries were abolished
once and for all.

Before dealing with the reforms of Kleisthenes we must
pause to consider the effects of the growth of property on the
internal structure of the clan. Down to the beginning of the
sixth century the ownership of property, both real and personal,
was still vested, at least nominally, in the clan. The individual
enjoyed only the usufruct. When a man died, his wealth
reverted to his fellow clansmen, among whom it was distributed
in portions no doubt determined by their degree of affinity to
the deceased. It is probable that males benefited more largely
than females, and of course by this period membership of the
clan was transmitted in the male line.

The Attic law of inheritance, as established under the
democracy, was attributed to Solon; and, while there is no
reason to question the accuracy of this tradition, it must be
remembered that some time would necessarily elapse before
the full effects of the new system became apparent. We may
say therefore that the democratic practice in regard to inheritance had grown up gradually in the sixth century. In order to
understand it, we must compare it with what is known of the
inheritance of property in other parts of Greece.[3] The Code of
Gortyna, dating from the fifth century, has survived, and we
know something of the Spartan practice in the time of Aristotle.
This evidence, though meagre, is sufficient to set the Attic
Code in evolutionary perspective, because Gortyna was
economically more backward in the fifth century than Athens
was in the sixth, and Sparta, even in the fourth, was more
backward still.

In Attic law, the right of bequest was recognised only in
default of legitimate issue, and it was exercised by means of
adoption. If a man had no issue, he might adopt a son, who
thereby became his heir. The primitive custom of adoption was
thus put to a new use. If he died without children, legitimate
or adopted, his property reverted to his kin in the following
order of priority: the father, the brothers and their children,
the sisters and their children, the paternal cousins and their
children, the maternal cousins and their children. The exclusion

of the mother, as well as her brothers and sisters, shows that the unilateral conception of kinship characteristic of the clan had not yet succumbed to the narrower but bilateral conception characteristic of the family. If a man had issue of both sexes, the property was divided by the sons on condition that they maintained their sisters till marriage and furnished them with a dowry, the amount of which was limited. If he had only daughters, they inherited but were obliged to marry his next-of-kin, who would be in the first instance his brothers, and the inheritance passed to their sons as soon as they came of age. Thus, the rule of exogamy was violated. Moreover, if the heiress was already married, she was obliged to divorce her husband in order to marry the next-of-kin, and the next-of-kin divorced his wife in order to marry her. These restrictions on the liberty of the women in the interests of property correspond to the Attic law in respect of adultery, which was regarded as a crime so serious that a man might kill an adulterer caught in the act without incurring the guilt of homicide.

At Gortyna, the wife retained her rights over the property she had brought with her as a dowry, and, if divorced on her husband's responsibility, she received in addition five *statêres* of money. When a man died, the property was disposed as follows. The town house and its contents, and the livestock, were divided among the sons; the remainder—the country estate, including the serfs tied to it and the houses and livestock belonging to them,—were divided among the sons and daughters, each daughter receiving half as much as a son. If there were no sons, the whole of the property went to the daughter, who could refuse to marry the next-of-kin, provided that she indemnified him by surrendering half the estate.

At Sparta the laws were not codified, and therefore the rules of inheritance are not so easy to determine. They can, however, be deduced from Aristotle's remarks on the subject in the light of Attic and Gortynian law. The Spartan economy was based on the same system of family estates as the Cretan, but at Sparta, owing to the absence of money and the repression of industry and trade, there was no property apart from the estate, the serfs tied to it, and its produce.

Aristotle notes as one of the characteristics of Spartan society the liberty and influence of the women.[4] His account of this matter is confirmed by other writers. The women were free to go about in public; adultery was not punishable or even discreditable; a woman might have several husbands. Of all this Aristotle severely disapproves, but we must remember that he writes from the standpoint of an Athenian bourgeois, to whom the subjection and seclusion of women appeared as a dispensation of nature. Then he proceeds to comment on the Spartan rules of inheritance:[5]

> Some have managed to acquire too much land, others very little, and so the land has fallen into the hands of a small minority. This has also been badly arranged by the laws; for while the lawgiver quite rightly made it dishonourable to buy or sell land, he did not restrict its alienation by gift or bequest, and so the same result necessarily followed. Owing to the number of heiresses and the size of the dowries, nearly two-fifths of the land are owned by women. It would have been better to prescribe no dowry at all or only a small one. As it is, a man can give the heiress to anyone he chooses, and if he dies without having disposed of her, his heir can do so.

At first sight this passage seems to imply that the Spartans recognised the right of free testamentary disposition, and that is how it has been commonly understood; but a little reflection serves to show that this is a misinterpretation. It is impossible to suppose that a right which was not admitted in the Code of Gortyna, nor in the Attic Code, nor in any other ancient code before the development of mature law, could have been recognised by the reactionary aristocracy of Sparta, which had not reached the stage of codifying the laws at all. What, then, is the alternative? Aristotle is judging Spartan practice from the standpoint of an Athenian, and what he means, when he speaks of alienation by gift or bequest, and again when he says that a man could give the heiress to anyone he chose, is simply that in Sparta, unlike Athens, Gortyna, and other Greek states, the heiress was not required to marry the next-of-kin, and consequently there was no means of ensuring the transmission of the family property to the descendants in the male line.

The social life of Sparta has already been described (pp. 103–5).

At the age of seven the boy was taken from his parents and enrolled in the *agéla*; at nineteen he came of age and took up residence in the Men's House, eating and sleeping with the other men and spending the day in military exercises. When he married, he did not live with his wife, but merely visited her clandestinely from time to time. It is to be presumed that the bride lived with her parents, as in Crete. Plutarch says that the men continued to live in this way "for a long time" —perhaps until they obtained exemption from military service.[6]

The girls, too, were organised in *agélai*, but there is no evidence that they were segregated like the boys. In these circumstances, the Spartan home must have consisted of the father (old enough to be excused residence in the Men's House), the mother, the daughters married and unmarried, and the children of both sexes under seven. In the absence of the grown sons, the daughters were at an advantage in asserting their claims on the inheritance. Not only did they obtain substantial dowries, but, owing to the continued absence of their husbands, the administration of the estate was in their hands. They were, of course, excluded from political life, but, thanks to their economic position, their influence was so great that Aristotle speaks of Sparta as a country "ruled by women."[7] Finally, if it is asked how this system had arisen, the answer may perhaps be found in the special conditions of the conquest. We know that the Spartan settlers had intermarried with the conquered population, and, since they were compelled to maintain a standing army composed of all the adult male citizens, the new state arose on the basis of a division of labour between the sexes. The men fought, the women administered the estates.

If we compare these three systems—the Spartan, the Gortynian and the Athenian—it becomes clear that they represent three successive stages in the development of property and in the subjection of women. Moreover, if the subjection of women in Attica was a consequence of the development of property, it follows that in earlier times the women must have enjoyed a greater measure of liberty; and this is strikingly confirmed by Attic tradition.[8] Down to the reign of Kekrops, the women had enjoyed the right of voting with the men in the popular assembly, there had been no formal marriage, each woman had children by several men, and the children were named after the mother. Thus, the status of women in Attica had once been higher than it was in historical Sparta, and, moreover, this was remembered in Attic tradition. This double contrast, between contemporary Attica and contemporary Sparta and between contemporary Attica and Attic tradition, explains why Attic writers—Æschylus, Sophokles, Euripides, Aristophanes, Plato, Aristotle—were so deeply concerned with the social relations of the sexes.

Thus, during the sixth century the men of property had completed the work of the Eupatridai by whittling away what remained of the primitive structure and functions of the clan. In order to counteract the influence exercised by the nobility through their clan cults, Kleisthenes continued the policy of Peisistratos in developing the popular state festivals, but in his hands this policy was not sufficient, perhaps was not even designed, to eliminate completely the power which the noble families derived from their wealth and prestige. That will appear in the next chapter. The immediate struggle centred in the phratry, in which, as we have seen, the nobility were still strong enough to threaten the security of the middle class. If that threat was to be removed—and the supporters of Kleisthenes were insistent—the phratry had to be rendered politically impotent, and, since it had become the pivotal point in the tribal system, that system had to be reconstituted.

The way in which this was done was characteristic. Tribal reconstruction was nothing new. It had been done at Kyrene, as we remarked in an earlier chapter, and it had been done at Sparta as part of the military reorganisation. Yet the imprint on men's minds of the social structure under which their ancestors had lived continuously since human society had first taken shape out of the primitive horde was so deep—it had already, as we have seen, moulded their conception of the structure of the physical universe—that it was still accepted without question as the natural and necessary foundation for any form of social order. Accordingly, in Attica, as elsewhere, when the primitive tribal system was superseded, the external features of the old order were faithfully reproduced in the new;

and when a modern historian remarks that "a system more artificial than the tribes and *trittyes* of Kleisthenes it might well pass the wit of man to devise,"[9] it may be replied that, whatever we may think about it, to Greeks of this period it was the most natural thing in the world.

The vital unit in the new system was the *dêmos*, or parish. As a territorial unit, the *dêmos* had existed since prehistoric times. In a great many cases it bore the name of a clan— Eupyridai, Aithalidai, Semachidai. Moreover, the word itself means properly a division, being cognate with *dasmós*, whose significance in relation to land tenure has already been examined. It follows from our conclusions on that subject that in its original form the *dêmos* was the *moîra* of land allotted to a particular clan. It had therefore a traditional association with the clan, although of course by the end of the sixth century, owing to the dissolution of the clan system of land tenure, the original connection had largely been effaced.

Kleisthenes organised the men residing in each *dêmos* as a corporation with an elective chief (*démarchos*) and with important corporate functions, including the maintenance of a register in which was entered the name of every male as soon as he came of age. Enrolment on this register carried with it the rights of citizenship. The original members of the *dêmos* were the adult males resident within its borders at the time the reforms of Kleisthenes passed into law—to that extent the principle of kinship was relaxed; but in subsequent generations membership was determined by descent. No matter where he might happen to reside, the son always belonged to the same *dêmos* as his father. And so, after a couple of generations, this unit grew into a body of genuine kinsmen, with its own chief, its own corporate life and its own sentimental attachments. Kleisthenes could not have devised a better way of filling the void which had been left in the minds of the people by the destruction of the primitive clan.

The number of the *dêmoi* at this period is unknown. It was probably between 150 and 200. They were divided into thirty groups, called *trittyes*, or ridings. As a group of *dêmoi*, the *trittys* bore the same relation to the phratry as the *dêmos* bore to the clan. It had no corporate existence at all; it was a purely geographical unit, but it provided the reformers with a cover under which they were able to introduce unobtrusively the really revolutionary feature of the new system. Of these thirty *trittyes*, ten were composed of *dêmoi* situated in or near the city, ten of *dêmoi* situated in the maritime districts, ten of *dêmoi* situated in the interior. The purpose of this arrangement will become clear when we see how the *trittyes* were grouped in tribes.

Hitherto there had been four Attic tribes. That number was now raised to ten. And each of these ten tribes contained three *trittyes*, one from the urban area, one from the maritime districts, and one from the interior. This meant that the urban population was securely entrenched in each tribe, and, since all political meetings took place in the city, it was in a position to muster a voting power out of proportion to its numbers. Thus the middle class of merchants, manufacturers and artisans secured a permanent advantage over the landowners, farmers and peasants, and at the same time the interests of the country were subordinated to those of the town.

Such was the new order of society which Kleisthenes had constructed on the pattern of the old. The old clans and phratries were not interfered with, but they had been effectively supplanted, and so they withered away. The effect of the new system, and the object for which it was designed, was, of course, to remove the last remaining obstacles to the development of property by the most advanced section of the community—the middle class. That is generally recognised, but it does not explain why these essential changes were embodied in so conservative a form. It has been said that "the substitution of the *dêmos* for the clan meant in effect the transition from the principle of kinship to that of locality or residence."[10] This is true, but it does not explain why membership of the *dêmos* was hereditary. What had happened was that the *old* system of kinship, controlled by the aristocratic clans, had been replaced by a new system in which the clans were ignored but the principle of kinship was so far as possible preserved. In other words, what the democrats had done was to abolish the old tribal system, which had been perverted by the aristocracy into an instrument of class oppression, and to set up in its place

a new tribal system, which, being modelled on the old but at
the same time democratic, was readily accepted by the people
as a reassertion of their ancient tribal rights—not a break with
the past but a revival of the past.[11]

Why was the number of tribes raised to ten? This innovation
was connected with a reform of the calendar which was introduced at the same time. Hitherto Attica had retained the
primitive lunar calendar based on twelve months with periodical intercalations controlled by the priesthood and designed
to reconcile the lunar with the solar year. Under the democracy,
the lunar reckoning was retained for religious purposes, just as
it has been in modern Europe for the feasts of the Church; but
for secular purposes Kleisthenes introduced a solar calendar
based on ten periods of thirty-six or thirty-seven days. At the
same time, the Council of Four Hundred instituted by Solon
was raised to 500—fifty from each of the ten tribes; and these
ten tribal groups of fifty members acted in rotation through the
year as a standing committee of the Council. It would be in
harmony with the spirit of the new constitution to suppose that
this correlation between the new tribal system and the new
calendar was designed to supersede a similar correlation
between the old tribal system and the old calendar; and there
is some evidence that this was in fact the case.

According to Aristotle, the primitive Attic system had
consisted of four tribes, each of which contained three phratries.[12]
He goes on to say that each phratry contained thirty clans and
each clan thirty men. And he adds that the four tribes corresponded to the seasons, the twelve phratries to the months, and
the thirty clans in each phratry to the thirty days in each month.
The fictitious character of this arrangement is so palpable that
many modern scholars have discredited the whole statement,
even to the point of denying that the phratry was a group of
clans. Yet, whether he is discussing the origin of democracy or
the origin of tragedy, Aristotle's handling of historical tradition
is so firm and clear-sighted that his conclusions should not be
lightly brushed aside. In the present instance, his view of the
relation between the phratry and the clan is certainly right,
and the tradition regarding the relation of the old tribal system
to the seasons, though obviously schematised, is likely at least

to be ancient, because it is based on the old lunar calendar; and indeed it may quite well be essentially correct, at least to the extent that each tribe and phratry had performed certain functions by rotation in successive periods of the year. Such an arrangement would be entirely in keeping with the elaborate ritual co-operation characteristic of tribal society, and it explains the connection between the new tribal system and the reform of the calendar.

The members of the new Council of the Five Hundred were elected by lot, and the same method was extended a few years later to the election of the highest officers of State, the *árchontes*. The use of the lot served the same purpose in the new democratic constitution as it had originally served in the democracy of the primitive tribe; it was a safeguard of equality. Ancient democracy was a reversion to tribal democracy on a higher evolutionary plane.

The watchword of the new constitution was *isonomía*—equality of civic rights, equality before the law. Yet, as a later Greek historian shrewdly observed, political equality is futile without economic equality.[13] That was a bitter lesson which Athenian democrats had yet to learn, and rather than learn it they ceased to be democrats. At this period, however, thanks to the expropriation of the landlords by the tyrants and the rapid expansion of industry and trade, this contradiction was still hidden; and in the same way the still deeper contradiction latent in the development of slave labour had not yet penetrated society to the point of forcing itself on the consciousness of honest men.

On the other hand, there was one point at which the constitution of Kleisthenes fell short even of its professed ideal. Admission to the office of *árchon* was still subject to a property qualification, which excluded the lower classes. This restriction reveals the essential character of the democratic revolution. It was a middle-class revolution. Having rallied the whole people in the name of equality, the middle class proceeded to entrench itself in a constitution which denied equality to the masses that had enabled it to prevail. This contradiction had an effect on middle-class thought, which, since it was instinctively suppressed, was all the more profound.

The first great exponent of democratic thought was Pythagoras, a citizen of Samos who emigrated about 530 B.C. to
the colony of Kroton in southern Italy.[14] The accounts of his
birth are conflicting and partly fabulous. The most probable is
that he was the son of a Samian engraver of gems. At this
period Samos was under the tyranny of Polykrates, which,
until it was cut short by the Persian conquest of Ionia, was
one of the most brilliant that Greece had seen. Polykrates
overthrew the landed aristocracy, opened up direct trade with
Egypt, executed enormous public works, including a mole for
the harbour and a subterranean aqueduct, experimented with
the coinage, and aspired to the commercial hegemony of the
Ægean.

Thus, Pythagoras came from one of the main centres of the
urban revolution, and his life in Italy coincided with the
development of coinage in the west. According to Aristoxenos,
it was Pythagoras who introduced weights and measures to the
Greeks; and, though this tradition cannot be accepted in the
form in which it has come down to us (we do not possess the
actual words of Aristoxenos), it is likely enough that he was
interested in the standardisation of weights and measures which
was being effected at this time under the pressure of overseas
trade. At any rate, there can be no doubt of the origin of his
interest in mathematics, for Aristoxenos says that he was the
first to develop that study beyond the necessities of trade.[15]

At Kroton he founded a secret society, which differed from
the Orphic *thíasoi* in being organised as a political party.
About 510 B.C., after a political reverse, Pythagoras migrated
to Metapontion, where he seems to have remained until he
died. During the first half of the fifth century the Pythagoreans
extended their influence all over southern Italy. Then, in one
city after another, beginning with Kroton, the order was
suppressed and its members persecuted.

It is obvious that, being organised as a political party, the
Pythagoreans must have had a political programme related to
the economic and social developments of their time. It is
amusing to observe that Condorcet, the Girondin, who had a
political programme of his own which bore very directly on
the French Revolution, took it for granted that the early

Pythagoreans were democrats.[16] The Pythagorean harmony of opposites made an immediate appeal to him because it so closely resembled the idea of social reconciliation expounded by the Girondins. But the majority of modern scholars, being less conscious than Condorcet of their own relation to society, have taken the view that the Pythagoreans formed the nucleus of the aristocracy. In support of this view, they quote a statement of Diogenes of Laerte that at Kroton the disciples of Pythagoras, "about three hundred in all, administered the government so well (*árista*) that their rule was as it were an aristocracy (*aristokratía*)."[17] It is quite clear, however, that the word *aristokratía* is here employed in its literal and philosophical sense of the rule of the best. That the control of the state should have been in the hands of 300 persons certainly implies that their social basis was narrow, but it does not follow in the least that they were aristocrats in the sense of representing the interests of the landed nobility. On the contrary, it is hard to see how a colonist from Samos could have found himself at the head of the hereditary landowning oligarchy in a state which had been founded nearly 200 years before his arrival.

The first to reject the accepted view was Burnet, who argued that the Pythagoreans were democrats, but that their main concern was with the cult of holiness.[18] This is a step in the right direction; but there is other evidence which shows that the statement that they were democrats needs qualification; and, if they were not concerned with a good deal more than the cult of holiness, why did they play such a strenuous part in the political struggles of the time, and why were they hunted down?

According to Apollonios, the opponents of the Pythagoreans were two—Kylon the aristocrat, who is described as the leading citizen in wealth and birth, and Ninon the democrat; and, moreover, the Pythagoreans are said to have resisted proposals for extending the franchise and making the magistrates responsible to the people. It follows that, if they were democrats, they were moderate democrats, representing the interests of the big merchants, and therefore opposed by the nobility on the one hand and the workers on the other.

It must be admitted that the political history of southern

Italy in this crucial period has not yet been clarified, but the hypothesis I have advanced not only seems to account for the evidence better than any other, but it is strongly supported by an examination of the religious aspect of Pythagoreanism.[19]

The Pythagoreans believed in reincarnation, which they described as the Wheel of Necessity. They were severely ascetic and much addicted to silent meditation. They invented the symbol of the "ox on the tongue," corresponding to the Orphic "door on the tongue" and the Eleusinian "key on the tongue." They observed numerous taboos, some of them primitive, to which they attached an ethical significance: for example, "Don't step over the beam of a balance"—that is to say, don't transgress the bounds of equity. They believed in the moral responsibility of the individual for his actions, and when they returned home after the day's work, they said to themselves, "Where have I erred? What have I accomplished? What have I left undone that I ought to have done?" They taught that the soul was immortal and something different from life; that the souls of the pure ascended to the upper region of Hades, while those of the impure were bound by the Erinyes in unbreakable bonds; that the air was full of guardian spirits which visited men in dreams, for the soul awakes when the body sleeps; and that the man who was possessed of a good soul was blest. Their rites of burial were peculiar to themselves and designed to secure their personal salvation. Admission to the society was by some form of initiation, with a probationary period of five years.

It is plain that this creed, so far from being aristocratic, has the closest affinities with Orphism, for which Pythagoras is said to have had an intense admiration. Bury indeed goes so far as to say that "the Pythagoreans were practically an Orphic community,"[20] but this is an exaggeration. All the fundamental elements—initiation, purification, salvation, the differentiation of body and soul—were common, but there were also important divergences. The patron god of the Pythagoreans was Apollo, not Dionysus. The Orphic cult of holiness was entirely, or almost entirely, ritualistic; the Pythagoreans had an elaborate code of social and moral conduct. In its intellectual content Pythagoreanism was far superior to Orphism, indicating that it was a cult of the *élite* rather than of the masses. And most significant of all, while the Orphics were quietistic, content to renounce the world, the early Pythagoreans were strenuously engaged in changing it by the prosecution of a radical political programme. While Orphism had drawn its impetus from the dispossessed peasantry and the new urban proletariat at a time when they were still politically unorganised, the Pythagoreans represented the active and class-conscious section of the popular movement—the men of money, the merchants, who, already enriched by the growth of overseas trade, found the path to further enrichment blocked by the opposition of the hereditary landowning oligarchy. Their rule at Kroton may therefore be described as a commercial theocracy.

At this point it may be helpful to consider a modern analogy.[21] The feudal system of mediæval Europe was based on the land, and it was destroyed by the growth of trade. It was maintained in the interests of the landowning barons, supported by the leaders of the established Church, who were themselves big landowners. Consequently, the attack on it, led by the rising bourgeoisie, necessarily involved a break with the Church— the Reformation. The basis of the Lutheran movement is thus described by Tawney. The peasants of South Germany—

> found *corvées* redoubled, money-payments increased, and common rights curtailed, for the benefit of an impoverished noblesse, which saw in the exploitation of the peasant the only means of maintaining its social position in face of the rapidly growing wealth of the bourgeoisie.

Meanwhile a parallel movement had been developing in the towns. Like Lutheranism, it was directed against the established religion, but it was also consciously organised for the attainment of a political objective:

> Where Lutheranism had been socially conservative, deferential to established political authorities, the exponent of a personal, almost quietistic, piety, Calvinism was an active and radical force. It was a creed which sought, not merely to purify the individual, but to reconstruct Church and State, and to renew society by penetrating every department of life, public as well as private, with the influence of religion. . . . Its leaders addressed their teaching,

P▲

not of course exclusively, but none the less primarily, to the classes engaged in trade and industry, which formed the most modern and progressive elements in the life of the age.

This is how Tawney describes the Calvinist state of Geneva:

> The principle on which the collectivism of Geneva rested may be described as that of the omnicompetent church. The religious community formed a closely organised society, which, while using the secular authority as police officers to enforce its mandates, not only instructed them as to the policy to be pursued, but was itself a kind of state, prescribing by its own legislation the standard of conduct to be observed by its members, putting down offences against public order and public morals, providing for the education of youth and for the relief of the poor. The peculiar relations between the ecclesiastical and secular authorities, which for a short time made the system possible at Geneva, could not exist to the same degree when Calvinism was the creed, not of a single city, but of a minority in a national state organised on principles very different from its own. Unless the state itself were captured, rebellion, civil war, or the abandonment of the pretension to control society, was the inevitable consequence.

The same distinction between Luther and Calvin is drawn by Pirenne:

> While Luther confined religion to the domain of the conscience, and left the temporal power to organise the Church and follow its political interests after its own fashion, Calvin submitted all human actions to theology. . . . The State, being willed by God, had to be transformed into an instrument of the divine will. It was not subordinated to the clergy, and did not derive its power from them, but it acted in conformity with the end for which it was created only by associating itself intimately with the clergy in order that the mandate of the Most High should triumph here on earth. . . . Such a system of ideas, if it is fully applied, inevitably leads to theocracy, and under the inspiration of Calvin the government of Geneva did actually constitute a theocracy.

There were, of course, profound differences between the democratic movement of ancient Greece and the rise of the modern

bourgeoisie, but, except for those who like H. A. L. Fisher can
see no sequence in human history, "only one emergency following upon another as wave follows wave,"²² a study of the social
and religious movements of sixteenth-century Europe makes it
clear—for the first time, as it seems to me—why, after seizing
power in the highly commercialised cities of southern Italy, the
Pythagoreans were suddenly and violently expelled.

With these considerations in mind, let us now turn to the
fundamental conception which lies at the root of Pythagorean
philosophy—the doctrine of the fusion of opposites in the mean.

On the relation of this doctrine to Milesian philosophy
Burnet wrote:²³

> Now this discovery of the Mean at once suggests a new
> solution of the old Milesian problem of opposites. We know
> that Anaximander regarded the encroachment of one
> opposite on the other as an "injustice," and he must therefore
> have held that there was a point which was fair to both.
> That, however, he had no means of determining. The
> discovery of the Mean suggests that it is to be found in a
> "blend" (*krâsis*) of the opposites, which might be numerically
> determined, just as that of the high and low notes of the
> octave had been. The convivial customs of the Greeks made
> such an idea natural to them. The master of the feast used
> to prescribe the proportions of wine and water to be poured
> into the mixing-bowl before it was served out to the guests.

Since he described the encroachment of one opposite on the
other as an injustice, Anaximander must presumably have
regarded justice (if he defined his idea of it at all) as a state in
which each opposite keeps to itself. There is no evidence that
"he held that there was a point which was fair to both," and,
if he had done so, he would not have been prevented from
determining it by ignorance of music or mathematics, because
the doctrine of the mean had already been propounded by
Solon. The truth is that Anaximander simply did not look at
the problem from that point of view. According to Burnet, the
idea of fusion was deduced by Pythagoras from his theory of
the mean; yet, as we shall see immediately, that theory presupposes it. And this deduction sprang to his mind because the
idea was "natural" to the Greeks. This slipshod thinking, which

glides with a deceptive facility past all the crucial issues, is the result of attempting to interpret Greek philosophy as a closed system of pure thought, endowed like the Platonic Soul with a power of self-movement independent of its material environment.

What Pythagoras discovered was the relation between the four fixed notes of the octave, represented by the numerical series 6—8—9—12. The terms 6 and 12 are regarded as opposites; 8 is the subcontrary or harmonic mean $\left(8=12-\dfrac{12}{3}=6+\dfrac{6}{3}\right)$ and 9 is the arithmetic mean $(9=12-3=6+3)$. What led Pythagoras to this discovery? In the first instance, no doubt, his interest in mathematics, which had its roots, as we have seen, in the social movement of his time. But, while there is no doubt that the medical and other applications of the mean were merely extensions of the musical theory, the musical theory itself is not fully explicable in terms of the phenomena it was designed to interpret. From the point of view of music or mathematics, there is nothing in the nature of the numbers 6 and 12 which demands that they should be regarded as opposites. That notion is a preconception, and at the same time it is essential. The relation between these terms is constantly described in Pythagorean writings as one of dissension or hostility, which is resolved or reconciled by their fusion in the mean. Thus, we are told by Theon of Smyrna that the Pythagoreans described concord (*harmonía*) as "an attunement of opposites, a unification of the many, a reconciliation of dissentients." The last phrase is found again in a fragment attributed to Philolaos.[24]

What was the origin of this preconception? It may be said that it was derived from Anaximander, who spoke of the encroachment of one opposite on the other as an "injustice" to which a "penalty" was attached. But the Pythagorean terminology was different. The terms *dícha phronéein* "dissension" and *symphrónasis* "reconciliation" are Doric, and their Attic equivalents are *stasiázein* and *homónoia*, corresponding to the Latin *certamen* and *concordia*. Both these terms are derived from social relationships: *stásis* means party strife or civil war, *homónoia* means civil peace or concord. Thus, the *symphrónasis* or *homónoia* of the Pythagoreans expressed the subjective attitude characteristic of the class which claimed to have resolved the old class-struggle in democracy. The doctrine of the fusion of opposites in the mean was generated by the rise of the middle class intermediate between the landowners and the serfs. And of this development in Greek philosophy we have a striking piece of independent evidence in the poetry of Theognis, who had lived to see his native Megara pass into the control of the hated democrats.[25]

> In our rams, asses and horses we endeavour to preserve a noble breed, and we like to mate them with a good stock. Yet the nobleman does not scruple to marry a low-born wife, so long as she brings him money, nor does a woman refuse the hand of a low-born suitor, preferring riches to nobility. What they honour is money. The nobleman marries into a family of base birth, the base-born into a noble family. Wealth has blended breed. So do not wonder that the breed of the citizens is dying out; for noble is being blended with base.

In these words we have in epitome the whole history of the fall of the hereditary nobility and the rise of the middle class. Theognis was not a philosopher—he is merely describing, as one bitterly opposed to them, the changes he saw taking place in the society of his time, and what did he see? He saw the opposites, *esthloí* and *kakoí*, whom as an aristocrat he wished to keep apart, being blended by the wealth of the new middle class.

This conclusion does not, of course, affect in any way the objective value of the mathematical discovery made by Pythagoras. Its importance is that it shows how social progress had resulted in an extension of knowledge by inducing those engaged in it to adopt a fresh point of view. Just as the advancement of knowledge enables man to extend his control of matter, so material advancement enables him to extend his knowledge.

The doctrine of the mean was applied to medicine by a younger contemporary of Pythagoras himself, Alkmaion of Kroton, who declared that "health consisted in the enjoyment by the powers—the wet and dry, the hot and cold, the bitter and sweet, and so on—of equal rights (*isonomía*), while the monarchy of one or other of them was conducive to sickness."²⁶ Here the political significance of the conception is undisguised. The reference of *monarchía* is probably to tyranny, because that is the word used of the tyranny in the Ionic dialect, and the state of health is described explicitly as *isonomía*—the watchword of democracy.

The final stage in the scientific development of this theory, which the Pythagoreans applied to mathematics, medicine and astronomy, was reached when Hippokrates, who was deeply influenced by Alkmaion, applied it to the evolution of the human race.²⁷

If the sick had benefited by the same diet and regimen as the healthy—if there had been nothing better to be found, the art of medicine would never have been discovered or sought after—there would have been no need for it. What forced men to seek and find medicine was sheer necessity, because the sick do not, and never did, benefit by the same regimen as the healthy. To go still further back, I maintain that even the mode of life and diet which we enjoy at the present day would never have been discovered, if men had been content with the same food and drink as the other animals, such as oxen and horses, which feed, grow up and live without pain on fruit, wood and grass, without the need for any other diet. Yet in the beginning, I believe, this was the diet of man himself. Our present mode of life is in my opinion the outcome of a long period of invention and elaboration. So long as men partook of crude foods strong in quality and uncompounded, their brutish diet subjected them to terrible sufferings—just the same as they would suffer now, attacked by acute pains and diseases quickly followed by death. In former ages no doubt they suffered less, because they were used to it, but severely even then. Many of them, whose constitutions were too weak to stand it, naturally perished, but the stronger resisted, just as now some men dispose of strong foods without difficulty, others only with severe pain. And that I think is the reason why men sought for a diet in harmony with their constitutions until they discovered the diet which we use now.

It was the Orphics who, following Hesiod, had first thought of human life as a struggle, because for the masses whose aspirations they voiced it *was* a struggle; but, since those masses were unconscious of their strength and therefore unable to exert it, they had placed the prize of victory the other side of death. Since then, however, the new middle class had thrown itself into the struggle and won the prize of democracy; and accordingly the world order appeared to them as a cessation of the agelong strife of opposites, which by blending and merging into one another had ceased to *be* opposites; and these ideas were then applied to the historical process which had engendered them. Human civilisation appeared in retrospect as a dynamic and progressive conflict, in which men had been compelled by their material needs to extend their mastery of their material environment. All this is implicit in the words just quoted, but already a generation before Hippokrates the same ideas had been worked out in poetry by Æschylus, who was himself a Pythagorean and a democrat.

XIII

ATHENS AND PERSIA

THE earliest inhabitants of Mesopotamia were Semitic nomads from the Arabian desert who had begun to clear the swamps and till the soil by irrigation when they were subjugated by Sumerian invaders from the east. For a short time after the conquest the whole area was ruled under a centralised monarchy, but before long it broke up into a number of agricultural city-states, each ruled by a hereditary priest-king. With the rapid advance of agriculture and metallurgy, the competition between these states became intense, and in each state there arose a merchant class opposed to the ruling priesthood. The role of such usurpers as Urukagina of Lagash seems to have resembled that of the Greek tyrants. But these Sumerian city-states developed differently from the Greek. The needs of irrigation imposed a check on the development of property in land and the freedom of communication facilitated expansion by means of war. The first imperialist unification of Babylonia was effected by Sharrukin and his successors, a dynasty belonging to the Semitic stock, but it was followed by a period of civil wars in which the Sumerian nobility recovered their position. Then, towards the end of the third millennium, Hammurabi of Babylon built up an empire which extended as far as Armenia in the north and Palestine in the west. The Babylonian dynasty was overthrown by the Assyrians, who however made no attempt to organise their conquests, and their empire broke up. The second great imperialist movement took place under the Persian dynasty of the Achaimenidai, who by the end of the sixth century had subjugated Lydia, Ionia, Babylon and Egypt.

The Persian Empire was far too strong for the Greeks to attack it, and they were therefore unable to unite on the basis of imperialist expansion in the east. Similarly, in the west, expansion was restricted by the growing power of Carthage.

Hemmed in on both sides, the Greek city-states were forced along the path of internal development. The competition between them was so keen that there was no possibility of organised resistance to the Persian conquest of Ionia. After the fall of Miletos, a large part of her trade went to Athens and Corinth. The Persian capture of Samos, at a time when it was heading under Polykrates for the commercial hegemony of the Ægean, removed an obstacle from the path of the Athenian tyrants, who were aiming at the same objective. Consequently, when in 499 B.C. the Ionian Greeks revolted, they received little help from the mainland, and the revolt was suppressed. The mainland Greeks then found themselves threatened by the same fate. The effect was to intensify the internal contradictions in each state.

The Athenians knew that, if they submitted, they would be subjected to tribute and to the rule of a tyrant in the Persian interest. The democratic movement would therefore be arrested. On the other hand, if they resisted, they would have to seek help from Sparta, whose attitude to the democracy they had already experienced. In these circumstances the only chance of preserving the democracy was to fight Persia with Spartan assistance in the hope that victory would give them sufficient strength to stand up to their former ally. This policy was eventually adopted, with signal success, but only because the people were strong enough to force it through.

The democratic revolution effected under the leadership of Kleisthenes was the outcome of a three-cornered struggle in which the opposition to democracy was divided. After this defeat, the reactionaries closed their ranks. The differences between the followers of Hippias and of Isagoras, both intent on overthrowing the democracy, so far disappeared that in the year 506 Sparta sent another expedition to Attica with the object of restoring Hippias. The expedition broke up owing to the withdrawal at the last minute of Corinth, who had no desire to see Spartan influence extended north of the Isthmus or to weaken the Athenians at a time when they were engaged in a trade-war with her own commercial rival, Aigina.

While Hippias appealed to Sparta, Kleisthenes appealed to Persia. Without consulting the people, he offered to submit to the Persians, no doubt on the understanding that he would be installed as tyrant. This action on his part is not adequately explained by fear of Sparta. The lower classes, whom he had excluded from the franchise, were already beginning to make their influence felt, and so, as leader of the middle class, Kleisthenes was faced with the choice of retreating from democracy or being ultimately swept aside. When the nature of his negotiations with Persia became known, he attempted to cover himself by repudiating his envoys, apparently without success, because shortly afterwards he dropped out of Athenian politics entirely. What happened to him is obscure, but he is said to have been sentenced to exile.

Weakened by the loss of their leader, the Alkmaionidai moved still further to the right. It was probably with their support that the adherents of Hippias secured the election as *árchon* of Hipparchos, a close relative of Hippias himself (496 B.C.). Meanwhile, having lost confidence in Sparta, Hippias went to Sardis to press his claims, in which his ancestral rivals the Alkmaionidai had now acquiesced, as the prospective tyrant of an Athens subjugated by Persia. The moderates had drifted over to the reactionaries.

During the next three years, while the Persians were crushing the Ionian revolt and laying plans for a campaign against the mainland, two new figures appear on the scene. One is Themistokles, the new leader of the radical democrats, who was elected to the archonship in 493. Themistokles was the first political leader at Athens who did not belong to one of the old noble families. He had risen to power by detaching the lower middle class from the Alkmaionidai, but he was not yet strong enough to pursue an independent line, and contented himself with playing off his opponents against each other. The other was Miltiades, whose father had been installed by Peisistratos as tyrant of the Thracian Chersonese (Gallipoli) after its annexation by Athens. Miltiades had succeeded his father, but he had broken with the Peisistratidai by supporting the Ionians, and now, after the failure of the revolt, he was back at Athens as a fugitive. Miltiades belonged to the illustrious clan of the Philaidai. He was not, of course, a democrat, but he saw the opportunity of rallying to himself the support of the people against the reactionary and defeatist policy of the Peisistratidai and the Alkmaionidai by placing before them the alternative of fighting Persia with Spartan aid. His opponents tried to forestall him by impeaching him on a charge of misgovernment in the Chersonese, but Miltiades was acquitted. His acquittal shows that Themistokles had decided, for the time being, to support him.

After mopping up Ionia, the Persians closed in on Euboia and landed a division at Marathon. The Athenians sent an urgent appeal to Sparta, but the Spartans procrastinated. Evidently there were many of them who thought that, notwithstanding the risk to themselves, the best course was to leave Athenian democracy to the Persians. Meanwhile, at the head of the Athenian army, Miltiades attacked at Marathon. The battle was short, but long enough for Hippias, watching from a Persian flagship, to see a flash from a shield on the heights overlooking the bay. It was a signal to him—a wink from the Alkmaionidai to say that they were ready to betray the city to the tyrant from whom they had delivered it twenty years before. The Athenians fought well and drove the Persians into the sea, then rushed back to the city to meet the danger of an enemy landing at Phaleron. The Persians did in fact cruise into Phaleron, awaiting a signal to land, but, thanks to the result of Marathon, the Alkmaionidai did not venture to wink again. In the evening the Spartan army arrived, to be informed by the victorious Athenians that their assistance was no longer required. There was nothing for the Spartan commander to do but to present his compliments and retire. Once more the Spartans had miscalculated.

A few months after Marathon, Miltiades led an expedition against the island of Paros, which had gone over to the Persians. The circumstances of the expedition are obscure, but its object was probably, as Walker has suggested, to organise the Cyclades as an outer line of defence against the Persians, for whom the defeat at Marathon had not been in any way decisive. The expedition ended in a complete fiasco, and on his return Miltiades was impeached by Xanthippos, the brother-in-law of Megakles, who was the new chief of the Alkmaionidai. Miltiades was already dying of a wound he had received during the expedition. But for that he would have been sentenced to death. As it was, the sentence was reduced to a fine, and he died shortly afterwards.

Walker says that the failure of this expedition "was a blow to the cause which Themistokles had at heart, and he must have used his influence to secure the acquittal of Miltiades, or at least the mitigation of the sentence."[1] This view renders the course of events unintelligible. On this occasion, as at the previous trial two years before, the prosecutors of Miltiades were the Alkmaionidai. At the previous trial, as we have seen, Miltiades, then a newcomer with no organised following, was acquitted. Since then the Battle of Marathon had been won; Miltiades had been acclaimed as the saviour of Athens, while the Alkmaionidai had suffered a crushing defeat and lay under a suspicion of treachery which it took them a generation to live down. It is incredible that they could have secured the condemnation of Miltiades in these circumstances without the support of Themistokles. Nor are the motives of Themistokles far to seek. He had supported the anti-Persian policy of Miltiades because he was not yet strong enough to pursue it independently, but he knew that the ultimate objective of this scion of the Philaidai was no more democratic than that of other wealthy noblemen who had offered their services to the people. The radicals were beginning to learn their lesson. Therefore, at the first opportunity, he took advantage of the division between Miltiades and the Alkmaionidai to get rid of Miltiades. And shortly afterwards he succeeded in getting rid of the Alkmaionidai. In 487 their nominee, Hipparchos, was banished; in the following year their leader, Megakles, was banished; in 484 Xanthippos, the prosecutor of Miltiades, was banished; in 482 Aristeides, one of their most influential adherents, was banished. Thus, in the years following Marathon, one after another of the opponents of Themistokles was swept off the board. Thanks to the promptitude with which they had dealt with Miltiades, the people were able to take the defence of their country into their own hands.

Themistokles saw that, notwithstanding the victory of Marathon, the real struggle with Persia was still to come, and he saw that the only hope of final victory lay in the construction of a navy. This policy was opposed by the Alkmaionidai, because it meant an access of power to the poorest class of the city and the ports, from which the personnel of the navy would have to be drawn. Themistokles carried it through in spite of them. Even so, their opposition was very nearly fatal, because, when the decisive moment came, the new navy was still not strong enough for Athens to carry her claim to the supreme command at sea.

Meanwhile the Emperor Xerxes, who had succeeded his father, Darius, was preparing a full-scale invasion of Greece. The army he had mustered was too large to be transported across the Ægean, and accordingly it marched overland by a bridge of pontoons over the Hellespont and thence along the Thracian coast into Thessaly. Its advance was to be covered by the fleet, which could be used to land troops in the enemy's rear if he ventured to resist. It was a formidable armada, and the position of Sparta and Athens, both marked out for exemplary punishment, might well have seemed desperate.

On the situation created by the Persian Wars Bury wrote:[2]

The Persian war, in its effects on Greece, illustrates the operation of a general law which governs human societies. Pressure from without, whether on a nation or a race, tends to promote union and cohesion within. In the case of a nation the danger of foreign attack increases the sense of unity among individual citizens and strengthens the central power. In the case of a race, it tends to weld the individual communities into a nation or federation. In the latter case, the chance of realising a complete or permanent unity depends partly on the strength and duration of the external pressure, partly upon the degree of strength in the instinct for independence which has hitherto hindered the political atoms from cohesion.

It is not often that modern English historians venture to formulate general laws of human society, and this exception is not a very happy one. Indeed, it is difficult to see what relation it bears to the events in which its operation is said to be illustrated. When the Ionian cities were first threatened with the loss of their independence, there was mooted, it is true, a proposal for a pan-Ionian union, but nothing came of it. When these cities endeavoured to throw off the Persian yoke, they appealed for assistance to Sparta and Athens, but the response was chilling, and the revolt collapsed owing to defections among themselves. We have already seen how first Kleisthenes and then Hippias had offered to sell Athens for their own advantage, and the pressure that prompted these offers was internal. Late in the year 481, when the Persian plans were complete, delegates from a number of Greek states met at the Isthmus to concert their defence under the leadership of Sparta, who, thanks to her unrivalled army, was still the most powerful state in Greece. Corinth and Athens were willing to co-operate, and Athens reached an agreement with Aigina. The Thessalians and Bœotians also joined the confederacy, but they were known to be unreliable. The ruling aristocracy of Thebes was pro-Persian, and so was the Thessalian clan of the Aleuadai. In the Peloponnese itself, Argos, who had recently been defeated but not conquered by Sparta and was now leaning towards democracy, refused to join, and so did the Achæan cities along the northern coast. Across the Gulf of Corinth, the Delphic Oracle was more than ever equivocal, and there were grounds for suspecting that it was ready to go over to Xerxes. Further north, the city of Kerkyra, which was a commercial rival of Corinth for the trade with the west, promised to send assistance, but failed to do so. Emissaries were sent from the congress to the Ægean and to the west, but the results were negative. There was no question of winning over the Ionians, who, thanks to the conciliatory policy astutely adopted by Persia after the revolt, were now furnishing contingents to the Persian fleet. The cities of Crete devoutly sheltered behind an oracle from Delphi. In the west, probably as a result of Persian diplomacy, Gelon, the tyrant of Syracuse, found himself preoccupied with a war against Carthage, and perhaps too he paused to reflect that the fall of Corinth and Athens might react not unfavourably on Syracusan trade. It must be admitted that the response to this pan-Hellenic clarion call from the Isthmus was discouraging. Apart from the class divisions inside each "political atom," the smaller states were evidently actuated by one or both of two motives—the belief that the external pressure was so strong as to render resistance futile, and the fear that unity under Spartan rule would prove hardly more congenial than the present lot of Ionia.

The Greeks were heavily outnumbered both on land and sea. Neither their army nor their fleet could afford to offer resistance except in narrow positions where the enemy would be unable to deploy his forces. On the other hand, if they could inflict a defeat on the enemy at sea, they would be able to draw off his army by harrying the coast of Asia Minor. The difficulty was to decide where to meet him. The Spartans had strong reasons for awaiting the enemy at the Isthmus. If they sent their troops further north, they would be exposed to a Persian landing on the coast of Argos, which, if it was followed, as it well might be, by a rising of the serf population of Sparta itself, would be fatal. On the other hand, if the defence were confined to the Peloponnese, Athens, being unprotected, would probably come to terms, and without the Athenian fleet the Spartans would soon be forced back from the Isthmus. Accordingly, Themistokles proposed that the Spartan army should march north and hold the pass of Tempe, the gateway of Thessaly, while the fleet sought an engagement with the enemy at the northern entrance to the Euripos.

The Spartans accepted this plan, but without the energy necessary to make it a success. They sent a small force to Tempe, but withdrew without fighting. Then they sent a still smaller force to Thermopylai, the pass leading from Thessaly into Boiotia, which the Persians caught in the rear and annihilated. Boiotia and Attica were now defenceless. After an inconclusive engagement off Artemision, the Greek fleet withdrew to the channel between the Attic mainland and the island of Salamis. The population of Attica was hastily evacuated to Salamis, Aigina and Troizen. Shortly afterwards the Persian army entered Attica, ravaged the countryside, seized the Akropolis, and burnt the temples to the ground.

The Greek defence was now cracking up. The Spartans wanted to withdraw the fleet to the coast of Megara and revert to their original plan of making a stand at the Isthmus. This meant abandoning the Athenian refugees on Salamis and relinquishing the one remaining chance of meeting the Persian fleet in narrow waters. Themistokles rose to the occasion. He declared that, if Salamis were abandoned, the Athenians would take their refugees on board their ships and migrate *en masse* to Italy. Meanwhile he sent a message to the Persians suggesting that they should attack immediately, as the Greek fleet was planning to escape. It was now late in the autumn, and the Persians, impatient of delay, fell into the trap. Caught between Salamis and the mainland, their ships fell into disorder and they suffered a crushing defeat. Xerxes withdrew his fleet to Asia for the winter, leaving his army under Mardonios in Thessaly.

At the beginning of the following year (479), Aristeides, who had been recalled with other exiles at the outbreak of the war, was elected to the command of the Athenian forces in place of Themistokles. This suggests that the Athenian resistance (Attica was still evacuated) was near breaking-point; but, when Mardonios offered Athens a separate peace, the offer was fiercely rejected and a citizen who supported it was lynched, together with his wife and family. Another urgent appeal was sent to Sparta, and after an agonising delay a Spartan army under Pausanias crossed the Isthmus. Mardonios met it in Boiotia, and the result was a decisive victory for the Spartans. The crisis was now over. The Ionians rose in revolt and were organised under Athenian leadership in an anti-Persian confederacy.

The next few years were occupied in harrying the Persians throughout the Ægean as far as Cyprus and the coast of Phœnicia. There now opened before the victors a new and alluring prospect of commercial expansion. On the Athenian side, these operations were conducted by Aristeides and Kimon, the son of Miltiades, who had married a granddaughter of Megakles. The rival clans of the Philaidai and the Alkmaionidai were thus reconciled, and between them, in 471, they secured the banishment of Themistokles, who fled to Argos and there engaged in anti-Spartan intrigues. At first, under Pausanias, the Spartans had taken an active part in the Ionian operations, but in 476 Pausanias was recalled and accused of intriguing first with Persia and later with Themistokles for the overthrow of the Spartan constitution by means of an insurrection among the serfs. Pausanias was put to death, and in response to a

Spartan protest Themistokles was summoned home to answer a charge of treason. Failing to appear, he was hunted from Argos to Kerkyra, from Kerkyra across the mountains to the Ægean coast, and thence to Ephesos, where he found safety under the protection of the Persian Emperor.

This is a startling *bouleversement*. What had happened? We are told that Pausanias had his head turned by success, and that as a *novus homo* Themistokles was no match for the combined prestige of his high-born opponents;[3] but this is mere tittle-tattle of the same order as the explanation offered by Plutarch, who says that Themistokles fell from power "because the people were fed up with him."

The political alignments at Athens and Sparta had changed because the situation had changed. The objectives remained in each case the same. When Persia had been strong, the Alkmaionidai had counselled submission, but Themistokles had carried through the alternative policy of resisting her with the aid of Sparta. Now Persia is weak. The Alkmaionidai are all for organising Ionia in an anti-Persian crusade. Themistokles, on the other hand, is determined to oppose Sparta, if necessary with Persian assistance.

The war had left Athens at an advantage. Thanks to her fleet and to her commercial organisation, she was able to follow up the victory. The wealthy commercial houses seized this opportunity of securing the economic control of the Ægean and at the same time they were anxious to cultivate friendly relations with the anti-democratic government of Sparta. That government had been shaken. Unless it were to abandon its traditional policy, it stood to gain comparatively little from the war, but it could not embark on a policy of commercial expansion without endangering the supremacy at home of the landowning aristocracy whose interests it represented. It was forced therefore to recall Pausanias, who was evidently aiming at a tyranny. Themistokles perceived that, in the new situation, the danger threatening Athenian democracy was not the might of Persia, which had now been broken, but the anti-democratic régime of Sparta, and therefore he supported the attempt of Pausanias to overthrow it. But the Athenian people, whose nationalist passions had been inflamed by the war, could not

QA

be persuaded that Persia was no longer the enemy, especially as the prospect of enrichment offered by the conservative opposition was substantial. They were caught off their guard, and consequently they were induced to drop their pilot. They paid the price seventy years later, when, with a Spartan army at their gates, their democratic rights were torn from them in a bloody counter-revolution (404 B.C.).

Seven years after the banishment of Themistokles the town of Sparta was destroyed by an earthquake (464 B.C.). Hundreds of citizens perished. It seemed to the serfs that at last the hour of their deliverance was come. In many parts of Laconia and all over Messenia they rose in revolt. The Spartans were saved by a contingent of troops from Mantineia in Arcadia, where they had installed a régime friendly to themselves after the war. The rebels retreated to the fastness of Mount Ithome in Messenia, where they held out for several years. The Spartans were not trained for siege operations, and they appealed to Athens to send them troops. The appeal met with strenuous opposition from Ephialtes, the new leader of the radical party and, like Themistokles, a commoner. The radicals saw that they had now an opportunity, which was not likely to recur, of retrieving the blow they had suffered by the loss of Themistokles. On the other side, the conservatives were equally intent on responding to the appeal, and the influence of Kimon prevailed. The Assembly voted him a force of 4,000 heavy-armed troops, with which he hastened to Messenia to lay siege to Mount Ithome. But still the siege made no progress, there was friction between the Athenian and Spartan troops, and eventually the Spartan Government was obliged to request their allies to return home. The causes of the friction are not stated, but it has rightly been conjectured that Kimon was unable to restrain the sympathy of his rank and file for the insurgents. When Kimon returned to Athens, he found both himself and his party utterly discredited. The alliance with Sparta, which had been maintained since the Persian War, was annulled, and an alliance was concluded with her rival, Argos, instead. In the following year Kimon was banished.

The radicals were again in power. It was too late for effective intervention in Sparta, but they were able to introduce some important reforms at home. Since the year 480, when the conservatives had regained the ascendancy, the Council of the Areopagus, which had always been the most reactionary body in the state, had recovered a large measure of its influence. At the instance of Ephialtes, all the powers of the Council, excepting its jurisdiction in cases of homicide, were divided between the Council of the Five Hundred, the Assembly, and the popular courts of law. The significance of this reform is shown by the fact that it was repealed by the counter-revolutionaries at the end of the Peloponnesian War; nor was it lost on the conservatives at the time, for a few months later Ephialtes was assassinated. The radicals replied by removing the last remaining restrictions on the franchise. The offices of state were thrown open to the lowest property class but one, and the lowest class of all, though still formally disqualified, were in practice admitted by a legal fiction. This was in 456 B.C., the year in which Æschylus died.

Meanwhile the structure of Athenian society was being surreptitiously but rapidly transformed by the development of slave labour and the conversion of the anti-Persian confederacy into an Athenian Empire. By the middle of the century Athens had entered irrevocably on the path of imperialist expansion. This development will be examined in a later chapter. Its immediate effect was to relieve the class tension among the citizen population by joint exploitation of slavery and empire. The conflict underlying the democratic revolution was now to be solved by the negation of democracy. Of this negative aspect of the revolution, except to some extent in his latest work, Æschylus was hardly aware; but he was intensely conscious of its positive aspect, which was indeed the inspiration of his art. For him, who was old enough to remember the tyranny of Hippias, the struggle had been won, the opposites had been reconciled.

XIV

TETRALOGY

THE festival of the City Dionysia, as reorganised by Kleisthenes at the end of the sixth century, lasted five or six days. The programme of the first day has been described in Chapter X. The order of events during the remainder of the festival is uncertain. The regulations governing the competitions were as follows.[1]

Ten dithyrambs were performed, one from each tribe. The training of the choir devolved on a wealthy citizen nominated by and from the tribe and known as the *choregós*. If a citizen nominated for this purpose considered that the choice should have fallen on another member of his tribe, he could challenge him either to take his place as *choregós* or to exchange properties. A panel of judges was elected by the Council of Five Hundred with the assistance of the *choregoí*, and from this panel ten names were selected by lot. The prize, as we have already remarked, was a bull.

The dramatic performances were independent of the tribal system. It was open to any citizen to compete. The citizen who wished to do so submitted to the *árchon epónymos* four plays, consisting of three tragedies and one satyr play. The nature of the satyr play will be explained later. This group of four plays was known in later times as a tetralogy, and the three tragedies taken by themselves were known as a trilogy. Throughout the fifth century there was never a dearth of competitors. From the applicants the *árchon* selected three, to each of whom he assigned a *choregós* nominated by him from the citizen body as a whole. The rules relating to the *choregoí* and the judges were the same as for the dithyramb. The prize was a goat. The word *tragoidía* means properly "goat-song."

The reason why the dithyrambic competition was tribal and the dramatic non-tribal is not clear. It seems probable that the tribal character of the former was anterior to the reorganisation of the festival by Kleisthenes, because otherwise it is hard to see why he should have discriminated between them. The hypothesis that suggests itself is that the dithyrambic contest existed in some form before the tyranny of Peisistratos, who in taking it over left its tribal character undisturbed, but took care to place the dramatic contest, which was new, on a more popular basis.

More important is the wider question why all the performances at this festival, dithyrambic and dramatic alike, were competitive. There is nothing corresponding to this feature in mediæval drama. The competition was very keen. Rich citizens vied with one another as *choregoí* for the sake of political prestige. Not only was the *árchon* who selected the three tetralogies a political officer who changed from year to year, but the method of assigning them to the three *choregoí* nominated by him did not preclude the possibility of collusion between the *choregós* and the poet. In 493 B.C. a tragedy called *The Sack of Miletos* was produced by Phrynichos. Its subject was the fall of that city at the close of the Ionian revolt. The play aroused great indignation—evidently among the adherents of the pro-Persian Alkmaionidai—and the author was fined. Seventeen years later Themistokles dedicated a votive tablet commemorating a victory won at the tragic contests by him as *choregós* and Phrynichos as poet.[2] We cannot affirm that Themistokles was *choregós* to *The Sack of Miletos*, but it is impossible not to suspect that he had a hand in its production. It was, of course, unusual for the subject of a tragedy to be drawn from contemporary life, but in many of the extant tragedies, especially by Æschylus and Euripides, the myths are handled with open reference to political events, and it follows that both the choice of the *árchon* and the verdict of the judges must have been influenced, consciously in some cases, by political bias.

What, then, was the origin of this element of civic rivalry represented by the institution of the *choregía*? It was not the only institution of its kind. Besides the *choregós*, there was the *gymnasíarchos* and the *hestiátor*, both nominated in the manner described, the former for training boys for the athletic festivals, the latter for giving public feasts to the members of his tribe. The generic term for services of this kind was *leitourgía*, which is derived from *léiton* or *láiton*, the Æolic equivalent of *prytaneîon*. These "services in the Men's House" carry us back to the days before Theseus, when every Attic village settlement had its own *prytaneîon* (pp. 74–5), in which the tribesmen met under the presidency of the local chief for ritual celebrations, preparing boys for initiation, and communal meals. The *leitourgíai* are the form in which these primitive customs had been reorganised under the democratic constitution—reorganised rather than revived, because there is evidence that they had lingered on under the aristocracy in the practice of keeping open house. Thus, we are told by Plutarch, with references to Aristotle and Kratinos, that Kimon the son of Miltiades used to keep at home a table plain but sufficient for a large number, to which all members of his *dêmos* had free access:[3]

> Kimon's generosity outdid all the old Athenian hospitality and liberality. . . . By offering the use of his house as a *prytaneîon* and by permitting travellers to eat the fruits growing on his estate, he seemed to restore to the world that community of goods which is fabled to have existed in the reign of Kronos.

In thus acting as a *hestiátor* on his own account, Kimon, who was very proud of his aristocratic traditions, was evidently maintaining an old family custom, in which Plutarch rightly recognises a relic of primitive communism.

Our next task must be to solve, if possible, the problems presented by the tetralogy. Why was the candidate for the tragic prize required to offer three tragedies and a satyr play?

The satyr play resembled tragedy in its structure, but in tone it was burlesque, and its chorus always represented a band of satyrs. The satyrs were mythical creatures part man, part beast. Their origin is at present unknown. The evidence relating to them has been assembled by Pickard-Cambridge together with a full statement of the insuperable objections to the theory (based on a misunderstanding of Aristotle) that the satyr play represents the original element in the art of tragedy,

from which tragedy proper was an offshoot.⁴ Pickard-
Cambridge's treatment of this question leaves nothing to be
desired, but, since it is possible in my opinion to extract from
the evidence a more positive conclusion than he has done, it
is necessary to deal briefly with certain points.

First of all, let us take the ancient tradition. It was
Arion at Corinth who "first introduced satyrs speaking in
verse," and it was Pratinas of Phlious (a few miles south of
Corinth) who "first produced satyr plays." Pratinas had
settled at Athens, where he competed with Æschylus for
the tragic prize between 499 and 496 B.C. He is said to have
written fifty plays, of which thirty-two were satyric. It follows that
he must have been competing at Athens before the rule of the
tetralogy came into force, otherwise the ratio between these
two figures cannot be explained. Now, we know that the
festival was reorganised during the last decade of the sixth
century—probably in 502/1 B.C., and it is therefore very likely
that the rule of the tetralogy was instituted then. This conclusion, that, so far from representing the kernel of tragedy, the
satyr play was a late accretion, is confirmed by a consideration
of its structure, which, so far as can be judged from the extant
remains, followed exactly the same lines as tragedy. If the
satyric chorus is regarded as a survival of the primitive form of
the tragic chorus, it becomes impossible to explain why there are
no other primitive features in the structure of the satyr play.
Nothing further need be said here regarding the other arguments adduced for this theory, which have been rebutted by
Pickard-Cambridge. My conclusion is therefore as follows.
Of the early history of satyric drama at Corinth and Phlious,
nothing is known beyond the bare facts recorded in the tradition already mentioned. It was imported into the Athenian
convention by Pratinas during the last quarter of the sixth
century B.C. and its structure was then assimilated to that of
tragedy, which was already approaching maturity. Finally,
in the last decade of the century, when the City Dionysia was
reorganised, it was given a permanent place in the new convention of the tetralogy, which it retained almost without exception throughout the ensuing century.

Before proceeding further, we must pause to deal with a

difficulty which has been raised—gratuitously, as it seems to me—by Pickard-Cambridge himself. Aristotle's statement that "tragedy arose from the leaders of the dithyramb" has been discussed at length in a previous chapter, where it was found to accord both with the internal Greek evidence and with the conclusions drawn from our general study of primitive ritual. Aristotle continues in the same passage as follows:[5]

> Beginning with small plots and humorous diction, on account of its satyr-like origin (*ek satyrikoû*), tragedy eventually became serious, and the iambic trimeter was substituted for the trochaic tetrameter, the latter having been employed at first on account of the satyr-like (*satyrikén*) and dance-like character of the poetry.

The question turns on the meaning of *satyrikós*, literally "satyr-like." This word had two applications. First, in general, it meant "like a satyr" or "pertaining to a satyr," just as *basilikós* meant "kingly" or "pertaining to a king." The satyrs were lascivious creatures, and the nearest equivalent to *satyrikós* in this sense was *hybristikós*, "lewd," "wanton," "obscene," "boisterous," "full of animal spirits." Secondly, it was used in a technical sense with special reference to satyr plays, which were commonly called *sátyroi* but also sometimes *satyrika drámata*. Both senses follow naturally from the formation of the word. The first is not found earlier than Plutarch, while the second is attested by Plato, but, since the word does not occur more than a dozen times in all, this discrepancy is insignificant, and in fact it can be shown that the first sense was almost certainly familiar to Plato, who speaks of a *sátyros hybristés*, a "wanton satyr," just as Plutarch describes someone as *satyrikos kai hybristikós*, "wanton and satyr-like."[6]

Which, then, did Aristotle mean—that tragedy was originally boisterous, wanton, obscene, or that it originated in the satyr drama? Since either interpretation is linguistically possible, the point must be decided in the light of the general probabilities of the case. There is no evidence that the dithyramb had any connection with satyr drama, or that Aristotle thought it had. Therefore, if we understand him to mean that tragedy originated in the satyr drama, we are imputing to him a

contradiction. The alternative interpretation involves no difficulty at all. Originally, he says, tragedy was not serious; its plots
were petty, its diction was comic—it was low, lewd, obscene.
We are reminded of the dithyramb of Archilochos, performed
when the leader was "thunderstruck with wine." It seems clear,
therefore, that this is what Aristotle meant.

I have dwelt on this question at some length, because
Pickard-Cambridge's treatment of it is a very serious blemish
on an excellent book.[7] After admitting that "we cannot tell"
in which sense the word is used by Aristotle, he expresses the
opinion that "the balance of probability is in favour of the
literal interpretation," i.e. the technical sense, referring to
satyr drama, but repeats his caveat that this interpretation
"cannot be held to be beyond dispute." Then, throwing his
own caveat to the winds, he proceeds to argue as though the
alternative interpretation did not exist, and so, having convicted
Aristotle of self-contradiction, reaches the following conclusion:[8]

> We have, in short, to admit with regret that it is impossible
> to accept Aristotle's authority without question, and that he
> was probably using that liberty of theorising which those
> modern scholars who ask us to accept him as infallible have
> certainly not abandoned.

It is not necessary to believe in the infallibility of Aristotle in
order to see that the method by which Pickard-Cambridge
sets aside his authority at this vital point is thoroughly falla-
cious; and it is a matter for regret that a critic who has exposed
so many pitfalls underlying current theories of the origin of
tragedy should have stumbled into a ditch of his own digging.

It is more than likely that the celebrations of the Dionysiac
thíasos contained much that we should describe as obscene.
Primitive ritual abounds in sexual self-expression of all kinds,
because its function is to make things grow by means of mimetic
magic; and at the same time it is quite serious, because the
fulfilment of that function is a stern necessity. But, as the real
technique of production develops, the magical element decays,
and then two things may happen. The ritual may pass into the
official liturgy of a ruling class. In that case it becomes repressive, and the element of sexual self-expression is either eliminated

or else confined within prescribed limits. Or, alternatively, abandoned by the ruling class, it survives among the peasantry, for whom it provides a release from the inhibitions induced by social repression through obscene and riotous behaviour. In an earlier chapter it was argued that this was the stage which the Dionysiac passion play had reached at the time when it was adopted by the state as part of the City Dionysia. This created a new tension, which had an important effect on its development. While the middle class strove to refine its intellectual content and to remove it from direct contact with reality, the peasantry and urban proletariat continued to seek in it the fulfilment of its earlier function. The result was that, as Aristotle says, it took a long time to become serious. Indeed, the comic element was never entirely eliminated. While it was being extruded from the tragedies, it reappeared in the satyr play, and on this basis at the end of the sixth century the art-form attained a final equilibrium, which owed its stability to the fact that in the meantime the comic element was finding a new and independent outlet. Thus the evolution of tragedy and the emergence of comedy were both directly related to the interplay of internal tensions which is the dynamic of society.

In regard to comedy, I shall confine attention to those aspects which illustrate most clearly its connection with the art of tragedy. Starting from a comparison of the structure of Aristophanic comedy with the peasant festivals of modern Macedonia, which contain one or two specifically Dionysiac elements, Cornford has argued that Attic comedy is founded on the ritual pattern of death and resurrection which has been interpreted in the present work in the light of primitive initiation—the same ritual, in fact, to which I have traced the origin of tragedy.[9] Cornford's theory is in need of modification at certain points. Assuming that both the Macedonian ritual and the structure of Attic comedy were more coherent than they really were, he has endeavoured in my opinion to prove too much. On the other hand, I am convinced that his general thesis—that comedy is derived from primitive ritual of the type which I have discussed in Chapter VIII—is sound. It is necessary to insist on this, because his theory has been challenged *in toto* by Pickard-Cambridge, who has no difficulty in pointing out incidental defects but shows himself quite unable to appreciate its essential significance.[10] Pickard-Cambridge's point of view is that several of the features of comedy which Cornford has sought to explain are "natural." Thus, discussing the part of the Cook in the *Knights*, who, as Cornford perceives, is related to the traditional doctor who restores the dead to life, he answers Cornford as follows:[11]

> The rejuvenation by cooking is surely no more than a reminiscence of the story of Medea and Pelias in a comic context—a variation on the rejuvenation of an elderly person which certainly does occur in several plays, and is natural enough in a comedy in which the old rustic was a traditional character and would be granted his heart's desire best by becoming young again. It needs no ritual to explain this.

To this criticism, it may be suspected, Cornford would reply, quite rightly, that it leaves unexplained all the things that require to be explained. What is the significance of the myth of Medea and Pelias? Why was the old rustic a traditional character? Why does the theme of rejuvenation occur in several plays? For Pickard-Cambridge it is sufficient to say that these things were "natural." The same point of view is expressed in his comment on the evidence relating to the animal disguises of the comic chorus.[12]

> Indeed, the practice of dressing up in the guise of animals is world-wide; in some countries it may go back to a totemistic origin; in others (or in the same) it may be connected with magic rites for securing the fertility of the ground or of the human species; and very often, probably oftener than anthropologists always allow, it may have been done just for fun, either because any religious reason for the custom has long been forgotten, or (perhaps more often) because the child in mankind dies hard.

It is world-wide, it may have been this or that, or it may have been just for fun. Such remarks as these show that Pickard-Cambridge's mind moves within a narrow circle. Within that circle, no student of Greek drama is more thorough and acute; outside it, he does not think at all. The last remark, that the child in mankind dies hard, is to me unintelligible.

Like the dithyramb, comedy developed in Attica under influences from the Peloponnese. The medium through which these influences were conveyed was probably immigration, which, as we have seen, was going on throughout the sixth century. Unfortunately we know very little about Peloponnesian drama.[13] There is evidence from an early period of a ritual drama connected with the cult of Artemis Orthia at Sparta and comprising two traditional figures, the quack-doctor and the old woman, which we meet again in Attic comedy; but these figures have a wide distribution, both in antiquity and in the Middle Ages, and it cannot therefore be assumed that Attic comedy derived them from the Peloponnese. There is also a record—probably from Sikyon, but the locality is not certain—of a band of mummers who entered the orchestra improvising a hymn to Dionysus. Their leader, whose face was smeared with soot, carried the phallus. After the hymn was finished, they ran up to individuals among the audience and mocked at them. It is tempting to recognise in the phallus the prototype of the modern maypole. The Black Man, whom we have already met at Eleutherai as Melanthos, is another traditional figure. The mocking of the bystanders is clearly related to the function of the Aristophanic *parábasis*.

It was in Megara, however, that Peloponnesian drama developed most rapidly and fully; and, since Megara is only a few miles across the Attic frontier, it may be regarded as certain that Attic comedy owed a good deal to this source. Moreover, we are expressly told that Megarian comedy developed under the democracy, which was established about 580 B.C.; and, since Megara was the first Peloponnesian state (perhaps, in the sixth century, the only one) to attain this stage, we have here a plain indication that comedy no less than tragedy was bound up with the democratic movement.

Attic comedy originated at the Dionysiac festival of the Lenaia, celebrated in December and probably identical with the Country Dionysia which was held about the same time in the Attic villages.[14] In 487/6 B.C. competitions in comedy were officially instituted at the City Dionysia on the same basis as the tragic contests, except that the comic poet competed with a single play. It is noteworthy that this date falls at a time when Themistokles, the leader of the radical democrats, was at the height of his power. It is possible that similar competitions were already being held unofficially at the Lenaia, but these did not receive state recognition until 442 B.C.

The Lenaia was originally a feast of the Lenai or "mad-women": that is to say, it was based on the ritual of a Dionysiac *thíasos*. It began, like the City Dionysia, with a *pompé*, the character of which can be partly deduced from Aristophanes' parody of the *pompé* at the Country Dionysia.[15] The procession was headed by girls carrying sacrificial baskets and followed by a male choir whose leader carried the phallus. As they marched, the choir improvised a hymn, in the course of which they jeered at individuals among the crowd of spectators. An animal was sacrificed, and probably at this point a priest pronounced the words "Call the god!" to which the congregation responded, "Dionysus, son of Semele, giver of wealth!"[16] It is to be presumed that the sacrifice was followed by a *kômos*. The word *komoidía* means "*kômos*-song." Thus, the ritual of the Lenaia reveals the same sequence—*pompé, agón, kômos*—which we have already traced at the City Dionysia; and the possibility suggests itself that the latter festival had been consciously modelled on the Lenaia.

The comedies of Aristophanes (444–388 B.C.) are based on a structural pattern subject to considerable variation, but nevertheless clearly marked. The principal elements are the *párodos* or entry of the chorus: the *agón*, an altercation or debate sometimes preceded by a fight; the *parábasis*, in which the poet addresses the audience through his chorus on personal and political matters; and the *éxodos*, which usually has the character of a *kômos*. Interspersed between these are scenes of iambic dialogue in which one or more characters take part, and the *párodos* is preceded by a prologue.

Aristotle says that comedy arose "from the leaders of the phallic hymn," just as tragedy arose from the leaders of the dithyramb.[17] What he means is clearly that it was the leader of the phallic hymn who by speaking in character transformed the ritual into drama, just as it was the leader of the dithyramb who became the tragic actor. It is generally agreed by modern critics that the prologue and other iambic scenes, in which the dramatic element is concentrated, are of later origin than the other parts; and, when these are eliminated, we are left with the *párodos*, which we recognise as the *pompé*, the *agón*, the *parábasis*, and the *éxodos* or *kômos*. Apart from the character of the *agón*, which is clearly founded on a ritual mock-fight, and the *parábasis*, which is peculiar to comedy, this is the sequence we have already identified as the substructure of tragedy. The two art-forms go back to a common origin.

The comic element in the tragic convention, represented by the satyr play, has now been accounted for, and it remains to be considered why the tragedies were composed in groups of three. On this question I wrote in my edition of the *Oresteia*:[18]

> I do not believe that Æschylus invented the trilogy. The practice of composing tragedies in groups of three, even though they dealt with different themes, is not likely to have arisen from the innovation of a particular dramatist, nor would it have persisted after its significance had disappeared unless it had formed an ancient and fundamental part of the tragic convention.

This argument is demonstrably unsound. Why the Æschylean practice of composing tetralogies on a single theme was eventually abandoned is a question which will be considered in due course; but, since all the evidence goes to show that the satyr play was a late accretion, the assumption that the trilogy was primitive cannot be sustained.

In this matter I was misled by the seductive hypothesis, suggested by Murray, but unsupported by the evidence, that the trilogy was designed to represent the birth, death and resurrection of the god.[19] That the art of tragedy goes back to ritual of this type seems to me certain, and the credit for discovering it belongs mainly to Jane Harrison, whose study of Greek religion was the starting-point for Cornford's work on comedy and Murray's on tragedy; but, whereas Cornford rightly looked for ritual vestiges in the basic structure of comedy, Murray concentrated his attention mainly upon the tragic plots, which from this point of view are a superficial element, and consequently in his case the hypothesis broke down. The trilogy is capable of a simpler explanation.

The plots of early tragedy, so Aristotle tells us, were small. How were they enlarged? A serious obstacle was presented by the chorus. The actor might change characters, but the chorus necessarily remained the same throughout the play. The only way in which this difficulty could be surmounted was to multiply the number of the plays. The several plays of the Greek trilogy corresponded functionally to the several acts of the Elizabethan play: they served to extend the scope of the plot by effecting complete breaks in the action. Without the trilogy, it would have been impossible for Æschylus to treat at length the myth of Œdipus, which was one of the themes he handled in this way. The first play dealt with the father, the second with the son, the third with the son's sons. Thus, the whole trilogy covered three generations. Sophokles, it is true, covered the first two generations in a single play, the *Œdipus Tyrannus*, but he was only able to achieve this masterpiece of concentration because he had behind him his predecessor's achievements on the larger scale.

To the question, did Æschylus invent the trilogy, all that can be replied is that he is known to have been writing not more than six years after the date at which the rule of the tetralogy was probably established in its final form, and therefore it is likely enough that he had a hand in fixing it. What is certain is that it was Æschylus who brought the tetralogy to perfection. We have seen how it had grown out of the social history of the period. Æschylus worked at it and fashioned it into a dramatic form which for breadth of scope, organic unity, and cumulative intensity, can only be compared with the symphony of Beethoven.

Some doubt has been expressed in modern times regarding the artistic propriety of the satyr play, and it must be admitted that the *Ichneutai* of Sophokles and the *Cyclops* of Euripides (the only ones that survive) cannot have done much to enhance the effect of the tragedies that preceded them. In the case of Æschylus, however, there are two reasons, apart from the paucity of the evidence, why we should withhold judgment. As a writer of satyr plays, he was regarded by the ancients as so far superior to Sophokles and Euripides that, while he was placed first, the second place was given to a dramatist whose work is unknown to us, Achaios of Eretria. Furthermore, the Æschylean satyr play was an organic part of the tetralogy. Thus, the *Proteus*, which followed the trilogy of the *Oresteia*, dealt with the adventures of Menelaos after the Trojan War as a *scherzo* to his brother's tragic homecoming; and it is not difficult to imagine a *Proteus* charged with the romantic atmosphere of the *Odyssey* which would round off in a whirl of irresponsible gaiety the liturgical grandeur of the *Oresteia*.[20]

Even more significant was his treatment of the trilogy itself. In his hands, as we shall see in the next chapter, it became a vehicle perfectly adapted to the natural movement of his thought, being designed to express the offence, the counteroffence, and the reconciliation—strife and the reward of strife, the resolution of discord into harmony, the triumph of democracy.

XV

ORESTEIA

ÆSCHYLUS was a native of Eleusis. His father's name was Euphorion. We do not know the name of his clan, but his family belonged to the Eupatridai. This is important, because it means that he was heir to an aristocratic tradition going back to the tribal society of primitive Attica. The year of his birth was 525 B.C. He was therefore old enough to remember the tyranny of Hippias and to vote on the democratic reforms of Kleisthenes. He made his *début* at the City Dionysia in the year 500, but did not win the prize until fifteen years later. He fought at Marathon, where his brother Kynegeiros was killed, and again at Salamis. He is said to have composed about ninety plays in all, of which only seven have survived. Most of his life was spent in Attica, but he paid at least two visits to the court of Hieron, tyrant of Syracuse, where some of his plays were produced—the first about 471 B.C. and the second after the production of the *Oresteia* in 458. He died at Gela two years later, leaving a son, Euphorion, who won four victories with tetralogies which his father had composed but not produced.[1]

He is described by Cicero as being "a Pythagorean as well as a poet—such is the tradition."[2] Cicero had studied at Athens, so that, even if it were not abundantly confirmed by the internal evidence of the surviving plays, there would be no reason to reject this tradition, and Wilamowitz's attitude on this point —he dismisses the statement as a "lapse of memory" on Cicero's part—can only be described as perverse. It is also clear that Æschylus was deeply imbued with the mystical traditions of his birthplace. According to one tradition, not very well authenticated, some of the costumes he had designed for the tragic stage were taken over by the high priests of Eleusis. It might appear on the face of it that the borrowing would rather have been the other way, but we must remember that the

Eleusinian Mysteries were being reorganised in this period no
less than the City Dionysia, and therefore the tradition may
be accepted as evidence of interaction between them. According to another, which goes back to Aristotle, Æschylus was
prosecuted for revealing in his plays some of the mystical
secrets, but was acquitted on the plea that he was unaware
that they were secrets. We shall see that the dramatic use of
mystical ideas is an outstanding feature of the *Oresteia*.

Of the seven surviving plays, the *Suppliants* is generally agreed
to be the earliest and is usually assigned to the first decade of
the century. The *Persians* was produced in 472, the *Seven against
Thebes* in 467, and the *Oresteia* in 458. The date of the *Prometheus Bound* is still controversial, but for reasons which I have
given elsewhere I believe that this is the latest of the extant
plays, and the possibility cannot be excluded that it was one
of those produced posthumously by Euphorion.[3]

The *Suppliants* and *Prometheus* were the first plays in their
respective tetralogies, the *Persians* was the second, and the
Seven was the third. The *Oresteia* is a complete trilogy—the only
one we possess. Moreover, with the exception of the *Persians*,
all these plays belonged to tetralogies of the interconnected or
unitary type. The *Suppliants* and *Prometheus* are first acts, and
the *Seven against Thebes* is a third act, in dramas of which the
remainder has in each case been lost. Without the *Oresteia*, we
should have no means of determining how Æschylus welded
his three tragedies into a whole; with it, we have indirect
evidence of considerable value for the problems presented by
the other plays. For these reasons it is expedient, despite the
chronological order, to give first place to the *Oresteia*.

When Pelops died, he left two sons, Atreus and Thyestes,
who disputed the succession. Atreus drove his brother out of
the country, but some time later, on the pretext of a reconciliation, he recalled him and entertained him to a feast at which
he served up to him the flesh of his children, whom he had
secretly murdered. When Thyestes discovered the crime, he
cursed the House of Pelops. After the death of Atreus, the
kingdom was divided between his sons, Agamemnon and
Menelaos, who had married two sisters, Clytemnestra and
Helen. Menelaos was visited by Paris, a son of the King of

Troy, who fell in love with Helen and eloped with her. That was the occasion of the Trojan War. The Greeks assembled at Aulis under the leadership of Agamemnon, but the departure of the expedition was delayed by a storm. Agamemnon was told by his prophet Kalchas that the storm was due to the anger of Artemis, who could only be appeased by the sacrifice of his daughter Iphigeneia. Accordingly, Odysseus was sent to Argos to fetch the girl from her mother on the pretext that she was to be married to Achilles, and she was slaughtered by her father. The expedition then sailed for Troy. Shortly afterwards, Clytemnestra began an intrigue with Aigisthos, a son of Thyestes who had escaped the feast which Atreus had given to his father. In order to facilitate her intrigue, she had her son Orestes, then a child, sent away to Phokis. The war lasted ten years. When Troy fell, the Greeks incurred the anger of the gods by plundering the temples, and consequently the fleet was scattered by thunder and lightning. Menelaos and Odysseus disappeared and did not return for many years. Agamemnon returned in safety, but was murdered by his wife with the complicity of her paramour. Kasandra, a daughter of the Trojan King, whom he had brought home as a concubine, was murdered at the same time. Some years later, Orestes received a command from Apollo's oracle at Delphi to avenge his father's murder. Returning in secret with his friend, Pylades, the son of his host at Phokis, he revealed himself to his surviving sister, Elektra, and with her assistance killed both his mother and Aigisthos. Pursued by his mother's avenging spirits, the Erinyes, he fled to Delphi, where he was purified by Apollo. Still harried by the Erinyes, who refused to recognise the validity of his purification, he continued his wanderings until at last he was tried and acquitted on the charge of matricide at the Athenian Court of the Areopagus, founded for this purpose by Athena.

Such is the story of Orestes as told by Æschylus.[4] The same story is told in the Homeric poems, but with no mention of the feast of Atreus, the sacrifice of Iphigeneia, the Delphic oracle, the persecution by the Erinyes, the purification by Apollo, or the trial for matricide. In judging the significance of these omissions, it has to be remembered, on the one hand, that Homer does not purport to tell the story in full and, on the other, that there is a general tendency in epic to modify popular tradition in the interests of the monarchy. The feast of Atreus is a myth of the same type as the feast of Tantalos discussed in an earlier chapter (p. 113); the custom of human sacrifice at the inauguration of a campaign is attested elsewhere as a feature of early monarchy combined with a politically powerful priesthood;[5] and the persecution of Orestes by his mother's Erinyes points to matrilineal descent. Of these three elements, which may all be regarded as primitive, the third survived independently in various local traditions.[6] In one of these, Orestes was cured of his madness by sitting on a stone fetish called Zeus Kappotas, which was evidently a thunderstone; in another, he was cured after gnawing away one of his fingers, and dedicated a thank-offering of hair to the Erinyes. In a third, he was purified by nine men of Troizen at a holy stone in front of a temple of Artemis. In all these traditions Apollo plays no part, and in the third the idea of purification seems to have been superimposed on a pre-anthropomorphic cult like that of Zeus Kappotas. It may be inferred therefore that the purification by Apollo belongs to the period of the landed aristocracy, and this inference is supported by other evidence. It was during this period that the Spartans procured an oracle from Delphi authorising the removal of Orestes' bones from Tegea to Sparta in order to reinforce their claim to the political hegemony of the Peloponnese,[7] and there is reason to believe that the lost *Oresteia* of Stesichoros was designed to serve Spartan interests. Lastly, the trial at the Areopagus is clearly an Athenian accretion, developed in conscious opposition to the Spartan version. It was probably Æschylus himself who assigned the rôle of prosecutors to the Erinyes and made the trial of Orestes the occasion for the institution of the Court. In the *Elektra* of Euripides the Erinyes simply vanish into the ground, overcome with grief at their defeat. In the *Eumenides*, too, they vanish into the ground, but conducted amidst popular rejoicing by Athena's escort. We may take it then that the escort and all that it implies was added by Æschylus. Thus, as he tells it, the story of Orestes is a stratified piece of social history embodying

the accumulated deposits of the primitive tribe, the early
monarchy, aristocracy and democracy.[8]

The opening of the *Agamemnon* is designed with reference to
a distinctive feature of the plot. Clytemnestra is a conspirator
and cannot speak her mind. Shakespeare would probably have
revealed her purpose, as Seneca did, in a dialogue with
Aigisthos or in soliloquies and asides; but the method of
Æschylus is more economical. We hear her before we see her;
we see her long before she speaks. Each time she appears at
the threshold of the palace, the words of the Chorus provide
an unconscious comment on what is passing in her mind, so
that, when at last she speaks, we are ready to catch the hidden
meaning in her words and are thus prepared for the final
revelation of her motive, which is the more impressive because
so long deferred.

The hour is shortly after midnight, the season late autumn,
marked by the setting of the Pleiades, when it became
dangerous to cross the sea. The Watchman has been on duty
since the beginning of the year, the tenth of the war and,
according to prophecy, the last.

He is tired, and longs to be released (1–2):

> I've prayed God to deliver me from evil
> Throughout a long year's vigil.

A little later this prayer is repeated, but in consequence of
what has intervened its significance has changed—it has
become a prayer, not merely for his own release, but for the
deliverance of the House he serves from the curse that hangs
over it (16–21):

> And when I start to sing or hum a tune,
> And out of music cull sleep's antidote,
> I always weep the state of this great House,
> Not in high fettle as it used to be.
> But now at last may good news in a flash
> Scatter the darkness and deliver us!

"Deliverance from evil" or "from labour" was one of many
phrases which had passed into common speech from the

language of the mysteries, in which, as we have seen, it denoted the means whereby the mystic hoped to attain that state of spiritual bliss which was the reward of purification from the evils of mortality. The Watchman has no thought of this significance, but in the course of the trilogy it is gradually brought out.

The conquerors are asleep in the captured city, unconscious of the disasters that await them (347-9):

> Free from the frosty sky,
> From heaven's dew delivered—O how blest
> Their sleep shall be, off guard the whole night long!

While Orestes is murdering his mother, the Trojan serving-women, who have fondly persuaded themselves that the House has at last been purified, chant a hymn, which, as will be seen later, is based on Eleusinian ritual (Cho. 941-4):

> Cry alleluia, lift up in the house a song,
> Deliverance from ill and from the waste of wealth
> By the unholy sinners twain,
> From rough thorny ways.

Soon afterwards the purifier is himself in desperate need of purification (Cho. 1057-8) and he is instructed by Apollo to go to Athens (Eum. 81-3):

> For there,
> With judgment of thy suit and palliatives
> Of speech, we shall find out at last a way
> From all these evils to deliver thee.

Hunted down by the Erinyes, the fugitive throws himself on the mercy of Athena (Eum. 297-8):

> O may she come—far off, she still can hear—
> And from these miseries deliver me!

The Watchman prayed to the gods. The second play opens with another prayer, to Hermes, the intermediary between the living and the dead; and at the beginning of the third the Delphic priestess prays to Pallas (Athena), Loxias (Apollo) and

other deities, ending with Zeus the Perfecter (*Eum.* 28). It was
the custom after supper to offer a grace of unmixed wine, first
to the gods of Olympus, next to the spirits of the dead, and
finally to Zeus the Third, also called the Perfecter or Deliverer;
and in the *Agamemnon* the Chorus relate how, in the happy
days before the war, the girl Iphigeneia used to sing a hymn
of thanksgiving for her father at the performance of this ceremony (254–8). But Iphigeneia has been murdered, and standing over the dead body of her murderer the triumphant mother
cries (1384–6):

> Then on his fallen body
> I dealt the third blow, my drink-offering
> To the Zeus of Hell, Deliverer of the dead.

Intent on murdering his mother and her paramour, Orestes
takes up the blasphemy (*Cho.* 574–6):

> My steel shall strike and make a corpse of him,
> And so a Fury never starved of slaughter
> Shall drain her third draught of unmingled blood.

The Fury is the Erinys. After much suffering Orestes is delivered
(*Eum.* 757–63):

> O Pallas, O deliverer of my house,
> I was an outcast from my country, thou
> Hast brought me home again; and men shall say,
> Once more he is an Argive, and he dwells
> In his paternal heritage by the grace
> Of Pallas, and of Loxias, and third
> Of him who orders all, Deliverer.

Let us now return to the *Agamemnon*. The Watchman's task
has been imposed on him by the sanguine hopes of a woman
(10–11), the wife of Agamemnon (26), Clytemnestra (84), who
is now dreaming of victory. When at daybreak she announces
that Troy has fallen, the news will be dismissed by many as an
idle dream, too good to be true (286, 496); but, after its truth
has been proved, the deepening conviction that she is working
for another victory will turn this dream into a nightmare (966–
84). At the beginning of the second play this woman will dream,

not of victory, but of retribution (*Cho.* 32–41), and again her dream will come true (*Cho.* 928); and, finally, the dreamer will herself become a dream, stirring the drowsy Erinyes to revenge (*Eum.* 116).

This woman has the will of a man (11). Her personality is masculine (363), though she herself ironically disclaims it (361, 1661, *Cho.* 668–9); and she lacks the modesty that becomes her sex (618–19, 847, 931, 1372, *Cho.* 627–8). Yet her feminine charm, when she cares to exercise it, is irresistible (932–4). Her story of the beacons is scoffed at as a piece of woman's folly (489–93), but she is not deflected from her purpose (595–9). When her suspicions are aroused by the disguised Orestes, Aigisthos is inclined to discount them as the scare of a frightened woman (*Cho.* 844–5), but when the moment comes for action, it is the woman who cries, "Bring me a man-axe!" (*Cho.* 888).

Unlike his mistress, the Watchman dares not dream (12–15). To keep awake, he sings, but his song turns into a lament for the House of Atreus. Then, after his prayer for deliverance, he sees the beacon flash. The blessed light has shone, the darkness has been scattered, tears are turned into joy.

Having hailed the beacon, the Watchman calls the Queen to raise the alleluia, and begins to dance for joy—but breaks off abruptly, arrested by some unexpressed misgiving. His joy is indeed delusive. Later in the day the inspired imagination of a prophetess will see the Erinyes dancing on the roof where he has danced (1185–9) and hear their fearful alleluias (1105–7). Again and again such premature rejoicing will pass into brooding premonition. The Chorus of old men enter with firm confidence in the past, but before long they are seeking to allay their fears for the future (99–103). Reverting to the past, they recall the auspicious beginning of the war, but then they remember the terrible price paid for it, the sacrifice of Iphigeneia, so that, when the dawn breaks at last, it seems to herald, not the deliverance for which the Watchman prayed, but worse calamity (259–69). After the Queen's announcement, they begin a joyful hymn of thanksgiving for the punishment of Paris (367), but the hymn ends with anxiety for Agamemnon (465–76). The Herald salutes the rising sun in an ecstasy of joy (513, 580) but he is soon forced to confess that victory has

already been overtaken by disaster. The Elders are at pains to
greet Agamemnon in a spirit befitting the occasion (774–800),
then they have to watch helplessly while he walks into the trap;
and after a final struggle between hope and fear (966–1018)
they surrender themselves in fascinated horror to the inevitable.
So in the second play. The Chorus of serving-women, confident
of victory, urge the brother and sister to pray for revenge; but
later, losing heart, they can foresee nothing but disaster (461–
73). While Orestes is at his task, they rejoice in the deliverance
of the House (934–70), but at the close of the play they are
asking in despair when will its afflictions cease. Not until
the end of the trilogy will tribulation issue in true and lasting
joy.

All this is latent in the Watchman's speech. Overcome with
doubts, he seeks refuge in silence (36–9):

> The rest is secret—a heavy ox has trod
> Across my tongue. These walls, if they had mouths,
> Might tell tales all too plainly. I speak to those
> Who know, to others—purposely forget.

The mystery is for "those who understand." With these words
the Watchman disappears into the palace, and then, as if in
response, we hear out of the darkness "Alleluia!"—Clytemnestra's cry of joy.

In the *párodos*, and again in the first *stásimon*, the poet begins
by taking our minds back ten years to the beginning of the war.
Together they form the longest choral passage in his extent
work, and of the *stásima* which follow each is shorter than the
last—a device by which the *tempo* is quickened as we approach
the crisis. Absorbed in the past, we forget the present, and when
the action is resumed, the plot advances so rapidly that we
accept without question the poet's time-scheme, in which
widely separated events are compressed within a single day.

The *párodos* provides a background for the first appearance
of the Queen. The sons of Atreus, in their anger at the rape of
Helen, are likened to two eagles robbed of their young. The
discrepancy is striking and deliberate. The eagles appeal to the
gods, who visit the transgressor with an Erinys (59). At this
point Clytemnestra comes out of the palace and begins to

sacrifice in silence at the shrines standing at the gates. Meanwhile, still thinking of Paris, the Elders declare that the sinner's sacrifice is vain. Then they speak of themselves; too old to fight, they have been left at home, as feeble as children or dreams floating in the daylight (79–82). Finally, they catch sight of Clytemnestra, turn to her and ask what is her news (99–103). Their question is left unanswered. The Queen silently leaves the stage on her way to the other altars of the city. We expected to hear her speak, but the climax has been postponed.

If the Elders are too old to fight, they are not too old to sing; and they sing of the sign from heaven which appeared at the departure of the expedition, and the prophet's reading of it. Two eagles appeared, devouring a hare in the last stages of pregnancy. The eagles are the kings (we observe that these are now the oppressors, not the oppressed), and the hare is Troy, destined to fall in the tenth year just as the hare was to have been delivered in the tenth month. But Artemis, goddess of childbirth and protectress of the wild, is offended, and demands in recompense another sacrifice. The first part of the prophet's interpretation was plain enough, but now he seems to foresee dimly things which even he does not understand (161–3):

> Terrible wrath that departs not,
> Treachery keeping the house, long-memoried,
> children-avenging.

At this point the fluent narrative is interrupted by a slow and grave meditation on the sovereignty of Zeus, who has laid down the law that man must learn wisdom by suffering (186–91):

> He to wisdom leadeth man,
> He hath stablished firm the law,
> Man shall learn by suffering.
> When deep slumber falls, remembered sins
> Chafe the sore heart with fresh pain, and no
> Welcome wisdom meets within.

The old Hesiodic proverb that suffering teaches sense, which was merely a warning to the man who sought too much, has here been charged with a new and positive value.

Conacher

When the story is resumed, the rhythm has become constrained and tense. The storm blows, Agamemnon wavers, the fleet is wasting, the voice of God has spoken, until, without pausing to question the priest's authority, the King is driven by imperial ambition to kill his own child, stifling her cries of evil omen.

> The arts of Kalchas achieved their purpose.
> But Justice leads man to wisdom by suffering
>   Until the morrow
> Appears, afflict not thy heart; for vain it is
> To weep before trouble comes.
> It shall be soon known as clear as daybreak.

During these words (260-6) Clytemnestra reappears on the threshold of the palace, standing against the background of her past.

Again, what news? This time she deigns to answer (276-9):

> Good news! So charged, as the old proverb says,
> May Morning rise out of the womb of Night!
> It is yours to hear of joy surpassing hope.
> My news is this: the Greeks have taken Troy!

And at the end of the dialogue, asked what time the city fell, she replies (291):

> The night that gave birth to this dawning day.

Her language is coloured by ten years of brooding over her murdered child. Then, impatient of her questioners, she breaks into an outburst of flamboyant rhetoric, tracing the course of the beacons relayed across the Ægean. Like the sun, or the moon, or a trailing comet, the light rises out of the darkness, and as it leaps from peak to peak it seems to change its character, swooping on the roof of the palace like a thunderbolt. Then, in a more sombre vein, the Queen describes what she imagines to be happening in Troy. The captives are mourning the death of those they loved, the conquerors are at rest. The Greeks have won, but they must respect the sanctuaries of the fallen city. Actually, like the Persians who plundered Attica, they did not. Like the prophet Kalchas (136), Clytemnestra qualifies her good news with a warning (353–6), to which she adds a thinly-veiled threat (357–9):

> And if they came guiltless before the gods,
> The grievance of the dead might then become
> Fair-spoken—barring sudden accident.

The second *stásimon* draws a subtly elaborated parallel between Paris and Agamemnon. Emboldened by riches, Paris grew proud and so incurred the jealousy of the gods. The spirit of Persuasion or Temptation raised his hopes, made him reckless, and so induced him to commit an overt act of insolence leading directly to his fall. All this, as we have seen, is traditional. The originality of the ode lies in the skill with which these traditional ideas are dramatised. As Headlam wrote:

> It opens with a confident Te Deum after triumph; by the time you reach the end you have gradually been plunged into the deepest gloom of apprehension: and the result has been achieved by the consummate skill of the transitions, which carry you from shore to shore, from thought to thought, as boldly and rapidly as the reflections of a rapid mind.

The opening meditation on the danger inherent in excessive prosperity (381–91) is ostensibly a comment on the fate of Paris, though the general terms in which it is couched invite a wider application; the fate of those who trample on inviolate sanctities (382–4) recalls Clytemnestra's warning (353–4); the compelling power of Temptation (396–7) reminds us of the sin of Agamemnon (232–3); and the sinner's prayers which win no hearing (406) are also familiar (69–71). The spirit of Temptation is embodied in Helen, who lured Paris and his people to destruction (413–24), and was mourned by Menelaos (425–34). And, just as he, bereft of the substance, was left with a dream (429–34), so all the Greeks who sent their loved ones to the war are repaid in urns and ashes (445–51). The people mutter in resentment against the war-lords who ordered all this bloodshed (456–8). Thus, by the end of the *stásimon*, our attention has been surreptitiously shifted. At the beginning (379–95):

By Zeus struck down, 'Tis truly spoken,
With each step clear and plain to track out. . . .
Help is there none for him who, glutted with gold, in wanton
Pride from his sight has kicked the great altar of watchful
  Justice.

That was Paris; but now it is Agamemnon (468–76):

> The black
> Furies wait, and when a man
> Has grown by luck, not justice, great,
> With sudden overturn of chance
> They wear him to a shade, and cast
> Down to perdition, who shall save him?
> In excess of fame is danger.
> With a jealous eye the lord Zeus in a flash shall smite him.

The old men conclude by pointing the moral—a prayer recalled
from the beginning (389–91) that they may be permitted to
lead the middle life, neither conquerors (like Agamemnon) nor
captives (like Kasandra).

  In language which mockingly reflects the imagery of her
beacon-speech the old men declare their doubts about Clytemnestra's story (482–507), only to be refuted by the arrival of
a Herald from the army. With tears of joy springing from bitter
memories of war he salutes the gods of his fatherland, which
he had never hoped to see again, and he bids the Elders prepare
a fitting welcome for his master (530–5):

> Him who with mattock of just-dealing Zeus
> Has levelled Troy and laid her valleys waste . . .
> Great son of Atreus, master, sovereign, blest.

"Call no man blest until he is dead." That was the proverb.
In the stress of emotion the Herald has applied to his master
the same invidious epithet which Clytemnestra has already
used with deliberate malice (348). Then comes a moment of
embàrrassment, as the Elders inadvertently let fall a hint of
treachery at home, but the Herald's anxious enquiries are
impulsively brushed aside: "Now it were joy to die" (555). In
his second speech he is more pensive. As he calls to mind the
hardships of war and the comrades who have not returned,

he falters, rallies, falters and with an effort rallies again. Scarcely has he recovered his serenity when the ominous figure of the Queen reappears at the palace door. Instead of promising him the expected largess for his good news, she declares that she has no need of him—she will welcome her master herself, being "as loyal as he left her . . . to enemies unkind, and in all else the same" (612–14); and after further menacing allusions to her secret intentions she retires abruptly into the palace. The Herald turns in dismay to the Elders, who, with an unlucky change of subject, enquire after Menelaos. It is now his turn to answer unwelcome questions. He is compelled to reveal that the fleet has been scattered by a storm, and the scene ends in deep gloom, which he endeavours in vain to dispel (676–7):

> And now, if any of those others live,
> Why, they must deem that *we* are dead and gone.

Menelaos is destined to survive, Agamemnon is not.

The Chorus resume the slow, meditative music which we heard in the first *stásimon* (170–93). Their theme is Helen, taken from the middle of the second *stásimon* (413–27) and aptly reintroduced after the news of Menelaos. The parallel between Paris and Agamemnon is now to be completed by another between Helen and Clytemnestra. Just as Helen tempted Paris, so her sister will tempt Agamemnon. She was like a lion-cub reared by a herdsman, at first the darling of old and young; at first tender and seductive, but in the end (746–8):

> With the guidance of the stern wrath
> Of Zeus she came as a bridal-bewailing Fury.

Her sister is again standing at the palace door, ready to welcome Agamemnon; and the old men continue as though in a dream, or like seers unaware of the meaning of what they see (762–5):

> Behold, whenever the time appointed come,
> A cloud of black night, spirit of vengeance irresistible,
> Horror of dark disaster hung brooding within the palace!

Then the conclusion, in which the conclusions of the two preceding *stásima* are combined and reinforced (767–73):

And where is Justice? She lights up the smoke-darkened hut,
Yea, she loves humility.
From gilded pinnacles of polluted hands
She turns her eyes back unto the dwelling of the pure in heart;
So, regarding not the false
Stamp on the face of wealth, leads all to the end appointed.

Agamemnon enters in the royal chariot at the head of a
triumphal procession, followed by another chariot in which is
seated the captive Kasandra. To the greeting of the Elders,
studied in its moderation and designed to warn him of his
danger, he replies (801–4):

> First, it is just to greet this land of Argos
> With her presiding gods, my partners in
> This homecoming, as in the just revenge
> I dealt to Priam's city.

With these words Justice, the leading motive of the trilogy,
steps from the orchestra to the stage, and with unconscious
irony the King couples together, as both ordained by heaven,
the fall of Troy and his own return to Argos. He acknowledges
the warning of the Elders as though already on his guard, but
then, secure in the sense of his own greatness, dismisses them
(842–5):

> But now, returning to my royal hearth,
> My first act shall be to salute the gods
> Who led me hence and lead me safely home.
> Victory attends me; may she rest secure!

Clytemnestra stands silent, waiting for her opportunity. Her
purpose is to induce him to commit an overt act of pride which
will symbolise the sin he is about to expiate. That is the
significance of the sacred tapestries on which she makes him
tread.

He addressed the assembled people, ignoring her. She retorts
by doing the same. There has never been any love between
these two. She begins slowly, in language cold and colourless,

as she describes the lot of the wife, left alone at home; she speaks too of her fears for his safety, though secretly she means her longing for his death; then, with an unobtrusive transition to direct address, she excuses the absence of Orestes; then, in a heightened tone, she reaffirms her love, her language becomes richer and more highly coloured, and after a magnificent crescendo of adulation, in which one extravagant image is piled upon another, she commands her servants to spread out the purple at their master's feet (896–904):

> And now, beloved,
> Step from the chariot, but do not plant
> Upon the ground those feet that trampled Troy.
> Make haste, my handmaids whom I have appointed
> To strew his path with outspread tapestry.
> Prepare a road of purple coverlets
> Where Justice leads to an unhoped-for home;
> And there the rest our sleep-unvanquished care
> Shall order justly, as the gods ordain.

That is her answer to his challenge. The issue of the trilogy is knit: "With Strife shall Strife join in battle, Right with Right" (*Cho.* 459). We have already learnt from the Chorus that this, the rule of the vendetta, is not justice, but another generation must pass away before the House of Atreus finds it out.

The Queen stands behind the gorgeous display of wealth, inviting. All eyes are turned to Agamemnon.

With frigid formality he acknowledges her address and declines her homage (916): "Honour me as a man, not as a god." He has refused to be tempted; her plan has failed. Having led us within sight of the climax, the dramatist now takes us back to where we started and begins again.

Clytemnestra changes her tactics. She abandons rhetoric and argues with him. She understands his character, and plays upon his weakness. Her arguments are a woman's, illogical but nimble. She is too quick for him. She makes a gesture of deference to his authority (922), extracts from him a conditional consent (924–5), touches his pride (926–7), and as he begins to weaken, she flatters him (931–2):

Ag. It is not for a woman to take delight in strife.
Cl. Well may the victor yield a victory!

The business of men is war, and women are for their recreation. Sure of their own superiority, they take pleasure in humouring feminine caprice. Agamemnon hesitates:

Ag. Do *you* set store by such a victory?
Cl. Be tempted, freely vanquished, victor still!

She has won. "With her much fair speech she caused him to yield, with the flattering of her lips she forced him." After ordering his sandals to be untied, because he is about to tread on holy ground, he draws attention to the captive Kasandra and with unperturbed effrontery asks his wife to extend her welcome to his concubine. Then, as he sets foot on the sacred purple, the flow of imagery bursts out afresh, suggestive of the dangers of abundance, of blood about to be shed and of a girl's blood shed ten years before. Agamemnon comes like the star of summer after the long winter's cold (961–3):

> So, when Zeus from the bitter virgin-grape
> Draws wine, then coolness fills the house at last,
> As man made perfect moves about his home.

The stage is now empty, save for the silent figure seated in the chariot. The slow music begins again (966), now tense and sinister. The theme of the *stásimon* is fear, which has routed hope, and it is expressed in the language of divination. When the music ceases, we are at a loss to know what is to happen next: are we to hear the death-cry from the palace or the voice of Kasandra? Then to our astonishment Clytemnestra reappears at the door of the palace. The Greek dramatists, tied to traditional themes, had little use for the element of surprise; but sometimes, after insistently impressing on our minds a sense of the inevitable, they give a sudden turn to the situation which could not have been anticipated.

Clytemnestra has determined that her husband's paramour shall share his death. Once more she exerts her powers of persuasion, assisted this time by the Chorus, who, cowed with terror, behave as though in a trance. And as she speaks we realise that she is using the language of the Mysteries. With blasphemous audacity she imagines Kasandra as a candidate for initiation, herself as the officiating priest, and the impending murder as a holy mystery (1034–6):

> Nay, if she speak not like the chattering swallow
> Some barbarous tongue which none can understand,
> With winning words I'll charm the heart within.

But her second victim knows what is to come, and, deaf alike to appeals and menaces, she neither speaks nor moves. Clytemnestra has no time to lose, and returns into the palace.

After a long pause we hear a low moan. It is Kasandra crying to Apollo. Then, in a delirious flood of prophecy, she sings of the children slaughtered long ago, sees the murder that is being done within, hears the Erinyes chant for joy and sees them dancing on the roof; and, finally, with poignant grief she mourns her own death and the passing of the House of Priam. When the trance has left her, she interprets the song of the Erinyes—they are celebrating the sin of Atreus; and she goes on to relate how Apollo inspired her with the art of prophecy (1177–1212). Suddenly the ecstasy returns: the children of Thyestes appear before her eyes—this is the crime for which Aigisthos is now exacting retribution; then she calmly tells the Elders that, like the *epóptai*, they are about to look on Agamemnon's death (1213–54); but the Elders are at a loss—they cannot understand (1252). Suddenly the ecstasy returns. Predicting once more her own death, she foretells the homecoming of the exile, who "to avenge his father shall kill his mother" (1280); and with a last cry to Priam and his sons she approaches the door, but recoils sick with horror, then approaches again, but still she lingers, staying to repeat her assurance of retribution to come (1316–19), and her last words are a passionate lament for her fate and Agamemnon's, captive and captor, slave and king, both confronted by the same death.

After she has gone, our attention is recalled to Agamemnon (1334–6):

> Unto him heaven granted the capture of Troy,
> And he enters his home acclaimed as a god.

These words show that the triumphant return of Agamemnon is regarded as a *kômos*. His deification is his death.

The effect of the scene as a whole is to concentrate on Kasandra the compassion we might otherwise have felt for Agamemnon, to set Clytemnestra's crime in relation to the past and future, and by delaying the action to intensify the climax.

The Elders confer in anxious whispers, but do nothing. That is in keeping with the proverbial view of old age—wise in counsel, weak in action. But the artistic purpose of the dialogue is to relieve the tension in order that we may respond to the culmination of the play, which is still to come. At the end of the dialogue, when the Elders approach the palace, the illusion intended is that they actually break in and discover the scene that follows. The stage doors are thrown open, revealing a tableau—the dead bodies of Agamemnon and Kasandra laid out on the bloodstained purple, with Clytemnestra standing over them. Exultantly she describes how her husband fell, entrapped in his own wealth, and now at last she is free to proclaim her motive (1415–18):

> To exorcise the storms,
> As though it were a ewe picked from his flocks
> Whose wealth of snowy fleeces never fails
> To multiply, unmoved, he killed his own
> Child, born to me in pain, my best-beloved.

The revelation of Clytemnestra's character is now complete. In the course of ten years her love for her first-born has been transformed into hatred of the man who wronged her, and the whole of her passionate nature devoted to revenge. Yet this hate was the outcome of love. Her crime is terrible, but her motive is adequate to explain it. And the reason why Æschylus, unlike Homer, has made her the prime agent in the murder is now plain. The man who killed her child must die by her hands alone. That Aigisthos has a feud of his own with Agamemnon is of no concern to her, and when she mentions her paramour it is not as an accomplice, but as her protector after the act (1435–8).

Slowly the horrified denunciation of the Elders turns to grief. Clytemnestra, too, becomes more tranquil, declaring that when she did this thing she was possessed by the avenging spirit, the hereditary *daimon* of the House, which demanded blood for blood (1476–81, 1498–1505, 1528–31). For her the murder was a necessary rite of purification, a perfect sacrifice by which the family has been purified of its hereditary madness; and now that her task is done all she asks is to live in peace (1567–76). That, however, is not the view of the Elders, who turn her own plea against her (1562–3):

> The law abides yet, as long as Zeus shall reign,
> The sinner must suffer—so 'tis ordered.

To this scene the epilogue (1577–1672) is a pendant and a contrast. If Clytemnestra is masculine in her strength of purpose, Aigisthos is a woman-hearted coward. She remains noble despite her depravity, but he is entirely contemptible. There was awe as well as accusation in the attitude of the Elders towards her, but the spiteful bombast of this upstart sets them beside themselves with indignation, leading to the defiant cry (1646–8):

> Oh, does Orestes yet
> Behold the light of life, that he may come
> Favoured of fortune home, and prove himself
> The sovereign executioner of both?

Our sympathies already lie with the exile far away. The vulgar truculence of Aigisthos, into whom the dramatist has put all his hatred of the tyranny, makes us feel that, after all, this was only a senseless and sordid crime; and Clytemnestra, too, as she listens in silence, seems to feel the same. Harassed and oppressed she pleads for peace. But the Elders remain defiant to the end, and peace will be denied to her. The discord is unresolved.

The fate of Agamemnon has been illustrated by the figure of the hunting net, which was first cast over the city of Troy and then became a disastrous robe, symbol of his excessive wealth, in which he was trapped and slain. So in the next play Clytemnestra is figured as a snake which, after strangling the eagle in its eyrie and leaving its nestlings to starve, is itself slain by the snake to which it has given birth. And in the last play Orestes becomes a flying fawn or hare with the hell-hounds hot upon his tracks. Apart from these leading figures, the *Agamemnon* is characterised by a profusion of incidental imagery. The sun and moon, the stars and interstellar spaces, the sea, with its inexhaustible riches, now sunk in midsummer calm, now lashed to fury by hail and lightning, the snows of winter in which the birds drop dead, budding corn, ripening grapes, the harvest and the vintage, and, above all, the beacons which flash across the darkness and fade into the dawn—the whole pageantry of Nature is displayed as a background to the conflict of man with man. In contrast to this, the image of the *Choephoroi* will be less lavish and more sombre—a withered forest oak, meteors, dragons and monsters of the deep. But at the end of the *Eumenides* the bright colours will return, when the maledictions of the Erinyes break into sunshine and gentle breezes bringing fruitful increase to crops, to cattle and to men.

The interval between the action of the first two plays is not stated, but it is evident that several years have elapsed. The boy whom Clytemnestra sent from home, now a young man, brave, devout and ambitious, has secretly returned to Argos, accompanied by Pylades, the son of his host in Phokis. Standing in the morning twilight at his father's grave, he hears from the palace a sudden shriek. As the play proceeds, the dawn breaks unnoticed. By the time his task is done, it will be dusk again, and, once more an exile, he will flee from home with his mother's avenging spirits at his heels.

As before, the prologue falls into two parts, divided this time by the cry from the palace, which is a cry of panic in contrast to the joyful "Alleluia!" heard in answer to the Watchman. The text is badly mutilated, and the gist of what is lost must be restored in the light of considerations drawn from the rest of the play. Two points in particular are invested in the sequel with such significance that we may be sure they were at least foreshadowed here.

First, Orestes has received from Apollo an express command to avenge his father by killing his mother and her paramour (268–304, 1027–31). "Whoso sheddeth man's blood, by man shall his blood be shed" (311–13, 434–6, 645–8, 835–7). This law, which Clytemnestra and the Elders have already invoked, the one in justification for the murder of Agamemnon, the others in anticipation of her own, has now received divine sanction; and, if Orestes is to be convicted of murder in the time to come, his guilt must be shared by Apollo, who has not only promised to exculpate him for obeying his command, but has threatened him with the direst penalities if he should disobey (275–95). Orestes has no option: he is an agent of the gods, and, knowing this, he faces his task with confidence. We are thus prepared for the final conflict of the trilogy, in which the feud between mother and son will become a feud between the deities of Heaven and of Hell affecting the welfare of all mankind.

Secondly, the death of the two sinners is necessary to cleanse the House of sin. The partisans of Orestes regard him as a divinely appointed purifier or deliverer (159–63, 865–7, 1044–5). What neither he nor they foresee is that in purifying the House he must take its pollution on himself (1015).

After a prayer to Hermes and to his father's spirit, Orestes lays a lock of his hair upon the tomb, and then we hear the cry—"heavy, haunting shriek of fear" (34–5). Presently he sees a company of women, dressed in black, coming from the palace, and stirred by the sight of his sister, walking among them bowed in grief, he calls upon the name of Zeus (18–19):

> O Zeus, may I avenge
> My father's death! Defend and fight for me!

The women are beating their breasts and tearing their hair in an Oriental dirge. The Queen has had bad dreams, in which the dead have signified their anger, and she has sent these serving-women with propitiatory offerings to her husband's tomb. But when blood has once been shed, there is no cure for it (47, 69–73; cf. *Ag.* 1004–6) and no escape from Justice, who visits some in this life, others in Purgatory and Hell. Clytemnestra is destined for a violent death, and her murderer will barely be saved from her avenging spirits dragging him down to eternal torment. In conclusion, the women reveal their own identity—they are captives from the sack of Troy. They obey their masters by compulsion; their goodwill is reserved for the avenger, when he comes.

Though older than her brother, Elektra is still only a girl, whose gentle nature has not yet been embittered by her unhappy upbringing. She cannot ask a blessing of her father for the wife who murdered him, but it does not occur to her, until the serving-women suggest it, to pray for revenge. Even then she is reluctant to comply, and the thought of her mother's wickedness prompts her, not to anger, but to a prayer that to her may be granted greater purity of heart.

During her prayers at the tomb she discovers the lock of hair, which resembles her own, and at once she thinks of Orestes. Presently she observes in the ground, leading away from the graveside, two sets of footprints.[9] Planting her feet in the first, she finds they match her own. Torn between hope and doubt, she follows them up step by step to the spot where, unknown to her, her brother is standing, and as she approaches him she cries out in her perplexity (210): "What agonies are here, what shattered wits!" It is as though these words were addressed to him, and they are an unhappy augury.

Orestes comes forward, and Elektra draws back in alarm. He tells her who he is. She cannot at first believe him. With gentle raillery he chides her, and at the same time offers proof of his identity—the *gnorísmata* or tokens, a garment she wove for him before he left home. Face to face with the brother, on whom, bereft of father and sister and estranged from her mother, she has lavished in absence the full devotion of a loving nature, Elektra forgets everything save the happiness of this moment. But Orestes is already uneasy at the danger in which this reunion has placed them, and presently the Chorus remind him of the future (242–4):

> Trust in thy courage, and thou shalt repossess
> Thy father's heritage, if only Might
> And Right stand by thy side, and with them third,
> Of all the greatest, Zeus Deliverer.

Orestes at once responds:

> Zeus, Zeus, look down upon our state, regard
> The eagle's offspring orphaned of their sire,
> Whom the fell serpent folded in her coils
> And crushed to death.

With implicit faith in the Delphic oracle—"Apollo will not break his faith" (268)—and fully determined to obey, he seems at the end of the scene almost light-hearted in his confidence.

The chant at the tomb which follows is technically a *thrênos*, or lament, the ritual basis of which was examined in Chapter XI. It is a capital example of the manner in which primitive ritual was raised by Æschylus to the level of dramatic art.

The choral odes of Sophokles are always relevant and serve dramatic purposes, but within each ode there is usually little movement. The Chorus comments, anticipates, points a moral or a contrast, but in general it does not directly contribute to the advancement of the plot. The Æschylean ode, on the other hand, is at its best highly dynamic. It moves and grows within itself. The action of the play is at a standstill, yet as we listen to the music we feel that something is happening within our minds. We have already come across two of his masterpieces in this kind—the first two *stásima* of the *Agamemnon*. But the chant at the tomb which we have now to consider is even more remarkable. Like those, it effects a revolution in our attitude of mind; but, being set for two voices in addition to the Chorus, it affords greater scope for dramatisation. Each of the three parts is a little drama in itself; the participants react upon each other, and out of their successive changes of mood is evolved a highly complex and organic whole. If we compare it with the invocation of Darius in the *Persians*, we have a striking measure of the artist's progress. There we are impressed by the magical incantations of the Elders and by the appearance of the ghost in answer to them; but these effects are external and spectacular —there is nothing inherently dramatic in the chant itself. Here the dramatist has dispensed with magic and the ghost remains invisible; yet, listening to the prayers of the brother and sister, we feel their father's spirit slowly entering their hearts. The action is wholly internal, yet for that very reason more moving and impressive.

Orestes and Elektra begin with a lament for their father's death (314–21 = 331–8, 344–52 = 362–70) but at the persistent instigation of the Chorus (305–13, 322–30, 374–8) this lament is transformed into a passionate appeal, in which the Chorus join, for the punishment of the murderers (379–98).

Meanwhile, as the Chorus observe the effect of their incitement on the other two, their own confidence begins to waver, and they are assailed with doubts (409–16). Elektra then takes the lead, recalling her own sufferings and the maltreatment of her father's body (417–21, 428–32, 443–8). Thereupon Orestes, who has himself felt a momentary dismay (404–8), is spurred to a renewal of his determination (433–7) and the Chorus now return to the attack, joining with Elektra in urging him to action (438–42, 449–53). We are thus brought to the second climax, in which all three are once more crying out for vengeance (454–8); but then the Chorus again lose faith (461–3) and they break off the chant with a lament for the future sufferings of the House of Atreus (464–73). It was they who first raised the cry of blood (311–12) and dictated it to the others (385–8); now they are weeping over what they have done. It is a fine conclusion, and essentially musical in conception.

The music ceases, the chant is at an end. In the hands of a less accomplished artist, the invocation too would have ended there, but Æschylus still has a *coda*. The son and daughter remain at the graveside; deaf to the ominous lamentation of the Chorus, they continue to cry out for vengeance, but alone. The curse of Atreus has risen from the tomb and lives again in them.

The effect upon Orestes is to confirm his resolution. After hearing the particulars of Clytemnestra's nightmare—she dreamt that she gave birth to a snake, which drew from her breast milk mixed with blood—he interprets it with ruthless assurance (546–8):

> Then surely, as she gave that monster life,
> So she must die a violent death, and I,
> The dragon of her dream, shall murder her.

Henceforward his whole mind is devoted to the successful execution of the plot, though, as we shall see, he will falter once again.

The effect upon Elektra is to transform her. The girl who a short time ago could hardly bring herself even to pray for retribution has now boasted that she will prove as savage and relentless as her mother (420–1). Under the irresistible force of the ancestral curse, she has become a second Clytemnestra, and conversely we might infer that there had been a time when Clytemnestra was as innocent as she. Modern critics have almost all misunderstood the character of Elektra in this play, and the reason is their failure to recognise that human character changes with its environment.

After explaining his plan of action, Orestes gives his final instructions to the serving-women (579–82):

> To you a tongue well-guarded I commend,
> Silence in season and timeliness in speech.
> The rest is for my comrade's eyes alone,
> To supervise this ordeal of the sword.

The phrase "silence in season" is another of those that passed into common speech from the language of religion; and its origin lies in the vow of secrecy imposed on the candidate for initiation at Eleusis. At a later stage, as we have seen, the initiate became an *epóptes*, one who was admitted to the secret rites performed in the Hall of Initiation and who superintended the initiation of others (p. 125). So here, the serving-women have been admitted into the secret of the plot, but its execution is a higher mystery which is not for them to behold. The act itself, which will take place inside the palace, is for Orestes to perform under the guidance of Pylades, who will stand over him and watch.

As they dwell on the enormity of Clytemnestra's crime, unparalleled in the annals of female wickedness, the Chorus recover their faith in the avenger (645–8):

> There comes to wipe away with fresh
> Blood the blood of old a son,
> Obeying some inscrutable
> Fury's deadly purpose.

It is now late evening. Orestes approaches the palace, accompanied by Pylades and disguised as a Phocian pedlar. He asks to speak with someone in authority—"a woman, or more fittingly a man" (660). His plan is to kill Aigisthos first. Scarcely has he spoken, when Clytemnestra, the real master of the house, appears in person, accompanied by Elektra, who is acting in accordance with her brother's instructions (577–8).

The Queen addresses the newcomers with cautious reserve. She is ready to give them hospitality, but, if their business is for men to deal with, then she will send for men. Orestes delivers his message, announcing his own death, and Elektra supports the deception with a feigned lament (687–95):

> O Curse of this sad House, unconquerable,
> How wide thy vision! Even that which seemed
> Well-ordered, safe beyond the reach of harm,
> Thou hast brought down with arrows from afar,
> And left me desolate, stripped of all I loved.
> And now Orestes—he who wisely thought
> To keep his foot outside the miry clay,
> Now that one hope of healing which might yet
> Have exorcised the wicked masquerade
> Within this palace, mark it not as present.

These words contain a double irony. Elektra tells her mother to count Orestes as dead, although in fact he stands before her eyes, and she does this without actually pronouncing the ill-omened word. But to the audience she conveys a deeper meaning. Orestes has been caught at last by the curse of his fathers. He was wise to keep out of the way: his return will be his ruin. And then her own desolation will no longer be a fiction.

Orestes continues in the same vein of sinister equivocation, asking pardon for being the bearer of bad news and at the same time affirming his determination to carry out the task he has undertaken. Clytemnestra replies with an equally guarded welcome, but reveals her elation at the news, if true, in a spiteful taunt at Elektra, whom she orders as though a slave to wait upon the strangers (711–14). Throughout this tense dialogue her attitude to the strangers is profoundly suspicious. But she does not suspect Elektra, and that is her undoing. By treating her as a slave, she plays into her hands.

Her next step is to convey a message to Aigisthos, asking him to return at once and bring his armed bodyguard. The messenger she chooses is the old family nurse, who, left to herself, would have suspected nothing and so enabled her mistress to defeat the conspiracy; but on her way she encounters the

Chorus, who instruct her to deliver the first part of the message and suppress the second. This nurse is garrulous, simple-minded and affectionate, but her reminiscences of the infant Orestes are strictly dramatic, being designed to forewarn us against the extravagant acclamations with which Orestes is soon to be saluted and to prepare us for the moment when his mother will plead for mercy (895-7):

> O stay, my son! Dear child, have pity on
> This bosom where in slumber long ago
> Your toothless gums drew in the milk of life!

In the previous *stásimon* the Chorus sang of the wickedness of Clytemnestra; now they pray for the success of the heaven-sent deliverer who is to slay the monster. Orestes is engaged in a chariot race, and the prize of victory is his ancestral heritage. They have forgotten their fears and urge him to show no mercy (829-36).

Aigisthos appears in answer to the summons. He is inclined to discredit the report of Orestes' death, not, however, because he suspects the messenger, but because it seems too good to be true. Conceited and self-assured, he walks straight into the trap. The excitement grows, and as they await the issue, the Chorus utter a final prayer for victory (865-7):

> So much is at issue, and single he goes,
> Orestes the god-like, and twain are his foes;
> O grant that he goeth to conquer!

We recall the old saying that Agamemnon had on his lips but not in his heart: "Honour me as a man, not as a god."

While the issue is in the balance, the serving-women draw aside, fearing to compromise themselves in the event of defeat (871-3; cf. 77-9). Then the man-servant comes to the door, displaying the same hesitancy, but now it is a register of success (874-9). He calls for help to the women's quarters, but the doors are bolted. This is Elektra's doing (577-8). Then he pauses to reflect. If Aigisthos is dead, he must prepare for a change of masters. His third cry is less a call for help than a summons to justice:

What is Clytemnestra doing?
Where is she? Now at last, it seems, her head
Shall touch the block beneath the axe of Justice.

At last she comes: "What is the meaning of that shout?" The answer is grimly oracular: "It means the living are being killed by the dead." Orestes, reported dead, has killed Aigisthos. But she recognises at once the fulfilment of her dream. Meeting the crisis with all her old defiance, she calls for an axe, but before she can get it Orestes confronts her, sword in hand, the body of Aigisthos at his feet. This is the crucial moment. He hesitates. Lowering his sword, he turns helplessly to his companion: is he to spare his mother? And Pylades speaks for the first and last time (899–901):

> What then hereafter of the oracles
> And solemn covenants of Loxias?
> Let all men hate thee rather than the gods.

Clytemnestra pleads for her life. Reminded by her son of Aigisthos, she reminds him of Kasandra (917–20):

Cl. No, no—remember too *his* wantonness!
Or. Accuse him not—for you he toiled abroad.
Cl. It is hard for a woman, parted from her man.
Or. What but his labour keeps her safe at home?

Failing to persuade, she threatens him (923): "Beware the hell-hounds of a mother's curse!" But Orestes is not to be moved again. "Ah me, I bore a serpent, not a son." "Turned dragon," as he said himself, her son drives her in and kills her.

The last *stásimon* is a hymn of mystical exultation, springing from the conviction that, by means of the ordeal of blood now being enacted in the palace, the House of Atreus has died and is born again, thus throwing off the incubus of sin which has so long lain upon it. The Chorus have already prayed that the House may be divested of its veil and adorned with the crown of glory (804–7):

> Let us rejoice and set a crown on the palace;
> O let it swiftly appear,
> Gleaming and friendly and free,
> Out of the veil of encircling darkness!

Now the struggle is over, the House of Atreus is delivered, it
will err and stray no more (941–4):

> Cry alleluia, lift up in the house a song,
> Deliverance from ill and from the waste of wealth
> By the unholy sinners twain,
> From rough thorny ways!

Then they greet the blessed light and call upon the House to
arise like a sinner who has been purified (959–62). It will soon
be made perfect, and the inmates, whose weeping has been
turned to joy, shall behold the usurpers laid low like the
prostrate multitude of the uninitiated (963–9).

One of the ceremonies of mystical religion (not, probably,
Eleusinian, but clearly in the same tradition) is described as
follows:[10]

> Upon a certain night an image is laid upon a couch and
> mourned with cries of grief disposed in numbers; next, after
> they have had enough of their feigned lamentation, a light
> is brought in; and thereupon the throats of all those who
> wept are anointed by the priest, who then whispers in a slow
> murmur:

> > Take courage, mystics, for our God is saved:
> > Deliverance from evil shall be yours.

The Chorus have already acclaimed the deliverance of the
House and saluted the light; and finally they sing (967–9):

> With kind fortune couched and fair-eyed to see
> For all those that weep
> Shall aliens within be laid low again.

Night has fallen, and, while the Chorus chant this hymn of
deliverance, the doors of the palace are thrown open, revealing
a blaze of torchlight, in which Orestes, the deliverer, is seen standing over a couch on which is laid the dead body of his mother.

The intensity imparted to the climax by this sustained
parallel with the ritual of Eleusis must have made a deep
impression on all those to whom that ritual was the symbol of
a living faith; and it is characteristic of Æschylus that the

parallel is enforced not so much by similarity as by contrast. The rising spirits of the Chorus have reached their highest point just when they are to be plunged into disillusionment and disaster.

Orestes spreads out for all to see, as the testimony that shall vindicate him at the day of judgment, the purple robe in which this monster who was his mother once displayed the body of his father. The Chorus, however, are already filled with misgivings, and Orestes too begins to lose confidence (1014-15). As the struggle becomes more acute, revealing the first signs of approaching insanity, he reminds himself of the command of Apollo and announces his intention of seeking sanctuary at Delphi; and the Chorus recall, though no longer with conviction, the heroic nature of his achievement (1044-5):

> Thou art deliverer of the land of Argos,
> With one light stroke lopping two dragons' heads.

While they speak, Orestes catches sight of the Erinyes (1046-8):

> What are those women? See them, Gorgon-like,
> All clad in sable and entwined with coils
> Of writhing snakes!

It is as though a fresh crop of monsters had sprung from the blood of the dragons he has slain. The Chorus seize in desperation on the name of Apollo, which now rings out, much as the name of Orestes himself rang out at the end of the *Agamemnon*, with the promise of deliverance to come (1057-8):

> Thou shalt be purified! Apollo's touch
> From these disasters shall deliver thee!

In the *Agamemnon*, the Watchman, the Herald and the Chorus, in one ode after another, find themselves constrained as by some hidden power to turn from rejoicing to ever-deepening apprehension, and by this recurrent rhythm a tremendous impetus is imparted to the plot. Then, when all is ready for the crisis, the action is delayed by one expedient after another, until the suspense seems interminable; yet the accumulated pressure is so great that the tension is never relaxed, with the result that the climax, when it comes, is almost more than we can bear. The movement of the *Choephoroi* is different. It depends on repeated contrasts of mood, in which the Chorus play the leading part. When Elektra is at a loss, the Chorus dictate a prayer for vengeance. When Orestes is embracing his sister after years of absence, the Chorus remind him of his patrimony. When Orestes and Elektra are weeping beside the tomb, the Chorus are crying out for blood. When Orestes and Elektra are bent on vengeance without mercy, the Chorus are weeping for the Curse of Atreus. That is the first movement of the play. After that the *tempo* is relaxed, then gathers pace again; and in the last scene of all, when victory is swept away in horror and despair, the Chorus turn in rapid succession from rejoicing to dismay, from dismay to half-convinced assurance and desperate consolation. This ever-shifting interplay of conflicting moods is like an elaborate piece of counterpoint, in which two themes, continually varied, are played in two long crescendos one against the other.

The theme of the trilogy—the murder of Agamemnon and its consequences—is treated in the third play in such a way as to become much more than that. Its significance is steadily extended and enriched until the vicissitudes of the House of Atreus appear in retrospect as the battle-ground of human progress. The fate of Orestes concerns us still, but with it is now bound up the future of humanity at large. The issue is not merely whether the matricide is to be absolved, but whether mankind is to succeed in its struggle towards a new social order.

Before proceeding further, it will be as well to guard against possible misunderstanding by some general remarks on the nature of primitive symbolism. For, though Æschylus belongs to a period in which the development of scientific thought was already considerable, he has chosen to express himself through the more primitive medium of mythology. Objectively regarded, myths are symbols of reality. They are the forms in which reality presents itself to the primitive mind. It follows that to the primitive mind, as distinct from ours, the symbol and the reality are indistinguishable—they are one and the same thing.

Take the evolution of the goddess Athena. The city of Athens derives its name from entities called "athenas"—evidently sacred objects (possibly birds) or persons disguised to represent those objects, which eventually crystallised into the anthropomorphic abstraction Athena.[11] According to an Attic tradition, Erichthonios, the ancestor of the royal clan of the Erechtheidai, was born from the seed which Athena brushed from her person to the ground after Hephaistos had attempted to ravish her.[12] There can be little doubt that what this means is that Athena was originally regarded as the mother of Erichthonios, who was naturally fatherless, because his clan was matrilineal, and that the intervention of Hephaistos (assisted by the popular etymology of Erichthonios from *éris*, "strife," and *chthón*, "ground") is a derivative element introduced after the adoption of patrilineal descent had rendered the lack of paternity unintelligible. In another tradition, when Athena and Poseidon disputed the possession of the Akropolis, Athena was supported by the women and Poseidon by the men.[13] Here again the matrilineal function of the goddess is unmistakable. Later, when matrilineal descent had disappeared, Athena became a virgin goddess, affiliated to Zeus by a nativity myth which is clearly a symbol of re-birth or adoption, and endowed with attributes as masculine as her sex, determined by her origin, permitted. The same process can be traced in the history of Artemis, who began as a matrilineal mother-goddess with attributes derived from the totemic hunting clan, and ended as the chaste virgin huntress described by Homer.

The question is, how did these developments present themselves to the mind of Æschylus? It is, of course, obvious that Æschylus did not think in terms of social anthropology. At the same time he must have been conscious in some form of the antecedents of his contemporary Athena, because, as has just been pointed out, those antecedents were embodied symbolically in a series of Attic myths. The answer is therefore that his consciousness of these developments took precisely the form in which he expresses it. The degree of objectivity he displays in expounding the underlying significance of the myths is the measure of the extent to which he had emancipated himself from primitive modes of thought. Nevertheless, in analysing his mythological symbolism, it is for us, not only legitimate,

T A

but absolutely necessary to treat it scientifically, because that is the only way in which it can be rendered intelligible to minds which have almost entirely outgrown that mode of thinking.

The parties to the dispute over the fate of Orestes are Apollo and the Erinyes. Apollo is the Interpreter of Zeus (17–19)— that was traditional; and he claims that his testimony is incontrovertible, because it comes from Zéus (619–21). The doctrine of Delphic infallibility was familiar at Athens in the fifth century, but it was resisted by the more advanced democrats, who saw that it was used to support an attitude to contemporary society which they regarded as reactionary. Therefore, as spectators at the City Dionysia, Athenian citizens would be prepared to see the doctrine vindicated and they would be equally prepared to see it challenged. Actually, in the play, Apollo's claim is ultimately endorsed by Athena, but in circumstances redounding to her credit rather than his, and only after his whole position has been challenged by the Erinyes.

If Apollo appeals to Zeus, his opponents appeal to the Moirai, whose ministers they are (392–6); in particular, they have been entrusted with the task of punishing those guilty of shedding kindred blood (335–9). They contend, therefore, that in opposing them, Apollo is destroying the authority of the Moirai (172–3), who are older than Zeus; and they recall his conduct on another occasion, when he cheated the Moirai of a life which was their due (730–1). Thus, behind the feud between Apollo and the Erinyes there lies a deeper discord. Zeus and the Moirai are at variance. It was pointed out in an earlier chapter that the cult-epithet *moiragétes* or "leader of the Moirai," applied to Zeus at Olympia and to Apollo at Delphi, corresponded to the subordination of tribal rights to the authority of the state (pp. 53–4).[14] And that is how the feud between the Erinyes and Apollo is treated by Æschylus—as a symbol of the conflict between tribal custom in respect of homicide and the reorganisation of the law of homicide effected under the rule of the aristocracy; only, the solution of the conflict is presented characteristically, not as the submission of one party to the other, but as the reconciliation of the two. At the end of the trilogy the Erinyes will be reinvested,

in the new circumstances created by Athena, with the ancient
privileges which Apollo has sought to override.

The issue is therefore this. The Erinyes stand for the tribal
order of society, in which kinship, traced through the mother,
had been a closer bond than marriage and the murder of a
kinsman had been punished instantaneously and absolutely by
the outlawry of the murderer. Their attitude on these points,
as we shall see shortly, is stated explicitly. Apollo, on the other
hand, whom the Athenians worshipped as "paternal" (*patrôios*),
proclaims the sanctity of marriage and the precedence of the
male. And the issue turns on the fate of Orestes. The dilemma
in which he has been placed reflects the struggle of divided
loyalties characteristic of the period in which descent was being
shifted for the sake of the accompanying succession and inheritance from the mother's to the father's side, and his acquittal
will mark the inauguration of the new order which is to
culminate in democracy.

In persecuting Orestes for the murder of his mother, the
Erinyes are performing the function of the ancestral curse,
which, as explained in Chapter II, has its roots in the life of
the primitive clan; but, in keeping with the parallel with
mystical religion which runs right through the trilogy, this
function is described in terms of the role assigned to these
deities as "angels of torment" in the Eleusinian and Orphic
Hades. They are daughters of Night and ministers of the
supreme judge of the dead, who allots to each soul its *moîra* or
portion of felicity or chastisement. They threaten their victim
in language which reminds us of the mystical Eurynomos, an
infernal demon "with blue-black skin, like the flies that settle
on meat, showing his teeth, and seated on the outspread hide
of a vulture," which devoured the flesh of the dead, leaving
nothing but the bones. The place where they propose to work
their will on him is one (389–90)—

From whence the gods are barred
By dark corruption foul, region of rugged ways—

like the Eleusinian and Orphic wilderness of mire in which
the soul of the sinner strays and perishes. And there he shall

"make a feast for fiends" (302), abandoned by all and knowing not "where in the bosom joy resides"—the joy of the initiates in Elysium. In the same way, the long and circuitous journey which Orestes undertakes on his way to Athens after his purification at Delphi corresponds to the wanderings of the soul in search of salvation. As Tierney has pointed out,[15] purification does not "immediately confer the longed-for salvation; it merely gives, both to the mystic and to Orestes, knowledge of the right *way* which leads to the judgment-seat, and the assurance of a favourable judgment." And consequently, by the time he is brought to trial, the Court of the Areopagus has become surrounded with all the grandeur and terror of the judgment seat of Minos, at which the Erinyes stood waiting impatiently to carry off the lost soul as soon as it had been condemned. Further, just as the Orphic was taught to declare his purity as his claim to deliverance or salvation—"From the pure come I, pure Queen of the Dead" —so, on his arrival at the shrine of Athena, Orestes declares (276–98):

> Taught in the school of suffering, I have learnt
> The times and seasons when it is right to keep
> Silence and when to break it; and in this matter
> A wise instructor has charged me to speak.
> The blood upon my hands has sunk to sleep,
> The matricidal stain is washed away . . .
> And now with lips made pure and reverent
> I call to my defence this country's Queen . . .
> O may she come—far off she still can hear—
> And from these miseries deliver me!

And, finally, after the trial is over, he is readmitted to the phratry (659) and so becomes "once more an Argive" (760). His purification is vindicated as a regeneration. He has died and is born again.

The opening scene is laid before the temple of Apollo at Delphi. Having finished her prayers, the Priestess enters the temple, and immediately afterwards we hear a cry of horror. Though its meaning is as yet unknown to us, it falls on the ear like a note of destiny, startling and yet familiar. The three prologues of the trilogy have been designed according to a common plan.

Half-paralysed with fear, the Priestess returns and describes what she has seen. Then the interior of the temple is revealed in a tableau—Orestes clinging to the sanctuary, the Erinyes asleep on the thrones, and standing over them the commanding figure of Apollo. The god assures his suppliant that he will keep faith with him (64; cf. 232–4) and instructs him to go to Athens. Escorted by Hermes, the guide of souls, the pilgrim sets out on his journey. Apollo remains, a silent witness to what follows.

The ghost of the murdered mother appears. She picks her steps among the prostrate Erinyes, recalling them with bitter reproaches to their forgotten purpose. This is the woman who dreamt of victory at the fall of Troy, and of retribution at the coming of Orestes; now, as her avenging spirits dream of her, they wake with whimpering cries and creep into the sunlight, only to find that their quarry has escaped. Then they catch sight of Apollo, and point accusing fingers at the thief. In a speech of violent denunciation, he commands them to depart. His attitude is too passionate to be final, and in contrast their own is studied in its restraint: they do not denounce, they reason with him. And their reasoning is consistent. They are persecuting Orestes in virtue of the powers assigned to them (208–10); they did not persecute Clytemnestra because the blood she shed was not a kinsman's (211–12); and they have no concern with the sanctity of wedlock. Apollo's reply, on the other hand, is not consistent, being an attempt at compromise between two incompatible principles. He uses the law of retribution to condemn Clytemnestra (203), the law of purification to protect Orestes (205): but, if Clytemnestra forfeited her life by murdering her husband, then by murdering his mother Orestes has forfeited his own. Apollo's attitude is transitional. He has challenged the old order, but it is not for him to construct the new (224).

The scene changes, and we find ourselves at a shrine of Athena in the city of Athens. During the interval Orestes has travelled far and wide (75–7) and now he claims that his penance is complete and seeks refuge with the goddess who is to decide his fate.

The Erinyes, however, are still upon his trail. They gather round him and begin to dance and sing their binding-song which is to bind him like the souls of the damned in unbreakable bonds (332–4):

> Hymn of hell to harp untuned,
> Chant to bind the soul in chains,
> Spell to parch the flesh to dust.

We remember the vision of Kasandra (*Ag.* 1185–9):

> On yonder housetop ever abides a choir
> Of minstrels unmelodious, singing of ill;
> And deeply drunk, to fortify their spirit,
> In human blood, those revellers still abide,
> Whom none can banish, Furies congenital.

And the premonition of the Argive Elders (*Ag.* 980–2):

> Still I hear a strain of stringless music,
> Dissonant dirge of the Furies, a chant uninstructed
> Quired in this trembling breast.

And the Watchman's cry (*Ag.* 22–4):

> Hail, lamp of joy, whose gleam turns night to day,
> Hail, radiant sign of dances numberless
> In Argos for our happy state!

Apart from the refrains, which form the magical element in the chant, the Erinyes expound once more the authority on which their powers rest. The decrees of everlasting Moira (335–6) enjoined upon them when they first came into being (348) the task of exacting vengeance from those who have shed the blood of kith and kin (356–7). Orestes is prostrate with terror and fatigue, like a hare (327) that cowers motionless while the hounds close in for the kill.

To the poets of the democracy, Athena, the daughter whom Zeus loved best, and born of the father that begot her, was greater than Apollo. She was the divine projection of their ideals—bravery in battle, which had enabled them to defeat the Persians; skill in the arts of peace, which had made their city the most brilliant in Greece; and above all that sense of moderation and restraint (*sophrosýne*) which corresponded exactly to the aspirations of the middle class as embodied in the constitution established after the overthrow of the tyranny. She was pre-eminently a mediator and a peacemaker, endowed with the gift of clear, persuasive speech, which, in a city where the extension of the franchise had made the art of public speaking a dominant feature of social life, appeared as a vital condition of human civilisation. As Isokrates said:[16]

> It is by the power of persuading one another that we have raised ourselves above the level of the beasts, founded cities, laid down laws, and discovered arts.

And again:

> Finding the Greeks living without laws in scattered communities, oppressed by tyrants or perishing in anarchy, our city delivered them from these evils, either by taking them under her protection or by offering herself as an example. So much is clear from the fact that those who preferred the earliest charges of homicide, desiring to compose their differences by reason instead of violence, tried their cases according to Athenian law.

This, of course, is a conscious allusion to the trial of Orestes, and shows how the work of Æschylus had served to mould Attic tradition. It is in this spirit that Athena now addresses herself to the task of leading mankind from barbarism to civilisation. And she accomplishes her purpose by persuading the agents of the Moirai to accept freely and without compulsion the will of Zeus.

She confronts them with serene and majestical reserve, very different from the passionate indignation of Apollo. She listens to their statement with courteous deference. Only when they venture to argue their case does she adopt a sterner tone, rejecting the suggestion that the case can be decided by appeal to the primitive ordeal by oath (432–5). The Erinyes accept the rebuke, and offer to submit to her decision (437–8). With the same impartiality, she then turns to Orestes, who declares that he has sought her sanctuary as one already purified, and he too

beseeches her to judge (471–2). By consent of both parties the
decision now rests with her, but she immediately declines it.
The issue is too grave for mortal judgment, too fraught with
passion for her own. The suppliant has a claim on her protection; yet, if his pursuers are frustrated, they will vent their
displeasure on her people (485–91):

> But be it so; since it is come to this,
> Judges I will appoint for homicide,
> A court set up in perpetuity.
> Meanwhile do you call proofs and witnesses
> As sworn supports of Justice; then, having chosen
> The best of all my people, I shall come
> To pass true judgment on the present cause.

In these words she forecasts the institution of the Court of the
Areopagus, which is to be the symbol of the new order. And
of that order one feature is already clear. Hitherto the homicide
has been punished summarily; henceforward he is to be tried
before a jury of his fellow men.

The task of these judges will, of course, be to try the case of
Orestes; but Athena seems to have suggested that she hopes to
find in them a means of solving the divine dispute as well—that
the foundation of the new Court will have the *effect* of concilia-
ting the Erinyes. We look to the sequel to see how this can be.

The origin of the Council of the Areopagus was the subject
of diverse traditions, from which Æschylus has selected those
which best serve his purpose.[17] The Court was founded by
Athena for the object of trying Orestes, his accusers were the
Erinyes, and his judges a committee elected by lot from the
Athenian people. The Athenians claimed that their city was
the first to establish laws; that of their laws those relating to
homicide were the oldest and best; and that of all their legal
institutions the Court of the Areopagus was the most venerable,
distinctive and august. It was the "overseer of all things" and
"guardian of the laws"; it had in its keeping "the secret deposi-
tions wherein lay the salvation of the city"; it was charged to
uphold sobriety and good conduct, on the principle that good
government depends, not on a multiplicity of legal enactments,
but on the maintenance of justice within the hearts of men; it

was grave, severe, and incorruptible; and in a later generation Isokrates counts it as one of the virtues of his forefathers that they had been slow to tamper with their ancestral institutions, deterred by their respect for the Council of the Areopagus.

Such was the tradition associated with the Court which is now to be established. It is clearly a conservative tradition, and it is reproduced point by point in the play. The Erinyes contend (520–34):

Times there be when fear is well;
Yea, it must continually
Watch within the soul enthroned.
Needful too straits to teach humility.
Who of those that never nursed
Healthy dread within the heart,
Be they men or peoples, shall
Show to Justice reverence?
Choose a life despot-free,
Yet restrained by rule of law. Thus and thus
God doth administer, yet he appointeth the mean as the master
   in all things.

After this profession of faith from the Erinyes, Athena has little difficulty in showing that her new Court is exactly designed to achieve their aims, which therefore will not, as they imagine, be jeopardised by the acquittal of Orestes. She is giving her direction to the judges before they record their votes (684–713):

People of Athens, hear my ordinance
At this first trial of bloodshed. Evermore
This great tribunal shall abide in power
Among the sons of Aigeus. . . .
      Here Reverence
And inbred Fear, enthroned among my people,
Shall hold their hands from evil night and day,
Only let them not tamper with their laws. . . .
I bid my people honour and uphold
The mean between the despot and the slave,
And not to banish terror utterly,
For what man shall be upright without fear?
And if you honour this high ordinance,
Then shall you have for land and commonweal

> A stronghold of salvation. . . .
>   I establish
> This great tribunal to protect my people,
> Grave, quick to anger, incorruptible,
> And ever vigilant over those that sleep.

It is highly significant that Æschylus should have defined his attitude to the Court in these terms only a few months after it had been deprived of all its specific functions excepting its jurisdiction in cases of homicide—a reform which excited the greatest opposition among conservatives, so great that its sponsor, Ephialtes, was assassinated shortly afterwards. Since Athena founds the Court for the express purpose of trying the homicide Orestes, and since in her introductory reference to its members she describes them as "judges of homicide" (486), it may be inferred that Æschylus acquiesced retrospectively in the curtailment of its powers; but his insistence on the respect due to it and more particularly on the principle that the deterrent effect of laws is an essential aspect of the mean, which, as we have seen, is the basic doctrine of democracy, shows plainly that, at least at the end of his life, he was opposed to the advanced policy of the radical democrats.

We have seen that Athena meets the contention of the Erinyes, that the acquittal of the matricide will result in anarchy and lawlessness, by investing the Court with such a character that, so far from being in danger, their aims are identified with hers and so safe for ever. She has cut the ground from under their feet, and all that remains for her to do is to invite them to accept the divine presidency of the new Court. As we discern her ulterior purpose, a new prospect opens before us, leading to the conclusion of the trilogy. But for the present we are preoccupied with the trial of Orestes.

Athena has returned, accompanied by her chosen judges, probably ten or twelve in number, and followed by the citizens of Athens, who are eager to witness the first trial at law in the history of man; and presently Apollo appears to give evidence for the accused.

In accordance with the actual procedure of the Court, the Erinyes begin by addressing to Orestes three questions—

whether he did what he is accused of doing, how, and why. This means that the judges are going to consider, not merely the act itself, but the circumstances and the motive. The automatic adjustments characteristic of primitive morality are to be superseded by the power of discrimination.

The examination advances rapidly to the point where the controversy was suspended earlier in the play (607–8; cf. 211–12); then, after a false step (609) which will be retrieved later by Apollo, Orestes turns to his protector, beseeching him to pronounce whether his act was *just* (614–16). Apollo, whose role in relation to Orestes is that of an *exegetés* (612), a priest appointed at Athens for supervising the purification of homicides, comes forward for his second encounter with the Erinyes and declares in bold and ringing tones that it was *just* (617–18). He soon finds, however, that to defend this plea against the sharp wits of his opponents is not an easy matter. His first attempt, an appeal to the authority of Zeus, is abortive, because appeals to authority are useless when there is a conflict of authority; and so we are brought back to the dilemma with which the controversy began—Orestes has avenged his father by dishonouring his mother (625–7; cf. 202–3). Apollo makes a second attempt. He contends that, since the murder of Agamemnon was a crime, the execution of the murderess was not. This is a plea of justifiable homicide, seeking to discriminate between acts similar in effect but different in motive; but the Erinyes reply with the caustic comment that such a plea comes ill from the spokesman of Zeus, who bound in chains his own father Kronos (643–5). Apollo indignantly retorts that chains can be loosed, whereas blood once shed is irrecoverable; but this, as the Erinyes are quick to point out, is the very offence of which Orestes is guilty.

By this time it is plain that no progress can be made until a solution has been found for the dilemma with which we have been confronted from the outset. To which parent does the son owe the prior duty? The Erinyes champion the mother; Apollo, who has already urged that the tie between mother and son is no more sacred than the tie between husband and wife, now goes further and declares that the child is more closely related to the father than to the mother (660–4). This argument is not an improvisation: it is the Pythagorean doctrine of paternity. And in this issue, now at last clearly stated, lies the crux of the whole matter.

Why then does Athena give her casting vote to Orestes? Because she gives precedence to the male over the female, to the husband over the wife (737–43):

> The final judgment is a task for me;
> So for Orestes shall this vote be added.
> No mother gave me birth, and in all things
> Save marriage I, my father's child indeed,
> With all my heart commend the masculine.
> Wherefore I shall not hold of higher worth
> A woman who was killed because she killed
> Her wedded lord and master of her home.

The reason could not have been more clearly stated, and it touches the crucial point at issue. On the question of paternity Athena endorses the attitude of Apollo, thus laying down the cardinal principle of the Attic law of inheritance, in which not only was the liberty of the wife narrowly circumscribed in the interests of the husband but, so far as the transmission of property was concerned, the mother was not reckoned among the kinsfolk at all. And if we ask why the dramatist has made the outcome of the trial turn on the social relations of the sexes, the answer is that he regarded the subordination of woman, quite correctly, as an indispensable condition of democracy. Just as Aristophanes and Plato perceived that the abolition of private property would involve the emancipation of woman, so Æschylus perceived that the subjection of woman was a necessary consequence of the development of private property.[18]

Not only is the plain interpretation of Athena's words demanded by the nature of the issue in which the trial has culminated, but it brings the trial to its full and proper conclusion. Those critics who have been puzzled by a decision so out of keeping with our ideas of the administration of the law forget that, at the time when this crime was committed, there were no laws, only divine sanctions diverse and incompatible, and Athena's decision constitutes a ruling on the very point at which they were in conflict. So much for the past, but the future

will be different. Such a case as this can never arise ag
because henceforward the criminal will be tried before a c
of justice. The reign of law has begun. As we followed the
fortunes of Orestes, we were in effect watching the growth of
law through successive stages of social evolution. Regarded
originally as a tort to be redressed by the kinsmen of the victim,
and subsequently as a pollution to be expiated by the pre-
scriptions of the aristocratic priesthood, the offence of homicide
is now a crime to be submitted to the judgment of a legally
appointed committee of the people. The conflict between tribal
custom and aristocratic privilege has been resolved in democracy. So too the principle of male precedence, now formally
ratified as the basis of democracy, is accompanied by the
declaration that the wealth of the community is now equitably
distributed (997). In the dispute between the Erinyes and
Apollo over the fate of Orestes, and in the feud between Zeus
and the Moirai, who are now to be reconciled by Athena, we
see as it were mirrored in heaven the terrestrial process that
began with the primitive tribe and ended with the emergence
of a state in which the common people had recovered in a new
form the equality denied to them during the rule of the aristocracy.

To all those critics who have assumed that the question at
issue is simply a moral one, the ground on which Athena bases
her decision has been a stumbling-block. It would have been
easy for the dramatist to make her say that she is going to vote
for Orestes out of compassion or humanity (*philanthropía*),
because that was one of her traditional qualities;[19] but he has
chosen not to base her decision on these grounds, and that
makes the grounds on which he does base it all the more
significant. And it may well be asked whether there is even an
initial plausibility in the assumption which these critics have
accepted. Is a man justified in avenging his father by killing his
mother at the command of God? If the trilogy had been made to
turn on that sterile speculation, they would have been hardly
less perplexed than they are now. Æschylus was not interested
in the solution of an insoluble conundrum.

The significance of the acquittal is not primarily moral at
all but social, and it provides the answer to a question which

has been prominent in our minds from the beginning of the trilogy. What is Justice? Is it the rule of the vendetta? Is it the law of blood for blood? Does it permit of absolution? Does it lie in the act or in the motive? All these considerations have been suggested, and therefore we are impelled to look for the poet's final answer.

To Plato, who regarded the material world as an unreal image of the ideal and sought to stabilise human society on the basis of the exclusive domination of a leisured class, the idea of justice was something absolute and immutable which expressed itself politically in the doctrine that "the cobbler must stick to his cobbling." "When," he declared, "each class in the state fulfils the function assigned to it, and minds its own business, this is what makes the state just—this is justice."[20] Such was the idealist conception; but the materialists took an entirely different view, which may be illustrated from Epicurus, who was strenuously opposed to the whole system of class-domination embodied in the city-state of his time:[21]

> There never has been an absolute justice, only an agreement reached in social intercourse, differing from place to place and from time to time, for preventing the injury of one man by another. . . . All those elements in what is recognised at law as just possess that character in so far as they are proved by the necessities of social intercourse to be expedient, whether they are the same for everyone or not; and if a law turns out to be incompatible with the expediencies of social intercourse, it ceases to be just. And should the expediency expressed in the law correspond only for a time with that conception, nevertheless for that time it is just, so long as we do not trouble ourselves with empty phrases but look simply at the facts.

The notion that justice is relative can be traced in the democratic thought of the fifth century. Thus, justice was defined by Thrasymachos as "the strong man's interest," and, though this view was grossly misrepresented by Plato in his *Republic*, it is quite clear that what Thrasymachos meant is that justice is the interest of the ruling class.[22] It will be observed that all these thinkers, including Plato, regarded justice as a matter of social relations, and that Plato's absolute conception corresponds to his own position as a member of a class whose power he wished to see perpetuated.

What, then, was the position of Æschylus? He was an early Pythagorean, a moderate democrat. Plato, too, was deeply influenced by Pythagoreanism, but the Pythagoreans of his day, at least in Greece proper, had gone right over to the reaction—the usual fate of moderate progressives when the class struggle has progressed beyond the point at which it serves their interests. In the middle of the fifth century the issues on which Athenian democracy was to split were still embryonic. Therefore, as a Pythagorean, Æschylus was nearer to Hippokrates than to Plato, and, steeped though he was in the mystical traditions of Eleusis, he was not a mystic in his attitude to society, because he had no need to seek refuge from a reality in which his aspirations had been fulfilled. Accordingly, asked to define his idea of justice, he would, it may be suspected, have replied in one word—democracy. That answer is implicit in his treatment of the story of Orestes. The matricide is acquitted by an appeal to historical expediency, and the trilogy ends with the ratification of a new social contract, which is just because it is democratic.

Orestes has been acquitted, but the divine antagonism has still to be resolved. The nature of the settlement proposed by Athena has already been indicated, but we have still to see how she will work it out.

Just as the Erinyes stand for the blood feud (the rule of tribal society) and Athena for trial by jury (the rule of democracy), so Apollo stands for the practice of purification, the origin of which has been explained in Chapter V. Apollo, therefore, represents in this trilogy the rule of the landed aristocracy, intermediate between the primitive tribe and the democratic state of contemporary Athens. After the overthrow of the tyranny, the punishment of homicide had passed into popular control along with the archonship, from which the Court of the Areopagus was recruited; but the practice of purification persisted, and the *exegetaí* who performed it continued to be drawn from the ranks of the Eupatridai. The old nobility, to which, we remember, Æschylus himself belonged, retained its

ritual office side by side with the popularly elected officials who
had taken over the administration of the law, and, moreover,
election to the office of *exegetés* continued to be subject to the
ratification of the Delphic Oracle. Thus, in the democracy
established by Athena, Apollo will remain in control of the
exegetaí. That is his part in the new order.

At the Court of the Areopagus both prosecutor and defendant
bound themselves to tell the truth by an oath in which, as the
penalty of perjury, they invoked destruction on themselves,
their houses and their families; and this oath was taken in the
name of the Semnai, a trinity of female divinities worshipped
in a cave on the slopes of the Areopagus as the presiding deities
of the Court. The origin of the Semnai has never been fully
investigated; but it seems clear that, like the Horai, the
Charites, the Eumenides of Argos, and the Erinyes themselves,
they were descended from matrilineal ancestral spirits of the
same type as the Moirai, whose origin we investigated in
Chapter III. Æschylus himself was evidently conscious to some
extent of these affinities, for what he does is to make Athena
persuade the Erinyes to identify themselves with these Semnai,
thus accepting the presidency of the Court, and in their new
guise they will still be required to visit the perjurer with the
penalties which have been theirs to inflict since the beginning
of the world (933–8). That is their part in the new order, which
is not new in the sense that it supersedes the old, but in the
sense that in it the conflicts of the old are blended and reconciled—the fusion of opposites in the mean.

The significance of this solution is so clear that it may
reasonably be supposed that the dramatist himself was directly
conscious of its social and political implications as distinct from
the symbolical form in which it is cast. There is only one point
at which there is any serious discrepancy between his exposition
and the reality. In historical fact, the Court of the Areopagus,
which he has presented as being established by Athena at the
inauguration of democracy, was an ancient institution going
back to the primitive Attic monarchy. It was the council of
chiefs founded according to Attic tradition in the reign of
Theseus. From a historical point of view there is undoubtedly
a confusion here, but it is one which is easy to accept for the

purposes of imaginative drama, and moreover it is readily explained by the fifth-century tradition, to which we referred in a previous chapter (p. 75), that the founder of Athenian democracy was Theseus. That the dramatist has been influenced by this tradition appears from his description of the women and children who take part in the procession at the end of the trilogy as "the eye of the land of Theseus" (1025-6). This incidental discrepancy does little to detract from the profound historical insight of the *Oresteia*, in which not only is social evolution conceived as an organic process, a progressive conflict of cumulative tensions which subsequently merge in a new unity, but some of the primary characteristics of ancient society are clearly apprehended.

At first the Erinyes are blinded by passion to the advantages of Athena's offer. But Athena is unrivalled in her power of persuasion (797-9):

> Let me persuade you from this passionate grief.
> You are not vanquished; the issue of the trial
> Has been determined by an equal vote.

Unmoved, the Erinyes repeat their maledictions. Still serene, Athena repeats her invitation (835-6):

> Calm the black humours of embittered rage,
> Reside with me, and share my majesty.

Menaces give place to impotent despair, and Athena speaks again (886-92):

> Nay, if Persuasion's holy majesty . . .
> Is aught to thee, why then, reside with me . . .
> Since it is in thy power to own this soil
> Justly attended with the highest honours.

This is the spirit which tempted Agamemnon to commit the crime which we have seen visited on him and his children; which tempted Paris to plunge the world in war; which was embodied in Helen and again in Clytemnestra, and was summoned to the support of Orestes when he plotted to kill his mother. Now the same spirit, embodied in Athena, brings the sufferings of three generations to an end (971-6):

Uᴀ

To the eye of Persuasion I give all praise,
That with favour she looked on the breath of my lips
As I strove to appease these powers that once
Were averted in anger; but Zeus who is lord
Of the eloquent word hath prevailed, and at last
In contention for blessings we conquer.

Versed from time immemorial only in the language of malediction, the Erinyes are at first at a loss for words to express their change of heart, and so these "singers of ill" are taught a new song (904–7):

A song of faultless victory: from earth and sea
From skies above may gentle breezes blow
And, breathing sunshine, float from shore to shore.

Quick to learn, the converts call down a shower of blessings on the people whom they have threatened to destroy. They pray that the people of Attica may be blessed by sun and earth, in allusion to the present reconciliation between the upper and nether powers; that the spring blossoms may be protected from the storms, in allusion to the "Spirits who hush the Winds" (Heudanemoi) worshipped on the slopes of the Akropolis; that flocks and herds may multiply by the grace of the goat-god Pan, whose shrine may still be seen on the same hillside, just above the theatre where the drama was performed; that the precious metals of the earth may be brought to light, in allusion to the silver mines of Laurion; that husband and home may be found for each of the daughters of Athens, and that her sons, free from the curse of civil strife,[23] may be brought up in amity and good-will, the whole community being cemented by ties as close as those which had formerly united fellow members of the clan.

Their curses have melted into blessings; Athena has prevailed. But having prevailed, she introduces a note of warning, reminding her people that these divinities are still to be feared by the perjurer (936–8):

He is led unto these to be judged, and the still
Stroke of perdition
In the dust shall stifle his proud boast.

When the Erinyes threatened, Athena sought to assuage; now, when the Erinyes bless, Athena warns. It is like a duet in which, after the bass has taken up the theme of the treble, the treble imitates the bass.

Since the beginning of the century, there had grown up in the city and its environs, attracted by the opportunities of trade, a class of resident aliens (*métoikoi*) whom it was the policy of the government to encourage, although as foreigners they were excluded from civic rights and from the public ceremonies of the state religion. Once a year, however, at the national festival of the Panathenaia, these aliens were not only permitted to take part, but were accorded special marks of honour. The climax of the festival came on the night of the anniversary of Athena's birth, when a robe of saffron, woven by the women of the city, was carried up to the Akropolis in a torchlight procession, led by a band of *épheboi* chosen for the occasion and attended with cries of "Alleluia!" by all the citizens, men and women, old and young, and there hung on the statue of Athena Polias, the goddess of the city-state. In this procession, to mark the purpose of the festival, which was to proclaim peace and good will to all who dwelt under the goddess's protection, the resident aliens were clothed in robes of crimson and attended by a special escort.

The Erinyes have consented to become co-residents with Athena, partakers and joint owners of the soil, and accordingly they now assume the title of *métoikoi* (1012, 1019), accepting the goodwill of the citizens and offering their own. The dominant mood of the Panathenaic festival was rejoicing—not the wild transport of the Bacchants, but deep, restrained, almost solemn joy, the prize of grief and suffering; and accordingly the Erinyes sing (997–1001):

> Joy to you, joy of your justly appointed riches,
> Joy to all the people, blest
> With the Virgin's love, who sits
> Next beside her Father's throne.
> Wisdom ye have learned at last.

At this point a company of women enters the orchestra, carrying lighted torches and crimson robes. Meanwhile Athena returns the greeting (1004–10):

Joy to you likewise! Walking before you,
To the chambers appointed I show you the way,
Led by the sacred lights of the escort.
Come with me, come, and let solemn oblations
Speed you in joy to your homes in the earth.

The Erinyes repeat their greeting, and again Athena thanks
them (1022–32):

I thank you for these words of benison,
And now with flames of torchlit splendour bright
Escort you to your subterranean home,
Attended by the wardens of my shrine,
And justly so; for meet it is that all
The eye of Theseus' people should come forth,
This noble company of comely maids
And women wed and honourable in years.
Adorn them well in robes of crimson dye,
And let these blazing torches lead the way,
So that the goodwill of these residents
Be proved in manly prowess of your sons.

At this point the band of young men takes its place at the head
of the procession. The Erinyes put on their new robes; and in
the light of the torches black gives place to crimson. This blaze
of light and this feast of colour are both fitting symbols to mark
the close of a spectacle in which again and again lights have
been lit only to be quenched in darkness and in which we have
twice gazed in horror on displays of bloodstained purple.

The procession begins to move away, and the women of the
escort invite the Erinyes to accompany them (1041–4):

Gracious and kindly of heart to our people,
Hither, O holy ones, hither in gladness,
Follow the lamps that illumine the way.
O sing at the end, Alleluia!

This "Alleluia!" first raised by Clytemnestra in answer to the
Watchman, heard by Kasandra from the Erinyes on the house-
top, raised again by Clytemnestra over her husband's dead
body and by the friends of Orestes over her own—now, as it
is heard for the last time, it signifies that the spirit of man has

passed through suffering into true and lasting joy; and in the closing words of the trilogy we are reminded of the new harmony in heaven in virtue of which these changes on earth have been effected—Zeus and Moira are reconciled.

By his introduction of the Panathenaic procession, the poet has brought his story out of the darkness of antiquity into the brilliant light of the Athens of his day. It began in the remote and barbarous past, it ends here and now. It is as though at the close of the trilogy he invited his audience to rise from their seats and carry on the drama from the point where he has left it.

Of all the features of the *Oresteia*, the most conspicuous is this organic union between the drama and the community out of which it had emerged and for which it was performed—this perfect harmony between poetry and life. In this respect it is almost unique. The audience of the Globe Theatre which witnessed Shakespeare's plays was a cross-section of the community, ranging from the Court to the proletariat, but the audience at the City Dionysia was more than that—it was the community itself, assembled for the performance of a collective ritual act. The great plays of Shakespeare were not immediately and consciously related to the social movement of his time; in the *Oresteia* the citizens of Athens witnessed the history of their civilisation, culminating in a festival in which all of them annually took part. The only thing in my experience which seems to me comparable is what I saw one evening a few years ago at a dramatic festival in Moscow. It was also a festival of youth. On our way through the streets, our car was held up by throngs of children in pageant costume who greeted us with songs and peals of laughter and pelted the car with flowers. When we got to the Red Square, we found ourselves marooned in a sea of colour as thousands of children from all parts of the city assembled for the pageant. Eventually we reached the Bolshoi Theatre, where we saw the first performance of a new opera, the theme of which was inspired by the emancipation of woman consequent on the abolition of private ownership, and all parts of the auditorium, including the old Imperial Box, were packed out with an alert and critical audience of workpeople. It was then that I realised for the first time the nature of the inspiration behind the *Oresteia*.

XVI

EARLIER PLAYS

THE myth of Io has been discussed in a former chapter, where it was suggested that the extension of the heroine's wanderings to Egypt was a consequence of her identification with the Egyptian Isis (p. 146). How and when this feature of the myth was developed we do not know. It may have originated in the mystical traditions of Demeter, which, both at Argos and at Eleusis, show signs of Egyptian influence; or it may have been introduced by the early Pythagoreans, in whose mystical teaching the same influence can be traced. Its effect was to bring the myth of Io into relation with another—the story of the daughters of Danaos—with which it had no original connection.

Danaos and Aigyptos were brothers, descended from Epaphos, the son whom Io had born to Zeus in Egypt. Danaos had fifty daughters and Aigyptos had fifty sons. The sons of Aigyptos sought their cousins in marriage, but the daughters of Danaos refused and fled overseas to Argos, pursued by their unwelcome suitors. Commending themselves to the people of Argos by their claim to descent from Io, they at first found protection from their pursuers, but eventually they were forced to marry them. In revenge, at their father's command, they murdered their husbands on the wedding night—all except one, Hypermnestra, who by sparing hers became the ancestress of a famous line of kings. According to one tradition, Hypermnestra was brought to trial for having disobeyed her father and acquitted. According to another, the father himself was prosecuted by Aigyptos, who came from Egypt for the purpose, and the feud was resolved through the mediation of Lynkeus, who had married Hypermnestra. It was said that Danaos made the hitherto barren soil of Argos "well-watered"—that is, it may be presumed, he introduced the practice of irrigation. One of his daughters, Amymone, gave her name to a stream in the marshes of Lerna, where Herakles, the most famous of the descendants of Io, slew the Lernean hydra; and the Danaides are said to have expiated their crime in Hades by eternally drawing water in leaking pitchers.[1]

The murder of the sons of Aigyptos by their brides seems to rest on a confusion of traditions. It was the custom at Argos, as at Sparta, for the bride to dress in men's clothes, and at the Argive festival of the Hybristika the men used to dress as women and the women as men. As Halliday has shown,[2] the sexual interchange of clothes is especially associated with initiation, marriage and mourning; and therefore it is to be interpreted as symbolising the change of identity which is necessary in order that the individual may be born again. But this is hardly sufficient to explain why the Danaides were so unwomanly as to murder their husbands. It was said that the women of Argos had once taken up arms and vanquished a force of Spartan invaders in a battle mentioned in a Delphic oracle beginning with the words, "When the female shall conquer the male";[3] and if this is a folk-tale, as it appears to be, rather than a historical tradition, it may have some bearing on the myth, because there are indications—not very clear, it is true—that the Danaides were regarded as female warriors.[4] More to the point, however, is the legend of the women of Lemnos.[5] When the Argonauts landed on that island, they found it "ruled by women" under Queen Hypsipyle, because a short time previously all the women of the island, with the exception of Hypsipyle, who spared her father Thoas, had murdered their fathers and their husbands. This myth was interpreted by Bachofen as pointing to some form of matriarchy, and the crime of the Lemnian women closely resembles that of the Danaides. It would, however, be unwise to press the details further, and perhaps the most we can say is that both legends sprang out of changes in the social status of women. The question that immediately concerns us is how the story of the Danaides was interpreted by Æschylus, and here we are on firmer ground.

The tetralogy which he devoted to this theme began with the *Suppliants*. The other two tragedies were the *Aigyptioi* and the *Danaides*. The satyr play was the *Amymone*.

Accompanied by their father, the Danaides (who form the Chorus) have landed in Argos, and after a prayer to Zeus, the god of suppliants and strangers, they proclaim the Argive origin of their ancestress Io, and implore the gods to overwhelm their pursuers with thunder and lightning before they can bring their ship to harbour. In the *stásimon* which follows, this prayer is repeated in an intensified form. They call upon Epaphos, the "calf-man" born of Io, and the inscrutable power of Zeus to punish the insolence of their suitors, declaring that, should Zeus fail them, they will appeal to the other Zeus, the Zeus of the Dead—in other words, kill themselves. Meanwhile Danaos has descried a company of Argives approaching and instructs his daughters to take their stand as suppliants at the altars. He declares that in seeking this forced match their cousins are sinners, and reminds them that the sinner has to render an account on the day of judgment to Zeus of the Dead.

Interrogated by the King of Argos, the suppliants reveal their descent from Io, thus claiming kin with the Argive people, and explain why they are in flight. They appeal to him for protection, even though it may mean war, because justice is on their side, and to this appeal they add the threat that, if justice is denied to them, they will hang themselves at the altars. Faced with this choice between war and pollution, the King reserves his decision until he has had an opportunity of consulting his people.

Again the Danaides appeal to Zeus, reminding him at length of the wanderings of Io and their consummation in the birth of Epaphos. It is evidently their purpose to persuade Zeus by this means to bring their own wanderings to an equally happy end, but they overlook the deeper significance of the parallel, which is that Io's sufferings concluded in a forced union with her lover.

The King returns, announcing that an assembly of the people has decided to grant the suppliants protection. The resolution was passed by a formal show of hands, and it is couched in legal terms designed to recall the specific conditions on which rights of residence were granted to aliens in contemporary Athens. The Danaides call down blessings on their benefactors, but through their rejoicing there runs a suggestion of strife to come, and they conclude by recalling that it is the duty of children to honour their parents—an allusion to the command which they will receive in the sequel from their father.

At this point Danaos catches sight of the pursuing ship approaching harbour, and hurries off to the city for assistance. His daughters are in despair. "Left alone," they cry, "woman is nothing—there is no fight in her." In the sequel that proverb will be belied. While they are praying for death rather than marriage, a Herald appears from the sons of Aigyptos and begins to drag them off by the hair. He is interrupted by the reappearance of the King, who meets his claim to rightful possession of the fugitives by pointing out that he is guilty of sacrilege and has failed to observe the legal formalities incumbent in such circumstances on a foreigner. The Herald retires, threatening war. The suppliants again bless their saviour and are reminded by their father of the need to conduct themselves with womanly decorum in their new home. As they move away, their rejoicings are mingled with misgivings that the marriage they have averted may be forced on them after all, and their final prayer is set to a rhythm which has acquired a dramatic significance from its association in earlier passages of the play with the idea that such a marriage would be worse than death.[6] From this and other indications it is evident that they have not succeeded in winning the will of Zeus to their side.[7]

—Would that truly the purpose of Zeus . . .
—Who can untangle his path out of the maze of the thicket?
Dark is it everywhere,
Even thrown against Night's blackness, dark to the mortal
    seeker.
Though it fall to the ground seven times,
Yet shall it rise up again, should Zeus will to accomplish.
Hard to search is his mind,
Darkness-wrapt his unknown, winding paths in the trackless
    forest.

Why are the Danaides opposed to marriage with their cousins? It is not merely that their suitors are proud and violent. These qualities have been manifested only in consequence

of their refusal, and it must be remembered that the contrast in this play between the righteousness of the women
and the wickedness of the men is to be followed in the next
with an act of even more violent retaliation. The objection of the
Danaides is of a more concrete nature: it is that the match is
unlawful, unholy—what we should call incestuous. The answer
to our question is therefore likely to be found in the history of
Greek marriage. Now, in Attic law, not only was there no bar to
the marriage of first cousins, but in certain circumstances,
which have been explained in Chapter XII, it was positively
enjoined. If a daughter inherited, as she did in default of sons,
she was claimed in marriage by her father's next-of-kin—his
brothers or their sons; and there was nothing to prevent the
father from bestowing his presumptive heiress in this way
before he died. Consequently, the match proposed by the sons
of Aigyptos is already permissible and proper, and, as soon as
Danaos dies, it will become a legal claim. In fleeing from Egypt
to Argos, the daughters of Danaos are plainly seeking to evade
their obligations. That is the light in which the dispute would
inevitably have been regarded by a contemporary audience;
and, moreover, it is clear that the dramatist has been at pains
to present it in that light, for one of the most striking features of
the play is its wealth of allusions to the procedure and phraseology of contemporary Attic law.[8]

The King himself is dissatisfied with the grounds on which
the suppliants reject the match.[9] "If," he argues, "the sons of
Aigyptos are your masters by the law of the land, claiming to
be your next-of-kin, who would wish to oppose them?" This
passage, with its unmistakable reference to the Attic law of the
heiress, places the dramatist's intention beyond question. It
also suggests that a similar law was believed to exist in Egypt.

One of the characteristics of Egyptian marriage was the
extensive practice of endogamy, especially in the royal family.[10]
Many instances are recorded, from this and earlier periods, of
marriage with a sister or a brother's daughter. Further, it is
agreed by Egyptologists that this practice arose from the desire
to retain succession or inheritance, both of which were partly
transmitted through women, in the male line. And this, as we
have seen, is the motive underlying the Attic law of the heiress.

It would, of course, be a mistake to infer, as Ridgeway has done, that the dispute in the *Suppliants* has anything to do with the conflict between matrilineal and patrilineal inheritance. Of that, in this play, there is no trace. Nevertheless, the analogy which Æschylus has suggested between Athenian and Egyptian practice in this matter is sound, because in the special circumstances of the heiress Attic law prescribed marriages of the same type, and for the same reason, as the Egyptian. The heiress must marry her father's next-of-kin.

The story of the Danaides was told again by Æschylus in the *Prometheus Bound*, where he says that they sought refuge at Argos "fleeing from kindred marriage with cousins."[11] Now, these are precisely the grounds on which, in the *Suppliants*, the sons of Aigyptos justify the marriage—they claim the daughters of Danaos as theirs by right because they are their cousins.[12] It is clear, therefore, that the women reject the match for the very reason that the men demand it—because they are of the same kin. The issue turns on marriage within the kin.

All that is necessary to complete our argument is to show that the same point is made with equal clarity by the Danaides themselves. The difficulty here is that the text of the play is very corrupt; but, with the passages just quoted to guide us, this difficulty can be overcome.

In their appeal to Zeus at the beginning of the play the Danaides declare that they have fled from Egypt "in abhorrence of sinful wedlock of near kindred with the folly-prating sons of Aigyptos." That is how Headlam restored the passage, as against Wilamowitz, who took it to mean that the Danaides reject the match "because they were born to shun men"; and Headlam's interpretation is supported by the almost identical expression in the *Prometheus*, which Wilamowitz ignores.[13]

The King is interrogating the fugitives.[14] "What," he asks, "is your request of me?" "That I may be saved from bondage to the sons of Aigyptos." Why the Danaides regard marriage with their cousins as tantamount to bondage will appear in due course. "Is it because you hate them, or do you mean it is unholy?"

The crux lies in the answer to this question, and unfortunately the text is again corrupt. The choice lies between two interpretations. The first is this: "Who would object to masters that they loved?" The second is this: "Who would buy a kinsman to be her master?" Against the first it may be urged that it implies that the objection to the match is not that it is unholy, but merely that the suitors are personally unacceptable, and this view is contradicted by other passages in the play. Moreover, as we shall see immediately, it does not provide a satisfactory starting-point for the King's next remark. I am convinced that the second interpretation is correct. The Danaides hate the marriage *because* it is unholy, and it is unholy because, for the sake of the accompanying inheritance, the sons of Aigyptos are seeking to marry within the kin. In confirmation of this view, it may be added that exactly the same point is made by Euripides in a passage where Medea, who has been deserted by Jason, gives the woman's attitude to the inferior status of the wife: "We have to buy husbands with money and accept them as masters of our bodies."[15] They take our money, and we become their slaves.

Why, then, is marriage within the kin equivalent to bondage for the woman? This point is explained by the Danaides in answer to the King's next remark. "And yet," he says, "by this means mortal wealth is multiplied." Exactly: the way to accumulate wealth is to keep it "in the family," and that can only be done by keeping the heiress "in the family." This remark of the King's goes straight to the heart of the matter, and shows that Æschylus understood correctly the economic basis of the Attic law of inheritance. The Danaides cannot deny the force of this contention, but what they do is to point out its effect on the position of the woman: "Yes, and when things go badly, divorce is easy!" Under the rule of exogamy, when husband and wife had necessarily belonged to different clans, the wife could appeal, in case of conjugal difficulties, to her kinsmen for protection; but, when the woman marries a member of her own clan, her kinsmen are his and will take his side against her.[16]

The reason why this interpretation, which in the main is Ridgeway's, has not found general acceptance lies in misapprehension regarding the nature of Æschylean art.[17] Those critics who judge Greek poetry from the standpoint of our own, which for the most part holds aloof from social problems, because the social system under which we live is one we are all consciously or unconsciously ashamed of, are not unnaturally disconcerted to find a poet of acknowledged greatness devoting his art to the exposition of a theme so apparently unpoetical as the status of women in contemporary society; but the fault lies in themselves. To Æschylus, social struggle was the means of human progress, and one of the forms which that struggle assumed—the conflict between the sexes—was, as he apprehended, an essential feature of the transition from barbarism to civilisation. Nor is that all. For him and his contemporaries it was still a living issue. If that had not been so, Euripides would not have written the *Medea* nor Aristophanes the *Lysistrata*. As a matter of legislation, the issue had been decided by the laws of Solon, but there must have been many contemporaries of Æschylus whose grandfathers had known Solon; and when we turn to other Greek states, less advanced than Athens, we find that this very issue—the law of the heiress—was still being fought out. Discussing the causes of political disturbances, Aristotle writes:[18]

> And in general disputes among the nobility often embroil the whole state, as at Hestiaia after the Persian Wars, when two brothers quarrelled about the division of their patrimony, the one espousing the popular cause, because his brother had failed to produce a clear statement of his father's wealth, while the other, being rich, sided with the party of the rich. . . . At Mitylene, a quarrel about heiresses led to a series of calamities, including the war with Athens. A wealthy citizen, Timophanes, had left two daughters, whom Doxandros tried but failed to obtain in marriage for his sons, and being thus thrust aside he fomented a civil war and incited the Athenians, whose official representative he was. At Phokis, it was a quarrel about heiresses between Mnaseas, the father of Mnason, and Euthykrates, the son of Onomarchos, that started the Sacred War.

Having grasped the social nature of the issue, we may recognise without danger of misunderstanding its moral aspect. On this point, D. S. Robertson writes:[19]

What did Æschylus mean by the trilogy as a whole? He must have raised some moral problem which he felt to be fundamental, and I cannot believe, with Ridgeway, that this was the question of exogamy. So far as I can follow the thought of the *Suppliants* (and I claim no novelty for my view), the real issue seems to be the right of women to refuse to be forced into marriage. The Danaids' hatred of marriage is indeed meant to be fanatical . . . but fundamentally they are justified. The crime of the sons of Aigyptos is their determination to force themselves on unwilling brides.

If that was the crime of the sons of Aigyptos, it was a crime enjoined in democratic Athens by an express provision of the law and committed regularly by the dramatist's contemporaries in the happy belief that by so doing they were serving simultaneously the gods, the state and their own interests.[20] Robertson has not thought out the implications of his argument, and it is instructive to observe that this interpretation of the play, which is still the most generally accepted, breaks down on a point of the same nature as the conventional interpretation of the *Oresteia* (p. 289). In both cases the moral issue has been isolated from its social context. The influence of private property on the morals of the proprietors raises issues which contemporary critics are instinctively reluctant to explore, and so they "cannot believe" it is fundamental. To Æschylus, however, living in the heyday of ancient democracy, the subjection of women was not only just, but preferable to the liberty which they had formerly enjoyed. In all stages of society the prevailing code of morals is at once a reflection and a justification of the established social order. The reason why the Egyptians regarded marriage with one's sister as right and proper is simply that in Egypt private ownership had developed in such a way as to make such marriages expedient; and in the case of Æschylus the social basis of his moral judgments is exceptionally clear, because he himself was conscious of it. The work of such a poet necessarily presents difficulties to those who have not analysed their own relation to contemporary society.

The extant evidence is insufficient to indicate more than the outlines of the remainder of the trilogy; but, if our interpretation of the first play is correct, the conclusion to which the drama is tending is already fairly clear. The murder of the bridegrooms probably took place in the second play, and the trial in the third. A few lines from a speech by Aphrodite in the *Danaides* have been preserved:[21]

> The pure Sky yearns with love to wound the Earth,
> The loving Earth yearns likewise to be wed,
> And from the heavenly bridegroom showers descend
> Upon the bride, who brings forth for mankind
> The grazing cattle and Demeter's corn,
> With precious moisture ripening the fruits
> To autumn fulness. In this I too have part.

These words were evidently spoken by the goddess of love in vindication of Hypermnestra, who, we are told in the *Prometheus*, was moved by love to spare her husband.[22] Aphrodite is to Hypermnestra what Apollo is to Orestes. The daughter who chose to cleave to her husband rather than obey her father is justified at law, and in this way the institution of matrimony, involving the subordination of the woman to the man, is formally established.

It follows that the defendant at the trial must have been Hypermnestra and not Danaos. This does not mean, as Robertson supposes, that Æschylus regarded her sisters as either obviously guiltless or obviously unpardonable. The struggle between the Danaides and their suitors was not a conflict between right and wrong, but between two rights, one old and the other new. The acquittal of Hypermnestra does, of course, condemn her sisters by implication, and that, in Robertson's opinion, would be "a lame conclusion."[23] But, in the first place, we cannot be sure that it *was* the conclusion, because the insistence in the first play on the idea of the judgment of the dead suggests the possibility that the trilogy concluded with a reference to the fate of the Danaides in the other world. And, in any case, the important thing is not the condemnation of the others, who acted, like the Erinyes, on a principle which has only now been superseded, but the acquittal of Hypermnestra, who is vindicated, like Orestes, by an appeal to historical expediency.

We saw that at the end of the *Oresteia* the old order

represented by the Erinyes was not simply abolished, but adapted and merged into the new, and that by this means Athena secured their goodwill. Now, according to Herodotus, the Danaides brought to Greece from Egypt a mystical cult of Demeter.[24] After the Dorian invasion, this cult disappeared from most parts of the Peloponnese, but it survived in Arcadia, and also at Athens, where it formed the basis of the festival of the Thesmophoria, which was reserved to women. Attention was first called to this evidence over a century ago, but the editors of Æschylus have ignored it, and the credit for reasserting its importance belongs to Robertson, who rightly observes that "on the analogy of the *Eumenides* we might expect to find the final solution symbolised by Æschylus in the foundation of some religious institution safeguarding the dignity of women." Accordingly, he suggests that this trilogy ended with the institution of the Thesmophoria, just as the *Oresteia* ended with the institution of the Court of the Areopagus. There can be little doubt that this view is correct. The women were reconciled to their changed status by the foundation of a festival in which they enjoyed exclusive rights. It is, moreover, not improbable that, as an epithet of Demeter, the word *thesmophóros* refers to the institution of marriage. This is disputed, although, as Robertson points out, the epithet was certainly interpreted in that way by Latin writers. However that may be, the festival had another significance which Æschylus would not have overlooked. It was essentially, as Jane Harrison has shown,[25] an act of agrarian magic, and in Attic tradition it was Demeter who, by means of her mysteries, had introduced the art of agriculture. We have already remarked that in the Argive tradition the Danaides were associated with the introduction of irrigation, and therefore, if this trilogy concluded with the foundation of the Thesmophoria, we may be sure that Æschylus took the opportunity to stress what was in fact an achievement of the female sex as well as a historic landmark in the material progress of mankind.

We see therefore that from the outset of his career Æschylus was concerned with the evolutionary process which had transformed the primitive Attica of tradition into contemporary Athens, and already revealed an attitude to the problem which we have identified as characteristic of his own position in the world he was endeavouring to explain.

The *Persians* was the second tragedy in a tetralogy of which the first was the *Phineus* and the third the *Glaukos Potnieus*, followed by a satyr play called the *Prometheus Pyrkaeus*. These titles show that, whether or not there was any homogeneity in the treatment, there was no continuity of plot. Each play dealt with a different theme. This therefore is the earliest known example of a disconnected tetralogy.

It was produced in 472 B.C.—the year before the banishment of Themistokles. Four years earlier, probably with Themistokles as his *choregós*, Phrynichos had produced a tragedy called the *Phoinissai* on the subject of the victory at Salamis. It is therefore significant that, when Æschylus expounded the same theme in his *Persians*, his *choregós* was Perikles of the Alkmaionidai, the future leader of Athenian democracy. At this time Perikles was a young man, not much more than twenty, and a supporter of Kimon, whose naval operations in Ionia were laying the foundations of the Athenian Empire. It may be inferred that Æschylus too supported the policy of Kimon, and this harmonises with the other evidence that he was a moderate democrat.

The play opens with a long passage from the Chorus of Persian Elders, who, like the old men in the *Agamemnon*, have been left at home, awaiting news of the war. The flower of Asiatic manhood, drawn from all the fabulously wealthy cities of the East, is *gone*. This word, insistently repeated, carries in Greek the ominous implication that the strength and opulence of Asia is gone, never to return. The old men are anxious, and the wives and mothers of the Persian capital are counting the days. News has already reached them of the passage of the Hellespont—how the young king Xerxes forced the sea-god to do his bidding by lashing pontoons across the narrow waters. The might of Persia has been hitherto invincible, but never before has it faced the perils of the sea: can it be that jealous gods are luring it to destruction? These are the forebodings that make many a bride bathe her deserted bed in tears.

The King's mother, Atossa, at the threshold of the palace, reveals that her sleep has been disturbed by a dream which

WA

seems to signify that, while her son has mastered Ionia, Greece will throw off the yoke. In reply to her anxious questions the Elders tell her that Athens lies far away in the sunset, and that the Athenians, who serve no despot, have already proved their fighting spirit. These replies bring no comfort to the mother of an absent son.

A breathless messenger brings news from Salamis. The Elders break into lamentation as they hear of the disaster which will make the hated name of Athens memorable for ever. Then the Queen, who has controlled her grief, asks the names of the survivors and the fallen. Xerxes lives, but Artembares and Dadakes and Tenagon—one by one, the Messenger names all the king's vassals who have died a brave man's death in battle. The city of Athens has been sacked, but the men of Athens live. The disaster began when an avenging demon in the guise of a Greek deluded Xerxes into believing that the enemy was about to take to flight (p. 228). After the description of the battle, which is, of course, as it is claimed to be, an eye-witness's account, the Queen cries out against the fiend which enticed the fleet to its destruction, and to crown her grief she hears how the retreating army has been decimated by cold and famine.

The Elders continue their lamentation, contrasting the young king's fatal impetuosity with the wisdom of his father, and, when the Queen returns with offerings for her husband's tomb, they take on the character of the Persian Magi, chanting a necromantic invocation, in response to which the ghost of Darius rises from the earth to ask what calamity it is that has disturbed his rest. The Queen repeats for him the news of Salamis, and after condemning the harnessing of the Hellespont as an act of pride inviting the jealousy of Heaven, he declares that Salamis is not the end, predicting the rout of the Persian army in the ensuing year. When he has gone, the Elders sing a hymn in praise of the dead king who raised Persia to greatness and extended her empire from sea to sea but wisely refrained from attempting more. At the end of the hymn Xerxes himself appears, uncontrolled in his grief, dishevelled, his robes torn, and the play concludes with an Oriental dirge.

The central theme of the play, apart from the patriotic senti-
ment which animates the whole, is the idea that wealth breeds
pride, which is punished by the gods. This, as we have seen,
is the old aristocratic tradition, which Æschylus has systematised
and elaborated, developing its latent implications and enrich-
ing the imagery associated with it, but substantially he has
added nothing new. Consequently, in intellectual content this
play is the poorest of the seven. It is an eloquent homily on
a rather tedious text.

Even from a more narrowly dramatic point of view, it is
not altogether a success. It begins with a dynamic opening
which makes a magnificent prelude to the entry of Atossa and
by the same impetus carries us to the exultant rhetoric of the
Messenger's report. All this is very like the opening of the
Agamemnon. But it is not followed up. Atossa, on whom our
attention has been fixed, recedes before the figure of Darius,
and he in turn gives place to Xerxes. The appearance of Darius
is theatrically effective, but he does little more than reinforce
a lesson we have already learnt, and by this time the rhetoric
is becoming monotonous. It is difficult for us to take much
interest in the humiliated Xerxes, and in the concluding dirge
even the diction flags, sinking to the level of mere ritual. The
trouble is that the dramatist has chosen a theme whose conclusion is necessarily unconstructive. To make up for this
deficiency, he has appealed insistently to the nationalist feelings of his audience, and in this he was evidently successful,
because he won the prize; but we are left with the impression
that he was not at home in the disconnected tetralogy, and
for my own part I would willingly have exchanged the *Persians*
for the lost sequel of the *Suppliants* or the *Prometheus*.

The Seven against Thebes, produced five years later, was preceded by the *Laios* and the *Œdipus*, and followed by the *Sphinx*.[26]
Unfortunately, it is doubtful whether the form in which we
have it is intact. Most students of Æschylus are agreed that
the concluding scene between the Herald and Antigone is
spurious, being added at a time when the work of Sophokles
and Euripides on the same theme had made it difficult to
ignore the fate of Antigone, as Æschylus had done; and it is

at least probable that this spurious conclusion has ousted something else.

Laios was King of Thebes, and he received an oracle from Delphi commanding him "to save the state by dying without offspring." The terms of the oracle are recalled explicitly in the surviving play. They imply that the welfare of the community is dependent on the conduct of the king who rules it —a primitive notion which has been discussed in connection with the magical functions of the early kingship (p. 117). They also imply a conflict between the interests of the state and those of the ruling dynasty. As King of Thebes, Laios should have died childless, but by so doing he would have failed to fulfil his obligations as the leader of his clan.[27] Accordingly, "prevailed upon by the folly of his kinsmen," he became by Jocasta the father of a son, Œdipus.[28] After the child was born, the parents took fright and exposed it; but Œdipus grew up unknown to them. Returning to Thebes as a young man ignorant of his parentage, he fell in with his father on the road from Thebes to Delphi, quarrelled with him, and killed him. Then, having read the riddle of the Sphinx, he was acclaimed King in place of Laios and married the widowed Queen. Some time later the royal pair discovered their true relationship. In Sophokles, the discovery follows from a public pestilence consequent on the double crime which Œdipus has committed; and if, as seems likely, Æschylus used the same tradition, it provided a manifestation of the working of the oracle and of the principle that the welfare of the people was vested in the King's person. After the discovery, Jocasta hanged herself. Œdipus put out his eyes, and was held a prisoner by his sons, Eteokles and Polyneikes, in the palace dungeon. One day, at table, Œdipus was served by his sons with a haunch instead of the shoulder, which was the royal *géras* or portion; and, enraged by this affront, he cursed them, praying that they should divide their paternal heritage by the sword.[29] After his death, the brothers quarrelled over the succession, and Polyneikes fled to Argos, whence shortly afterwards, like the tyrant Hippias, he returned to recover his patrimony by force of foreign arms. It is at this point that the surviving play begins.

Eteokles regards himself as the pilot of the state. This idea of the ship of state, which recurs throughout the play, is intended to imply that the ship will weather the storm so long as the captain keeps his head. Having been informed of the approach of the invaders from Argos, Eteokles summons the people to the defence of their native land, and, after hearing a scout's report of the enemy's plan of attack, he prays to the gods for victory:[30]

> O Zeus, and Earth, O gods who guard this city,
> And thou, Erinys, my father's mighty Curse,
> Vouchsafe that this my people, Greek in speech,
> Be not uprooted from their hearths and homes
> Nor bent beneath the yoke of slavery!

The Erinys is here regarded as the King's ancestral spirit, and the allusion to the people of Thebes as Greek in speech (in fact, of course, the enemy was the same) means that we are to regard the expedition against Thebes in the light of the Persian invasion.

After the King has hurried off to supervise the defences, the orchestra is filled with a chorus of panic-stricken women, terrified by the thought that the gods have deserted the city. Harassed, but without losing his presence of mind, the King returns to restore order. Rebuking them sharply for their lack of confidence, he prays sarcastically that never in good fortune or in bad may he consort with woman—a point which is important for the sequel, because it implies that he is un-married.[31] The frightened women explain that their ears are filled with the din of passing chariots, and the King retorts:[32]

> What of it? When did a seaman ever save
> His ship from foundering in the hurricane
> By scuttling from the helm into the prow?

Having succeeded at last to some extent in calming them, he returns to his task of organising the defence. There are seven gates to the city, and he will appoint seven champions, includ-ing himself, to man them. Meanwhile the women address a hymn to the gods, imploring them not to forsake their worshippers and still harping on the horrors that are enacted in a conquered city. In this, too, the dramatist is evidently appealing to memories of the Persian occupation.

So far the King's conduct of affairs has been admirable. His military preparations are well in hand, and, though the indiscipline of the non-combatants has threatened to hamper his plans, he has kept his head. We are almost lulled into forgetting that this capable leader is under a curse. The Erinys is asleep.

The attack is now imminent. The enemy champions are taking up their positions, one at each gate, and as they do so they are described in detail from a point of vantage by a scout in order that for each of the assailants the King may appoint a defender. In contrast to the enemy champions, who are loud in their boasts, defying God and man alike, the King replies by asserting his confidence in the justice of his cause.

Five of the gates have now been disposed of. The sixth is being attacked by the prophet Amphiaraos, who has denounced Polyneikes for taking up arms against his country and foresees his own death on the disastrous expedition in which he has participated against his will and judgment. Eteokles replies:[33]

> Alas, what evil augury in mortal life
> Unites a righteous man with the ungodly!
> Of all things worst, no matter what the task,
> Is wicked fellowship. It bears no fruit—
> A crop of madness harvested in death . . .
> Maybe he will not move to the assault,
> Not lacking courage or a manly spirit,
> But knowing that he goes to meet his death,
> If the oracles of Apollo are fulfilled,
> Who speaks to the purpose or else holds his peace.

As the enemy champions are named one by one, followed by the names of their opponents, we realise with growing horror that the two brothers have independently reserved the seventh gate for themselves. Eteokles alone is in the dark, and, when he perceives the truth, the ancestral curse is once more awake in him, confounding his sense of right and wrong:[34]

> O lamentable race of Œdipus,
> Infatuate, abominable, abhorred,
> At last it is fulfilled, our father's curse!

The name of Justice, which Polyneikes has emblazoned on his shield, is flung back in his teeth.[35]

> I place my trust in justice, and I myself
> Shall fight him—what antagonist so just?
> King against king and brother against brother.

It is now the women's turn to plead for reason, and they plead in vain. Eteokles has gone mad.[36]

> The Curse of Œdipus has broken out.
> Too true those visions that foretold by night
> How we should share our father's heritage!

While the battle is being fought, the Chorus review the whole history of the curse from the time when Apollo spoke to Laios down to the present moment, and then a Messenger brings news of victory:

> The state is saved, but Earth has drunk the blood
> Of royal brothers, slain by each other's hand.

Eteokles and Polyneikes have died without offspring. The ancestral spirit of the royal dynasty has now been laid to rest, because the dynasty itself is extinct. The oracle given to Laios has been fulfilled.

In seeking to interpret the general significance of the conclusion, we are hampered by the presence of contradictions due to interpolation of the text, and the spurious elements are not always easy to delimit. It seems clear, however, that, as Æschylus wrote it, the end of the story was marked by a striking deviation from the epic tradition, which he has closely followed hitherto. In that tradition, both brothers had sons, and the son of Polyneikes avenged his father by a second expedition against the city, which resulted in its destruction. By bringing the story to an end with the death of the two brothers, he has reduced its compass from four generations to three, thus adapting it to the form of the trilogy; and by the same means he has produced a conclusion, in which, while the clan has perished, the state survives, thus developing the full implications of the oracle. The Theban kings were under an ancestral curse which brought successive calamities on the people as well as on themselves, and therefore it is necessary that the primitive system of kinship, which the ancestral curse implies, should be superseded by the higher organisation of the state, in which the clans lose their identity in common citizenship.[37] Owing to the condition of the text, this interpretation is necessarily conjectural and probably incomplete, but, if it is substantially correct, it means that Æschylus was already moving towards the general theory of the origin of the state which he formulated nine years later in the *Oresteia*.

XVII

PROMETHEIA

PROMETHEUS, it was once said, is the patron saint of the proletariat.

It was Prometheus who bestowed on man the gift of fire, which he had brought down from the sun stored in a fennel stalk. That is the primitive nucleus of the myth, which can be traced in this or similar forms all over the world. It is a genuine folk-memory of the earliest and one of the most revolutionary steps in the advancement of material technique. Its significance in this respect has been well described by Gordon Childe.[1]

> In the comparatively short evolutionary history docu-mented by fossil remains, man has not improved his inherited equipment by bodily changes detectable in his skeleton. Yet he has been able to adjust himself to a greater range of environments than almost any other creature, to multiply infinitely faster than any other near relative among the higher mammals, and to beat the polar bear, the hare, the hawk, and the tiger at their special tricks. Through his control of fire and the skill to make clothes and houses, man can, and does, live and thrive from the Arctic Circle to the Equator. In the trains and cars he builds, man can outstrip the fleetest hare or ostrich. In aeroplanes he can mount higher than the eagle, and with telescopes see farther than the hawk. With firearms he can lay low animals that a tiger dare not tackle. But fire, clothes, houses, trains, aeroplanes, telescopes and guns are not, we must repeat, part of man's body. He can leave them and lay them aside at will. They are not inherited in the biological sense, but the skill needed for their production and use is part of our social heritage, the result of a tradition accumulated over many generations, and transmitted, not in the blood, but through speech and writing.

In the myth of Prometheus, the first of these technical advances became a symbol for the rest. Fire stands for the material basis of civilisation. That is the one constant element in the myth. The others vary, because this myth has a history of its own, being continuously reinterpreted and adapted to new developments in the process of which it is a symbol. The higher stages of that process were conditional, as we have seen, on the division of society into economically unequal classes—into those that performed the actual labour of production and those that enjoyed the wealth and leisure thus produced. This division created, among the rulers, the need to justify their privileged position, and, among the ruled, a sense of frustration springing from the perception that their own wealth and leisure had not kept pace with the increasing productivity of their work. The primitive form of the myth, which simply registered the pride of the community in the success of its collective struggle against its material environment, was no longer adequate, because out of the struggle between man and Nature had now emerged the struggle between man and man. Accordingly, it was complicated and elaborated.

The peasants of Hesiod were hungry and oppressed. Why were they condemned to toil so hard and enjoy so little? Because man had sinned against his masters. Once the human race had lived in happiness without sickness or labour or the need to win their bread in the sweat of their brows. That was the Reign of Kronos, when the untilled earth had brought forth of itself abundance of good things, which all men enjoyed in common; and in those days, of course, they had possessed the gift of fire. This happy state of things was brought to an end through the culpability of Prometheus, who, at a banquet of the gods, tried to cheat Zeus of the special portion which was his due. In punishment for this offence Zeus deprived man of fire. Prometheus replied by stealing it from heaven and restoring it to man. Zeus then impaled him on a rock, where he was tormented by an eagle, which visited him daily to devour his liver, until he was released by Herakles. Meanwhile, the human race remained in possession of the gift of fire, but to it was added another gift—Pandora and her box, which, when the lid was removed, let loose over the world labour, sorrow, sickness and a multitude of plagues. And so, Hesiod tells his listeners, had it not been for Prometheus, who provoked the gods into withholding from men their means of living, "you would have been able to do easily in a day enough work to keep you for a year, to hang up your rudder in the chimney corner, and let your fields run to waste."[2]

Thus, for the peasants of Hesiod, Prometheus, the pioneer in man's conquest of nature, had been degraded to the level of a common malefactor. Material progress has been complicated by the class struggle in such a way that for them, instead of enlarging, it has diminished the sum of human happiness. Such was the form which the myth had assumed under the aristocracy. But that form was not final any more than the aristocracy itself.

The story of Prometheus is not mentioned in the Homeric poems, nor, so far as we know, was it treated in choral lyric. It was not the sort of story to appeal to members of the aristocracy. In our records, its next exponent after Hesiod is Æschylus himself; but, while his version was doubtless to a large extent his own creation, it contains certain structural features which clearly have their roots in the mystical teaching of the Orphics. At the beginning of the trilogy, Prometheus describes himself as banished from the company of the gods and as about to endure an agony that will last thousands of years; throughout the first play his torments are described with reference to the idea of Ananke or Necessity; at the end of it he is hurled down into Hades, whence, at the opening of the second, he has been brought up again to earth; and, finally, after his penance has lasted for a total period of 30,000 years,[3] he is readmitted to Olympus. This is the Orphic Wheel of Necessity—the cycle that leads the soul from divinity to birth and death and thence back to divinity. In the words of Empedokles:[4]

> There is an oracle of Necessity, an ordinance of the gods, ancient, eternal and sealed by broad oaths, that whenever one of the *daímones*, whose portion is length of days, has sinfully stained his hands with blood or followed strife or forsworn himself, he shall be banished from the abodes of the blessed for thrice ten thousand seasons, being born throughout the time in all manner of mortal shapes, exchanging one toilsome path for another. . . . One of these am I now, an exile

and a wanderer from the gods, because I put my trust in
insensate strife.

Alas, unhappy race of men, bitterly unblest, such are the
groans and struggles from which ye have been born!

But at the last they appear among mankind as prophets,
poets, physicians and princes; and thence they arise as gods,
exalted in honour, sharing with the other gods a common
hearth and table, free from the miseries of mortality, without
part therein, untroubled.

Set against this background, the sufferings of the Æschylean
Prometheus appear as the sufferings of man himself, cast down
from heaven into misery and death but destined to rise again.

The cults of Prometheus were few and insignificant. At
Athens, he was worshipped in the Academy together with
Athena and Hephaistos, who were also closely associated with
the handicrafts that man had learnt from his control of fire.
All three were honoured with torch races, run by the *épheboi*
from some point outside the city to one of the altars within it
with the object of renewing the sacred fire.[5] In origin, these
races were probably ordeals of initiation, like the foot-races at
Olympia.

Prometheus was delivered by Herakles, a figure far more
prominent both in myth and cult, and far too complex to be
discussed in detail here. He was a son of Zeus by Alkmene, a
descendant of Io, and he was sent into the world to clear it of
primeval monsters for the benefit of man. The last of his
labours was a descent into Hades, for which he prepared himself by initiation at Eleusis, and after it he ascended into heaven
and received in marriage Hera's daughter, Hebe. Here, too,
we can discern traces of the mystical sequence of strife, death,
and deification.[6]

Turning to the *Prometheus Bound*, the first question that we
ask ourselves is, where does the poet intend our sympathies to
lie as between the two antagonists? It is a vital question, because the answer to it necessarily reveals so much both in the
poet and his critics. If modern readers of the play have given
sharply divergent answers to this question, it is not, as we shall
see, because there is any ambiguity in the play itself, but
because, on an issue so crucial as that of rebellion against the

established order, they have been forced to disclose their own attitude to contemporary society. Thus, Mahaffy expressed himself as follows:[7]

> Despotic sovereignty was the Greek's ideal for himself, and most nations have thought it not only reconcilable with, but conformable to, the dignity of the great Father who rules the world. No Athenian, however he sympathised with Prometheus, would think of blaming him for asserting his power and crushing all resistance to his will.

What Mahaffy has done is to shut his eyes to the democratic tradition and to present as the Greek's ideal for himself Mahaffy's ideal for himself—the ideal of the Anglo-Irish aristocracy, as formulated by another member of the same class, Edmund Burke:[8]

> Good order is the foundation of all good things. To be enabled to acquire, the people, without being servile, must be tractable and obedient. The magistrate must have his reverence, the laws their authority. The body of the people must not find the principles of natural subordination by art rooted out of their minds. They must respect that property of which they cannot partake. They must labour to obtain what by labour can be obtained; and, when they find, as they commonly do, the success disproportioned to the endeavour, they must be taught their consolation in the final proportions of eternal justice.

I still remember my dismay, when, after reading the play for the first time at school, I was asked to accept Mahaffy's view, and the comfort I derived from Shelley's reassuring words: "But in truth I was averse from a catastrophe so feeble as that of reconciling the Champion with the Oppressor of mankind." Later we shall examine Shelley's treatment of the myth, and see where and why it differed from the Æschylean; but, so far as the first play of the trilogy is concerned, Shelley's intuition was sound—there Zeus *is* the "oppressor of mankind" and their champion's "perfidious adversary." And the reason why Shelley came nearer to the truth than classical scholars, who have studied the evidence far more closely than he did, is

that Shelley was, like Æschylus himself, what they never were—
a revolutionary poet.

Zeus is a tyrant and his rule is a tyranny. We learn this from
his own ministers, who are proud of it (10); from Prometheus,
who denounces it (238, 321, 373, 762, 782, 941, 974, 988–90,
1028); from the Ocean Nymphs, who deplore it (201); and
from the God of Ocean, who is resigned to it (326). The fact is
incontestable, and the only question is how the dramatist
intended his audience to interpret it.

The history of the tyranny at Athens has been reviewed in
an earlier chapter, where we saw how the progressive character
of its opening phase became obscured in retrospect by the
reactionary tendencies which it subsequently developed
(p. 93). We also saw that, when the Athenians had to face a
Persian landing at Marathon, the exiled Hippias was on the
Persian side; and, even after the Persian menace had been
removed, Athenian democrats found it necessary to remain
constantly on their guard against the danger that some influential aristocrat, a Miltiades or an Alkibiades, might make
a bid for the position which Hippias had lost. The result was
that, in the fifth century at Athens, there grew up a traditional
conception of the tyrant, endowed with all the qualities which
the people had experienced in Hippias; and eventually, owing
partly to similar experiences elsewhere and partly to the
dominant influence exercised by Attic writers in the development of thought, this tradition became fixed.[9] Thus, Herodotus
describes the tyrant as irresponsible, with a dangerous tendency
towards pride, suspicions of his best citizens, and, above all,
violent, a ravisher of women. Similar arguments are repeated
by Theseus in his dispute with the herald from Argos in the
Suppliants of Euripides. The tyrant is a law to himself; he cuts
off his leading citizens as he might the tallest ears of corn (in
accordance with the advice which, so Herodotus tells us, was
actually given by one tyrant to another); and, lastly, parents
cannot safeguard their daughters from his violence.

The tragedians were naturally quick to turn this tradition to
dramatic advantage. In the *Antigone*, for example, the heroine
bitterly declares that one of the privileges of the tyranny is to
do and say what it likes; and in the *Persians* Atossa raises her

defeated son above the reach of popular reproach with the significant reminder that he is not responsible to his people. In the *Œdipus Tyrannus*, as Sheppard has shown, the character of the king is thrown into ominous relief by a number of such allusions, which, though for the most part implicit, were readily appreciated by an audience made familiar with such technique by Æschylus.

The ministers whom Zeus has appointed to escort Prometheus to his place of confinement are Might and Violence, the one signifying his power, the other the method by which he exercises it. He is described as harsh (202, 340), as irresponsible (340), as unconstitutional, acknowledging no laws but his own, a law to himself (159, 419, 202-3); he is suspicious of his friends—a feature described expressly as characteristic of the tyrant (240-1); implacable and impervious to persuasion (34, 199-201, 349); and, above all, in his treatment of Io, he reveals his violence (761-3). The brutality of this episode is not, as in the *Suppliants*, veiled in lyric poetry; on the contrary, the poet seems to be at pains to fill his audience, like his own Oceanids, with abhorrence. Zeus tried first persuasion and then threats to bend the unhappy girl to his will. This is the method Prometheus expected of him, and it is typical of the tyrant. Hence there can be no question where the sympathies of an Athenian audience must have lain—or, indeed, of any popular audience—when Prometheus breaks off his prediction of Io's future agonies with the impassioned cry (761):

> Is it not plain to you
> That the tyrant of the gods is violent
> In all his ways alike?

In view of this evidence, it is fairly clear that those critics who can pass judgment against the hero who has dared to rebel against this heartless despotism have been influenced by factors independent of the dramatist's intention.

The characterisation of Prometheus is more complex. In the opening scene, the sinister figure of Violence eyes the prisoner in silence. Might assails him with insults as he spurs Hephaistos to the task of binding him, but does not address him directly till he flings at him his parting taunt (82-7). Hephaistos alone is filled with compassion. He recognises his crime, by which indeed, as god of fire, he has been particularly affected; yet he forgets his own loss in sympathy for the sufferer. Prometheus is silent.

The compassion of Hephaistos is that of kin for kin (14, 39). The same feeling prompts the visit of the Ocean Nymphs (130–1) and is professed by their father Ocean (305–6), who counsels moderation, but with an underlying subservience to authority that marks him as a type of the trimmer or conformer; and Prometheus dismisses him with politely veiled contempt. The Ocean Nymphs have said nothing in the presence of their father, but after his departure they are forced to confess that with them, too, sympathy is tempered with disapproval. So far the indignation of Prometheus has been controlled; but during his discourse with Io we feel the anger rising in him, and, when his enemy's victim is carried away in a sudden agony of pain, the reaction is immediate. The Nymphs, horrified and terrified, bow down in helpless submission. Prometheus, on the other hand, hurls at his antagonist a speech of reckless denunciation and defiance. Yet he does not forfeit our sympathy, because this change of attitude corresponds to our own reaction to the brutality of Zeus manifested in the spectacle of Io. The Nymphs remonstrate, but he is deaf to their appeals. Hermes arrives with a peremptory demand that he shall reveal the secret with which he threatens his master's supremacy; yet even Hermes, when he perceives the prisoner's state of mind, joins with the Nymphs in a sincere attempt to reason with him. But Prometheus, who received the insults of Might in silence, himself assails Hermes with insults; and in dramatic fulfilment of his own prayer (161–8, 1083–6) he is cast into the pit of Tartarus. The ambivalent effect of the last scene on the audience is faithfully reflected in the attitude of the Chorus, who, while disapproving as strongly as Hermes of the prisoner's lack of restraint, nevertheless refuse to desert him.

Thus, the play ends in a deadlock. The ruler of the gods is a tyrant, the champion of mankind has been reproved by his own friends for exceeding the bounds of moderation. The wrath of Zeus is a disease, and the unrestraint of Prometheus is a disease. This metaphor, which is of course intended to suggest the hope of a cure to come, recurs again and again throughout the play. The world is out of joint, and only a change in both antagonists can set it right.

While insisting on the tyrannical nature of the rule of Zeus, Æschylus is careful to impress on us at the outset, and to remind us repeatedly, that his power is new. He is displaying the world not as it is now but as it was in the beginning. In the course of 30,000 years, taught by experience, the adversaries will be reconciled. So we are told, early in the play, by Prometheus himself, whose vision is as yet unclouded by passion (206-8). Later, forgetting his own prophecy, he can foresee nothing in store for his enemy but destruction (939-59); but the truth re-emerges in his final altercation with Hermes (1011-14). Reminded of his lost bliss, Prometheus inadvertently utters a cry of grief—"Ah me!"—of which Hermes is quick to take advantage:

> "Ah me!"—that is a cry unknown to Zeus.

At the mention of his enemy, Prometheus recovers himself:

> All things are being taught by ageing Time.

But again Hermes is ready with his retort:

> Yes, *you* have yet to learn where wisdom lies.

With this allusion to the doctrine of wisdom through suffering, the scattered hints of an impending change in both antagonists are significantly brought together at the end of the play.

It is clear, therefore, that in the sequel both antagonists will learn by experience; but of course that is very far from saying that Prometheus ought not to have done what he has done. It is true that, when they hear of his theft of fire, the Oceanids exclaim, shocked by his audacity, that he has sinned; but, if so, it is a sin which has saved humanity from annihilation, and, if any further doubt remain as to the dramatist's attitude on this point, it is dispelled by the hero's narration of the conse-quences of his sin for the destiny of man (458-522):

> No more of that, for it is known to you,
> But listen to the sufferings of mankind,

XA

In whom, once speechless, senseless, like a child,
I planted mind and the gift of understanding . . .
At first, with eyes to see, they saw in vain,
With ears to hear, they heard not, groping through
Their lives at random, like figures in a dream,
All in a blind confusion, without the skill
To carve in wood or build against the sun
Houses of brick, but sheltering like ants
In sun-forsaken subterranean caverns,
With no sure sign of approaching winter's frosts,
No herald of spring-blossoms or the ripe
Fruits of the harvest, labouring without wit
In all their works, till I instructed them
In the mysterious courses of the stars,
In the art of number, a most excellent
Invention, in the written alphabet,
The Muses' mother, the world's memorial.
And I first tamed the wild beasts of the field,
Enslaved in pack and harness, to relieve
The human labourer of his heaviest loads,
And yoked in chariots, quick to obey the rein,
Proud, prancing ornaments of high estate,
And I it was contrived the mariner's car
On hempen wing riding the trackless ocean . . .
Nay, hear the rest, and you shall marvel more
At the resource of my imagination.
Of all the chief was this—when men fell sick,
They knew no remedy, no shredded herb,
No draught to drink or ointment—in default
Of physic their strength was wasting, until I
Discovered gently tempered medicines
To shield them from all manner of disease . . .
All this I gave, and more—beneath the earth,
Long-buried benefits of humanity,
Iron and bronze, silver and gold, who else
Can claim to have discovered these but I?
None, I know well, unless an idle chatterer.
In these few words learn briefly my whole story:
Prometheus founded all the arts of man.

All this, as the details of the passage show, belongs to the
tradition of the Pythagoreans—the same tradition which we

have illustrated from Hippokrates' account of the origin of medicine (p. 218); and the striking thing about it is its bold materialism. This combination of materialism with mysticism, which we have already noticed in the work of Æschylus, was evidently characteristic of the early Pythagoreans. We find it again in Empedokles, whose preoccupation with the revival of magical practices and beliefs did not prevent him from making solid contributions to science. How the Pythagoreans reconciled these two sides to their teaching, we do not know; but it seems clear that, while the first was derived from the Orphic movement, of which their own was an offshoot, they owed the second to their political activity in the initial stage of the democratic revolution; and from them it was transmitted through Hippokrates and the sophists to Demokritos and Epicurus.

The mystical form in which Æschylus has clothed this tradition does not disguise its essential significance—on the contrary, the myth itself has been reinterpreted so as to throw into relief the underlying doctrine that progress is the outcome of conflict. If Prometheus has erred, it is because *es irrt der Mensch solang' er strebt*. The champions of a new order offend inevitably against the old. If Prometheus has to suffer, it is because man himself has suffered in the course of his advancement. Without suffering he would have lacked the stimulus to invention. The truth which both Æschylus and Hippokrates, in different ways, were seeking to express was one that had been grasped in practice by primitive man from the earliest stages of his history and was eventually formulated by Epicurus in the words:[10]

Human nature was taught much by the sheer force of circumstances, and these lessons were taken over by human reason, refined and supplemented.

The view of human progress expressed by Æschylus is therefore not far removed from the position of modern dialectical materialism:[11]

Until we acquire knowledge of the laws of nature, which exist and act independently of our mind, we are slaves of "blind necessity." When we acquire knowledge of them, we acquire mastery of nature.

Intelligence, the gift of Prometheus, had made man free, because it had enabled him to comprehend, and so to control, the laws of nature. Freedom consists in the understanding of necessity.

The *Prometheus* contains very little action; yet it is intensely dramatic. Technically, it is the most accomplished of the extant plays, and shows that by the end of his life Æschylus had become an absolute master of his craft. It is therefore worth examining in some detail from this point of view.

The play contains three marked pauses. The first is at the end of the *párodos* (208) after Prometheus' first prediction of the future, which carries us, without revealing the intermediate steps, to the ultimate reconciliation, and at the same time lets fall the first allusion to his secret. The second comes at the end of the second episode (541), where he declines to reveal this secret, which, we are now told, is to be the means of his deliverance. And the third comes at the end of the next episode (912), after he has predicted the actual coming of his deliverer. These pauses divide the play into four movements. In the first, Prometheus is nailed to the rock; in the second he relates the past history of gods and men; in the third he predicts the future; in the fourth he is cast into Tartarus.

Each of these movements has an internal structure of its own. Each falls into three parts, except the third, which falls into two such sets of three. Further, in each set of three, there is an organic relation between the first and third parts, the second being in the nature of a digression or development. Thus, in the first movement, Prometheus is punished by his enemies; he delivers his soliloquy; and he is visited by his friends, the Ocean Nymphs. In the second, he relates the story of the war among the gods and his own services to Zeus; he is interrupted by the visit of the God of Ocean; and he proceeds to relate his services to man. In the first part of the third movement, Io appears and entreats him to reveal her future; at the request of the Oceanids she tells the story of her past; and then, after predicting her wanderings as far as the borders of Asia, Prometheus hints at the fall of Zeus and his own deliverance. In the second part, he continues his prophecy as far as her destination in Egypt; then, in proof of his veracity, he reverts to her past (thus completing her own account); and, finally, he predicts her ultimate fate and the coming of his deliverer. In the fourth movement, he alludes once again, more openly, to his secret, which, he now declares, will effect his enemy's downfall; the emissary of Zeus seeks in vain to extort his secret from him; and Prometheus is cast into Tartarus.

Now turn to the choral odes, which are integral links in this development. In the *párodos*, the Oceanids offer the sympathy of the gods (169–70): Prometheus goes on to relate his services to the gods. In the first *stásimon* (413–51) they sing of the compassion of mankind: Prometheus relates his services to humanity. In the second *stásimon* (413–51) they sing of the helplessness of man and contrast his present state with the happiness of his wedding day: Io appears, helpless mortal persecuted by a brutal suitor (765–6). The theme of the third *stásimon* (913–38) is wisdom; and this prepares us for the final scene, in which they join with Hermes in an appeal to the sufferer to follow the course of wisdom.

Thus, the subject of the first movement is the binding of Prometheus—the present; of the second, the history of the past; of the third, the destiny of Io and the birth of Herakles—the future; and the fourth movement, with its increase of the penalty, balances the first. Yet, throughout the play, these threads of present, past and future are interwoven with such skill that at each turning-point our attention is thrown with increasing emphasis on the future. The opening speech of Might ends with a declaration that Prometheus must be taught by suffering to accept the tyranny of Zeus (10–11) while the speech of Hephaistos which follows ends with a suggestion that the tyrant himself, in course of time, will change his ways (35); and both these themes will be developed in the *párodos* (180–201). In the middle of his task Hephaistos utters the impassioned cry, "Alas, Prometheus! it is for you I weep" (66). The retort of Might comes at the close of the scene, where our attention is redirected to the future (85–7):

> Your name is false, Prometheus, God of Foresight!
> Now you need all your foresight for yourself
> To shuffle off this piece of craftsmanship!

And again this parting insult will be answered at the end
of the first movement, where we are permitted a glimpse
of the final reconciliation, welcomed by both antagonists
(202–8).

We are brought back abruptly to the past (209). At the
request of the Nymphs, who entreat him to "reveal all things,"
Prometheus reluctantly begins his exposition. Later, shocked
by his audacity, the Nymphs are anxious to change the subject
(277–8); but now it is Prometheus who insists on continuing,
urging them to listen to his revelation of the future (288–9).
Then comes the interlude—the visit of the God of Ocean. After
his departure the exposition is resumed, leading to the end of
the second movement, where, eagerly questioned about the
secret to which he alluded at the end of the first, Prometheus
draws back, refusing to disclose it (538–41):

> No, think of other things. This is no time
> To speak of that. That is my secret, which
> Must be kept closely veiled. By guarding that,
> From agony and shame I shall escape!

To resume, we have seen that the opening speeches of the
play ended by directing our attention to the future, thus
anticipating the close of the binding scene and the climax at
the end of the first movement, the last speech of the *párodos*.
The second movement began by taking us back into the past;
but at the end of the first of its three parts and still more
intently at the end of the third we looked once again to the
future. Then comes the Io scene, so divided as to throw the
future into still greater prominence: future, past, future; future,
past, future. Hence the tremendous effect, like a goal to which
the whole exposition has been straining, of the prophecy of the
coming of Herakles (897–9), which, again, is abruptly broken
off, and then crowned at the opening of the last movement
(939–59) by the completion of that other motive, the fatal
secret, which marked the culmination of the first movement
and again of the second. The narrations and predictions of
Prometheus have been handled with such artistic mastery of
the material as to concentrate at the end of the play our whole
attention on the sequel.

That sequel has been lost, but some important fragments of the second play, the *Prometheus Unbound*, have survived.

The play began with the entry of the Chorus of Titans. Many thousands of years have elapsed, giving time for many changes, on earth and in heaven. Prometheus is still chained to his rock, but he has been restored from Tartarus to the light of day. The Titans describe their voyage from the banks of Ocean, where the Sun waters his horses after their day's labour, to the borders of Europe and Asia. They are brothers of Prometheus—bound to him therefore by ties closer than those which wrung compassion from Hephaistos and brought the God of Ocean and his daughters to his solitary rock. In the war against Kronos they had sided with the old order, and for this offence Zeus cast them, with Kronos, into Tartarus. They have now been released; and Kronos, too, we may presume, in accordance with the tradition, has been removed to his new home in the Islands of the Blest. Zeus has learnt to temper his power with mercy. No doubt the Titans recount these events to their brother. They can hardly fail to make a deep impression on him; but, as at the beginning of the first play, Prometheus is silent.

His opening words have survived in a Latin translation by Cicero. He appeals to them to bear witness to his agony. Pierced by cruel bonds and tormented by the eagle whose coming Hermes had predicted, he longs for the death which is denied to him. The speech is as notable for the speaker's absorption in physical pain as his speeches in the first play are notable for his indifference to it. There is not a word of his deliverer, not a word of his secret. And he longs to die. In the first play, which represented a time when the will of Zeus had been weaker than the Moirai (531–4), he had dared Zeus to do his worst, defiantly declaring that he was fated not to die (1086). Now he laments that he is being kept alive by the will of Zeus himself. The implication is that during the interval Zeus and the Moirai have come together. The old and the new are being reconciled.

The ensuing scenes must have acquainted the audience with the changes that have taken place in the interval between the two plays; but it is likely that on this occasion the narrator is not Prometheus himself, who is hardly in a position to know what has happened, but the Titans, who, we may suppose, relate for their brother's benefit both the advances which Zeus has made in the consolidation of his power and the mercy he has begun to extend to his former enemies. In the first play we learnt that, but for the intervention of Prometheus, Zeus would have destroyed the human race; but we may be certain that any such intention has been abandoned, because, as we shall see, the greatest of his sons is shortly to be sent down to earth for the improvement of their lot. Thus, if Prometheus remains obdurate, his motive can no longer be fear for the future of mankind: it can only be resentment for past wrongs. And if the Titans proceed to advise their brother to prepare the way for his own release by surrendering the secret which Zeus demands of him, appealing, like the God of Ocean, for wisdom and restraint (325–6), their advice, unlike his, will not be ignoble: they will urge him to submit to his old enemy, not merely because he rules the world, but because he now rules it well. Nor can Prometheus reply, as he did to the Oceanids, that advice comes ill from those who are not themselves in trouble (279–81), because his brothers' sufferings have been hardly less terrible than his own. Yet, in view of further evidence, we must, I think, assume that Prometheus rejects their appeal. He cannot yet bring himself, by revealing his secret before his release, to "unsay his high language."

In the Medicean manuscript of Æschylus, the list of *dramatis personæ* prefixed to the *Prometheus Bound* includes the names of Ge, the Goddess of Earth, and Herakles. As it is known that Herakles appeared in the *Prometheus Unbound*, it is generally agreed that both names have been inserted by mistake from another list, which gave the characters of the second play or of the two plays together.

The Goddess of Earth was traditionally regarded as the most ancient and in some ways the most august of the divinities of Greece—the origin of all things into which all things return, and the fountain of all wisdom, from whom all prophets, divine and human, drew their inspiration. And she was the mother of Prometheus. It was to her that he appealed in his opening soliloquy and again at the end of the first play to bear witness

to his wrongs. From her he learnt the destined course of the **war in** heaven, and at her advice he took the part of Zeus. It **was she** who foretold to him the coming of his deliverer, and **it was** she who imparted to him his secret.

It has already been noted how in the first play both Hephaistos and the God of Ocean stressed their kinship with the prisoner, and how at the beginning of the second he is visited by still closer kinsmen, the sons of Earth. Their visit is followed by a visit from the Goddess of Earth herself, which will thus mark the culmination of a motive introduced at the beginning of the trilogy. And we may infer that her purpose is similar to theirs—to offer him her sympathy, and at the same time to urge upon him the wisdom of submission. The voice of his mother is now added to the entreaties of the rest of his kin, beseeching him to soften his obduracy and remove the bar to his deliverance.

His secret is this. If Zeus unites with Thetis, she will bear him a son who will overthrow him. Now, in the tradition recorded by later writers, Zeus was actually in pursuit of Thetis when the revelation of the secret deterred him. Thus, the situation is highly dramatic. Prometheus has only to hold out a little longer, and the downfall of his enemy is assured. On the other hand, his mother pleads with him to submit, before it is too late, not merely in order to effect his own release, but to prevent the fall of Zeus, who, no longer the vindictive tyrant who sought the extinction of the human race, has already, in the birth of Herakles, taken them under his care. Prometheus is asked, not to quail before his adversary, but to sacrifice his pride for the sake of that very race for which he has already sacrificed far more.

With regard to the actual manner of the revelation, it should be observed that, since the Goddess of Earth is as well acquainted with the secret as Prometheus himself, all she requires is his permission to divulge it. There is no need for it to pass his lips. And, further, if she is intent on such a mission, she will take advantage of the occasion to urge Zeus to deliver Prometheus in return for his own deliverance. And what more influential mediator could be found than the goddess who is the author of the being of Zeus himself, as of all created beings, who helped him to his supremacy, who is, moreover, the personification of Right?

It is at this point, I believe, that Prometheus yields: but one further agony awaits him. After his mother's departure, he hears a rush of wings. We remember the alarm in which he awaited the coming of the Ocean Nymphs, and how they hastened to reassure him. This time his fears are well-founded. The eagle is returning to its feast. Prometheus bends his gaze in the direction from which it is approaching. From the opposite direction appears a warrior, armed with bow and spear and clad in the famous lion skin. He draws his bow and, with a prayer to Apollo, whose gift it is, he shoots the eagle down. Recognising his deliverer, Prometheus greets him as "a hated father's son beloved," and we may suppose that he followed up this greeting with an appeal to Herakles to release him from bondage in accordance with his destiny. Herakles, however, who has now learnt who the sufferer is, may well be reluctant to assist his father's inveterate enemy. Prometheus will then explain that he has already removed the main obstacle to their reconciliation, and will doubtless recall the services which he rendered many centuries before to his ancestress on that very spot. Moreover, he can direct him on his travels and foretell what the future holds in store for him when his labours are at an end. He is now eager to let flow the fount of prophecy, which he unsealed so reluctantly to Io, if only his own request is granted in return. Herakles "pities the suppliant." Prometheus is to predict his future, and in return Herakles will release him. An arrangement of this kind, parallel to the bargain struck by Prometheus with Io and the Oceanids (804–11), would enable the dramatist to reserve the climax of the actual release for the end of the scene.

The surviving fragments suffice to show that, just as the wanderings of Io covered the eastern and southern limits of the world, so those of Herakles will extend to the north and west. The two prophecies are complementary, embracing the whole surface of the earth. In particular, we know from other sources that it was Prometheus who directed Herakles to the Garden of the Hesperides and instructed him how to get the Golden Apples with the help of Atlas, to whom we were introduced in the first play. We also know that in the second the dramatist explained the origin of the constellation called the Kneeling Herakles. During his fight with the Ligurians on his way to the Hesperides, the hero's weapons gave out and he was forced to his knees. This means that Prometheus predicted that, in memory of this encounter, the image of Herakles, like that of other departed heroes, would be set after his death among the stars. That being so, the prophecy can hardly have ended with the quest of the Golden Apples, or even with the last of the hero's labours, the descent into Hades, without some allusion to his final destiny—his ascent into Heaven. It must have been carried to its proper conclusion in the deification of the hero, in harmony with the prediction to Io, which concluded with his birth.

Prometheus has now fulfilled his part of the agreement; it remains for Herakles to fulfil his. The hero mounts the rock and shatters the handiwork of Hephaistos.

We still await the result of Earth's mission to Zeus, and we also remember that at the close of the first play Zeus declared through the medium of his emissary that the sufferings of Prometheus could not end until he had found another god to surrender his immortality in his stead (1058–61). It is possible, therefore, that Hermes reappears. He announces first of all that the mediation of Earth has been successful. With the revelation of the secret the cause of offence has been removed, although, for reasons which will appear immediately, it is probable that the formal reconciliation has still to be effected. Further, it is possible that Zeus transfers part of his displeasure to his son, who, as predicted of him, has delivered the prisoner without the Father's consent (797). Herakles is said to have bound himself with olive—probably in allusion to the olive planted by Athena in the Academy at Athens; and the motive for this act appears to have been his desire to avert his father's anger by binding himself vicariously on the prisoner's behalf. This point is dramatically important, because it provides a starting-point for the third play. In the regular manner of the trilogy, one difficulty is solved by the creation of another. Finally, the prisoner must find a substitute. At this point Herakles comes forward and explains that he has accidentally wounded the Centaur, Cheiron, who, suffering incurable pain, longs to die, but cannot: let him, therefore, relinquish his immortality in place of Prometheus. His offer accepted, Herakles departs, with the blessings of all present, to fulfil the remainder of his historic destiny.

If we consider the situation in which the dramatist has left us, we see that, just as in the first play the prophecy to Io raised an expectation which has only been satisfied by its fulfilment in the second—namely, the coming of Herakles—the prophecy to Herakles has now raised an expectation no less far-reaching, his deification; and our minds will not be at rest until we are assured that this, too, has been realised. It is therefore difficult to resist the conclusion that the plot of the third play was concerned, not merely with the readmission of Prometheus to Olympus, but with the future of Herakles. The destinies of the two heroes have become interlocked, and at the close of the second play our interest has been transferred in some measure to the latter.

Before leaving the *Prometheus Unbound*, let us compare its structure, so far as it can be recovered, with that of the *Prometheus Bound*. The silence of Prometheus at the opening of the first play is balanced by his silence at the opening of the second; the visit of the God of Ocean in the first by the visit of the Goddess of Earth in the second; the Daughters of Ocean, the chorus of the first play, by the Sons of Earth, the chorus of the second; the wanderings of Io in the east and south by the wanderings of her descendant in the north and west; the prophecy of the birth of the great benefactor of mankind by the prophecy of his deification. Thus, it appears that the two plays were constructed with that organic symmetry which the study of his other work has led us to expect.

The third play was entitled *Prometheus the Fire-bearer*. This epithet probably refers to the torch which Pausanias saw (mistaking it for a sceptre) in the right hand of the archaic image of Prometheus in the Academy, where, as already noted, the god was worshipped as one of the three divinities who had taught man the use of fire and were honoured with annual torch races.

We have already made some progress with the conclusion

of the trilogy. In the first place, Prometheus is a suppliant, seeking readmission to Olympus. In the *Oresteia*, the suppliant was saved by the intervention of Athena, the goddess of wisdom and patroness of the city which claimed to uphold that virtue among men. The same goddess had an ancient connection with Prometheus. We are told that Prometheus assisted at her birth, when she sprang fully armed from the head of Zeus, and that the two collaborated in the creation of mankind. But above all Prometheus was granted a place in the Academy— an honour which he could not have won without the goddess's consent. Of the three fire gods, we made the acquaintance of the two elder at the opening of the trilogy, and I believe, there-fore, that in the conclusion we were introduced to the youngest and greatest of the three. It is she who reconciles Prometheus with her father and invests him with the human honours that are his due.

Before his descent into Hades, Herakles visited Eleusis with the intention of becoming an initiate, but he was unable to behold the mysteries until he had been cleansed of the blood of the Centaurs: accordingly, he was purified at Agra and then initiated. We are also told that the Lesser Mysteries of Agra were founded by Demeter for the express purpose of purifying Herakles after the slaughter of the Centaurs. These traditions, preserved by Apollodoros and Diodoros, relate to Æschylus's birthplace. They must have been known to him, and it is extremely probable that they were derived by the later writers from him. It appears, therefore, that here again the poet was working with an ulterior purpose—namely, the inception at the end of the trilogy of another and far more important feature of Athenian ritual, the Lesser Mysteries of Demeter.

The agony of Io was due in part to the jealousy of Hera, and her descendant suffered much from the same cause. Ultimately, however, when Herakles was admitted to Olympus, he was reconciled with Hera and received in marriage her own daughter, Hebe, the goddess of eternal youth. Furthermore, if the marriage of Herakles and Hebe signifies the reconciliation of Hera with the House of Io, it signifies just as clearly her reconciliation with her lord. Her hostility to Io and Herakles was prompted by conjugal jealousy, of which Zeus was the guilty cause. In the first play we saw Zeus heartlessly pursuing a mortal girl; in the second we saw him in pursuit of Thetis; but in the third, when he joins with Hera in blessing the union of their son and daughter, the two stand together as guardians of the sanctity of marriage, thus marking a further step in the advancement of humanity.

In the beginning, Zeus crucified Prometheus for the salvation of mankind. In the course of time, which taught wisdom to them both, Prometheus saved Zeus from destruction and was himself saved by the son of Zeus, who, under his father's guidance, carried on the work of Prometheus, clearing the path of human progress; and the divine feud was eventually resolved by Athena, who completed her father's purpose by her patronage of the city which stands at the summit of human civilisation. Hence, at the close of the trilogy, these three—Prometheus, Herakles, Athena—appear together as representatives of the inception, development and consummation of the idea of God, and as the founder, promoter and perfecter of the destiny of man.

If this view of the trilogy is essentially correct, it means that, for all the profound differences in their interpretation of the myth, Æschylus was continuing the work which Hesiod had begun. The story of Prometheus has now been infused with an intellectual content far beyond the compass of the tale told by the rude peasants of Boiotia; but the advance which the new interpretation marks over Hesiod, no less than his advance on the primitive nucleus of the myth, has only been rendered possible by the underlying advancement of society itself. As the material basis of human life is extended and enriched, there emanates from it an ever-growing profundity and fertility of thought; but, since the material process is continuous, the new being at first secreted within the old, intellectual progress takes the form of incessant adaptations of traditional ideas. Of this truth the legend of Prometheus is a clear example. The work of Æschylus on this subject was so widely known and admired that it might well have fixed the tradition, if anything could have fixed it; but this tradition was no more capable of rest than the world it so vividly reflected. It is therefore interesting to see how the story of Prometheus was subsequently interpreted.

The following passage is from a lost play by Moschion, a
writer otherwise unknown:[12]

And first I shall unfold from the beginning
The early origin of the life of man.
There was an age long since when mortals dwelt
Like beasts in mountain caverns and ravines
That seldom saw the sunshine, for as yet
They had no vaulted houses and no towns
With walls of stone securely fortified,
No ploughshares to cut deep into the sod
And make it mother corn, no blade of iron
To tend row upon row the blossoming vine.
The earth was still a virgin without child,
And men fed on each other's flesh, for then
The place of Law was lowly and Violence
Was throned on high at the right hand of Zeus.
But when at last Time, who brings all to birth,
Transformed the manner of our mortal life,
Whether through the contrivance of Prometheus,
Or through Necessity, or whether long
Practice had learned from Nature's own instruction,
Then men discovered how to bring to fruit
Demeter's gift, discovered too the draught
Of Dionysus, then, furrowing the soil
With teams of oxen, raising roofs above
Their heads, and founding cities, they
Forsook the beasts and became civilised.

This passage provides just the link in the development of the
tradition that our argument has led us to expect. On the one
hand, the mythical integument has been shed, the surviving
vestiges being no more than poetical embellishments; and one
of them, the allusion to Violence, is clearly a conscious reminiscence of the *Prometheus Bound*, showing that the writer has
correctly interpreted the intention of Æschylus in introducing
Might and Violence as ministers of the god who was in the
beginning "a law to himself." On the other hand, the mention
of Necessity points just as clearly to the fourth-century materialists. The tradition has been stated in a form which would have
been equally acceptable to Æschylus and to Epicurus.

Our next evidence is another dramatic fragment—from a play by Plato's uncle, Kritias:[13]

> There was a time when human life was ruled
> By force, being brutal and disorderly,
> When there was no reward for righteousness
> And wickedness went unpunished. Then, I think,
> Men laid down laws as penalties to make
> Justice supreme and insolence her slave;
> But even then, although the laws restrained
> Mankind from deeds of open violence,
> They still did wrong in secret, until some
> Shrewd and far-sighted thinker had the wit
> To invent gods, that all who did or said
> Or even imagined evil might be afraid;
> And so he introduced the Deity,
> Teaching men faith in an eternal spirit
> Who sees and hears with his intelligence
> And pays close heed to all men say and do.

Here we find ourselves in a different atmosphere. Kritias was one of the Thirty Tyrants who instituted a reign of terror at Athens in the closing years of the Peloponnesian War (404 B.C.). As an active and class-conscious counter-revolutionary, he openly avows the repressive function of "law and order" and recognises with cynical frankness the value of religion as a means of keeping the masses in ignorance and subjection. This analysis of the idea of God, which, if we look to the essence rather than the manner in which it is expressed, is sound, would perhaps have shocked Æschylus; yet his own master Pythagoras is reported to have declared that, realising the need for justice, men had assigned the same function to Themis in Heaven, Dike in Hell, and Nomos on earth, in order that those who committed the sin of disobedience might appear as offenders against the whole structure of the universe;[14] and Æschylus himself had taught that God, as well as man, was a product of evolution, the two processes being closely parallel. Further, when we hear that the function of the law is to intimidate, we are reminded of the words which Æschylus put into the mouth of Athena when she instituted the reign of law in the

PROMETHEIA 341

Oresteia—"What man shall be upright without fear?" The later
work of Æschylus has brought us to a point in the history of
Athens at which the *isonomía* of the middle-class supporters of
Kleisthenes is being revealed with increasing clarity as an
instrument to be used by that class for the enforced maintenance of its own privileged position.

Returning to Prometheus, the story of his services to man is
told again by Plato in a new version which he puts into the
mouth of Protagoras in the dialogue of that name.[15] It seems to
me that this version owes more to Plato himself than to Protagoras, but, without entering into that question, we may agree
with Burnet that it is the work of "a strong believer in organised
society." It may be summarised as follows.

Living creatures were made by the gods out of earth and
fire. After they had been created, Prometheus and his brother
Epimetheus (a foil to the god of Foresight, ignored by Æschylus
but going back to Hesiod) bestowed on them their appropriate
faculties, giving them hoofs or wings or underground dwellings,
so that each species might have the means of self-defence;
wrapping them in furs and skins for shelter against the cold;
ordaining that some should be the natural prey of others and at
the same time ensuring their survival by making them exceptionally prolific. All this was done by Epimetheus under his
brother's direction, but at the end of his task he found that he
had inadvertently bestowed all the available faculties on the
animals, leaving none for man. Faced with this difficulty,
Prometheus gave men fire, which he stole from its owners,
Hephaistos and Athena, and he was subsequently prosecuted
for theft. Being akin to the divine, men were distinguished from
the other animals by their innate belief in God and by their
faculty of speech. They began to make clothes and shoes, to
build houses and till the soil, and eventually, for protection
against the animals, they founded cities. Unfortunately, however, after gathering together in cities, citizen began to prey
on citizen; and so, fearing that the race might perish, Zeus
commanded Hermes to confer on them the gifts of shame and
justice. Asked whether these were to be bestowed indiscriminately or assigned to selected individuals like the specialists in
the handicrafts, Zeus replied, "Let them be given to all in

common, and give them too a law from me that any man who cannot partake of shame and justice shall be put to death as an infection in the body politic."

The author of this interpretation is at one with Kritias in his attitude to justice and the law, but shows superior insight in acknowledging that strife between man and man—the class struggle—only began with the inauguration of city life; and he discreetly places man's belief in God far back in the very origins of his existence. In contrast to Æschylus, the divine government of the world is fixed and stable, and the credit for human progress is transferred from Prometheus, whose part is subordinate, to an all-wise, omnipotent and unchanging Zeus.

Let us now see how these things appeared to the lower orders. Philemon was a comic dramatist of the fourth century, and, like the majority of comic dramatists at that time, he was a resident alien, not an Athenian citizen.[16] It was Philemon who said:

> The slave has human flesh the same as ours.
> Indeed, in Nature all men were born free.

And this is what he said of the gifts of Prometheus which had raised man above the level of the beasts:

> Thrice blest and happy are the beasts that have
> No reason in these things, no questioning,
> Nor other harmful superfluities—
> Their law is their own nature; but the life
> Of man is more than he can bear—he is
> The slave of fancies, he has invented laws.

A similar view was expounded at length by Diogenes the Cynic, a popular philosopher whose social outlook is indicated by his condemnation of the lectures given by Plato to rich young men in the Academy as "a waste of time," and by a remark he is said to have made in Megara, where he saw sheep protected from the weather by leather jackets, while the backs of the children were bare—"It is better," he said, "to be a Megarian's ram than his son."[17]

Diogenes declared that it was luxury that had made human life more miserable than that of the animals. The animals drink water, eat grass, go about naked for the most part all the year round, never enter a house or make use of fire, and so, unless they are slaughtered, they live out the term of years that Nature has appointed for them in health and strength without any need for medicines or physicians. Men, on the other hand, are so attached to life and so ingenious in prolonging it that most of them never reach old age and live burdened with diseases too numerous to mention. It is not enough for them that the earth furnishes them with natural medicines—they must have surgery and cautery as well. . . . As soon as they came together in cities, they began to commit the most terrible crimes against one another, as though that were what they had come together for. Accordingly, he understood the story of how Prometheus was punished by Zeus for the discovery of fire to mean that this was the origin and starting-point of human luxury and fastidiousness; for Zeus, he declared, did not hate mankind nor would he have grudged them anything that was for their good.[18]

Prometheus has now become an upstart justly punished for the gift of what is regarded, not as a blessing, but as a curse. Diogenes's view of the corrupting effects of civilised life brings us back to Hesiod—it is the fable of the successive ages of man, each more degenerate than the last, in a new form; and it shows that in his day the struggle between rich and poor in the decaying city-state had bitten into human consciousness as deeply as the old struggle between the landowner and the serf.

It would be an interesting and profitable task to pursue the history of this myth in its successive reinterpretations through the Middle Ages down to our own day;[19] but for the present it must suffice to conclude the subject with some remarks on what Shelley made of it.

Gilbert Murray, who believes that "the strong tradition in the higher kind of Greek poetry, as in good poetry almost everywhere, was to avoid all the disturbing irrelevances of contemporary life," and can see "no evidence of any political allusions" in the *Oresteia*, remarks that "it is surprising that out of material so undramatic as a mere contest between pure evil and pure good Shelley has made such a magnificent poem."[20] It would indeed be surprising, if it were true, but, unlike Æschylus, Shelley was in the habit of writing prefaces to his poems with the object of explaining what they were about, and in his preface to the *Prometheus Unbound* he wrote as follows:

> We owe the great writers of the golden age of our literature to that fervid awakening of the public mind which shook to dust the oldest and most oppressive form of the Christian religion. We owe Milton to the progress and development of the same spirit; the sacred Milton was, let it ever be remembered, a republican, and a bold enquirer into morals and religion. The great writers of our own age are, we have reason to suppose, the companions and forerunners of some unimagined change in our social condition or the opinions which cement it. The cloud of mind is discharging its collective lightning, and the equilibrium between institutions and opinions is now restoring, or about to be restored.

If we are curious to know what these institutions were that Shelley found in conflict with his opinions, we have only to read his *Mask of Anarchy written on the Occasion of the Massacre at Manchester*:

> 'Tis to work and have such pay
> As just keeps life from day to day
> In your limbs, as in a cell
> For the tyrants' use to dwell
>
> So that ye for them are made
> Loom and plough and sword and spade
> With or without your own will bent
> To their defence and nourishment.

This conflict was something more substantial, as well as more disturbing, than "a mere contest between pure good and pure evil," and it was also inherently dramatic, because it sprang straight out of contemporary strife.[21] Only those who have studied the brutality, duplicity and hypocrisy of the ruling class of that date as revealed in their Enclosure Acts and Game Laws, their Speenhamland system and their truck system, and who stand where Shelley would have stood in relation to the sufferings no less great that are the common lot of all but a fraction of mankind to-day, are in a position to appreciate the indignation which burns in the challenge of Prometheus:

> Fiend, I defy thee! with a calm, fixed mind,
>   All that thou canst inflict I bid thee do;
> Foul Tyrant both of Gods and Human-kind,
>   One only being shalt thou not subdue.

During Shelley's lifetime, the last of the English peasants had been turned out of their common fields on to the roads, and from there herded into the workhouses, prisons, cotton-mills and coal-mines, where they worked, men, women and children, in conditions still paralleled in such places as Jamaica, Johannesburg and Bombay. It was the period of the Industrial Revolution, which enriched the rich and impoverished the poor —the period in which the new manufacturing class was engaged in overthrowing the privileges of a corrupt landowning oligarchy, while the new proletariat, notwithstanding hunger and squalor and police persecution, was slowly and painfully learning how to organise for action.

Æschylus was a moderate democrat, who had seen the long struggle between the landowners and the merchants culminate in a *concordia ordinum*, marked by the abolition of aristocratic privilege and the extension of the franchise to the whole of the citizen body. It is essential, however, to remember that this *concordia* owed its completeness to the fact that there was another class which was not free. The slaves were the proletariat of ancient democracy, and if they had not been slaves, incapable of organisation and therefore politically powerless, the overthrow of the landed aristocracy would have been followed by a struggle between them and their masters. It was only by excluding this class from his very conception of democracy that Æschylus was able to regard the democratic revolution as a fusion of opposites symbolised in the reconciliation of Zeus and Prometheus.

Shelley was a member of the upper middle class who had transferred his allegiance to the proletariat. But this was not a slave proletariat; it was free, and already clamouring for the suffrage. Between this class and the capitalists there was no room for compromise, because their interests were contradictory, and that is what made it impossible for Shelley to accept the Æschylean conclusion. He was bound to revolt against the idea of reconciling the champion with the oppressor of mankind. As for his alternative, even in those early days there were a few who saw more or less clearly that the only possible solution of the conflict was the expropriation of the ruling class by the class which it had expropriated; but, owing partly to the immaturity of the proletariat, which at this time was hardly conscious of its future, and partly to his own middle-class outlook, which he had not entirely outgrown, Shelley shrank from the idea of revolutionary action. Accordingly, his Jupiter is overthrown, but only by the mystical power of passive resistance.

In fairness to Shelley, it must be added that, whereas Æschylus was celebrating a revolution which he had already seen accomplished, Shelley's revolution was at this time no more than a hope of the future; and so, for a century, it remained.

AFTER ÆSCHYLUS

THE latest work of Æschylus marks a turning-point in the evolution of Greek tragedy. In the first place, it concludes that process of expansion and co-ordination which had begun when the tetralogy first took shape. At this point the tetralogy ceases to develop and splits into its component parts. The satyr play persists, but with diminishing vitality. The new unit is the single tragedy, now self-contained. Thus, in the hands of Sophokles (495–405 B.C.) and Euripides (480–405 B.C.), the art-form reverted to an earlier phase of its development; but at the same time this single tragedy is marked by certain features which can be traced to the distinctive function of the third play of the Æschylean trilogy. It is therefore not simply a reversion to type, but a reversion to type on a higher plane.

In the second place, it is only at this stage that the art developed what came eventually to be regarded as one of its primary characteristics. According to Aristotle, the tragic plot should consist of a change from good fortune to bad.[1] This principle has only a very limited application to the work of Æschylus, because the normal conclusion of his trilogy was a change in the reverse direction. From this point of view, therefore, his work is still archaic, preserving the primitive sequence of the passion play, in which the god's death had been followed by his resurrection.

These structural changes in the art can only be explained by reference to external factors; and therefore, before passing on to the work of Sophokles and Euripides, we must pause to consider the developments that were taking place in Athenian society.

The data for the population of Attica in the fifth century B.C. are too fragmentary and uncertain to permit of more than a conjectural estimate.[2] For the time of the Persian Wars all that can be said is that the number of citizens was probably less, the number of resident aliens and slaves certainly much less, than at the outbreak of the Peloponnesian War. In 431 B.C., according to the most recent estimate, there were at least 172,000 citizens, including their women and children, at least 28,500 resident aliens, and not more than 115,000 slaves. This means that the slaves already amounted to over half the free population, and that little more than a quarter of the total number of adults were in possession of the franchise.

Slave labour became one of the most productive fields for the investment of capital. Nikias owned 1,000 slaves, whom he hired out for labour in the mines; Hipponikos owned 600, whom he employed for the same purpose. Of the number employed in the mines, all we know is that in the year 413 B.C. over 20,000 slaves deserted to the Spartans, and it is probable that most of these were miners. Slaves were also employed in large numbers in quarrying and transport.

As the supply of slave labour increased, the demand for free labour declined, with the result that the free labourer was either unable to find employment or else compelled to work in conditions which reduced him to the economic level of a slave. Against this destructive competition, the resident alien had no protection, because he did not possess the franchise, and consequently the poorer aliens sank to a status which Aristotle describes as "limited slavery."[3] But the position of the citizen was different. The lower classes used their newly won political rights to force the state to maintain them without working at all. During the twenty years from 450 to 430 B.C., under the leadership of Perikles, the principle of payment for public services, including attendance at the law courts, was adopted and extended as a permanent policy of state, with the result that, at the end of that period, over 20,000 citizens —that is, between one-third and one-half of the whole citizen body—were supported in one way or another at the public expense. This was the price at which Perikles retained popular support.

Where did the money come from? The fact that the policy was carried through without effective opposition is enough to show that the burden did not fall on the rich. It came partly from imposts on trade and taxes levied from the resident aliens, in whose hands trade was concentrated; and it came partly from the empire into which Athens had now converted the league of free cities which she had organised for the war of liberation against Persia some thirty years before. The internal revenue at this period has been estimated at 400 talents, most of which was raised by taxes of the kind just mentioned, and the average annual assessment of the tribute exacted from the subject states was probably 460 talents.[4] Thus, the wealth of the community was administered by that section of it which had the least part in its production. The citizens of Athens became a class of *rentiers*, living parasitically on the labour of others.

These measures, of course, did nothing to eliminate the tendency, inherent in an economy based on private ownership, for wealth to concentrate at one pole of society; and consequently they only served to intensify the inequalities which they were designed to remove. Fed by cheap corn imported from Athenian dependencies overseas, the city populace was swollen by a constant influx of peasants from the Attic countryside, for whom, owing to the competition of foreign corn, farming had ceased to pay; and so the demand for imported food only grew with the supply. In the same way, many of the impoverished citizens whom the state tried to get off its hands by settling them overseas on lands seized from the subject states, found it profitable to sell their holdings and return to Athens. The state could only maintain itself on this basis by continuous expansion. It had entered on a path which led inevitably to war. And the strongest advocates of this policy were naturally the radicals, representing all those who were struggling to maintain their standard of living against the growing menace of slavery. It was therefore the advanced democrats that now became the most ardent imperialists. So long as their own incomes were not affected, the rich citizens acquiesced, but, when the empire revolted, they were not slow to act. Shortly before the end of the war, when the empire was collapsing, the democracy was overthrown and replaced by a régime whose policy was "to secure for high civil offices men of special competence, to reserve the privileges of the commonwealth to Athenians who could afford them, and deny a voice in political decisions to such as lacked an appreciable property-stake in the community"[5]—in other words, rather than surrender their wealth, the rich aimed at holding the poor in check by depriving them of the franchise, which was their only protection against the competition of slave labour.

Such were the insoluble contradictions on which Athenian democracy wrecked itself. The constitution which had been founded at the beginning of the century in the name of equality was overthrown at the end by the class that had founded it in the name of inequality. The class which had risen to power on the strength of its claim that the state should be ruled by those who produced its wealth now saw its unearned income threatened by rival claimants to the proceeds accruing from the taxation of traders and the exploitation of a multitude of slaves. The cry of liberty, which had been raised with such fervour against the Persian invader, had taken on a hollow ring, because, though Perikles might clothe it in fine words, the policy for which he stood meant that liberty was to be maintained at home by suppressing it abroad. Democracy had been transformed into the negation of democracy.

These contradictions produced in the human consciousness an underlying sense of disillusionment and frustration which it sought to escape by formulating ideas designed to cast a veil over the reality—the idea that Athens was destined to be the "school of Hellas"; the idea that the slave was naturally inferior to the freeman; and, above all, the idea of *sophrosýne*, that virtue of moderation or restraint which was embodied in Athena. The notion of *sophrosýne* is the old aristocratic "nothing too much" in a new guise, but with one difference. In the aristocratic tradition, the man who sought too much had been simply blasted by the thunderbolt of Zeus. What happened to the man whose ambitions or desires led him beyond the limits of *sophrosýne* is that he got the opposite of what he was striving after. This notion, which from the fifth century onwards becomes a dominant element in Greek thought, must be traced back to its origin.

The social contradictions which came to a head after the democratic revolution were insoluble, because they were inherent in an economy based on private property, and it was the growth of private property which through the democratic revolution had brought them to a head. And further, what had facilitated and accelerated the growth of private property was the development of money. In his discussion of this subject, which for depth of insight is one of the most remarkable in the whole range of his work, Aristotle says that the original function of money was to facilitate the process of exchange—selling in order to buy. So long as it was confined to this purpose, the use of money was limited by the fact that it was merely a means to an end—the satisfaction of immediate needs. This use of money (here his own social preconceptions come into play) is regarded as natural and just. But it was not long before money came to be used for a new purpose—buying in order to sell: the merchant buys cheap in order to sell dear. Money-making has become an end in itself, and in this form it has no limit.[6] The same truth has been formulated in modern times by Marx:[7]

> The simple circulation of commodities (selling in order to buy) is a means for carrying out a process which lies outside the domain of circulation—a means for the appropriation of use-values, for the satisfaction of wants. The circulation of money as capital, on the other hand, is an end in itself, for the expansion of value can only occur within this perpetually renewed movement. Consequently, the circulation of capital has no limits.

This, in effect, is what Solon had said at the beginning of the Athenian monetary revolution: "Riches have no limit." And, as Aristotle points out, owing to various causes, such as depreciation in the value of money, the pursuit of wealth for its own sake is liable to result in the opposite of the intention: a man may amass money only to find himself like Meidas starving in the midst of his gold.

Under the landed aristocracy, the economic relations between peasant and landowner had been simple and clear. The peasant had paid over so much of his produce to his lord, and this relation was expressed in the simple formula, Nothing too much. But with the development of money economic relations became increasingly complex and obscure. The producer took his goods to market only to find them unsaleable, because others had produced more of the same goods than there were purchasers to buy them. The speculator put his capital into an industrial enterprise only to find that a monetary crisis, which he had unwittingly helped to precipitate, robbed him of the expected return. He found himself the victim of a process which lay outside his understanding and control.

When money was first introduced, it was recognised as a new power destined to increase in an unprecedented degree man's control over Nature. "Man is money": such was the saying of a citizen of one of the first Greek states to strike a coinage.[8] There is nothing money cannot buy; there is nothing the man with money cannot become. But this new power was soon seen to be ambivalent. As Sophokles wrote:[9]

> Money wins friendship, honour, place and power,
> And sets man next to the proud tyrant's throne.
> All trodden paths and paths untrod before
> Are scaled by nimble riches, where the poor
> Can never hope to win the heart's desire.
> A man ill-formed by nature and ill-spoken
> Money shall make him fair to eye and ear.
> Money earns man his health and happiness,
> And only money cloaks iniquity.

And so we find the same poet denouncing money as the root of all evil:[10]

> Of all the foul growths current in the world
> The worst is money. Money drives men from home,
> Plunders great cities, perverts the honest mind
> To shameful practice, godlessness and crime.

The invention has returned to plague the inventor.

As money extended the range of its operations, penetrating every department of human life with its subversive influence, men came to perceive that this yellow slave had become their master; and, since its operation lay outside their control, they could only explain it by idealising it as a universal law. From this time forward there runs through Greek literature the persistent tradition that the excessive pursuit, not only of riches, but of health, happiness and all things good and desirable in themselves, is liable to produce their opposites.[11] As Isokrates said, men who have acquired great riches cannot rest content, but risk what they have by reaching after more. As Bakchylides said, the spirit of pride or excess bestows on man his neighbour's wealth only to plunge him in the gulf of calamity. As Hippokrates said, extreme conditions of physical well-being are dangerous, because they cannot remain stable. Æschylus said the same of health and happiness:

> If a man's health be advanced over the due mean,
> It will trespass soon upon sickness, who stands
> Close neighbour, between them a thin wall.
> So doth the passage of life,
> Sped by a prosperous breeze,
> Suddenly founder on reefs of disaster.

The idea received its most precise and comprehensive formulation in the words of Plato: "In the seasons, in plants, in the body, and above all in civil society, excessive action results in a violent transformation into its opposite."

Æschylus had been able to take the tide of democracy at the flood. His conception of progress as the result of conflict reflected the positive achievement of the democratic revolution; but in his last years, when he urged his fellow citizens to leave their laws unchanged, his outlook was ceasing to be progressive. He failed to see that his reconciliation of opposites was but a transitory equilibrium out of which new opposites must arise. And so the tide began to turn. In his hands, the tragic chorus had still preserved something of its primitive function: it was designed to evoke and organise the attitude of mind appropriate to the ensuing action. In Sophokles, it loses this dynamic quality, and in Euripides it tends to become a musical interlude unrelated to the action. Similarly, the Æschylean trilogy split up into a group of single tragedies, and the reconciliation survived only in the atrophied form of the *deus ex machina*, a summary conclusion bearing no organic relation to the plot.[12] The centre of interest had shifted from the reconciliation to the conflict. And at the same time there emerged the figure of the tragic hero in its mature form—a good man destroyed by his own self-will; and this reversal of his fortune is brought about on the principle of *peripéteia*, which Aristotle defines as "the

transformation of the action into its opposite."[13] The hero
brings disaster on his own head by doing something which
results in the reverse of what he had intended. His tragedy is
therefore the tragedy of the community which has created him.

The principle of *peripéteia* can, of course, be traced in Æschylus. Xerxes lost his empire because he overreached himself,
and the circumstances in which Eteokles met his death were of
his own making; but the blindness of Xerxes is merely a manifestation of the pride that goes before a fall, and, although the
position in which Eteokles finds himself is not what he anticipated, he has the opportunity to withdraw and makes his
choice with full knowledge of the consequences. In these plays,
therefore, the principle is still rudimentary. To see it in its
prime, we must turn to the finest work of Sophokles.

Sophokles raised the single tragedy to a level of technical
perfection as high as the Æschylean trilogy, and what makes
this achievement still more remarkable is that, so far from seeking to shun comparison with Æschylus, again and again he
chose as his material the same myths which his predecessor
had already dramatised. Just as he adapted the form of the
art to his own outlook, so, by reinterpreting its content, he
made it thoroughly his own. Further, since his own interpretation was new, he was in a position to exploit the work of
Æschylus, which was, of course, familiar to his audience, by
consciously appealing to it in order to economise an effect or
to point a contrast. A firm grasp of this principle is indispensable to the understanding of Sophokles. Where the corresponding work of Æschylus has perished—for example, his *Œdipus*
and his *Philoktetes*—our appreciation of the Sophoclean plays
on those subjects is necessarily incomplete; but fortunately we
possess in the *Elektra* a play which covers exactly the same
ground as the *Choephoroi*, and, as Headlam pointed out many
years ago, "in the *Elektra* of Sophokles there is hardly any
touch which in one form or another is not already to be found
in Æschylus."[14]

To Sophokles, meditating on the *Oresteia*, the question
presented itself: What happened to Elektra? Æschylus had
shown how, through the agency of the ancestral curse, an
innocent girl had been transformed into a second Clytemnestra;

but there he had left her, because the plan of his trilogy demanded that the attention of the audience should be concentrated on the consequences to Orestes of obeying the oracle of Apollo. Sophokles was not interested in working out the implications of the oracle, which accordingly, in striking contrast to Æschylus, he states in such terms as to throw on Orestes the responsibility for interpreting it as a command to kill his mother. By this means the theological issue, which for Æschylus had been fundamental, is carefully excluded. In the same way, he is not interested in the ancestral curse, or, rather, only in the reality of which it is a symbol—the effects of upbringing and environment on the characters of a young man and his sister.

In the case of Orestes, the function of the curse is performed by the Tutor, who accompanies him back to Argos. This energetic and heartless old man, who has been in charge of Orestes ever since he was sent away from home and has brought him up of set purpose for the mission on which he is now engaged, is a fitting embodiment of the political interests of the royal dynasty. It is he who, after pointing out to the boy the wealthy palace of his fathers and rehearsing him in the details of the conspiracy, roughly orders him out of the way when he hears his sister weeping in the early morning twilight; and it is he who interrupts their sobs of joy when the forlorn pair are for a moment happily united. He realises that, despite all his coaching, he has his work cut out to screw this tenderhearted boy up to the pitch of murdering his mother; and it is made quite clear that, without his constant vigilance and timely intervention, the plot would have ended in fiasco. In all this we recognise a development of one of the functions assigned by Æschylus to his chorus; and it is characteristic of Sophokles that this dynamic element is transferred to one of the actors.

The difference between Orestes and Elektra is that, whereas his conduct has been virtually dictated to him by the manner of his upbringing, hers is her own choice, obstinately maintained in face of tremendous opposition. By turns sullen and defiant, never ceasing to denounce the murderers and constantly reminding them of the hope on which she has staked everything—the coming of Orestes—she is subjected to every insult and indignity and lives in misery and squalor like a slave, fortified by the conviction that only by refusing to compromise can she remain true to her father's memory. The knowledge that in so doing she is forced to behave in a manner of which she is herself ashamed is a torment to her. Her sense of decency, which makes it impossible for her to condone her father's murder, has involved her in a situation in which decency is impossible. She perceives the contradiction herself, but there is no escape from it.[15] When her sister Chrysothemis pleads with her to be sensible, she retorts that to be sensible is to betray her father. Chrysothemis is what Elektra has deliberately chosen not to be—one who has decided "to obey her masters in all things in order that she may be free."[16] This allusion to the proverb quoted by Æschylus in the *Choephoroi*—"Slave, obey your masters right or wrong"—expresses the heart of the dilemma. One sister enjoys a life of freedom because she has the spirit of a slave; the other is treated like a slave because she refuses to submit. And therefore, when the Chorus of her friends warn her that persistence in her attitude can only result in some fatal calamity, she does not deny it, but insists that her attitude has been forced upon her by sheer necessity. Confronted by her mother—a woman hardened by success in crime against all sense of shame (although even she will feel a momentary pang at the news of her son's death, showing that her depravity, too, has a history)—Elektra becomes strident and aggressive. "You admit you killed my father," she declares. "What could be more damning, whether it was justified or not?" To the audience the answer to this question is so obvious that it is left to speak for itself in the sequel of the play. The accusations which Elektra levels against her mother sound unpleasantly like the arguments with which Clytemnestra seeks to justify her murder of her husband, making us feel that what the mother is the daughter may become; and, indeed, the same feeling seems to disturb Elektra herself, for she says:[17]

> Though you will not believe me, of all this
> I *am* ashamed—I see that it is wrong,
> Unlike myself. I have been driven to it
> By your misdeeds and by your hatred of me.
> Dishonour is a teacher of dishonour.

The plan of action on which Orestes and his Tutor have agreed has been very thoroughly worked out; yet, when put to the test, it is all but wrecked by an unforeseen contingency. In the *Choephoroi*, when Orestes delivers the report of his own death, Elektra knows that it is false, because his identity has already been revealed to her. Sophokles reverses the order of these events. The Tutor dare not let Orestes reveal himself beforehand, because he does not trust him; and therefore he has to leave to chance the effect of the report on the girl who has declared that her hope in her brother is the one thing that enables her to go on living. The Tutor, of course, is quite indifferent to the feelings of Elektra, but not so Orestes. Had he possessed more imagination and initiative, he would have foreseen this contingency, which, as it is, takes both him and his adviser by surprise.

The message is that Orestes has been killed by a fall from his chariot when he was leading in the last lap of a race at the Pythian Games at Delphi. This is the mystical charioteer of the *Choephoroi*, who again runs his race under the direction of Apollo (p. 272); but Sophokles gives a novel turn to the theme by reminding us through his Chorus of the story, ignored by Æschylus, of the race of Pelops at Olympia; and with this in mind, as we listen to the headlong career of the latest champion of the House of Pelops, we realise that he is doomed.

It is at this point that Sophokles introduces the *motif* of the discovery of the lock of hair which Orestes has laid on his father's tomb, and it is Chrysothemis, not Elektra, who discovers it. But when she brings the joyful news to her sister, she is met with the blank assurance that their brother is dead. Meanwhile Elektra, exerting all her strength of will to recover herself after the destruction of her sole hope, has conceived the desperate expedient, in which she now appeals to her sister for assistance, of killing Aigisthos herself. Chrysothemis, of course, will not hear of such a thing—as she says quite rightly, it is madness; and so Elektra, who had hardly expected any other answer, declares that she will make the attempt single-handed, since the worst that can come of it is her own death. By this time we share the feeling of Chrysothemis and the Chorus that her mind is becoming unhinged.

Za

Orestes appears in disguise, carrying an urn supposed to
contain his own ashes. This, too, is part of the prearranged plan,
being designed to reinforce the message already delivered in
case it should have failed to carry conviction. Elektra takes the
urn to her breast and breaks into lamentation. This is too much
for Orestes. Disregarding his instructions, he tells Elektra, who
has been pouring out her heart in a flood of passionate despair,
that the brother, whose ashes she is still clasping in her arms,
stands before her. It was a foolish thing to do, not because it
jeopardises the conspiracy, but because this last stroke drives
his sister mad. A few moments ago she heard that he was dead,
and on meeting that situation she has spent the last ounce of
her strength. The news that he is not dead after all is more
than she can bear. She throws herself into his arms, then, tearing herself away, shouts at the top of her voice to all and sundry
that Orestes has come home. Her brother strives in vain to
calm her, and the situation is only saved by the resourceful
Tutor, who, waiting until her fit of hysteria is over, keeps a
close watch on the palace door.

The crisis has now come. Aigisthos, who is out in the country,
has been sent for. Clytemnestra is at home. Orestes goes in,
accompanied by his tutor. After they have gone, there is a
short *stásimon* in which the Chorus, who show as little foresight
in this play as in the *Choephoroi*, describe them as "hounds un-
escapable on the trail of crime," reminding us, both in words
and in rhythm, of the opening of the corresponding *stásimon* in
the *Choephoroi*. A woman's screams are heard—"Oh, I am
struck!"—and Elektra shouts back, "Strike, if you have the
strength, again!"

Their mother's body is brought out, and a shroud thrown
over it. Aigisthos returns. He has heard the report of Orestes'
death, and is anxious to have proof. The son and daughter
point to the body lying at the door. Aigisthos asks them to call
Clytemnestra. Meanwhile he goes up to the body and lifts
the veil. "Did you not know," the murderer says, smiling, "you
have miscalled the living as though dead?" It is to Aigisthos
that Sophokles gives the reading of this riddle: "Surely, it must
be Orestes that addresses me?" He asks leave to speak a few
words, but Elektra intervenes: "For God's sake no more talk.

Kill him at once and throw his body into the fields." Ordered into the house, Aigisthos continues to prevaricate, evidently in the hope of catching Orestes off his guard. After some further badinage, he goes in, followed by Orestes, and Elektra remains on the stage alone, while the Chorus brings the tragedy to an end with the words: "O seed of Atreus, after much suffering thou hast come forth in freedom, by this enterprise made perfect." These words recall the last *stásimon* of the *Choephoroi*, where the deliverance of the house was acclaimed in an ecstasy of ill-timed jubilation.

In order to bring out the full effect of this last scene, it would be necessary to study it in detail, showing how almost every line vibrates with memories of Æschylus; but enough has perhaps been said to indicate the method which the dramatist has adopted; and, when that has been understood, we shall hardly be in danger of falling into the egregious blunder of supposing that Sophokles really imagined that these two unhappy creatures were justified in murdering their mother. It is true that he does not expressly tell us that the next thing that happened was that Orestes saw the Erinyes, but that is because he does not wish to distract our attention from the silent figure of Elektra. So far as the future of Orestes is concerned, he leaves the audience to draw their own conclusions from the *Oresteia*. But what does the future hold in store for Elektra? Her hope has been fulfilled, she has won her deliverance, but the result is her utter desolation:

> O Curse of this sad House, unconquerable,
> How wide thy vision! Even that which seemed
> Well-ordered, safe beyond the reach of harm,
> Thou hast brought down with arrows from afar,
> And left me desolate, stripped of all I loved.[18]

It is not an accident that Sheppard, the first modern scholar to explain this play correctly,[19] was also the first to produce it on the stage; for the stagecraft of Sophokles, who in this respect excelled, is unanswerable. Nor is it an accident that, notwithstanding Sheppard's interpretation, the play continues to be misunderstood, because of all Greek tragedies it presents that sense of contradiction which is the essence of mature tragedy, in

its sharpest and most inescapable form. Sophokles and his contemporaries could stand it, but for our dyspeptic culture it is
too tough. Of those who seek refuge in the view that Sophokles
regarded the murder simply as a justifiable homicide, it must
be said that they have been deaf to his appeals to the *Choephoroi*,
and that they have no right to father on Sophokles their own
predilection for an easy answer to an insoluble problem. Others,
less crudely, but with no more success, have tried to find some
compromise, some middle point between Elektra and Chrysothemis, which will enable them to say that the heroine failed in
some way to do what she ought to have done; but these critics
(who might well be asked what they would have done in the
circumstances themselves) are apparently unaware that they
are attempting that very task of reconciling the irreconcilable
in which Elektra so heroically failed. There is no way out, and
that is where the tragedy lies—the tragedy of a passionate
nature which by the very exercise of its vitality is caught as in
a vice and crushed.

Let us now turn to the *Œdipus Tyrannus*, which Aristotle
regarded as the type of all Greek tragedy.

Laios and Jocasta were King and Queen of Thebes. Kreon
was Jocasta's brother. To the south of Thebes lies Corinth; to
the west, cradled in the cliffs of Parnassus, the Delphic Oracle
of Apollo, on whose temple were inscribed the words, "Know
thyself." To Laios and Jocasta was born a son, Œdipus, of
whom the Oracle predicted that he was destined to murder
his father and marry his mother. Rather than rear such a child,
Jocasta handed it over to one of the men-servants with instructions to leave it to perish in the hills. The man-servant, who
was a shepherd, took pity on it and gave it to another shepherd, a Corinthian, who took it home with him. The King
and Queen of Corinth were childless, and reared it as their
own.

Some twenty years later the young Œdipus was taunted by
one of his companions with not being the true son of his father.
He consulted his supposed parents, who sought to reassure him
without revealing the truth. Dissatisfied with their assurances,
Œdipus made a pilgrimage to Delphi and consulted the Oracle.
The only reply he got was a repetition of the old prophecy, of

which he now heard for the first time. Resolving never to set foot in Corinth again, he took the road to Thebes.

At this time the people of Thebes were afflicted by the ravages of the Sphinx, which took a daily toll of human life until some one could be found to read the riddle it had set them. Laios was now on his way to Delphi to consult the Oracle. He was driving a chariot, and one of his attendants was his man-servant, the shepherd. Meeting Œdipus, he tried to force him off the track. A quarrel ensued. Laios struck at Œdipus with his whip. Œdipus struck back and killed him. He killed the attendants, too—all except the shepherd, who took to his heels and brought back to Thebes the panic-stricken story that the King had been murdered by a band of robbers.

Pursuing his journey, Œdipus reached Thebes, where the first thing he did was to deliver the people by reading the riddle of the Sphinx. The answer, as we have seen, was Man. Œdipus knew himself. And yet he did not know himself: that he was yet to learn. The grateful people acclaimed him as their King. At this point the shepherd, who recognised in the deliverer of Thebes his master's murderer, but resolved to keep the truth to himself, obtained Jocasta's leave to spend the rest of his days in retirement in the hills. The new King married the widowed Queen.

Many years passed, and children were born to them. Then once more the Thebans were afflicted, this time with a plague. Determined not to fail them, Œdipus sent Kreon to consult the Oracle. The reply was that the plague would cease when the murderer of Laios had been expelled. Œdipus immediately instituted a search for the unknown criminal in their midst, on whom he pronounced a curse. There was one other besides the shepherd who knew the truth and, like him, had decided to keep it dark—the aged prophet, Teiresias. Questioned by Œdipus, he refused to answer. Œdipus lost patience and accused him of disloyalty to Thebes. Then Teiresias lost patience, too, and denounced Œdipus as the murderer. Œdipus flew into a passion, accused Teiresias of having been suborned by Kreon, and accused Kreon of conspiring against the throne. The quarrel was brought to an end by the intervention of Jocasta, who, in reply to her husband's questions, told him what she had heard of the death of Laios—that he had been killed on the road to Delphi by a band of robbers. The road to Delphi—Œdipus remembered. But a band of robbers— Œdipus had been travelling alone. Jocasta assured him that the second point could be proved by sending for the sole survivor, the old shepherd in the hills. This Œdipus instructed her to do in the hope that his evidence would clear him.

At this point a messenger arrived from Corinth with the news that the King of that city was dead and Œdipus his successor. Œdipus was now at the height of fortune—king of two cities; and Jocasta acclaimed the news as proof that, since his father had died a natural death, the old prophecy was falsified. Reassured on that point, Œdipus nevertheless insisted that he would never return to Corinth for fear of marrying the Queen. Eager to reassure him on this point, too, the messenger explained that he was not her true son, but a foundling.

Meanwhile the old shepherd had arrived and at once recognised the messenger from Corinth as the shepherd he had met long ago in the hills. He tried hard to evade the King's questions, but was forced to answer by the threat of torture. The truth was out at last: Œdipus knew himself. Rushing into the palace, he put out his eyes with brooches torn from the dead body of his mother, who had already hanged herself.

> Ah, generations of men!
> I count your life as nothing.
> None that mortal is hath more
> Of happiness than this—
> To seem and not to be, and then, having seemed, to fail.[20]

Since the beginning of the play, objectively nothing has changed, but subjectively everything has changed. All that has happened is that Œdipus has come to know what he is as apart from what he seemed to be. He ends life as he began it—as an outcast. The interval was only seeming. And yet, if seeming is being, this outcast who became a king, this king who has become an outcast, has twice become the opposite of what he was. And these strange mutations have been brought about against the intention, yet through the unconscious agency, of the persons concerned. The parents exposed the child to avert the prophecy. The shepherd saved it out of pity, with the result that it grew up ignorant of its parentage. When doubt was cast on his parentage, Œdipus consulted the Oracle, and, when the Oracle revealed his destiny, he sought to escape it by taking the road that led to Thebes. He killed his father in self-defence. When the shepherd recognised him, he said nothing, thus leaving him free to marry his mother. When the Oracle demanded the expulsion of the murderer, Œdipus led the search and followed up each clue until he was brought face to face with himself. Teiresias would not have denounced him if he had not denounced Teiresias. His charges against Teiresias and Kreon were unjustified. His vehemence at this point was the error that brought about his fall. And yet this error was but the excess of his greatest quality—his zeal in the service of his people. And, finally, the old shepherd, summoned to disprove the charge that he had killed his father, played into the hands of the Corinthian messenger, who, by seeking to relieve Œdipus of the fear of marrying his mother, proved that what he feared to do he had already done. This constant transmutation of intentions into their opposites, carried on to the catastrophe with the automatic precision of a dream, is the motive that governs the whole conception. The Œdipus of Sophokles is a symbol of the deep-seated perplexity engendered in men's minds by the unforeseen and incomprehensible transformation of a social order designed to establish liberty and equality into an instrument for the destruction of liberty and equality.

This play differs from the *Elektra* in that the crisis is followed by an epilogue, which culminates in the prayer dictated by the sufferer to his children:[21]

> Children, out of much
> I might have told you, could you understand,
> Take this one counsel: be your prayer to live,
> Where fortune's modest measure is, a life
> That shall be better than your father's was.

The purpose of this epilogue is, of course, to relieve the tremendous tension created by the crisis, and that purpose it serves perfectly; but the release it provides is, as it was meant to be, purely emotional. If the lesson to be drawn from what has happened is the "modest measure" of conventional morality, the sufferer might have answered his god in the words of Augustine, "Thou hast counselled more wisely than thou hast permitted." But the strength of Œdipus is spent. Defeated and crushed by an irresistible and impenetrable power, which out of his own goodness has made the net that has enmeshed him, his wounded spirit instinctively seeks refuge in the simple, idle phrases that he learnt as a child.

Sophokles came of an aristocratic family, and in his conscious life he accepted the conventional outlook of his class.[22] This is shown by his active support of the anti-democratic constitution which placed restrictions on the franchise in the last years of the Peloponnesian War (411 B.C.). It is also shown by his attitude to the Delphic Oracle, to which, owing to its reactionary policy, the democrats were hostile. In the *Œdipus*, as in the *Elektra*, he evades the religious issue, insisting that the oracle given to Laios is the interpretation put on the will of Apollo by his human agents, who are not infallible. For him, of course, that issue is dramatically irrelevant, but the fact that, unlike Æschylus and Euripides, he has chosen to make it irrelevant signifies that he accepted the aristocratic view of Apollo, or at least was not prepared to challenge it.[23] It is also true, as Webster has remarked, that he accepted the conventional attitude, which Euripides was already challenging, to slaves and women. These social prejudices were certainly limitations, and more severe in him than in Æschylus, because their true character was becoming increasingly apparent; but Webster is entirely mistaken in supposing that they constituted the essentials of his thought.[24] As one who acquiesced in the privileges of his class, he was bound to accept the moral values designed to protect them, but where he differed from other members of his class, less intellectually gifted, was in his profound sense of the contradictions which those values involved; and this is the conflict that he sublimated in his art. He was far less conscious than Æschylus had been of his relation to society, but of course this does not mean that the relation was any the less close—merely that it was passive rather than active; and indeed it was partly because of this that he was able to express the conflict in a symbol so true to the reality as the tragedy of Œdipus.

Euripides, like Æschylus, was actively conscious of his relation to society; but for that very reason his work was fundamentally different, because society had changed. Reared from the cradle in the democratic ideas of liberty and equality, he was dismayed to see them flouted by reality. He saw the decay of the state religion in consequence of the deepening division of interests among the worshippers; he saw the degradation of family life in consequence of the subjection of women; he saw the demoralising effects of imperialist aggression, waged in the name of democracy; and he even dared to challenge the validity of the distinction between freeman and slave, thus laying bare the irremediable evil which from this time forward was to gnaw at the vitals of ancient society—the condition both of its growth and its decay. Hence his outspoken individualism, the speculative inconsistency of his thought, and the experimental variety of his technique.

As a democrat, he delivered, in the *Ion*, a scathing denunciation of the unscrupulous chicanery by which the Delphic priesthood maintained its hold over the masses. As a rationalist, he boldly declared, in the *Madness of Herakles*, that, in the absence of moral responsibility, the pollution of homicide was merely physical. But, like other rationalists, he failed to see that the evils of society could never be cured by an appeal to reason, because their origin lay, not in ignorance or unenlightenment, but in a conflict of interests. It is therefore not surprising that at the end of his life he turned to mysticism. In his *Hippolytos*, an early play, he had shown little sympathy with the Orphic way of life; but in the *Bacchants*, written shortly before his death in Macedonia, where the worship of Dionysus still survived in its primitive, orgiastic form, his position has changed. The self-abandonment of the mystic is attractive to one who has thought long and earnestly on the riddle of reality, but without achieving any positive result; yet at the same time it is repulsive, because he cannot bring himself to renounce the faculty which has made man what he is. Agaue and her Bacchants escape from the city into the wilds, where, in communion with the divine, they dance their night-long dances, but she returns to the city carrying in her arms the head of her son, whom she has torn to pieces.

We have seen how the position of women at Athens had deteriorated. Lysias gives a picture of Athenian family life in his speech *On the Murder of Eratosthenes*, and it is not a pleasant one. All that was permitted to the wife was housework in the company of slaves and fidelity to a husband who spent most of his time away from home and was free to associate with other women. The result was the rapid growth of concubinage, prostitution and also male homosexuality. This institution, which seems to have been particularly widespread among the aristocratic intellectuals, was an adaptation of the primitive relationship between the newly-initiated boy and the young man who had supervised his initiation—a relationship which, in the conditions of Athenian city life, became predominantly sexual. The extent to which the relations between husband and wife were poisoned by these developments may be judged from the complacent remark of another Athenian orator:[25] "We have courtesans for our pleasure, concubines for the daily needs of our bodies, and wives to keep house for us and bear us legitimate children." And, finally, having been reduced to this condition in the interests of the men, the woman was told to accept it as a dispensation of Nature. Perikles, who had divorced his own wife for an Ionian courtesan, and consequently quarrelled with his son, who then spread scurrilous reports about his father's private life, delivered a public oration in which he exhorted the widows of the men who had died for Athens to make the best of their inferior natures by behaving with such self-effacement as to excite neither applause nor censure.[26] The attitude towards women corresponded to the attitude towards slaves. One wonders how Perikles explained matters to Aspasia, who, being an alien, was free from disabilities declared to be inherent in her sex; and one wonders how Plato felt on the day when by an unlucky stroke of fortune he was sold into slavery himself.[27] The story was that Dionysios of Syracuse, who ordered the sale, told him that no harm would come to him, because, being a just man, he would be happy though a slave. However, the philosopher's capacity to practise

what he preached was not put to the test, because, being rich,
he was able to buy himself out.

> All trodden paths and paths untrod before
> Are scaled by nimble riches.

There was an Attic proverb that women had no fight in
them. Jason returned home with Medea, a woman he had
fallen in love with on his travels. After his return he ceased to
care for her. She was a foreigner, his children by her were
illegitimate, and he wanted a son who would be able to inherit
from him. So he made a match with the King's daughter, and,
in case Medea should cause trouble, she was told to leave the
country and take her children with her. Medea obeyed, but not
before she had murdered the bride and her own children by the
bridegroom. The arguments advanced by Jason in defence of
his conduct are such as would be entirely acceptable to Athenian convention. As Medea says, we have to buy husbands with
our money and serve them with our bodies like slaves.

In the year 416 the Athenians delivered an ultimatum to the
islanders of Melos, who wished to remain neutral in the war,
and, according to Thucydides, this is what the representatives
of democratic Athens told the people of Melos:[28]

> As therefore it is not our purpose to amuse you with
> pompous details—how, after completely vanquishing the
> Persians, we had a right to assume the sovereignty, we shall
> waive all parade of words that have no tendency towards
> conviction, and in return insist from you that you reject all
> hopes of persuading us by frivolous remonstrances. Let us
> lay all stress on such points as may on both sides be judged
> persuasive; since of this you are as strongly convinced as we
> ourselves are sensible of it, that in all human competitions
> equal wants alone produce equitable determination, and, in
> whatever terms the powerful enjoin obedience, to those the
> weak are obliged to submit.

Since the people of Melos refused to submit, the adult male
population was put to the sword and the women and children
sold into slavery. In the following year Euripides produced his
Trojan Women, portraying the helpless misery of the captives
and the cynical insolence of the conquerors, who are destined
to be destroyed on the voyage home by thunder and lightning.

Thus, in the hands of Euripides, the age-old story of the Trojan War became prophetic, for a few years later Athens lost her empire as a result of her disastrous expedition to Sicily.

Euripides was a democrat who saw that democracy was being driven to self-destruction. That is the contradiction that underlies his work. He saw the evils inherent in contemporary society, and courageously exposed them. His influence was therefore disruptive: he helped to undermine the edifice which Æschylus had laboured to construct. But it was also, and for the same reason, progressive: the edifice was crumbling of itself.

After the war, the Greek city-state entered on its last phase, and Athenian thought became sharply divided in accordance with the cleavage between the few who had an interest in maintaining it and the many who had not. On the one hand, the idealists clung to their faith in the city-state at the cost of accepting social inequalities which were becoming less and less compatible with honest thinking. They were driven to deny the validity of the senses as a criterion of truth and to teach that happiness lay, not in pleasure, but in something called "virtue," which involved the acceptance of pain. Plato (428–348 B.C.) made slavery the basis of his ideal state, modelled on the parasitic communism of backward Spartan landowners, and, true to his model, passed imaginary laws narrowly restricting the activities of painters and poets, in whose creative imagination and fertile sense of human possibilities he recognised a danger to the established order; while, for the further security of his ruling class, he drew up a fantastic system of education designed to poison the minds of the people by dissemination of calculated lies.[29] Plato's Republic is an implicit confession of the intellectual bankruptcy of the city-state. Similarly, the contradictions in which even Aristotle (384–322 B.C.), less reactionary and more honest than Plato, entangled himself in his justification of slavery are a measure of the extent to which the intellectual integrity of the ruling class was compromised by the maintenance of its privileges. He justified the subordination of slave to freeman by appealing to the subordination of woman to man and of body to soul; but the subordination of woman was a phenomenon of the same nature as slavery, and the subordination of body to soul, or of matter to form, was a

projection on to the plane of ideas of the cleavage that confronted him in society. The early Orphics had asserted the
independence of the soul as a protest against the enslavement
of their bodies; now the same dichotomy was used to reconcile
the unfree to permanent subjection. We are reminded of those
nineteenth-century thinkers, beginning with Malthus, who,
accepting the manufacturers' demand for cheap labour,
justified the poverty of the workers by inventing laws of the
struggle for existence and the survival of the fittest, and, when
on this basis Darwin had founded a new science of biology, they
acclaimed his theories as a final proof that the poverty of the
workers was a law of nature.[30]

Conversely, the materialists were only able to reaffirm the
validity of sense-perception and to maintain their conviction
that happiness lies primarily in the satisfaction of material
needs, by renouncing their part in a society which no longer
conformed to reason and by preaching the self-sufficiency of the
individual. Epicurus (342–268 B.C.) taught that justice was
relative, rescued the human soul from metaphysical abstractions (even his gods were material), and so completed the work,
which Demokritos had begun, of formulating the Atomic
Theory. The atomism of the Epicureans was the complement
of their individualism. They made the elements of the universe
impassive and imperturbable, because, in a society torn by
discord, that is what they themselves strove to become. Their
definition of pleasure as the absence of pain reveals the social
desperation of the dying convulsions of the city-state, but it
had a positive value in their insistence that the aim of human
endeavour *is* pleasure and not self-frustration for an intangible
idea or an illusory hereafter. Thus, between the rise and fall of
the city-state, idealism and materialism had changed places.
At the beginning of the urban revolution, when the Orphics
were proclaiming the divinity of the soul, the philosophers of
Miletos maintained the primitive notion that the soul is an
activity of matter; but now, when the Greek city-states were
about to dissolve like crystals into the cosmopolitan empire,
the Epicureans suffered persecution in their endeavours to free
the masses from the fables of infernal torment with which their
rulers cowed them. The heir to Orphic mysticism was Plato;

the heir to Ionian materialism was Epicurus. In this, despite their limitations, the Epicureans were in the true line of progress; for at least they recognised that "the supreme being for man is man himself, and consequently all relations, all conditions in which man is humiliated, enslaved, despised, must be destroyed."

There was, however, one tradition which the Epicureans had inherited indirectly from the Orphics. We have seen in a former chapter how, in consequence of the transition from collective to private ownership, Moira had been transformed into Ananke (p. 158). During the maturity of the city-state, the idea of Ananke was developed and extended. Not only was the slave under the absolute control of his master and denied all share in the surplus product of his labour, but the master himself, in the conditions of a monetary economy, was at the mercy of forces which he was unable to control; and so the freeman, too, was enslaved to the blind force of Necessity, which frustrated his desires and defeated his efforts. But, if Necessity is supreme, and her action incalculable, all change appears subjectively as chance; and so by the side of Ananke there arose the figure of Tyche—opposite poles of the same conception.[31] The belief that the world is ruled by Tyche can be traced through Euripides to Pindar, who declared that she was one of the Moirai and the strongest of them all;[32] and during the next two centuries the cult of Tyche became one of the most widespread and popular in Greece.

It was precisely at this point that Epicurus made his most important advance over the cosmology of Demokritos. Parmenides, the forerunner of Plato, had taught that there was no empty space and consequently no motion; that the universe was one and unchanging, its apparent diversity and mutability being an illusion of the senses. Demokritos, the forerunner of Epicurus, had reasserted the existence of empty space and attributed the properties of the Parmenidean One to each of an infinite number of atoms, indivisible, indestructible, without weight, falling vertically through the void and by their collisions and combinations creating the world. The result was a mechanistic theory of the universe in which every event is the product of necessity—the slave of Ananke.

In the view of Epicurus, this theory was inadequate, because it failed to take account of one of the faculties which differentiate man from the other animals—what we call freedom of the will. He agreed with Demokritos, as against Plato, that matter, not mind, is the *prius*, but he recognised that the human consciousness was capable of reacting on its environment, and hence, by applying what it had learnt from science, of controlling it. Accordingly, endowed in his theory with the property of weight, the atom possesses in itself the cause of its own motion; and, moreover, it possesses, besides the vertical, an oblique motion or swerve from the straight line. Thus, in his system, necessity was superseded by chance, Ananke by Tyche, and in this way the atom became free.

In keeping with this rift in society and thought there was a corresponding rift in art. The old type of comedy, perfected by Aristophanes, which had been intensely political, passed into the comedy of manners, composed almost entirely by resident aliens and devoted to the intrigues of illicit lovers and foundlings, who after many vicissitudes are restored by fortune to their lost heritage. The only other art form that remained popular at Athens after the end of the Peloponnesian War was the dithyramb, which was now developed as an extravagant musical spectacle supplying an opiate to the people's unsatisfied desires. As for tragedy, which by its very nature was at the same time serious and collective, there was no scope for it in a community driven by internal dissensions to seek escape from a conflict that was to remain insoluble until the economic possibilities of slave labour had been exhausted; and, before that point was reached, it was necessary that Imperial Rome should bestride the world like a clay-footed colossus. The tragic festivals were maintained, but with a shift of interest to the stagecraft and the acting, and with an increasing dependence on revivals of the old masters, especially Euripides, whose prophetic individualism appealed far more strongly than the obsolete collectivism of Æschylus to an audience that had lost faith in social life. As a creative force, the art of tragedy ceased to exist, until the bourgeois revolution of modern Europe brought it once more into being out of conditions similar in certain essential respects to those which had prevailed under the merchant princes of early Athens.

XIX

PITY AND FEAR

ARISTOTLE's account of Greek tragedy contains certain
weaknesses, due to limitations inherent in his subjective
attitude to the problem. It is in keeping with his general
doctrine of the relation of matter to form that he treats the
evolution of the art as a wholly internal process without reference to the history of the community of whose life it was a part.
For this reason he is content to explain how tragedy assumed
its final form without explaining why it assumed that particular
form or why after that it ceased to develop. Again, his predilection, shared with his contemporaries, for the single tragedy, in
which the element of reconciliation was atrophied or eliminated,
makes it difficult for him to appreciate the work of Æschylus:
indeed, he omits all mention of the Æschylean tetralogy, which,
on his own assumptions, might well have been regarded as the
highest point in the formal evolution of the art.

Notwithstanding these limitations, his work has a great
positive value, which consists, first, in his conception of the
drama as a product of organic development to be studied
objectively like other natural phenomena, and, secondly, in his
scrupulous attention to the known facts. In the latter respect,
he reveals the same regard for detail that we find in his other
work, scientific and historical, and for that reason we should
beware of rejecting his statements of fact without good reason,
even where we cannot check them. The theory of the origin of
tragedy which has been propounded in these pages was worked
out in its initial stages on the basis of the anthropological data
at a time when I was inclined to accept Pickard-Cambridge's
estimate of the *Poetics*, but in the course of further study it was
slowly borne in on me that the conclusions to which the
evidence was tending were precisely those which had been
formulated by Aristotle. The man I had been cold-shouldering
turned out to be my best friend. I had much the same experience

with the *Politics*. Even in this field, where, of course, his preconceptions are more active and disturbing, Aristotle reveals an insight into primitive institutions which the study of comparative anthropology shows to be far superior to that possessed by those modern historians who have rejected his authority. For these reasons, I feel entitled to claim as a confirmation of my argument the fact that it coheres so closely with the evidence of Aristotle.

There is one important statement of Aristotle's that remains to be examined.[1] He says that "tragedy is a representation . . . which by means of pity and fear effects the purgation of such emotions." Plato had expelled the tragic poets from his ideal state because he considered them to be socially dangerous. Aristotle replies that the function of tragedy is socially useful. It will be noticed that both are agreed on one point: that the function of poetry is social.

Aristotle's conception of purgation or purification (*kátharsis*) is closely allied to the use of that term in medicine. In the doctrine of the Hippocratic school, disease is a disturbance of the bodily humours, leading to a crisis, in which, in the event of recovery, the morbid matter is evacuated or expelled, and the physician's aim is to induce the crisis in conditions which will have that result. But Aristotle's statement goes further than that, implying that, before the morbid affections can be expelled, they must first be artificially stimulated. To understand this point, we must trace it to its origin in the primitive treatment of epilepsy and hysteria.

Epilepsy was known in Greek as the "sacred disease," and, according to Aretaios, it was so called because its cause was believed to be the entry of a god or spirit into the body.[2] That this interpretation of the term is correct appears from what is said in the Hippocratic treatise on the disease of the "sorcerers, purifiers, charlatans and quacks" who attempted to cure it "by purifications and incantations."[3]

If the patient imitates a goat, if he roars, or is convulsed in the right side, they say that the Mother of the Gods is the cause. . . . If he foams at the mouth and kicks, the cause is assigned to Ares. If the symptoms are fears and terrors at night, delirium, jumping out of bed and rushing out of doors, they are described as attacks of Hekate or assaults of spirits of the dead.

This implies that the patient is "possessed" (*kátochos*)—he has "a god in him" (*éntheos*).

The purifications in vogue among these magicians are described by the writer as consisting of abstention from baths and certain foods, the wearing of black as a sign of death and the observance of certain taboos. When the purification has been successfully accomplished, the off-scourings "are buried in the ground or thrown into the sea or carried into the mountains where no one can touch them or tread on them." This means that through purification the spirit with which the patient has been possessed is expelled. The writer of this treatise does not specify the nature of the other part of the procedure—the incantations; but these can be studied in evidence from other sources.

The ritual of the Korybantes, whom we have seen reason to regard as a primitive magico-medical secret society, consisted of an orgiastic dance, to the accompaniment of flutes and drums, which induced in the participants what would be described in modern terminology as a fit of hysteria. Now, the Korybantes were credited with the power, not only of inducing madness, but of curing it, and the cure was effected by the same means as the inducement—by incantations, or songs "sung over" the patient, like the song which the Erinyes of Æschylus sang over Orestes in order to drive him mad. In the *Kriton*, after explaining the reasons why he refuses to escape from prison, Sokrates says that these reasons are ringing in his ears like the music of the flute in the rites of the Korybantes and make it impossible for him to hear any others.[4] The effect of the music was hypnotic. In the *Symposium*, speaking of the eloquence of Sokrates, Alkibiades says: "Whenever I listen to him, my heart throbs harder than it does in those who take part in the rites of the Korybantes, and his words evoke in me floods of tears."[5] Here the effect is not so much hypnotic as hysterical.

The evidence relating to the Korybantes is fragmentary, but, so far as it goes, it accords exactly with the psychiatric functions of primitive secret societies in all parts of the world. The following remarks are from a summary of the anthropological evidence by Fallaize.[6]

Among the primitive theories of disease, causation by spirits who enter into and torment the patient holds a prominent place. The therapeutic measures of the medicine-man, in so far as they are not purely materialistic, like the extraction of a bone or pebble, are largely directed towards driving out or propitiating the demons or spirits responsible for the disease. . . .

The Bathonga hold that possession in the form in which it is recognised among them is caused by the spirits of the dead. . . . The preliminary symptoms are a nervous crisis, persistent pain in chest, hiccough, extraordinary yawning, and emaciation. If, after consultation of the divinatory bones, the medicine-man decides that the patient is possessed, the spirit is exorcised. In the course of the elaborate series of ceremonies which follows the patient in a frenzy declares the name of the spirit which possesses him. . . . He is given drugs which act as an emetic and the spirit is declared to have left him.

The pathological character of those affections which are regarded by primitive peoples as evidence of possession is such that the symptoms of the disease or weakness would recur at more or less frequent intervals. It is therefore not surprising to find that those who are subject to such nervous crises come to be regarded as a class apart—a class of peculiar sanctity. . . . The Bathonga who had been exorcised for possession, after a period of probation himself became a fully-initiated medicine-man and exorcist. The Melenau woman who has been under the influence of the *toh* [spirit], when she has undergone the full ceremony of exorcism, becomes a medicine-woman with full powers to summon the spirits to assist her in healing others. . . . Among some Siberian tribes the office of shaman tended to become hereditary, but the supernatural gift was a necessary qualification, and the shamans also adopted children who appeared suitable to succeed them, i.e. those who showed signs of an epileptic or neurotic tendency. . . . On the other hand, even where a predisposition or the actual

symptoms of previous disease were not a condition of becoming a priest, diviner or soothsayer, the novitiate often
imposed conditions which could not fail to lead to an
abnormal or unhealthy frame of mind. . . . Among the
Chukchi, Koryak and Gilyak, during the long periods of
seclusion in the forests, not only did the shamans learn and
practise their professional arts—singing, dancing, ventrilo-
quism, and playing the drum—but they endured hardships
of cold and hunger which could not but intensify their
natural predisposition towards hysteria. . . .

The theory of possession is not applied solely to those
intermittent manifestations of abnormality to which it owes
its origin. It could hardly be expected that those who are
subject to attacks should not take advantage of the power
given them by the feelings of awe and terror aroused by
their supposed relation to the spirit world. But, as a crisis
of their disease cannot be relied upon to coincide with the
moment when their advice may be sought or their assistance invoked by the ordinary member of the community,
possession is superinduced voluntarily by an artificial
stimulus. . . .

A condition of the success of an attempt to exorcise the
possessing spirit is that it should be compelled to declare
through the mouth of its victim either its name, thus giving
the operator power over it in accordance with a generally
recognised rule of magical practice, or its desires (usually
a request for offerings), knowledge of which makes it possible
for it to be expelled by propitiation. It requires only a slight
extension of the argument that these sayings are an expression
of the will of the gods to transform them into a channel for
the revelation of the future. There is abundant evidence in
the recorded instances of possession to show that this is not
merely an *a priori* view but is in accordance with the facts. . . .
Those who are subject to possession by entering voluntarily
into the state of exaltation at the request of their consultants
attain the position of oracles. Analogies more or less close
to the priestess of Apollo at Delphi and the Sibyl at Cumæ
are found in almost every part of the world.

This evidence throws a flood of light on several fundamental
eléments in Greek life and thought—the close relation between
manía, "madness," and *mantiké*, "prophecy," the psychical

associations of the musical modes, and the original nature of poetical inspiration; but what immediately concerns us is its significance for the ritual of the Dionysiac *thíasos*.

The primitive attitude to possession may be interpreted as follows. In the earliest stage, epilepsy and hysteria were treated simply like other diseases: the patient was subjected to a rite of initiation, in the course of which he died and was born again. The essential part of this process was the act of expulsion or purification, by means of which the spirit which had taken possession of the patient was first aroused into activity and then expelled. There is no reason to doubt that, granted implicit faith on the patient's part, this cure by abreaction, to use the Freudian term, was to a considerable extent successful. The idea of possession was not originally confined to these diseases, but it came to be especially associated with them because of the peculiar violence of their symptoms and their tendency to recur. In this way there arose a special class of initiates, consisting of persons who had a predisposition to some form of dementia. These persons were organised in a magical society, modelled on the structure of the clan. At this stage, the pathological nature of their condition becomes increasingly obscured by the magical ideas to which it has given rise. The faculty of possession is regarded as a sign of exceptionally free and intimate intercourse with the spirit-world. Consequently, in pursuance of these magical powers, the members of the society are addicted to artificially inducing the symptoms in themselves, and, instead of curing them in others, they initiate the patient into their own mode of life, in which the disease is fostered because it is regarded as socially useful.

It is now clear why the Korybantes were credited with the power of both inducing and curing madness. They induced it in order to cure it and cured it in order to induce it. The same ambivalence is found in the cults of Dionysus. As Dionysos Bakcheios, he induced hysteria in his worshippers, who, being possessed by him, called themselves by his name, becoming *bákchoi* or *bákchai*; as Dionysos Lysios, he withdrew from them and so restored them to their right mind. Similarly, in myth, driven mad by the god, the daughters of Proitos were pursued by the medicine-man, Melampous, who purified them by an ecstatic dance and threw the off-scourings into a river.[7] By this means they recovered their senses, but by the same means they had become initiates of Dionysus. The descriptions of the Dionysiac *sparagmós*—for example, the rending of Pentheus in the *Bacchants*—show that the participants were acting under the influence of artificially induced hysteria; and, conversely, the madness of Herakles, which, as related by Euripides, exhibits the symptoms of a hysterical seizure, is described in terms borrowed from the orgies of the Korybantes and the Dionysiac *thíasos*.[8]

The prominence of hysteria and allied disorders among primitive peoples is not to be explained by the artificial value placed on them in consequence of the hypertrophy of magic. Rather, that hypertrophy is itself a response to the need for organising socially an existing tendency. Thus, as Fallaize points out, the areas where arctic hysteria is prevalent are precisely those in which the mediumistic functions of shamanism are most highly developed. The truth seems to be that in primitive society, the division of labour being still rudimentary, the members of the community are proportionately deficient in individuality and consequently lack the stability to withstand those acute maladjustments between the individual and society which are the recognised causes of these disorders. This point has been well expressed by Caudwell. After explaining that the contradictions generated by the development of society are necessarily reflected in man's consciousness in such forms as moral problems and feelings of sin, he goes on:[9]

> In a primitive society, where man is as yet undifferentiated, conscience and consciousness are similarly simple, direct and homogeneous, and for this very reason lacking in depth and vividness. . . . When this consciousness is attacked, there is no complexity or balancing of forces to soften the blow; the collapse is complete. The primitive who is once convinced that he has sinned or is bewitched will promptly die—a fact well-attested by field-anthropologists. The shallowness of his consciousness is revealed in the simplicity of his dissociation, the ease with which his psyche can be precipitated in hysteria, his high degree of susceptibility and the "all-or-none" nature of his emotional reactions—all symptoms

pointing to a mentation more unconscious and instinctive
than that of "civilised" differentiated man.

These considerations suggest that the disposition to these disorders in modern tribes has been accentuated by impact with
European culture, the effect of which is seen in the familiar
police-court cases of lascars "running amok."

In Chapter IX it was argued that the Orphic movement drew
its impetus from the peasantry uprooted by the urban revolution. After the tribal ties of cult and kinship had been severed,
they were recreated on the mystical plane in these religious
brotherhoods. The form of the new cult was derived from
Thrace, where the orgiastic features of Dionysiac worship were
particularly prominent. Next to Thrace, the most fertile centre
for the dissemination of orgiastic religion was Phrygia, the
home of Attis and Kybele, the mother-goddess of the Korybantes, who was closely associated with Dionysus. And, next to
Thrace, Phrygia was the principal area for the mining of gold
and silver. The development of these industries must have
induced among the neighbouring tribes, which supplied the
labour, a spiritual crisis of the same kind as that which the
urban revolution precipitated among the Attic peasantry.
Speaking of one of the Thracian tribes, the Trausoi, Herodotus
says:[10]

> When a child is born, its kinsfolk sit round it lamenting
> the sufferings it must undergo and recounting all the sorrows
> of mankind; but, when a man dies, they bury him with
> rejoicing and merry-making, because they consider that he
> has been delivered from all those evils and lives in perfect
> bliss.

This attitude to life and death is not primitive. It is the attitude
characteristic of mystical religion, which we have studied at
Eleusis. It is the cry of a primitive people caught in the vortex
of industrial exploitation.

The Orphic brotherhoods were modelled, as we have seen,
on the earlier Dionysiac *thíasos*, which, as all the mythological
data go to show, had its origin in the Mycenean period; and
therefore we look for some analogous disturbance to account

for the emergence of the Dionysiac *thiasos* out of the primitive clan. The wide distribution and remarkable uniformity of this cult indicate that the need which it was evolved to satisfy was general and fundamental; and the fact that, apart from the priest or medicine-man at the head, the initiates were women, suggests that its origin lies in the stress imposed on women by the abolition of matrilineal institutions and the consequent decline in the social status of their sex.

It appears therefore that, whether he was aware of it or not, when Aristotle declared that the function of tragedy was "through pity and fear to effect the purgation of such emotions," he was describing correctly the essential function of the Dionysiac ritual out of which tragedy had evolved; and his use of the term "purgation" or "purification," referring to the expulsion of the indwelling disease in order to induce newness of life, shows that in his view the function of tragedy was essentially akin to that of initiation, from which it was in fact derived.

I am inclined to think that he was aware of it. Several Greek writers describe in detail the emotional effects of mystical initiation, and the uniformity of the symptoms shows that they were recognised as normal. They consist of shuddering, trembling, sweating, mental confusion, distress, consternation and joy mixed with alarm and agitation.[11] These are the characteristics of religious hysteria, such as might be extensively paralleled from the literature of Christianity. Now, Aristotle is quoted as saying that "the initiates were not required to learn anything but to experience certain emotions and to be put in a certain disposition."[12] In view of what has just been said concerning the emotions of initiation, it may be inferred that what Aristotle meant by this statement was that through the artificial excitation of fear and distress these emotions were so to speak discharged from the system, and so the mental disposition of the subject was readjusted to its environment.

How, we are led to ask, did an Athenian audience react to the performance of their tragedies? In our own London theatres, the members of the audience usually keep their emotional reactions (other than laughter) to themselves; but in the cinemas of the west of Ireland, where the spectators are peasants, the atmosphere is far more intense. At the critical moments of the plot, almost every face wears a terrified look and continuous sobbing may be heard. In this respect, an Athenian would undoubtedly have felt more at home in the west of Ireland than in the West End of London. In one of Plato's dialogues, a professional reciter of the Homeric poems describes the effect of his performances on himself and on his audience.[13]

> When I am describing something pitiful, my eyes fill with tears; when something terrible or strange, my hair stands on end and my heart throbs. . . . And whenever I look down from the platform at the audience, I see them weeping, with a wild look in their eyes, lost in wonder at the words they hear.

This was a recital of Homer. At the dramatic festivals the excitement must have been even greater. No wonder there was a panic in the theatre at the first performance of the *Eumenides*.

What this reciter did in his public performances—working himself into a frenzy and inducing some measure of the same condition in his audience—was not essentially very different from what was done by the Korybantes in their ecstatic dances. Indeed, the resemblance is pointed out in the same dialogue by Sokrates:[14]

> All good epic poets are able to compose good poetry not by art but because they are divinely inspired or possessed. It is the same with good lyric poets. When they compose their songs they are no more sane than the Korybantes when they dance. As soon as they start on rhythm and concord, they become frenzied and possessed, like the Bacchants who in their madness draw milk and honey from the streams. . . .
> Poets are simply interpreters of the gods, being possessed by whatever god it may happen to be.

The tone of this dialogue is light and playful, but that does not alter the fact that Sokrates has correctly identified the poet as a descendant of the priest-magician, medicine-man, or exorcist, whose hysterical cries appeared as the voice of an

immanent god or spirit. At the present day, the art of poetry
has left its magical origin so far behind that, when we speak
of a poet as inspired, it is only an empty phrase; but the ancient
Greeks had the orgies of Dionysus to remind them that the
art had grown out of ritual.

The actor was regarded in the same light. In the fourth
century, when the profession was highly organised, actors were
granted exemption from military service and their persons were
treated as sacred.[16] Evidence is lacking for the fifth century,
but there is no reason to doubt that they were held in the same
regard, because their sanctity flowed from their origin. They
were mediums for expressing what had once been the voice of
a god. The actor who spoke the part composed for him by the
poet was descended from the poet-actor; and the poet-actor,
who spoke the words which he had been inspired to compose,
was descended through the leader of the dithyramb from the
priest at the head of the *thíasos*, who, since the god had entered
into his body, *was* the god.

It may therefore be concluded that, in keeping with their
common origin, these three rites—the orgy of the Dionysiac
thíasos, initiation into the Mysteries, and tragedy—fulfilled a
common function—*kátharsis* or purification, which renewed
the vitality of the participants by relieving emotional stresses
due to the contradictions generated in the course of social
change. And this purpose was achieved by the expression of
what had been suppressed. The different forms which this
function assumed are explained by the increasing complexity
of the social structure which rendered the mode of expression
progressively less violent. In the Dionysiac orgy, all the participants were subjected to an actual hysterical seizure, involving automatism, paroxysms, and analgesia. When the orgy
became a passion play, the active part was restricted to the
performers, who may have exhibited acute symptoms themselves, like the ecstatic dancers of many modern tribes, but in
the spectators they excited nothing more than feelings of terror
and floods of tears. In the Mysteries, the initiates still have to
participate actively in many of the rites, but the chief of these
is a mystical drama performed for them by others; and at the
tragic festivals the role of all but a fraction of those present has

become entirely passive, being confined to expressing those emotions of pity and fear which are evoked in them by the climax of the plot. And, lastly, although the stresses have not grown less severe, the intensity of the symptoms has steadily diminished, because the growing individuation of society, resulting from the more manifold divisions of labour, has so deepened and enriched the emotional and intellectual life of the people as to render possible a proportionately higher level of sublimation.

The principle of *kátharsis* is accepted by modern psychologists. It provides relief by giving free outlet to repressed emotions through such channels as the practice of confession or participation in public festivals.[16] The citizen who has purged himself in this way becomes thereby a more contented citizen. The emotional stresses set up by the class struggle are relieved by a spectacle in which they are sublimated as a conflict between man and God, or Fate, or Necessity. Plato banned tragedy because it was subversive of the established order; Aristotle replied that a closer analysis showed it to be conservative of the established order. For, like modern psychologists, he assumed that, where there is maladjustment between the individual and society, it is the individual that must be adapted to society, not society to the individual. Modern psycho-analysts have only been able to maintain this attitude because the majority of their patients have belonged to the wealthy classes. Applied to the community as a whole, their therapy would necessarily involve them in the task of investigating the laws governing the social environment with a view to adapting it to the patients. The psycho-analyst would become a revolutionary.[17]

One of the effects of civilisation is undoubtedly to multiply the possibilities of nervous disorders. As society grows more complex, it develops fresh contradictions. If this were the whole of the matter, we should have reason to curse Prometheus; but it is not. The relation between the two processes is not a mechanical one, but dialectical. These internal maladaptations resulting from social development accumulate to a point at which they precipitate a reorganisation of society itself; and, after they have been thus resolved, there emerges a new set of contradictions operating on the higher level. This reciprocal pressure between the members of the organism and its structure as a whole is the dynamic of evolution, both biological and social. Man learns by suffering. And it is these contradictions that find expression in the arts. The artist may endeavour to reform the world, like Shelley, or to escape from it, like Keats, or to justify it, like Milton, or simply to describe it, like Shakespeare, but it is this discord between the individual and his environment, which, as an artist, he feels with peculiar force, that impels him to create in fantasy the harmony denied to him in a world out of joint. And since these works of art embody the spiritual labour that has gone to their production, they enable the other members of the community, through the experience of seeing or hearing them, which is a labour less in degree but similar in kind, to achieve the same harmony, of which they too are in need, but without the power of constructing it for themselves. Therefore, the arts are conservative of the social order, in that they relieve the pressure on its members, but at the same time they are subversive, because they promote a recurrence of the stresses which they stimulate in order to relieve. They are a form of the organisation of social energy, and the flood which they set in motion may at any moment, in favourable conditions, reverse its direction. The artist leads his fellow men into a world of fantasy where they find release, thus asserting the refusal of the human consciousness to acquiesce in its environment, and by this means there is collected a store of energy, which flows back into the real world and transforms the fantasy into fact. This, then, is the connection between such masterpieces of human culture as Greek tragedy and the mimetic dance, in which the savage huntsmen express both their weakness in the face of nature and their will to master it.

APPENDIX I

NOTE ON THE CLASSIFICATORY
SYSTEM OF RELATIONSHIP

IT is not the purpose of the present note to consider the general validity of Morgan's theory of group marriage beyond pointing out tnat, so far as it is based on the classificatory system, it is internally consistent. What I want to consider is whether the classificatory system can be explained in any other way.

The first to reject Morgan's theory was McLennan, who argued, quite correctly, that what the classificatory terms denote is not consanguinity but social status; but, as Rivers pointed out, he was mistaken in supposing that this constituted an objection to the theory.[1] McLennan's own view was that the classificatory system is merely a system of mutual salutations or modes of address, and therefore unrelated to rules of marriage.[2] This view, which still leaves the salutations unexplained, has long been abandoned.

In the present century, Morgan's interpretation has been attacked from several points of view. Thomas claimed to have reduced it to an absurdity by demonstrating its application to the relationship of mother and son.[3]

If we are entitled to conclude from the fact that a man's wife bears the same name for him as all the other women he might have married, that he at one time was the husband of them all, then we are obviously equally entitled to conclude, from the fact that a woman's son is known to her by the same name as the sons of other women, either that during the period of group marriage she actually bore the sons of the other women or that the whole group of women produced their sons by their joint efforts. Finding that the term which is translated *son* is equally applied by the remainder of the group of women to the son of the individual woman whose case we have been considering, we may discard the former hypothesis and come to the conclusion that, if there was a period of group marriage, there was also one of group motherhood. This interesting fact may be commended to the attention of zoologists.

[1] Rivers in AEPT 319f.   [2] McLennan SAH 270.
[3] Thomas KMA 123.

In putting forward this frivolous argument, which has been rebutted by Rivers,[1] Thomas shut his eyes to the fact that, as interpreted by Morgan, the classificatory terms denote collective relationships. It may seem strange to us that the individual relationship between mother and child should not be recognised, but, since it is not recognised in the classificatory system, no matter how it is to be interpreted, it is merely specious to pretend that Morgan's theory is vulnerable at this point. Perhaps the best answer to Thomas is Kleintitschen's account of a native of New Britain, who boasted of having three mothers, and these likewise asserted, "All three of us bore him."[2]

More recently an attempt has been made to cut the ground from under Morgan's feet by an expedient even more drastic than McLennan's. Kroeber claims to have demonstrated that the accepted distinction between the classificatory and descriptive systems is entirely illusory and therefore devoid of social or historical significance.[3] He begins by distinguishing the various kinds of relationship which are expressed in terminologies of kinship, and by this means he establishes the following categories: (1) the distinction of generations, e.g. between father and son; (2) the distinction between relatives by blood and relatives by marriage; (3) the distinction between lineal and collateral relationships, e.g. between son and nephew; (4) the distinction of sex of the relative; (5) the distinction of sex of the person through whom the relationship exists, e.g. between the father's and the mother's brother; (6) the distinction of sex of the speaker (in many languages different terms are used according as the speaker is a man or woman); (7) the distinction of age within the same generation, e.g. between elder and younger brother; (8) distinctions based on external conditions, e.g. in some languages the term for wife's father varies according as the wife is alive or dead. These results are then applied to a comparison of the two types of system. For this purpose English is assumed to be typical of the descriptive system, while the classificatory is represented by five North American languages and seven Californian. The extent to which the above-mentioned categories are represented in these languages is then set forth in the following table. The languages are (1) English, (2) Arapaho, (3) Dakota, (4) Pawnee, (5) Skokomish, (6) Chinook, (7) Yuki, (8) Pomo, (9) Washo, (10) Miwok, (11) Yokuts, (12) Luiseño, (13) Mohave.

[1] Rivers in AEPT 317. See further Briffault M 1. 747.
[2] Kleintitschen quoted by Frazer TE 1. 305.
[3] A. L. Kroeber in JRAI 39. 77.

Language:													
	1	2	3	4	5	6	7	8	9	10	11	12	13
No. of terms:													
	21	20	31	19	18	28	24	27	28	24	28	34	35
Category:													
1	21	20	31	11	13	23	24	21	27	24	22	30	26
2	21	19	31	17	18	26	24	27	28	24	28	32	34
3	21	10	20	5	11	25	24	21	28	18	26	34	28
4	20	18	29	17	2	12	16	21	20	20	17	18	22
5	0	6	6	2	0	20	13	13	14	10	14	19	21
6	0	3	18	4	0	15	3	3	10	2	12	10	14
7	0	3	7	2	2	2	3	4	4	4	4	12	8
8	0	0	0	0	8	1	0	0	0	0	0	0	1

From this array of statistics, Kroeber draws the following conclusions:

> While in English the degree of recognition which is accorded the represented categories is indicable by a percentage of 100 in all cases but one, when it is 95, in Pawnee corresponding percentages range variously from about 10 to 90, and in Mohave from 5 to 95. All the other languages, as compared with English, closely approach the condition of Pawnee and Mohave. It is clear that this difference is real and fundamental. . . . Judged from its own point of view, English is the less classificatory, inasmuch as in every one of its terms it fails to recognise certain distinctions often made in other languages; regarded from a general and comparative point of view, neither system is more or less classificatory. In short, the prevalent idea of the classificatory system breaks down entirely under analysis.

And finally:

> If it had been more clearly recognised that terms of relationship are determined primarily by linguistic factors, and are only occasionally, and then indirectly, affected by social circumstances, it would probably long ago have been generally realised that the difference between descriptive and classificatory systems is subjective and superficial.

In reaching this conclusion Kroeber has forgotten that the science of historical linguistics starts from the postulate that the evolution of

language is ultimately determined by social factors; and his attitude
on this point is symptomatic of the extent to which the theoretical
basis of anthropology has disintegrated since Morgan's time. He
also appears to have forgotten that English is not the only type of
the descriptive system nor his twelve American languages of the
classificatory. As soon as his method is applied to other languages,
his whole basis of comparison crumbles away.

As Morgan pointed out, the purest of the descriptive systems are
Celtic, Norse and Semitic. All of these belong to the same type,
which may be illustrated from modern Irish.[1] Modern Irish contains only twelve terms of relationship: *sean-ahir* grandfather,
seana-mháhir grandmother, *ahir* father, *máhir* mother, *driohúir*
brother, *driofúr* sister, *col ceahar* cousin, *mac* son, *iníon* daughter,
fear husband, *bean* wife, *céile* husband or wife. All other relationships are expressed by combination, e.g. *driohúir ahar*, father's
brother, *fear iníne*, daughter's husband.

Applying Kroeber's analysis to this system, we find that, if the
compound terms are to be included in the total number along with
the simple terms, no total can be fixed in Irish or in any other
language, because in all languages such combinations can be formed
at will indefinitely. If, on the other hand, we confine our attention
to the primary terms, the total is 12, lower than Skokomish, and,
moreover, a number of relationships are not expressed at all. The
result is that, on Kroeber's showing, the differences between Irish
and the other languages, American and English, are far more "real
and fundamental" than the differences between English and the
American. In short, Kroeber's method breaks down.

Further, these twelve American languages are even less representative of the classificatory system than English is of the descriptive.
In systems of the Dravidian type, a common term is used for the
mother's brother and the father-in-law. This is not because distinct
relationships have been confused, but because, owing to the practice of cross-cousin marriage, which still survives among the Dravi-
dian-speaking peoples (see p. 405), these two relationships are or
may be united in a single person. This is a feature of the classificatory system, which Kroeber's second category, based on the assumption that blood and marriage are mutually exclusive, is incapable of
expressing. Similarly, in systems of the Australian type, we find
terms denoting relationships connected with the speaker by two,

[1] This list has been compiled from my own knowledge of the West Kerry
dialect, of which I am a fluent speaker. I have omitted the terms *úncail* and
aintín, which are recent borrowings from English and only used when the
speaker is not concerned to be precise.

three or four intermediate relatives of different sexes. Applied to
these, Kroeber's fifth category, based on the assumption that there
is only one connecting relative, is meaningless.

The classificatory system is most highly developed in the Australian languages, and of the Australian systems there is none more
elaborate than the Arunta. Let me give the Arunta system in full,
because it is a marvel of complexity and coherence. These black-
fellows, not having cattle to keep or corn to measure, cannot count
beyond five, but they carry the facts of kinship in their heads with a
facility which makes the white man seem stupid.

The data from which this table has been compiled are given by
Spencer and Gillen A 41f. Variants, such as *yurumbura* for *unkulla*
(woman speaking) and *urumba* for *ilchella*, have been omitted. There
is also one descriptive term, *quaia-nurra*, applied by a woman to her
husband's actual mother.

Column I gives the terms of relationship. Where different terms
are used, or the same terms used differently, according to the sex of
the speaker, the distinctions are marked by the signs m (male
speaking) and f (female speaking). The other duplicate terms mark
distinctions of external conditions, in most cases of residence, e.g.
anua is used only of those who live in a local group different from the
speaker's, while the corresponding use of *apulla* is confined to those
who live in the speaker's own local group (see Notes and References
p. 423) and only those called *anua* are marriageable to the speaker.

Column II gives the moiety (A or B), section (1 or 2) and sub-
section (a or b) to which each set of relatives belongs. It is assumed
that the speaker belongs to B1a.

The remaining columns give the relationships covered by each
term or pair of terms, grouped so far as possible according to the
degree of affinity and abbreviated as follows: B brother, s sister, B^s
brother or sister, Ee elder, Yy younger, F father, m mother, S
son, d daughter, S^d son or daughter, H husband, w wife. Thus,
FFEBSS is the father's father's elder brother's son's son.

(The table follows on the next page.)

The reader is now able to judge for himself how far the difference
between the classificatory and descriptive systems is "subjective and
superficial." Yet, despite its apparent complexity, the principle on
which this structure rests is quite simple.

As has been explained in Chapter II, the classificatory system was
evolved to express the relationships characteristic of a community
divided into two exogamous and intermarrying groups. The effect
of this division is that I must marry a daughter of my mother's

kullia	B1a	EB	FEBS	mesS	FFEBSS	FmesSS	mFEBdS	mmesdS
guaia m	B1a	es	FEBd	mesd	FFEBSd	FmesSd	mFEBdd	mmesdd
ungaraitcha f	⎱							
itia	B1a	YBˢ	FYBSᵈ	mysSᵈ	FFYBSSᵈ / FFsdSᵈ	FmysSSᵈ / FmBdSᵈ	mFYBdSᵈ / mFsSSᵈ	mmysdSᵈ / mmBSSᵈ
ipmunna	B1b							
unkulla	A1b		FsSᵈ	mBSᵈ	FFBdSᵈ	FmsdSᵈ	mFBSSᵈ	mmsSSᵈ
chimmia m	⎱							
umbirna m	A1a	wB	sH	⎱ sHB				
anua f	A1a	⎱ H	⎱ HB		FFsSS	FmBSS	mFsdS	mmBdS
apulla f	A1a							
anua m	A1a	⎱ w	ws					
apulla m	A1a			⎱ Bws				
indinga f	A1a	⎱ Hs	Bw		FFsSd	FmBSd	mFsdd	mmBdd
apulla f	A1a							
okilia	B2a	F	FB	FFBS	FmsS			
winchinga	B2a		Fs	FFBd	Fmsd			
uwinna	⎱							
mura	B2b	wm	Hm	wmBˢ	HmBˢ	mFsSᵈ	mmBSᵈ	
mia	A2a	m	ms			mFBd	mmsd	
gammona	A2a		mB			mFBS	mmsS	
umba	⎱							
irundera m	A2b	wF	HF	wFBˢ	HFBˢ	FFsSᵈ	FmBSᵈ	
nimmera f	⎱							

arunga	B1a	FF	FFB^s	wFm	HFm		
ipmunna	B1b	mm	mmB^s	wmF	HmF		
apulla	A1a	Fm	FmB^s	wFF	HFF		
chimmia	A1b	mF	mFB^s	wmm	Hmm		

allira	B2a	S^d(m)	BS^d	FBSS^d	msSS^d		
mura	B2b	dH(f)	Sw(f)	FsdS^d	mBdS^d		
gammona	A2a	dH(m)		FsSS	mBSS		
mia	A2a	Sw(m)		FsSd	mBSd		
umba	A2b	S^d(f)	sS^d	FBdS^d	msdS^d		

arunga	B1a	SS^d(m)	BSS^d(m)	FBSSS^d	msSSS^d	FsSdS^d	mBSdS^d
ipmunna	B1b	dS^d(f)	sdS^d(f)	FBddS^d	msddS^d	FsdSS^d	mBdSS^d
chimmia	A1b	dS^d(m)	BdS^d(m)	FBSdS^d	msSdS^d	FsSSS^d	mBSSS^d
apulla m	A1a			FBdSS^d	msdSS^d	FsddS^d	mBddS^d
anua f / *apulla* f	A1a	SS	sSS	FBdSS	msdSS	FsddS	mBddS
indinga f / *apulla* f	A1a	Sd	sSd	FBdSd	msdSd	Fsddd	mBddd

okilia	B2a	SSS(m)	SdS(f)
wvinchinga / *uwinna*	B2a	SSd(m)	Sdd(f)

	Class				
mura	B2b	ddS^d(m)	dSS^d(f)		
gammona	A2a	dSS(m)	ddS(f)		
mia	A2a	dSd(m)	ddd(f)		
irundera m *nimmera* f	} A2b	SdS^d(m)	SSS^d(f)		
itia	B1a	SSSS^d(m)	dddS^d(f)	dSdS^d(m)	SdSS^d(f)
ipmunna	B1b	SddS^d(m)	SSdS^d(f)	ddSS^d(m)	dSSS^d(f)
umbirna m	A1a	dddS	SdSS		
anua f *apulla* f	} A1a	SSSS	dSdS		
anua m *apulla* m	} A1a	dddd	SdSd		
indinga f *apulla* f	} A1a	SSSd	dSdd		
unkulla m	A1b	SSdS^d	dSSS^d		
unkulla f	A1b	SddS	ddSS		
ilchella f	A1b	Sddd	ddSd		

brother and father's sister. That is the rule of cross-cousin marriage.

This rule presupposes, of course, that marriage is restricted to members of the same generation. In many tribes this restriction is expressed concretely by dividing each of the two moieties into two sections. My father belongs to one section of moiety A (A1); my mother belongs to one section of moiety B (B1). With patrilineal descent, I belong to my father's moiety but to the other section (A2); and similarly my wife belongs to the other section of my mother's moiety (B2). I marry into my mother's moiety, but not into her section.

In the Arunta and allied tribes, instead of the normal type of cross-cousin marriage, in which husband and wife are cross-cousins of any degree, marriage is forbidden between cross-cousins of the first degree. My wife is therefore a daughter, not of my mother's brother and father's sister, but of my mother's mother's brother's daughter (who is also my mother's father's sister's daughter) and of my father's father's sister's son (who is also my father's mother's brother's son). And this rule is expressed by dividing each section into two subsections, with the result that my cross-cousins of the first degree are separated from my cross-cousins of the second.[1] It is hard to see how one could desire a more definitive proof of the direct connection between the classificatory system of relationship and the marriage system.

Let me re-state briefly the essential differences between the descriptive and classificatory systems. In English, my father and mother, my brothers and sisters, and my sons and daughters, are sharply distinguished, in each generation, from their collaterals. Outside these limits, the terminology is less precise: my father's brother is equated with my mother's as my uncle, my father's brother's children with my father's sister's children as my cousins. Further, each of the terms father, mother, husband, wife, denotes a specific individual. A nomenclature of this type corresponds to the basic unit of civilised society, which is the individual family, consisting of two parents and their children. In the classificatory system, my father and mother, my brothers and sisters, my sons and daughters, are each equated with certain of their collaterals in an

---

[1] Thus, referring to the sixth and following lines of the table, the reader will see that my cross-cousins of the first degree (the children of my father's sister and mother's brother) belong to A1b, whereas those cross-cousins of the second degree who stand to me in the relation of wife (husband), wife's brother (husband's brother), wife's sister (husband's sister), etc., belong to A1a. Without the division of the section into subsections, all these would belong indiscriminately to A1.

infinite series. On the other hand, my father's brothers and sisters are distinguished from my mother's, my father's brother's children from my father's sister's children, and so on. Further, in the more primitive forms of the system, my father-in-law is equated with my mother's brother, my mother-in-law with my father's sister, my wife with the daughters of my mother's brother and my father's sister. Such a nomenclature can only be explained as the product of a society based on the collective intermarriage of two exogamous groups.

The question of the significance of the classificatory system has recently been re-opened by Radcliffe-Brown, who, so far from agreeing with Kroeber that there is no connection between kinship terminology and social institutions, maintains that, at least in Australia, the classificatory system can be completely explained by reference to the present social institutions of the Australian tribes.[1]

> As against Morgan and those who follow him, it can be shown that there is a very thorough functional relation between the kinship terminology of any tribe and the social organisation of that tribe as it exists at present. If this is so, there is no reason whatever to suppose that the kinship terminology is a survival from some very different form of social organisation in a purely hypothetical past.

It will be understood that the point which Radcliffe-Brown is attacking here is that part of Morgan's theory in which he maintained that marriage was collective between all the members of the corresponding groups. Radcliffe-Brown's arguments require to be closely examined, because they represent the first attempt to offer an alternative to Morgan which will bear more than a moment's examination.

According to Radcliffe-Brown, "the active principles at work in determining the system are the result of the strong solidarity of the individual family," which he defines as "the group formed by a man and his wife or wives and their dependent children."[2] The argument proceeds as follows:

> The most important of these principles may be spoken of as that of the equivalence of brothers. It applies of course equally

[1] A. R. Radcliffe-Brown in O 1. 34, 202, 322, 426.
[2] O 1. 435, cf. 438: "While the family is the primary economic unit in both production and consumption, the horde unites a number of families in a wider economic group in which there is regular co-operation in hunting and other activities, and a regular sharing of food." The truth is, of course, that the family has grown out of the horde, not the horde out of the family.

to two sisters. Now this principle is universally applied in all Australian systems of terminology. Everywhere the brother of a father is called a father, and therefore his children are called brother and sister, and similarly the sister of a mother is called mother and her children are also called brother and sister. This principle is not merely a matter of terminology. It is a most important sociological principle which runs through the whole of Australian life. It depends on the fact that there is a very strong, intimate and permanent bond between two brothers born and brought up in the same family. This solidarity between brothers, which is itself an expression or result of family solidarity, is a very obvious thing to anyone who studies the aborigines at first hand. It shows itself, moreover, in certain institutions.

Radcliffe-Brown goes on to describe the rule of the levirate, which entitles a man to marry his deceased brother's wife or wives, and the rule of the sororate, which entitles a man to marry two or more sisters. "In this custom of the sororate," he says, "we have sisters treated as being socially equivalent, just as with brothers in the levirate."

The argument continues thus:

The principle of the equivalence of brothers as an active principle in determining social structure may be regarded as a special example of a more general tendency, the presence of which is readily discovered in the social structure of the simpler cultures. Wherever the structure includes small groups of strong solidarity and having important and varied functions, when an individual is brought into some close social relation with one member of the group, there is a tendency to bring him into close relation with all the other members of the group. . . . If there is a strong, intimate and permanent bond between two persons A and B, then, when a third person C is brought into an important social relation with B, there is a tendency to bring him into close relation with A. The resulting relation between C and A will depend of course on the kind of relation between A and B.

His conclusion is therefore as follows:

Without considering in any way how the Australian social organisation may have arisen in a distant past about which we shall never obtain any direct knowledge, we may say that as it exists at present an analysis of it reveals this important active principle of the solidarity of brothers, and we may say that on this principle the existing system is built.

Thus, according to Radcliffe-Brown, the social unit on which the classificatory system is based is the individual family. Now, we have already seen that the descriptive system of modern Europe is also based on the individual family. It is therefore pertinent to enquire how a similar cause has produced such different results.

If the classificatory system is based on the individual family, it should follow that a clear distinction is drawn between those who are members of my family and those who belong to other families. In the descriptive system this distinction is drawn; in the classificatory system it is not. That is precisely the difference between them. I am bound to my brother by a strong, intimate and permanent bond. Our father is bound to his brother by a similar bond. Therefore, it is argued, we apply to our father's brother the same term as we apply to him, and we apply to our father's brother's sons the same term as we apply to each other. But neither our father's brother nor our father's brother's sons belong to our family. Instead of reflecting the solidarity of the family, the classificatory system cuts right across it. And this contradiction reveals itself most sharply in what Radcliffe-Brown regards as the keystone of the system—the relation between brothers:

> The basic principle of the classification is that a man is always classed with his brother and a woman with her sister. If I apply a given term of relationship to a man, I apply the same term to his brother.

What is here described as the basic principle is not in accordance with the facts. In most forms of the classificatory system, both in Australia and elsewhere, there are two entirely different terms for elder and younger brother and for elder and younger sister. Thus, I have one term for my elder brother and another for my younger brother, and the term I apply to my elder brother I also apply to my father's elder brother's son, while the term I apply to my younger brother I also apply to my father's younger brother's son. In the Arunta language, my elder brother and my father's elder brother's son are *kullia*, while my younger brother and my father's younger brother's son are *itia*. So far from reflecting the solidarity of brothers, the classificatory system contradicts it by dividing sons of the same family and uniting sons of different families.

If the classificatory system is to be explained on the principle of the equivalence of brothers, that principle must be interpreted in another way. The wife applies the same term to her husband's brothers as she applies to him, and the husband applies the same term to his wife's sisters as he applies to her. The husband and his brothers are treated as equivalent by the wife; the wife and her sisters are treated as equivalent by the husband. "If," we are told, "there is a strong, intimate and permanent bond between two persons A and B, then, when a third person C is brought into an important social relation with B, there is a tendency to bring him into close relation with A. The resulting relation between C and A will depend, of course, on the kind of relation between A and B." What, then, is the close relation between a man (A) and his wife's sister (C) and how does it depend on the kind of relation between the man and his wife (B)? We have seen that by the rule of the sororate a man marries two sisters. As Radcliffe-Brown remarks, "in many Australian tribes the ideal arrangement is considered to be that a man who marries the eldest of the sisters should also marry the second, and that he should then transfer his right to the third and fourth to his younger brother." Why then does the husband apply the same term to his wife's sister as he applies to his wife? Radcliffe-Brown says it is because his wife's sister is "socially equivalent" to his wife. But, in the case of the sororate, the usage is capable of a simpler explanation. She *is* his wife. The sororate marks a point at which the classificatory system still coincides with present practice. But why does the wife apply to her husband's brother the same term as she applies to her husband? It is recorded by Howitt that in the Dieri tribe, when two brothers married two sisters, they commonly lived together in a group marriage of four.[1] In such a case the woman called her husband's brother husband because he *was* her husband; and similarly the father's brother was a father, the mother's sister a mother—the correspondence between the nomenclature and the reality was complete. In this evidence of Howitt's we have an instance of the actual practice of the form of marriage which Morgan had deduced from the classificatory system.

The Dieri practice was as follows. Each man, besides his "primary wife" (*tippamalku*), had one or more "secondary wives" (*pirrauru*), each of whom might be the "primary wife" of another man; and each woman had, besides her "primary husband," one or more "secondary husbands," each of whom might be the "primary husband" of another woman. These relations, both primary and

[1] Howitt NTSEA 181. This explicit statement seems to have been overlooked by Malinowski when he wrote (FAA 113): "If groups of men and women, who are pirraurus to each other respectively, normally and permanently live in marital relations, no one of our authorities, who plead so strongly for the character of group marriage in the relation in question, would omit to mention such an important feature, which would support their views in the highest degree." See further Briffault M 1. 726.

secondary, were confined to those men and women who stood to one another in the relationship of husband and wife. Again, the husbands were all "brothers," the wives were all "sisters," the father's brothers were all "fathers," the mother's sisters all "mothers" and so on. If we disregard the distinction between primary and secondary, which is readily explained as a development in the direction of individual marriage, this practice *is* group marriage, neither more nor less. Similar customs have been recorded over a wide area of Australia, also from North America, Siberia and Tibet.[1]

These facts, which establish the general character of the Dieri practice, are not in dispute. There are, however, certain difficulties regarding the precise nature of the necessarily complex relations which such a form of marriage involves; and these difficulties were seized on by Thomas, followed by Malinowski, to discredit the value of the evidence as a whole. I do not propose to examine their criticisms now: it must suffice to say that they are not nearly so destructive as they are claimed to be and to draw attention to some remarks on this subject by Radcliffe-Brown:

> Some of the earlier writers, such as Howitt and Spencer, have given a false picture of the Australian family by entirely neglecting the economic aspect and regarding marriage as only a matter of sexual union. . . . We have nothing like complete or even satisfactory information about the *pirrauru* and *piraungaru* customs of the tribes round Lake Eyre, and it is now perhaps too late to make any thorough investigation, but we can be quite satisfied that, when Spencer and Gillen say that "a group of women of a certain designation are actually the wives of a group of men of another designation," they are using the word wife in a way in which it cannot be used if we are to apply it to the ordinary marriage relation either in Australia or among ourselves.

It is not true that Howitt and Spencer entirely neglected the economic aspect of Australian marriage. Howitt described at length the rules among the Kurnai which required a man to supply food to his wife's relatives, and Spencer did the same for the Arunta.[2] Moreover, Howitt pointed out that the *pirrauru* marriage itself had an economic function in that the man was provided with food by his secondary wives when their primary husbands were away.[3] It is true that our information is not complete nor entirely free from

---

[1] Bancroft NRPSNA 1. 81, Ridgeway EAG 2. 105. The whole subject is dealt with by Briffault M 1. 614–781.

[2] Howitt NTSEA 756 (see p. 423), Spencer and Gillen A 491.

[3] Howitt NTSEA 184–5.

difficulties, but the evidence collected by Howitt and Spencer is far too substantial to be dismissed with the remark that it is now perhaps too late to make a thorough investigation. The thoroughness with which those observers did their work can be judged from a comparison of their books on the *Native Tribes of South-East Australia* and the *Arunta* with Radcliffe-Brown's on the *Andaman Islanders*. And, lastly, since the word "wife" must necessarily mean something different according as it is applied to group marriage or to individual marriage, this objection seems to rest on a mere misapprehension—a misapprehension, moreover, against which Howitt expressly warned his readers when he wrote: "In speaking of the marriage relations, I shall have occasion to use the terms husband and wife, and it must be clearly understood that in so doing I do not use them in the sense in which we use them."[1] It is, of course, easy to define the marital relation in such a way as to exclude group marriage, but such definitions add nothing to the argument.

The difference between Morgan and Radcliffe-Brown in this matter springs from a fundamental difference of method. Morgan explained the classificatory system by means of the hypothesis that, in so far as it includes under a single term relationships now regarded as distinct, it reflects an antecedent condition of society in which those relationships were not differentiated. Radcliffe-Brown explains the system by referring it to his principle of equivalence, and he seeks to give this principle a basis in reality by correlating it with the solidarity of the family. But, as we have seen, this correlation is illusory, and the principle is left in the air. Morgan believed that the structure of society at any stage can only be understood by studying the changes in virtue of which it has become what it is. Radcliffe-Brown believes that, with the help of "active principles," the present structure of Australian society, at least so far as the classificatory system is concerned, can be understood without reference to its past. Yet Morgan's attitude, so far from giving a "false lead," as Radcliffe-Brown says it did, represents the attitude of progressive thinkers in all branches of modern science, and in the present instance it enabled Morgan to explain consistently what Radcliffe-Brown has only explained by contradicting himself.

[1] Howitt NTSEA 175.

APPENDIX II

THE INDO-EUROPEAN TERMS OF RELATIONSHIP

THE importance of the classificatory system for the history of Indo-European culture was pointed out by Morgan himself, who was convinced that the descriptive systems characteristic of those languages in their historical form are not original;[1] but subsequent workers in this field have been more concerned to refute his conclusions regarding primitive marriage than to apply them to their own languages.

It is an interesting illustration of the neglect of the subject of relationship by sociologists that only recently has any attempt been made to use European systems of relationships as instruments for the study of social organisation. When the lesson taught by the study of the classificatory system has been learnt, much light will be thrown on the nature of Indo-European and Semitic social organisation by means of the terminology of relationships.[2]

The result of this neglect is that, while recent progress in comparative linguistics has sufficed to establish the form of the kinship terminology of common Indo-European, it contains a number of admitted anomalies which have never been explained. It is these anomalies which I propose to examine here, and I shall take up the problem from the point where it was left in Chapter II. It was shown there (1) that the I.E. *bhrātēr and *suesōr were displaced in Greek by adelphós and adelphé, which were originally descriptive epithets, owing to the influence of matrilineal institutions; and (2) that the Greek phrátēr was employed in a sense which indicates that its original usage had been classificatory.

As Kretschmer observed, analogous displacements are found in Spanish, Catalan and Portuguese.[3] Thus, the Spanish fraile and sor denote a brother or sister in religion, the terms for brother and sister in the descriptive sense being hermano and hermana, i.e. Latin (frater) germanus and (soror) germana, "own brother" and "own

---

[1] Morgan AS 481.   [2] Rivers in Hastings 7. 703.
[3] Kretschmer in G 2. 210.

sister." Exactly the same displacement has occurred in Irish. The
Modern Irish *bráthair* and *siúr* denote a brother or sister in religion,
the terms for brother and sister in the descriptive sense being *dearbh-
bhráthair* and *deirbh-shiúr*, properly "true brother" and "true sister."

There was no common I.E. term for cousin. The Greek is *anepsiós*,
used also of a nephew; and in the other languages the same term,
representing I.E. **anépōtios*, fluctuates between the nephew and the
grandson. What this term denoted originally is a question to which
I shall return. On the other hand, the Old Irish *bráthir* was applied
both to the brother and to the father's brother's son, and in the
Slavonic languages the terms for cousin are simply the terms for
brother and sister with the addition of a descriptive epithet denoting
the degree and at the same time distinguishing them from the true
brother and sister. In parts of Yugoslavia, however, the term for
brother is restricted to those who belong to the same *bratstvo* or
phratry[1]—that is to say, it is used exactly like the Greek *phráter*.

If we compare the Greek and Latin terminologies, we find that
the Greek is on the whole the less primitive of the two. Greek has
lost the primitive terms for brother, sister, grandfather, grandson,
and many of its other terms are derivatives of *adelphós*. Latin has
preserved the primitive terms for these relationships, and its terms
for the children of the father's brother and mother's sister, although
derivative in form, are based, as we shall see, on a primitive distinction. On the other hand, it has lost the primitive terms for son
and daughter. Another remarkable feature is the designation of the
mother's brother by a diminutive of the term for grandfather
(*avonculus—avos*).

It is a world-wide rule among primitive peoples that a man may
marry the daughter of his father's sister or of his mother's brother,
but not the daughter of his father's brother or of his mother's sister;[2]
and this rule, known as cross-cousin marriage, corresponds, as we
have seen, to the social structure presupposed by the classificatory
system—the bisection of the community into exogamous and intermarrying groups. In the more primitive forms of the classificatory
system the daughters of my father's sister and of my mother's brother
are actually called my "wives" if I am a man or my "husband's
sisters" if I am a woman; and similarly the sons of my father's sister
and of my mother's brother are called my "husbands" if I am a
woman or my "wife's brothers" if I am a man.[3] In the more

[1] Durham TOLCB 151.
[2] Frazer TE 1. 181, 491, 572, 2. 141, 224, 244, 249, 250, 256, 271, 365,
399, 405, 581, 607, 615, 3. 350.
[3] Howitt NTSEA 180.

advanced forms of the system these terms are replaced in this connection by terms denoting a male or female marriageable cousin. On the other hand, in all types of the system, the children of my father's brother and of my mother's sister, whom I am forbidden to marry, are my "brothers" and "sisters." The parents of my cousins are distinguished on the same principle. My father's sister and my mother's brother are denoted by terms which may be translated "aunt" and "uncle," but my father's brother is my "father" and my mother's sister is my "mother."

In classical Latin, there are no specific terms for the children of my father's sister or of my mother's brother, but the children of my father's brother are my *patrueles* and the children of my mother's sister are my *consobrini*.[1] These terms are properly epithets of *frater* and *soror*, which indeed are frequently expressed—*frater patruelis* or *frater consobrinus* as opposed to *frater germanus*.[2] Moreover, the epithets are not indispensable: *frater* and *soror* often stand alone for the children of the father's brother or of the mother's sister[3]—that is to say, they are used in the classificatory sense.

Further, in the classificatory system, as we have just remarked, my father's brother is my "father" and my mother's sister is my "mother," but my father's sister is my "aunt" and my mother's brother is my "uncle." Similarly, in Latin, my father's brother is my *patruus*, which is merely an extension of *pater*, and my mother's sister is my *matertera*, which is an extension of *mater*, but my father's sister is my *amita* and my mother's brother is my *avonculus*.

Two features of the Latin terminology remain to be accounted for. In the first place, the primitive terms for son and daughter have disappeared. They have also disappeared in Celtic, and, as Vendryes has remarked, this feature of the Italo-Celtic group must have originated in some social change which took place before the differentiation of Celtic and Italic.[4] The Latin *filius* and *filia* are properly adjectives, which have been conjecturally connected with *felo*, "suck."[5] They are therefore analogous to the Latin *patruelis* and *consobrinus* and the Greek *adelphós*, whose function as descriptive

---

[1] The term *consobrinus* was sometimes used generally of any first cousin, but its original sense is fixed by its etymology (**consuesrinus*). The terms *matruelis* for the mother's brother's son and *amitinus* for the father's sister's son are late, being formed by analogy during the codification of imperial Roman law.

[2] Cic. *Planc.* 11. 27, *Fin.* 5. 1. 1, Plaut. *Aul.* 2. 1. 3.

[3] Cic. *Clu.* 24. 60, *Att.* 1. 5. 1, Cat. 66. 22, Ov. *M.* 1. 351.

[4] Vendryes PLC 26.

[5] Walde VWIS 1. 830.

epithets has already been explained; and it may be added that differentiation of the classificatory terms by descriptive epithets is found in all parts of the world as a means of transition from the one system to the other.[1] It may therefore be inferred that the Latin *filius* and *filia* originated as epithets of the primitive terms, which they subsequently supplanted.

In the second place, why is the term for mother's brother (*avonculus*) a diminutive of the term for grandfather (*avos*)? In the classificatory system, the father's father is normally included under the same term as the mother's mother's brother. This is because, in the conditions of cross-cousin marriage, he *is* the mother's mother's brother. I shall have more to say on this point later, but it is already clear that, if my mother's mother's brother was my *avos*, my own mother's brother might naturally be called my *avonculus*.

All the principal features of the Latin terminology have now been explained on the hypothesis that they are derived from the classificatory system; and this, in conjunction with the preceding analysis of the Greek terms for brother, creates a presumption that the Indo-European terminology as a whole is to be explained in the same way.

It was pointed out in Chapter II that a comparative analysis of the linguistic data has established that common Indo-European was spoken by a predominantly pastoral people with some knowledge of agriculture, and that marriage was patrilocal—that is to say, the woman went to live with her husband's people. With this evidence to guide us, let us compare the Indo-European terminology with a typical form of the Dravidian.

The classificatory systems of the Dravidian languages of India were collected and analysed by Morgan, and, as Rivers has shown, some of them are still associated with the actual practice of cross-cousin marriage, on which, as we have seen, the whole system is based.[2] The example I have chosen is Telugu. The Telugu terminology conforms to a type of the classificatory system which has a particularly wide distribution, being common not only to Telugu, Tamil and Canarese, but to a very large number of languages in North America.[3]

[1] Morgan SCAHF 313, 533, Spencer and Gillen NTCA 85, A 41f, Rivers T 492, Frazer TE 2. 509, 553.

[2] Rivers in JRAS 1907. 621.

[3] The Telugu system is given in full by Morgan SCAHF 523f. The duplicate terms serve in most cases to indicate the age of the person in question in relation to the speaker, e.g. *anna* elder brother, *tammudu* younger brother. The accepted interpretation of the I.E. terms is given by Meillet IECLI 389.

The table which follows contains three columns. The first gives all the terms of relationship which have been traced in common Indo-European. The second gives the terms of relationship in Telugu. The third gives, first, the accepted meaning of each I.E. term in its descriptive sense, which is also one of the meanings of the corresponding term in Telugu, and this is followed by the other meanings also borne by the same term in Telugu. It will be understood that these last are not exhaustive, because each category is infinite, but they are sufficient to define the category in question.

*aṵos	tata	grandfather, father's father's brother, mother's mother's brother.
*au̯ia	avva	grandmother, father's father's sister, mother's mother's sister.
*pǝtḗr	tandri	father, father's brother, father's father's brother's son, mother's sister's husband.
*māter̃	talli	mother, mother's sister, mother's mother's sister's daughter, father's brother's wife.
*su̯ékuros { mama / menamama		father-in-law, mother's brother, mother's mother's brother's son, father's sister's husband.
*su̯ekrū̃s { atta / menatta		mother-in-law, father's sister, father's father's sister's daughter, mother's brother's wife.
*bhrā́tēr { anna / tammudu		brother, father's brother's or mother's sister's son, father's sister's daughter's or mother's brother's daughter's husband.
*su̯esōr { akka / chellelu		sister, father's brother's or mother's sister's daughter, father's sister's son's or mother's brother's son's wife.
*daiu̯ḗr { bava / maradi		brother-in-law, father's sister's or mother's brother's son, father's brother's daughter's or mother's sister's daughter's husband.
*g(e)lōu– { vadine / maradalu		sister-in-law, father's sister's or mother's brother's daughter, father's brother's son's or mother's sister's son's wife.
*sunus	koduku	son; brother's son, sister's daughter's husband, father's brother's son's son, mother's sister's son's son, father's sister's daughter's son, mother's brother's daughter's son (man speak-

ing); sister's son, brother's daughter's husband, father's brother's daughter's son, mother's sister's daughter's son, father's sister's son's son, mother's brother's son's son (woman speaking).

*dhughtěr kuthuru daughter; brother's daughter, sister's son's wife, father's brother's son's daughter, mother's sister's son's daughter, father's sister's daughter's daughter, mother's brother's daughter's daughter (man speaking); sister's daughter, brother's son's wife, father's brother's daughter's daughter, mother's sister's daughter's daughter, father's sister's son's daughter, mother's brother's son's daughter (woman speaking).

*gem(e)- { alludu / menalludu } daughter's husband; sister's son, father's brother's daughter's son, mother's sister's daughter's son, father's sister's son's son, mother's brother's son's son (man speaking); brother's son, father's brother's son's son, mother's sister's son's son, father's sister's daughter's son, mother's brother's daughter's son (woman speaking).

*snusós { kodalu / menakodalu } son's wife; sister's daughter, father's brother's daughter's daughter, mother's sister's daughter's daughter, father's sister's son's daughter, mother's brother's son's daughter (man speaking); brother's daughter, father's brother's son's daughter, mother's sister's son's daughter, father's sister's daughter's daughter, mother's brother's daughter's daughter (woman speaking).

*anépōtios manamadu grandson, brother's or sister's grandson.

*anepōtia manamaralu granddaughter, brother's or sister's granddaughter.

———— magadu husband.

———— pendlama wife.

*įenətēr todikodalu husband's brother's wife.

———— saddakudu wife's sister's husband.

(The Telugu terms for the generations above the grandparents
and below the grandchildren are based on the terms for grandparents and grandchildren, like the Latin *proauos, abauos, pronepos,
abnepos.*)

The striking feature of the I.E. terminology is that, while it
recognises no less than five different relationships by marriage, it
appears to have no terms at all for cousins, nephews, nieces, uncles
and aunts. Even more puzzling is the lack of a designation for the
mother's brother, because in primitive society this relationship is
universally of special significance. Delbrück supposed that the
mother's brother was originally equated with the grandfather;[1] but
while he was right in refusing to believe that there was no term for
this relationship, his explanation involves the assumption, which, as
Schrader has pointed out, is unsupported by the evidence, that the
term for grandfather was specially associated with the mother's
father.[2] On the accepted interpretation of the I.E. system, it is
necessary to suppose either that it had evolved no terms for these
important relationships, which is incredible, or else that it had lost
them, which is to say that the accepted interpretation is inadequate.

If we compare the Telugu terminology with other types of the
classificatory system, we see that it belongs to a fairly advanced
type. The terms for husband, wife, husband's brother's wife, and
wife's sister's husband, are descriptive, and there is no distinction,
such as we find in Australian languages, between the father's parents
and the mother's, or between the son's children and the daughter's.[3]
It is however, significant that, while the mother's mother's brother
is included under the term for grandfather, the father's mother's
brother is not; and conversely, the father's father's sister is included
under the term for grandmother, but the mother's father's sister is
not. With cross-cousin marriage, the mother's mother's brother is the
father's father and the father's father's sister is the mother's mother,
while the father's mother's brother is the mother's father and the
mother's father's sister is the father's mother. It may be inferred that
the two Telugu terms for grandparents were originally confined to
the father's father and the mother's mother. The other two terms,
for the mother's father and the father's mother, have been lost.

On the other hand, in common with Tamil and Canarese,

[1] Delbrück IV 501.
[2] Schrader *s.v.* Oheim.
[3] Howitt NTSEA 160, 169; see above, p. 393. The two categories of
grandparents are shown in the diagram on p. 24 by the arrangement of the
lines connecting the grandparents with the great-grandparents, and the
two categories of grandchildren are shown in the same way.

Telugu has duplicate terms for brother and sister, distinguishing the elder and younger in each case. This is a primitive feature, which has disappeared from other Indian languages, and in Australia it is associated with the rule that a man must marry the daughter of his father's elder sister or his mother's elder brother.[1] Lastly, although, as normally in the classificatory system, the father's brothers are equated with the father and the mother's sisters with the mother, in practice they are usually distinguished by descriptive epithets—*pettandri* or "great gather" for the father's elder brother and *pinatandri* or "little father" for his younger brother.

In those parts of the Dravidian area where the practice of cross-cousin marriage survives, the nomenclature is natural, because it coincides with the reality; but, where that form of marriage has been abandoned, the classificatory system has become an encumbrance, because it treats as identical relationships now entirely distinct. The nomenclature is contradicted by the facts it was designed to represent. For this contradiction to be resolved, it is necessary that the terminology should be reorganised on the descriptive principle. The special features of the Telugu system which have just been mentioned are all steps in this direction, but for the complete transformation we must turn to Indo-European. The I.E. evidence is sufficient to establish not only the fact of the transition but the manner in which it was carried out. Each term was restricted to one of its several applications, the nearer relationships being preferred to the more remote and relationships through the husband to relationships through the wife. The result was that many relationships were left without a designation. These were eventually re-named, but in most cases only after the parent-language had broken up.

Let us begin with I.E. *$a\underset{\sim}{u}os$*, corresponding to the Telugu *tata*, which was applied to the grandfather and the mother's mother's brother. In Latin, as we have remarked, this term was used to denote both the grandfather and also, in a modified form, the mother's brother (*avonculus*). It appears therefore that, like *tata*, the I.E. *$a\underset{\sim}{u}os$* originally denoted the father's father, who was equated with the mother's mother's brother. Its subsequent history may be reconstructed as follows. On the one hand, in the Latin

[1] Spencer and Gillen NTCA 64–6. This, the only age distinction characteristic of the classificatory system, may have referred originally to seniority in respect of initiation: see Rivers SO 187–9. In Arunta and many other Australian languages, while the elder brother is distinguished from the elder sister, there is only a single term for the younger brother and sister; i.e. the latter, not having reached puberty, were treated as sexless.

avos, Armenian *haw*, and Old Norse *afi*, it was applied to the grand-father. On the other, in the Latin *avonculus*, Old Irish *amnair*, Old High German *oheim*, and Lithuanian *avýnas*, it was modified by an element *–en* affixed to the stem[1] and transferred from the mother's mother's brother to the mother's brother. The corresponding term for the mother's father and father's mother's brother was lost. Finally, in the French *oncle*, Welsh *ewythr*, and Modern German *Oheim*, the modified form has been generalised as "uncle."

The transference of **ayos* to the mother's brother implies the loss of some other term which had previously denoted that relationship. The lost term was **suékuros*, comprising the mother's brother, the father-in-law, and the father's sister's husband. This term was appropriated by the father-in-law. The feminine **suekrũs* was appropriated in the same way by the mother-in-law, with the result that no term remained for the father's sister. This was supplied in Latin by *amita*, which is probably based on the "baby-word" **ama*. We also find Old High German *ano*, "grandfather," and *ana*, "grand-mother," Old Prussian *ane*, "grandmother," and Lithuanian *anýta*, "mother-in-law"—all based on the baby-word **ana*. Now, with cross-cousin marriage, the father's sister is identical with the mother-in-law, and in the Telugu type of the classificatory system both are included under the same term. It is therefore probable that the Latin *amita* and Lithuanian *anýta* are of common origin, both being formed by extension of the stem from a primitive I.E. term (**ama* or **ana*) for the mother's mother and father's father's sister, just as the Latin *avonculus* and Lithuanian *avýnas* were formed from the primitive I.E. term for the father's father and the mother's mother's brother. Thus, the I.E. terms for grandparents developed in the same way as the Telugu.

The father's brother was distinguished from the father by exten-sion of the stem: Latin *patruus*, Greek *pátros*, Old High German *fatureo*, Sanskrit *pitrvyah*.[2] The analogous term for the mother's sister is confined to Italo-Celtic: Latin *matertera*, Welsh *modryb*.

The I.E. **bhrãtër* and **suesõr* continued in Latin to include the children of the father's brother and mother's sister, though even-tually they were supplanted in this connection by their descriptive epithets. In Greek they ceased to be used as terms of relationship. In Slavonic, on the other hand, they were extended to the children of the father's sister and mother's brother. In the other languages

---

[1] Ernout-Meillet *s.v.* Avonculus. The Anglo-Saxon *eam* was used both of the uncle and of the grandfather: Morgan SCAHF 32.

[2] The Greek *métros*, "mother's brother," has no parallel in the other languages and was formed by analogy from *pátros*.

they were restricted to the true brother and sister, with the result that new terms had to be found for the two categories of cousin which they had denoted.

The I.E. *daiu̯ér, comprising the brother-in-law and the son of the father's sister or mother's brother, was appropriated by the brother-in-law (Latin *levir*, Greek *daér*, Armenian *taygr*, Sanskrit *devár*, Old Slavonic *deveri*, Lithuanian *deveris*). The feminine *g(e)lōu– was appropriated in the same way by the sister-in-law (Latin *glos*, Greek *gálos*, Russian *zolva*). This removed the remaining terms for cousin.

The I.E. *sunus and *dhughter were appropriated by the true son and daughter, except in Italo-Celtic, where they disappeared. This removed the designations for a man's brother's children and a woman's sister's children. The I.E. *gem(e)–, which had comprised the daughter's husband, a man's sister's son and a woman's brother's son, and its feminine *snusós, were appropriated by the daughter's husband and son's wife respectively (Latin *gener nurus*, Greek *gambrós nyós*, Sanskrit *jāmātar snusā*, Old Slavonic *zeti snuxa*, Armenian *nu*, Anglo-Saxon *snoru*). This removed the remaining terms for nephews and nieces.

We have seen that, with cross-cousin marriage, my father's father is my mother's mother's brother. So, speaking as a man, my son's son is my sister's daughter's son. Therefore, just as I.E. *au̯os was divided between the grandfather and the mother's brother, the latter being eventually generalised as "uncle," so its reciprocal, *anépōtios, was divided between the grandson and the sister's son, the latter being generalised as "nephew." But, whereas the second use of *au̯os was marked by modification of the stem, the second use of *anépōtios was not, and consequently the division was less definite. In Sanskrit it was restricted to the grandson (*napāt*, fem. *napti*); in Old Irish it was transferred to the sister's son (*nia*, fem. *necht*); in Greek (*anepsiós*), Old Norse (*nefi*, fem. *nipt*), Old High German (*nevo*, fem. *niftila*) and Old Slavonic (*netiji*, fem. *nertera*) it was generalised as "nephew"; in Latin (*nepos*, *neptis*), Old Lithuanian (*nepōtis*), Anglo-Saxon (*nefa*) and Albanian (fem. *mbese*) it fluctuated between the grandson and the nephew.[1]

There remains the I.E. *ienəter "husband's brother's wife," corresponding to the Telugu *todikodalu*.[2] This term, which is alien to the

---

[1] The Italian *nipote* is used indiscriminately of the grandson and the nephew. The English *nephew* and *niece* were used of grandchildren as late as the sixteenth century, and the Dutch *neef*, like the Greek *anepsiós*, covers the nephew, grandson and cousin: Morgan SCAHF 31, 35.

[2] Latin *ianitrices*, Greek *eináteres*, Sanskrit *yātar*, Old Slavonic *jetry*.

classificatory system, probably belongs to the latest period of the parent language, in which, as we have seen, the social unit was the group of brothers living with their wives, who came from other groups.

All the I.E. terms have now been examined, and they are seen to have constituted originally a coherent and comprehensive terminology closely similar to the Telugu type of the classificatory system.

Reverting to Greek and Latin, we observe that several terms are based on *Lallwörter*, or "baby-words," e.g. Latin *amita*, Greek *pappós* "grandfather," *theîos* "uncle." Similar formations are common in the other languages: Old High German *muoma* "mother's sister," Welsh *tad* "father," and *mam* "mother," Russian *otets* "father," and *djadja* "uncle." These *Lallwörter* probably originated as terms of intimate address applied to close relatives. They have supplied formal terms of relationship in many primitive languages, and probably underlie I.E. *pətḗr* and *mātḗr*. These two, however, are the only I.E. terms that have been traced to this origin. The remainder were formed in other ways. It is therefore remarkable that they should have been supplanted in so many cases by *Lallwörter* during the period in which the derivative languages were evolved. There is no parallel to this process in the evolution of the Romance languages out of Latin. It may therefore have resulted from the instability of the formal terms during the disintegration of the classificatory system.

It is worth considering more precisely how far the classificatory system had been superseded at the time when common Indo-European broke up.

On the one hand, the primitive distinction between elder and younger brother had already disappeared, and this in itself implies a system of a fairly advanced type. Further, the consistency displayed in the subsequent development of *suékuros*, *suekrūs*, *daiuḗr*, and *g(e)lōu-*, indicates that these terms were already established in the descriptive sense. On the other hand, the history of *bhrātḗr* and *suesōr* in Greek, Latin and Slavonic, and the ambivalence of the reciprocals *auos* and *anépōtios*, suggest that these had not entirely divested themselves of the classificatory usage.

If the Latin *filius* and *filia* originated as descriptive epithets, they must have done so at a time when the primitive terms were still current in the classificatory sense; and, since they bear no relation to the corresponding terms in Celtic, the primitive terms must have remained classificatory as late as the differentiation of Celtic and Italic. This hypothesis, that the Italo-Celtic group was characterised by the exceptional persistence of the classificatory usage, accords with other indications that it was the first group to emerge.

We have seen that one of the features of the I.E. classificatory system during the period of its disintegration was a tendency to distort existing terms by extending their meaning without regard to distinctions of generation. The term *ayos, which properly belonged to the second ascending generation, was extended to the mother's brother, and the term *anépōtios, belonging to the second descending generation, to the sister's son. And this development was due in both cases to the need for new terms to designate the relatives by blood as distinct from the relatives by marriage. Here may perhaps be found the key to one of the unsolved problems of the American Indian terminologies.

In the languages of the Rocky Mountain Nations and the Eastern and Western Tinneh the cross-cousins have been differentiated from the brothers-in-law and sisters-in-law by assigning them to the category of straight cousins—that is, by equating them with the brothers and sisters. In Seneca-Iroquois, Ojibwa, and Dakota they have been kept distinct from the straight cousins and at the same time differentiated from the brothers-in-law and sisters-in-law by the development of distinctive terms. In Dakota the terms for the cross-cousins are simply the terms for brother-in-law and sister-in-law with the addition of a suffix. In all these languages the contradiction arising from the abolition of cross-cousin marriage has been resolved with the minimum of change, and the result is that in them the system of relationships has remained relatively stable.

In many other languages, however, including those of the Missouri, Upper Missouri, Gulf, Prairie, Great Lake, and parts of California, the cross-cousins have been transferred to categories outside their own generation, and by this means a fresh contradiction has been introduced, which has had more or less extensive repercussions on the other denominations, leading in some cases to the dislocation of the whole system.

In Punca, the father's sister's children are classified with the son and daughter (woman speaking) or with the sister's son and daughter (man speaking). Consequently, the father's sister's grandchildren are equated with the grandchildren, the father's sister's son's wife is equated with the son's wife, the father's sister's daughter's husband with the daughter's husband. A similar series of interrelated displacements is found in Winnebago. Again, in Minnitaree, the mother's brother's children are equated with the son and daughter, the mother's brother's grandchildren with the grandchildren, the mother's brother's son's wife with the son's wife, and the mother's brother's daughter's husband with the daughter's husband. The same series, more or less extended, is found in Creek and Pawnee.

In Minnitaree, the father's sister's children are equated with the father and mother,[1] and consequently the father's sister is equated with the grandmother. The proper term for the father's sister has accordingly disappeared. Further, in pursuance of the same principle, the father's sister's husband is equated with the grandfather, the father's sister's daughter's husband with the father, the father's sister's son's wife with the mother, and the father's sister's son's children with the brother and sister. Again, in Miami, the mother's brother's son is equated with the mother's brother, the mother's brother's daughter with the mother, the mother's brother's son's wife with the mother's brother's wife, the mother's brother's daughter's husband with the father, the mother's brother's daughter's children with the brother and sister. This series is also found in Punca and Arapaho, where, on the same principle, the mother's brother's son's wife is equated with the mother's brother's wife and the father's sister.

In Minnitaree, where the mother's brother's children are equated with the son and daughter, the mother's brother is equated with the elder brother. This is because, as normally in the classificatory system, the term for son (man speaking) includes the brother's son. If my mother's brother's son is my "son," my mother's brother is my "brother." And further, if I call my mother's brother "elder brother," he calls me "younger brother." Accordingly, in this language the sister's children (man speaking) are equated with the younger brother and sister.

In Two-Mountain Iroquois the cross-cousins are equated with the brother and sister. If my father's sister's children are my "brother" and "sister," my father's sister is my "mother." Accordingly, the term for the father's sister has been supplanted by the term for mother. Further, if I call my father's sister "mother," she calls me "son" or "daughter." Accordingly, in this language the brother's children (woman speaking) are equated with the son and

---

[1] If I call my mother's brother's son "son," he calls me (his father's sister's son) "father." The terms are reciprocal and hence the two dislocations are complementary to one another.

daughter.[1] The same equation is found in Cayuga, Crow, Mandan, Pawnee, Achaotinneh (Slave Lake), Hare Indian and Kutchin, and in all save the last two it is accompanied by the corresponding equation of the father's sister with the mother. Similarly, in Chickasa, where the father's sister is equated with the grandmother, the term for granddaughter includes the brother's daughter (woman speaking); and in Chocta and Achaotinneh, where the parents-in-law are equated with the grandparents, the term for granddaughter includes the son's wife.[2]

[1] This analysis shows that Rivers (SO 182) was mistaken in supposing that the Two-Mountain Iroquois terminology supported his objections to Morgan's interpretation of the Polynesian type of the classificatory system. I have not attempted to deal with these systems here, because they have not yet been properly collated. In some (not all) of the Polynesian languages, the mother's brother is equated with the father, the father's sister with the mother, all cousins with the brother and sister, all nephews and nieces with the son and daughter. This is Morgan's "Hawaiian system," which he believed to be the original form of the classificatory system, corresponding to the endogamy of the primitive horde (his "consanguine family"). Against this, Rivers maintained that those languages which lack the above-mentioned distinctions have lost them (HMS 2. 173, SO 175); but this view is not borne out by the evidence, so far as it has been collected. The terms for "mother's brother" and "father's sister," where such exist, are either isolated forms, confined to one language or locality and therefore not referable to the primitive Polynesian system, or else compounds based on the Polynesian words for the primary relationships of father, mother, brother, sister, which are distributed with remarkable uniformity over the whole area, e.g. *tuatina* "mother's brother," from *tua* "brother" and *tina* "mother," *nganeitama* "father's sister," from *ngane* "sister" and *tama* "father." Similarly, the Tongan term for the mother's brother's son or daughter is compounded of the three primary terms for mother, brother, son or daughter, while the Fijian for cross-cousin is a word meaning *concumbens*. All these terms are manifestly derivative, and so therefore are the distinctions they serve to mark.

[2] Other instances of the identification of reciprocal terms are GF = GS (Spokane, Yakama), gm = gd and mF = dS (Spokane), wF = dH (Seneca), wm=dH (Yakama), and HF =Sw (Mandan). The equations HF =Sw and Hm = Sw are also found in the system of the Kingsmill Islands, which belongs to the Polynesian type. It seems probable that this principle is derived from a very primitive stage of the classificatory system, in which the second ascending and second descending generations were designated by the same terms—that is, the grandparents were equated with the grandchildren. It is applied consistently in the Arunta system (see pp. 392–4), where the father's father is equated with the son's son and the mother's mother with the daughter's daughter. This explains why, in the same system, the son's son's son is equated with the father, the daughter's daughter's daughter with the mother, and the children of the son's son's son and daughter's daughter's daughter with the brother and sister.

It will be found that this principle of consecutive dislocation, arising from the need for differentiating the primitive relationships, suffices to explain almost all the characteristic irregularities of the American Indian terminologies, and so turns the tables on those who have derived encouragement from these anomalies in their opposition to Morgan's theory of the classificatory system.

In the Dakota language, according to Riggs, there is only one word for grandfather and father-in-law. Following the mode of reasoning sometimes employed, it might be deduced from this that these two relationships were once identical. Worked out to its implications, the absurd conclusion would be that marriage with the mother was once customary among the Sioux.[1]

If Kroeber had been less preoccupied with abstractions and more intent on objective analysis of the available data, he would have hesitated before committing himself to this superficial criticism. The only difference at this point between Dakota and Indo-European is that, whereas Dakota has transferred the father-in-law to the grandfather and left the mother's brother where he was, Indo-European transferred the mother's brother to the grandfather and left the father-in-law where he was. So far from constituting a *reductio ad absurdum* of Morgan's theory, this evidence confirms it by showing that, when the classificatory system began to collapse, the process followed the same course in different hemispheres. And the reason why these dislocations went much further in the American Indian languages than they did in Indo-European is that the American Indians have failed to advance beyond the tribal system, whereas the Indo-European-speaking peoples advanced so rapidly that, after a period of instability which was relatively brief, their whole terminology was reconstructed on an entirely new foundation.

All this and other related problems require of course much closer and more comprehensive treatment than has been attempted here, but it may be suggested that their solution will be found by

[1] Kroeber in JRAI 39.82. Similar dislocations are found in the Banks Islands, New Hebrides, and parts of Africa (Rivers HMS 1. 28-31, 192, Seligman MBNG 707, PTNS 117, 258), and they may have been promoted to some extent by the practice, which occurs sporadically, of marriage with the father's sister, mother's brother's wife, or wife's brother's daughter (Rivers HMS 1. 47-9, 100, Eggan SANAI 274, Frazer TE 2. 387, 510). Such marriages, which by their nature are necessarily exceptional or occasional, cannot have been the cause of the dislocations, but they may have determined their direction.

the reapplication and extension of Morgan's methods rather than by accepting the standpoint of Malinowski, who declares (in *Man* 30. 22) that "the plain fact is that classificatory terminologies do not exist and never could have existed."

NOTES AND REFERENCES

Pronunciation of Greek Words. The simple vowels *a e i o* are pronounced as in Italian; *y* is equivalent to French *u*. Of the diphthongs, *ou* is equivalent to Italian *u*; in the others, each component vowel has its proper value (*a+i*, *e+u*, etc.). *Ch* is guttural; *g* is always hard. In a few of the more familiar names, such as Æschylus, Hecuba, Thucydides, the Latin spelling has been used in deference to the English convention. The accents mark the intonation of the voice, which rises with the acute accent (´) and first rises and then falls with the circumflex (^). Diphthongs carry the accent-sign on the second vowel. In pronouncing Greek most English scholars ignore the accent.

INTRODUCTION

1 (p. 1). Thuc. 1. 6. 6.
2 (p. 1). Cf. Glotz SF 408.
3 (p. 3). Pickard-Cambridge DTC 159.
4 (p. 4). This should be remembered in connection with the theory, propounded by Perry in his CS, that ancient Egypt is the centre from which human culture has radiated all over the world. He finds the origin of Egyptian culture in the unique conditions of the Nile Valley, but recently evidence has been adduced to show that the distinctive institutions of the primitive Egyptians were evolved before they entered the Nile Valley: Wainwright SRE 8f.
5 (p. 4). Ferguson EHCS 257.

CHAPTER I

1 (p. 11). Hobhouse, Wheeler and Ginsberg MCSISP 16. For the sake of simplicity I have omitted their grade of Dependent Hunters, which is not necessary for my argument. The general scheme adopted by these writers is in some respects over-simplified, and their data are incomplete, but the results are of great value. They have been applied, again with important results, by Diamond in his PL. The current views of totemism are summarised and discussed by Van Gennep in his EAPT. On mixed farming, see Childe MMH 85, Heichelheim WA 48f.
2 (p. 11). It is important to observe that the totemic taboo is directed primarily against eating the totem species, not against killing it, and in some tribes the distinction is clearly drawn: Spencer and Gillen NTCA 149, 202, Elkin in O 3. 257f. Conversely, a man who catches the totem species of another clan is expected to refrain from eating it until he has obtained permission to do so from members of that clan: NTCA 159, 323. On the distribution of totemism, see Lowie PS 131. He ignores the question of Indo-European

totemism, which Frazer discusses, though very inadequately (TE 4. 13). On Semitic and Chinese totemism, see Robertson Smith RS, Granet CC 180.

3 (p. 12). Of more than 200 Australian totems enumerated by Spencer and Gillen, over 150 are edible plants or animals: NTCA 768, cf. Elkin in O 3. 282. The development of totemism beyond these limits is correlated with developments in the organisation of the totemic tribe. In some Australian tribes, notably those of S.E. Queensland, the totem-species are distributed among the exogamous groups according to their mutual affinities: trees belong to the same moiety as the birds that nest in them, water to the same moiety as water-fowl and fish. See Kelly in O 5. 465, and cf. Radcliffe-Brown, ib. 1. 63: "Just as each human being has his own place in the social structure, so each of the important natural species is allotted its place as belonging to a particular moiety, section or clan." The world of nature is reduced to order by reflecting on it the system imposed by nature on society.

4 (p. 12). Instances of totem centres at breeding places of the species are given in the authorities cited by Frazer T 59, 62, 69, 70, 99, 185, 189, 204, 238, cf. Spencer and Gillen NTCA 147, 288, 296. Of many increase-ceremonies, we are expressly told that they took place annually at the beginning of the breeding season of the species: Frazer T 72, 78, 195. It is perhaps unnecessary to explain that the example of wallabies, which I have used in this and the following paragraphs, has been chosen for the sake of illustration only, and is not intended to imply that this particular species, which cannot be hunted without skilful spearmanship, goes back to the initial stage of totemism. The specialised diet characteristic of that stage must have consisted of such species as witchetty-grubs, beetle-grubs, molluscs, etc.

5 (p. 13). Ritual eating of the totem: Spencer and Gillen NTCA 323, NTNTA 198, A 81.

6 (p. 13). The Arunta tell of a fish man fishing in a pool for the fish on which he lived, of a beetle-grub man who fed on beetle grubs, and an opossum man who carried the moon as a lantern to help him catch opossums: Spencer and Gillen NTNTA 208, NTCA 321, A 331–52. The Kaitish tell of a grass-seed man who fed on grass seed, and of an edible bulb which formed the staple diet of the woman whose totem it was: NTCA 321, 394, 405. A clan of S.W. Australia explained the origin of its totem, the opossum, by saying that opossum was formerly its principal article of food (Grey VDSWA 4); and the Karadjeri tell of a married couple who fed exclusively on fish until they found it disagreed with them, when they advised people not to live on fish alone: Piddington in O 2. 380. Even more explicit is a tradition of the Unmatjera tribe. In former days there were some beetle-grub men who lived on beetle grubs, because at that time there was nothing in the country at all except beetle grubs and a little white bird. One day the men reflected that if they went on eating beetle grubs the supply might fail. Nevertheless, they persisted, with the result that one of them fell sick and died: Spencer and Gillen NTCA 324. The reason for the presence of the little white bird, which belonged to the species known to the natives as *thippa-thippa*, is evidently that it acts as a guide to them in their search for grubs: see Frazer TE 1. 256.

7 (p. 14). On the rise of ancestor worship, see the authorities cited by Landtman OISC 125. The "primitive horde," which corresponds to

Howitt's "undivided commune" and Morgan's "consanguineous family," may be defined as a small, self-contained, undifferentiated, nomadic band of food-gatherers—probably not more than two or three dozen individuals: see Hobhouse 46.

8 (p. 15). Cf. Spencer and Gillen NTCA 327: "The fundamental idea common to all the tribes is that men of any totemic group are responsible for the maintenance of the supply of the animal or plant which gives its name to the group, and that the one object of increasing the number of the totemic animal or plant is simply that of increasing the general food-supply." Instruction of youth: Spencer and Gillen NTCA 328f, Landtman OISC 21, 31, Webster PSS 27, 32, 60, 140.

9 (p. 15). Hartland PP 1. 256.

10 (p. 15). Hobhouse etc. MCSISP 150f.

11 (p. 15). Division of labour in hunting tribes: Malinowski FAA 275f; Bancroft, NRPSNA 1. 66, 131, 186, 196, 218, 242, 261–5, 340, Heichelheim WA 1. 14. The need for the men to travel unencumbered except for their weapons explains why the women carry the baggage: Basedow AA 112, Landtman OISC 115.

12 (p. 16). Cattle-raising: Westermarck ODMI 1. 634, 2. 273, Landtman OISC 15. Garden-tillage: Hobhouse etc. MCSISP 22, Heichelheim WA 1. 14. Men in agriculture: Lowie PS 71, 174, 184, Childe MMH 138.

13 (p. 16). Howitt NTSEA 119, 142. The typical Australian tribe is divided at the present day into local groups or "hordes." In the great majority these local groups are patrilineal, and so are the totemic clans—that is to say, each local group consists of the men born in it, all belonging to the same clan, together with the women who have married into it from other clans. But in a number of tribes, while the local group is patrilineal, the clan is matrilineal. This means that the members of each clan are scattered in different groups all over the tribal territory. Yet, as we have already seen, the clan was originally concentrated at a particular locality, and the matrilineal clans cannot be regarded as a development of the patrilineal, because as such they are impossible to explain. It seems probable, therefore, that originally both the local group and the clan were matrilineal, being in fact identical. Subsequently, owing to the decline in the status of women and in the economic functions of the clan, there emerged patrilocal groups independent of the clans, which were still matrilineal, and, finally, in the stage reached by the majority of tribes to-day, the identity of local group and clan was restored by introducing patrilineal descent into the clan. The evidence on this subject is collected by Radcliffe-Brown in O 1.

14 (p. 16). Recent development of exogamy in Australia: Frazer T 5.

15 (p. 16). Spencer and Gillen A 491: "In the Arunta and other Central Australian tribes, in which descent is counted in the male line, a man continues as it were to pay a kind of tribute to his wife's group. . . . This is further the one important feature, so far as the Arunta are concerned, which appears to indicate in any way a former condition in which a man owed allegiance to the group of his wife." There is, however, strong evidence to show that among the Arunta the relations of the sexes have changed; for they assert that women formerly took part in ceremonies which they are now forbidden even to witness: A 150, cf. 167, 328, 340, 346. Among the Kurnai, if a man killed five opossums, he had to give two to his wife's

parents and two to her brothers; if he killed one sloth-bear, he had to give it to his wife's parents; if two, he had to give the other to his own parents; if three, two to his wife's parents and one to his own, keeping only the liver for his wife and himself: Howitt NTSEA 756–64. Cf. Rivers ETS 5. 148, Eggan SANAI 215. The evidence for matrilocal marriage and matrilineal descent is collected by Briffault M 1. 268–430.

16 (p. 16). Yukumbil: Radcliffe-Brown in JRAI 59. 403.

17 (p. 17). The endogamy of the primitive horde is still remembered in tradition; for in the ancestral legends of the Arunta the intermarriage of members of the same totem is represented as having been the normal practice: Spencer and Gillen A 331–52, NTCA 393f. This is a further indication that totemism originated in *pre*-tribal society, because the structure of the tribe is based on exogamy. Morgan explained the development of exogamy by the progressive limitation of inbreeding, which he assumed to be injurious, and this is one of the few of his conclusions to commend themselves to bourgeois writers. It is also one of the most questionable. It seems to have little or no support in modern genetics, and it does not explain the facts; for one of the striking things about the rule of exogamy in its simplest form is that, while in certain directions it prohibits the intermarriage of kindred to an infinitely remote degree, in other directions it permits marriage between first cousins and even between parents and children. The genetical evidence is discussed at length by Briffault (M 1. 204–40), who in other respects is one of Morgan's strongest supporters, mercilessly exposing the theoretical fallacies of his "orthodox" opponents and assembling in his favour a mass of concrete data far more comprehensive and cogent than they have ever adduced against him. Briffault himself, who recognises that the totem-species was originally the staple diet, though without explaining the taboo, accounts for exogamy on the hypothesis that the matriarchal constitution of the primitive group, determined by biological factors and necessary for its survival, could only be preserved by systematically expelling the grown males. But there is no reason why these conditions should have resulted in more than a peripheral existence on the part of the males, such as he notes among some of the anthropoids (1. 179); and, if the females were strong enough to expel the males, it is not clear why they should not have been strong enough to control them. Moreover, his hypothesis does not square with the evidence of the classificatory system, which points to an original state of endogamy. This seems to me one of the weak points in what must be regarded as the most important theoretical contribution to social anthropology since the beginning of the century.

18 (p. 17). The percentages for slavery among modern tribes are computed by Hobhouse etc. MCSISP 236 a follows: Lower Hunters 2, Higher Hunters 32, First Agricultural 33, Second Agricultural 46, Third Agricultural 78. As they remark: "Ignoring the pastoral peoples, for whom the numbers are too small to be of any value, we find that the practice of killing some or all of the vanquished predominates and is nearly constant till we reach the highest agricultural stage, where it drops by 50 per cent," and "the drop in the practice of killing prisoners in Agricultural III is the reverse side of the equally sudden rise in the practice of enslavement." Cf. Plekhanov FPM 35.

19 (p. 17). The position of the elder in the lower hunting tribes is well illustrated by the Punans of Borneo, described by Hose and McDougall PTB 2. 182.

DDA

20 (p. 18). Prayer and propitiation: Rivers HMS 2. 405, cf. Spencer and Gillen A 146, NTCA 491, Howitt NTSEA 500. The first stage in the evolution of an anthropomorphic god may be studied in Howitt's account of the sky-spirit Biamban, who was simply a projection of the natives' idea of a headman: Howitt NTSEA 506, cf. Moret et Davy CE 133.

21 (p. 18). Royal totems: Moret et Davy CE 143f. Tribalisation of clan-cults: Durkheim FEVR 406. Gods evolved out of totems: Frazer TE 1. 81, 2. 139, 151, 166, cf. 2. 18. Of course, it is not to be understood that every particular case of the association of a god with an animal is a direct totemic survival, but merely that the principle underlying such associations is derived from totemism.

22 (p. 19). Zeus Lykaios: Farnell CGS 1. 41f. Zeus of Praisos: CGS 1. 37.

23 (p. 19). Erechtheidai: Eur. *Ion* 20–9, 1421–31, Paus. 1. 24. 7, Hyg. *Astr.* 2. 13. In the historical period the clan had disappeared, and the name was used, like Kekropidai, of the Athenian people.

24 (p. 19). Totem marked on the person: Frazer TE 1. 196, 2. 28, 37, 3 353. A Maenad on an Attic *kÿlix* has the figure of a fawn tattooed on her right arm: Harrison T 132. The Spartoi of Thebes had two emblems, a snake and a spear. The latter was traditionally explained as a birthmark (Arist. *Poet.* 1454b. 22, Dio Chr. 1. 149R, Hyg. *Fab.* 72, Plut. *M.* 563B) but in reality it was probably a totemic tattoo: Harrison T 435. See further Cook Z 2. 122.

25 (p. 20). Spartoi: Tzetzes *ad* Lycoph. 495, Pind. *P.* 5. 101 sch., Paus. 8. 11. 8.

26 (p. 20). Attic clan-emblems: Seltman AHC 24, 30, 49. The hind-quarters of a horse, which may have belonged to the Philadai (AHC 37)—an emblem described by Seltman as extraordinary—were evidently a "split" totem due to segmentation of the clan: Frazer TE 1. 10, 58, 77, 2. 397, 520, 536, 3. 100, 4. 175.

27 (p. 20). Diipolia: Robertson Smith RS 288, Farnell CGS 1. 89. Euneidai: *Anth. Pal.* 3. 10, cf. Eur. fr. 765; Toepffer AG 181. Ioxidai: Plut. *Thes.* 8. On totemic taboos observed by Roman *gentes* see the article by Kagarov in VIDO 619, which contains the best work on the Roman *gens* since Morgan and Engels.

28 (p. 21). Cattle used for milk: Robertson Smith RS 269.

29 (p. 21). Nestor: Hom. *Od.* 3. 4–8.

30 (p. 21). Initiation: see Chapter VII. Group-marriage: see Chapter II.

31 (p. 21). Robertson Smith RS 406.

32 (p. 22). Secret sodalities: see Chapter VII.

33 (p. 22). Ritual of the god-king: Hooke MR, Wainwright SRE.

CHAPTER II

1 (p. 23). Immigration of Greek-speaking tribes: Nilsson HM 82.

2 (p. 23). Identification of Indo-European people: Childe A 94. Primitive Indo-European culture: Childe A 78, Meillet IECLI 391.

3 (p. 25). Classificatory system: see further Appendix I and II. The distribution of the dual organisation (moieties) is world-wide (Rivers HMS 2. 500, SO 205, Morgan AS 79–83, 162–3, Eggan

SANAI 268, 287, Frazer TE 1. 256–71, 314–514, 2. 274, 3. 33, 90,
119, 121, 125, 131, 266, 280, etc.), and so is that of cross-cousin marriage
(Briffault M 1. 563–84). Yet, dismissing the explanation of the classificatory
system on the basis of exogamous moieties, S. Tax (in Eggan SANAI 279)
asserts that "the distribution of moieties is comparatively limited." What
is his standard of comparison? Similarly, cross-cousin marriage has been
described by Kroeber (in JRAI 39. 82) as "utterly opposed to the basic
principles of almost all [American] Indian society." Cross-cousin marriage
has been recorded of the Western Tinnehs, Hopis, Arawaks, Naskapis,
Crees, Ojibwas, and other tribes of North, South and Central America
(Briffault M 1. 572, Eggan SANAI 95).

4 (p. 26). Howitt NTSEA 173, Spencer and Gillen NTCA 73, 95, Rivers
SO 175; Thomas KMA 110, Malinowski FAA 108, Kroeber in JRAI 39. 77,
Lowie PS 57, Radcliffe-Brown in O 1. 34, 202, 322, 426; Briffault M
1. 614. None of those who claim to have overthrown Morgan's theory
of group marriage has put anything constructive in its place, and some
have affirmed the impossibility of doing so. Thus, Goldenweiser (in JAFL
23. 179) argued that the resemblances between totemic institutions in
different parts of the world are the result not of common origin or of
parallel development but of what he called "convergent evolution." The
differences are primary, the resemblances secondary; the diversity is fundamental, the unity superficial. Subsequently, he modified this view to the
extent of admitting a fundamental correlation between totemism and the
clan-system, thereby incurring the disapproval of Lowie, who, after
rejecting Goldenweiser's second thoughts, sums up his own position by
announcing that he is "not convinced that all the acumen and erudition
lavished on the subject has established the reality of the totemic phenomenon" (PS 137). This is indeed a triumph of bourgeois agnosticism: the
problem is solved by denying its existence. To Lowie, Morgan's belief in
social progress, culminating in his memorable forecast of the socialist
revolution, "was a natural accompaniment of the belief in historical laws,
especially when tinged with the evolutionary optimism of the seventies of the
last century" (PS 427). That is true, in the sense that Morgan's work was a
product of the rise of American capitalism; but it is equally true that
Lowie's disbelief in social progress, expressed in his concluding aphorisms
about "that planless hodge-podge, that thing of shreds and patches called
civilisation" is a product of capitalism in the last stages of decay.

5 (p. 27). Morgan AS 481; see Appendix II.

6 (p. 27). Evolution of the phratry: Morgan AS 171, Frazer TE 3. 41,
44, 79, 214.

7 (p. 27). The Latin *curia* was regularly equated by Greek writers with
phratria. The Irish evidence is abundant and would repay scientific analysis:
Joyce SHAI 1. 166, Hubert GDC 198.

8 (p. 28). Apatouria: Mommsen FSA 322. *Kásios, káses:* Hesych. *s. vv.*

9 (p. 28). Kretschmer 'Die griechische Benennung des Bruders' in G 2. 210.

10 (pp. 28–9). Lycia: Hdt. 1. 173, Müller FHG 5. 461, cf. Polyb. 12. 5.
Bellerophon: Hom. *Il.* 6. 192–5. Temenos: Apollod. 2. 8. 5. See further
Thomson AO 2. 264. Meleager: Apollod. 1. 8. 2. Attic tradition: Varro
ap. Aug. C. D. 18. 9. Lycia and Crete: Paus. 8. 3. 4; Hall CGBA 135.

11 (p. 29). Position of women in Crete: Hall CGBA 272, Glotz CE 142.
Minoan mother-goddess: Glotz CE 161, 239, 266, Hall CGBA 275, Childe
DEC 25, Evans PM 1. 151, 495. While the Minoan male costume is quite

different from the Mycenean, the Minoan female costume was taken over entirely by the Mycenean women (Glotz CE 73, 76). This means that the dominant element in Mycenean culture was transmitted largely through the women.

12 (p. 30). Cook in CR 20. 365, 416.

13 (p. 30). Arist. *Meteor.* 1. 14 p. 352, Frazer on Paus. 3. 20. 6.

14 (p. 30). Hesych. *s. vv. éor, éores.*

15 (p. 30). Kretschmer in G 2. 210.

16 (p. 31). Ridgeway EAG 2. 14, 18.

17 (p. 31). Spencer and Gillen A 52, 490, NTNTA 36, NTCA 73, Howitt NTSEA 756, Bancroft NRPSNA 1. 118, 417, 506, Malinowski FAA 283, Rivers SO 108, Williamson SPSCP 3. 235, Hobhouse etc. MCSISP 244, Landtman OISC 7. It seems probable that the English *kind*, Greek *gennaîos*, Latin *generosus*, Irish *cinéalta*, all of which are ,derived from tribal relationships, connoted originally communal customs of this kind. In Samoa the word for *generous* is (or was) *mata-ainga*, literally *gentem reverens*: Williamson 3. 236.

18 (p. 31). Collective hunting of certain animals was general throughout N.W. Queensland: Roth ESNWQA 96, 100, cf. Mathew TRTQ 87.

19 (p. 31). On primitive inheritance in general see Fallaize in Hastings 7. 295. One of the commonest methods of evading the rule that property reverts at death to the kin is the practice of bestowing it before death on one's children: Frazer TE 2. 195, 3. 174, 245, 4. 131, 290.

20 (p. 31). Tribal co-operation: Morgen AS 95, Spencer and Gillen NTCA 164, Frazer TE 1. 75, 3. 275, Landtman OISC 70.

21 (p. 32). Potlatch: Frazer TE 3. 262, 300, 342, 344, 519, 545. Exchange of gifts: Bancroft NRPSNA 1. 192, 217, 2. 711. In China: Granet CC 165, 267. In Homer: *Il.* 6. 234–6, cf. *Od.* 1. 315–18. See further Glotz TGA 54, Hubert GDC 54, 193, 220, Grönbech CT 2. 8, 87.

22 (p. 32). Heichelheim WA 1. 47.

23 (p. 33). Jewish law of inheritance: H. P. Smith in Hastings 7. 306, Ridgeway EAG 2. 123, Seebohm SGTS 27.

24 (p. 33). *Mishpaha*=clan: Robertson Smith RS 276.

25 (p. 33). Pre-Dorian genealogies: Thomson AO 2. 265. Cf. p. 302.

26 (p. 33). Incest and witchcraft: Diamond PL 289, cf. Robertson Smith RS 264. Homicide (general) Diamond PL 144; (Germanic) Grönbech CT 1. 55, 283; (Greek) Glotz SF 47, Diamond PL 149, Calhoun GCL 9, 41, Chadwick HA 353.

27 (p. 34). The vendetta: Glotz SF 271.

28 (p. 34). Prosecution and defence: Calhoun GCL 64.

29 (p. 34). Prosecution initiated by victim's kinsmen: Dem. 43. 57.

30 (p. 34). Labour-service for homicide: Pherecydes *ap.* Eur. *Alc.* 1 sch., Apollod. 2. 6. 2, 3. 4. 2. The word *poiné* is commonly connected with *timé* (Boisacq 801, Glotz SF 105) but it seems worth pointing out that the series *poiné—pónos—pénes* corresponds to the series *moîra—môros—méros.*

31 (p. 34). Chadwick HA 346, 359, Grönbech CT 1. 35.

32 (p. 35). Grönbech CT 1. 283.

33 (p. 35). Adoption of the homicide: Grönbech CT 1. 343, 2. 99.

34 (p. 35). Erinyes: Harrison PSGR 213, Nilsson HGR 142, cf. Farnell CGS 1. 300. Spirits of the dead embodied in snakes: Frazer GB 4. 1. 82, Karsten CSAI 289. On the snake as a symbol of immortality see Briffault M 2. 641–51.

35 (p. 35). Æsch. *Th.* 710–12, 751, 771, 776, Soph. *O.C.* 1434, Pind. *O.* 2. 42–6, Hdt. 4. 149; Hom. *Od.* 11. 279–80; *Il.* 9. 565–72, Apollod. 1. 8. 3, 3. 7. 5.

36 (p. 36). Erinyes and perjury: Thomson AO 1. 51, 2. 269. Ordeal by oath: Diamond PL 52, 350, 364.

37 (p. 36). Rhadamanthys: Plat. *Ll.* 748 B-D. Aristotle (*Pol.* 2. 10. 2. 1271b) says that the Dorian settlers in Crete adopted the constitution of the earlier inhabitants, who continued to be governed by the laws of Minos.

CHAPTER III

The general evidence relating to land tenure among modern tribes has been analysed by Hobhouse, etc., whose conclusions are as follows (MCSISP 253): "We may express the whole tendency best by saying that the communal principle predominates in the lower stages of culture and retains a small predominance among the pastoral peoples, and that private ownership tends to increase in the higher agricultural stages, but partly in association with the communal principle, partly by dependence on the chief, or in some instances by something in the nature of feudal tenure. We seem in fact to get something of that ambiguity as between signorial and popular ownership that we find at the beginning of our own history. Over and over again, at the stage in which barbarism is beginning to pass into civilisation, the communal, individual, and signorial principles are found interwoven . . . and it seems to be the next stage upward in civilisation which gives its preponderance to the lord." On the Homeric evidence, see Esmein in RHDFE, 14. 821, Pöhlmann GSFS 1. 12, Guiraud PFG 36, Ridgeway in JHS 6. 327, Glotz SF 5, TGA 35, Toutain EA 12. In Greece, as elsewhere, the transition must have been a gradual and complex process, varying from district to district and from class to class. If we remember that, we shall avoid the mistake made by Toutain in assuming that, if property is not common, it must be private. There are several well-recognised gradations—tribal ownership, gentile ownership, family ownership, ownership vested in the head of the family— and it is only when the land has become alienable that we have full private ownership. What we want is a comparative study of land tenure on the lines of Diamond's PL, but meanwhile it is impossible to acquiesce in Adcock's statement in CAH 4. 42: "The Greeks had long outlived the stage, if it ever existed, when property had been held in common by the clan and private ownership was unknown." Are we to understand that private ownership may be as old as the enclosure of the Garden of Eden? About the year 580 B.C. the islands of Lipara were colonised from Rhodes and Knidos. The account which follows is from Diodoros (5. 9): "Being well received at Lipara, the settlers were induced to share the land with the natives, who were the surviving descendants of Aiolos, about five hundred in all. In course of time, owing to the depredations of Tuscan pirates, they built a fleet and divided their occupations, some of them continuing the collective tillage of the soil, others being organised for defence against the pirates. They held property in common and ate at common meals. After leading this communal life for some time, they divided Lipara itself, where the city was, but continued to cultivate the other islands collectively; and eventually they divided all the islands for periods of twenty years, reallotting them at the end of each." The reference to common meals shows that the organisation was tribal (see p. 70), and the rest of the account reveals three successive stages in the transition from common to private property: (1) collective cultivation of all the arable land; (2) division of the land in the vicinity of the *pólis*; (3) division of all the land and periodical re-distribution. That seems plain enough. This evidence is ignored by Adcock, ignored by Toutain. Bury mentions it, but hastens to add that the original system was subsequently modified and treats the whole thing as though it were an isolated "communist experiment" (HG 297). Guiraud mentions it, too, but sets it aside with a piece of casuistry: these settlers, he says, were pirates themselves, and therefore their institutions are devoid of political or social significance (PFG 13). Being no better than robbers abroad, they had naturally failed to develop at home that sense of private property which is the hall-mark of civilisation. Even more incorrigible, and with less excuse, were the Vaccaei of Spain, also described by Diodoros, who not only reallotted the land every year, each receiving his share of the fruits, which were common property, but punished appropriation with death (5. 34); and the Germans described by Tacitus (*G.* 26), who exchanged their fields every year, the common land remaining over (see Marx-Engels B 236); and the common people of Peru, who worked the land on the basis of family holdings subject to annual reallotment (Prescott CP 29); and the people of Mexico, where the land was the common property of the clan (*calpulli*) and allotted to individuals on condition that they cultivated and improved it (Bancroft NRPSNA 2. 226). Similarly, in the English strip-system, "the common meadow-land was divided up by lot, pegged out, and distributed among the owners of the strips" (Hammond VL 4), and the Celtic run-rig system, which survived in Devon and Cornwall, involved periodical re-distribution of the soil (Vinogradoff OHJ 309, Hubert GDC 216, Joyce SHAI 1. 168). On the significance of this evidence for the interpretation of Hom. *Il.* 18. 541f see Ridgeway in JHS 6. 327f and Seebohm SGTS 104. Further study along these lines would probably show that the whole complex of institutions and ideas centred in the Greek *klêros* was a heritage from common Indo-European; but, if it is to be productive, such a study must be undertaken by scholars who, like Morgan, believe that "a mere property career is not the final destiny of mankind."

1 (p. 37). Enclosure Acts: Hammond VL 1–81, Marx K 803.

2 (p. 37). Nilsson HM 275.

3 (p. 37). *Il.* 12. 421. Modern commentators: Glotz TGA 9, Guiraud PFG 38. It is true, as Toutain observes (EA 15), that Hes. *Op.* 37f points to individual ownership, which was doubtless developing rapidly by the time of Hesiod; but, as Seebohm remarked (SGTS 123), the case of Hesiod and his brother, sons of an immigrant, cannot be assumed to be typical.

4 (p. 37). It is of course possible that the men were dividing the land in order to appropriate it, but that only implies that the land had previously been common. Nilsson remarks on this passage (HM 242): "It is uncertain whether the word *epíxynos* means 'communal'; it may signify simply 'common,' viz. of disputed ownership, and the quarrel may be one of the quarrels concerning boundaries common among farmers." One would like to know (1) what is the difference between "communal" and "common,"

and (2) by what mental process "common" comes to mean "of disputed ownership."

5 (p. 38). Joh. Diac. *Alleg.* 886, cf. Aesch. *Eum.* 173, 730.

6 (p. 38). Boisacq 469, Ridgeway 330. Similarly, the Irish *crann* "lot" is identical with *crann* "tree." Another synonym of *moîra* is *pótmos*, that which falls (*píptei*) to one's lot, cf. Latin *casus.*

7 (p. 38). Hdt. 5. 57, cf. 4. 145. With *moîra* as applied to land may be compared *dêmos*, properly a "division" (*daîo*) either of the land or of the people, i.e. either the land occupied by the clan or the clan itself (see p. 206). That is why so many Attic *dêmoi* bear the names of clans. The Arabic *hayy* was similarly applied both to the tribe and to the land belonging to it: Robertson Smith KMEA 39.

8 (p. 39). See Chap. II n. 24.

9 (p. 39). Pind. *O.* 7. 74, Hom. *Il.* 2. 654, 668; Cornford RP 15.

10 (p. 39). Helios: Pind. *O.* 7. 58.

11 (p. 39). Pind. *O.* 7. 64. The use of *láchos* in this passage explains the common use of *lancháno* in reference to the association of a god with a particular region or city: Hom. *H.* 19. 5, Hdt. 7. 53. cf. Pind. *N.* 11. 1, Plat. Tim. 23D.

12. (p. 39). Hom. *Il.* 15. 185–204. Pindar's version of the myth connotes the distribution of land among tribes—that is clear from its context. In Homer, however, we are told that Olympus and the Earth were not distributed but held by the brothers in common (193). This shows that the myth is regarded in the light of succession to a deceased father's property, the real estate (the house and the land) being held jointly, while the personal estate was divided by lot; and the implication that the land was not divided is further evidence that in the Homeric poems, apart from the *témenos* and the *eschatié*, individual ownership of land is not recognised.

13 (p. 39). Hekate: Hes. *Th.* 411–28, cf. Hom. *H.* 4. 427–8.

14 (p. 39). Apollod. 2. 8. 4. The question of the historical authenticity of this tradition does not affect its value as evidence of primitive custom.

15 (p. 39). Hom. *Od.* 6. 9.

16 (p. 40). Hdt. 4. 159. Cf. Plat. *Ll.* 745B–C; Moret et Davy CE 62.

17 (p. 50). Re-division of the land: Arist. *Ath. Rp.* 11. 2.

18 (p. 40). Lesbos: Thuc. 3. 50. Thus, at *O.* 9. 26f Pindar is describing himself as a priest of the Charites tilling his *témenos*; cf. Plut. *M.* 993D.

19 (p. 40). From *Il.* 22. 489 and *Od.* 7. 149–50 it appears that these gifts of land were bestowed for life only.

20 (p. 40). Bellerophon: Hom. *Il.* 6. 193f. Aeneas: 20. 185f. Meleager: 9. 577f. Cf. Ridgeway in JHS 6. 335. The elders (*gérontes*) were *basilêes*, i.e. chiefs of the clans: Glotz SF 12.

21 (p. 41). Hom. *Od.* 11. 533, *Il.* 15. 189, 195, cf. Hes. *Th.* 202. The words *moîra*, *géras*, *timé* are all synonymous in this connection—hence the use of *moîra* in the sense of "honour" or "esteem." The primitive meaning of *timé* appears to have been the reward, in the form of a *géras* or *láchos*, which each of the tribesmen received at the distribution of the products of their labour. The term *géras* is used in the same way, but, since it has also yielded *geraiós* "old", it may have connoted originally those special rights in the distribution of food which are universally enjoyed by the elders, who cannot hunt for themselves, in the early stages of tribal society: Westermarck ODMI 2. 319.

22 (p. 41). *Dasmós: Il.* 1. 166. *Témenos* "set apart" (*exaíreton*): Pind. *O.* 9. 26,

Æsch. *Eum.* 405, Hdt. 4. 159, Thuc. 3. 50. Chosen gift: Hom. *Il.* 1. 368–9, 2. 226–8, Od. 14. 232. Æsch. *Ag.* 945, Eur. *Tro.* 248, 273. Cf. Robertson Smith KMEA 65.

23 (p. 41). Hom. *Il.* 1. 123.

24 (p. 41). *Il.* 9. 330, 367.

25 (p. 41). Telemachos: *Od.* 1. 394–8, cf. Chadwick HA 379. Deiphontes: Apollod. 2. 8. 5. Election to the kingship: cf. Chadwick HA 368, Hubert GDC 220.

26 (p. 41). Hdt. 7. 144.

27 (p. 42). Plut. *M.* 644 A. *Daîs = dasmós*: ci. Hom. *Od.* 8. 470, Hes. *Th.* 544.

28 (p. 42). *Moîrai* of meat equally divided: *Od.* 20. 280–2. By lot: Hom. *H.* 4. 128.

29 (p. 42). Menelaos: *Od.* 4. 65, cf. *Il.* 7. 321, *H.* 4. 122. Eumaios: *Od.* 14. 433.

30 (p. 42). Plut. *M.* 644A, cf. Theogn. 677–8.

31 (p. 42). On the communal feasts of ancient Greece see Fustel de Coulanges CA 3. 179, and cf. Nilsson HGR 255. Guiraud, having dismissed the evidence for common ownership in early Greece, derives the communal feasts from the idea that the gods of the city must eat with the citizens just as the spirits of the dead must eat with the family (PFG 15); but, as Robertson Smith has explained (RS 282), the reason why the god eats with the citizens is that he was originally the ancestor of a tribe or clan—that is, a kinsman, and, as such, entitled to eat with the rest of his kin.

32 (p. 42). Hom. *Il.* 12, 310–21; Ridgeway in JHS 6. 335.

33 (p. 42). Royal honours: Nilsson HM 219, Morgan AS 246. Among the Germans, the kingship was more highly developed in the warlike than in the sedentary tribes: Chadwick HA 367.

34 (p. 42). The lot was democratic (Hdt. 1. 80, Arist. *Pol.* 6. 2. 1317b); it was employed in connection with colonial emigration (Hdt. 4. 153), in determining priority of approach to the Delphic Oracle (Æsch. *Eum.* 32), and possibly for election to the chieftaincy of Attic clans (Toepffer AG 21, 125). It is still used by fishermen in Ireland and elsewhere to divide the catch.

35 (p. 43). See pp. 207–9.

36 (p. 43). Terminology of inheritance: Hes. *Th.* 606, *Op.* 37, Æsch. *Th.* 929, Soph. *O.C.* 1396, *Tr.* 161, Dem. 43, 51; Dareste etc. RIJG xvii. 10. Hom. *Od.* 14. 209, cf. Isae. 6. 25. Attic law: pp. 201–2. Law of Gortyna: Woodhouse in Hastings 7. 305. See further Diamond PL 235.

37 (p. 43). Morgan AS 232. Cf. Diamond PL 241f: "The earliest rules of inheritance arise simply from the fact that the property of the group remains in the group. . . . In the Third Agricultural grade the spread of patrilocal marriage and the weakening of the clan begin to concentrate in the person of the head of the family the control over the members and the property held by them. . . . In systems where the eldest surviving brother succeeds to the property of the family, with a duty to support the members, he maintains the daughters and receives the bride-price in respect of them. In other cases the bride-price usually goes to the sons who 'keep' their sisters. . . . The clan disappears and a narrowed family group emerges as the basic social and economic unit."

38 (p. 43). Testamentary disposition: Diamond PL 249; see p. 201.

39 (p. 44). Hes. *Th.* 73, 112, 383–403, 883, Æsch. *P.V.* 244. This legend is

clearly related to the myth and ritual of the god-king in Egypt and Babylonia: Hooke MR 1–14.

40 (p. 44). Hephaistos: Æsch. *P.V.* 38. Atlas: Hes. *Th.* 520. Nymphs: Hes. *Th.* 348. Apollo and Hades: Stes. 22. Aphrodite: Hes. *Th.* 202, Nonn. *D.* 24. 274–6. Erinyes: Æsch. *Eum.* 173, 335, 730. Asklepios: Æsch. *Ag.* 1004.

41 (p. 44). Hesych. *s. vv.*, Toepffer AG. There were a number of craft-clans in Sparta: Hdt. 6.60.

42 (p. 44). Hdt. 7. 134, cf. Rose PCG 217. The development of hereditary crafts seems to have been a factor in the decline of matrilineal succession and descent, cf. Landtman OISC 83.

43 (p. 45). Gardner in CAH 3. 585.

44 (p. 45). Grönbech CT 1. 35.

45 (p. 45). Hesych. *s. vv.*, Toepffer AG.

46 (p. 46). Wade-Gery in CQ 25. 82.

47 (p. 46). Hdt. 2. 53.

48 (p. 46). Hom. *Od.* 7. 197. The trinity first appears in Hes. *Th.* 218. That the concept of Klothes was already ancient in the Homeric period appears from the generalised use of *epiklótho* (*Il.* 24. 525, *Od.* 1. 17). Another stereotyped expression of the same kind is *theôn en goúnasi keîtai* (*Il.* 17. 514, *Od.* 1. 267) which originally connoted the unworked wool lying on the knees of the spinners: Onians in CR 38. 2.

49 (p. 47). I have rolled up: *Isaiah* 38. 12.

50 (p. 47). I have not yet succeeded in tracing this idea in Greek or Latin literature at all, though it seems to be implied in Verg. *A* 10. 814. In Graeco-Roman art, Klotho is represented as seated and spinning, Lachesis as drawing lots with averted eyes, and Atropos as writing on a tablet: Roscher 2. 3095.

51 (p. 47). She who cannot be turned back: Æsch. *Eum.* 335 (see my note), Plat. *Rp.* 620E, *C.I.G.* 956, Callim. *L.P.* 103, Nonn. *D.* 25. 365, 40. 1, Luc. 2. 638, Eur. fr. 491, Joh. Diac. *ad* Hes. *Sc.* 236.

52 (p. 47). Lucan. *Orph.* fr. 3 (Kern OF 70), *Anth. Pal.* 7. 5, Erinna 23.

53 (p. 47). Hom. *Il.* 20. 127–8, *Od.* 7. 197, Æsch. *Eum.* 348, Eur. *Hel.* 212, *I. T.* 203, *Ba.* 99. cf. Plut. *M.* 637F.

54 (p. 47). Karsten CSAI 1–197, Robertson Smith RS 335; see Chap. I n. 25.

55 (p. 48). Roman children wore round the neck a small box (*bulla*) containing a phallus—the boys until they assumed the *toga virilis*, when it was dedicated to the Lares, the girls probably till marriage: Daremberg-Saglio *s. v.* Bulla. What happened to the Greek *gnorísmata* is not so clear, but it is evident from the case of Orestes that they were carefully preserved, and in at least one instance they were dedicated by a girl at marriage (Long. 4. 37).

56 (p. 48). Cyrus: Hdt. 1. 111. 3.

57 (p. 48). Robertson Smith KMEA 213.

58 (p. 48). Boisacq 704. This same base, which has yielded the I. E. terms for mark and name, is cognate with another, which has yielded Latin *gnosco* and *gens*, Greek *gignósko* and *génos*, English *know* and *kin*. What is the connection between knowledge and kinship? Boisacq assumes that it can only be (1) to know (2) to know how (3) to be able (4) to beget. And this, quite rightly, he rejects. In primitive thought the fact is not deduced from the idea: the idea is deduced from the fact. The starting-point in this case is the fact of kinship. My kinsmen are known to me—*gnotoí* in Greek; and,

since social relations are confined to the circle of kin, strangers are unknown —*uncouth* in English. And the kinsman is known by the sign he wears and by the name he bears—by his totem. We remember how the sons of Hypsipyle claimed kin—that is, made themselves known to her—by revealing the totem of their clan (p. 20).

59 (p. 48). The name was magical, because it embodied the totem or ancestor of the clan. That the peoples of Europe were no exception in this respect is proved by the Germanic evidence, cf. Grönbech CT 1. 258: "Name and fate interpenetrate. The name was a mighty charm, because it carried the history not only of the bearer but of his ancestors and of the whole clan. ... When a new man came into the family, the Norsemen said expressly, Our kinsman is born again—so-and-so has come back. And they confirmed their saying by giving the old name to the young one." So in Greece. In the *Dionysiaka* of Nonnos, which, late though it is, is a storehouse of primitive ideas, Dionysus says to Pentheus (the "Mourner") (46. 73): "A fair name indeed have the Moirai given unto thee, a harbinger of thy death"; cf. Pind. *O*. 10. 49, Æsch. *Ag*. 686. See further Chap. VII n. 3, 7.

60 (p. 49). Spartoi: Chap. I n. 25-6. The Boeotian ships at Aulis carried figureheads representing Kadmos, the ancestor of the Spartoi, holding a snake (Eur. *I.A*. 253).

61 (p. 49). Æsch. *Cho*. 230 sch.

62 (p. 49). Men. 181 Kock (Allinson p. 46), 872 Kock (Allinson p. 260). Cf. Philostr. *Imag*. 1. 26, where we are told that the Horai scattered flowers on the swaddling-bands of the newborn Hermes "in order that they might not lack markings."

63 (p. 49). Reinach O 16, 86, 103. Cf. Headlam in Thomson AO 2. 156, Moret et Davy CE 8, 145, Bancroft NRPSNA 1. 277, Webster PSS 125, Schoolcraft ITUS 196. On the relation of the *manitoo* to the clan-totem see Webster PSS 154.

64 (p. 50). Æsch. *Ag*. 1478, 1568.

65 (p. 50). Æsch. *Th*. 493, *Cho*. 511, Emped. *ap*. Plut. *M*. 474B, Eur. *I.T*. 203, cf. *Hel*. 212, Hom. *Il*. 3. 182. The *daímon genéthlios* of Pind. *O*. 13. 105, is the *pótmos syngenés* of *N*. 5. 41.

66 (p. 50). Childbirth in general: Pind. *N*. 7. 1, *O*. 6. 42, Paus. 8. 21. 3, Plat. *Sym*. 206D. *Deuterópotmos*: Plut. *M*. 265A, Hesych. *s.v.*

67 (p. 50). Marriage of Zeus and Hera: Ar. *Av*. 1731, cf. Pind. fr. 30 Schroeder. Offerings of hair to the Moirai at marriage: Poll. 3. 38. Antiphon fr. 49 Diels.

68 (p. 50). Æsch. *Pers*. 917, *Ag*. 1463, Hom. *Il*. 4. 170, Hes. *Th*. 607.

69 (p. 51). Robertson Smith KMEA 39.

70 (p. 51). Chadwick HA 359, Meillet et Vendryes GCLC 390, Buck CGGL 341.

71 (p. 51). Marett A 196, Briffault M 1 309.

72 (p. 51). Cult of Moirai and Erinyes reserved to women: Eur. *Mel. Vinct.* 18 (Hunt TGFP).

73 (p. 52). Nornen: Paul GGM 3. 282, Mannhardt GM 576, 609. Whether the idea of Moira can be traced in other I.E. languages is more than I can say, but it is worth noting that the Greek *moîra* (1) "share" (2) "esteem" (3) "fate" corresponds to the Irish (1) *cion* (a) "share" (b) "affection" (2) *cinneamhaint* "fate."

74 (p. 52). Matres Deae: Roscher *s.v.*

75 (p. 52). Aesch. *P.V*. 532.

76 (p. 53). Æsch. *Th.* 962–5; Hom. *Il.* 19. 86; Soph. *Aj.* 1389–92, cf. 1326, *Ant.* 1070–5; Æsch. *Eum.* 514–15; Pind. *P.* 4. 145; Plat. *Ll.* 943E, cf. Hes. *Op.* 256f; Heracl. fr. 94 Diels.

77 (p. 54). Æsch. *P.V.* 534. Sarpedon: Hom. *Il.* 16. 433.

78 (p. 54). Hom. *Od.* 11. 292, 22. 413, 1. 17, cf. *Il.* 19. 87.

79 (p. 54). *Moiragétes*: Paus. 5. 15. 5, 8. 37. 1, 10. 24. 4, cf. 1. 40. 4, Eurfr. 620, *El.* 1247, Mel. fr. adesp. 5, Orph. H. 59. 11, fr. 248. 5. The Erinyes were subordinated to Zeus in the same way: Cook Z 2. 1001–2.

80 (p. 54). *Nòmos*: Cornford RP 27. Exactly parallel is the development of *éthos* (1) "haunts" (2) "custom."

CHAPTER IV

1 (p. 59). Earliest settlers in Crete: Hall CGBA 25. Legends of Argos and Attica: Nilsson MOGM 36, 176.

2 (p. 59). Thuc. 1. 4. 1.

3 (p. 59). Judgment of the dead: Thomson AO 2. 191.

4 (p. 60). Distribution of dialects: Nilsson HM 86, Myres WWG 159. Ægean loan-words: Meillet AHLG 65, Glotz CE 386.

5 (p. 60). On the cult of Earth in general see Dieterich ME. At Dodona: Farnell CGS 1. 39, cf. Cook in CR 20. 365. At Delphi: Farnell 3. 9. Poseidon in Attica: Farnell 1. 270. At Argos: Paus. 2. 15. 5, Apollod. 2. 1. 4. In Arcadia: Farnell 3. 50. Zeus and Hera at Olympia: see p. 116. Poseidon was closely associated with the Ionians: Farnell 4. 18, Nilsson HGR 120, MOGM 155, HM 92. Demeter seems to have been connected in origin with the Erinyes. The type of the Erinyes on vases has a snake held in either hand (Roscher 1. 1331–4), like the statuette of the snake-goddess from Knossos, which is one of a pair (Hall CGBA 127–8). The other one answers exactly to Æschylus' description of the Erinyes (*Cho.* 1047–8) and wears a tall hat resembling the *kálathoi* of the *pappádes* discovered at Eleusis and believed to represent Demeter (Farnell CGS 3. 215). In a terra-cotta at the Louvre, Demeter appears with corn-stalks in her hands and snakes coiled round either uplifted arm (Roscher 2. 1359). On a gem in Leningrad she holds poppies, corn and cornucopia, and rides a bull, like the Cretan Europa (Farnell 3. 220): there was a cult of Demeter Europa in Boiotia (Paus. 9. 39. 4). Finally, at Thelpousa in Arcadia she was worshipped as Demeter Erinys. All this requires closer investigation, but it may be suggested provisionally that the evolution of Demeter Erinys was parallel to that of Zeus Moiragetes (p. 54) and reflected the transition from pre-Hellenic Ægean tribal societv to the matrilineal Minoan state.

6 (p. 61). Social organisation of the Achæans: Nilsson HM 212, Chadwick HA 344. Belerophon: Hom. *Il.* 6. 179f. Phoinix: *Il.* 9. 479f. Odysseus: Procl. *Chr.* p. 103 Allen.

7 (p. 62). Chadwick HA 365, Nilsson HM 230.

8 (p. 62). Homeric allusions to tribal organisation: Glotz SF 14. The phratry as a military unit: Morgan AS 237.

9 (p. 62). Cf. Hom. *Il.* 9. 406–9. Thersites: *Il.* 2. 212f.

10 (p. 62). The Homeric Olympus: Nilsson HM 267.

11 (p. 63). Nilsson HGR 158.

12 (p. 63). Cf. Chadwick HA 397. Royal insignia of early Egypt: Moret et

Davy CE 128–44, Peet in CAH 2. 203. Babylonian pantheon: Robertson Smith RS 73, cf. Tylor PC 1. 248: "Among nation after nation it is clear how, man being the type of the deity, human society and human government became the model on which divine society and government were shaped."

13 (p. 64). Chadwick HA, GL 2. 595.

14 (p. 65). Achilles: Hom. *Il.* 9. 189. Contemporary themes: *Od.* 1. 351–2. Minstrel of Mycenae: *Od.* 3. 267f.

15 (p. 66). Sarpedon: Hom. *Il.* 12. 322f.

16 (p. 67). Nilsson HM 130.

17 (p. 67). The decline of the kingship can be traced most clearly in the Attic tradition. Kodros was the last king, his successors being merely *árchontes* for life: under the twelfth of these the office became decennial (752 B.C.) and seventy years later it was made annual and distributed among nine persons elected from the Eupatridai: Grote HG 3. 48.

18 (p. 68). Hes. *Op.* 382.

CHAPTER V

1 (p. 69).Hom. *Il.* 9. 149–56.

2 (p. 69). The Spartan constitution did not assume its historical form until the latter part of the seventh century, when, after a revolt of the serfs, it was reorganised on a more strictly military basis. The principal change was the substitution of five tribes, based on locality, for the three tribes of the primitive Dorian system (Wade-Gery in CAH 3. 560). These changes, together with the institution of all the characteristic social and political features of historical Sparta, such as the *gerousía* and *apélla*, the *pheidítion* and the *agéla*, were traditionally ascribed to Lykourgos who was said to have introduced them from Crete and was dated far earlier than the end of the seventh century. It is clear, however, that the institutions mentioned are much older than that and are primitive Dorian rather than borrowings from Crete. It is questionable whether the militarisation of Sparta was really so abrupt as it was represented to be, but there is no doubt that the early Sparta was as famous for her culture as the later for her lack of it. This contrast is abundantly confirmed by archaeological remains. The early history of Sparta is at present very obscure, but the foreign origin of Alkman of Sardis, Terpandros of Lesbos and Thaletas of Crete suggests that Spartan culture in this period was a development of the same nature as Mycenean, being due to the influence, as intense as it was short-lived, of a highly cultivated indigenous population on their semi-barbarian conquerors.

3 (p. 70). Fifty per cent.: Tyrt. 5. The difference in spirit between Alkman and Tyrtaios is very striking. After Kallinos, an older contemporary at Ephesos, Tyrtaios is the first Greek poet to extol the glory of dying for the fatherland, which is a sure sign of the consolidation of the state. The very word "fatherland" embodies an attempt to invest the state-power with the sanctity of kinship.

4 (p. 70). The danger from the serfs: Arist. *Pol.* 2. 9. 1269b.

5 (p. 70). Thessaly: Bury HG 59. Crete: Wade-Gery in CAH 2. 537. The outlook of the Cretan nobles may be judged from the fragment of a song in which Hybrias addresses his weapons (Diehl 2. 128): "With these

I plough, with these I reap, with these I tread my sweet wine from the grape, with these I make my serfs call me lord."

6 (p. 71). Sikyon and Argolis: Wade-Gery in CAH 2. 536.

7 (p. 71). Economic advantages of the *témenos*: Ridgeway in JHS 6. 335.

8 (p. 71). *Eschatié:* Glotz TGA 35.

9 (p. 71). Glotz TGA 29. Turned adrift: Hes. *Op.* 602. Appropriation of the land: Glotz TGA 35.

10 (p. 72). In post-Homeric Greek the use of *témenos* is confined almost exclusively to a piece of land attached to a temple. The intermediate stage is illustrated by Hdt. 4. 159, where we are told that *teménea* and priestly functions were assigned to the king.

11 (p. 72). Cf. Robertson Smith RS 147, 250.

12 (p. 72). Hosioi of Delphi: Parke in CQ 34. 88.

13 (p. 73). Grönbech CT 1. 343.

14 (p. 73). Odysseus: Hom. *Od.* 7. 142–71, cf. Thuc. 1. 136. 3.

15 (p. 73). There is no trace of purification for homicide in the Homeric or Hesiodic poems (Calhoun GCL 16f). It was not a primitive practice, in Greece or elsewhere (Diamond PL 144f), and it was developed under the landed aristocracy. It is possible, however, that, in regard to pollution, a distinction was drawn between inter-clan homicide and homicide within the clan. The man who was pursued by the Erinyes for the murder of a kinsman, as distinct from the man who had merely killed a member of another clan, may have been regarded from early times as being in some sense polluted: at any rate he was under a curse. For this reason I am inclined to qualify my statement in AO 1. 9 that, "in believing that the idea of blood-pollution was as old as society itself," Æschylus was "essentially at fault." According to Apollo, Clytemnestra was polluted by the blood of Agamemnon (*Eum.* 603), but the Erinyes reject this view on the ground that she was not his kinswoman (606, 608); and this, taken in conjunction with the constant association in his plays of blood-pollution with the Erinyes, suggests that he may have regarded blood-pollution as ancient only in respect of the murder of a kinsman.

16 (p. 74). We are all one kin: cf. Æsch. *Eum.* 986–7.

17 (p. 74). On the influence of the Delphic priesthood in propagating the aristocratic view of homicide see Parke HDO 370.

18 (p. 74). Wade-Gery 'Eupatridæ, Archons and Areopagus' in CQ 25. 1, 77.

19 (p. 74). Thuc. 2. 15.

20 (p. 74). Wade-Gery 11.

21 (p. 76). Ure OT 321.

22 (p. 76). Theagenes: Ure OT 267.

23 (p. 76). On the practice of banishing the whole kin see Glotz SF 473.

24 (p. 76). Aristotle says that almost all legislators belonged to the middle class (*Pol.* 4. 11. 1296a). On the Code of Drakon see Glotz SF 473.

25 (p. 77). Oriental art: Nilsson HM 122.

26 (p. 77). Plat. *Ll.* 735E. "When the have-nots, lacking a livelihood, organise to attack the haves, the lawgiver rids the state of their infectious presence by despatching them under the most favourable auspices to found a colony." Much is still obscure in the early history of Ionia, but the general development of the class-struggle has been well described by Glotz TGA 71.

27 (p. 78). Hes. *Op.* 248f, 307f, 366f, 694, 218.

28 (p. 78). Chaucer *Parson's Tale* 763, cf. Tawney RRC 23.

29 (p. 78). Hom. *Il.* 15. 195.

30 (p. 78). Cf Theocr. 16. 35.

31 (p. 78). Plat. *Prot.* 343B.

32 (p. 79). Pindar: Wilamowitz P 445.

33 (p. 80). Cf. Bowra GLP 142.

34 (p. 80). Thales: Diog. L. 1. 26.

35 (p. 80). Egypt and Babylonia: Burnet GPTP 19, cf. Childe 'The Oriental Background of European Science" in MQ 1. 105.

36 (p. 81). In the Indo-European family of languages the future tense was not evolved until after the dispersal, being formed independently in each group: Meillet IECLI 214. In Homeric Greek it is still immature, as also in modern Russian. There is no future tense in the Australian languages described by Spencer and Gillen NTNTA 449, cf. Mathew TRTQ 214.

37 (p. 81). Similarly, the Russian *mir* means (1) village community (2) peace (3) world. There is evidence that the Latin *mundus* was used originally in reference to the tribal settlement (Cornford RP 53); and in the later Empire, owing to the development of Roman citizenship, it was transferred back again from tne world-order to the social order (French *monde*, cf. Modern Greek *kósmos*). A similar connection between the world-order and the social order can be traced in Chinese: Granet CC 195.

38 (p. 83). Burnet held that Anaximander's *ápeiron* meant spatially infinite, not qualitatively indeterminate (EGP 58); but this view is contradicted by Theophrastos, whose testimony Burnet himself described as specially reliable (73).

39 (p. 82). Cornford RP 7.

40 (p. 83). Calhoun GCL 11.

41 (p. 83). The observation of fossilised sea-shells is ascribed to Xenophanes, not Anaximander: see Burnet EGP 124. Advance of the coast-line: Cadoux AS 8. A gift from Poseidon: Aristid. 17. 16, cf. 15. 378.

CHAPTER VI

1 (p. 85). Meidas and Gyges: Ure OT 133, 143. Evolution of the coinage: Glotz TGA 67.

2 (p. 85). Heracl. fr. 90 Diels. In propounding his theory of the *tension* of opposites Herakleitos seems to have been countering the Pythagorean theory of *fusion* (see pp. 215-17); and, if so, he represents the aristocratic reaction to the popular movement. The first to put forward this interpretation was, I believe, Eleutheropoulos WP 1. 103.

3 (p. 86). Early tyrants: Ure OT 194, 265, cf. Bowra GLP 154. Aristotle says (*Pol.* 5. 5. 5. 1305a): "Most of the early tyrants were originally demagogues: they are not so now, but they were then."

4 (p. 86). On the effects of the introduction of money on prices see Glotz TGA 80. Cf. Bury HG 178: "The introduction of money, which was at first very scarce and led to the accumulation of capital in the chests of successful speculators, was followed by a period of transition between the old system of the direct exchange of commodities and the new system of a metallic medium; and this transitional period was trying to all men of small means." This, though beautifully vague, is true so far as it goes, except for the implication that the system of a metallic medium ceased to be "trying"

to the small man after the transition was over. What the small man felt about it may be illustrated from a remark in Sir Thomas More's *Utopia* (Book II): "So easely might men gette their living if that same worthy princesse lady money did not alone stop up the waye betwene us and our lyving, which in goddes name was most excellently devised and invented that by her the way therto should be opened." See further Engels UFPS 125. For the difference between the old landowners and the new cf. Æsch. *Ag.* 1026–9.

5 (p. 87). Landed wealth comes from God: Thomson AO 2. 107.

6 (p. 87). Thomson AO 2. 48, 50, 104. Ixion: Pind. *P.* 2. 25–40.

7 (p. 87). The interpretation of the term *hektemóros* or *hektemórios* "sixth-partner" is disputed: it is either one who pays over a sixth of his produce (Arist. fr. 351, Plut. *Sol.* 13, cf. Adcock in CAH 2. 35) or one who retains a sixth of his produce (Phot. *s. v. pelátes*, cf. Bury HG 174, Glotz TGA 81). In favour of the latter interpretation, which I have provisionally adopted, it may be pointed out that all the analogous formations from the same root (*ámoros, isómoiros, dimoirítes, trimoirítes, tetramoiría*) denote the possessor or recipient, not the donor. But the matter remains in doubt.

8 (p. 89). Wade-Gery in CQ 25. 80.

9 (p. 89). Adcock in CAH 4. 55.

10 (p. 89). Sol. 5 Diehl.

11 (p. 90). In this account of Peisistratos I have followed in the main Ure OT 33f, particularly in regard to the identification of the Diakrioi with the miners and the location of Semachidai in the mining district.

12 (p. 92). Müller FHG 1. 395, Ure OT 65. This enterprise of the Alkmaionidai is not mentioned by Hasebroek SHAG 44f, although it has an important bearing on his argument. He is undoubtedly right in his view that many historians (including Ure) have exaggerated the extent to which trade was organised in this period of Greek history, but his own conclusions suffer from a failure to distinguish clearly between the initial phase of the commercial revolution and the period following, which was marked by the enormous growth of slave-labour. Thus, the Alkmaionidai, who contracted for the reconstruction of the Delphic temple, may be contrasted with Nikias, who made his money by dealing in slave-labour (Xen. *de vect.* 4. 14). By the end of the sixth century, in the more advanced states, trade had reached the point at which it could only develop further on the basis of an international organisation for the division of labour and the exchange of commodities as between one state and another; and what prevented it from passing that point was the growth of slave-labour.

13 (p. 93). It was perhaps one of these poets who compared the tyranny of Peisistratos to the Reign of Kronos (Arist. *Ath. Rp.* 16. 7); and what he had in mind was no doubt the re-distribution of wealth, particularly of the confiscated estates, which the tyrant had effected; for in Greek tradition the Reign of Kronos was the symbol of primitive communism (see p. 234).

14 (p. 93). Theogn. 291, 53, 847, 699, 425.

CHAPTER VII

This chapter should be read in connection with Hutton Webster's excellent study of *Primitive Secret Societies*. I have also learnt much from Harrison's T, and from Ridgeway's EAG and DDD, although I am convinced that Ridgeway was mistaken in isolating ancestor-worship **from** productive magic, with which it was originally identical. Harrison's method has recently been taken up by Jeanmaire.

1 (p. 97). Spencer and Gillen A 177, 178, 277, Webster PSS 60. The very young and the very old are unable to procure their own food. That is the economic basis of the system of age-grades in its simplest form.

2 (p. 97). Hambly OEPP 284. Another reason why, at least in Australia, initiation is less elaborate for girls may be the decline in the status of women which has already been noted as a tendency characteristic of hunting tribes (p. 16).

3 (p. 97). Frazer TE 2. 302, 3. 298, Daremberg-Saglio 7. 88, Dieterich ME 23, Seebohm SGTS 54. Cf. Karsten CSAI 417: "We must assume that the well-known Indian custom of naming children after certain objects of nature, especially after animals or plants, has a deeper foundation. When the Indians give their children such names, or even names after mountains, rocks, rivers and lakes, as was the custom for instance in ancient Peru, this is evidently originally due to the idea that the soul of the ancestor, re-born in the child, has previously been incarnated or materialised in some of these objects of nature." See Chap. III n. 59. The idea of reincarnation may possibly underly the practice, characteristic of many Australian classificatory systems and a few American (Spencer and Gillen A 41f, Kroeber in JRAI 39. 81), of applying a common term to the father's father and to the son's son, i.e. the grandfather uses the same term of relationship for the grandson as the grandson uses for him. The primitive idea of reincarnation is well explained by Karsten CSAI 416: "When a child is born, the life thus coming into being is not a new life in the strict sense of the word. A spirit which had existed earlier has again assumed that form. It is simply one of the forefathers that reappears in the new-born. And on the other hand, when an Indian dies, he does not by any means cease to exist. Death does not imply the extinction of life. It only implies a transition from one form of life to another. . . . Thus, the human life, including a part of the animal and the plant life, presents an eternal circular course where there is apparently no beginning and no end, where the only things changing are the successive incarnations and transformations through which the soul has to pass."

4 (p. 98). Cureau SMCA 167. The primitive interconnection of these ideas survives in the Greek *gignomai* (1) to be born (2) to become.

5 (p. 98). Webster PSS 38. Cf. D'Alviella in Hastings 7. 318: "Even to-day, in the profession of vows in use among the Benedictines, the novice is laid out on the ground between four candles, and covered with a winding-sheet, the service of the dead is performed over his body, and the whole congregation chants the *Miserere* for him." I am told that the corresponding ritual of the Orthodox Church is of the same nature.

6 (p. 98). Sexual interchange of clothes: Halliday in ABSA 16. 212. As Halliday shows, this custom is especially associated with initiation, marriage and death. Marriage was originally the immediate sequel to initiation (pp. 100, 127, 132) and initiation involved the "death" of the novice. Similarly, in Greece, the hair was cut at the attainment of puberty, marriage, and death (p. 108), and the veil was worn both at marriage and at death (p. 122). Conversely, the rites of burial were designed to ensure that the dead would be born again (p. 115). The interconnection of these ideas is one of **the** keys to the understanding of primitive ritual.

7 (p. 98). A new name means a new life—it makes the bearer a "new man." That is why a new name is given at initiation (Webster PSS 40, Frazer TE 1. 44, 3. 510, 555. Van Gennep RP 120) and in time of sickness (Frazer TE 2. 543); for, as we shall see in a later chapter (p. 377), primitive medicine is primarily concerned with securing that the patient is "born again." That, too, is why Herakles received a new name after purification for homicide (Apollod. 2. 4. 12), purification being a form of regeneration (p. 145); and similarly a new name is assumed at the profession of vows in the Christian Church.

8 (p. 98). Preservation o íthe amputated parts: Webster PSS 36.

9 (p. 100). Webster PSS 1f.

10 (p. 100). Webster PSS 75.

11 (p. 103). Plut. Lycurg. 16–27; Schurtz AM 110f. For primitive parallels to the Spartan "lover" see Jeanmaire CC 450–5, Meek SK 368, Earthy VW 120–1. The Spartan bouagór, leader of the boúa, corresponds to the Bathonga "shepherd," an initiated youth in charge of a group of novices: Junod LSAT 1. 75. Cf. also Hollis NLF 57: "The warriors then seize the boy by the left hand, fasten a leather thong to his little finger, and ask him a question, the answer to which is known only to persons who have been circumcised. . . . In order that the boy shall not forget the answer, the thong is given a sharp jerk, which nearly dislocates the finger." As Nilsson points out (MMR 433, citing Thomsen in AR 9. 397), the flagellation of the Spartan boys "was once a rite in which the boys were struck with the sacred bough, which conferred strength and good luck"—in other words, a rite of initiation. Yet, rejecting Jane Harrison's analysis of the Hymn of the Kouretes in terms of initiation, the same writer declares (477) that "the ideas by which Miss Harrison explains the hymn are peculiar to one period of the development of humanity, that of savagery." Thus do modern scholars preclude themselves from understanding ancient society by refusing to analyse their own. If Nilsson would only examine the history of those learned institutions which have conferred on him his well-merited degrees, or if, the next time he goes to church, he would pause in his devotions to reflect on the place of the font in the development of humanity, he would recognise the marks of "savagery" in the initials attached to his own name, both before and after. See pp. 107, 127, 439.

12 (p. 104). This is doubtless the origin of the fruit-stealer, one of the traditional characters in Spartan drama: Pickard-Cambridge DTC 229. Practices of this kind have a wide distribution and a general connection with primitive secret societies. The double function of Hermes, who is at the same time god of stealing and the god who conducts the soul from life to death and from death to life, is reproduced in the Germanic Wotan. Cf. Höfler KGG 1. 259: "Beim samischen Feste des Hermes Charidotes durfte man stehlen: ein solches Stehlrecht, an gewisse (zum Teil 'heilige') Zeiten gebunden oder auch sonst streng gesetzlich umschränkt, gehört zu den allercharakteristischsten Kennzeichen kultische Männerbünde." Höfler shows that the initiates steal food in their character as spirits of the dead, and conversely it may be conjectured that the food which the European peasantry is accustomed to put out at Christmas-time for the spirits of the dead was formerly consumed by members of these secret societies.

13 (p. 105). Pind. fr. 101, cf. Bowra GLP 40. Agélai in Ionia: C.G.I. 2892, 3326.

14 (p. 105). Arist. *Pol.* 2. 10. 5. 1272a. The education of boys in Crete: Strabo 10. 4; Busolt GG 1. 344.

15 (p. 107). More probably the purpose of the *gamelia* was to admit the bride after marriage to her husband's phratry: Deubner AF 233. Apatouria: Mommsen FSA 323f.

16 (p. 107). Athenian education: Daremberg-Saglio *s.v.* Ephèbe.

17 (p. 107). Oath of allegiance: Poll. 8. 105.

18 (p. 107). *Gymnasiarchos:* pp. 233–4.

19 (p. 107). Haircutting at Sparta: Plut. *Lycurg.* 15, 22. At Athens: Hesych. *s.v. koureôtis,* Suid. *s.v. koureôtes.* The ancients believed that *koûros* "youth" and *kourá* "haircutting" were etymologically connected, and they may have been right: Cook Z 1. 24. The practice of cutting the hair at initiation is also found among the Germans: Grönbech CT 1. 123.

20 (p. 108). Rouse GVO 240, Robertson Smith RS 248, Frazer GB 1. 1. 368.

21 (p. 108). Paus. 8. 34. 2. Amputation of a finger at initiation: Frazer TE 3. 401. As a sign of mourning and a cure for sickness: Crawley MR 1. 274. Has this anything to do with the name of the Idaioi Daktyloi?

22 (p. 108). Æsch. Eum. 760: see p. 280.

23 (p. 108). Cannibalism at initiation: Webster PSS 35.

24 (p. 108). Hes. *Th.* 453f, Apollod. 1. 4. 5, Paus. 8. 36. 3, 9. 2. 7, 9. 41. 16, 10. 24. 6.

25 (p. 109). Poseidon and the horse: Farnell CGS 4. 15. Zeus and the thunderstone: Harrison T 56.

26 (p. 109): Callim. *H.* 1. 52f, Strabo 10. 3. 11, Diod. 5. 20. 2–4. On the Kouretes in general see Lobeck A 1111.

27 (p. 109). Harris B 354.

28 (p 109). Hes. *Th.* 493f, Apollod. 1. 2. 1.

29 (p. 109). Harrison T 1–29.

30 (p. 109). Harrison T 19.

31 (p. 110). Webster PSS 200, 205. Jewish rite of circumcision: Barton in Hastings 3. 679.

32 (p. 110). Hom. *H.* 4. 17f, Callim. *H.* 1. 57, Arat. *Ph.* 32.

33 (p. 110). Korybantes: Lobeck A 640, 1139. Daktyloi: Lobeck A 1156. Iron: Hall CGBA 252, Childe A 29.

34 (p. 110). Birth of Dionysus: Hes. *Th.* 940f, Eur. Ba. 1f, 242f, 286f, Diod. 4. 2. 2, 5. 52. 2, Paus. 3. 24. 3, 9. 5. 2, Apollod. 3. 4. 3, Clem. *Protr.* p. 15 (Abel *Orph.* 196), Plut. *M.* 996c, Philod. *de piet.* p. 16 Gomperz Lycoph. 208 sch. The word *Titan* was originally equivalent to *basileús* or *ánax* (Solmsen in IF 30. 35) and perhaps therefore the Titans were the initiated youths of a royal clan.

35 (p. 111). On adoption as a rite of re-birth see Hartland in Hastings 1. 106. Cf. Grönbech CT 1. 305: "Such re-birth lay in the act of adoption, the seating on the knee, or as the Swedes called it, seating in the lap . . . (308). Adoption full and complete involves a radical change in the son, so that all his thoughts are given a new direction, and the fate or *aldr* that was implanted in him at his first birth is exchanged for that of his new friends." In the same way, at Athens, the man who returned home after being mourned as dead had to be re-adopted into the community by a rite of mimic birth which invested him with a new *moîra* (p. 50). The Athenian rite of adoption was the same as the ceremony for introducing

the true son into his father's phratry: Seebohm SGTS 36. Cf. *Corp. Gloss. Lat.* 4. 304. 44 adoptio pæne naturæ imitatio, Plin. *Paneg.* 8 non in cubiculo sed in templo, nec ante genialem torum sed ante pulvinar Iovis optimi maximi adoptio (*sc.* Traiani a Nerva) peracta est; *John* 3. 5. 3. "Verily, verily, I say unto you, Except a man be born anew, he cannot see the Kingdom of God: Nicodemus saith unto him, How can a man be born when he is old? can he enter a second time into his mother's womb, and be born? And Jesus answered, Verily, verily, I say unto thee, Except a man be born of water and the Spirit, he cannot enter into the Kingdom of God"; *Romans* 8. 13 "For if ye live after the flesh, ye must die; but if by the spirit ye mortify the deeds of the body, ye shall live: for as many as are led by the Spirit of God, these are the sons of God." The Christian baptism is at once an initiation, an adoption, and a regeneration: see further Van Gennep RP 132, Loisy MPMC 261.

36 (p. 111). *Exodus* 12. 48: "And when a stranger shall sojourn with thee, and will keep the passover to the Lord, let all his males be circumcised, and then let him come near and keep it; and he shall be as one that is born in the land."

37 (p. 111). Herakles: Diod. 4. 39. 2.

38 (p. 112). Diod. 5. 52. 2; Cook Z 2. 9.

39 (p. 112). Hom. *H.* 2. 231–62, cf. Frazer A 2. 311.

40 (p. 112). 1 *Cor.* 15. 44.

41 (p. 112). Apollod. 2. 1. 3.

42 (p. 112). Harrison T 14, 61, Lang CM 39, 51.

43 (p. 113). Marett in HJ 8. 394, quoted by Harrison T 63.

44 (p. 113). On the cauldron of apotheosis in general see Cook Z 2. 210 and 1. 676, where he relates it to the Orphic formula "A kid, I have fallen into milk"; Frazer GB 2. 372, 3. 96, A 2. 359, Mannhardt GM 71.

45 (p. 113). Medea: Diod. 4. 51. Ino: Apollod. 3. 4. 3, Paus. 1. 42. 6, 1. 44. 7, 2. 1. 3, 4. 34. 4. Thetis: Hes. *Æg.* fr. 2 *ap.* Ap. Rh. 4. 316 sch.

46 (p. 113). Pelops: Pind. *O.* 1. 23–51, Bacch. fr. 54 Jebb; Cornford in Harrison T 212, Weniger 'Das Hochfest des Zeus in Olympia' in K (1905) 1. I have now rejected Weniger's explanation of the rule for fixing the date of the Games: see my article, 'The Greek Calendar', JHS 63. 52. My explanation of the three foot-races run at the Heraia (p. 117) must also be rejected, being based on a mere miscalculation.

47 (p. 115). Paus. 8. 2. 2.

48 (p. 115). Plut. *Lycurg.* 27, cf. Frazer GB 1. 1. 101, Dieterich ME 49. We still plant flowers on the grave.

49 (p. 116). Physkoa: Paus. 5. 16. 6.

50 (p. 117). Frazer LEHK, GB 1.

51 (p. 117). Hocart K 70. This writer shows that coronation is a form of initiation, but his view that coronation is the primitive form, from which initiation is derived, is absurd.

52 (p. 117). Agrarian magic associated with the kingship: Frazer LEHK 112, Chadwick HA 367, Hubert GDC 219, Moret et Davy CE 147, cf. Hes. *Op.* 225f.

53 (p. 118). Plut. *M.* 675c.

54 (p. 119). Farnell CGS 5. 382. Mannhardt BG 534 derives the torch-race from agrarian magic, and, if this is correct, these races of the Athenian *épheboi* are analogous to the spring and summer festivals discussed in the next chapter.

55 (p. 119). Eleusinian Mysteries: Mommsen FSA 179, Foucart **ME,** Farnell CGS 3. 126.

56 (p. 119). Discovery of agriculture: Isocr. 4. 28. Thesmophoria: **Hdt.** 2. 171 (see p. 308).

57 (p. 120). Adoption: Farnell CGS 3. 153. Peisistratos: Robertson **GRA** 619.

58 (p. 120). Arist. *Pol.* 6. 4. 1319b.

59 (p. 120). Foucart ME.

60 (p. 121). Democratisation of Osiris: Peet in CAH 2. 196.

61 (p. 121). Plut. fr. 23; Cornford in ESPWR 154.

62 (p. 121). Herakles at Eleusis: Apollod. 2. 5. 12, Diod. 4. 14.

63 (p. 122). Ar. *Pl.* 846 sch. Similarly, the Cretan boys used to wear the same cloak summer and winter: Heracl. Pont. 3. 3.

64 (p. 122). The veil of mystical initiation appears on the funerary urn reproduced by Harrison PSGR 547. Veil of marriage: Æsch. *Ag.* 1177–8, Plut. M. 138D, Luc. *Conv.* 8, Poll. 3. 36; Harrison PSGR 520, 532. Veil of mourning: Hom. *H.* 2. 42, 197, *Il.* 24. 93. Veil on the face of the dead: Soph. *El.* 1468, Eur. *Tro.* 623, *Hec.* 432, *Hipp.* 1428, Plat. *Phædo* 118A. Veil of primitive initiation: Fest. p. 128, "The Sacred Spring (*ver sacrum*) was a rite of dedication among the Italians. In times of calamity they vowed to sacrifice all things born to them in the following spring; but, since it seemed barbarous to slaughter innocent boys and girls, when they came of age they veiled them and drove them out beyond the boundaries of the state." The meaning of this ritual will become clearer in the next chapter.

66 (p. 123). Key on the tongue: Thomson AO 2. 7. Opening of the Mouth: Baly in JEA 16. 173, Budge M 172. Ox on the tongue: Thomson *l.c.*

67 (p. 123). Spencer and Gillen AA 2. 290, 382.

68 (p. 124). Plut. *de anima* 6. 4.

69 (p. 124). Plat. *Phaedr.* 247–8.

70 (p. 125). Plut. *M* 561A, Porph. *de abs.* 1. 30.

71 (p. 125). 1 *Cor.* 9. 24.

72 (p. 125). Thomson AO 2. 227; see pp. 272, 357.

73 (p. 125). Orph. fr. 32C Kern. See my article, 'The Wheel and the Crown,' CR 59. 9.

74 (p. 125). Theo Sm. *Math.* p. 14 Hiller.

75 (p. 126). *Epóptes* at Olympia: Headlam in Thomson AO 2. 221, and cf. Paus. 5. 9. 5.

76 (p. 126). Plut. *M.* 593D.

77 (p. 126). *Hebrews* 12. 1.

78 (p. 127). Plat. *Rp.* 363C.

79 (p. 127). Æsch. *Eum.* 214, Ar. *Th.* 973–6 sch., Suid. *s.v. téleios,* Poll. 2. 3, Mullach 2. 57; Harrison in Hastings 7. 322.

80 (p. 129). Plut. *Prov. Al.* 16, Dem. 18. 259.

CHAPTER VIII

1 (p. 130). Farnell CGS 2. 481, cf. 427.

2 (p. 130). Nietzsche GT 37f.

3 (p. 132). Robertson Smith: see Chap. I n. 32.

4 (p. 132). Granet CC 170, 161.

5 (p. 134). Jeanroy OPL. On the Irish *Natureingang* see Jackson ECNP 154.

6 (p. 134). Schmeller CB no. 47.

7 (p. 134). For a general account of these festivals see Mannhardt AWF, Frazer GB 3. 205, 220, 246.

8 (p. 135). Transylvania: Frazer GB 1. 2. 75. Upper Lusatia: G.B. 3. 247. Bohemia: GB 3. 237. Spachendorf: GB 3. 250. Harvest May: GB 1. 2. 47.

9 (p. 136). Kostrubonko: GB 3. 261.

10 (p. 137). Phallic origin of the maypole: Mannhardt BG 416, 469, 521.

11 (p. 137). Saxony: GB 3. 214. Magic doctor: Chambers MS 1. 185, 213.

12 (p. 139). Samos: Diehl ALG 2. 192.

13 (p. 139). Tree-stump: Max. Tyr. 8. 1. Oschophoria: Plut. *Thes.* 22, Procl. *Chr.* 28; Mommsen FSA 282, Harrison T 317.

14 (p. 139). *Pharmakós:* Frazer GB 6. 255.

15 (p. 140). Eur. *Ba.* 1114, 1169, 1180. A. G. Bather 'The Problem of the *Bacchae*' in JHS 14. 244. See further E. R. Dodds 'Maenadism in the *Bacchae*' in HTR 33. 155.

16 (p. 141). *Ba.* 68f, 683f. *Agón: Ba.* 964, 974, 1162. *Pompé:* 965. *Kômos:* 1167, 1173. *Mákar, eudaímon:* 1171, 1180, 1242, 1258.

17 (p. 142). Plut. *M.* 291A.

18 (p. 142). Nilsson GF 274.

19 (p. 143). Plut. *M.* 717A, 299E.

20 (p. 143). Paus. 8. 23. 1.

21 (p. 144). Tanagra: Paus. 9. 20. 4.

22 (p. 144). Diod. 5. 50.

23 (p. 144). Ikaros: Hyg. *Fab.* 30, *Astr.* 2. 4. Perseus: Hom. *Il.* 14. 319 sch.

24 (p. 144). Hom. *Il.* 6. 130f, Soph. *Ant.* 955.

25 (p. 144). Apollod. 3. 5. 1, cf. Hyg. *Fab.* 132.

26 (p. 145). Argos: Plut. *M.* 364F.

27 (p. 145). Nuptial bath: Poll. 3. 43, Eur. *Ph.* 344. Life-giving waters: Eur. *Ph.* 347 sch., Nonn. *D.* 3. 88. Scamander: Ps. Æschin. *Ep.* 10. 3.

28 (p. 145). Cf. Verg. *A* 11, 340 genus huic materna superbum nobilitas dabat, incertum de patre ferebat.

29 (p. 146). Koronis: Diod. 5. 52. Ariadne: Diod. 5. 51. Olympia: Paus. 5. 15. 6. Athens: Arist. *Ath. Rp.* 3. Proitides: Apollod. 2. 2. 2, cf. 1. 9. 13; Paus. 5. 5. 8.

30 (p. 146). Apollod. 2. 2. 2.

31 (p. 146). Proitides transformed into cows: Verg. *E.* 6. 47, Lact. Pl. *ad* Stat. *Th.* 3. 343; Nilsson MOGM 62. Io priestess of Hera: Æsch. *Sup.* 291, Apollod. 2. 1. 3, Hesych. *s.v. Kallithýessa*, Clem. *Str.* 1. 418, Aristid. 2. 3. 8 sch.

32 (p. 146). Euboia was one of the sites of the birth of Epaphos (*Et. Mag. s.v. Euboía*, Strabo 10. 1. 3, cf. Eust. *ad* Hom. 278. 30) and also of the sacred marriage of Zeus and Hera (Steph. Byz. *s.v. Kárystos*). The bull, cow and calf appear on fifth-century coins from Karystos: Head HN 357. The myths of the pursuit of Io and of the marriage of Zeus and Hera are probably duplicates, both being founded on the sacred marriage of the priest of Zeus with the priestess of Hera: Cook Z 1. 453. 458. Apollod. 2. 1. 2.

33 (p. 147). Plut. *de fluv.* 18.

34 (p. 147). Cook Z 1. 437.

35 (p. 148). Plut. *M.* 295b. This argument from the Heraeis cannot be

relied on, because the name may be no older than the Corinthian occupation of the district: see Payne P 21.

36 (p. 148). Harrison T 132.

37 (p. 148). Phot. *s.v. nebrízo.*

38 (p. 149). Meliastai: Paus. 8. 6. 5. Dionysiastai: *C.I.G.* 2525b. Patrai: Paus. 7. 20. 1. The presence of a man, even as leader, in the Dionysiac *thíasos,* calls for further explanation. It is agreed that the costume of the tragic actor, including the high boot or *kóthornos,* is derived from the cult of Dionysus (Haigh AT 239); and it appears that in ordinary life the *kóthornos* was worn principally by women (Ar *Lys.* 657, *Ecc.* 346, Hdt. 1. 155) —another sign that the art of "the buskined stage" originated in a society of women. Dionysus himself wears the *kóthornos,* also the *krokotós,* a woman's over-mantle, and the *mítra,* a headband used by women for fastening the hair (Ar. *Ran.* 46, 557, Ath. 198c, Poll. 4. 116): that is his attire in the vase-painting reproduced on p. 95. It is also known that men participating in Dionysiac rites wore female dress (Lucian 3. 147, Eur. *Ba.* 821–36). If, then, the leader of the *thíasos* was a man in woman's dress, we may infer on general grounds with some confidence (see Briffault M 2. 531 f) that the leader had once actually been a woman, and the change of sex is explained as the first step towards male control of what had been originally an exclusively female cult.

39 (p. 149). The association of Satyroi and Silenoi with Dionysus seems to have originated in Attica and Ionia: Kühnert in Roscher *s.v.* Satyros.

40 (p. 149). Oleiai: Plut. *M.* 299E. Thyiades: Paus. 10. 4. 3. Dionysiades: Paus. 3. 13. 7. Dysmainai: Hesych. *s.v.* cf. Paus. 3. 20. 4.

41 (p. 149). Diod. 4. 3.

42 (p. 149). Lenaion: Farnell CGS 5. 317. There was also a cult of Dionysos Leneus at Mykonos: Dittenberger SIG 615. 25. The ancients derived *Lénaia* from *lenós* "wine-press" (Clem. *Protr.* 1. 2. 2 sch.) and this etymology has been accepted by Mommsen FSA 377 and Foucart CDA 102. The objection advanced by Ribbeck AEDA 13, that *lenós* would have yielded *leneîos,* like *oikeîos* from *oîkos,* whereas *lenaîos* presupposes *léna* (cf. *anankaîos, biaîos*) is not decisive because this rule is not without exceptions, e.g. *nesaîos* from *nesós* (Buck CGGL 318); but what is decisive is the positive evidence pointing to *lénai* = *bákchai*: Heracl. fr. 15, Hesych. *s.v. lenaí,* Strabo 468, etc.

CHAPTER IX

1 (p. 151). Periandros: Hdt. 1. 23.

2 (p. 151). Kleisthenes: Hdt. 5. 67.

3 (p. 152). Arion: Hdt. 1. 23.

4 (p. 152). Dionysus on shipboard: Farnell CGS 5. 358; Philostr. *V.S.* 1. 25. 1, Aristid. 1. 373, 440, Hdt. 1. 150. Orpheus as a singer: Æsch. *Ag.* 1630, Eur. *Med.* 543, *Alc.* 357, *I.A.* 1211, Plat. *Prot.* 315A; Kern OF 14f. Death of Orpheus: Kern OF 33f. Tainaron: Kern OF 65. Head of Orpheus at Lesbos: Philostr. *Her.* 2. 306. Head of Dionysus: Paus. 10. 19. 3. The head was perhaps regarded as the seat of the soul: Cook Z 2. 290.

5 (p. 153). Kretschmer GGS 241. I have not expressed any opinion as to the date at which the cult of Dionysus emerged as such, because it is a difficult question and from my point of view the important thing is not the

association of the cult with his name but the cult itself. It may be remarked however that the coming of Dionysus is not proved to be post-Homeric by the fact that he is almost wholly ignored in the *Iliad* and *Odyssey*, because the same is true of Demeter, whose worship is admitted to be far older than Homer. The reason why these two deities have no place in the Homeric Olympus is probably that, as agrarian deities of the pre-Achæan population, they had no place in the worship of the Achæan ruling chiefs. The myths relating to the opposition encountered by Dionysus on his wanderings may, it is true, reflect state resistance to what was essentially a pre-state cult, but their significance may also be ritual rather than historical: Bather in JHS 14. 244, Tierney in JHS 57. 19.

6 (p. 153). Orpheus and Pangaion: Kern OF 33, 35, 37, 42, 57. Mines of Pangaion: Arist. *Ath. Rp.* 15, Hdt. 5. 17, Strabo 331. 34, Liv. 45. 29, Justin 8. 3, Oros. 3. 12.

7 (p. 153). Onomakritos: Kern OF 53. Lasos: Pickard-Cambridge DTC 22.

8 (p. 153). Ure OT 33, 307.

9 (p. 154). Cf. Gomperz GD 1. 135, Glotz SF 399. Guthrie speaks of the worship of Dionysus as "spreading like wild-fire through Greece" (OGR 48) but does not seek a cause for the conflagration.

10 (p. 155). Hes. *Op.* 256, *Th.* 901, Plat. *Ll.* 943E, Pind. *O.* 13. 6.

11 (p. 156). Kern OF 94.

12 (p. 156). Sol. 3. 14.

13 (p. 156). Empedokles: Burnet GPTP 73.

14 (p. 157). On the conservative influence of the Eumolpidai under the democracy see MacKendrick in HSCP 49. 271.

15 (p. 157). Plat. *Phædo* 62B–D.

16 (p. 158). Heracl. fr. 8, Parmen. 1. 14, 8. 14, 8. 37, 10. 6.

17 (p. 158). Plat. *Rp.* 616c.

18 (p. 158). Thomson AO 2. 345.

19 (p. 158). Sisyphos: Guthrie OGR 190.

20 (p. 159). Kern OF 106.

21 (p. 159). The Orphic Wheel: Kern OF 244; Diog. L. 8. 14. Wheel of torture: Anacr. 54. 7, Ar. *Pl.* 875, *Pax* 452, Dem. 39. 40, Andoc. 1. 43, Plut. *M.* 19E, 509B, Plat. *Rp.* 361E, *Gorg.* 473C.

22 (p. 160). Slave-revolt in Attica: Diod. 34. 2. 19, Ath. 6. 272F.

23 (p. 160). Thuc. 7. 27; Bury HG 485, Gomme PAFFC 20.

24 (p. 160). Diod. 3. 11.

25 (p. 161). Dutt IT 362.

26 (p. 161). Diod. 5. 38.

27 (p. 162). Plat. *Phædo* 114B–C.

28 (p. 162). Burnet EGP 223: "The 'cave' is not originally Platonic but Orphic." And it was of course older than Orphism: Knight CG.

29 (p. 162). Guthrie contends that the Orphics cannot have practised the Dionysiac *omophagia* because they preached abstention from meat, but this argument is disproved by Eur. fr. 472, where the initiate claims to have abstained from meat and to have participated in the *omophagia* as well. Even among Christians, there are total abstainers who drink wine at communion.

30 (p. 163). Kern OF 34.

31 (p. 163). Branchidai: Farnell CGS 4. 226. Parke HDO 21 doubts the authenticity of the traditions relating to the intoxication of the Delphic

priestess, at least for the pre-Hellenistic period; but some of his assumptions are open to question, and he has made no attempt to treat the problem from the standpoint of comparative religion: see Fallaize in Hastings 10. 125.

CHAPTER X

1 (p. 165). The data for the City Dionysia will be found in Haigh AT 6. Deubner insists that the order of events given in *I.G.* 2. 1006. 12, 1011. 11. must be taken as it stands, and he treats the sacrifices mentioned in these two inscriptions as distinct, with the result that Haigh's sequence of *pompé—thysia—kômos* is duplicated. But the words *eis to théatron* are against this, and it is clear from other examples that these regulations were sometimes worded rather carelessly. In the law of Euegoros (Dem. 21. 10) the *kômos* is mentioned after the dithyrambs; in an inscription from Eleusis referring to the Country Dionysia the *thysia* is mentioned before the *pompé* (*I.G.* 2. 949. 31); and see further *I.G.* 2. 1245. 3, 1247. 7.

2 (p. 166). Worthy of the god: *C.I.A.* 2. 470.

3 (p. 166). Beds of ivy-leaves: Philostr. *V.S.* 2. 1.

4 (p. 166). *Pompike hodós:* Paus. 5. 15. 2, 5. 15. 7.

5 (p. 167). Dem. 21. 10.

6 (p. 167). Plut. *M.* 364F.

7 (p. 167). Plut. *M.* 299B.

8 (p. 167). The vase-painting is reproduced by Pickard-Cambridge DTC 113.

9 (p. 168). *Agôn:* C.I.A. 2. 307. The following account of the mature dithyramb is based on the data collected by Pickard-Cambridge DTC 5f.

10 (p. 169). Archil. 77.

11 (p. 269). Æsch. fr. 355.

12 (p. 170). Simon. 145 Bergk, *Anth. Pal.* 6. 213.

13 (p. 170). Pind. *O.* 13. 18.

14 (p. 170). Hymn of the Kouretes: Harrison T 7.

15 (p. 171). Payment of the flute-player: Plut. *M.* 1141D.

16 (p. 271). Bergk PLG 3. 496.

17 (p. 171). Paus. 1. 20. 3, 1. 29. 2; Suid. *s.v. Melanaigís.*

18 (p. 172). Cf. Ar. *Vesp.* 270 sch.

19 (p. 172). Arist. *Poet.* 4. 14. 1449A.

20 (p. 173). All the extant tragedies of Sophokles and Euripides begin with a prologue in iambic trimeters, and all except two end with a passage in anapæsts or trochaic tetrameters. The exceptions are the *Trojan Women*, which ends in lyric, and the *Iphigeneia at Tauris*, the end of which is doubtful. Further, all these conclusions except one (in the *Trachiniæ*) are delivered by the Chorus. The *Choephoroi* and *Prometheus Bound* of Æschylus conform to the same type; and so does the *Agamemnon*, except that there the tetrameters are spoken by an actor. The *Seven* begins with an iambic prologue; the conclusion is doubtful. The *Eumenides* begins in the same way, but ends with an anapæstic parœmiac appended to a passage of lyric. On the other hand, in the *Suppliants* and *Persians*, the two earliest of the extant plays, not only is the conclusion in lyric (in the former a processional, in the latter a lament) but there is no prologue. Both begin with an anapæstic *párodos* delivered by the Chorus as it enters the orchestra.

CHAPTER XI

1 (p. 176). Arist. *Poet.* 4. 16. 1449A.

2 (p. 176). Kranz S 16. Kranz's view that tragedy began with the bisection of the dithyrambic chorus rests on the assumption that the Herald of the *Suppliants* is the leader of a Chorus of Egyptians; and that assumption is unsupported by the evidence.

3 (p. 178). Arist. *Rh.* 3. 1.

4 (p. 180). Arist. *Poet.* 4. 17. 1449A.

5 (p. 180). Pickard-Cambridge DTC 117.

6 (p. 180). Xanthos and Melanthos: Ar. *Ach.* 146 sch., Plat. *Sym.* 208D sch.; Usener in AR (1904) 303, Farnell CGS 5. 234 and in JHS 29. 47, H 17. 21.

7 (p. 180). Chambers MS 1. 212.

8 (p. 181). Eur. *Ba.* 934f; Bather in JHS 14. 250.

9 (p. 181). Arist. *Poet.* 4. 17. 1449A. Trochaic was one of the rhythms employed in the ecstatic dances of the Korybantes and the Bakchai: Plut. *M.* 759A.

10 (p. 181). On current theories of the significance of *hypokritēs* see Bywater AAP 136, Pickard-Cambridge DTC 110.

11. (p. 181). Hom. *Il.* 12. 228, *Od.* 19. 535, 555, 15. 170.

12 (p. 182). Plat. *Tim.* 72A–B.

13 (p. 183). Webster PSS 178.

14 (p. 184). The origin of antiphony is traced by Wallaschek AT 257 to co-operative tribal ritual.

15 (p. 185). Hom. *Il.* 24. 720, cf. 18. 49, 316.

16 (p. 185). *Skólion*: Bowra GLP 402. It is not certain that the melody was repeated in identical form, but the structure of the extant *skólia* shows that in rhythm at any rate there was little variation. The compelling power of the incantation survived in the ritual structure of the prayer (Bowra GLP 192) as used by Sappho in her Ode to Aphrodite, where she first prays to the goddess to come and console her, then *envisages* her as coming and consoling her, and finally repeats the prayer. The central theme, creating the illusion of the desired reality, is directly descended from mimetic magic, and in virtue of its origin it imparts to the prayer, when repeated at the end, an added force which it did not possess at the beginning. This consideration may throw light on the origin of three-part form, which is almost as prominent in ancient Greek poetry as it is in modern music. Further, the last five syllables of the Sapphic stanza consist of an Adonius, which was probably used in the traditional dirges for Adonis (Diehl ALG 1. 334), and Sappho is known to have written songs for this cult (*A.P.* 7. 407). Is the cadence a lingering echo of the lost refrain?

17 (p. 186). Plut. *M.* 299B.

18 (p. 187). Phrygian mode: Arist. *Pol.* 5. 6. 23. 1340b, cf. 5. 7. 9. 1342b. The Phrygian mode was employed by the Bakchai and the Korybantes: Plut. *M.* 759A.

19 (p. 188). Arist. *Poet.* 10. 1–4. 1452a, 11. 4. 1452a.

20 (p. 188). Chambers MS 2. 1.

21 (p. 189). Æsch. *Sup.* 473.

22 (p. 189). Æsch. *Cho.* 886–7.

23 (p. 190). Schulz in Pauly *s.v.* Rätzel.

24 (p. 190). Klearchos: Ath. 448c.
25 (p. 190). Sheppard OTS p. xvii.
26 (p. 190). Sphinx: Paus. 9. 26; Frazer A 1. 347, Robert O 48, 97.
27 (p. 191). Ath. 457c, 451B, Plut. *M.* 717A.
28 (p. 191). Flickinger GT 57f.
29 (p. 192). Hor. *A.P.* 276. Thespis: Pickard-Cambridge DTC 97.
30 (p. 193). Chambers MS 2. 68.
31 (p. 194). Pickard-Cambridge DTC 32.

CHAPTER XII

1 (p. 200). The *phylé* and *dêmos* were military units: Isæ. 2. 42.
2 (p. 200). Gardner in CAH 3. 584.
3 (p. 201). A convenient summary of the Attic and Gortynian Codes will be found in Hastings 7. 304; see further Diamond PL, Dareste, etc. RIJG.
4 (p. 202). Status of Spartan women: Grote HG 2. 383.
5 (p. 204). Arist. *Pol.* 2. 9. 1270a. The last sentence in this passage from Aristotle I take to mean that daughters shared in the inheritance as well as sons and were given in marriage by the father or his male heir. It may be inferred that there was nothing corresponding to the Attic law of the *epíkleros,* and this is confirmed by Hdt. 6. 57.
6.(p. 204) Plut. *Lycurg.* 15.
7 (p. 204). "Ruled by women": Arist. *Pol.* 2. 9. 7. 1269b. This view about the original Dorian settlement of Sparta cannot be pressed without further investigation. If sound, its paralleled by what Tacitus says of the Germans: *G.* 15.
8 (p. 204). Justin. 2. 6., Suid. *s.v. Prometheús;* Varro *ap.* Aug. *C.D.* 18. 9 isto Cecrops oraculo accepto, cives omnium utriusque sexus (mos enim tunc in eisdem locis erat ut etiam feminæ publicis consultationibus interessent) ad ferendum suffragium convocavit. . . . Triplici supplicio dicit idem auctor ab Atheniensibus affectas esse mulieres: ut nulla ulterius ferrent suffragia, ut nullus nascentium maternum nomen acciperet, ut ne quis eas Athenæas vocaret. Varro is a late author, but this is a tradition which nobody would have thought of inventing.
9 (p. 206). Walker in CAH 4. 143.
10 (p. 207). Walker in CAH 4. 144.
11 (p. 208). The Athenian institution of ostracism, found also at Syracuse under the name of *petalismos,* was probably another modified survival or revival of tribal custom: Glotz SF 483f.
12 (p. 208). Arist. *ap.* Plat. *Ax.* 371D sch. The whole subject of tribal co-operation in production, administration and ritual would repay closer study.
13 (p. 209). Diod. 2. 39; Farrington DS 37.
14 (p. 210). On the political significance of early Pythagoreanism see Delatte EPP (who however assumes that it was aristocratic) and Thomson AO 2. 346.
15 (p. 210). Aristoxenos: Stob. *Anth.* 1. p. 20. 1, quoted by Burnet EGP 99. Cf. Head HN li: "The coinage appears simultaneously in all the Greek cities of southern Italy during the supremacy of Kroton, but still some time before the destruction of Sybaris." More recently the whole problem, including the numismatic evidence, has been reinvestigated by von Fritz, who

writes: "Kroton exercised a widespread economic and probably also political influence in southern Italy towards the end of the sixth and throughout the first half of the fifth century" (PPSI 85)—the period of the Pythagorean ascendancy. The implication is that under Pythagorean leadership Kroton pursued a vigorous policy of commercial expansion with the aim of uniting the cities of S. Italy in some sort of federation. von Fritz concludes that, while the later Pythagoreans were extreme conservatives, there had been a time when they were opposed to the established order represented by the aristocracy (97–8). His political analysis is not altogether clear, but he agrees with me in recognising that after the initial period there was a radical change in Pythagorean politics—a change from progressive to conservative. The Pythagorean aim of centralising the Italian cities may be compared with the proposal attributed to Thales, urging the Ionians to form themselves into a single state centred at Teos (Hdt. 1. 172). Both failed: see Chap. VI n. 12.

16 (p. 211). Condorcet EPEH.
17 (p. 211). Diog. L. 8. 3.
18 (p. 211). Burnet EGP 90.
19 (p. 212). Diog. L. 8. 14f. On the Pythagorean "ox on the tongue" see Thomson AO 2. 7.
20 (p. 212). Bury HG 317.
21 (p. 213). Tawney RRC 87, 102, 104, 124; Pirenne HE 580.
22 (p. 215). Fisher HE preface.
23 (p. 215). Burnet GPTP 48.
24 (p. 216). Theo Sm. *Math.* p. 12 Hiller, Philol. *ap.* Nicom. *Ar.* 2. 19, cf. Plat. *Sym.* 186D.
25 (p. 217). Theogn. 189.
26 (p. 218). Alcmæon *ap.* Aet. 5. 30. 1, cf. Galen. 19, 343 Kühn.
27 (p. 218). Hipp. *Ant. Med.* 3.

CHAPTER XIII

1 (p. 224). Walker in CAH 4. 265.
2 (p. 225). Bury HG 322. If I have laboured this point against Bury, it is not because his text-book is highly esteemed by specialists, but because it is still widely used in English schools and universities, and the passage quoted is an instance of the sort of nonsense on which the younger generation looks up but is not fed.
3 (p. 229). Walker in CAH 5. 47; Plut. *Cim.* 5.

CHAPTER XIV

1 (p. 232). The regulations governing the *choregía* are given in full by Haigh AT 31.
2 (p. 233). Themistokles and Phrynichos: Walker in CAH 4. 172.
3 (p. 234). Plut. *Cim.* 10.
4 (p. 235). Pickard-Cambridge DTC 90, 124, 131, 149, 167.
5 (p. 236). Arist. *Poet.* 4. 1449a.

6 (p. 236). Plat. *Sym.* 221E, Plut. *Cat. Ma.* 7.
7 (p. 237). DTC 124.
8 (p. 237). DTC 128.
9 (p. 238). Cornford OAC.
10 (p. 239). DTC 329.
11 (p. 239). DTC 347.
12 (p. 239). DTC 245.
13 (p. 239). Peloponnesian drama: DTC 225, 253.
14 (p. 240). Lenaia: DTC 237.
15 (p. 241). Ar. *Ach.* 247f.
16 (p. 241). Ar. *Ran.* 482 sch.
17 (p. 241). Arist. *Poet.* 4. 1449a.
18 (p. 242). Thomson AO 2. 352.
19 (p. 242). Murray in Harrison T 341.
20 (p. 244). On the *Proteus* see Headlam in CP 112, Mazon E 2, 34.

CHAPTER XV

The next three chapters are devoted to an analysis of the surviving plays of Æschylus, in which the *Oresteia* and *Prometheus* are dealt with fully, the other three much more summarily and briefly. The reasons for this discrimination are, first, that the *Oresteia* and *Prometheus* are the greatest of the seven and the most interesting to modern readers, and secondly that, not having published my work on the others, I am not in a position to discuss them in detail without entering into problems too technical for a book of this kind. The plays are cited by Wecklein's numeration, which is followed by Headlam in his prose translations and by me in my editions of the *Oresteia* and the *Prometheus Bound*. Those editions include verse-translations. I hesitate to recommend my translation of the latter, which in many respects is faulty, and, if I recommend my version of the *Oresteia*, it is mainly for the sake of the textual recension on which it is based. Apart from this, R. C. Trevelyan's rendering of the *Oresteia* (he has also done an excellent rendering of the *Prometheus*) is in many ways more adequate than mine.

1 (p. 245). The data for the life of Æschylus will be found in Wilamowitz-Moellendorff AT 3. The name Aischylos occurs in the genealogy of the royal clan of the Kodridai: Petersen QHGA 90.

2 (p. 245). Cic. *T.D.* 2. 23; Wilamowitz-Moellendorff AT 11.

3 (p. 246). On the date of the *Prometheus* see Thomson APB 38, where the views of Bethe PGTA 159 and of Schmid UGF are discussed, and Yorke in CQ 30. 152. The linguistic and metrical evidence is ignored altogether by the latest editor, Rapisarda. Kranz S 226 maintains that the second and third *stásima* are post-Æschylean, but his arguments do not bear examination. He says that "das zweite und dritte Stasimon sind von einer für die aischyleische Tragödie unerhörten Kürze." This is untrue. Divided according to the Alexandrian *kôla*, the second contains 39 verses, the third 35; divided in the same way, the last *stásimon* of the *Choephoroi* (934) contains 40 verses, while *Sup.* 422 contains only 22. Referring to the theme of the second—"der Erinnerung an glücklichere Zeit, glücklichere Stimmung, Gamos und Hymenaios"—he says that "es ist der Stil, der Gedanke der *Antigone*- und *Medeazeit*"; but the same contrast, including the *gámos* and *hyménaios*, is found at *Ag.* 703–16. Finally he remarks that "die Anadiplosis

des Eingangs . . . entspricht ganz der späteren Weise"; but a similar anadi-plosis has been restored by Weil at *Ag.* 1483, and, whether this restoration is sound or not, there is no reason to suppose that such a use of language is post-Æschylean.

4 (p. 247). On the history of the tradition see Wilamowitz-Moellendorff AO 3, Bowra in CQ 28. 115, Parke HDO 309, Thomson AO 2. 355.

5 (p. 248). Among the Incas of Peru: Karsten CSAI 402.

6 (p. 248). Paus. 3. 22. 1, 8. 34. 2, 2. 31. 4.

7 (p. 248). Hdt. 1. 68.

8 (p. 249). The following account of the *Oresteia* is taken from Thomson AO 1. 13, where full references are given.

9 (p. 267). In recognising her brother's footprints Elektra displays the sort of knowledge that all primitive peoples possess, cf. Junod LSAT 2. 54–5. I have myself seen Irish peasant girls round the fire comparing their family likenesses in feet. The same consideration applies to the lock of hair, for "hair patterns in olden days were tribal marks" (Earthy VW 89).

10 (p. 274). Firm Mat. *de. err. prav. rel.* 22.

11 (p. 277). Athena was associated with various birds, especially the owl, and bird-cults were prominent in Minoan religion: Nilsson HGR 27. On this subject Halliday writes in CAH 2. 622: "The evidence for the direct worship of birds as pre-anthropomorphic deities is purely hypothetical, and comparative anthropology must give a verdict against its inherent probability. . . . Recorded examples of any definite cult of a bird are exceedingly rare in any stage of culture in any part of the globe." One has only to glance at the evidence amassed by Frazer in his TE to see that this statement is baseless. The Australian totems enumerated by Spencer and Gillen NTCA 768 include 31 species of mammals, 8 of fish, 24 of insects, 22 of plants, 53 of reptiles, and 46 of birds. At all stages of culture and in all parts of the globe totemic cults of birds and totemic taboos on birds are just as common as the totemic cults and taboos relating to other animals.

12 (p. 277). Apollod. 3. 14. 6; see Frazer *ad loc.*

13 (p. 277). Varro *ap.* Aug. *C.D.* 18. 9.

14 (p. 278). Paus. 10. 28. 7; see p. 54.

15 (p. 280). Tierney in JHS 57. 20f.

16 (p. 283). Isocr. 15. 254, 4. 39, cf. Æl. *V.H.* 3. 38.

17 (p. 284). Thomson AO 1. 58.

18 (p. 288). So too Engels declared that "the emancipation of woman will only be possible when woman can take part in production on a large, social scale, and domestic work no longer claims anything but an insignificant amount of her time" (UFPS 184, cf. Lenin SW 9. 494f). Hence the liberty enjoyed by women in the U.S.S.R.: see Webb SC 805f.

19 (p. 289). Thomson AO 2. 300.

20 (p. 290). Plat. *Rp.* 434c.

21 (p. 290). Epic. *ap.* Diog. L. 10. 150, 152.

22 (p. 290). Thrasymachos: Plat. *Rp.* 338c.

23 (p. 294). So Athena says (vv. 861–7):

> Lay not upon my territories the spur
> Of civil strife . . .
> Let battle rage, for every heart possessed
> By love of glory, abroad! That shall be theirs
> In plenty.

Having carried civil war to the point of placing themselves in power, the

middle class denounce it and turn to wars of conquest (see p. 231). Cf. 1 *Henry IV* 1. 1:

> No more the thirsty Erinnys of this soil
> Shall daub her lips with her own children's blood . . .
>   Therefore, friends,
>   As far as to the sepulchre of Christ . . .

How closely great minds think alike!

CHAPTER XVI

1 (p. 299). Hyg. *Fab.* 168, Nonn. *D.* 3. 308–9; *Sup.* 715–17; see Thomson AO 2. 269. Hypermnestra: Paus. 2. 19. 6, 2. 20. 7, 2. 21. 1–2. Aigyptos: Eur. *Or.* 871 sch. Danaos and irrigation: Hes. *Cat.* fr. 16, Strabo 8. 6. cf. Müller FHG 2. 258; Semple GMR 462. Amymone: Paus. 2. 37. 1. Danaides: Harrison PSGR 613.

2 (p. 299). Halliday in ABSA 16. 212; see p. 98.

3 (p. 299). Hdt. 6. 77.

4 (p. 299). Kinkel EGF 78.

5 (p. 299). Lemnos: Apollod. 1. 9. 17; Bachofen M 84.

6 (p. 301). On the rhythmical design of the trilogy see Thomson GLM 81.

7 (p. 301). *Sup.* 88f.

8 (p. 302). On legal phraseology in this play see H. G. Robertson in CR 50. 104.

9 (p. 302). *Sup.* 392–4.

10 (p. 302). Royal endogamy in Egypt: Griffith in Hastings 8. 443. Among the Hebrews: Rivers SO 217. Cf. p. 33, and see further Briffault M 1. 384.

11 (p. 303). Æsch. *P.V.* 880–5.

12 (p. 303). *Sup.* 944.

13 (p. 303). *Sup.* 6–10; see Headlam and Wilamowitz *ad loc.*

14 (p. 303). *Sup.* 335–41.

15 (p. 304). Eur. *Med.* 232–3, cf. 236–7, 252–8.

16 (p. 304). Marett A 196.

17 (p. 304). Ridgeway in CP 156, OT 190. Against this interpretation G. H. Macurdy in *Class. Phil.* 39. 95 argues that in Attic law a man who had no sons could leave his daughter, together with his estate, to anyone he liked, not necessarily a kinsman. True, but only by adopting the legatee as his son, thereby evading the claim of the next-of-kin. The legal fiction testifies to the strength of the obligation which it was designed to . circumvent. Miss Macurdy goes on to remark that at v. 339 the choice between *onotto* and *onoito* is "almost anybody's guess." But not quite. Apart from everything else, the reading *onotto* is textually the more probable; for the verb *ónomai* is found nowhere else in Attic, and the same corruption occurs at Eur. *Alc.* 59. I think Miss Macurdy might have noticed this, seeing how ready she is to believe that I have allowed my "preconceived views" to run away with my judgment.

18 (p. 305). Arist. *Pol.* 5. 4. 1303b–1303a.

19 (p. 305). D. S. Robertson in CR 38. 51.

20 (p. 306). That the Athenians regarded marriage with a kinswoman as entirely right and proper appears from Isæ. 7. 12: "Matrimonial unions, not only with one's own kin but even with other persons, have the effect of heal-

ing serious disputes, if the contracting parties entrust one another with their closest interests." Similarly, in Plat. *Ll.* 924, the legislator arranges matches for women in a way which shows that he is solely concerned with the nearness of kin and the preservation of the property.

21 (p. 307). Æsch. fr. 44.

22 (p. 307). *P.V.* 891. Later writers give a different version: see E. Harrison in PCPS 160–2. 8. Harrison asserts that the interpretation "desire for children" is more consonant with the tragic usage of *pais*. On the other hand, the interpretation "one of the children" seems to be more consonant with the order of the words: see Thomson AO 2. 383.

23 (p. 308). D. S. Robertson in CR 38. 50.

24 (p. 308). Hdt. 2. 171.

25 (p. 308). Harrison PSGR 120.

26 (p. 311). On the legend of Œdipus as treated in this trilogy see Robert O 252. The interpretation offered here owes a good deal to Solmsen in TAPA 68. 197. On the question of interpolation see Schmid-Staehlin 1. 2. 215, Page AIGT 30.

27 (p. 312). Plato says (*Ll.* 721B) that by means of marriage mankind partakes of immortality, which all desire. Marriage was compulsory in Crete and officially encouraged at Sparta: see pp. 104–6.

28 (p. 312). *Th.* 735. The words might also mean "prevailed upon by his (own) sweet folly," and that is how Mazon understands them, but the rendering given in the text seems to me the more natural.

29 (p. 312). *Th.* 770–1, Soph. *O.C.* 1375 sch. A different version is given in Ath. 465E.

30 (p. 313). *Th.* 69–75.

31 (p. 313). Cf. 813, where the two brothers are described as having died childless—a passage which is likely to be authentic, because it contradicts the received version of the legend; and for the same reason I agree with Verrall in rejecting the allusion to the Epigonoi at 886, which violates the strophic correspondence as well as being incompatible with 813.

32 (p. 313). *Th.* 192–4.

33 (p. 314). *Th.* 584–606.

34 (p. 314). *Th.* 640–2.

35 (p. 315). *Th.* 659–62.

36 (p. 315). *Th.* 696–8. The Chorus plead (687) that, when Eteokles has sacrificed to the gods, the Erinys will quit his house, implying that release from the clan-curse can be found in state-religion. Similarly, in *Phædr.* 244D, Plato says that men can be cured of madness by seeking refuge in prayers and services to the gods, and in the Hippocratic *de morbo sacro* 50 we are told that "it is the divinity that purifies, sanctifies and cleanses us from the greatest of our sins."

37 (p. 316). Solmsen in TAPA 68. 208: "Whereas Eteokles' fate is determined by the family curse and by religious factors of an archaic non-political nature, the city survives and triumphs."

CHAPTER XVII

1 (p. 317). Childe MMH 27, cf. Engels DN 1 7, 288.

2 (p. 319). Hes. *Op.* 42–6.

3 (p. 319). *P.V.* 94 sch.

4 (p. 319). Emped. 115, 124, 146, 147.

5 (p. 320). Torch-races: Farnell CGS 5 .381.

6 (p. 320). The following account of the *Prometheia* is taken for the most part from my APB 6, where references are given.

7 (p. 321). Mahaffy HCGL 1. 260. A similar view is taken by Schmid-Staehlin 2. 296. Mahaffy's remarks are dutifully retailed to schoolboys by Sikes and Willson in the introduction to their edition p. xxiv. Rapisarda (EPL p. xxix) saves the credit of modern scholars at Æschylus' expense: "se il poeta poi avesse voluto manifestare una sua partecipazione in sede morale per alcuno dei due antagonisti dovremmo ammettere che sia stato tanto maldestro da rendere possibile le opinioni e le impressioni cosi contrastanti di gran numero di filologi e di poeti." He subjoins a list of those who have sided with Prometheus and those who have sided with Zeus. The first consists of Augustine, Byron, Bacon, Calderon, Cammelli, Croiset, Eusebius, Fuochi, Goethe, Gomperz, Graf, Guzzetta, Hermann, Herder, Lactantius, Lipiner, Longfellow, Mancini, Monti, Quinet, Rabano, Mauro, Romagnoli, Schlegel, Shelley, Schütz, Tertullian, Voltaire; the second of Coman, Dissen, D'Annunzio, Delff, Errante, Haines, Hermann, Mazon, Prickard, Schoemann, Terzaghi, Wecklein. I have not checked these lists, which are far from complete, but it is interesting to note that the only poet on the side of Zeus is the fascist D'Annunzio.

8 (p. 324). Burke RRF 359.

9 (p. 322). Thomson APB 6. To the passages cited there may be added Æschin. *Tim.* 5, Isoc. *de pace* 112, Plat. *Ll.* 661B, Arist. *Pol.* 5. 11. 1314a, Max. Tyr. 4. 3. Plut. *M.* 152A, 166D, Paus. 6. 22. 2, Porph. *V.P.* 54, Hdt. 3. 80, Thuc. 1. 130, Max. Tyr. 11. 5

10 (p. 327). Epic. *ap.* Diog. L. 10. 75.

11 (p. 327). Lenin ME 156.

12 (p. 339). Moschion: Nauck TGF 812.

13 (p. 340). Kritias: Nauck TGF 770.

14 (p. 340). Iambl. *V.P.* 9. 46.

15 (p. 341). Plat. *Prot.* 320–2; Burnet GPTP 117.

16 (p. 342). Philemon: Kock CGF fr. 93, 95, cf. 2, 3, 88, 89.

17 (p. 342). Diog. L. 6. 24, 21.

18 (p. 343). Dio Chr. 6. 204R.

19 (p. 343). On the myth of Prometheus in European literature see Heinemann TGGW 12.

20 (p. 344). Murray A 75, 97.

21 (p. 344). Massacre of Peterloo: Hammond TL 89. Enclosure Acts: Hammond VL 19. Game Laws: VL 163. Speenhamland system: VL 137. Truck system: TL 40.

CHAPTER XVIII

1 (p. 347). Arist. *Poet.* 13. 6. 1453a.

2 (p. 347). Gomme PAFFC; see Thomson AO 2. 357.

3 (p. 348). Arist. *Pol.* 1. 13. 13. 1260b.

4 (p. 349). Tod in CAH 5. 29, 45.

5 (p. 350). Ferguson in CAH 5. 339.

6 (p. 351). Arist. *Pol.* 1. 8–9. 1256a–1257b.

7 (p. 351). Marx K 1. 137.

8 (p. 352). Alcæ. fr. 101 Diehl.

9 (p. 352). Soph. fr. 85.

10 (p. 352). Soph. *Ant.* 295. Cf. Engels UFPS 125: "When men invented money, they did not think that they were again creating a new social power, the one general power before which the whole of society must bow. And it was this new power, suddenly sprung to life without knowledge or will of its creators, which now, in all the brutality of its youth, gave the Athenians the first taste of its might."

11 (p. 352). Isocr. 8. 7; Bacch. *Epin.* 14. 59; Hipp. *Aph.* 1. 3; Æsch. *Ag.* 990; Plat. *Rp.* 563E.

12 (p. 353). The connection between the *deus ex machina* and the Æschylean epiphany is particularly clear in such plays as the *Hippolytos*, which end with the institution of a historical cult. My attention was called to this point by my pupil R. F. Willetts.

13 (p. 354). Arist. *Poet.* 11. 1. 1452a.

14 (p. 354). Headlam in Thomson AO 2. 217.

15 (p. 356). Soph. *El.* 307–9.

16 (p. 356). *El.* 339–40, cf. 396; Æsch. *Cho.* 77; Thomson AO 2. 170.

17 (p. 356). *El.* 616–21

18 (p. 359). Æsch. *Cho.* 688–91.

19 (p. 359). Sheppard in CR 41. 2, 163.

20 (p. 362). Soph. *O.T.* 1186–92 tr. Sheppard.

21 (p. 363). *O.T.* 1511–14 tr. Sheppard.

22 (p. 364). Webster IS 54.

23 (p. 364). On the Athenian attitude to the Delphic Oracle see Farrington SPAW 75.

24 (p. 364). Webster IS 48.

25 (p. 366). Ps. Dem. 59. 122.

26 (p. 366). Thuc. 2. 45.

27 (p. 366). Plut. *Dio.* 5. Some scholars have discredited this story because Plato says nothing about it in his *Letters*, but his silence is capable of a different interpretation. Taylor, in his lengthy monograph on Plato (PMW), follows his master's example and ignores it.

28 (p. 367). Thuc. 5. 89 tr. W. Smith.

29 (p. 368). In Cornford's version of the *Republic* the phrase *gennaîon pseûdos*, "noble lie," is translated as "a bold flight of invention," and the accepted interpretation is dismissed as "a self-contradictory expression no more applicable to Plato's harmless allegory than to a New Testament parable or the Pilgrim's Progress." It is regrettable that so fine a scholar should have lent his name to this perversion of the Greek. The word *gennaîos* means (1) true-born, high-born, noble; (2) honest, genuine; (3) of good quality, high-grade; (4) whole-hearted, sincere, intense, vehement. There is no evidence that it could mean "on a generous scale," and the phrase *mázas gennaías*, which he quotes from *Rep.* 372b in support of this interpretation, means probably something equivalent to our "plain bread and butter" (cf. our "good, honest beer"), *máza* being the traditional type of a simple diet (Thomson AO 2. 109–10). The expression is certainly self-contradictory, but such expressions are familiar to every Greek student under the name oxymoron, and the present example is merely a variant of the proverbial *kalon pseûdos*, a lie which brings an immediate advantage but is nevertheless unprofitable because it does not last (Thomson AO 2. 74). Cornford adduces no evidence to show that *pseûdos* could mean

"allegory," and in any case this fable cannot be so described. It is of the very nature of an allegory that it does not, as such, require to be believed—it is merely a symbolical illustration of an alleged truth. But Plato admits that it will take several generations before the people can be got to accept this *pseûdos*, which shows that he wants them to accept it, not as an allegory, but as a fact. And he admits himself it is not a fact. It is, in other words, a lie, and noble only to those who share his class prejudices.

30 (p. 369). Hammond TL 201, Engels DN 208, Prenant BM 179.

31 (p. 370). Cf. Engels UFPS 199–200: "With commodity production . . . the products necessarily change hands. In exchanging his product, the producer surrenders it; he no longer knows what becomes of it. When money, and with money the merchant, steps in as intermediary between the producers, the process of exchange becomes still more complicated, the final fate of the products still more uncertain. The merchants are numerous and none of them knows what the other is doing. . . . Products and production become subjects of chance. But chance is only one pole of a relation whose other pole is named 'necessity.' In the world of nature, where chance also seems to rule, we have long since demonstrated in each separate field the inner necessity and law asserting itself in this chance. But what is true of the natural world is true also of society. The more a social activity, a series of social processes, becomes too powerful for men's conscious control and grows above their heads, and the more it appears a matter of pure chance, then all the more surely within this chance the laws peculiar to it and inherent in it assert themselves as if by natural necessity. Such laws also govern the chances of commodity production and exchange; to the individuals producing or exchanging, they appear as alien, at first often unrecognised, powers, whose nature must first be laboriously investigated and established. These economic laws of commodity production are modified with the various stages of this form of production; but in general the whole period of civilisation is dominated by them. And still to this day the product rules the producer; still to this day the total production of society is regulated, not by a jointly devised plan, but by blind laws, which manifest themselves with elemental violence, in the final instance in the storms of the periodical trade crises." This is the significance underlying the Greek idea of the interrelation of Tyche and Ananke. Cf. Bailey GAE 142. On the relation between Demokritos and Epicurus, which Marx was the first modern scholar, and until recently the only one, to understand, see Marx DDEN, Nizan MA, and Bailey in CQ 22. 205. On the social significance of Epicureanism see Farrington SPAW.

32 (p. 370). Pind. *ap.* Paus. 7. 26. 8.

CHAPTER XIX

1 (p. 373). Arist. *Poet.* 6. 2. 1449b.

2 (p. 373). Aret. *Caus. M. Diut.* 1. 4.

3 (p. 373). Hipp. *de sacro morbo* 1–4. The magical origins of Greek medical therapy appear also in Plutarch's definition of the physician's task (*Lycurg.* 5): "After dissolving and readjusting the existing temperament of an unhealthy body, infected with all manner of disease, by means of medicines and purgations, he institutes a new and different diet." This is not far

removed from the newness of life to which the initiate attained by purification.

4 (p. 374). Plat. *Crito* 54D.

5 (p. 374). Plat. *Sym.* 21E.

6 (p. 375). Fallaize in Hastings 10. 122, relying principally on Junod
LSAT 2. 436, Callaway RSA 185, 289, Hose and McDougall PTB 2. 130,
Czaplicka AS 169; add Karsten CSAI 18, Webster PSS 151, 175.

7 (p. 378). Apollod. 2. 2. 2.

8 (p. 378). Eur. *H.F.* 892–3, 894–5.

9 (p. 378). Caudwell IR 194.

10 (p. 379). Hdt. 5. 3.

11 (p. 380). Thomson AO 2. 239.

12 (p. 380). Arist. *ap.* Synes. Dion. 48A.

13 (p. 381). Plat. *Io* 535.

14 (p. 381). Plat. *Io* 533E–534B. So in early Arabia poets were believed
to be possessed by the *jinn*, i.e. *daímones*: Macdonald RALI 18.

15 (p. 382). Status of the actor: Haigh AT 278.

16 (p. 382). McDougall OAP 479.

17 (p. 383). Caudwell IR 184.

BIBLIOGRAPHY

Where an English translation of a foreign work is specified, the references are to its pages and not to those of the original.

American Anthropologist.

Annual of the British School at Athens.

Anthropological Essays Presented to E. B. Tylor. Cambridge, 1906.

Archiv für Religionswissenschaft.

ASHLEY, W. J. *Economic Organisation of England.* London, 1922

BACHOFEN, J. J. *Das Mutterrecht.* Stuttgart, 1861.

BAILEY, C. *Greek Atomists and Epicurus.* Oxford, 1928.

BANCROFT, H. H. *Native Races of the Pacific States of North America.* London, 1875–6.

BASEDOW, H. *The Australian Aboriginal.* Adelaide, 1929.

BERGK, T. *Poetæ Lyrici Græci.* 4 ed. Leipzig, 1900–15.

BETHE, E. *Prolegomena zur Geschichte des Theaters im Altertum.* Leipzig, 1896.

BOISACQ, E. *Dictionnaire étymologique de la langue grecque.* 3 ed. Paris, 1938.

BOWRA, C. M. *Greek Lyric Poetry.* Oxford, 1936.

BREASTED, J. H. *History of Egypt.* 2 ed. New York, 1910.

BRIFFAULT, R. *The Mothers.* London, 1927.

BUCK, C. D. *Comparative Grammar of Greek and Latin.* Chicago, 1933.

—— *Introduction to the Study of Greek Dialects.* 2 ed. Boston, 1928.

BUDGE, E. A. W. *The Mummy.* Cambridge, 1893.

BURKE, E. *Reflections on the Revolution in France.* 4 ed. London, 1790.

BURNET, J. *Early Greek Philosophy.* London, 1920.

—— *Greek Philosophy, Thales to Plato.* London, 1928.

BURY, J. B. *History of Greece.* 2 ed. London, 1913.

BUSOLT, G. *Griechische Geschichte.* Gotha, 1873.

BYWATER, I. *Aristotle on the Art of Poetics.* Oxford, 1909.

CADOUX, C. J. *Ancient Smyrna.* Oxford, 1938.

CALHOUN, G. M. *Growth of Criminal Law in Ancient Greece.* Berkeley, 1927.

CALLAWAY, H. *Religious System of the Amazulu.* London, 1870.

Cambridge Ancient History. Cambridge, 1923–39.

Cambridge Prælections. Cambridge, 1906.

CAUDWELL, C. *Illusion and Reality*. London, 1937.
CHADWICK, H. M. *The Heroic Age*. Cambridge, 1912.
—— *Growth of Literature*. Cambridge, 1932–40.
CHAMBERS, E. K. *The Mediæval Stage*. Oxford, 1903.
CHILDE, V. G. *The Aryans*. London, 1926.
—— *Dawn of European Civilisation*. 2 ed. London, 1927.
—— *Man Makes Himself*. London, 1936.
Classical Quarterly.
Classical Review.
CONDORCET, J. A. *Esquisse d'un tableau historique des progrès de l'esprit humain*. Paris, 1794.
COOK, A. B. *Zeus*. Cambridge, 1914–40.
CORNFORD, F. M. *From Religion to Philosophy*. London, 1913.
—— *Origin of Attic Comedy*. London, 1914.
—— *Plato's Cosmology*. London, 1937.
CRAWLEY, E. *The Mystic Rose*. 2 ed. London, 1927.
CUREAU, A. L. *Savage Man in Central Africa*. London, 1915.
CZAPLICKA, M. A. *Aboriginal Siberia*. Oxford, 1914.
DAREMBERG, C., *et* SAGLIO, E. *Dictionnaire des antiquités grecques et romaines*. Paris, 1877–1919.
DARESTE, R., HAUSSOUILLER, B., *et* REINACH, T. *Recueil des inscriptions juridiques grecques*. Paris, 1891–8.
DAUBE, B. *Zu den Rechtsproblemen in Aischylos' Agamemnon*. Zurich, 1939.
DELATTE, A. *Essai sur la politique pythagoricienne*. Li ge, 1922.
DELBRÜCK, B. *Die indogermanischen Verwandtschaftsnamen (Abhandlungen der königlichen sächsischen Gesellschaft der Wissenschaft, phil.-hist. Kl., Bd.11, Nr. 5)*, 1889.
DEUBNER, A. F. *Attische Feste*. Berlin, 1932.
DIAMOND, A. S. *Primitive Law*. London, 1935.
DIEHL, E. *Anthologia Lyrica Græca*. Leipzig, 1925.
DIETERICH, A. *Mutter Erde*. Leipzig–Berlin, 1905.
DITTENBERGER, G. *Sylloge Inscriptionum Græcarum*. 2 ed. Leipzig, 1903–5.
DOPSCH, A. *Wirtschaftliche und soziale Grundlagen der europäischen Kulturentwicklung*. Vienna, 1923–4. *Economic and Social Foundations of European Civilisation*. London, 1937.
DURHAM, M. E. *Tribal Origins, Laws and Customs of the Balkans*. London, 1934.
DURKHEIM, E. *La division du travail social*. 2 ed. Paris, 1902.
—— *Les formes élémentaires de la vie religieuse*. 2 ed. Paris, 1912.
DUTT, R. P. *India To-day*. London, 1940.
—— *Native Tribes of the Northern Territory of Australia*. London, 1904.

EARTHY, E. D. *Valenge Women.* Oxford, 1933.

EGGAN, F. *Social Anthropology of N. American Tribes.* Chicago, 1937.

ELEUTHEROPOULOS, A. *Wirtschaft und Philosophie.* Berlin, 1900.

ENGELS, F. *Anti-Dühring.* (*Marx-Engels Gesamtausgabe*). *Anti-Dühring.*
London, 1934.

—— *Dialektik der Natur* (*Marx-Engels Gesamtausgabe*). *Dialectics of Nature.* London, 1940.

—— *Der Ursprung der Familie, des Privateigentums und des Staats* (*Marx-Engels Gesamtausgabe*). *Origin of the Family, Private Property and the State.* London, 1940.

ERNOUT, A., *et* MEILLET, A. *Dictionnaire étymologique de la langue latine.* Paris, 1932.

Essays and Studies Presented to William Ridgeway. Cambridge, 1913.

EVANS, A. J. *Palace of Minos.* London, 1921–35.

FARNELL, L. R. *Cults of the Greek States.* Oxford, 1896–1909.

FARRINGTON, B. *Diodorus Siculus.* Swansea, 1937.

—— *Science and Politics in the Ancient World.* London, 1939.

FERGUSON, A. *Essay on the History of Civil Society.* Basel, 1789.

FISHER, H. A. L. *History of Europe.* London, 1936.

FLICKINGER, R. C. *The Greek Theater.* 4 ed. Chicago, 1936.

FOUCART, P. *Le culte de Dionysos en Attique.* Paris, 1904.

—— *Les mystères d'Eleusis.* Paris, 1900.

FRAZER, J. G. *Apollodorus.* London, 1921.

—— *Golden Bough.* London, 1923–7. 1. *The Magic Art and the Evolution of Kings* (2 vols.). 2. *Taboo and the Perils of the Soul.* 3. *The Dying God.* 4. *Adonis, Attis, Osiris* (2 vols.). 5. *Spirits of the Corn and of the Wild* (2 vols.). 6. *The Scapegoat.* 7. *Balder the Beautiful, the Fire Festivals of Europe, and the Doctrine of the External Soul* (2 vols.).

—— *Lectures on the Early History of the Kingship.* London, 1905.

—— *Myths of the Origin of Fire.* London, 1930.

—— *Pausanias's Description of Greece.* London, 1898.

—— *Totemica.* London, 1937.

—— *Totemism and Exogamy.* London, 1910.

FRITZ, K. VON. *Pythagorean Politics in Southern Italy.* New York, 1940.

FUSTEL DE COULANGES. *La cité antique.* 7 ed. Paris, 1878.

Glotta.

GLOTZ, G. *La civilisation égéenne.* Paris, 1923. *Ægean Civilisation.* London, 1925.

—— *La solidarité de la famille dans le droit criminel en Grèce.* Paris, 1904.

—— *Le travail dans la Grèce ancienne.* Paris, 1920. *Ancient Greece at Work.* London, 1926.

GOMME, A. W. *Population of Athens in the Fifth and Fourth Centuries B.C.* Oxford, 1933.

GOMPERZ, T. *Griechische Denker.* Leipzig, 1896. *Greek Thinkers.* London, 1901–12.

GRANET, M. *La civilisation chinoise.* Paris, 1929. *Chinese Civilisation.* London, 1930.

GREY, G. *Vocabulary of the Dialects of S.W. Australia.* London, 1840.

GRÖNBECH, V. *Culture of the Teutons.* Oxford, 1931.

GROTE, G. *History of Greece.* 2 ed. London, 1869.

GUIRAUD, P. *La propriété foncière en Grèce.* Paris, 1893.

GUTHRIE, W. K. C. *Orpheus and Greek Religion.* London, 1935.

HAIGH, A. E. *The Attic Theatre.* 3 ed. Oxford, 1907.

HALL, H. R. *Ancient History of the Near East.* 7 ed. London, 1927.

—— *Civilisation of Greece in the Bronze Age.* London, 1928.

HAMBLY, W. D. *Origins of Education among Primitive Peoples.* London, 1926.

HAMMOND, J. L. and B. *The Town Labourer.* 2 ed. London, 1925.

—— *The Village Labourer.* 4 ed. London, 1936.

HARRIS, J. R. *Boanerges.* Cambridge, 1913.

HARRISON, J. E. *Prolegomena to the Study of Greek Religion.* 3 ed. Cambridge, 1922.

—— *Themis.* Cambridge, 1912.

HARTLAND, E. S. *Primitive Paternity.* London, 1909–10.

Harvard Studies in Classical Philology.

Harvard Theological Review.

HASEBROEK, J. *Staat und Handel im alten Griechenland.* Tübingen, 1928. *Trade and Politics in Ancient Greece.* London, 1933.

HASTINGS, J. *Encyclopædia of Ethics and Religion.* Edinburgh, 1908–18.

HEAD, B. V. *Historia Numorum.* 2 ed. Oxford, 1911.

HEICHELHEIM, F. *Wirtschaftsgeschichte des Altertums.* Leiden, 1939.

HEINEMANN, K. *Die tragischen Gestalten der Griechen in der Weltliteratur.* Leipzig, 1920.

Hermathena.

Hibbert Journal.

HOBHOUSE, L. T., WHEELER, G. C., and GINSBERG, T. *Material Culture and Social Institutions of the Simpler Peoples.* London, 1930.

HOCART, A. M. *Kingship.* Oxford, 1927.

HÖFLER, O. *Die kultischen Geheimbünde der Germanen.* Frankfurt-am-Main, 1934.

HOLLIS, A. C. *The Nandi, their Language and Folklore.* Oxford, 1909.

HOOKE, S. H. *Myth and Ritual.* Oxford, 1933.

Hose, C., and McDougall, W. *Pagan Tribes of Borneo*. London, 1912.

Howitt, A. W. *Native Tribes of S.E. Australia*. London, 1904.

Hubert, H. *Greatness and Decline of the Celts*. London, 1934.

Hunt, A. S. *Tragicorum Græcorum Fragmenta Papyracea*. Oxford, 1912. *Indogermanische Forschungen*.

Jackson, K. *Early Celtic Nature Poetry*. Cambridge, 1935.

Jeanmaire, H. *Couroi et Couretes*. Lille, 1939.

Jeanroy, A. *Les origines de la poésie lyrique*. 2 ed. Paris, 1904.

Journal of American Folklore.

Journal of Egyptian Archæology.

Journal of Hellenic Studies.

Journal of the Royal Anthropological Institute.

Journal of the Royal Asiatic Society.

Joyce, P. W. *Social History of Ancient Ireland*. London, 1903.

Junod, H. A. *Life of a South African Tribe*. London, 1913.

Karsten, R. *Civilisation of the South American Indians*. London, 1926.

Kern, O. *Orphicorum Fragmenta*. Berlin, 1922.

Kinkel, G. *Epicorum Græcorum Fragmenta*. Leipzig, 1877.

Kitto, H. D. F. *Greek Tragedy*. London, 1939.

Klio.

Knight, W. F. J. *Cumaean Gates*. Oxford, 1936.

Kock, T. *Comicorum Græcorum Fragmenta*. Leipzig, 1880–8.

Kranz, W. *Stasimon*. Berlin, 1933.

Kretschmer, P. *Einleitung zur Geschichte der griechischen Sprache*. Göttingen, 1896.

Landtman, G. *Origin of the Inequality of Social Classes*. London, 1938.

Lang, A. *Custom and Myth*. London, 1884.

Lenin, V. I. *Materialism and Empirio-criticism*. London, n.d.

—— *Selected Works*. (12 vols.) London, n.d.

Lobeck, C. A. *Aglaophamus*. Königsberg, 1829.

Loisy, A. *Les mystères païens et le mystère chrétien*. 2 ed. Paris, 1930.

Lowie, R. H. *Primitive Society*. New York, 1929.

Macdonald, D. B. *Religious Attitude and Life in Islam*. Chicago, 1909.

Mahaffy, J. P. *History of Classical Greek Literature*. London, 1880.

Malinowski, B. *The Family among the Australian Aborigines*. London, 1913.

Mannhardt, W. *Antike Wald- und Feldkulte*. Berlin, 1877.

—— *Der Baumkultus der Germanen*. Berlin, 1875.

—— *Germanische Mythen*. Berlin, 1858.

MARETT, R. R. *Anthropology*. London, 1927.

MARX, K. *Das Kapital (Marx-Engels Gesamtausgabe). Capital*. London, 1930.

—— *Ueber die Differenz der demokritischen und epikurischen Naturphilosophie (Marx-Engels Gesamtausgabe)*.

Marx-Engels Briefwechsel (Marx-Engels Gesamtausgabe). Selected Correspondence of Marx and Engels. London, 1934.

MATHEW, J. *Two Representative Tribes of Queensland*. London, 1910.

MAZON, P. *Eschile*. Paris, 1920–5.

McDOUGALL, W. *Outline of Abnormal Psychology*. London, 1926.

McLENNAN, J. *Studies in Ancient History*. London, 1886.

MEEK, C. K. *A Sudanese Kingdom: an Ethnographical Study of the Jukun-speaking Peoples of Nigeria*. London, 1931.

MEILLET, A. *Aperçu d'une histoire de la langue grecque*. 4 ed. Paris, 1935.

—— *Introduction a l'étude comparative des langues indo-européennes*. 8 ed. Paris, 1937.

—— *et* VENDRYES, J. *Traité de grammaire comparée des langues classiques*. 2 ed. Paris, 1927.

Modern Quarterly.

MOMMSEN, A. *Feste der Stadt Athen*. Leipzig, 1898.

MORET, A., *et* DAVY, G. *Des clans aux empires*. Paris, 1923. *From Tribe to Empire*. London, 1926.

MORGAN, L. H. *Ancient Society*. New York, 1877.

——– *Systems of Consanguinity and Affinity of the Human Family*. New York, 1871.

MÜLLER, C. *Fragmenta Historicorum Græcorum*. Paris, 1868–83.

MURRAY, G. *Æschylus*. Oxford, 1940.

MYRES, J. L. *Who Were the Greeks?* Berkeley, 1930.

NAUCK, T. *Tragicorum Græcorum Fragmenta*. 2 ed. Leipzig, 1889.

NIETZSCHE, F. W. *Die Geburt der Tragödie (Gesammelte Werke)*.

NILSSON, M. P. *Griechische Feste von religiöser Bedeutung mit Ausschluss der Attischen*. Leipzig, 1906.

—— *History of Greek Religion*, Oxford, 1925.

—— *Homer and Mycenæ*. London, 1933.

—— *Minoan-Mycenean Religion*. Lund, 1927.

—— *Mycenean Origin of Greek Mythology*. London, 1932.

NIZAN, P. *Les matérialistes de l'antiquité*. Paris, 1936.

Oceania.

PAGE, D. L. *Actors' Interpolations in Greek Tragedy*. Oxford, 1934.

PARKE, H. W. *History of the Delphic Oracle*. Oxford, 1939.

PAUL, H. *Grundriss der germanischen Mythologie*. Strassburg, 1900.

PAULY, A. *Realencyclopädie der klassischen Altertumswissenschaft.* Stuttgart, 1842–66.

PAYNE, H. G. G. *Perachora.* Oxford, 1940.

PERRY, W. J. *Children of the Sun.* London, 1923.

PETERSEN, W. *Quæstiones de historia gentium Atticarum.* Schleswig, 1880.

PICKARD-CAMBRIDGE, A. W. *Dithyramb, Tragedy and Comedy.* Oxford, 1927.

PIRENNE, H. *Histoire de l'Europe.* Brussels, 1936. *History of Europe.* London, 1939.

PLEKHANOV, G. F. *Fundamental Problems of Marxism.* London, 1937.

POEHLMANN, R. VON, *Geschichte der sozialen Frage und des Sozialismus in der Antiken Welt.* 3 ed. Munich, 1925.

PRENANT, M. *Biologie et Marxisme.* Paris, 1936. *Biology and Marxism.* London, 1938.

PRESCOTT, W. H. *Conquest of Peru.* Everyman ed. London, 1908.

Problemy Istorii Dokapitalisticheskikh Formatsi. Moscow/Leningrad, 1934.

Proceedings of the Cambridge Philological Society.

RAPISARDA, E. *Eschilo, Il Prometeo Legato.* Turin, 1936.

REINACH, S. *Orpheus: histoire générale des religions.* Paris, 1909. *Orpheus.* London, 1931.

Révue historique du droit français et étranger.

RIBBECK, O. *Anfänge und Entwickelung des Dionysoscultus in Attika* Kiel, 1869.

RIDGEWAY, W. *Dramas and Dramatic Dances.* Cambridge, 1915.

—— *Early Age of Greece.* Cambridge, 1901–31.

—— *Origin of Tragedy.* Cambridge, 1910.

RIVERS, W. H. R. *Expedition to the Torres Straits.* Cambridge, 1908.

—— *History of Melanesian Society.* Cambridge, 1914.

—— *Social Organisation.* London, 1932.

—— *The Todas.* London, 1906.

ROBERT, C. *Oidipus.* Berlin, 1915.

ROBERTSON, D. S. *Greek and Roman Architecture.* Cambridge, 1929.

ROBERTSON SMITH, W. *Kinship and Marriage in Early Arabia.* 2 ed. London, 1903.

—— *Religion of the Semites.* 3 ed. London, 1927.

ROSCHER, W. H. *Ausführliches Lexikon der griechischen und römischen Mythologie.* Leipzig. 1884–1937.

ROSE, H. J. *Primitive Culture in Greece.* London, 1925.

ROTH, W. E. *Ethnological Studies among N.W. Queensland Aborigines.* Brisbane/London, 1897.

Rouse, W. H. D. *Greek Votive Offerings*. Cambridge, 1902.

Schmeller, A. J. *Carmina Burana*. Stuttgart, 1847.

Schmid, W. *Untersuchungen zum gefesselten Prometheus*. Stuttgart, 1929.

—— *und* Staehlin, O. *Geschichte der griechischen Literatur*. Munich, 1929.

Schoolcraft, H. J. *Indian Tribes of the United States*. Philadelphia, 1853–6.

Schrader, O. *Reallexikon der indogermanischen Altertumskunde*. 2 ed. Berlin/Leipzig, 1917–28.

Schurtz, H. *Altersklassen und Männerbünde*. Berlin, 1902.

Seebohm, H. E. *Structure of Greek Tribal Society*. London, 1895.

Seligman, G. C. *Melanesians of British New Guinea*. Cambridge, 1910.

—— *Pagan Tribes of the Nilotic Sudan*. London, 1932.

Seltman, C. T. *Athens, its History and Coinage*. Cambridge, 1924.

Semple, E. C. *Geography of the Mediterranean Region*. London, 1932.

Sheppard, J. T. *Œdipus Tyrannus of Sophocles*. Cambridge, 1920.

Spencer, B., and Gillen, F. H. *Across Australia*. London, 1912.

—— *The Arunta*. London, 1927.

—— *Northern Tribes of Central Australia*. London, 1904.

Tawney, R. H. *Religion and the Rise of Capitalism*. London, 1926.

Taylor, A. E. *Plato, the Man and his Work*. 2 ed. London, 1927.

Thomas, N. W. *Kinship and Marriage in Australia*. Cambridge, 1906.

Thomson, G. *Æschylus, Oresteia*. Cambridge, 1938.

—— *Æschylus, Prometheus Bound*. Cambridge, 1932.

—— *Greek Lyric Metre*. Cambridge, 1929.

Toepffer, J. *Attische Genealogie*. Berlin, 1889.

Toutain, J. *L'économie antique*. Paris, 1927. *Economic Life of the Ancient World*. London, 1930.

Transactions of the American Philological Association.

Tylor, E. B. *Primitive Culture*. 3 ed. London, 1891.

Ure, P. N. *Origin of Tyranny*. Cambridge, 1922.

Van Gennep, A. *L'état actuel du problème totémique*. Paris, 1920.

—— *Les rites de passage*. Paris, 1909.

Vendryes, J. *Langage*. Paris, 1921.

—— *La position linquistique du celtique*. London, 1937.

Vinogradoff, P. *Outlines of Historical Jurisprudence*. London, 1920–2.

Voprosy Istorii Doklassovovo Obshchestva. Moscow/Leningrad, 1936.

Wainwright, G. A. *The Sky-Religion in Egypt*. Cambridge, 1938.

Walde, A. *Vergleichendes Wörterbuch der indogermanischen Sprachen*. 2 ed. Leipzig, 1928–33.

Wallaschek, R. *Anfänge der Tonkunst*. Leipzig, 1903.

WALLON, H. *Histoire de l'esclavage.* 2 ed. Paris, 1879.

WEBB, S. and B. *Soviet Communism.* London. 1935.

WEBSTER, H. *Primitive Secret Societies.* 2 ed. New York, 1932.

WEBSTER, T. B. L. *Introduction to Sophocles.* Oxford, 1936.

WESTERMARCK, H. H. *History of Human Marriage.* London, 1901.

—— *Origin and Development of Moral Ideas.* London, 1906–8.

WILAMOWITZ-MOELLENDORFF, U. VON. *Æschyli Tragoediæ.* Berlin, 1914.

WILAMOWITZ-MOELLENDORFF, U. VON. *Æschylos Interpretationen.* Berlin, 1914.

—— *Aischylos Orestie: Das Opfer am Grabe.* Berlin, 1896.

—— *Aristoteles und Athen.* Berlin, 1893.

—— *Pindaros.* Berlin, 1922.

WILLIAMSON, R. W. *Social and Political Systems of Central Polynesia.* Cambridge, 1924.

CHRONOLOGICAL TABLE

I. HISTORICAL

B.C.

c. 3300.	Beginning of the Bronze Age in the Ægean area (p. 59).
c. 1800.	Beginning of Greek immigration (p. 60).
c. 1450.	Fall of Knossos. Coming of the Achæans (pp. 59–60).
c. 1400.	Reoccupation of Knossos. Rise of Mycenæ (p. 61).
c. 1230.	Theseus King of Athens (p. 75).
c. 1213.	Argive expedition against Thebes (p. 59).
c. 1184.	Fall of Troy (p. 60).
c. 1050.	Beginning of the Iron Age. Dorian invasion. Ionian colonisation of Asia Minor (p. 60).
900–800.	*Iliad* and *Odyssey* (pp. 65–7).
750–650.	Greek colonisation of Italy and Sicily (p. 77).
c. 700.	Meidas King of Phrygia (p. 85).
687–652.	Gyges King of Lydia. Spread of coinage in Ionia (p. 85).
c. 640.	Kypselos Tyrant of Corinth. Theagenes Tyrant of Megara (p. 86).
632.	Kylon attempts a *coup d'état* at Athens (p. 76).
621.	Legislation of Drakon at Athens (p. 76).
c. 610.	Thrasyboulos Tyrant of Miletos (p. 86).
c. 600.	Pittakos Tyrant of Lesbos (p. 86). Periandros Tyrant of Corinth (pp. 151–2).
594.	Reforms of Solon at Athens (pp. 87–9).
c. 590.	Kleisthenes Tyrant of Sikyon (pp. 151, 169).
586.	Aristocratic counter-revolution at Corinth
585.	May 28th, Solar eclipse, predicted by Thales (p. 80).
561–560.	Peisistratos becomes Tyrant at Athens (pp. 90–4).
556–555.	First exile of Peisistratos
550–549.	Restoration and second exile of Peisistratos.
548–547.	Temple of Apollo at Delphi burnt down (p. 92).
546.	Cyrus, King of Persia, captures Sardis (p. 90).
546–545.	Persian conquest of Asiatic Greece (p. 220).
540–539.	Second restoration of Peisistratos (p. 90).
538.	Cyrus captures Babylon (p. 220).
c. 530.	Polykrates Tyrant of Samos. Pythagoras emigrates to Kroton (p. 210).

528–527. Death of Peisistratos (p. 91).
525. Persian conquest of Egypt (p. 220).
521. Darius becomes King of Persia.
514. Assassination of Hipparchos (p. 91).
512. Persian conquest of Thrace (p. 92).
510. Expulsion of Hippias (p. 92).
508–507. Beginning of the reforms of Kleisthenes (pp. 205–9).
499. Outbreak of the Ionian revolt (p. 221).
496. Miltiades returns to Athens from the Thracian Chersonese (p. 222).
494. Persians recapture Miletos (p. 233).
493–492. Themistokles *árchon* at Athens (p. 222).
490. Battle of Marathon (p. 223).
489. Expedition of Miltiades to Paros (p. 223).
485. Xerxes becomes King of Persia (p. 225).
480. Battle of Salamis (pp. 227–8).
471. Flight of Themistokles (p. 228).
464. Revolt of Spartan serfs (p. 230).
463–461. Reform of the Council of the Areopagus (p. 231).
462–460. Introduction of payment for public services at Athens (p. 348).
431. Outbreak of the Peloponnesian War.
429. Death of Perikles.
416. Subjugation of Melos (p. 367).
415. Athenian expedition to Sicily (p. 368).
411. First counter-revolution at Athens.
410. Restoration of democracy at Athens.
404. Second counter-revolution at Athens: the Thirty Tyrants.
403. Spartan garrison in Athens.

II. BIOGRAPHICAL

Achaios of Eretria, Athenian dramatist, born *c.* 482.
Æschylus (Aischylos) of Eleusis, Athenian dramatist, 525–456.
Alkaios of Lesbos, aristocratic poet, *fl.* 630–600.
Alkman of Sardis and Sparta, choral poet, *fl.* 630–600.
Anaximander (Anaximandros) of Miletos, Ionian scientist, 611–547.
Anakreon of Teos, lyric poet, 550–464.
Antiphon of Rhamnous, Athenian orator, 480–411.
Apollodoros of Athens, antiquarian, born *c.* 140.
Apollonios of Rhodes, poet, born *c.* 260.

Aratos of Soloi, poet, born *c.* 270.

Archilochos of Paros, poet, born *c.* 735.

Aretaios of Cappadocia, physician, born *c.* A.D. 180.

Aristeides of Bithynia, rhetorician, born *c.* A.D. 120.

Aristophanes of Athens, comic dramatist, 444–388.

Aristotle (Aristoteles) of Stageira, scientist and philosopher, 384–322.

Aristoxenos of Taras, philosopher and pupil of Aristotle, *fl.* 330.

Bakchylides of Keos, choral poet, *fl.* 450.

Demokritos of Abdera, scientist and philosopher, 460–360.

Demosthenes of Paiania, Athenian orator, 384–322.

Diodoros of Sicily, historian, *fl.* 40.

Diogenes of Laerte, historian of philosophy, *fl.* A.D. 150.

Diogenes of Sinope, Cynic philosopher, 404–323.

Dion Chrysostomos of Prousa, rhetorician, born *c.* A.D. 50.

Empedokles of Akragas, Orphic philosopher and scientist, born *c.* 490.

Epicurus (Epikouros) of Gargettos, scientist and philosopher, 342–268.

Euripides of Salamis, Athenian dramatist, 480–405.

Herakleitos of Ephesos, Ionian philosopher, *c.* 535–475.

Herodotus (Herodotos) of Halikarnessos, historian, died *c.* 424.

Hesiod (Hesiodos) of Askra, Boeotian epic poet, *fl.* 750.

Hesychios of Alexandria, lexicographer, *fl.* A.D. 375.

Hippokrates of Kos, physician and scientist, born *c.* 460.

Iamblichos of Syria, neoplatonist philosopher, died *c.* A.D. 330.

Kratinos of Athens, comic dramatist, 520–423.

Kritias of Athens, one of the Thirty Tyrants.

Lysias of Athens, orator, 445–368.

Menander (Menandros) of Athens, comic dramatist, 342–290.

Nonnos of Panopolis, poet, *fl.* A.D. 450.

Parmenides of Elea, idealist philosopher, born *c.* 510.

Pausanias of Lydia, geographer, *fl.* A.D. 150.

Philemon of Soloi or Syracuse, Athenian comic dramatist, born *c.* 362.

Philolaos of Thebes, Pythagorean philosopher, *fl.* 450.

Photios of Constantinople, lexicographer, died A.D. 891.

Pindar (Pindaros) of Thebes, choral poet, 522–442.

Plato (Platon) of Athens, idealist philosopher, 428–348.

Plutarch (Ploutarchos) of Chaironeia, biographer and essayist, born *c.* A.D. 50.

Porphyry (Porphyrios) of Syria, neoplatonist philosopher, A.D. 233–304.

Pratinas of Phleious, Athenian dramatist, *fl.* 500.

Sappho of Lesbos, poetess, *fl.* 620–580.

Simonides of Keos, poet, 556–468.
Sophokles of Kolonos, Athenian dramatist, 495–405.
Stesichoros of Himera, choral poet, born *c.* 630.
Suidas (Souidas), lexicographer, *fl.* A.D. 970.
Thales of Miletos, Ionian scientist, *fl.* 585.
Theognis of Megara, aristocratic poet, *fl.* 510.
Theon of Smyrna, mathematician, *fl.* A.D. 130.
Thucydides (Thoukydides) of Athens, historian, *c.* 471–395.
Tyrtaios of Sparta, poet, *fl.* 630.

INDEX

ACADEMY: *see* Akademia.
Achæans, 21, 41, 60–7, 79, 157
Achaimenidai, 220
Achaios, 244
Achilles, 40, 41, 53, 61, 62, 65–7, 69, 113, 247
Actor, 103, 173–9, 241, 382. See *Hypokrités*.
Adcock, 89, 425, 426
Adonis, 191
Adoption, 35, 44, 50, 73, 74, 111, 112, 120, 121, 201, 277
Adrastos, 151
Adultery, 202, 203
Æneas, 40
Æschylus: his life, 245, 246; attitude to blood-pollution, 433; to the Mysteries, 246, 274, 291; to Pythagoreanism, 219, 245, 291, 340; to society, 1, 2, 5, 219, 231, 291, 305, 345; on the dithyramb, 169; treatment of the actor, 178; of the chorus, 253, 268, 353; of the tetralogy, 243, 244; view of justice, 291. *See* titles of plays.
Africa, 12, 97, 101, 102, 375, 416
Agamemnon XV, 41, 53, 65–7, 69, 176
Agamemnon: see *Oresteia*.
Agaue, 140, 141, 167, 365
Age grades, 97, 104, 107, 436
Agéla, 28, 103–6, 204, 432
Agón, 117, 141, 166–8, 173, 192, 241
Agra, 121, 122, 125, 337
Agriculture, 11, 22, 54, 119, 121, 154, 308
Agrionia, 143, 145, 146, 191
Aigina, 76, 221, 226, 227
Aigisthos, 189, 247, 249, 252, 262–4, 271–3, 357–9
Aigyptos, 298–308
Aithalidai, 45, 206
Aither, 155
Ajax, 53, 66
Akademia, 165, 320, 335–7, 342
Akamantis, 171
Aleuadai, 226
Alkaios, 80, 86, 184, 186
Alkibiades, 322, 374
Alkmaion of Athens, 90
— of Kroton, 217, 218
—, son of Eriphyle, 35

Alkmaionidai, 20, 76, 90, 92, 222–5, 229, 233, 309
Alkman, 78, 80, 184, 185, 432
Alkmene, 320
Alphabet, 77
Althaia, 35
American Indians, 32, 34, 64, 101, 102, 183, 388–90, 400, 413–16, 43
Amphiaraos, 314
Amymone, 298
Anagnórisis, 188, 189, 192
Anakálypsis, 113, 192
Anánke, 158, 159, 319, 356, 370, 371
Anaximander, 81–4, 156, 215, 216
Ancestor worship, 14, 18, 63, 102
Andromache, 185
Antigone, 311
Antigone, 176, 311, 322
Antistrophic form, 184–7
Apatouria, 28, 106
Aphrodite, 44, 63, 307
Apollo: at Delphi, 60, 72, 74, 163, 248, 376; relation to Dionysus, 130, 212, interpreter of Zeus, 278; Moiragetes, 54, 278; musician, 44, 65, 130; *patróios*, 279; prophet, 45, 46, 130; at Samos, 139; in the *Oresteia* XV, 176, 307
Arabia, 48, 455
Archilochos, 169, 171, 237
Archon, 74, 75, 88, 209, 233
Archon basileús, 75, 146
— *epónymos*, 232
Areopagus, 88, 89, 231, 247, 248, 284, 291, 292, 308
Ares, 130, 373
Argonauts, 299
Argos, 28, 59, 70, 107, 146–8, 153, 226, 228, 230, 292, 299, 300, 312
Ariadne, 146
Arion, 151–3, 168, 169, 235
Aristeides, 224, 228
Aristophanes, 119, 241, 288, 305, 371
Aristotle: *Poetics*, 175, 372; *Politics*, 373; on Æschylus, 246, 372; on comedy, 241; on Crete, 105, 425; on democracy, 120; on early Attica, 74, 200, 208; on legislators, 433; on money, 351; on the Mysteries, 380; on quarrels about heiresses, 305; on resident aliens, 348; on slavery, 368;

Aristotle—*contd.*

on Sparta, 202, 203; on tragedy, 6,
172, 175–80, 187, 193, 236–8, 243,
347, 354, 360, 372, 373, 380, 383;
on tyrants, 434

Aristoxenos, 210

Army, organisation of, 62, 70, 81, 199

Artemis, 50, 104, 106, 126, 130, 240,
247, 248, 254, 277

Artemision, 227

Arunta, 123, 391–5, 409, 420, 421

Asklepios, 44, 45, 122

Aspasia, 366

Assembly, 69, 88, 199, 231

Atalanta, 29

Athena: in Attic tradition, 276, 277,
282, 283; as a bird, 449; her birth,
337; goddess of handicrafts, 44, 320,
337; Polias, 76, 91, 295; in the
Oresteia XV, 176, 308, 337, 340

Atlas, 44, 334

Atossa, 309–11, 322

Atreus, 63, 246–8, 252, 253, 262, 269,
273, 276, 359

Atropos, 46, 47

Attis, 127, 379

Augustine, 364

Australia, 4, 6, 12, 13, 16, 100, 101,
112, 113, 123, 131, 132

Autonoe, 140

BABYLONIA, 22, 63, 80, 120, 220

Bacchants, 139–42, 167, 168, 171, 180,
365, 378

Bachofen, 299

Bakchiadai, 86

Bakchiadas, 169

Bakchylides, 184, 194, 353

Barter, 32, 85

Basilidai, 86

Bather, 140, 142, 146, 180

Bathonga, 375

Beethoven, 243

Bellerophon, 28, 40, 61

Birds, cults of, 449

Boiling, mythical, 113

Boukolion, 146

Boutes, 20, 144, 145, 170

Bouzyges, 45, 46

Branchidai, 72, 163

Briffault, 400, 421

Bringing in the Summer, 135–8

Bull-roarer, 112, 113

Burke, 321

Burnet, 211, 215, 341, 434

Bury, 212, 225, 426, 434, 447

CALENDAR, 114, 147, 208, 209, 439

Calhoun, 83

California, 388, 389, 413

Calvinism, 213, 214

Cannibalism, 108, 141, 143

Cape Flattery Indians, 102

Carrying out Death, 135–9

Carthage, 220, 226

Catechism, 99, 104, 191

Cattle-raising: *see* Pastoral society.

Caudwell, 378

Cave, Platonic, 162

Celtic, 390, 403, 404, 410–12

Centaurs, 336, 337

Chadwick, 64

Chambers, 193

Chance and necessity, 454

Charites, 167, 171, 292

Chaucer, 78

Cheiron, 336

Childe, Gordon, 317

China, 32, 132–4, 145, 434

Choephoroi: see *Oresteia.*

Choral lyric, 79, 80, 184–7

Choregia, 232, 233

Christianity, 124, 159, 380, 437, 439

Chryseis, 41

Chrysothemis, 356, 357

Cicero, 245, 331

Circumcision, 98, 110, 111

Classificatory system, 6, 25–7, 132,
387–417

Clothes, magic of, 47, 48, 98, 104, 105,
107, 122, 139, 140, 299, 374

Clytemnestra XV, 35, 176, 189, 354,
356, 353

Comedy, 238–42, 371

Common meals, 20, 21, 42, 70, 72, 104,
113, 140, 234, 425–6

Communism, primitive, 6, 43, 68, 234,
425–6, 435

Condorcet, 210, 211

Cook, A. B., 3, 29, 112, 147

Co-operation, tribal, 14, 17, 31, 82,
209, 396

Corinth, 86, 151–4, 168, 194, 221, 226,
235, 360

Cornford, 113–19, 238, 239, 242, 453–4

Coronation, 22, 115–18, 124, 125, 131,
273

Costume, 245, 465, 466

Council, 62, 63, 69, 74, 75, 88, 208–9,
231, 232

Counting, 391

Craft clans, 44–6

Crete, primitive, 59; Dorian, 70, 105–6,
204. *See* Minoan culture.

Cross-cousin marriage, 395, 403–5, 411,
423

Cureau, 97
Cyclops, 243
Cyrus, 48

Daímon, 49, 50, 101, 126, 129, 212, 264
Daís, 42, 50
Daktyloi, 110, 115, 438
Danaides, 298–308
Danaos, 178, 298–308
D'Annunzio, 451
Darius, 177, 225, 268, 310, 311
Darwin, 369
Defence, Attic term for, 34
Deification, 22, 112, 117, 118, 127, 164, 263
Deiphontes, 29, 41
Delbrück, 408
Deliverance from evil, 124, 128, 157, 159, 162, 249, 250, 274, 359, 379
Delos, 149
Delphi, political attitude of, 72, 74, 226, 248, 278, 364. See Apollo.
Démarchos, 206
Demeter, 60, 112, 119–22, 308, 337, 431, 443
Demodokos, 65
Demokritos, 327, 369–71
Demophoon, 112
Dêmos, 206, 429, 446
Descent, 15, 16, 23, 28, 30, 31, 51, 120, 201, 248, 277, 279, 429
Deubner, 444
Deus ex machina, 353
Deuterópotmos, 50, 129
Dialects, Greek, 51, 60, 83, 216, 234
Dialogue, tragic, 176–8
Diamond, 36, 421, 428
Dieri, 399
Diipolia, 20, 21
Dike, 53, 156, 158, 340. See Justice.
Diodoros: on adoption, 111; on democracy, 209; on Dionysus, 149; on the Lesser Mysteries, 337; on the mines, 160–2; on primitive communism, 425, 427
Diogenes the Cynic, 342, 343
Diomedes, 32
Dione, 30
Dionysia, City, 91, 93, 152, 165–72, 192, 194, 195, 232, 235, 238–41
—, Country, 240, 241
Dionysiac sacrament, 21, 141, 148, 162, 195
Dionysiades, 143, 149, 171
Dionysiastai, 149
Dionysios, 366
Dionysus: his name, 153; birth, 110–12, 188; marriage, 116, 145, 146; death,

111, 155, 188; resurrection, 111, 188, 189, 191; as a bull, 21, 166–8; other totemic forms, 142, 148; his relation to Ares, 130; to Osiris, 110, 120; at Alea, 143; at Argos, 144–6; at Elis, 167; at Naxos, 144; at Orchomenos, 144; at Patrai, 443; at Tanagra, 144; Bakcheios, 377; Eleuthereus, 165, 171, 172; Iakchos, 122; Lysios, 377; Melanaigis, 172, 180; Melpomenos, 20; Zagreus, 111; costume, 442
Dithyramb X, 6, 151, 153, 179, 183–7, 194, 195, 232, 233, 236, 237, 241, 371, 382
Division of labour, 15, 46, 50, 61, 204, 378, 383
Doctor, magic, 137, 138, 239, 240
Dodona, 30, 60
Dokimasía, 107, 192
Dorians, 27, 28, 39, 60, 61, 65, 67, 69–71, 106
Dörpfeld, 191
Douleía, 158
Drakon, 76
Dravidian, 390, 405–9
Drios, 144–6
Dryas, 144
Dysmainai, 149, 150

EARTH goddess, 19, 60, 332–4, 336
Edonoi, 144, 153
Egypt, 22, 49, 59, 60, 63, 80, 120, 121, 123, 146, 160, 210, 220, 298, 302, 306, 418
Eiren, 104, 126, 190
Eiresióne, 139
Elegiac, 79
Elektra, 267–72, 276, 354–60
Elektra of Euripides, 248
— of Sophokles, 354–60, 363, 364
Eleusinian Mysteries, 119–29, 156, 157, 159, 163, 246, 250, 270, 274, 279, 280, 291, 380, 382
Eleutherai,165,166,171,172,180,183,240
Elis, hymn of, 167, 170, 171, 186
Empedokles, 50, 156, 319, 327
Enclosure Acts, 37, 344
Engels, 449, 453, 454
Epameinondas, 20
Epaphos, 112, 298, 300
Ephebos, 107, 119, 122, 139, 143, 165, 166, 295, 320
Ephesos, 86, 130, 149, 229
Ephialtes, 230, 231, 286
Epic, 64–8, 79, 91, 194, 248
Epicurus, 290, 327, 339, 369–71
Epikaste, 190
Epilepsy, 373, 375, 377

Epimetheus, 341
Epóptes, 123, 125–7, 262, 270
Erechtheidai, 19, 277
Erechtheus, 20, 63
Erichthonios, 20, 277
Erinyes XV, 35, 36, 44, 51–3, 108, 186, 212, 307, 308, 313, 314, 359, 374, 431
Eriphyle, 35
Eschatié, 71
Eteoboutadai, 20, 90
Eteokles, 312–5, 354
Ethos, 431
Euboia, 146, 223
Eudaimonía, 125, 127, 129, 141, 250, 256
Eumaios, 42
Eumenides, 292
Eumenides: see Oresteia.
Eumolpidai, 72, 119, 120, 122
Euneidai, 20, 44
Eupatridai, 75, 76, 86–9, 200, 205, 245, 291
Euphorion, 245, 246
Eupyridai, 45, 206
Euripides, social attitude, 365, 368, 371; treatment of chorus, 353. See titles of plays.
Eurynomos, 279
Exárchon, 169, 183, 185
Exegetés, 182, 287, 291, 292
Exogamy II, 15, 16, 17, 21, 202, 304, See Marriage.

FALLAIZE, 375, 378
Family, 31, 41, 43, 54, 70–2, 75, 79, 202, 366, 395, 396, 428
Farnell, 131, 180
Fatherland, 432
Ferguson, 3, 4
Fisher, H. A. L., 215
Food-gathering, 11, 21
Foucart, 120, 121
Frazer, 114, 117, 134, 136, 137, 139, 140, 409
Fritz, von, 447
Funeral customs, 98, 108, 115, 119, 122, 299
Fusion of opposites, 215–9, 292, 345
Future tense, 436
Game Laws, 344
Gardner, 45
Gela, 245
Gelon, 226
Génos, 27, 46
Gephyraioi, 38
Géras, 41, 44, 53, 312, 427
Germans, 34, 52, 61, 64, 65, 136, 193, 426, 430, 437, 438, 446

Glaukos, 32
Gnorísmata, 48, 49, 188, 267
God, idea of, 18, 63, 117, 340
God-king, 22, 117, 118
Golden Age, 68, 234, 318, 435
Golden Apples, 112, 334, 335
Goldenweiser, 423
Gortyna, 36, 43, 70, 201, 202
Granet, 132
Green George, 135
Grönbech, 34, 45, 432, 438
Group marriage: see Marriage.
Guardian spirit: see Daímon.
Guiraud, 426, 428
Guthrie, 443
Gyges, 85
Gymnasíarchos, 107, 233
Gytheion, 108

HAIR-CUTTING, 104, 107, 108, 266, 357
Haliakmon, 147, 148
Halliday, 299, 449
Hammurabi, 220
Harris, Rendel, 109
Harrison, E., 451
Harrison, J. E., 3, 109, 242, 308, 437
Harvest May, 136, 138
Hasebroek, 435
Head, 446
Headlam, 6, 256, 303, 354
Hebe, 320, 337
Hebrews: see Jews.
Hector, 185, 186
Hecuba, 185
Heichelheim, 7
Hekate, 39, 374
Helen, 185, 246, 247, 256, 258, 293
Helios, 39
Hephaistos, 44, 63, 277, 320, 323, 324, 329, 331, 333, 335, 341
Hera: at Argos, 60, 63, 146, 148; Parthenos, 116; relation to Dionysus, 111; to Herakles, 30, 111, 337; boôpis, 148. See Zeus.
Heraeis, 148
Heraia, 116, 117
Herakleitos, 53, 85, 158, 434
Herakles, 30, 111, 121, 299, 318, 320, 329, 330, 332–8, 378, 437
Hermes, 45, 46, 110, 250, 266, 281, 324, 325, 331, 335, 341, 430, 437
Hermione, 153
Herodotus, 40, 44, 46, 152, 168, 308, 322, 379
Hesiod, 29, 39, 46, 62, 77–9, 113, 126, 142, 155, 156, 219, 318, 338, 341, 343, 426
Hesperides, 112, 334, 335

Hestidtor, 233, 234
Hieron, 245
Hipparchos, 91, 154, 222, 224
Hippias, 91-3, 199, 221-3, 226, 231, 245, 312, 322
Hippodameia, 114, 116, 117
Hippokrates, 218, 219, 291, 327, 353, 371, 451
Hippolytos, 163, 365, 453
Hipponikos, 348
Historical linguistics, 4, 389
Hittites, 36, 110
Hocart, 117
Höfler, 439
Homeric pantheon, 63, 130
Homeric theogony, 29, 46, 443
Homeridai, 44, 45, 66
Homicide, 33-5, 73, 74, 83, 89, 122, 125, 231, 278, 287, 289, 291, 365, 433
Homosexuality, 366
Hooke, 120
Hopi Indians, 102
Horace, 192
Horai, 171, 292, 430
Howitt, 26, 399-401, 421
Human sacrifice, 102, 141-3, 248
Hunting, 11, 12, 16, 31, 43
Hybrias, 432
Hybristika, 299
Hypermnestra, 298, 307
Hypodikos, 194
Hypokrités, 181-3
Hypsipyle, 20, 299, 430
Hyrnetho, 29
Hysteria, 373, 377, 378, 380

IAKCHOS, 122
Iambic, 181, 236, 444
Iamidai, 44, 45, 115
Ichneutai, 243
Idealism, 157, 216, 290, 368
Ikarios, 144, 145
Ikhnaton, 121
Immersion in water, 133, 144-7
Imprecation, ritual, 122, 144, 147
Improvisation, 169, 170
Inachos, 147
Incantation, 186
Incest, 33
India, 12, 27, 405. *See* Dravidian.
Indo-European, 23, 27-31, 35, 51-3, 60, 402-17, 426, 429, 436
Inheritance, 33, 43, 199, 201-5, 279, 288, 302-6, 427, 446
Initiation VII, 21, 29, 50, 73, 131-3, 137, 139, 141, 145, 163, 166, 190-2, 212, 238, 270, 299, 320, 377
Ino, 113, 140

Io, 146-8, 172, 298-300, 320, 323, 324, 328-30, 334-7
Ion, 19, 49, 188
Ion of Euripides, 365
— of Plato, 381
Ionians, 27, 76, 80-2, 106, 149, 220, 221, 225, 226, 228
Ioxidai, 20
Iphigeneia, 50, 247, 251, 252
Iphigeneia at Tauris, 444
Iron-working, 110
Irrigation, 298, 308
Isagoras, 92, 199, 200, 221
Isis, 120, 146, 298
Isokrates, 283, 285, 352
Isonomía, 209, 218, 341, 350
Ithome, 230
Ixion, 87

JASON, 304, 367
Jealousy of the gods, 63, 87, 256, 309-11
Jews, 32, 38, 110, 111, 450
Jocasta, 312, 360-2
Judgment of the dead, 59, 123, 157, 279, 280, 300, 307
Justice, 156, 215, 290, 291, 340, 342, 369

KADMOS, 20, 38, 39, 110, 190, 430
Kagarov, 422
Kalchas, 247, 255
Karmanor, 147
Karsten, 436
Kasandra, 176, 247, 257, 259, 261-3, 273, 282, 296
Kátharsis, 373, 382, 383
Keats, 384
Kekrops, 22, 29, 74, 204
Kerkyra, 226, 229
Kerykes, 44, 45, 119, 122
Kimon, 228, 230, 234, 309
Kingship, 18, 23, 32, 41, 42, 46, 61, 67, 74, 75, 117, 118, 248
Kleintitschen, 388
Kleisthenes of Athens, 92, 200, 201, 205-9, 221, 222, 226, 232, 233, 245, 341
— of Sikyon, 151, 169
Kléros, 38, 39, 44, 104, 129, 426
Klerouchía, 40
Klotho, 46, 114
Klytiadai, 115
Knights, 239
Knossos, 59, 66
Know thyself, 78, 360, 361
Kodridai, 448
Kommós, 187, 192

Kômos, 166, 167, 169, 173, 192, 241, 263
Koronis, 144, 145
Korybantes, 110, 374, 377–9, 381, 445
Kósmos, 81
Kostrubonko, 136, 137
Kóthornos, 466
Kouretes, 109, 110, 115, 126, 149, 167, 170
Koûros—kourá, 438
Kranz, 178, 187, 448
Kreon, 176, 360, 361, 363
Kreousa, 19
Kretschmer, 28, 30, 153
Kritias, 340, 342
Kriton, 374
Kroeber, 388–91, 396, 415
Kronos, 39, 46, 108, 111, 155, 287, 331
Kronos, Reign of: *see* Golden Age.
Kroton, 210, 211, 213, 217, 446
Kybele, 379
Kylon of Athens, 76
— of Kroton, 211
Kynegeiros, 245
Kypselos, 86
Kyrene, 40, 205
Kyzikos, 149

LABOUR SERVICE, 32, 34
Lachesis, 38, 39, 41, 46, 47
Laios, 35, 190, 312, 315, 360–2
Lallwörter, 410, 412
Lampadophoria, 130
Lampoon, 181
Lampsakos, 149
Land tenure, 37–41, 70–3, 78, 90, 202, 206, 425–6
Lang, Andrew, 112
Lasos, 153, 194
Laurion: *see* Mines.
Law, codification of, 36, 76, 203
Leaves, ritual contact with, 104, 115, 118, 131, 138, 139, 141, 166, 167
Leitourgía, 234
Lemnos, 299
Lenaia, 149, 150, 240, 241
Lenin, 327
Lesbos, 40, 80, 151, 153
Lesser Mysteries: *see* Agra.
Levirate, 397
Lipara, 425
Lot, 38–44, 199, 209, 426
Love and Strife, 155, 156, 164
Love, Orphic conception of, 156
Lover, initiatory, 104, 105, 366
Lowie, 418, 423
Lutheranism, 163, 213
Lycia, 20, 28, 29, 40, 42, 59, 60, 61
Lydia, 77, 85, 220

Lykourgos of Athens, 20, 90, 153
— of Sparta, 432
— of Thrace, 144, 153, 170
Lynkeus, 298
Lysias, 366
Lysistrata, 305

MACURDY, 450
Madness of Herakles, 365, 378
Magi, 310
Magic, basis of, 13, 102
Magnificat, 160
Mahaffy, 321
Mainades, 150
Malinowski, 399, 400, 417
Malthus, 369
Man is money, 352
Mannhardt, 134, 140, 439
Mantineia, 230
Marathon, 223, 224, 245
Mardonios, 228
Marriage, 21, 25, 28, 33, 50, 52, 99, 104–8, 110, 122, 127, 129, 131, 145, 279, 299, 302–8, 338, 395–401, 403, 405, 429
Marx, 351, 454
Mask of Anarchy, 344
Materialism, 83, 158, 290, 327, 369–71
Matres Deæ, 52
Mazon, 450
McLennan, 387, 388
Mean, idea of the, 90, 215–8, 285, 286, 292
Medea, 113, 239, 304, 305, 367
Medicine, primitive, 373–7, 454
Megakles, 90, 92, 153, 223, 224, 228
Megara, 76, 86, 148, 217, 227, 240, 342
Meidas, 85, 351
Melampous, 146, 377
Melanesia, 12, 16, 27, 101
Meleager, 29, 35
Melenau, 375
Meliastai, 149
Melikertes, 113
Melisseus, 109
Melleîren, 104, 107, 122
Melos, 367
Menander, 49
Menelaos, 42, 53, 181, 244, 246, 247, 256, 258
Men's House, 100, 105, 119, 204, 234
Mentes, 32
Messenger, character of, 179
Metapontion, 210
Methymna, 151, 153
Métoikoi, 295, 300, 342, 348
Métron, 53, 78, 82, 164, 364
Mexico, 49, 102

Miletos, 81, 86, 106, 157, 163, 221, 233, 369
Millar, 3
Miltiades, 222–4, 228, 234, 322
Milton, 344, 384
Mimetic ritual, 13, 18, 21, 64, 102, 131, 148, 183, 196, 237, 384
Mines, 41, 88, 90, 153, 154, 160–2, 294, 379
Minoan culture, 29, 36, 59, 66, 70, 427, 433, 449
Minos, 59, 280
Minyas, 143, 146
Mixed farming, 11
Modes, musical, 187, 377
Moîra, 38–55, 78, 83, 129, 158, 159, 166, 206, 279, 282, 297, 370
Moirai, 6, 36–55, 278, 292, 331
Money, 85–6, 93, 351–3
Monody, 80, 185
Monostrophic form, 184, 185
More, Sir T., 436
Morgan, 3, 6, 26, 27, 43, 387, 388, 390, 396, 399, 401, 402, 405, 414, 421, 426
Moschion, 339
Moscow, 297
Mother goddess, 29, 30, 110, 277, 373, 379
Mumming-plays, 180, 193
Murray, 242, 343
Mycenæ, 59, 61, 65, 67
Mysteries of Agra: *see* Agra.
— of Eleusis: *see* Eleusinian Mysteries.
Mystery-plays, 188, 193
Myth and ritual, 62, 63, 103, 130

NAMES, 48, 97, 98, 111, 113, 375, 376
Natureingang, 134
Nausithoos, 39, 40
Naxos, 144–6, 168
Necessity: see *Anánke*.
Nestor, 21
Next-of-kin, 202, 302, 303, 450
Nietzsche, 130
Nikias, 348, 435
Nilsson, 37, 67, 142, 146, 426, 437
Ninon, 211
Noble lie, 453–4
Nómos, 54, 340
Nonnos, 142, 432
Nornen, 38, 52
Nothing too much, 78, 89, 118, 254, 350, 351
Nymphs, 44, 145

OATH, ordeal by, 36, 283
Obscenity, 122, 181, 237

Ocean, god of, 155, 322, 324, 328, 330–3, 336
Octave, 215, 216
Odysseus, 42, 61, 62, 73, 181, 247
Œdipus, 35, 53, 190, 243, 312, 360–5
Œdipus Tyrannus, 243, 323, 360–4
Oinomaos, 114
Ojibwa, 102
Oleiai, 143, 149
Olympia, 54, 60, 113–9, 126, 131, 146, 147, 166, 278, 320
Olympus, 28, 29, 44, 46, 62, 63, 111, 319
Onomakritos, 153, 155
Orchomenos, 59, 142, 143, 145, 146
Ordeals, 36, 99, 104, 106, 126, 137, 141, 143, 283, 320
Oresteia of Æschylus XV, 53, 108, 176, 186, 189, 242, 244, 306–8, 337, 354, 356–60, 374, 381, 433, 444, 448
— of Stesichoros, 248
Orestes XV, 35, 49, 108, 176, 188, 191, 307, 355–9, 374
Orestes, 179
Orpheus, 144, 145, 152, 153, 163
Orphism IX, 6, 7, 21, 49, 111, 120, 125, 210, 212, 213, 219, 279, 280, 319, 327, 369, 370, 379
Orthagoras, 86
Oschophoria, 139
Osiris, 120, 121, 146
Ostracism, 446

PALAIKASTRO, 109
Palaimon, 113
Pan, 294
Panathenaia, 91, 295, 297
Pandora, 318
Pangaion, 90, 144, 153, 154
Parábasis, 240–2
Parcæ, 38, 52
Paris, 246, 252, 254–8, 293
Parke, 443
Parmenides, 157, 158, 370
Párodos, 173, 186, 192, 241, 242
Paros, expedition to, 223
Pastoral society, 11, 15, 20, 21, 31, 32, 54
Pausanias of Sparta, 228, 229
Peisistratidai, 20, 90, 153, 154, 222
Peisistratos, 90, 91, 120, 151, 153, 155, 165, 194, 200, 205, 222, 233, 435
Pelias, 113, 239
Pelopidai, 188
Pelops, 113, 114, 117, 118, 246, 357
Penelope 47, 181
Pentheus, 139–42, 144, 167, 168, 180, 378, 430

Penthilidai, 86
Periandros, 151–3
Perigoune, 20
Perikles, 309, 348, 350, 366
Peripéteia, 6, 188, 192, 353, 354
Perjury, 36, 292
Persephone, 122, 155
Perseus, 144, 145
Persians, 177, 178, 242, 268, 309–11, 322, 444
Peru, 102, 449
Peterloo, 344
Phæacians, 39, 75
Phaleron, 223
Phallus, 137, 240, 241
Phanes, 111, 155
Pharmakós, 139, 145
Phemios, 65
Pherekydes, 142
Philaidai, 222, 224, 228, 422
Philemon, 342
Philolaos, 216
Phœnicians, 67, 77
Phoinix, 61
Phráter, 28, 30, 402
Phratry, 27, 31, 62, 106, 107, 200, 201, 205–8, 280, 439
Phrygia, 77, 85, 110, 187, 379
Phrynichos, 233, 309
Phylé, 27, 446
Phylobasileús, 200
Physkoa, 116
Phytalidai, 139
Pickard-Cambridge, 3, 168, 169, 180, 181, 234–9, 372
Pindar, 39, 41, 78–80, 87, 93, 118, 168, 170, 184, 194, 370
Pirenne, 214
Pittakos, 86, 153
Plato: on colonisation, 435; his ideal state, 368; on justice, 290, 291; on the Korybantes, 374, 381; on madness, 451; on marriage, 450; on the Mysteries, 124, 127; on poetical inspiration, 381; on property, 288; on prophétes, 182; on the soul, 157, 162; on tragedy, 373, 383; sold as a slave, 366
Pleiades, 249
Plutarch: on Dionysus, 142, 143, 191; on medicine, 454; on the Mysteries, 124, 126; on primitive feasts, 41, 234; on Spartan education, 103–5, 204
Poiné—pónos, 424
Polydamas, 181
Polykrates, 210, 221
Polyneikes, 312, 314, 315

Polynesia, 101, 102, 414, 415
Pompé, 141, 166, 167, 172, 173, 192, 241, 242
Population of Attica, 347, 348
Porphyry, 124, 125
Poseidon, 20, 21, 39, 60, 78, 83, 108, 109, 277
Possession, 374–7, 381, 382
Potlatch, 32
Praisos, 19
Pratinas, 235
Priam, 40, 66, 262
Private property, 31, 33, 37, 41, 43, 44, 54, 70, 74, 82, 199, 207, 351, 370, 425–6
Proitos, 130, 146, 172, 377
Prometheus XVII, 6, 383
Prometheus Bound XVII, 176, 246, 303, 307, 311, 444
Prosecution, Attic term for, 34
Protagoras, 341
Proteus, 244
Prytaneion, 74, 75, 115, 118, 119, 166, 234
Psycho-analysis, 383
Puchstein, 191
Purification, 73, 99, 122, 125, 145, 146, 173, 247, 248, 280, 291, 373, 374, 380, 382
Pursuit, ritual, 144–7
Pylades, 176, 265, 270, 273
Pythagoras: his life, 210; on justice, 340; on the mean, 216
Pythagoreanism, 6, 49, 83, 123, 210–19, 288, 291, 298, 326, 327, 340, 447
Pythian Games, 115, 357

Radcliffe-Brown, 396–401
Rapisarda, 452
Re-birth, 21, 97, 98, 102, 108, 111, 114, 123, 129, 132, 239, 242, 277, 280, 299, 377, 438–9
Reconciliation, 211, 216, 231, 244, 278, 283, 297, 308, 325, 333, 338, 345, 353, 372
Redemption, 160
Reformation, 213
Refrain, 169, 170, 184–7, 282, 445
Revenue, Athenian, 349
Rhadamanthys, 36
Rhea, 108, 109, 115, 155
Rhodes, 39, 41, 60, 149, 425
Riches have no limit, 351
Riddles, 143, 189–91
Ridgeway, 3, 37, 303, 304, 306
Rivers, 26, 387, 388, 402, 405, 415
Robertson, 305–8
Robertson Smith, 32, 46, 50, 132, 428

SABAZIOS, 110
Sacred disease, 373
Sacred Marriage, 21, 114, 116, 117, 146–8
Sacred Spring, 440
St. Augustine, 364
St. George, 180
St. Paul, 125
Salamis, 227, 228, 245, 310
Samos, 139, 149, 210, 221
Sappho, 80, 86, 184, 185, 445
Sarpedon, 53, 66
Satyr play, 232, 235–8, 242–4, 347
Satyrs, 149, 234
Scamander, 145
Schrader, 408
Schulz, 190
Secret societies, 22, 101–3, 110, 131, 139–43, 148–50, 172, 195, 374, 377, 437
Seltman, 422
Semachidai, 154, 206, 435
Semele, 110, 111, 241
Semitic, 48, 390
Semnai, 292
Seneca, 249
Serfdom: *see* Land tenure.
Seven against Thebes, 177–9, 246, 311–6, 444
Shakespeare, 249, 297, 384, 450
Shamanism, 375, 378
Sharrukin, 220
Shelley, 321, 343–6, 384
Sheppard, 6, 323, 359
Siberia, 375, 376, 378, 400
Sibyl, 376
Sigeion, 91
Sikyon, 70, 86, 151, 169, 194
Simonides, 93, 170, 194
Sisyphos, 158
Skené, 191, 192
Skólion, 185
Sky god, 19
Slavery, 32, 71, 120, 154, 155, 158–62, 209, 231, 342, 345, 348–50, 356, 364, 366, 368, 370, 371, 421, 435
Sleep of initiation, 98, 104, 115, 141, 166
Smyrna, 66, 83, 130, 149
Sokrates, 374, 381
Solmsen, 451
Solon, 40, 70, 87–90, 156, 200, 201, 215, 305, 351
Sophokles: attitude to the Delphic Oracle, 355, 364; on money, 352; treatment of chorus, 268, 353; use of Æschylus, 354. *See* titles of plays.
Sophrosýne, 283, 332, 350

Sororate, 397, 399
Soviet Union, 27, 346, 449
Sparta, 69, 70, 103–5, 202–4, 229
Spartoi, 20, 49, 188
Speenhamland system, 344
Spencer and Gillen, 26, 123, 400, 401
Sphinx, 190, 312, 361
Spinning, 46, 47, 52, 54, 158
Stage, 191, 192
Staphylodromia, 130
Stásimon, 172, 179, 186
Stealing, ritual, 437
Stesichoros, 80, 142, 184, 248
Stichomýthia, 189–92
Strophic form, 184–6
Strymon, 154
Suffering teaches wisdom, 78, 218, 254, 295, 297, 325, 327, 329
Suppliants of Æschylus, 176–9, 186, 187, 246, 298–308, 311, 444
— of Euripides, 322
Swaddling-bands: see *Gnorísmata*.
Sybaris, 446
Symbols, mystic, 99, 113, 122, 123, 189, 191, 212
Symposium, 374
Syracuse, 226, 245, 366, 446

TABOO, totemic, 11–16, 19–21
Tainaron, 152
Talthybios, 45, 46
Tanagra, 38, 39, 144, 145
Tantalos, 113, 114, 248
Taras, 152
Tattoo, totemic, 19, 48, 148
Tawney, 213
Taygetos, 149
Taylor, 453
Tegea, 248
Teiresias, 361, 363
Téleios, 127
Telemachos, 32, 41
Telugu, 405–12
Temenos, 28, 41, 69
Témenos, 40, 42, 69–72
Tempe, 227
Teos, 447
Terpandros, 80, 432
Testamentary disposition, 43, 203
Tetralogy, disintegration of, 347, 353, 372
Thales, 80, 447
Theagenes, 76, 86
Thebes, 20, 59, 60, 110, 130, 168, 190, 226, 312–4, 360
Themis, 340
Themistokles, 41, 222–30, 233, 309

Theognis, 93, 94, 217
Thermopylai, 227
Thersites, 62
Theseus, 20, 75, 146, 234, 292, 293, 322
Thesmophoria, 119, 308
Thespis, 180, 192
Thessaly, 60, 65, 70, 144, 145, 226–8
Thetis, 113, 144, 333, 338
Thíasos: see Secret societies.
Thirty Tyrants, 340
Thoas, 299
Thomas, 387, 388, 400
Thrace, 90, 92, 130, 144, 153, 154, 160, 222, 379
Thrasyboulos, 86
Thrasymachos, 290
Thucydides, 59, 74, 75, 367
Thyestes, 246, 247, 262
Thyiades, 130, 149, 150
Tibet, 400
Tierney, 280
Titans, 44, 111–3, 155, 157, 331, 332, 438
Tithes, 72
Torch races, 119, 336, 439
Totem, individual, 49, 101: see *Daímon.*
—, split, 424
Totemism I, 5, 48, 49, 52, 79, 83, 101, 159, 196, 239, 277, 449
Toutain, 425–6
Trachiniæ, 444
Tragoidía, 232
Trausoi, 379
Trevelyan, 448
Triadic form, 184
Tribes, Attic, 207–9
Triptolemos, 120
Triton, 144
Trittýs, 206, 207
Trochaic, 181, 236, 444
Troizen, 227, 248
Trojan Women, 367, 444
Troy, siege of, 60, 247
Truck system, 344
Tudors, 90, 193
Tyche, 370, 371
Tylor, 432

Tyranny VI, 76, 77, 81, 151–4, 199, 200, 209, 210, 218, 220–2, 229, 264, 322, 323
Tyrtaios, 432

UNIVERSITIES, 107, 127
Ure, 143, 435
Urukagina, 220
Usener, 180
Usury, 87

VASSALAGE, 61, 62, 69
Veil, 122, 136, 273
Vendetta, 34, 82, 83
Vendryes, 404
Verrall, 451

WADE-GERY, 46, 74, 75, 88
Waggon of Dionysus, 167, 192
Walker, 223, 224
Wealth, aristocratic idea of, 35
Webster, Hutton, 100, 119, 183
—, T. B. L., 364
Weniger, 113–6
Wheel, Orphic, 159, 212, 319
Wilamowitz, 245, 303
Wiradthuri, 112, 113
Witchcraft, 33
Women, status of, 16, 20, 54, 119, 133, 150, 172, 195, 199–205, 288, 297, 299, 304–6, 308, 364, 366–8, 380
Wotan, 437

XANTHIPPOS, 223, 224
Xanthos and Melanthos, 180, 240
Xerxes, 225, 226, 228, 309–11, 354

YUKUMBIL, 16

ZAGREUS, 111, 149, 170
Zeus: birth, 108–10, 115; king, 44, 62; relation to Dionysus, 111, 112, 130; to Hera, 29, 54, 116, 127, 147, 338; to the Moirai, 53, 54, 278, 289, 297, 331, 431; to the oak, 19; to Poseidon, 39, 78; at Dodona, 30, 60; Kappotas, 248; Lykaios, 19; at Praisos, 19; Teleios, 127, 251